Konrad Pędziwiatr

The New Muslim Elites in European Cities

Konrad Pędziwiatr

The New Muslim Elites in European Cities

Religion and Active Social Citizenship Amongst Young Organized Muslims in Brussels and London

VDM Verlag Dr. Müller

Impressum/Imprint (nur für Deutschland/ only for Germany)
Bibliografische Information der Deutschen Nationalbibliothek: Die Deutsche Nationalbibliothek
verzeichnet diese Publikation in der Deutschen Nationalbibliografie; detaillierte bibliografische
Daten sind im Internet über http://dnb.d-nb.de abrufbar.
 Alle in diesem Buch genannten Marken und Produktnamen unterliegen warenzeichen-, marken-
oder patentrechtlichem Schutz bzw. sind Warenzeichen oder eingetragene Warenzeichen der
jeweiligen Inhaber. Die Wiedergabe von Marken, Produktnamen, Gebrauchsnamen,
Handelsnamen, Warenbezeichnungen u.s.w. in diesem Werk berechtigt auch ohne besondere
Kennzeichnung nicht zu der Annahme, dass solche Namen im Sinne der Warenzeichen- und
Markenschutzgesetzgebung als frei zu betrachten wären und daher von jedermann benutzt
werden dürften.

Coverbild: www.ingimage.com

Verlag: VDM Verlag Dr. Müller GmbH & Co. KG
Dudweiler Landstr. 99, 66123 Saarbrücken, Deutschland
Telefon +49 681 9100-698, Telefax +49 681 9100-988
Email: info@vdm-verlag.de

Herstellung in Deutschland:
Schaltungsdienst Lange o.H.G., Berlin
Books on Demand GmbH, Norderstedt
Reha GmbH, Saarbrücken
Amazon Distribution GmbH, Leipzig
ISBN: 978-3-639-27026-6

Imprint (only for USA, GB)
Bibliographic information published by the Deutsche Nationalbibliothek: The Deutsche
Nationalbibliothek lists this publication in the Deutsche Nationalbibliografie; detailed
bibliographic data are available in the Internet at http://dnb.d-nb.de.
 Any brand names and product names mentioned in this book are subject to trademark, brand
or patent protection and are trademarks or registered trademarks of their respective holders. The
use of brand names, product names, common names, trade names, product descriptions etc.
even without a particular marking in this works is in no way to be construed to mean that such
names may be regarded as unrestricted in respect of trademark and brand protection legislation
and could thus be used by anyone.

Cover image: www.ingimage.com

Publisher: VDM Verlag Dr. Müller GmbH & Co. KG
Dudweiler Landstr. 99, 66123 Saarbrücken, Germany
Phone +49 681 9100-698, Fax +49 681 9100-988
Email: info@vdm-publishing.com

Printed in the U.S.A.
Printed in the U.K. by (see last page)
ISBN: 978-3-639-27026-6

CONTENTS

LIST OF TABLES

LIST OF FIGURES

4

In Memory of My Father

ACKNOWLEDGMENTS

"It takes a whole village to raise a child" - says the African proverb. It takes more than the population of a village to write a sociological monograph, especially if it is based, like this one, on fieldwork carried out in two different countries. In fact, this book has been a result of intensive interactions with the populations of several 'villages'. It was my 'intellectual journey of a thousand miles' during which I could not only discover 'new worlds' of sociological scholarship and broaden the horizons of my sociological imagination, but also learn a great deal about the multicultural realities of British and Belgian society and meet many extraordinary people. There is insufficient space here to acknowledge the assistance of all of the individuals that I have met during this journey. However, I would like to thank at least some of the people that have helped me either intentionally or unintentionally to carry out this project.

"The journeys of a thousand miles begin with one step" – is attributed to the Chinese philosopher Lao Tse. The first step in this journey was undertaken during my MA studies at the Jagiellonian University, University of Exeter and University of Oxford. These places stimulated my interest in the issues of migration, modernization, multiculturalism, individualization, secularization and religious minorities – at first Christians in the Middle East and then Muslims in Europe. Zdzisław Mach, Andrzej Flis, Beata Kowalska and Ireneusz Cezary Kamiński were some of my guides and mentors at the Jagiellonian University, Grace Davie and Bogdan Szajkowski at the University of Exeter, and Steven Vertovec and Cari Peach at the University in Oxford. I owe all of them a considerable debt of thanks.

I also took important steps in my explorations of the issues behind the Muslim presence in Europe while working as a Marie Curie Research Fellow at the University of Bradford. In the European Curry Capital, cruelly described by Bill Bryson in his *Notes From Small Island* as a city whose role in life is to make every place else in the world look better in comparison, I not only met great companions for dinners in the superb local curry restaurants but also made many friends, the discussions with whom provided me with plenty of food for thought. Amongst them there were Charlie Husband, Yunas

Samad, Philip Lewis, Yunis Alam, Sean McLoughlin, Mikołaj Stanek, Jérôme Jamin, Maria Sultan and Tamsin Fuller.

I have remained steadfast on the intellectual journey that has ended with the production of this book first and foremost thanks to my supervisor who has never doubted my capacity to accomplish this task. I would like to wholeheartedly thank Rudi Laermans not only for his extremely valuable comments, suggestions and advice, without which this work would be less refined and clear, but also for his constant support along the way. His patience, knowledge, experience but most of all, his humanity forms a precious combination few individuals, especially those in the extremely competitive world of academia, can ever hope to have.

This research project would not have been possible without the help of the numerous inhabitants of the 'European Muslim village'. I am profoundly grateful to Muslim men and women who agreed to devote their time to take part in my research. I will not name them in order to protect their identities and ensure their rights to privacy. However, I must say that gaining their trust and experiencing their honesty has been my great privilege. Their time, trust, enthusiasm, good humour and insights constitute an important part of this book. I remain indebted and hope that I have done justice to their views and voices.

I would also like to thank the many inhabitants of the 'professional village' or members of my community of practice with whom I have had the pleasure to discuss the issues behind this research and some of its findings. Amongst the colleagues and friends studying the processes within the Muslim populations in Europe with whom I have been in contact were: Jocelyne Cesari, Hassan Bousetta, Dirk Jacobs, Marco Martiniello, Johan Leman, Mark Swyngedouw, Nadia Fadil, Dilwar Hussain, Michael Privot, Jamil Sherif, John Eade, Yahya Birt, Brigitte Maréchal, Christiane Timmerman, Els Vanderwaeren, Anwar Alam, Nancy Venel and many others. Of course, any failings this book may have are entirely the responsibility of the author.

Last but not least, my most grateful and loving thanks go to my wife Justyna Woźniakowska who has supported me in the realization of this project over the years and my daughter Łucja who has provided me with the necessary distraction.

8

PREFACE

"Religion is Dead. God isn't religious - why should you be?" – asked the big yellow hoardings which were displayed in 400 railway stations across Britain in the first month of the new millennium. The billboards were part of a nationwide campaign run by Sir Cliff Richard's millennium charity Fanfare for a New Generation which had intended, first of all, to draw people's attention in the midst of the Millennium media hype to the religious aspect of the year 2000 and secondly, even more ambitiously, to *"stir the dormant faith of Britons"*.[1] The campaign was conducted by the minority of Christians on the British Isles who 'believe and belong' and want others to follow their example. The reality, however, and not only in Britain looks slightly different.

In Western European countries if people happen 'to believe', they very rarely 'belong' and actively practice their religion (Davie 1994). In Belgium, for instance, according to the recent surveys 42 per cent of people do not belong to any religious community (Le Soir 10.12.2004) and only 14,4 per cent of Flemings, 6,8 per cent of Walloons and 6,2 per cent of inhabitants of Brussels went to mass during the Christmas of 2006 (Laporte 2008). The general decline in membership of faith communities in this part of the world in the modern age has meant that the traditional authority of religion has retreated from many spheres of social life. The religious system is no longer an all-encompassing system of meaning, but is reduced to one of the social subsystems. Thus, religion has ceased to be not only the general point of reference, but also a source of civic duty and a means through which people learn how to be members of their societies or acquire citizenship skills. This is especially evident if one compares Western Europe with the United States, where religion still plays an important role in the political socialization of many of its citizens (Verba et al. 1995, Putnam 2000, Uslaner 2002).

21st century Europe is a place where people become citizens most commonly through employment. Thus, having a job means to have rights in a state because of the existence of more or less efficient welfare states (Steenbergen 1994, Rea 1995). This,

---

[1] Information about the Fanfare Foundation on http://www.zenadsl2125.zen.co.uk/page2.htm

9

however, does not mean that there are no groups of individuals who connect with the wider society through their faith communities and remain socially active because of their strongly held religious convictions. One such group are the young Muslims who are involved in various kinds of religious organizations that try to bring Muslim communities closer to the host societies' public life. Influenced by various traditions within reformist Islam, among others by the scholarship of European Muslim thinkers and preachers like Tariq Ramadan, these members of the second and third generations of immigrants who arrived in Europe after the Second World War, have been trying to put the ethos of civic engagement that is central to his project into practice. However, while the intellectual contributions of the grandson of the founder of the Muslim Brotherhood (ar. *al-Ikhwan al-Muslimun*) are well known (e.g. Ramadan 1999, 2001, 2004) and his religious authority has been relatively well researched (Frégosi 2000, Bouzar 2001, Mohsen-Finan 2002, Fourest 2003, Dassetto 2004, Ternisien 2005, Hamel 2007), very little attention has been paid to the exploration of various dimensions of active social citizenship of young European[2] Muslims (Mandaville 2003). This book aims to fill this gap and to shed light on this largely unexplored area of study by focusing on the analysis of the perceptions of citizenship by young Muslims involved in the activities of religious organisations in Brussels and in London. Its purpose is to reveal what young Muslims mean when they describe themselves as 'Muslim citizens', and thus explore relations between Islam, as a minority religion, and citizenship in two urban/national settings: one in which Muslims are mostly perceived as individuals (Brussels/Belgium) and a one in which they are usually viewed as members of religious, ethnic or other social groups (London/Britain). The assumption here is that the way in which young Muslims understand themselves as citizens is likely to have a significant impact on their perception of their rights and obligations and on whether they participate in wider social life, as well as, in what form and why. Furthermore it will be argued that the creation of a successful Muslim civil society implies specific views on religion and citizenship.

The main reason why this area of study is still largely underdeveloped is its novelty. It is only in recent years that Islam in Western Europe has ceased to be the

---

[2] The terms 'European' and 'Europe' refer in the book to the Western part of the continent unless it is clearly stated otherwise.

religion of immigrants and has begun to emerge as the religion of European born citizens. The generational change within Muslim populations marks a critical difference not so much in the legal citizenship status between generations but above all in terms of identity, participation and understanding of rights and duties. While immigrants of the first generation were either denizens[3] (they did not have any political rights - Belgium) or partial citizens (except for small elites, they lacked the cultural resources to choose between different courses of action - Belgium and Great Britain), their offspring in most cases can enjoy full citizenship rights. They possess not only full legal citizenship rights, but what is even more important, a range of forms of tacit knowledge[4], competences and taken-for-granted assumptions which allow them to engage in citizenship activities. As research into young Muslims in Europe has shown, citizenship (beside religion) is often central to their self-understanding and assertions of who they are (Cesari 2003: 264, Maréchal et. al. 2003, Lathion 2003). This book further explores this observation, and analyses how young organised Muslims in Brussels and London construct their notions of citizenship as a form of identity. It focuses on the new Muslim elites, namely the social actors of the second and third generations who participate directly or indirectly in the processes of decision making that are important for the future of Muslim communities and wider societies. It concentrates in particular on these young Muslims who try, through various projects, to tackle some of the issues faced by their communities and societies and thus at least partially solve the problem of collective uncertainty.[5] Through their social engagement, the young Muslim men and women begin to play in the analysed countries a role of the new religious brokers.[6] Felice Dassetto and Jorgen Nielsen suggest that these young people's approach can be on the whole described as constructive engagement with the local and national institutions (Nielsen and Dassetto 2003). This monograph will not only shed light on examples of this engagement but also provide some information about the elite formation within the Muslim populations in two global cities: Brussels and London.

---

[3] The notion of denizenship is taken from Hammar (1990).
[4] It involves among others basic working knowledge of the social and political systems, skills in accessing and processing information, interpreting political talk and debating public issues.
[5] For an overview of scholarship on local elites see for example Tilleux 2003 or Trivelin 2003.
[6] By religious brokers I mean individuals who play a key role in the articulation of the identity narrative, discourse.

The above mentioned transition from the Islam of immigrants to the Islam of citizens is not a smooth process. The deficit of institutional channels for acquiring Islamic knowledge and of intellectual endeavour in translating the key elements of this knowledge into the social realities of life in 21st century Europe are only two of out of many barriers which significantly slow this transition. In order to influence it, one needs to know exactly what mechanisms are in play. I believe learning how young organized Muslims mix religiosity with the elements of citizenship is one of the ways through which these transformations could be speeded up and smoothed. We must also better understand how young European Muslim perceive citizenship in relation to their faith, in order to more effectively promote an active Muslim citizenship that extends beyond the boundaries of ethnic and religious communities and leads to the development of bridging social capital which stretches over different social groups and improves social cohesion.

The debates about the rights and obligations of Muslims as minorities in the West which are currently animating Muslim and non-Muslim circles are part of the larger revival of discussions on the notion of citizenship. Globalization, the enlargement of the European Union and the related erosion of the boundaries and identities of the nation states; the presence of large migrant communities and issues concerning their integration and accommodation; the general disengagement of individuals from the political process caused among others by the lack of trust in elected officials, are only some of the factors that have contributed to this revival.[7] They have also marked a shift within public debates about citizenship from a discussion about what the state should do for the individual, to what the individual should do for the state. Not only are the rights and obligations of citizens being redefined, but also what it means to be a citizen has become an issue of central concern. This issue is of great importance for the children of Muslim immigrants born in Europe who are aware of their rights as citizens and have some resources (at least cultural) to exercise these rights. The book attempts to explore how young Muslims position themselves in these debates and how they construct their notion of citizenship. It is intended to be a contribution to the cumulative, ongoing effort to disentangle the problematics of citizenship in sociology and apply the concept to the study of the contemporary society and to the analysis of the Muslim activism in civil society in

---

[7] Other factors that have contributed to this revival will be elaborated more extensively in the chapter two.

particular. Too often the theoretical debates about the meaning of citizenship are conducted in an empirical void. This study aims to be a step towards reversing this trend.

The terrorist attacks on the Pentagon and WTC in 2001 and the revival of the debate about the clash of civilizations (Huntington 1998) are only two factors that have contributed to the contemporary plunge of the sacred at the heart of the politics in Europe. However, religion was politicized already in the 1980s when the Solidarity movement in Poland, allied with the Catholic Church, defeated communism; when the pupils were expelled from French school for wearing hijabs and when Muslims called for the ban on the publication of Salman Rushdie's "*The Satanic Verses*", to mention only a few significant events. Whereas religion as a topic was at the margins in the 1960s and 1970s, in the later decades it became to be seen as a constitutive feature of modern social movements (Casanova 1994: 5). An important but troublesome question for contemporary sociological theory is to understand the relationship between religious movements, politics and modernity[8]. While for Max Weber and Karl Marx the main issues were respectively, the influence of religion on the foundations of the capitalist economy, and its ability to contain the impact of radical working-class politics, the contemporary issue, that is being also addressed in this book, is the location of religion in the processes of globalization and the tensions between religion and modernity.

As a study shedding light on the contemporary tensions between Islam and modernity, through the analysis of the personal notions of citizenship among young organized Muslims, this book has clear empirical and theoretical limitations. Although some of its observations may apply to all members of the Muslim populations living in Western Europe, they most strictly concern only a small part of these population, namely young European Muslims living in two European capitals who are actively involved in the activities of specific Muslim organizations. The motives for the selection of these people are extensively explained in the later part of the book, so here it should suffice to say that they constitute an important part of the growing new Muslim elites that with every year have a stronger impact on the character of Islam in their respective countries, as well as in wider Europe. As far as the theoretical limitations are concerned, the

---

[8] If not stated otherwise the term "modernity" refers to the Western modernity. At the same time following Eisenstadt (2003) I accept the possibility of different paths toward and through modernity.

ambition of this monograph is to explore various dimensions of the sociological notion of citizenship among the chosen groups, but not to elaborate on political and juridical aspects of citizenship that have been extensively dealt with in other studies (e.g. Bousetta 1997, Saggar 1998).

The book consists of six chapters. The first chapter sets a general context for the study. It provides a brief overview of the existing research on Muslims in Europe with particular attention to the scholarship on the Muslim presence in Great Britain and Belgium and especially in their capitals. Then, it sheds light on the main transformations that have taken place within European Muslim populations in recent years.

The second chapter sketches a conceptual framework of the research and moves away from discussing the changes within the social landscapes of the Muslim populations to clarify the meaning of the concepts of identity and citizenship as used in the text. It critically reviews sociological literature on citizenship and proposes a new understanding of the concept that is more in line with the multicultural diversity of the Western European countries. The key research problem is operationalized and the research questions are formulated. exploring participatory, identity and normative dimensions of citizenship of young European Muslims. The chapter sheds also light on the relations between identity and modernity which are at the base of Muslims' efforts to rework images, assumptions and representations of their religion and their communities and to position themselves as citizens and full members of the European polities. It sketches the different possibilities of being a Muslim and sheds light on the target groups and target areas.

In the following chapter, which serves as a bridge between the more theoretical chapters and later empirical ones, the main issues related to the Muslim presence in Belgium and in Britain are discussed. In line with the comparative framework of the research, the chapter starts with the presentation of the most important similarities and difference of the multicultural regimes of the analysed countries. Then it portrays how both analysed countries have acquired substantial Muslim populations and describes the key areas and groups analysed in the book. It also explores the development of the policies of the incorporation of immigrants, the accommodation of Islam within existing Church and State structures and the main debates around Islam in both countries.

14

The fifth chapter makes extensive use of the fieldwork material and analyses the relationship between Islam and citizenship amongst organized Belgian Muslims. It explores the different dimensions of citizenship of the young Muslim Brusselers.[9] After a brief presentation of the main socio-economic features of the Muslim interviewees in the Belgian capital it moves to assess how these people conceive of their Muslim and civic identities and how they frame their belonging. These explorations of the religiosity and depth of citizenship of young organized Muslims are followed by the analysis of the extent of their citizenship. The two last sections are devoted to an assessment of the perceptions of civic rights and civic obligations by young Muslim Brusselers.

The following chapter, using the fieldwork material from London, has by and large the same structure as the former. It begins with the presentation of the key socio-economic characteristics of the British sample and then explores the religious and civic identities of Muslim Londoners. Having elaborated on the identity dimension of citizenship of the young British Muslims, it analyses the participatory dimension of their citizenship and in particular their resources and motivations for activism within Muslim organisations and wider civil society. In the last two sections it deals with the normative dimensions of citizenship. It looks into the perceptions of the civil rights and obligations of the young British Muslims and the relationship between Muslim ethics and perceived requirements of citizenship.

The concluding chapter sums up the key findings of the Belgian and British case studies and points out the main similarities and differences between the lived citizenship of the members of the new Muslim elites in Brussels and London. It also explores the major change in the public mobilisation of Islam in Europe in recent years and the development of the new type of project identity - the Muslim civicness - that is largely responsible for this change. It concludes with reflections about the relationship between Islam and modernity and social cohesion within the highly diverse and individualised Western societies.

---

[9] Here it has to be noted that the English language does not have a very good synonym of the French term 'Bruxellois' (Fr. inhabitant of Brussels). Traditionally the term 'Brusselers' (Brusseleers) refers to autochthonous inhabitants of Brussels speaking a particular mixture of Flemish and French. I have decided to use this term, however, to refer to my Belgian informants because they talked about themselves using the Dutch term 'Brusselaar' and because they are marked by strong local identity. These reasons are explored in depth in chapter 4.

CHAPTER I – European Muslims as Immigrants and Citizens: Overview of the Existing Research and Key Transformations

Le beur est mort et le musulman a pris sa place.
Xavier Ternisien (2005a)

*Islamic identity is rooted in a mode of being
and not merely in a mode of oppression.*
John Rex (1991)

"There will be a time when your religion will be like a hot piece of coal in the palm of your hand; you will not be able to hold it" - said to the people who embraced Islam Prophet Mohammad (Ahmad 2003: 1). It seems that this time has come especially for circa 15 million Muslims living in the Western Europe. After the terrorist attacks on 11 September 2001 (USA), 11 March 2004 (Spain) and especially those on 7 July 2005 (Great Britain) carried out by home-grown Muslims, Islam promoting in its mainstream form peace and benevolence has been widely associated by the European public with violence and bloodshed.[10] Although the aforementioned terrorist attacks were carried out only by a small group of followers of a specific form of Islam, it is all the Muslim populations in Europe that are being stigmatized and looked at with suspicion. Today it is not only Muslims' loyalty and a sense of belonging that are being questioned, but also their willingness of integration with wider European societies. In many influential circles in Europe it is widely held that Muslims pose a serious cultural and political threat. It is argued that although Muslim immigrants have now been in Europe for almost half a century, they have, unlike their past and present counterparts failed to integrate; they show no commitment to its democratic institution; mock its liberal freedoms; do not feel at home in European societies; prefer to live among themselves forming ghettos; keep

---

[10] A recently conducted survey in Germany has shown for instance that 80% of its citizens associate the word 'islam' with terrorism and persecution of women (Rzeczpospolita 08.03.2005). Similarly negative image of Islam and its followers have also other Europeans (Le Soir 10.12.2004). Even in Poland where the Muslim population consist of only 25 000 and where one-fifth of the Polish Muslims are descendents of the Tatars who settled in the country already in the 14th century, the anti-Muslim sentiment is widespread. The European Values Survey 2000 shows actually that the anti-Muslim sentiment among Poles is even stronger than among other European nations where Muslims make up significantly larger groups within the total populations.

making unreasonable demands and are more concerned about their fellow religionists in other parts of the world than their fellow citizens – to mention only the most commonly evoked arguments (Parekh 2006: 179). A powerful meta narrative on Islam, reinforced by the mediatic image of Islam (Said 1997, Allievi 2003), maintains that Muslims do not want and cannot integrate because their ways of life and thought are fundamentally incompatible with those of Europe (they are collectivists, intolerant, authoritarian, illiberal and theocratic) and because they want to convert others to Islam (Parekh 2006: 180). As Mohammed Arkoun aptly notices today it is almost impossible to pronounce a word 'islam' without evoking very strong imagery of all sorts of violence committed in the name of Allah (1994). It should not be surprising then that with this kind of imagery, as many studies show, the anti-Muslim and anti-Islamic sentiments are being widely accepted as 'natural' and 'unproblematic', whereas Islam has been increasingly viewed as a monolithic bloc, unresponsive to change, inferior to the West, barbaric, irrational, primitive, and sexist (e.g. Runnymede Trust 1997, Allen and Nielsen 2002, Geisser 2003, EUMC 2006)[11].

Against the background of this dramatisation of Islam in Europe, which according to some scholars (e.g. Van Der Veer and Munshi 2004, Werbner 2004 and Schiffauer 2006) shows all the symptoms of a moral panic[12] or collective hysteria, one may observe in recent years an increasing mobilization of young European Muslims around religious identity. Many of them declare to find in their religion not only answers to their quest for meaningful identity, but also a sense of empowerment that is denied to them by their marginalized existence. The Muslim identity which they declare to posses is often an identity which stresses not only the differences between Muslims and non-Muslims but

---

[11] Other features of the Islamophobia or 'unfounded hostility towards Islam' that according to the Runnymede Trust is becoming increasingly widespread are: a tendency to look at Islam as religion that does not have values in common with other cultures, is not affected by them and does not influence them; as the religion that is violent, aggressive, threatening, supportive of terrorism, and engaged in a clash of civilizations; as a political ideology, used for political or military advantage. It also argues that in this atmosphere criticisms made of 'the West' by Islam are rejected out of hand and hostility towards Islam is used to justify discriminatory practices towards Muslims and exclusion of Muslims from mainstream society (Runnymede Trust 1997).

[12] The key features of a moral panic according to the author of the term Stanley Cohen are: a strong concern 'over the behaviour of a certain group or category and the consequences which this behaviour presumably causes for the rest of society, an increased level of hostility towards that particular group implying a division between 'us' and 'them', a remarkable consensus between actors which usually hold widely divergent views (e.g. journalists, politicians, scientists), an exaggerated representation of the threats and a disproportionate reaction to them, and a certain volatility (1972).

also similarities. As Bousetta and Jacobs observe, paradoxically, the radicality of the jihadist discourse of bin Laden and his followers has stimulated a form of civic consciousnesses among Muslims (2006: 32-33). The key observation on which this study builds up is that, one may see in both analysed countries not only a development of a civic consciousness among certain segments of their Muslim populations, but also a construction of new type of identity - Muslim civicness - and a move from the politics of Muslim identity, largely based on the emphasis of 'otherness' to the politics of Muslim citizenship that increasingly stresses also elements of 'sameness'. This has been done by young Muslims inter alia by 'reversing the stigma' associated with Islam (Sayad 1991: 254-255) and 'positivisation of religion of their parents' (Babès 1997: 74) while participating in the public debates on Islam. The members of the new Muslim elites have been frequently joining these debates and skilfully challenging the dominant interpretative frameworks and some of the self-created myths and nightmares by strongly condemning any usage of violence in the name of Islam or by declaring their deep emotional attachment to their countries and other fellow citizens. One of the evidence of this attachment is their growing engagement with the wider civil society, which transgresses the ethnic and religious boundaries and replaces an inward-looking approach with the outward-looking one. With the help of their religion and a discourse on citizenship, which today is one of the major discourses of entitlement apart from the human rights discourse, they have been striving to influence the power structures in the countries in which they are living or to change the balance of power between the 'established' and the 'outsiders' (Elias & Scotson 1965) and at the same time reconnect with wider societies. While seeking space for their heritage and values in both the public and private sphere, they have been largely following the footsteps of other groups mobilizing around their identities and most notably ethnic minorities, women, gays and lesbians (Göle 2003: 812, Modood 2003: 102).

Before the aforementioned points will be developed further and the meaning of the terms 'citizenship' and 'identity' as used in the book will be clarified, one needs to draw a wider picture of the Muslim presence in Europe and research on it. The goal of this opening chapter is to locate this study within a wider context of scientific endeavour aiming at accounting for the transformations within Muslim populations in Europe, as

19

well as to elaborate on some of the most important instances of these transformations which are pertinent to the analysed issues. Thus, the review of existing work on the Muslim populations in Europe will be followed by analysis of the key changes within these populations.

1.1 OVERVIEW OF THE RESEARCH ON MUSLIMS IN EUROPE

Although a significant number of Muslims have been living in the countries of Western Europe for more than half a century their religious identity has not been academically recognized until very recently. For a long time they have almost exclusively been viewed in terms of secular labels such as nationality, language, ethnicity, political opinion or socioeconomic class, and their identities and loyalties have been considered to be almost exclusively tied up with one or a combination of these categories. Islam as a social issue emerged already during the recession in 1972-74, but first studies on Muslim experience in Europe had not appeared in the bookshops until a few years later (Hitchinson 1978, Nielsen 1979, Dassetto and Bastenier 1984). The reasons for this are rooted in a diversity of factors, among which the immigration policies of the national states and European Union, gradual changes within the Muslim communities themselves and a move from a sense of transience to one of permanence, have played the most important role. At the intellectual level a crucial role in changing researchers' perspective while looking at Islam played the publication of Edward Said's "Orientalism". Until Said's pioneering critique of the studies of Orient, orientalism was simply an academic label describing disciplines that studied 'Eastern' societies, histories and languages. Since then, it has come to denote an exercise in power/knowledge by which the 'non-Western' world is domesticated. With its book, Said has opened new areas of scientific inquiry and equipped the researchers of Islam with new analytical tools (Turner 1994a, Sayyid 1997, Zemni 2002).

With the residential permanence Muslim communities have become more vocal in articulating their needs and started to fight for their rights. The call for public recognition of their religious identities, made in recent years particularly strongly by the European-born and educated Muslims who refuse to practice their religion covertly have resulted not only in Islam gaining space within the public sphere but equally so in social, cultural, political and economic research. 1989, which saw two national affairs related to the Muslim presence in Europe, marks a turning point in the study of Islam in the EU. Both the Rushdie affair in Great Britain and the headscarf affair (affaire du foulard) in France resulted not only in politicising the Muslim presence in Europe, but also in attracting to it more systematic attention. This is also, one of the reasons why France and Britain are the countries where the studies on their Muslim communities are the most advanced. As Amiraux has rightly pointed out, the development of the study of Islam is to a certain extent contingent on the local situation (Amiraux 2001). Comparing German and French contexts, she has found remarkable differences with regard to both, the scientific and political attitudes towards Islam settled on their territories. Her research shows that while there is a plethora of knowledge about Islam in France, in Germany until very recently one could observe a quasi silence. These national differences in the scholarship on Islam can be explained among others by diverse histories of contact of European countries with Muslim societies[13] and the way how Islam is perceived by their political elites (as home or external issue).

In spite of the national differences in the scholarship on Islam, relating both, to its advancement and thematic focus, one may point out at the main subject areas that have been developed within this field across Europe so far. While mapping out these areas, a particular emphasis is paid to the research that has been carried out in Belgium and Britain, which are the main countries of interest of this study. It needs to be stressed, however, that this overview is not exhaustive and aims to delineate only the general thematic and conceptual frames of research on Islam in Europe[14].

1.1.1 RESEARCH ON MUSLIM INSTITUTIONAL DEVELOPMENT

One of the first areas which attracted considerable scientific attention within the scholarship on Islam in contemporary Europe was the research of institutional development within the Muslim communities. The process of the reunification of families that intensified in the 1970s had not only conservative influence on lifestyles within hitherto largely single-man Muslim communities in Europe, but resulted also in

---

[13] For instance, while France and Britain have a long history of colonial presence in the Muslim world Germany or Belgium lack such histories.

[14] For more elaborate overviews of the research on Islam in Europe see for example: Dassetto 1996, Bujis and Rath 2002 or Marechal et al. 2003.

establishment of large number of Muslim institutions varying from mosques, prayer halls, schools, halal butchers, religious radio stations, newspapers, right through to more or less successful political parties (e.g. Islamic Party of Britain or Parti de la Citoyenneté et Prospérité in Belgium). With the growing public visibility, the religion of immigrants was noticed also by social scientists. The first studies of Islam in Europe were mostly sociographic and had no or limited theoretical ambitions. They have consisted of descriptions of establishment of various Muslim communities and institutions and the responses of the governments to the new religion. With the exception of the study of Dassetto and Bastenier 'L'Islam Transplanté' (1984), which analysed in the systematic way the settlement of Muslims in Belgium, they were mostly based on a method of collecting heterogeneous information with little systematization.[15] The more recent studies on the institutional development, try not only to account for the rise of Muslim institutions in various countries (or cities and municipalities) but also to analyse how the receiving societies have created opportunities or impeded the development of such institutions (e.g. Rath *et al.* 2001 or Manço & Kanmaz 2005).

1.1.2 RESEARCH ON MUSLIM IDENTITY

The issue of religious identity constitutes another research area which has emerged, as soon as, it became clear that contrary to the popular expectations, the children of Muslim immigrants were not going to discard the religion of their parents but have continued to adhere to it. Several authors researching this problem have noticed that although religion is central to the self-definition of many members of the second and third generation, they perceive it differently than their parents. I shall elaborate in more details on these differences below, while here it suffices to point out that European-born Muslims, for example, unlike their parents, make a clear distinction between culture (ethnicity) and religion (Knott and Koher 1993, Cesari 1994, Jacobson 1997, Pędziwiatr 2003). In Britain for example, some of them 'use' Islam to question the legitimacy of certain South Asian ethnic customs and practices, which appear to be highly dysfunctional in the European context (e.g. cousin marriages popular among the South Asian Muslims - Knott

---

[15] Among the first studies of Islam in Britain one may point out the research on Muslim organisations in the country (Ally 1979), educational needs of young Muslims (Anwar 1988), settlement of Muslim immigrants (Nielsen 1984) or the study of Muslims in Birmingham (Joly 1987).

and Koher 1993, Jacobson 1997). This kind of 'positive reference' to Islam has been also indicated by several Belgian researchers (Kohen and Maréchal 1997, Ortmans 1996, Ouali 2000, Timmerman 1994, 1999).

One of the paradigms that has been advanced within this area is the *'between two cultures'* analysis. This perspective, rooted in assimilationist ideologies, sees Muslim young people as torn between the repressive traditional regimes of their parents and the more permissive freedoms of wider society (e.g. Watson 1977). This leads to 'culture clash' between Muslim parents and children, and to 'identity conflict' in trying to reconcile two opposing, and ultimately irreconcilable worldviews. The critics of this perspective stress the complexities of identity formation processes, possibility of cultural interaction and fusion, and the power relations that structure cultural hierarchies and conflict (e.g. Alexander 2000, Dwyer 2000 and Hopkins 2006). They propose to view ethnicity as only one axis of identity, which intersects with such factors as gender, class, sexuality, religion, locality, age and so on. The culture in this 'new ethnicity' approach is seen as part of a socially, historically and politically located struggle over meaning and identity (Hall 1991). Structures of power and inequality intersect and constrain subordinated identities, but do not wholly determine the forms they take. Identities become open ended, unpredictable and often contradictory in the ways they appear and are lived through.

Among the quantitative studies of different manifestations of religious identities of European Muslims the most significant include the one carried out by Tribalat (1995) in France, Modood and Berthoud (1997) in Britain, Lesthaeghe (2000) in Belgium and Phalet et al (2004) in the Netherlands. For example, the last study carried out between 1998 and 2002 by Karen Phalet et al. shows that religious identification is remarkably stable across generations and over time, while religious participation declines significantly in the younger generations, especially among the better qualified and the economically active, and it continues to decline after the terrorist attacks in USA on 11th September 2001. This research has also revealed that whereas a majority of Dutch Turks and Moroccans identifies strongly with Islam as a moral guide, cultural heritage and ethnic identity, only a minority actively participates in religious rituals and social life (ibid).

1.1.3 RESEARCH ON ISLAM IN THE POLITICAL SPHERE

The next research area that one can point out within the larger scholarship on Islam in Western Europe is research on Islam in the political sphere. The studies carried out within this area concern among others issues of the political participation of Muslims, formation of Muslim political organization or parties, political leadership, the recognition of Muslim organizations as dialogue partners of the state administration, and their participation in advisory and management structures. In contrast with the first studies on Islam in Europe that have had weak theoretical foundations, the studies carried out more recently possess firm conceptual frameworks. One of them is, for instance, a research of Geisser and Kelfaoui, examining how political parties in Marseille are courting Muslim voters (1998). Such studies are carried out both from the perspective of the Muslim populations, as well as from the angle of the host societies. For example, the politics of recognition of Islam, seen from the perspective of the autochthonous politicians was the subject of the study by Heckmann (1994) and by Manço and Kanmaz (2005).

In many European countries Muslims can now not only vote but also stand for local as well as national elections, hence their political participation has two dimensions. The latter dimension that is Muslim political leadership has been studied extensively especially in Britain where there are at the moment 4 Muslim MP and more than 220 councillors (e.g. Husband 1994 and Hussain 2004, 2006) of whom slightly above 60 are based in London. The experiences of local politics of the last group of people was in fact a subject of a doctoral dissertation (Purdam 1996). Although in Belgium the non-European immigrants have been granted the right to vote (but not to stand as a candidates) only recently (in February 2004), the Muslim political participation is also significant and well researched (e.g. Lambert 1999). Candidates with a Muslim background were elected in municipal election already in the 1980s. However, the real breakthrough with regards to Muslim political participation in the country came during the 2000 elections when in Brussels region only, 87 people of Muslim origin (77 of Moroccan and 10 of Turkish origin, including 23 women)[16] became local councillors (out

---

[16] The main reasons behind the differences in number of people of Moroccan and Turkish origin involved in politics are explained in the chapter III.

total number of 653 councillors) (Jacobs et al. 2002). In the communal elections in October 2006 the Muslim political representation in Brussels further increased to 94 councillors of Moroccan origin and 20 of Turkish origin (Le Soir 10.10.2006).[17] Fennema and Tillie (1999) on the basis of their research in Amsterdam formulated a thesis of a correlation between political participation and levels of social capital of ethnic minorities, that was later tested (on the example of Brussels) by Swyngedouw et al. (2002). The Belgian researchers have not found evidence that would uphold the thesis of Fennema and Tillie. In fact they have discovered that while the Turks are more active in associational life than the Moroccans, it is the latter group that is more politically involved. Thus their findings added strength to the theoretical argument that a distinction should be made between 'ethnic' social capital (embedded in ethnic associations) and cross-cultural social capital (embedded in mixed and more mainstream organisations).

In all European countries the authorities have sought to establish channels of communications with representatives of the Muslim populations. In some countries they were directly involved in the creation of the Muslim representative bodies (e.g. France or Belgium), while in other they have tacitly supported some of the existing Muslim organisations hoping that they would establish themselves as 'a voice' of all the Muslims in the country (e.g. Britain or the Netherlands). These endeavours from the part of the government as well as the Muslims have been analysed on the European level among others by Hussain (2003) and Pędziwiatr (2005). The efforts of one of the Muslim representative organisations in Britain, that is of Muslim Council of Britain to influence the foreign policy of the British government was a subject of the MPhil thesis (Radcliffe 2003), whereas its efforts to create Muslim public sphere and to influence the internal policies of the State was analysed by Pędziwiatr (2007a). The creation of the Executive of Muslims of Belgium (Fr. *Exécutif des Musulmans de Belgique),* as a representative organization of Muslims in Belgium (reported for example by Monique Renaerts - 1999) gave an incentive to significant mobilization within the Muslim population that was analysed by Hassan Bousetta. The main conclusion of his study grounded in the theory of social movements is that traditional understanding of ethnic politics is biased by an

---

[17] Although a small minority there are also amongst the people of Turkish origin in Belgium followers of the Syrian Orthodox Church and Assyrian Church of the East, so the actual Muslim political representation might be slightly smaller.

overemphasis on institutional channels of political demands and by an underspecification of internal differentiation within immigrant ethnic communities at both the level of strategy and of identity (Bousetta 2000). The same theoretical approach was applied to the study of Muslim political participation in several European countries by Fetzer and Soper who came to the conclusion that *"Muslim groups have been politically ineffective because they lack the resources necessary to bargain effectively with the state"* (2004: 8).

1.1.4 RESEARCH ON MUSLIM LEADERSHIP

The political mobilisation within Muslim populations and the emergence of Muslim political actors has also intensified research into religious leadership. This problematics was explored in depth on the examples from Belgium and from the wider Europe by Felice Dassetto (1996). One of the most popular approaches in studying religious leadership within the Muslim populations has been the research on different Muslim movements and organisations active in Europe (Pedersen 1999). To this genre belong for example research on Tablighi Jama'at in Belgium (Dassetto 1998), France (Khedimellah 2001) or Britain (King 1994) and worldwide (Sikand 2002), as well as studies on Jammat-t-Islami in the United Kingdom (Andrews 1993), or on Ikhwan Muslimun in France and in wider Europe (Ternisien 2005, Maréchal 2008).

One of the key developments in the area of the religious leadership in Europe in recent years analysed by students of Islam has been the emergence of the 'new religious leaders' who challenge the monopoly of religious power earlier enjoyed by classically trained religious scholars (*ulama*) (Roy 1994: 4, Dassetto 1996: 158, Lewis 2002, Werbner 2002, McLoughlin 2005). This has taken place in the context of destabilization of religious hierarchies resulted among others from the invention of electronic mass media (Piscatori 2000: 86). As Mandeville points out, a growing number of lay Muslims, who have started to read Qur'an and other religious scriptures in search for answers to questions that bother them, are bridging the knowledge gap which used to divide them from ulama (2002: 85). The electronic revolution has also resulted in the emergence of such truly global Muslim leaders as for example shaykh al-Qaradawi (Ternisien 2005, Pędziwiatr 2006c). The new religious leadership is characterized above all by its familiarity with the problems of youngsters from immigrant families and by and lack of official links with foreign agencies or governments (Mohsen-Finan 2002). It is not so much the key sources of Islamic authority (knowledge, actions, institutions and charisma) that distinguish them from traditional leaders, (although there are some differences), but above all the way how they are using their authority. The preaching of the traditional leaders is usually limited to the specific ethnic communities while this of the new leaders aims beyond ethnic boundaries (Pędziwiatr 2005: 216).

In recent years the great deal of attention has been paid in this field especially to the quality of the religious leadership. This issue came to the prominence especially after the terrorist attack in London on 7 July 2005, when several academics pointed at the imported imams and religious teachers not capable of explaining to the youth the contexts of the Qur'anic verses referring to the usage of violence, as one of causes of religious radicalisation of European Muslim youth (Abbas 2005, Sardar 2005). The character of religious training and changing social roles of *ulama* in Britain has been investigated among others by Philip Lewis (2006) and Sophie Gilliat-Ray (2006). In Belgium the issue of the quality of the Muslim religious leadership was addressed most comprehensively in two recent reports commissioned by the King Baudouin Foundation (see: El Battiui et al. 2004 and Husson 2006).

1.1.5 RESEARCH ON ISLAM IN THE EDUCATIONAL SPHERE

Yet another important area of research is Islam in the educational sphere. The central issue here is the transfer of knowledge about Islam and values (including the religious ones) to the young generation. While most of the studies in this area focus on one country one may also find amongst them multinational comparisons (e.g. Mohr compared the Islamic curricula in Germany and Austria - 2002). The provision for Islamic training and education and the content of this provision was researched by numerous authors in Belgium (e.g. Dassetto & Bastanier 1987), as well as in Britain (e.g. Anwar 1988). The teaching of Islam was introduced to the school curricula in Belgium already in 1978. Today there are more than 850 primary and secondary schools that organize courses of Islam for more than 30 000 pupils (Maréchal 2002). The role and status of Islamic teachers leading these courses, who are paid their salaries by the state, was examined among others by Monique Renaerts (1998). The issue of Muslim schools (at the moment

2 of which neither receives financial support from the state) has been discussed among others in the newsletter of the Centre Bruxellois d'Action Interculturelle (December 2005). In Britain there is no place for religious instruction of children in their own faith in the state schools. In such schools the religious education has been 'multifaith' for more than 3 decades. Out of more than 100 Muslim schools there are only 5 that receive public founding. The main attention of researchers has gone to the content and the quality of Islamic provision in the Qur'anic schools attended by the Muslim pupils after their school hours (e.g. Lewis 1994).

1.1.6 RESEARCH ON THE LEGAL ASPECTS OF ISLAM IN EUROPE

The legal aspects of the emergence of the significant Muslim communities in Western Europe were the subject of research of numerous lawyers and social scientists. While some of them focused on the specific aspects of the legal recognition of practices rooted in religion or religious traditions, others discussed such relatively abstract issues as human right (e.g. Poulter 1986), freedom of religion (e.g. Shadid and van Koningsveld 1995) or the neutrality of the state (e.g. Boender 2001,). The most numerous studies within this area concern the implementation of Islamic family law, and especially matters of marriage and divorce (e.g. Foblets 1996, Ferrari & Bradney 2000, Ferrari 2003). In Great Britain, as a result of the 'Rushdie Affair' a great deal of attention was devoted to the issue of freedom of speech and the law against blasphemy (CRE 1989). In Belgium, on the other hand, the main focus of the research in this area went to the formal recognition of Islam as one of the religions of the country (Panafit 1999) and the legal aspects of the subsidizing by the state of the recognized religions (Blaise & de Coorebyter 1993, Christians 1996, Husson 2000). Here a new area that has been developing should be mentioned, namely the research on the European market of *fatwas* and the application of the Islamic law to the minority situation of Muslims in the West, known also as research on the minority *fiqh*. One of the institutions that have been working towards development of such a fiqh is the European Council for Fatwa and Research[18] set up in 1997 by shaykh Yusuf al-Qaradawi. Its work has been critically analysed among others by Malik (2003), Caeiro (2003, 2006) and Ternisien (2005).

---

[18] More information about the organisation can be found on http://www.e-cfr.org (accessed 12.05.2008)

1.1.7 RESEARCH ON MUSLIM ENTREPRENEURSHIP AND RADICALISM

Among the less developed areas of scientific inquiry is research on Muslim entrepreneurship and economic institutions based on Muslim principles and scholarship on the Muslim radicalism. The first type of research has developed together with the growth of the size of the market of products destined to Muslims clients ranging from food and books through financial instruments to clothes. This research usually revolves around such establishments as slaughterhouses, Muslim libraries and publishing houses, financial institutions based on an interest-free principle (lariba banking), or Muslim unions and business associations (Kloosterman, van der Leun & Rath 1997, 1998). The new areas within the larger field of scientific inquiry into the Muslim economy in Europe include studies on the consumption of halal meat and other halal food products (Bergeaud-Blackler 2004, 2007, Bonne and Verbeke 2006), consumption of Muslim media (Ahmed S.T. 2003, El Asri 2006) Islamic banking in Europe (Matthews and Tlemsani 2004, Housby 2006) and Muslim clothing (Shadid & Koningsveld 2005, Haenni 2005).

The students of European Islam have for many years not paid much attention to the issues of Muslim radicalism for numerous reasons, among which the economic, methodological and ethical seem the most important ones. Having limited resources at their disposal they concentrated on the visible Islam, the Islam of the majority, which was relatively easily accessible and yet vastly under-researched. Secondly, as Dassetto notices, social science, in respect of its methods and its deontological principles, cannot conduct research in areas which almost by definition remain opaque to the questioning of a scientist. Thus, the methodological constraints made such an investigation a very difficult one. Thirdly, the students of Islam tended to turn a blind eye to the marginal phenomenon of radical Islam, since they were afraid that their work might be grist to the mill of public opinion or to policy positions hostile to immigration, which might use Islamophobia to support xenophobia (Dassetto 2003: 494).

In spite of the above mentioned constraints there was some academic endeavour trying to account for this phenomenon in the past (Kepel 1994, Werbner 1994, Grignard 1997, Roy 1999) and there is a great deal of interest in this area at present (e.g. Kapel

2002, Roy 2004, Coolsaet 2005). As a result of GIA attacks in France, the attacks on the Pentagon and the World Trade Center and other acts of violence committed in the name of Islam in Europe and elsewhere the research on Muslim groups that do not reject violence as means to achieve their goals has been now one of the fastest growing ones.[19] This strongly security oriented research concentrates mainly on monitoring different tendencies and movements within Western Islam (AVID 2002, 2004, Gringard 2006, Verheyden 2006) and rarely contributes to the scientific understanding of the mechanisms of religious radicalisation. One of the rare empirical studies which tries to test the existing knowledge about the Muslim Far Right in Europe with the reality, is the study of al-Muhajiroun (ar. Emigrants) by Quintan Wiktorowicz (2005). The American social scientist analysing the process of radicalisation of the Muslism in Europe from the perspective of theory of social movements has pointed out inter alia that in order to explain the process of religious radicalisation one needs to take into account not only depravation and frustration but also mobilization of resources, decision-making and framing processes. One of the drawbacks of the study is that social processes such as framing or socialization are mainly analysed from the social movement organization's (SMO's) perspective. As Dépelteau suggests the application of the concepts which do not come from the social movement theory – such as for example the one of habitus, could be very useful to see how the family, school, media, etc. influence the choices of Islamist recruits (2006).

1.1.8 RESEARCH ON ISLAM AND CITIZENSHIP

Finally, in recent years there has been a growing number of studies that look at the Muslim populations from the point of view of differently defined concept of citizenship. The vast majority of them deal with legal and political notions of citizenship[20]. One of the most important investigations in this field was carried out by Hassan Bousetta, who analysed the significance of citizenship frameworks in shaping the political opportunities

---

[19] For an overview of different sociological explanations of radicalization within the Muslim populations in Europe see for example Dassetto 2003: 489-530 or Pędziwiatr 2006g. Some of the most often mentioned causes of the 7/7 London bombing included for example: lack of intellectual leadership among Muslims in the country, weak political leadership, theological vacuum and Islamic 'cultural black hole' (Abbas 2005, Sardar 2005, Pędziwiatr 2005b).

[20] For extensive overview of the work that problematize the notion of citizenship in the context of migration studies see Vuddamalay 2002.

and constraints of Moroccans in France and the Netherlands (1997). He later enlarged his field of analysis to Belgium and using the Bourdieusian notion of field of integration, showed that the differences invoked by the classical models of integration and citizenship developed by authors such as Castles (1994) are largely overplayed. He pointed out that locally there are similar mechanisms of internal differentiation between actors which lead to a situation where only a minority of successful collective actors make a breakthrough in local policy communities while the general performance of the political mobilisation of Moroccans in three countries remains marginal and mainly introverted (2000a). The political notion of citizenship has been also comparatively investigated with reference to the Muslim populations by Dirk Jacobs who analysed the parliamentary debates on voting right for allochthons[21] in the Netherlands and Belgium explaining how the former country has managed to reach a consensus on the enfranchisement, which stimulated the active participation of immigrant minorities, while the latter one had been debating the question for more than two decades with very difficult step forwards. One of Jacobs's conclusions that is pertinent to this research is that we can observe the shift in the traditional conception of citizenship in both countries whereby nationality could not anymore be taken as an absolute requirement for local political rights and participation. More recently both researchers have noticed that the underdevelopment of a more inclusive citizenship and a overarching Belgian vision of multiculturalism is largely prevented by the multinational character of the country and the complex decision-making procedures devised to pacify the tensions between the two dominant communities. As a matter of consequence, if the Flemings and the francophones cannot reach a consensus in some issue (e.g. wearing a hijab by Muslim girls at school - Flemings are largely for, while the francophones influenced by France are mostly against) non-decision becomes the most likely perspective (Bousetta and Jacobson 2006: 28). Yet another important

---

[21] *Allochthon* – (In Dutch – allochtoon, plural: allochtonen) is an English version of the Dutch word (derived from Greek *allo-* other, and *khthon* - earth/land) literally meaning "originating from another country". The opposite of the *allochthon* is autochthon (derived from Greek auto-self) literally meaning "originating from this country". The term 'allochthon' referring to immigrants and their descendant is particularly popular in the Netherlands and Dutch-speaking Belgium. Here, however, it is worth mentioning that the category is not used by all the students of migrations in Belgium. Some of the scholars of migratory processes (e.g. Marco Martiniello) tend to refrain from using the term pointing out that today's autochthones are often former allochthons. It is with this point in mind that the category is being used in the research.

study dealing with the political notion of citizenship demonstrates the differences in the claims-making by Muslims in Britain and the Netherlands (Statham et al 2005).

The studies analyzing the relationships between social aspects of citizenship and Islam are very rare. One of them, based on the interviews with almost 1000 young Dutch Turks, Moroccans and autochthons was carried out in 2000 by Entzinger in Rotterdam. The Dutch researcher discovered that although young Muslims do not differ greatly from their non-Muslim compatriots in terms of tolerating signs of religious belonging in the public sphere or strength of the local identity, there are significant difference between the two groups as far as importance of religion in the public sphere, stand in the ethical issues and most importantly, national identity are concerned. The study has also found out that only 3% of Dutch Turks and 7% of Dutch Moroccans perceive themselves as Dutch, while 16 per cent of the first group and 22 per cent of the latter one feels equally Turkish or Moroccan and Dutch. Hence its author concludes that young Dutch Muslims are characterized by a very 'thin vision of citizenship' (Entzinger 2003: 108). Another study of social aspects of citizenship, this time a qualitative one, based on 35 in-depth interviews was carried out in France in the years 1999 – 2000 by Nancy Venel.[22] Its results were later published by the author in the book entitled "Musulmans et citoyens". "Muslims and citizens" explores the different ways of conceiving citizenship, by young French people of Maghrebian origin and proposes to divide them into four groups: the inheritors (*les héritiers*), the conciliators (*les accommodateurs*) the contractors (*les contractants*), and the neo-ethnics (*les néocommunautaires*) (Venel 2004). In Britain two important books dealing with the subjective aspects of citizenship, amongst other issues, were published by the Islamic Foundation in Leicester. "British Muslims: Loyalty and Belonging" (Seddon et al. 2003) and "British Muslims Between Assimilation and Segregation" (Seddon et al. 2004) are meant though not to provide a systematic analysis of how Muslims in Britain perceive citizenship, but rather to open up debate on rights and duties of Muslims as British citizens. Their Muslim contributors discuss not only Islamic perspectives on loyalty and belonging but also Muslim's socio-economic position, their involvement in politics and such obstacles to citizenship as racism or Islamophobia. The

---

[22] The research of Venel, alike this one, rely on the earlier elaborations of ordinary or banal representations of citizenship carried out especially by Sophie Duchesne (1997, 2003).

growth of anti-Muslim sentiment as a result of, inter alia, the 'vilification by the media' has been also viewed as one of the key drawbacks in attaining full citizenship by Muslims in the report entitled 'British Muslims' Expectations of the Government' (Ameli and Merali 2004).

So far, there have not been any studies in Belgium that would deliberately explore the social aspects of citizenship and Islam, and only two studies (qualitative and quantitative one) that have touched upon the subjective aspects of citizenship and immigrant populations. One of them analyzes with the aid of the subjective notion of citizenship the strategies of actions among immigrants (Hubert 1999), while the second one, based on large dataset (representative sample of 1380 people) examines social representations of citizenship among the Turks, Moroccans and working-class Belgians living in Brussels (Phalet and Swyngedouw 2002). The second research which is more pertinent to this investigation finds out inter alia that the social representation of citizenship of Belgian Turks and Moroccans is characterised by 'double absence' elaborated at length in the writings of Abdelmalek Sayad (1999). Their belonging to the distant Turkish or Moroccan nations lacks the participatory dimension, whereas their membership in the Belgian nation lacks the identitarian features. The authors conclude by noting that the multiplicity is a key feature of minority perspectives on citizenship, so that active participation in the national context of residence is complemented by enduring ethnoreligious identification in the national context of origin (Phalet and Swyngedouw 2002). The absence of research on the subjective aspects of what it means to be a Muslim citizen, that this book aims to address, was expressed among others by Daniele Joly and Karima Imtiaz (2002: 131) or Felice Dassetto (2005: 128).

1.1.9 RESEARCH ON ISLAM IN BRUSSELS AND LONDON
Before we conclude this overview it is important yet to mention the research that focuses on Muslims living in one of the two urban centres, Brussels or London, which set our geographical boundaries. The quick glance on the existing literature is enough to notice significant disparities between the scholarship on Muslims in the two cities. While there are numerous studies problematising the Islamic identity of the young Londoners (Ameli 2002, Glynn 2002, Alexander 2000, Jacobson 1997, Bauman 1996 - to name just a few)

or analysing developments within different Muslim communities in the city (e.g. Eade 1989, 2002, Berns McGown 1999, Smith 2000) there is relatively little research on Islam in Brussels.[23] If the existing studies do take into account the religious dimension of the identities of inhabitants of Brussels (e.g. Rea 2001, Jacobs 2004) they very rarely problematise it. The studies devoted to Islam in Brussels concern among others such issues as: the religiosity of the men of the second generation (Manço and Manço 2000), the religiosity of the city's adolescents (Abenchikar 1993), the notions of freedom and individuality among young Muslim women (Kohnen and Maréchal 1997), the celebrations and significance of the *Eid ul-Adha* (Hennart and Dassetto 1997), the 'hijabofobia' (Ben Mohammed 2000) or the Muslim institutional completeness of the district of Molenbeek (Verhoeven 1997). Among the new areas of sociological inquiry into the Islam in Brussels (or in Brussels among others) that have been recently developed are studies on the secularisation processes among Belgian Muslims by Nadia Fadil, the social role of mosques by Maryam Kanmaz, the visibility of Islam in the public sphere by Corinne Torrekens, and the cultural identity of European Muslims by Farid el Asri. Despite the growing strength of the Muslim civil society in both cities, reinvigorated by young Muslim activists, the issues of relations between active social citizenship and Islam have not been addressed in the literature.

To sum up this short overview of the research on Muslims in Europe it needs to be said that there is no dominant paradigm in this field. On the contrary there are a variety of different research approaches which are in constant competition with each other. The body of the research knowledge is divided by disciplinary, national, and theoretical boundaries. In spite of a significant number of books on Islam in Europe (usually compiled of essays on country studies by different authors – with the exceptions of monographs of Nielsen 1992 and Dassetto 1996), there are very few fully-fledged international comparisons, that is studies that empirically investigate similar phenomena in different countries on the basis of one and the same research design. The national context has remained the dominant research framework. The existing comparisons cover

---

[23] Among the reasons why the scholarship on Islam in Brussels (as well as in larger Belgium) is less developed than the one on Islam in London (or in Britain) are: weak orientalist tradition in Belgium (departments of Islamic studies marginal), no direct contact with the Islamic world during the colonial period and no scientific programmes financed by the state that would aim at improving the understanding of the Muslim reality in the country (Dassetto 2007).

34

such topics as conversion (Allievi 1999), the establishment of Muslim organisations (Doomernik 1991), the social responses to the establishment of Muslim institutions (Rath et al. 1991, Waardenburg 1991), religious education (Mohr 2002a), discourse of the Muslim individuals and organisations active in the European public sphere (Lathion 2003) and privatization of religion (Tietze 2002).

1.2 FROM THE ISLAM OF IMMIGRANTS TO THE ISLAM OF CITIZENS

Having briefly reviewed the current scholarship on Muslim populations in Europe and having shown the gaps in it that this study hopes to at least partially fulfil, it is time to point out at the key transformations that have taken place within Islam in this part of the world in recent years. Islam which was brought to Western Europe[24] by immigrants from almost all over of the Muslim world, thus contributing to one of the most important religious changes in this part of the continent since the Reformation (Lewis 2005) and significantly increasing its cultural diversity, is a faith which is very closely linked with the allochthons' ethnicity, private sphere of life and one that possess many features of a so-called 'low Islam'. The faith of their children who were born or spend their formative years in Europe is, on the other hand, characterized by weakening ties with the ethnic background of their parents. It is also increasingly becoming a matter of public sphere and acquiring a growing number of features of a 'high Islam'. I shall briefly elaborate on these differences between Islam of immigrants and Islam of citizens, and thus shed some light on the main processes within a wider transition from the 'transplanted' to the 'implanted' Islam to use the poetics of Felice Dassetto (2004), since they are crucial to the analysed phenomenon of active social citizenship of the young Muslims in Brussels and London.

1.2.1 IMMIGRANTS AND CITIZENS

First of all, it is the faithful of the two types of Islam that needs to be portrayed, that is those who had spent their formative years outside the continent, and brought Islam to

---

[24] Here it needs to be reminded that the presence of Islam in this part of the continent is not completely new phenomenon as Muslims ruled in Sicily (827-1091) and on Iberian Peninsula (711-1492) and have been living in (with interruptions) and travelling throughout the geographical region practically since the beginning of historical Islam itself (see for example Lapidus 1988: 378 – 389 or Fletcher 1998)

Western Europe as part of their 'cultural luggage', and their children whose process of socialization took place in the non-Muslim countries. Several researchers have shown that despite the passage of time, the Muslim immigrants like many other immigrants who left their home countries to improve their living conditions, do not fully discard the prospect of return. Even if they do not manage to turn this will into reality during their lifetime, many of them still manages to 'realize it' after their deaths, as the practice of sending deceased abroad among the Muslim populations in Europe although weakening is still observable. As Mohammed Anwar points out the plan of return to enjoy the fruits of the labour back home, or 'the myth of return', fulfils several social functions, among which the economic and cultural ones seem to be the most important. The 'mythologization of return' ensures the immigrants in their willingness to endure hardship in work and living conditions in order to generate as much savings as possible that could be later invested back home or send in the form of remittances to the members of their families who did not manage to migrate. It also legitimises continued adherence to the norms and values of their home countries and condemns assimilation into the culture of the host society (1979). Thus the immigrants who cherish the hope of return are less inclined to take actions in order to integrate with their new societies than those who have completely abandoned this hope. The first group of immigrants probably more than the second one is also characterized by the phenomenon described by the Algerian student of migrations Abdelmalek Sayad as 'la double absence' (Sayad 1999). Analysing the Maghrebian migration to France at the point of their departure and arrival[25], which is one of his key contributions to migration studies, Sayad noticed that immigrants neither fully belong to the receiving society, nor to the sending one which they have left. The immigrant, as he points out, is "*atopos, a quaint hybrid devoid of place, displaced, in the twofold sense of incongruous and inopportune, trapped in that 'mongrel' sector of social space betwixt and between social being and nonbeing*" (Sayad 1984, 1988). S/he is "*neither citizen nor foreigner, neither on the side of the Same, nor on that of the Other, s/he exists only by default in the sending community and by excess in the receiving*

---

[25] Sayad famously emphasized that the sociology of migration must start, not from the receiving society, but from the structure and contradictions of the sending communities or that the sociology of immigration cannot do without the sociology of emigration. Thus, one may say that he was promoting transnational approach to migration before it became institutionalized in the form of the research programmes such as for example The Transnational Communities Programme at the University of Oxford.

society, and s/he generates recurrent recrimination and resentment in both" (ibid). The key dilemma of immigrants can be summed up in the questions, 'how to be here (abroad) while at the same time mentally being there (in the home country)?' and 'how to be there, while physically being here?'. Out-of-place in the two social systems which define their (non)existence, the migrants force us, as Pierre Bourdieu and Loic Wacquant rightly point out, "*through the obdurate social vexation and mental embarrassment they cause, to rethink root and branch the question of the legitimate foundations of citizenship and of the relationship between citizen, state and nation*" (2000). I believe that even more bluntly the foundations of citizenship are being questioned by the children of immigrants, those who were born or have been living in Europe since very early age and yet they have been perceived by the majority groups as the others, or to use the words of George Simmel, as those who "*come today and stay tomorrow*" (1971: 143). The only problem is that the offspring of Muslim immigrants did not come to Europe today, but have been living on the continent for more than 20, 30 and sometimes even 40 years.

In contrast to their parents, children of the Muslim immigrants do not think about moving to their parents' countries of origin. Their usual answer to the calls of the European Far Right parties 'to go back home' is 'this is our home'. Their geographical contact[26] with Turkey or Morocco, to mention only the countries of origin of the largest Muslim groups in Europe, is usually limited to short holiday visits. As the research and this book demonstrate, even if the Muslim citizens in some of the countries might not identify strongly with the nation-states within which they are living (e.g. the Netherlands – Entzinger 2003: 108) they are frequently characterized by firm local identifications (e.g. Babès 1997: 165, Tietze 2002, Entzinger 2003: 108). They feel strong attachment to certain districts of their cities or to the whole cities and happily describe themselves as Londoners, Berliners, Parisians, etc. Their local identities bear not only many cultural marks, as they often speak European languages with strong local accents, but also participatory ones, as it is not uncommon to see them getting involved in projects of the local civil societies. While they often lack sufficient cultural capital to feel at ease in their

---

[26] I use the category of 'geographical contact' so as not to confuse it with other channels of communication through which the Muslim immigrants, as well as, Muslim citizens keep themselves informed about the situations in different parts of the Muslim world. This translocal politcs is analysed in depth by Peter Mandaville in his 'Transnational Muslim Politics: Reimaging the Umma' (2004).

parent's countries of origin, they possess numerous tools that enable them to get involved much more fully than their parents in the European public spheres. Speaking and writing skills, basic working knowledge of the social and political systems, skills in accessing and processing information, and interpreting political talk are only some of the tools that enable citizens to make use of their rights. These 'tools' are part of the civic skills that a great majority of poorly educated Muslims immigrants (with exception of minority of business people and professionals) who lived their formative periods outside Europe very often lack. Those born in Europe or who arrived in their early childhood, on the other hand, even if they have not managed to gain substantial amounts of cultural capital in the form of educational qualifications (institutionalised cultural capital), they still posses much wider knowledge than their parents of the mechanisms through which the European societies work (embodied cultural capital[27]), acquired during the process of socialization. The members of the new Muslim brokers on which this study focuses, posses in fact not only substantial amounts of the embodied cultural capital, but also the institutional form of it, as the majority of persons interviewed finished universities and sometimes very prestigious ones.

1.2.2 RELIGION AND ETHNICITY

Having pointed out the main differences between the Muslim immigrants and the Muslim citizens, it is time to present the key features of their religiosity. As it was mentioned above, one of the attributes of Islam as it is practiced by the immigrants is its profound ethnicisation. For the vast majority of Muslims who spent formative years outside Europe religion is inseparably linked with ethnicity. To be a Moroccan, Turk, Pakistani or Bangladeshi hence *ex definitione* means for them that one is a Muslim[28]. Thus, Islam of immigrants has been functioning largely within the ethnic symbolic boundaries. By

---

[27] Both terms are used in the sense given them by Pierre Bourdieu (1986) that is as *"long-lasting dispositions of the mind and body; individual's 'culture' or 'cultivation' assimilated or acquired over a long period"* (embodied cultural capital p. 243-245), and as *"educational qualifications"* (institutionalised cultural capital p. 248).
[28] Here it has to stressed that being a Muslim does not necessarily imply that a certain person is a devout believer – different ways of being a Muslim are elaborated in the third chapter.

attaching religious meaning to certain ethnic practices, Islam has been sacralizing[29] ethnicity, giving these practices additional importance. For example, by proclaiming such South Asian marriage customs like dowry and wearing of regional dress to the mosque to be Islamic, the Muslim immigrants in Leeds researched by Ron Geaves have been bolstering their ethnic identity (Geaves 1995: 13). Religion has been not only protecting ethnic practices from change but also if necessary, legitimising the changes that have already taken place[30] (Pędziwiatr 2003).

A crucial role in reinforcing ethnic boundaries have been playing also religious institutions, and amongst them mosques. As a symbolic representation of 'the land of Islam' in Europe, they have also been to a great extent representation of the immigrants' countries of origin. Like other religious institutions functioning within immigrant groups, mosques perform amongst Muslims in Europe two main functions: integrating - they have been *"assuring the group of the ability to sustain itself under the new conditions"* - and expressive - they have been *"easing living together with 'others'"* (Kubiak 1982: 49). They serve as a refuge for the immigrants from the receiving societies and as a focal point for the recollection of a personal and corporate identity that is rooted in their countries of origin. This recollection has been facilitated by the recruitment of imams from the same area from where the particular Muslim community originated. Similarly to Italian Catholic congregations in the USA as analysed by Andrew Greeley (1972: 90), Moroccan, Turkish, Pakistani or other mosques are thus community centres that help members preserve their sense of roots. Not only the religious but also the social life of different Muslim groups revolve around their mosques. This is because European mosques are not merely places of worship, but to much greater extent than in *Dar al Islam*, also places of social gatherings. The fact that the vast networks of Muslim organizations have been built along the ethnic lines is yet another aspect of ehnicisation of Islam of immigrants.

Although the relationship between ethnicity and religion in the Islam of citizens does not disappear, it significantly weakens. Muslims born in Europe easily distinguish

---

[29] By 'sacralisation' it is meant after Hans Mol *"the process by means of which man has pre-eminently safeguarded and reinforced this complex of orderly interpretations of reality, rules, and legitimations"* (Mol 1976: 15)

[30] This role of religion in reinforcing ethnic boundaries have been also noticed by researchers studying non-Muslim immigrant communities (See Marzec 1998 or Rutledge 1985).

between the realm of religion and the one of ethnicity. They sometimes call upon religion to question the legitimacy of certain ethnic customs and practices, which appear to be dysfunctional in the European social environment, and with its help try to reshape them so as they become more compatible with the surrounding reality.[31] Thus, the Islam of citizens functions not only within the symbolic boundaries of specific ethnic communities, but also beyond these boundaries. It draws its own symbolic boundaries which are the basis of the new forms of self-descriptions alternative to ethnic identity. As numerous studies have shown, the religious identification amongst the second and third generations seem to be more widespread than the ethnic one (e.g. Cesari 1994, Modood and Berthoud 1997, Peach and Vertovec 1997). Why has 'a Muslim' taken the place of 'a dead beur'[32] - as Xavier Ternisien puts it (2005a)? There is no room here to account at length for possible explanations, so I shall just refrain to mentioning the ones provided by the prominent Belgian and the British scholar. According to the anthropologist Eugeen Roosens religious identification is subsuming the ethnic (and the class one) because Islamic membership is 'more prestigious' than the ethnic one. The author of "Creating ethnicity" sees the sources for it in the fact that *"Islam is still a world power, whereas the Turkish or Moroccan proletariat are not. Thus, emphasizing Islamic membership becomes a means of social promotion for immigrant workers and their families"* (1989: 145). He also aptly notices that *"At present-day* (that is at the end of the 80s in Belgium – KP) *Turks and Moroccans are voiceless because they have no muscle"* and adds that *"ironically, claims must be formulated by people who are already equals in some way and who have power"* (1989: 154). One would like to add to this, that claims do not have to be made necessarily by people who have power, as this study is going to demonstrate, but by people who have some means of attaining power.

A different explanation proposes Jessica Jacobson, who argues that a beur looses its battle with a Muslims or that the ethnic identity is subsumed by the religious one, because the last one is firstly more universal. Claiming to be a part of the world-wide Muslim community gives the offspring of the Muslim immigrants an opportunity to

---

[31] This has been often done by young Muslim women who strive to redefine the role of woman within the highly patriarchal Muslim communities (Pędziwiatr 2006).
[32] A French slang term for a descendant of immigrants of North African origin living in France, Belgium or Spain. The word is a reversal of the word "Arab".

belong not only to the community that is larger than the ethnic minority to which they belong, but also bigger than the surrounding them majority. Thus, it offers the possibility of a wider world in which to live (Jacobson 1997b). The membership in the Muslim ummah, which is an important aspect of self-definition for European-born Muslims is thus more 'rewarding', to use Barth's (1969) category, than belonging merely to the ethnic minority. At the same time, the reference to the religious identity allows a person who bears various marks of identity to unite all of them in one. Jacobson argues also that Islam is a more significant source of identity for the British-born Pakistanis than ethnicity because it delineates very clearly the boundary between them and the rest of society and thus, it enables them to easily locate themselves within a wider social milieu, whereas the ethnic boundaries have lost their lucidity and ability to generate social distance between the ethnic minority and the majority (Jacobson 1997a: 127).

1.2.3 PLACE OF RELIGION

As it was mentioned above yet another feature of 'transplanted Islam' is its limitation to the private sphere. Although, the 'public visibility' of Islam has been steadily growing since the petrol crisis of the 1970s, and acceleration of the processes of family reunification that significantly widened the scope of immigrants interactions with the receiving societies, for the majority of Muslims situated in the lowest social strata of European societies the natural place of religion was home. They did not openly claim the recognition of their religion in the public sphere, being quite comfortable with the freedoms that European democracies had to offer them. The formal recognition of Islam in Belgium in 1974 as a faith of its citizens, that will be elaborated below, was for example not a consequence of the social mobilization of the Muslim immigrants, but a result of the diplomatic negotiations in the centre of which there was an issue of the oil supply for the country (Panafit 1997).[33] The growing visibility of Islam until the end of the 80s was an outcome of the international events such as Iranian revolution or the war between Iran and Iraq and national ones such as openings of new mosques. Although

---

[33] For this reason Panafit has pointed out that at this period (the 1970s) one had to do in Belgium with 'Islam without Muslims' (2003: 60)

41

they were rarely purposed-build edifices[34] (usually opened in the converted houses, warehouses, parkings etc.), from the very beginning they have met with a great deal of contention (e.g. Karakasoglu and Nonneman 1997 or Cesari 2005[35]). Thus, the Islam of immigrants had its public face mainly due to more or less distinguishable places of Muslim worship.

Islam has become a permanent element of public debates and fully entered into the public sphere only from the end of the 1980s, which saw the outbreak of two affairs, Rushdie's and hijab affair. At this time the Muslim populations in Europe consisted already of a substantial number of members who were socialized in Europe and began to ask for the rights that were already in possession of other religious groups also for their own faith. In France, young Muslim women began to call for the permission to wear hijab at school, as the Jewish pupils were allowed to wear kippahs. In Great Britain, Muslims demanded so as the law on blasphemy could apply not only to the Christian God (and more specifically the Anglican one) but also to God of other religious groups. Islam has gained a public face not only thanks to various demonstrations of Muslims but also due to numerous examples of active involvement of Muslims in the public life of the European societies. From the beginning of the 1990, one may observe a growing number of representatives of the new Muslim elites starting to dynamically shape the politics of the state at both local and national level. At the same time they have been increasingly influencing the growing number of Muslim organizations created by their fathers or setting up their own organizations and in this way giving a new character to the Muslim civil society.

1.2.4 CHARACTER OF RELIGIOSITY

Finally, the last key feature of the Islam of the first generation is its strong folk character. In order to fully comprehend it, one needs to remember that Muslim immigrants who settled down in Europe after WWII were often not only moving from one continent to the other, but what is even more important, from little towns and villages to large cities and

---

[34] On average there are no more than 10 per cent of purpose-build mosques in Europe (see Peach 2000, Gale and Nylor 2002)

[35] Please see the whole issue of the Journal of Ethnic and Migration Studies (hereafter JEMS) devoted to mosque conflicts in European cities (JEMS 2005, vol. 31, no.6)

metropolises. Religion that was transplanted by immigrants to Europe has been to a large extent a religion of the rural areas. It is characterized among others by the saint-veneration, presence of many elements of magic and numerous superstitions. This kind of Islam in which the faithful's attitudes towards the main religious dogmas are more emotional than rational was named by Gellner as 'low Islam' (Gellner 1968). In this kind of Islam an important role is played by the Sufi *tariqas*. In Great Britain, for examples, the institutional base for Sufism is made up of the largest network of mosques in the country that are affiliated to the Barelwi movement.[36] One of the distinguished Sufi leaders whose arrival had a great impact on the revival of Barelwis traditions was Pir Maroof. In 1987 and 1988, for example, he organised under the World Sufi Council umbrella celebrations of the Prophet' Birthday (*milad*) in Hyde Park, which drew 25.000 people from all parts of the country (Lewis 1994: 25).

The Islam of citizens, or the European-born and educated Muslims, in contrast to that of their parents is largely an urban religion. As such it possess numerous features of the 'high Islam' generally oriented in Gellner's definition towards puritanism and scripturalism. For young European Muslims religion is increasingly not a matter of ethnicity, but of identity, ethics and spirituality. Their Islam acquires the features of the 'high Islam' inter alia through the process of intellectualisation of faith which commonly takes place outside their family home, at the conferences and seminars organized by Muslim associations, meeting of religious study groups etc. Leila Babes argues very convincingly that young Muslims cut off from the traditional basis of religious culture of their parents, have very little chances of rediscovering low Islam, and are somehow predestined to rediscover high Islam (1997: 137). Their approach to the faith that they have inherited from their parents is often deeply reflexive. This is not only a consequence of the fact that they are part and parcel of the societies which, as Giddens points out, *"are characterized by a growing capacity of active engagements with diverse sources of incoming knowledge"* (1996: 216), but also because being a Muslim outside *dar al-Islam*

---

[36] Brelwis are named after a village in India where the sect's founder Ahmad Raza Khan was born. Their teachings combine the fundamental tenets of Islam with the teaching of the international Sufi Orders. Brelwis believe, for instance, in intercession with God through pirs - holy men - both living and dead. In this tradition the person of the prophet Muhammad is extremely important. The great veneration for the Prophet Muhammad among the Brelwis is, inter alia, based on the belief in his miraculous powers. For more information about Brelwis and other Muslim movements in the UK see, for example, Rex 1991.

in not as straightforward as being a Muslim in the place where Islam is a religion of the majority. During the process of socialization Muslims born in Europe are being proposed various sets of allegiance. Religious and ethnic allegiances are just two out of many identity options. Thus, the way of being a Muslim and of practicing Islam is for the Muslim citizens a matter of private choice to a much greater extent than it was for the Muslim immigrants (Tietze 2002). The individualization of religiosity of European-born Muslims manifests itself not only in the personal tint of their religious practice (individualization of religious practice), but also in their own interpretation of religious beliefs (individualization of religious beliefs). However as Brigitte Maréchal observes, the individualization of religious beliefs does not necessarily need to result in questioning of the key religious dogmas, but only in the critical analysis of the traditional religious interpretations (2003: 13). The same point is making Nilufer Göle when she says that *'although there is a strong individualist component to the religious experience in modern times, this does not necessarily mean that the content will be individuating'* (2003: 814).

The students of the individualization processes within European Muslim populations advance two opposing theses. While some argue that religious individualization and related to it fragmentation of religious authority is leading to the 'liberalization of Islam' and emergence of 'critical Islam' (e.g. Schiffauer 2000, Mandaville 2004), other claim that in spite of individualization and the diversification of authority structures, the current situation is characterized by a relative stability of dogma and, in any case, not by a liberalization of Islam (e.g. Roy 1999, 2002, Wiktorowicz 2005). The proponents of the first thesis argue that the emergence of the critical Islam is to a large extent a reaction to the heightened intra-Islamic pluralism of the diaspora, which is increasingly valorized by Muslims in Europe, and that the main actors behind this development are young European Muslims *'dissatisfied with the Islam of their parents'* (Mandaville 2004: 121) and highly skeptical about the ability of the *ulama* to re-articulate the Islamic tradition in the vernacular (ibid: 124). Its opponents, on the other hand, believe that the individualized Islam only rarely brings forth a 'critical discourse' and instead remains tightly linked to the 'dogmatic affirmation of immutable principles' (Roy 2002: 90). While the careful observation of processes within the Muslim communities seems to suggest that both theses are actually to some extent valid, further research on these issues is definitely needed. This book is hoping to make a humble contribution in this matter by shedding light on views of the new Muslim elites on apostasy and on marrying outside the Muslim community by Muslim women.

Table 1.1 KEY FEATURES OF THE ISLAM OF IMMIGRANTS AND ISLAM OF CITIZENS

	Islam of immigrants	Islam of citizens
Religion and ethnicity	- Strong relationship	- Weakening relationship
Place of religion	- Mostly in the private sphere	- Increasingly in the public sphere
Character of religiosity	- Largely 'low Islam'	- Increasingly 'high Islam'

To sum up these reflections on different features of Islam of immigrants and Islam of citizens, as well as, on the transition from the former one to the latter one, which are at the background of the new Muslim claims of difference and sameness, one may point out that although we do not have to deal with Belgian or British Islam yet (and with their regional varieties), the processes of construction of such 'Islams' are well advanced. I agree with Stefano Allievi who writes that the European Muslim world is living through a process of extremely rapid transformation and that it will be of strategic interest to see how the process of restructuring of Muslim communities continues when they are no longer ethnic communities arriving from somewhere else. With the generational passage the Muslim communities are losing at least part their ethnic features and identification with their countries of origin, but are not autochthonous yet, at least not as communities (Allievi 2003a). In Belgium and Britain, however, the majority of their members are autochthonous as they were born in Europe and it is them who are most dynamically advancing the changes within their respective 'Islams'.

CHAPTER II – CITIZENSHIP, RELIGION AND IDENTITY

Parler de citoyenneté imparfaite ce n'est pas seulement suggérer que la citoyenneté est institution défectueuse, rectifiable, améliorable, c'est surtout suggérer que la citoyenneté est plutôt une pratique et un processus qu'une forme stable. Elle est toujours 'en devenir'.
Étienne Balibar (2001)

Without social identity there is no society, because without such frameworks of similarity and difference people would be unable to relate to each other in a consistent and meaningful fashion.
Richard Jenkins (1996)

Western European liberal democracies publicly proclaim an ethics of equality. Many of their citizens, especially those who trace their family origins to countries outside Europe, care deeply about being accepted as equals by others and resent any suggestions that they are untrustworthy or disloyal, that they are free riders or are less worthy of citizenship than others. They are especially resentful when these suggestions are based on matters central to their identity such as their religion. As Weithman notes, stigmata of this kind have profound effects on the way they think of themselves. They also have profound effects on their relations with others, especially when such stigmatizing claims are widely believed. Members of groups thought to be incapable of good citizenship are generally not accepted as equals and are often subject to exclusion from opportunities, both economically and politically if not legally, and may be treated with disdain or condescension (Weithman 2002: 12).

Although the young Muslims in the European cities on whom this study focused are citizens, equal before the law and with an equal voice and vote in the political arena, this does not necessarily mean that they are perceived as such by other compatriots or that they regard themselves as being so.[37] A poll carried out in Great Britain discovered that almost 70 per cent of British Muslims felt that the rest of society does not regard them as an integral part of life in Britain (ICM/Guardian 2002). A similar sense of exclusion has also been detected amongst Muslims in other parts of Europe (e.g. Tietze 2003, Choudhury et al. 2006). While there are a plethora of reasons for why many

---

[37] The perception of Muslim populations in Europe as entirely made up of immigrants, and not as made up of increasing number of citizens, is also not uncommon in the academic publications on Islam in Europe. See, for example, Paul 2004 or Tibi 2006.

European Muslims might feel that they do not fully belong to the Western European societies, many of them have to do with the fact that they do not equally share the benefits of economic growth in those countries and often live in economic insecurity[38] and, above all, that they do not feel that their non-Muslim compatriots view them as equal citizens. As the quantitative research shows, a growing number of Europeans fear Islam and its followers. While, for example, in October 2001 less than a third of Britons interviewed by the YouGov felt that Islam posed a threat to Western liberal democracy, in August 2006 more than half agreed with the statement (YouGov reports quoted in Johnston 2006). This growing level of distrust towards Muslims in Europe has a direct influence on the way they think about themselves since social identities are 'a matter of ascription': by individuals/groups of themselves, and of individuals/groups by other people and groups (Jenkins 1996: 98). In other words, what non-Muslims think about their Muslim compatriots is no less important than what European Muslims think about themselves. Stereotyping and attribution play an important role in these processes and the bigger the cultural distance between people, the more important their role. These are only two of the mechanisms of the process of identification that will be discussed in more detail below, as this dissertation moves from painting a larger context for this research to sketching its conceptual framework.

The key notions of this study which have been already mentioned several times without elaboration are citizenship and identity. This chapter sheds light on the understanding of both concepts that has informed this work and on different dimensions of citizenship through which the 'lived citizenship'[39] of young organized Muslim Brusselers and Londoners was analysed. It elaborates on the key research problem and formulates the main research questions exploring the participatory, identity and normative dimensions of citizenship of young European Muslims. The efforts of young Muslims to rework images, assumptions and representations of their religion and their communities within wider societies that they see as exclusive and marginalizing and to position themselves as citizens and full members of the European polities have to be

---

[38] The socio-economic profiles of the Belgian and British Muslim populations are presented in the following chapter.
[39] By 'lived citizenship' I mean after Ruth Lister, the meaning that citizenship actually has in people's lives and the ways in which people's social and cultural backgrounds and material circumstances affect their lives as citizens (Lister et al. 2005).

understood within a wider context of transformations of the ways in which people construct their personal biographies in the modern age and thus the relations between identity and modernity are also briefly discussed.

2.1 CITIZENSHIP IN SOCIOLOGY

Although there is an intellectual tradition that identifies the origins of the notion of citizenship (Fr. citoyenneté) in the ancient polis (e.g. Clarke 1994: 4-6, Pocock 1998), it is sociologically more appropriate to regard citizenship as a product of nationalism and political modernisation. As a modern concept it emerged with the creation of an international system of states and was formalized and institutionalised along the lines of state formation. Until recently the debate on citizenship has been dominated by normative political theory, as seen in the controversies between liberals and communitarians.[40] Although citizenship as social membership is central to the traditional question of sociology (namely the problem of social order) the founders of the discipline have not devoted much attention to it. Marx, for instance, objected to the notion that social membership and social participation could be defined merely in political or legal terms without a revolutionary transformation of the very basis of civil society. Weber and Durkheim showed more sympathy to the concept since while the first saw the origins of citizenship in the formation of infantry units, in the development of an urban militia and in the final collapse of the feudal principle of warfare (Turner 1993: 4-5), the second suggested in his "Professional Ethics and Civil Morals" that citizenship could be conceived as a set of civic ties that exist in the intermediary domain between the state and the individual (1957). The Durkheimian understanding of the concept was rooted in the author's scepticism about the state's ability to provide sufficient social integration. He believed that social integration depends crucially on such sources as the intermediary bonds of citizenship in association and civic forms of public service (Delanty 2000: 14).

Although, the concept of citizenship was problematized in different social science research before the 1980s (especially after the publication in 1950 of 'Citizenship and Social Class' by T. H. Marshall), sociology took greater interest in this notion only after

---

[40] For the overview of the political theories of citizenship see for example: Delanty 2000, Martiniello 2001 or Jones and Gaventa 2002.

this time. Citizenship studies established itself de facto as an interdisciplinary field in the humanities and social sciences in the late 1980s. Today this field includes a growing literature by specialists in feminist, queer, Aboriginal, African, diasporic, race and ethnic, migration, environmental and urban studies, who are exploring and addressing among others concepts of sexual citizenship, ecological citizenship, diasporic citizenship, multicultural citizenship, differentiated citizenship and cultural citizenship.

There are numerous reasons for the current revival of the concept of citizenship which as early as the 1970s was referred to as *"a notion that had gone out of fashion"* (Van Gunsteren 1978: 9). Although there is no place and room here to extensively elaborate on all of these reasons, it is essential to indicate some of the most important ones.[41] Amongst the most commonly mentioned factors that have contributed to the renaissance of the concept is the weakening of state power by the political, economic and social forces of globalization. With the growing consolidation of policy-making in the European Union the policy actions of the state have been circumscribed, which in turn creates a democratic deficit and problems of accountability. As Pattie et al. note, if citizens are unable to hold their governments to account it may in the long term result in the withdrawal of their allegiance from those governments (2004: 3). Some of the problems related to this include a decline in feelings of community and solidarity in the public, a growing public cynicism about politics, a widespread disaffection with political institutions and a decline in the institutions which underpin civil society and democracy. The political sovereignty of the state has been undermined not only by supra-national institutions but also by sub-national political movements seeking autonomy and, in some cases, independence from national governments. This is of particular relevance in the case of the two analysed countries where the governments have responded with policies of devolution and federalization to the autonomist aspirations of respectively the Scots (in particular, in the case of Britain) and the Flemings (in Belgium).

Some of the economic processes that have contributed to the erosion of national sovereignty and hence to the rebirth of the notion of citizenship in academic literature and

---

[41] In this part of the book the revival of citizenship is discussed briefly from the point of view of the transformations influencing the state and collective actors. The 'bottom up' erosion of the classical notions of citizenship in the wake of the process of reflexive modernization, or developments concerning individuals (e.g. transnationalisation of frames of belonging) are discussed below, in the sections of this chapter devoted to citizenship and identity in the high modernity.

public debates are the growing economic interdependence of countries worldwide through the increasing volume and variety of cross-border transactions in goods and services, freer international capital flows and more rapid and widespread diffusion of technology. All these processes are associated with the growing significance of multinational corporations and international economic institutions in the contemporary world and the weakening economic prerogatives of the state. The latter phenomenon is also closely linked to the crisis of welfare systems arising from demographic changes such as, for example, an aging population coupled with growing demands for state support amongst various groups.

As far as the social forces behind the current revival of the debates on citizenship are concerned, the growing social mobility across state boundaries resulting in the growing heterogeneity of state populations seems to be one of the most important. As societies become more heterogeneous[42] and new groups within them begin to demand the state's recognition, then also citizenship potentially becomes more problematic as the task of building a social contract becomes more difficult. The growing cultural diversity of European nation-states also calls for the redefinition of their founding myths and symbols that are the basis for identity formation. Another very important social force that leads to the erosion of classical notions of citizenship is the process of individualisation that will be elaborated in the last part of this chapter. What is common to all of the above mentioned reasons for the revival of the debates about citizenship is that they are constitutive of the 'runaway world' (Giddens 2000) that has dramatically changed the relationship between the individual and the state.

Despite the growing body of literature on citizenship within sociology, which in its approach to the phenomenon goes beyond the normative accounts of the political theory, there is no one agreement on an understanding of this major concept. The notion of citizenship is essentially contested both theoretically and normatively. At its lowest common denominator, citizenship means a membership in a legally constituted political community. It is commonly defined in narrow terms as a legal status recognizing formal

---

[42] The nation states like to present themselves as homogenous cultural entities, however even the least diverse are in fact very heterogeneous. One of the ways of managing this diversity has been developed in Belgium (as well as the Netherlands, Austria and Germany) on the model of 'vertical pluralism' or *verzuiling* (pillarisation, from the Dutch 'zuil' pillar) and will be elaborated in the chapter IV.

or associational membership of a nation state. The ensemble of duties and obligations of persons who participate fully in a political community constitutes citizenship. It is assumed that there is a high degree of correspondence between the obligations and entitlements of citizenship in terms of a relationship between taxation, national insurance contributions and entitlements to welfare, health and educational benefits. What we might call juridical citizenship is thus housed within nation states that have clear boundaries and specific criteria of membership.

One problem with the concept of legal citizenship is that it is too one-dimensional; this narrow juridical definition does not capture the breadth and significance of the concept. Therefore, if one is to understand the issues of social membership in the contemporary highly heterogeneous European societies, s/he needs an understanding of social rather than political citizenship. From a sociological point of view, citizenship involves the social inclusion of individuals in society through their membership of clubs, associations, groups and places of worship. While political membership as expressed primarily through the franchise is important, participation in civil society provides the substance of citizenship (Delanty 2000: 4, Turner 2003).

By locating the core of sociological citizenship within the civil society, that is an arena of non-governmental institutions and associations, which are nevertheless supportive of civic well-being and the sense of purpose, agency and freedom of citizens (McKinnon and Hampsher-Monk 2000:1),[43] this study deliberately follows the Durkheimian framework of social integration (social integration via corporations) that was more recently developed by Putnam, who emphasised integration through social networks (1993, 2000).[44] It does so because its author believes that the communitarian perspective on social integration is especially fruitful if one analyses the developments within the Muslim communities in Western Europe suffering serious levels of exclusion and disadvantage that are additionally strengthening their sense of separateness.

---

[43] This definition of civil society captures its dual character especially strongly emphasised by Antonio Gramsci: the fact that various institutions of civil society on the one hand prolong the dynamics of the state and, on the other, are deeply rooted among people which makes them a privileged terrain of political change by making it possible to seize the state without launching a direct, violent assault (Kołakowski 1981).

[44] At the same time the author remains aware of other views on social integration held for example by system theorists (e.g. Luhmann 1995), or theorists of the 'active welfare state' (e.g. Montanari 2001).

Individuals experience citizenship first-hand through social inclusion. This social and cultural involvement in the civil society is an important basis for access to social entitlements and forms the basis of social identities. Citizenship is not just the recognition of formal legal status; it creates and sustains identities. Thus, social citizenship crucially involves identity and participation. Together with rights and duties they make up the components of citizenship or 'the defining tenets of group membership' (Delanty 2000: 9) through which this study aims to analyse the issues of belonging for young European Muslims. However, before I elaborate on the four components of citizenship and pose the central sub-questions, it is important to explain in more detail how the concept of the citizenship is used in this work.

2.2 CITIZENSHIP AS A LEARNING PROCESS

The notion of citizenship has started to enter the public discourse together with the idea of learning in the last few years with many official initiatives for citizenship classes and learning civic duties. The view that citizenship is something that must be learnt and that rights must be accompanied by corresponding duties has gained significant attention among others in Great Britain, where citizenship became a compulsory part of the secondary school curriculum from 2002. In this study these two ideas, citizenship and learning, are also closely related but in a different way. Instead of talking about learning citizenship and formalised citizenship education, which entails the learning of the official values of the polity, this work focuses on citizenship as learning, that is a constructivist process through which everyone learns to be a member of legally constituted political communities.[45] Thus, the understanding of the concept adopted in this volume is much closer to the one of 'cultural citizenship' than to the one of 'disciplinary citizenship' (Delanty 2003).

The notion of 'disciplinary citizenship' is closely linked with the idea of citizenship from above, whereas in the earlier one it is conceived as a process from below

---

[45] This understanding of the concept of citizenship is close to that proposed by Felice Dassetto - the notion of 'citoyennisation' (in Dutch 'inburgering'), which stands for a multifaceted process (or rather processes) of becoming a citizen (Dassetto and Bastanier 1993, Dassetto 2001). The weak point of the theorisation of 'citoyennisation' by Dassetto is that he does not stress strongly enough that it is not only a process that concerns immigrants but everyone, and that he fails to elaborate on the fact that the process of becoming a citizen is also characterised by continuous redefinitions of what it means to be a citizen.

as defined by Turner (1994). Citizenship imposed from above as 'a ruling class strategy of incorporation' (Mann 1987) often implies a passive type of societal belonging, whereas its cultural form, generally defined as the right to be different while enjoying full membership of a democratic and participatory community (Rosaldo 1994)[46], conjures up an active type of citizenship. This last form of citizenship, when exercised by certain groups of people, often manifests itself in efforts to rework the images of these groups, as well as assumptions and representations judged by their members to be exclusive and marginalizing (Stevenson 2001: 4). It is a form of citizenship that has been exercised by many of the young European Muslims analysed in this research who, through various projects or simply by deconstructing certain myths about Islam in the media, have contributed to solving the problem of collective uncertainty in the places where they live. In contrast to Turner though, I do not think that citizenship from below needs inevitably take a radical form and involve social struggle (Turner 1994). As I am going to demonstrate, using the example of the organised Muslims in Brussels and London involved in the debates about the meaning of citizenship in the 21st century Europe, it may also take moderate forms, challenging and at the same time conforming to many of the elements of the traditional notion of citizenship.

The key idea behind the conceptualisation of citizenship as 'cultural citizenship' is that culture is, to some extent, fluid and flexible and does not necessarily denote particular forms of agency that have to be somehow managed. This understanding of the concept also emphasises that citizenship is not entirely about rights, but is a matter of participation in the political community and begins early in life. As Delanty points out *"citizenship concerns the learning of a capacity for action and for responsibility but, essentially, it is about the learning of the self and of the relationship of self and other* (all these processes concern, of course, the public and political sphere – KP). *It is a learning process in that it is articulated in perceptions of the self as an active agency and a social actor shaped by relations with others"* (2002). This view of citizenship as a learning process is also stressed by the contributors to the book "Culture and Citizenship" who suggest that citizens learn citizenship mostly in the informal context of everyday life and that this learning is heavily influenced by critical and formative events in people's lives

---

[46] For example, to be a Muslim and at the same time a fully recognized citizen of a non-Muslim country.

(Stevenson 2001). Thus, at the empirical level, this research looks into the ordinary and critical events that have shaped young Muslims understanding of their belonging to the specific local, national and subnational communities, their organisational activism and their understanding of rights and duties.

The important dimension of citizenship, conceptualised as a dynamic learning process, is the power of social actors to name, create meaning and construct personal biographies and narratives by gaining control over the flow of information, goods and cultural processes. It entails a cognitive process that allows information to be combined in different ways to provide a subject – individual, a group, a society – with the capacity for action. It shifts the focus of citizenship away from the formal aspects of membership of a polity onto common experience, cognitive processes, and forms of cultural translation and discourses of empowerment.

It is important to stress that citizenship is understood here as a life-long learning process, not only at the individual but also at the collective level. As Delanty notes, learning is processual and connective, differentiated into various levels which overall have a transformative impact on the learning subject that can be an individual or society (2003:602). Thus we can talk not only about individuals constructing their own meanings of citizenship but also about larger groups and societies.

The constructed notions of citizenship need to be recognized by others in order to be socially valid. Here the work of Mead (1967) and especially his theory of selfhood, comes in very handy since it allows us to see that citizenship is always rooted in the intersubjective nexus of the lifeworld. To be a citizen, Mead argues, one must recognize the perspective of specific and 'generalized others' (e.g. of the larger community) and this recognition, in turn, is dependent on a specific process of socialization. The individual 'I', in his theory, turns back upon and reflectively objectifies their self as 'Me' in a reflexive process which emphasizes agency. It explains how self-hood can integrate an individual into the community, equipping them with a sense of belonging, and also gives rise to responsible, reflective and argumentative agency. He also crucially points out that citizenship is dependent for its survival upon the basic processes of symbolic reproduction within the lifeworld and should not be taken out of this context (1967: 270). In other words, to be a citizen one must know what a citizen is and does. Thus,

55

'citizenship' must be a meaningful category in one's discursive repertoire, a category which one uses to make sense of one's place in the world. While the citizen's role is made up of a range of forms of tacit knowledge, competences and assumptions, citizenship is not just about taking things for granted. One of its key features at the level of the lifeworld is that it is always open to contestation and that is what many young Muslims are doing when they take up the role of a citizen and engaging with it from within their religious tradition.

Crossley proposes to supplement these important contributions of Mead to the sociology of citizenship with the notion of a symbol. He argues that, in order to perceive the notion of citizenship from the right angle, it should be understood as a 'symbol' in the sense given to the term by Alfred Schütz (Crossley 2001). A symbol, for Schütz, signifies a transcendent entity – that is, something which is not immediately given to our experience. In particular, it signifies those entities that we cannot experience *in toto* because we belong to them. Symbols do not just represent for Schütz, but function within 'we' relations to constitute or bind those relations (Schütz quoted in Crossley 2001). The icons of citizenship are symbols in the sense that they signify a transcendent phenomenon ('the generalized other') and at the same time function to constitute and bind this phenomenon, thus realizing it.

2.3 CITIZENSHIP AND RELIGION

While the role of religious factors in contemporary politics has been generally acknowledged, very little attention has been paid to the link between religion and citizenship and the influence of religion on the way how people view themselves as citizens. If religious identity was taken into account in the research on citizenship it has been usually viewed as a threat to civic self-definition, as if religious belonging automatically excluded the civic and vice versa. One of the reasons for this antagonistic vision of relationship between religion and citizenship may lie in the original understanding of civil society formulated by Thomas Hobbes as an alternative to kingdom and the church. The 17th century English political philosopher used the notion to describe a sphere of social activity distinguished from the state and out of reach of religious authority (Pietrzyk 2001).[47]

Hollenbach suggests that another reason could lie in the heightened awareness of religious diversity in contemporary societies and related to it an understanding of the difficulty, or even impossibility, of reaching an agreement on a common definition of the 'good life' (2002: 87). Members of today's individualized societies, as Beck and Beck-Gernsheim aptly note, tend to be wary or at least lukewarm to such concepts as 'common good', 'good society' or 'just society' (2002: X). I believe it is not only religious diversity that makes them sceptical of the chances of achieving a common definition of 'good life', but more the general cultural diversity and increasing functional differentiation or, as Giddens prefers to call it, the disembedding (1991: 18). As it will be argued below, the growth of individual freedoms and the increase in opportunities for greater self-interpretation made many social actors socially indifferent, as if the task of constructing personal biographies obscured them from a social reality without which, however, they are unable to perform this task[48].

The perceptions of relations between religion and citizenship as a zero-sum game have also been largely influenced by images of such places as Palestine, Kashmir, Iraq or Dharfur, to name only the main conflict areas on which the media focuses nowadays, where religion plays a divisive role, or more generally they are based on a knowledge of the history of religion. Worries about the conflict-prone tendencies of religion are thus not a product of the secularist bias but are well grounded and legitimate. Religious beliefs and loyalties have a marked proclivity to deepen social divisions which in some cases resulted in the outburst of violence. As numerous studies show, religions may build communal bonds that do not coincide with those linking the citizens of nation-state and thus threaten the basis of the unity of state and set subdivisions of the human race at odds with each other (e.g. Juergensmeyer 2003, Stern 2004). Huntington has systematized disparate cases of religious involvement in public life into a grand narrative that claims to tell the story of the future of global politics (1998). His much–noted thesis maintains that

---

[47] The relations between Islam and civil society are elaborated in depth by, for example, Esposito (2000) and Turam (2004).
[48] This phenomenon has been often referred to as a 'paradox of individualised citizens' – see for instance Beck and Beck-Gernsheim 2002.

world politics in the post-Cold War era will be driven by a clash of civilizations and cultures, rather than by ideology or economy, and raises the spectre of religious conflict on a global scale. It is a thesis though which has a very weak academic grounding as it is not based on representative sample of religious movements, but on the selective sample that cannot in any way exemplify the public role of religion in contemporary world[49].

In analyzing the public role of religion one should not overlook the other potential of such an ambiguous force as religion. The 'ambivalence of the sacred', or the 'paradox of religion' as it is often referred to in the literature (e.g. Appleby 2000), means that a religion can be both a cause of social divisions and disorder and a source of social cohesion and a stimulant for peaceful coexistence. In fact, religion can (and very often does) contribute to citizenship in all its dimensions. That is why many students of contemporary societies argue that citizenship is to a large extent an achievement that churches and religious organizations help to bring about (e.g. Verba et al. 1995, Putnam 2000, Weithman 2002). Although there is no space here to elaborate at length on how religions may empower citizenship, it is important to enumerate some of the potential religious contributions to different dimensions of citizenship.

At the level of identity and belonging, religion often serves as a powerful unifying force, bringing together people of different socio-economic statuses, races, and ethnicities and thus it fulfils the role of 'social glue' reserved for it by Durkheim. This aptitude of religion in forging connections across large segments of the population, spanning communities and regions, also fascinated de Tocqueville who saw the civility-enhancing role of religion mainly in the fact that it enables its followers to transcend egoistic and solipsist individualism and develop something that he called 'self-interest rightly understood' (1999). Thus, one can see that religious communities have both the capacity to strengthen people's sense of belonging and to enhance public activism, which becomes particularly important in a time when other social pressures encourage a retreat into privacy.

---

[49] Critics of Huntington's thesis point out, for instance, that the distinct cultural boundaries of civilizations do not exist in the present day (e.g. Berman 2003), that contrary to the description of Huntington, civilizations are fractured and show little internal unity (e.g. Bruce et al 2000) and that categorization of the world's fixed "civilizations" omits the dynamic interdependency and interaction of cultures (Said 2001). For a critical assessment of Huntington's thesis from the sociological point of view see Sutton & Vertigans 2005: 115- 140.

At the participatory level it not only provides an institutional basis for political mobilization (e.g. for the American Civil Rights Movement or the Solidarity Movement in Poland) but also acts as an educator, teaching people numerous civic skills such as writing letters, taking part in decision-making, planning or chairing meetings, giving presentations or speeches etc. In this way, religious organisations often serve as key domains of equal access to opportunities to learn civic skills. As Verba et al. have shown, religious membership encourages more equal political participation. by providing a counter-weight to the inequalities in public activism resulting from such factors as successful family background, a high level of education or a high paying job (1995: 320). Other researchers have proved, however, that when religion is understood as a purely private affair between an individual and his or her god, without the mediation of an institutional religious community with a public presence in society, little impact on civic participation can be detected (Wuthnow 1991: 156, Putnam 2000). Individualistic religious styles, in other words, seem to have a dampening effect on levels of civic voluntarism. As Putnam aptly observed, privatized religion may be morally compelling and psychologically fulfilling, but it embodies less social capital[50] which is important to carry out any political action (2000: 74). It seems that the Prophet Muhammad was well aware of this when he stated: *"It better to join another person and pray than to pray alone and it is more superior in the company of two men and the bigger the congregation the more liked it is by Allah."*[51]

Finally, religion contributes to the normative dimension of citizenship not only by inspiring many emancipatory movements such as those against slavery and racism, but also by nurturing sensibilities that give public life a philosophical and spiritual depth. In spite of the increasing secularization of the Western societies, *civisme,* or an ensemble of moral qualities which are considered necessary to the character of the 'good' citizen' (Leca 1992: 18), has been still to a large extent grounded in religious ethics. Thus, religions are still important sources of moral and social values. As Parekh points out, they continue to have much to say of great relevance about the good life, personal

---

[50] By 'social capital' I mean, after Putnam, *"connections among individuals – social networks and the norms of reciprocity and trustworthiness that arise from them"* (2000:19)
[51] Hadith about the importance of congregational prayer in Islam quoted on http://www.inter-islam.org/Actions/Congregation.html (accessed on 30.03.2008)

responsibility, family values, social justice, global redistribution of resources, the environment and other issues that dominate contemporary public agenda (1997). On the other hand secularism, which inter alia keeps religious passions at bay, avoids social authoritarianism and discourages moral absolutism, may also nurture moral positivism and cynical politics, undermine the wholeness of people's lives and homogenize public discourse (Ibid). Furthermore secularism, in contrast to religion, is not able to mobilize people's moral and spiritual energies. These energies are today being most commonly mobilized in three ways: in defence of traditional life-worlds against state and market penetration, in defence of traditional moral norms against the absolutist claims of states and markets to function according to their own intrinsic functionalist norms and, lastly, in defence of the principle of 'common good' against individualist modern liberal theories that would reduce the common good to the aggregated sum of individualist rational choices. These are the moments which, according to Casanova, are the most common when religion enters the public sphere of civil society to raise normative issues, participating in ongoing processes of normative contestation (1994, 2001).[52]

Religion is quasi-absent not only in research on banal citizenship or on citizenship to be found in the embodied habits of social life[53], but also in the scholarship of the theorists of difference and multiculturalism. As Tariq Modood indicates, in their theorizing there is usually a presumption in favour of secularism[54] (Modood 2000). Even if religious identities are problematised in studies on multiculturalism, then Islam is often identified as a faith to which multicultural arrangements do not apply. One of the most prominent scholars to do so is Charles Taylor. In his "Multiculturalism and 'the Politics of Recognition'" one can read that *"[f]or mainstream Islam, there is no question of separating politics and religion the way we have come to expect in Western liberal*

---

[52] For an overview of the political philosophical positions with reference to the role of religion in the public sphere see, for example, Loobuyck (2007).

[53] The notion of banality, as used in this book, is strongly influenced by the understanding of this concept by Michael Billing (1997).

[54] Secularism, as Talal Asad (2003) reminds us, does not simply insist that religious practice and belief should be confined to the space where they cannot threaten political stability or the liberties of a 'free-thinking' citizen, but builds on a particular conception of the world and of the problems generated by that world (e.g. need to control mutually hostile sects). It encourages religious faith in the private sphere (since without the idea of religion the concept of the secular cannot exist), tolerates religious organisation in the public spheres, but is highly critical of public organisations which are organized according to religious principles (e.g. religious political parties).

society. Liberalism is not a possible meeting ground for all cultures, but is the political expression of one range of cultures, and quite incompatible with other ranges ... as many Muslims are well aware, western liberalism is not so much an expression of the secular, postreligious outlook that happens to be popular among liberal intellectuals as a more organic outgrowth of Christianity" (1992: 95). The main reason for the incompatibility of the Muslim faith with multiculturalism is the lack of a division between the sphere of faith (ar. din دين) and that of state (ar. *dawla* دول) in Islam[55]. There is certainly no room here to adequately address this issue, but it is important to underline the arguments of a few scholars who have dealt with this problem.

Lapidus (1975) for example, who extensively studied the separation of state and religion in the development of early Islamic society, observed that contrary to the claims of today's conservative Islamists and Occidentalist critics alike, most Muslim societies displayed a significant separation of religious and state authority. Religious scholars learned to hold themselves at a distance from government despite the fact that official legal commentaries often spoke as if the ideal state was one in which the ruler is such an ardent defender of Islam that his interests are identical to those of the ulama (Lapidus 1975).[56] Furthermore, Eaton and Villalon point out that in fact it was not just Muslim scholars who developed the notable habit of distancing themselves from state authorities, but also so did many of the great mystical brotherhoods that served as vehicles for popular religious participation (Eaton 1993, Villalon 1995). Robert Hefner, another student of Muslim societies, noticed that not only do many Muslims regard their religion as a model for public order and personal ethics but that also many 'good Western democrats' view religion in an equally comprehensive manner, and that religion continues to play a significant role also in Western public sphere and politics (2001).[57] Taking only these few voices into account, it seems that it is not necessarily or entirely the problem 'a certain culture' (here Islam, and especially Islam in Europe), which makes it incompatible with the ideals of liberalism but that it might be, at least to some extent,

---

[55] Charles Taylor shares this view inter alia with Ernest Gellner (1996) and Samuel Huntington (1998).
[56] One may find also similar argumentation in 'Muslim Politics' by Eickelman and Piscatori (1996: 46).
[57] Here it is worth quoting Robert Bellah and his associates who pointed out that "*Yet religion, and certainly biblical religion, is concerned with the whole of life - with social, economic, and political matters as well as with private and personal ones (...) churches have continuously exerted influence on public life right up to the present time*" (Bellah et al. 1986: 220)

the problem also of liberalism. This is, in fact, what Charles Taylor himself acknowledges when he says later that *"liberalism can't and shouldn't claim complete cultural neutrality" and that "liberalism is also 'a fighting creed'"* (1992: 95).

One of the most powerful critiques of the aforementioned view on Islam and multiculturalism was provided by Tariq Modood who argued that *"the political demands of Muslims are not akin to conscientious objections, to principled exemptions from civic obligations, but – akin to other movements for political multiculturalism – are for some degree of Islamization of the civic; not for getting the state out of the sphere of cultural identities, but in some small way for an inclusion of Muslims into the sphere of state-supported"* (2000: 188). The British sociologist has also pointed out that Muslim assertiveness has emerged as a domestic political phenomenon in the specific political-intellectual climate of hitherto marginalized groups starting to confidently assert themselves in the public space. This development should be understood within a wider context of the blurring of the boundaries between the 'private' and the 'public' spheres. What would earlier have been called 'private' matters have become bases of the struggle for equality. In this respect the advances achieved by anti-racism and feminism (with its slogan 'the personal is the political') have acted as benchmarks for the entrance of subsequent political groups such as Muslims (2004: 247-248)[58]. I believe, however, that while analyzing Muslim public mobilization it is important to take into account not only the local context, which is undoubtedly crucial in this case, but also a wider perspective and in particular such developments as, for example, the emergence of Islam as a global symbol of opposition to the West. This is one of the ways in which this study into young Muslims' perceptions of their citizenship will try to contribute to the scholarship on Islam and multiculturalism and thus, at least minimally, fill the aforementioned semi-vacuum.

Although it is preoccupied with the question of 'what religion does' (a functional definition)[59], rather than with 'what it is' (a substantive definition), the understanding of religion on which it draws is a very broad one and could actually answer both questions. This is so in that it tries somehow to reflect the nature of religion in question which is, as

---

[58] The issues of public-private distinctions will be elaborated further in the concluding chapter.
[59] According to this approach - represented by Clifford Geertz (1966) - religion is *'a system of symbols which acts'* providing a blueprint for understanding the world'.

many Muslims like to stress, not only a religion but 'a whole way of life'[60]. Thus, by religion it will be meant a system of beliefs through which people organise and order their lives, and the central part of which occupies the belief that death does not imply the automatic annihilation of the individual self (Berger 1969: 133, Leach 1976: 71)[61]. Keith Roberts in 'Religion in Sociological Perspective' notices that among the wide range of various functions that religion performs in different social settings one may point out four main types of function that it serves in almost all social settings: meaning functions, identity functions, structural functions and cultural functions (1984: 54).

The importance of the identity function of religion, our main concern here, was especially emphasized by Durkheim who suggested that by defining and affirming personal and collective identities religion served as a sort of glue which bonds people of diverse self-interests (1915). Although this might be true of the non-industrial, homogeneous societies which were the subject of his examination, it does not hold in relation to industrial, pluralistic societies, at least if one thinks of them as not divisible entities. However, if one looks at the various groups of which they consist, his suggestion in many cases still might be accurate.

Hans Mol, following Durkheim, also stresses the role religion plays in defining man's identity at two levels. First of all, religion has an impact on identity at the personal level, through life cycles rites and the beliefs and practices which are related to them, and secondly at a social level, through traditions of religious authority and organisation. Thus, he continues, 'religion sacralizes man's identity' by providing him with a clear image of reality as well as with a list of rules that govern this reality and his place in it (Mol 1976: 15). It equips him with one of the forms of social identity, namely religious identity.

This study aims to analyse the relationship between religious and civic identities of organised Muslims and the role of religion in the process of learning of a capacity for action and for responsibility in the public sphere by them. It analyses the impact of religion on four components of citizenship: identity (main issue: how religion impacts on

---

[60] Islam (in Arabic الإسلام - the word means 'submission to the will of God') is treated here as a religion, not as a socio-political system; As a religion Islam is the faith of around one-fifth of the world population, circa 1.6 billion (343 million living in predominantly non-Muslim countries as a minority), and a faith whose historical origins can be located in and around Mecca in 7th century AD (Hinnells 1997).
[61] The definition of religion used in the book is a combination of the very broad understanding of religion proposed by Peter Berger and a so-called 'minimal definition of religion' of Edmund Leach.

the meanings of the civic identity and belonging of young Muslims), participation (how religion acts as an incentive for public engagement), rights (religion in the discourse of civic rights) and obligations (religion in the discourse of civic obligations).

2.4 DIMENSIONS OF CITIZENSHIP AND RESEARCH QUESTIONS

In the most general terms, the modern conception of citizenship has been based on the idea that membership in a legally constituted political community should rest on a principle of formal equality. This principle has been commonly defined in terms of a particular understanding of rights. Citizens' rights, which have been most extensively elaborated in the liberal tradition, were usually conceived as civil and political rights. These rights are formalized in law and claiming and exercising them is understood as a matter of choice for the individual. Liberalism considers the individual as the pre-eminent polity and citizenship as specific rights that protect the individual. The bearer of rights is the individual and the granter is the nation-state. This framework, however, is not alive to the rich variety of intermediate or alternative associational groupings actually found in human cultures, nor is it prepared to ascribe any rights not reducible either to the liberties of the citizen or to the prerogative of the state to such groups. It promotes a negative notion of freedom - 'freedom from' - which is commonly understood as the absence of coercion and interference, so the role of the state is limited to the protection of the freedom of individual citizens (Isin and Wood 1999). Such negative freedom does not enable citizens to claim rights since claiming requires resources, power and knowledge. A good illustration of this issue was provided by Anatole France who once observed that the rich and the poor had an equal right to sleep under the bridges of Paris. The point of his comment was obviously not to suggest that rights are always inconsequential, but rather that we should be careful not to over-interpret the importance of a basic equality of rights.

The notion of positive freedom, understood as social rights, was introduced into citizenship by T.H. Marshall (1950). For several decades the sociological analysis of citizenship was informed by his work. He has argued most importantly that the development of citizenship since the seventeenth century had involved the successive acquisition of civil rights, political rights and social rights. The emergence of civil rights,

64

such as the right to a fair trial, freedom from arbitrary detention and violence, freedom of speech, the right to hold property, and rights of contract was particularly associated with the development of the institutions of the judicial system and a free press. Political rights including the right to vote and to stand for election, developed along with the strengthening of such institutions as an elected parliament and payment for Parliamentary representatives. Finally, social rights that include rights to health care, education and a subsistence income arise with the development of the institutions of the welfare state. Marshall insisted that to limit citizenship to civil and political rights would exclude many from full membership of society, because people who were struggling with poverty or disease, or who were poorly educated, would not have the time, resources or capacity to exercise their citizenship rights in practice. He argued that social citizenship, when it eventually came with the modern welfare state, alleviated the social inequalities produced by capitalism. His vision of citizenship, which looks to the state rather than social actors as the arbitrators of social conflict, is usually associated with left-wing liberalism (Delanty 2000: 20).

2.4.1 CITIZENSHIP AND RIGHTS

While being very influential, the Marshallian theory of citizenship has been widely criticised on a variety of counts. There is no room here to present all the critical voices, so instead I would like to concentrate on the limits of his model that are pertinent to this research and which concern the main components of the citizenship, namely: rights, duties, identity and participation[62]. One of the major drawbacks of Marshall's model often highlighted by his critics is that it may be efficient when applied to relatively ethnically homogenous society (e.g. the Great Britain in the early 1950s), but it fails to address such salient issues of contemporary heterogeneous societies as politics of ethnicity and diversity. The issue missing in the Marshallian model of relationship between cultural pluralism and citizenship was addressed, inter alia, by Pakulski (1997) and Delanty (2002), who have argued that a fourth dimension of citizenship could be culture. They have pointed out that today there are other kinds of exclusion which cannot

---

[62] For extensive critique of the Marshallian theory see for example: Voet (1998), Isin & Wood (1999) or Delanty (2000).

be accommodated by a model of social rights. The recognition of these forms of exclusion has committed many people to the view that policies of universal equality would not be adequate and that therefore some kind of radical difference is necessary in the recognition of the group rights[63] (e.g. Young 1990, Kymlicka 1995, Isin and Wood 1999).

The emphasis on the last component of citizenship may also be found in the scholarship of Bryan Turner, who argues that citizenship confers not just a legal status but also *"a particular cultural identity on individuals and groups"*. He aptly notices that the main focus of citizenship struggles has shifted in recent decades from class to claims to cultural identity and cultural history. Today's struggles have been not about the access to the means of production, but inter alia about sexual identities, gay rights, gender equality and aboriginality (Turner 1997: 8). I believe that with the advancement of the European born generation of Muslims into the public sphere and their refusal to privatise Islam, we could also add religion to this list. Furthermore, I agree with Nilüfer Göle and Tariq Modood who point out that Muslims emerging into identity politics generally follow the example of ethnic minorities, women, gays and lesbians in seeking space for their heritage and values in both the public and private spheres (Göle 2003: 812, Modood 2003:102). The children of immigrants born in Belgium and Britain have been learning to take advantage of citizenship which is today one of the two, (besides the human rights) main discourses of entitlement. This exposes the growing tension between the discourse on equality (on civil, political and social levels), as a classical preoccupation of citizenship and recognition of difference, (equality on the cultural level) as a contemporary engine of citizenship.

The important question is: why has citizenship been such a valuable political tool for allowing various groups to make different demands? The answer can be found in the scholarship of T.H. Marshal who, in his classic exposition, spoke of *"an image of an ideal citizenship against which achievements can be measured and towards which aspirations can be directed"* (1950:29). It is thus nothing else but this 'ideal citizenship' that Muslims in various European countries have had in mind when demanding, for

---

[63] It refers to rights specific to particular groups of people (e.g. women, ethnic and religious minorities) which protect and enable realisation of the particular needs interests and priorities of these groups. These are the rights, which Isaac Berlin saw as embodiment of the third form of freedom.

instance, that state authorities allow Muslim girls to wear hijabs at school or to provide financial support to Muslim schools. The politics of citizenship has increasingly been a politics of recognition, in which claims are made for cultural rights and Islam has begun to play an important role in that politics.

This research into the social representations of citizenship amongst the young European Muslims sheds light on some of the mechanisms of this new politics of citizenship, and elaborates on various claims made in the two social contexts invoking the ideal of equality of rights embedded in citizenship. By looking into how organised Muslims view their rights as citizens, this study most importantly intends to find out what is the content of their lived citizenship. It accounts not only for their understanding of civic rights, but also for personal experiences of unequal treatment and key civic and religious demands.

Muslim demands can generally be divided into those that call for rights that are not already granted to other native cultural, minority or religious groups (e.g. the right to polygamy, or the right to wear *niqab* - full veil) and the ones that request for Muslims the same privileges and exemptions from duties already extended to other religions (e.g. provision of state-funding to religious schools). The first type of demand for exceptional group rights call for something substantively 'new' or a special exemption which, if realized, sets the specific group apart from all other groups hence I shall call them, after Statham et al., 'dissociative demands' (2005: 443). These kinds of demands often challenge a state's approach to minority and religious difference, by making a demand which goes further than or ignores current formulations. On the other hand, the second type of demands call for parity of rights or equality with other groups, often those already granted special treatment. In theory at least, parity demands should be less challenging and easier to accommodate than exceptional ones because they do not directly confront the logic of the category system used by a country's policies for cultural pluralism. Because they fit within a state' ways of managing cultural diversity, or policies of categorizing minority or religious groups, they can be perceived as essentially 'acculturative claims' (ibid.).

While inquiring about the perceptions of the civic rights by Muslim Brusselers and Londoners, the study also sought to find out what their views are on such rights, inseparably linked with modernity (or more precisely the socio-cultural dimension of it), as the free choice of religion and free choice of a future marriage partner. Thus, they were asked not only about their views on the right to apostasy but also about the right to marry non-Muslim men by Muslim women, both forbidden in Islam.[64] These questions were asked, inter alia, to assess the extent of the influence of modernity on perceptions of religious dogmas by the new Muslim elites and thus contribute to academic debates on the scale of the individualization of religiosity among European Muslims summarized in the introductory chapter.

2.4.2 CITIZENSHIP AND OBLIGATIONS

If citizenship has been a valuable tool for the claiming of different rights by various minority groups, it has been an equally useful instrument in demanding that minorities should quietly play by the majority's rules. Here also, it is the 'image of ideal citizenship' that is being used although not to extend the liberties of the minority groups, but rather to limit them and thus ensure the continuity of a society which otherwise is perceived as being under threat. The importance of the duties of citizenship has been most strongly emphasised by the conservatives. This has been done most commonly by building theoretical constructs of 'good citizenship'. In French this dimension of citizenship is usually described with assistance of the notion of *civisme* which, when applied to political actors, refers mostly to dedication to community work and, when used with reference to social actors, means the sense of collective obligations among members of a given society (Constant 1998: 32).

As the critics of T.H. Marshall have pointed out, this is yet another area that the English scholar failed to develop in his theory of citizenship. He defined the obligations of citizens in terms of civil obligations which can be imposed by the state, (e.g. obligations to pay taxes, mandatory schooling, obligatory voting – for example in Belgium) rather than as the civic obligations imposed by the society (e.g. active participation in the public debates, voluntary work for an NGO or voting where it is not obligatory – for example Great Britain) (Delanty 2000: 17). The limits of his conception

---

[64] The Qur'an talks about apostasy in the following suras and verses 3:72, 3:90-91, 16:106, 4:137, 5:54 and about marriage rules in the following 24: 3 and 60: 10.

of duty become especially apparent when he argues that *"a successful appeal to the duties of citizenship can be made in times of emergency, but the Dunkirk spirit cannot be a permanent feature of any civilisation"* (Marshall 1992: 46). The critics have pointed out that debates about qualities of 'good citizenship' are continuous and ongoing and that an appeal to these qualities is not only limited to the times of international tensions or war.

In the traditional models of citizenship (including the Marshallian one) a 'good citizen' is most commonly conceived as a 'good worker', since they take it for granted that a citizen is a worker. In current reality, however, the citizen is becoming primarily a consumer, and that is how it should be conceived (Delanty 2000: 127). The post-Fordist or post-industrial European societies are dominated less by production than by consumption and leisure.[65] As Richard Sennet has demonstrated, the job casualisation and labour flexibility has resulted in the 'corrosion of character' (1998) and the 'decline of respect' (2003).[66] The Western European 'thick communities' of the 1950s and the 1960s have gradually disappeared along with steel production, coal mining and car production as key sectors of economies. Furthermore, the traditional patterns of social solidarity have been disrupted and fragmented. The consequences for male identity are particularly important since the traditional foundations of working-class masculinity were associated with a society dominated by economic production, manual labour and the dignity of work. As Edmunds and Turner aptly point out, in contemporary society there is no corresponding ethic of consumption to match an ethic of hard work and the dignity of labour. The consequence of these developments is an important shift away from class politics to generational politics, a crisis in working-class masculinity and a turn towards the volatile politics of identity (Edmunds and Turner 2002).

In today's context of the risk society (Beck 1992), a new idea of responsibility has arisen which bears very little resemblance to the understanding of responsibility embedded in the traditional conceptions of citizenship. It puts an emphasis on the collective notions of responsibility rather than on an individualistic one. It does so

---

[65] The shift towards a consumer society has been possible among others by increases in productivity, by an expansion of the service sector and by credit arrangements that have made possible substantial increases in personal indebtedness.
[66] The decline of full time employment and stable careers have been also largely responsible according to other scholars for a loss of social capital and a decline of trust (see for example Putnam 2000 or Uslaner 2002).

through the introduction of the idea of co-responsibility (Apel 1993, Styrdom 1999), and is built on the assumption that individual responsibility is no longer able to find solutions to many of the problems facing today's society (e.g. emanating from technology). This idea has the advantage over the older frame in that it is able to reconcile the ideas of individual and collective responsibility. It is possible since the notion of co-responsibility does not preclude individual responsibility from some kind of collective responsibility but, as Delanty points out, it expresses the emergence of a moral consciousness that is beginning to have some effect on the cultural level of society (2000: 128).

This study attempts to shed light on the relationship between the obligations of faith and those of citizenship by looking into how organised Muslims perceive their obligations as citizens. It not only elaborates the diverse understandings of citizenship obligation by young European Muslims but also their image of a 'good' and a 'bad' citizen. Moreover, it tries to locate the role of Muslim ethics in young Muslim understanding of civic obligations. The young organized Muslims from Brussels and London were asked, during the in-depth interviews conducted by the author, about their understanding of the features of a 'good citizen', as well as, about their feelings of obligations towards their religious community and wider society. In the context of debates about Islam in Europe[67] religious obligations are often contrasted with civic ones and portrayed as a serious challenge to loyalty.[68] That is also why this study has paid particular attention to the issues of loyalty in worldly matters and in religious ones while exploring the normative dimension of my interviewees' citizenship.

In addition to questions about good citizenship, the young European Muslims were also asked to choose the most important, in their views, 'virtues of responsible citizenship' from the model of William Galston (1991) and explain their choices. The Galstonian model of responsible citizenship claims that liberal societies can function successfully only if their citizens possess 'general virtues' such as courage, law-abidingness and loyalty; 'social virtues' - independence, open-mindedness; 'economic virtues' that are constituted of the work ethic, the capacity to delay self-gratification and an adaptability to economic and technological change; and 'political virtues' which

---

[67] The main debates around Islam in the countries analysed will be outlined in chapter three.
[68] The issue of loyalty is particularly frequently brought up in public debates in Britain. For an overview of these debates see Hussain 2004.

translate into the capacity to discern and respect the rights of others, a willingness to demand only what can be paid for, the ability to evaluate the performance of those in office, and a willingness to engage in public discourse (Galston 1991: 221-4). The study used the aforementioned model of the liberal thinker in order to assess more accurately the subjective notions of citizenship obligations of the Muslim Belgians and Britons interviewed.

2.4.3 CITIZENSHIP AND IDENTITY

The limits of the Marshall's theory of citizenship have also been clearly visible when one carefully studies his understanding of such a crucial component of citizenship as identity. His theory follows the traditional way of thinking of civic identity as being synonymous with nationality. It conceptualizes citizenship at the level of the nation-state and perceives it as universal, while at the same time it views individual or group identities as particular (Isin and Wood 1999: 14). Thus, it does not question the ties of nation and state and views the state as the provider and guarantor of rights and the nation as the focus of identity. However, in the global age this linkage cannot be taken for granted. As numerous scholars have demonstrated, today there is no perfect equivalence between nationality and citizenship (e.g. Brubaker 1990, Soysal 1994, Castles & Davidson 2000). Although the marriage between citizenship and nationality has not ended in a 'full separation', as the nation-states continue to play a role of key centres of citizenship authority, the close link between them seems to have been definitively broken. The de-ethnicized conception of citizenship that has become increasingly popular challenges such tenets of traditional citizenship as the idea that a citizen is, above all, a national that belongs to a nation, that the state should be synonymous with this and that this belonging should be unitary. In light of this, to be a citizen does not need to connote membership in a particular cultural community. In fact, the only 'culture' that citizens are now most commonly asked to share is the political culture of political liberalism. Some of the manifestations of the popularity of this de-ethnicized citizenship are the resurgence of the *jus solis* as the basis of legal citizenship and increasing toleration of dual citizenship. Saskia Sassen suggests calling the processes described above as constitutive of the phenomenon of the 'denationalization of citizenship' (2002: 278). One of the implications of these developments is the growing popularity of such concepts as transnational citizenship (e.g. Soysal 1994, Jacobson 1996), cosmopolitan citizenship (Delanty 2000) and global citizenship (e.g. Falk 1994, Heater 1999).[69] There is no space here to elaborate on the phenomena described by these concepts at length[70], however it is important to point out some of the developments that underpin them.[71]

One of the most commonly mentioned developments is the emergence of multiple actors, groups and communities partly strengthened by the denationalization of citizenship and increasingly unwilling to automatically identify with the nation as represented by the state. The growth of the Internet and linked technologies has facilitated and often enabled the formation of cross-border networks among individuals and groups with shared interests that may be highly specialised (e.g. professional networks, various e-groups) or involve particularized political projects (e.g. human rights and environmental struggles). It has, for example, greatly empowered worldwide Muslim networks (not only the *jihadi* ones such as al-Qaeda, but also others) and made transnational Muslim activism as accessible as never before (Cooke and Lawrence 2005)[72]. At the same time it has filled the concept of *umma* with a new meaning, that of a cyber Muslim community or Muslims staying in touch through the means of the Internet and engaged in the production of 'digital Islam' or 'e-Islam' through the cultivation of the Muslim cyber land (Bunt 2000). The aforementioned transformations have both endangered and strengthened alternative notions of community of membership. While the locus of the identity of the members of elite groups has increasingly shifted from the nation state towards notions of 'post-national citizenship', at the same time many people adversely affected by globalisation have developed stronger senses of territorial citizenship and defensive patriotism.

---

[69] It must be noted that these concepts of post-national citizenship are not synonymous, and each of them points towards different transformations decoupling the citizenship and nationality.

[70] Here it needs to be stressed that there is no agreement on the assessment of the current condition of the citizenship authority of the nation state. Some authors rightly criticize the concepts of post-national citizenship by referring, for instance, to the continuous resilience of the nation states as a focus of identity (e.g. Kuisma 2001).

[71] For an exhaustive presentation of the transnational sources of membership see for example Soysal 1994: 143-156).

[72] One could observe the manifestations of it for example during the protests against the Danish cartoons of the Prophet Mohammad (February 2005), or during the protests against the speech of the Pope of Benedict XVI from Ratizbon (September 2006).

Another development that has had a crucial role in enlarging the framework of the identity dimension of citizenship was the emergence of locations for citizenship outside the confines of the nation state. I am thinking in particular of the establishment of the citizenship of the European Union by the Maastricht Treaty in 1992. Other processes that have disturbed the traditional relation in which nation states are viewed as the privileged location for identity, have to do with the growing importance of universal rules and conceptions regarding the rights of the individual, which are formalized and legitimized by a multitude of international codes and laws, or the international prominence of the international human rights regime.[73] Last but not least, the notions of the post-national citizenship have been fed by the reinvigorated cosmopolitanism (Nussbaum 1994, Turner 2000) and the proliferation of transnationalism (Basch et al. 1994, Smith 1997).

While assessing the identity dimension of citizenship of Muslim Brusselers and Londoners, this study follows Isin and Wood (1999), who argue that different claims to group identity should be conceptualized as forms of citizenship rights, such as gendered citizenship, ethnic citizenship, ecological citizenship or national citizenship, which is itself a form of group identity. In this formulation, citizenship is understood as an ensemble of different forms of belonging (1999: 21). Furthermore, drawing on Mouffe's (1992) conceptualization of identity, as 'an ensemble of subject positions' (e.g. female, Muslim etc) Isin and Wood argue that citizenship is not only differentiated across individuals, but that each individual person may experience and express different forms of citizenship (1999). One of the advantages of this conceptualization of civic identity is that it takes into account the importance of reflexivity in contemporary searches for 'authentic' identity elaborated below. Another is its insistence on the multiple forms of citizenship, which stresses the existence of a plurality of specific allegiances. This understanding is particularly useful while studying young Muslims who also fully participate in the contemporary searches for identity and, at the same time, often have to deal with a high diversity of allegiances, or multiply identities.

How young Muslims conceive of their civic and Muslim identities and frame their belonging is the key research question through which this study attempts to shed light on

---

[73] At the same time the bond with the state still remains meaningful since different forms of transnational identification/citizenship/civil society are not easy to anchor in political rights and obligations.

the identity dimension of the social representations of citizenship of Muslim Brusselers and Londoners. As Weithman states, an effective identification is a very important subjective condition of realized citizenship (2002: 14). The depth of the citizenship of the young European Muslims is being assessed, inter alia, by asking them about their understanding of the concept of a citizen and through the examination of the most meaningful (for them) levels of belonging (e.g. local, regional, ethnic community, religious community in the country, religious community worldwide, national or supranational). Through the analysis of the narratives of belonging, the research explores also the emotional and other links that connect young Muslims with the places in which they are living. In this way it also assesses the thesis about the growing popularity of post-national citizenship with regard to the people that, at the first sight, seem most likely to favour post-national forms of identification.

2.4.4 CITIZENSHIP AND PARTICIPATION

The last limitation of the Marshallian model that is pertinent to this book has to do with his treatment of participation. If we decided to use his model of citizenship it would not lead us far, since it almost completely ignores the salience of participation as a dimension of citizenship that is crucial for this study. The Marshall theory, which strives to account for the impact of citizenship on social classes, entails a very passive and highly privatised conception of the citizen that fails to account for the impact of social classes on citizenship. Numerous critics of his theory have pointed out that the rights of citizenship did not simply come automatically from a benevolent state, but arose from the historical struggles between capital and labour. Chantal Mouffe points out, for instance, that the democratic advances or the extensions of citizenship which provided new spaces for identity development have usually been the result of a process of displacement of rights along a double axis: either new groups have claimed access to rights already declared, or new rights have been demanded in social relations hitherto considered as 'naturally' hierarchical, such as those concerned with race, gender, etc. (1992: 4). Together with other scholars she argues that the question of rights cannot be posed aside from the question of participation, and thus puts an emphasise on the importance of active dimension of citizenship (Mouffe 1992, Eder 1993, Delanty 2000).

74

The challenge of substantive over formal citizenship, which is at the heart of the problem sketched above, has been most extensively elaborated by radical democracy theorists building upon the tradition of the civic republicanism and communitarianism. One of the key ideas advanced by these theorists is that participation in the public sphere is the best way of attaining rights, and that there is close link between participation and identity. Feminist and cultural pluralist writers have demonstrated that radical politics is not just a question of participation but a critical awareness about some of the assumptions about power and identity that were taken for granted in the communitarian and liberal theories. One of the leading feminist scholars, Ruth Lister, argues for example that citizenship as participation represents an expression of human agency in the political arena. Furthermore she asserts that "*human agency embedded in social relations is integrally related to consciousness – to act as a citizen requires first a sense of agency, the belief that one can act; acting as a citizen, especially collectively, in turn fosters that sense of agency. Thus agency is not simply about the capacity to choose and act but also about a conscious capacity which is important to the individual's self-identity*" (1997: 38). Before someone becomes active, though he or she needs to posses the capacity, some basic resources or dispositions are required to do so.

In this study the resources that allow the members of the new Muslim elites to choose between different courses of action and to move beyond the formal to more substantive forms of citizenship are assessed with the help of the notion of habitus and the Civic Voluntarism Model. By habitus I would mean, after Bourdieu, "*a system of acquired dispositions functioning on the practical level as categories of perception and assessment... as well as being the organizing principles of action*" or "*the durably installed generative principle of regulated improvisations ... [which produces] practices*" (1977: 78). The most important aspect of habitus that this work pays attention to are the cultural trajectories, which as Bourdieu has pointed out, make people disposed towards certain attitudes, values or ways of behaving, and which are transposable across different fields (Webb et al. 2002: 38). It is also important to note here that, while habitus is durable, it is also oriented towards the practical: dispositions, knowledge and values are always potentially subject to modification, rather than being passively consumed or reinscribed. As Webb et al. point out "*the habitus can tolerate social upheavals, and agents moving from one field to another, because there is a 'continuity of meaning' (or a doxa) that characterises and even permeates most national cultures, and is usually promoted by government, bureaucracies, the media and education systems"* (2002: 42-43). The study also takes into account a point made by Arjun Appadurai who argued that the unregulated flow of cultural texts, in concert with the continuous 'flowing of peoples' that characterizes the contemporary world, works to *"move the glacial forces of the habitus into the quickened beat of improvisations for large groups of people"* (Appadurai 1997: 6).

The Civic Voluntarism Model, the second conceptual tool used to analyse the means necessary for activism in the public sphere, draws heavily on the sociological theory of resource mobilization, and argues that the level of involvement in voluntary activities depends on three kinds of resources: time, money and civic skills (Verba et al. 1996: 4). As all social activism is time consuming, it therefore maintains that people who do voluntary work need to possess a surplus of free time that they are willing to devote to a particular activity. Apart from free time, they also need money since working *pro bono* means that they are at certain times not doing any paid work and, what is more, sometimes investing substantial amounts of their financial resources. Finally, Verba et al., who constructed the model on the basis of their research of political participation in the USA, point out that those who possess the requisite organizational and communications capacities, or civic skills, will find it less daunting to get involved. They demonstrate very convincingly that when inputs of time and money are coupled to civic skills people not only become more likely to participate but also more likely to be effective when they do so (ibid: 271). Furthermore they distinguish between the social positions from which the above mentioned resources derive – for example, the respondent's family background, occupation, education, organisational involvement, etc., - and the resources themselves. This allows them to focus on the processes by which resources are acquired in the context of social positions. Having applied this method to the analysis of American civic voluntarism they conclude that, depending on the nature of the institutions and the nature of extent of citizen's involvement with them, families, schools, jobs, voluntary associations, as well as places of worship (e.g. mosques) provide differential amounts of the three resources (ibid: 272).

This work will try to assess if the young Muslim Londoners and Brusselers uphold the main thesis of the Civic Voluntarism Model, which claims that there is a close link between people's level of involvement in voluntary activities and their level of reserves of time, money and civic skills. On the basis of their narratives of participation in the Muslim organisations and in a larger public sphere it will not only shed light on the circumstances in which these young people became active, and on the different factors that pushed them into Muslim and civic activism, but also on the main reasons why they continue to devote substantial amounts of time to this activism. Thus, it will try to answer how organised Muslims account for activism in the Muslim organisations and in the wider public sphere, as well as why they became religious actors.

Table 2.1 DIMENSIONS OF CITIZENSHIP AND MAIN RESEARCH QUESTIONS

Dimensions of Citizenship	Research Questions
Rights (Content of citizenship)	How do the organised Muslims view their rights as citizens?
Obligations (Content of citizenship)	How do the organised Muslims perceive their obligations as citizens?
Identity (Depth of citizenship)	How do the organised Muslims conceive of their civic and Muslim identities and frame their belonging?
Participation (Extent of citizenship)	How do organised Muslims account for activism in the Muslim organisations and in the wider public sphere?

While exploring the aforementioned research questions, this study will pay particular attention to the gender and geographical variables and thus it will try to account for the difference between the lived citizenship of the women and men, and Brusselers and Londoners.

To close this section of the book, which critical analysed T.H. Marshall's theory of citizenship and highlighted the main research problem and key research questions, I would like to note that in spite of all the differences between the classical and contemporary understandings of the main components of citizenship (identity, participation, rights and obligations), there are two issues that always remain in the centre of the discourse on citizenship. The first revolves around the question: 'what does it mean to belong to the society?', whereas the second one searches for an answer to the question 'how can our societies be more inclusive?'. These are also very broad issues which set the philosophical background for this study.

2.5 CITIZENSHIP AND A CITY

As this study focuses on two urban centres, the relationship between citizenship and a city needs to be at least briefly discussed. First of all it is important to recall that the word 'citizen' has for a long time meant simply the inhabitant of a town. In fact, both of the terms 'citizen' (English) and 'citoyen' (French) are derived from the word 'city' (French – cité) and indicate the idea of living in the urban space[74]. In medieval times the term did not mean the nationality with which it has become coterminous in modern times, but envisaged a specifically urban relationship concerning rights and duties in a town. A city dweller is historically a person with protection and entitlements which derive from the construction of an autonomous city and therefore the urbanization of population is related to the idea of the civilizing process where civility and citizenship have become combined (Turner 1993). As Max Weber (1958) has said of the medieval city, citizenship was a legal conception of the person and, as such, it stood in opposition to the word 'subject'. Thus, from the very beginning cities embodied freedom – as is testified by the saying derived from the medieval communes *'Stadt Luft macht frei'* ('City air is liberating'). As a consequence of this freedom, they not only became places of economic transactions but also the meeting places of cultures and the milieus of intellectual exchange.

The idea of a close relationship between the city and citizenship is also reiterated by scholars in regard to the contemporary context. Michael Ignatiev, for instance, maintains that *"to speak of citizens is to speak of cities. It is in the city where we live as civic beings: it is the urban environment what releases in every minute the sensation of belonging or not belonging to something called political society"* (quoted in Bianchini and Bloomfield 2001: 110). Also James Holston (1999: 189) emphasizes the importance of the urban experience for citizenship. He argues that as long as there are diverse

---

[74] In Dutch and German languages, in contrast, the origins of a modern citizen are linked with the idea of civil society – for more information on these differences see Turner 1993: 9-12.

populations' places and new politics of identity and difference *"the cities are challenging the nations, separating themselves and even replacing them, from an important space of citizenship to alive spaces, not only of their insecurities but also in their emergent ways".* The aforementioned authors share with many other scholars around the globe the same conviction that, although one of the essential purposes in the construction of a nation has been to disassemble the historical priority of the urban citizenship and to substitute it for the national citizenship, cities keep on being the strategic place for the development of the citizenship. The fact that numerous social scientific magazines (*Public Culture, Urban Studies, Innovation, and International Journal of Urban and Regional Research)* have lately dedicated special thematic numbers to questions related to cities and the citizenship is the best evidence of it.

One of the reasons why the position of cities in the discourse on citizenship does not seem to be weakening, but on the contrary celebrating its revival, is the far greater sensitivity of city governments than national ones to the issues of cultural and religious pluralism. As Gaetano Adinolfi has rightly pointed, this sensitivity makes the cities a live laboratory for democracy (CLRAE, 1992: 160-1). He has also observed that *"there is a new local citizenship that emerges as the cities of Europe go assuming the responsibility of the multicultural realities"* (CLRAE, 1992: 162). This book does not aim to analyze the multicultural policies of municipal authorities and the modes of citizenship among ethnic minority groups conceived from the institutional point of view, that was for example the goal of the research carried out in Brussels and other Belgian cities by Bousetta et al. (1999), but it hopes to account for the revival of the new local citizenship by looking at the social manifestations and practice of citizenship of the organized Muslim Londoners and Brusselers. For this reason it is also important to introduce a specific understanding of the urban contexts.

Following the suggestions of Gerard Delanty, a city is conceived in this study as a 'discursive space', that is the space of civic communication shaped by democracy and active social citizenship (2000: 102). I believe that this understanding of the contemporary space of the city which goes beyond the conceptions of the urban form as illustrated in the writings of Baudelaire, Joyce, Simmel and Benjamin (visible space[75]), as well as those which pervade in the designs of Le Corbusier or Baron Haussmann (representational space[76]), is more in tune with the current social realities of globalization, diversity, the postmodernization of culture and the information society and therefore, more productive. It emphasizes the invisible ties that bind citizens with the cities in which they are living. By doing so it presents the city as a symbolic space and a repository of memory and shared meanings.

The cities conceived as discursive spaces obviously form part of larger discursive arenas or they are embedded in the wider contexts of abstract flows. As such they constitute nodes in wider discursive contexts. The global cities analysed play the role of central nodes in these contexts.

2.6 SOCIAL IDENTITY IN HIGH MODERNITY

As I have noted at the beginning of this chapter, in order to better understand different aspects of the subjective notions of citizenship of young European Muslims and their efforts to construct a new identity that would more justly in their eyes position them vis-à-vis other social groups, it is necessary to elaborate on the features of identity and recent transformations in the processes of identity building. In recent years the debates on identity have become prominent not only in the public sphere, but also in the academic circles. The later development is, according to Craig Calhoun, directly related to an increasing recognition that social theory itself must be a discourse with many voices, not a monologue of a simple and unitary truth or its successive approximations (Calhoun 1994: 4). As for the cause of the revival of notion of identity in the public debates, the plethora of reasons could be summed up in one notion: high modernity or post–traditional order (Giddens 1991: 5) that is elaborated in the following subsection.

Although the notion of identity has been the basic research category in the study of the individual and of society for more than four decades there is no agreement on one understanding of the term. While personality theorists regard identity in terms of a sense

---

[75] This is a static conception of the urban form which has been highly influential in the making of the city of high modernity (Delanty 2000: 102)

[76] This more cognitive notion of the city refers to cultural constructions of space and entails an aesthetic orientation (Ibid)

of personal distinctiveness, personal continuity and anatomy, sociologists and social psychologists tend to emphasize that a sense of identity is formed from the dialectic between the individual and society (Banaszak-Karpinska 1998). Furthermore, within each discipline academics put emphasis on different features of the concept. In the most general terms identity is commonly understood as the way in which we describe ourselves. It answers the question 'who am I/who are we', and 'how do I/we differ from other men and women'. It is a concept which can be conceived both at the individual and the collective level. Consequently, one may distinguish analytically between individual and social identity, where the former stresses man's uniqueness and the latter his sameness with some other individuals (Jarymowicz & Szustrowa 1980). These two aspects of identity are, for example, signalled in the classical understanding of the concept by Henri Tajfel, according to which *"identity is a part of an individual's self-concept which derives from his knowledge of his membership of a social group (or groups) together with the value and emotional significance attached to that membership"* (Tajfel 1981). This study focuses on the latter aspect of identity, namely its social side.

The social nature of man is clearly visible in the way in which he constructs his identity. As Calhoun points out *"self-knowledge – always a construction no matter how much it feels like a discovery – is never altogether separable from claims to be known in specific ways by others"* (1994: 9-10). It is shaped in social interactions, 'dialogically' (Taylor 1992: 79), *"...in the process of exchange of messages which we send, receive and interpret until a general, relatively coherent image is achieved"* (Mach 1993). Without others the exchange cannot take place and consequently the individual's identity cannot be established. It may only emerge as a result of 'debate' between people, in which the action from one side meets the reaction from the other. One must also remember that people who participate in this 'debate' are the bearers of certain sets of moral, aesthetic, technical and legal rules that make up different cultures. Thus, the object world which helps to shape an individual's identity includes not only 'significant others'[77], but also the above mentioned rules. Like 'significant others' who expect the individual to act in a certain way, they make various demands upon him. The rules which are given priority by

---

[77] The concept is used in Meadian terms; it refers to those who have an important influence in shaping the behaviour of another

the religious believers tend to have religious character. In this way, religion has its own significant stake in the creation of man and his 'self-concept'. Here it is important to remember that the dialogical character of social identities means also that they are 'a matter of ascription', that was already noted at the beginning of this chapter (Jenkins 1996: 98). Thus, as Taylor importantly points out, our identities are partly shaped by recognition or its absence and often by the misrecognition of others. He argues that a person or a group of people might suffer real damage if the people around them mirror back to them a confining or demeaning or contemptible picture of themselves (Taylor 1992: 75). Non recognition or misrecognition can inflict harm, be a form of oppression, imprisoning someone in a false, distorted, and reduced mode of being (ibid).

The metaphor of 'debate' that was used above, in order to more clearly picture the nature of the process of construction of identity, also implies two main features of the concept as it is employed in the book: its situational, contextual character and - closely associated with it - dynamic, negotiable nature. Like a 'debate' which always takes place in a certain time and space (also cyberspace), and between certain people, both individual and group identity are impossible to think of without this essential frame, without the social context in relation to which they emerge and take certain shape. It is the context that establishes and continuously reshapes them. Both the individual and group are continuously confronted with new situations and new objects and must redefine their image of the world, and their place in it, in relation to these objects (Rex 1991: 13). While all identities come from somewhere and have their histories, they at the same time, like everything which is historical, undergo constant transformation. As Gupta and Ferguson point out they are subject to the continuous 'play' of history, culture and power (1997: 4).

The second feature of identity is its dynamism. It is a dynamic process, never a final or settled matter. This idea is clearly expressed by Stuart Hall, when he writes: *"identity is not as transparent or unproblematic as we think. Perhaps instead of thinking of identity as already accomplished fact, which the new cultural practices then represent, we should think instead of identity as a 'production' which is never complete, always in process, and always constituted within, not outside, representations"* (1991: 222), Some traits of peoples identities are, as arguments in one's speech, emphasised particularly strongly in a given situation whereas other are made less important or just ignored. As Friderik Barth points out, some aspects of our identities, (again, in a given moment) are used as *'signals and emblems of differences'* while other differences are *'played down or denied'* (Barth 1969: 14). The main objective in so doing is to delineate as clear boundary[78] as possible; which will separate 'us' with our distinctiveness from 'them'. Thus since the content of social identities is changeable, hence identities themselves are not fixed but flexible and malleable constructions. They are not primary identities and they can change over time.

In the modern age the notion of identity has gained yet another crucial feature, namely that of individualism or authenticity. From this time we have begun to speak about the individualised identity that is 'particular to me' and that I 'discover in myself'. This notion arises along with an ideal, that of 'being true to myself' and my own particular way of being. Charles Taylor traces the intellectual sources of this authenticity feature of social identities to two people: Jean-Jacques Rousseau and Johann Gottlob Herder. The first frequently presented the issue of morality in his writings as that of our following a voice of nature within us. According to Taylor, his idea, or rather his articulation of the idea that was already present in the culture, has greatly contributed to the displacement of the moral accent in the conceptions of 'being true to oneself', and consequently being in touch with our feelings took on an independent and crucial moral significance. It came to be something everyone is supposed to attain if he or she is 'to be true and full human being' (Taylor 1992: 77). Herder, the second person who has significantly pushed the ideal of authenticity forward, claimed that *"each of us has an original way of being human: each person has his or her own measure"* (Taylor 1992: 78). According to Taylor this innovative idea, which burrowed deeply into modern consciousness, gave a new importance to 'being true to myself'. In the new intellectual context if someone is not true to oneself then he or she misses the point of his her life. Furthermore he points out that being true to myself means *"being true to my own originality, which is something only I can articulate and discover"* (ibid). In articulating this originality people are also defining themselves and realizing a potentiality that is

---

[78] Following Barth (1969), by boundary I mean an ongoing product of social interaction that is to be found in interaction between members of different identities.

properly their own. This intellectual background to the modern ideal of authenticity, and to the goals of self-fulfilment and self-realization in which the ideal is usually couched, needs to be further extended by drawing a rough picture of the larger social context in which this ideal has arisen and transformed, since it is a crucial for understanding the efforts of young European Muslims in constructing original personal biographies.

The social context in which the ideal of authenticity was born is traditionally referred to by sociologists as modernity. In most general terms modernity can be understood as the institutions and modes of behaviour established first of all in post-feudal Europe, but which in the 20th century have increasingly become world-historical in their impact (Giddens 1991: 14-15). The theories of modernity usually distinguish between the simple (first or classical) modernity, linked with the rise of the industrial society and marked by the modernization of premodern tradition, and high (second or reflexive) modernity characterized by the modernization of the industrial design itself (Beck 1992: 10-11)[79]. While in the simple modernity social actors come under the sway of pre-given rules sourced in social institutions (a group- and role-wise differentiation) this is no longer possible in high modernity in which people live with the *"risk ... ambivalence and contingency [that] is forced upon them with the relative decline of institutions and organizations"* (Lash 1999: 3) (differentiation at the individual level)[80]. In other words, if traditional notions of fate (cases of being 'born into' certain identities) still exist in circumstances of high modernity, for the most part these are inconsistent with an outlook in which risk becomes a fundamental element and in which the determinism of social standing is replaced by compulsive and obligatory self-determination (Bauman 1995: XV)[81]. High modernity, to quote Anthony Giddens, one of the propagators of this term, is a 'runaway world' (2000). By this he means that it is not only the pace of social change that is much faster now than in any prior system but also its scope and the profoundness with which it affects pre-existing social practices and modes of behaviour (Giddens 1991: 16). From the point of this study the most important

---

[79] Here it has to be noted that some scholars locate modernity in time differently. See for example Wagner 1994: 201.
[80] The differences between the two modernities have been also explained by the notions of linear and non-linear individualizations (Beck & Beck-Gernsheim 2002: XXII)
[81] This applies also to religious identities – if someone's religious identity is supposed to be meaningful, it has to be reflexively constructed.

aspect of modernity is the emergence of new mechanisms of self-identity or the new 'ways of being true to oneself', which are shaped by – yet also shape – the institutions of modernity. The emergence of these mechanisms is directly linked to such key features of the modern social life which needs to be briefly explored as separation of time and space, disembedding mechanisms and reflexivity (ibid).

As Giddens demonstrates, one of the most crucial processes which contributed to the dynamic character of modern social life is the profound reorganization of time and space. While in the pre-modern setting time and space were connected through the 'situatedness of place', it is no longer the case in the modern age. Today "'when' markers" are neither connected to the "'where' of social conduct", nor to the "substance of that conduct itself" (ibid). The separation of time from space involves, according to the British sociologist, above all the development of an 'empty' dimension of time, the main lever which also pulled space away from place. This 'emptying' of time and space, which provided the very basis for their recombination in ways that coordinate social activities without necessary reference to the particularities of place, is also crucial for the second major influence of modernity's dynamism, that is disembedding of social institutions (Giddens 1991: 17).

The process of disembedding is defined by Giddens as *"'lifting out' of social relation from local contexts and their rearticulating across indefinite tracts of time"* (1991: 18). The same process underpinning modernity has also been observed by Beck who, in his model of triple individualization, talks about disembedding as a removal from historically prescribed social forms and commitments in the sense of traditional contexts of dominance and support (Beck 1992: 128). The reorganization of time and space and the disembedding mechanisms which have lead social life away from the hold of pre-established precepts or practices and radicalized and globalized pre-established the institutional traits of modernity, have deeply transformed the content and nature of day-to-day social life (Giddens 1991: 20). For social identity it means that its quite straightforward pre-modern relationship with locality, kinship and tradition radically changes and becomes increasingly ambiguous. This, however, is not the only way modernity influences identity. It also greatly impacts the contemporary 'ways of being true to oneself' through such key mechanism of modernity as reflexivity.

85

The third key feature of modernity, reflexivity, is defined by Giddens as "*the susceptibility of most aspects of social activity, and material relations with nature, to chronic revision in the light of new information or knowledge*" (Giddens 1991: 20). This feature of modernity is directly linked with the distinctive characteristic of social sciences which have to take into account the fact that the subjects of their inquiry - individuals and social collectivities - are capable of self-inquiry and adaptation. The logic of this mechanism is clearly portrayed by Lash who points out that "*modernization, understanding its own excesses and vicious spiral of destructive subjugation (of inner, outer and social nature) begins to take itself as object of reflections*" (1994: 112).[82]

From the point of view of this research probably the most important observation made by the theorists of modernity is that the reflexivity of modern institutions also extends to identity. They argue that the reflexivity of modernity is a twofold mechanism, which consists of not only structural reflexivity, which results in the core institutional responses of first modern society losing their self-evident, infallible or sacrosanct nature (Beck 2001: 23-24), but also of self-reflexivity or the individual reflection of changing institutional configurations and conditions. The self-reflexivity involves a shift in emphasis from heteronomous/socio-centric monitoring of agents to the autonomous, active and permanent self-organization of individual life narratives (Lash 1994: 115-116, Heelas 1996: 4). As Beck and Beck-Gernsheim notice, social relations, individual lifestyles and self-images are becoming 'reflexive' so that they have to be established, maintained, and constantly renewed by individuals (2002: 35). The same point is made by Giddens when he argues that 'the self', like the broader institutional contexts in which it exists, has to be 'reflexively made'. It means that everyone not only 'has', but 'lives' a biography reflexively organized in terms of flows of social and psychological information about possible ways of life (Giddens 1991: 14). The more tradition loses its hold and the more daily life is reconstituted in terms of the dialectical interplay of the

---

[82] Beck portrays how structural reflexivity breaks through when guiding ideas and core institutional responses of the first modernity (e.g. standardized full employment, gender-imbalanced nuclear family) no longer appear self-evident (Beck 2001: 23-24) and become a kind of 'zombie categories', which 'died yet live on' (Beck and Beck-Gernsheim 2002: 27). This point is further developed by Van Loon who demonstrates how all 'expert systems' of modern society have been forced to surrender their previously unchallenged claims to authority, what results in increased disembedding of individuals from positions assigned to them by these authoritative institutions within the structures of modern life (Van Loon 2002: 25-26).

local and the global, the more individuals are forced to negotiate lifestyle choices among a diversity of options (1991: 5). Identity in high modernity is a reflexive project which consists in the sustaining of coherent, yet continuously revised, biographical narratives. Beck and Beck-Gernsheim call this reflexive project, 'do-it-yourself [hereafter DIY] biography', while at the same time they stress that this 'DIY biography' is always a 'risk biography', which can swiftly turn into 'breakdown biography', if the wrong choice of career field is compounded by the downward spiral of private misfortune (2002: 3). The reflexive project of identity puts a particularly heavy burden on young people and especially on those who come from social milieus where social control, parental care and attention, and stable forms of socialization - crucial conditions for the development of personal identity - are lacking[83]. Many social milieus that are lacking these features are to be found amongst the Muslim populations in Europe, still largely of working-class background, which partially explains the difficulties encountered by numerous young European Muslims with 'carrying out the burden of DIY biography'.

The task of building its own original biography is 'risky' above all, because it has to be accomplished amid a puzzling diversity of options and possibilities. In circumstances of uncertainty and multiple choices, in which each person is required to steer his or her own individual course between the threats and the promises of modern society, the notions of trust and risk have particular application. While the former (trust) sustains a sense of 'ontological security' and serves as 'protective cocoon' in the face of the chaos that threatens the ordinariness of everyday conventions (Giddens 1991: 37), the latter (risk) implies that everyone must acknowledge that no aspects of our activities follow a predestined course, and all are open to contingent happenings (ibid : 28). Living in the 'risk society' (Beck 1992) means not only living with new forms of dangers (manufactured risks) unknown to earlier types of society, but also living with a calculative attitude open to the possibilities of action, positive and negative, with which, as individuals and globally, we are confronted in a continuous way in our contemporary social existence.

---

[83] The impact of developments in modern society on the conditions under which young people grow up are explored interestingly by Heitmeyer 2001.

Having sketched the main lines of social landscape in which the authenticity feature of identity has arisen and having explored some of the key mechanisms of the contemporary identity-building processes, it is time to introduce the understanding of the concept of identity that has clarified my usage of the term in this study. From the wide range of conceptualisations of this social phenomenon available, I find the one proposed by Manuel Castells the most promising analytically. Thus by identity it will be meant, after the author of 'The Information Age', *"a process of construction of meaning on the basis of a cultural attribute, or a related set of cultural attributes that is given priority over other sources of meaning"* (2004: 6), and where the meaning is defined as *"the symbolic identification by a social actor of the purpose of her/his actions"* (ibid: 7). However, in contrast with Castells, I would insist on the situational character of such a process of construction of meaning and its multidimensionality. Furthermore, taking into account the fact that the social construction of identity always takes place in a context marked by power relationships, it is essential to also introduce three main forms and origins of identity building: 'legitimizing, resistance and project' (ibid: 8).

The first form of the identity – 'legitimising' - is the one that is introduced by the dominant institutions of society to extend and rationalize their domination vis-à-vis social actors. It is the undifferentiated normalizing identity which rationalizes the sources of structural domination (ibid). This kind of identity is, for example, citizenship as it is understood in classical literature i.e. as synonymous with culturally homogenous nationality and where nationality is viewed as universal, and individual and group identities as particular (e.g. criticized above conception of citizenship by Marshall 1950).

'Resistance identity', as Castells explains, is a type of identity that is generated by actors who feel that they are in positions/conditions devalued and/or stigmatized by the logic of domination. This kind of identity-building leads to the formation of communes and constructs forms of collective resistance against dominant identities (Castells 2004: 9). Although it is traditionally utilised with minority groups, one may also observe it among majority groups. A form of such resistance identity is, for instance, 'defensive identity', which is constructed when members of the majority or a dominant cultural group feel threatened by the presence of other cultures (e.g. 'aggressive little

Englandism').[84] I believe the Muslim identity in Europe, which tries to resist the assimilationist pressures of the non-Muslim societies and their largely secular institutions by building trenches of resistance and survival and withdrawing from the mainstream social life can be seen as another example. A significant proportion of Muslims, who are involved in this kind of identity building, are those who cannot find their place in the 'runaway world', or those who are disempowered by stigmatizing representations of Islam. The case of many of them matches perfectly the classical explanation of the phenomenon of stigma by Erving Goffman, who argued that *"the discrepancy between individual's virtual and actual identity, when known about or apparent, spoils his social identity; it has the effect of cutting him off from society and from himself so that he stands a discredited person facing an unaccepting world"* (1968: 31).

Finally the last form of identity, 'project identity', is a situation when social actors, on the basis of whatever cultural materials are available to them, build a new identity that redefines their position in their society and by so doing seek the transformation of the overall social structure. Here Castells gives an example of the feminist movement when it moved out of the trenches of resistance of women's identity and women's rights, to challenge patriarchalism (Castells 2004: 9). In my opinion, another example of the 'project identity' are efforts of the Muslims (particularly the European-born ones) to maintain their religious identity and yet fully participate in a given society, or to be both Muslims and citizens, which challenges not only the traditional public-private sphere divide (e.g. the popular understanding of the role of religion in the public life), but also the existing power structures between the 'established' generating 'group charisma' and the 'outsiders' forced (by the established who have the upper hand in the 'relations of definition') to accept 'group disgrace' (Elias & Scotson 1965).[85] The members of the Muslim communities who engage in the construction of such a project identity, in contrast to the 'withdrawn Muslims' (of resistant identity) stressing mainly the elements of Muslim 'otherness', strongly emphasize the features of 'sameness' with other compatriots. Putting the emphasis on the

---

[84] Charles Husband analysed the construction of such defensive identity during the Rushdie affair through inspection of several newspapers. The editorial of one of them observed, referring to the anti-Rushdie demonstrations, for instance, that 'we do not burn books in this country, even symbolically' (1994).
[85] Further analysis of the Muslim project identity with reference to the study of Elias and Scotson (1968) is undertaken in the conclusion.

elements of 'sameness' (e.g. the fact of being citizens) opens up the way for the Muslims engaged in the creation of this type of identity to reconnect with wider society and be considered 'normal'[86]. Thus, they slowly, albeit consequently, divert the main stream of Muslim activism in the public sphere from the politics of Muslim identity, to the politics of Muslim citizenship, the mechanisms of which will be elaborated in more detail in the concluding chapter.

If Muslims constructing the resistance identity often withdraw from wider social life, disempowered by stigmatization, then those who build project identity are on the contrary frequently empowered by it, or to put it differently, they are able to work the stigmatization of Islam to their advantage. Thus, the experience of going 'through the eye of the needle of the other', to use the poetic language of Hall (1991: 21), is for them somewhat strengthening. It gives those who possess the tools to handle the stigma an opportunity to achieve fuller self-actualisation, both on the level of the individual and collectively. This is in line with the point made by Ainlay et al. who argued that the consequences of stigma might be both 'dehumanising and inspiring' (Ainlay et al. 1986: 7). By reversing the feelings of shame into dignity and self-esteem, stigma in their case turns into a source of empowerment. This is possible because, as it was explained earlier, religion provides an autonomous and an alternative space for Muslims self-definition and provides a framework for the orientation of identity, which means it incorporates a set of crucial qualitative distinctions, giving a sense of good and higher form of life (Taylor 1989: 16). I share in this regard the view of Nilüfer Göle who talks about the public face of Islam as a sort of 'management of spoiled identity' (Göle 2004: 820).[87] This kind of 'management' has to be understood against the social background of life in the 'runaway world', in which becoming a Muslim is not a result of the adoption of a ready-made socio-cultural pattern, but to a large extent a result of a long personal journeys, and

---

[86] Here it is useful to quote an important point made by Goffman who argued that "*[b]ecause of the great rewards in being considered normal, almost all persons who are in a position to pass will do so on occasion by intent*" (1968: 95).

[87] I do not agree with Göle, however, when she argues that Islamism is '*the work of those actors who have left their families and small towns to come to cities or to cross national boundaries, becoming migrants in Western counties in search of work, education and better living conditions*" (2004: 813). Although initially it might have been the case (in the 60s and 70s when Muslims were putting down their roots in Europe), today Islamism is no longer a 'migrant phenomenon' but a large extent a 'home-grown phenomenon' which I believe has to be understood against the background of the conditions of high modernity, and in particular contemporary searches for authenticity amid a puzzling diversity of options and possibilities.

tedious process of reflexive identity-building. As Göle rightly observes *"contemporary Muslims establish an individualized link with Islamic religion, which provides an ethical guidance for conduct in their daily life (...) offers a personal basis to construct themselves as moral citizens"* (ibid).

Before we move onto the next chapter, it is important to stress that although all identities in the high modernity, as it was argued above, are 'reflexively made' and hence they are to a larger or smaller extent 'reflexive projects' (Giddens 1991: 14), not all identities are 'project identities'. Project identities would be, according to Castells, only those which produce 'subjects'[88] and that are highly reflexive. He aptly pointed out that *"reflexive life-planning becomes impossible, except for the elite inhabiting the timeless space of flows of global networks and their ancillary locales"* (2004: 11). However, the difference in access to forms of self-actualisation and empowerment, which is crucial for this study, were already emphasised by Giddens who suggested that this is how class divisions and other fundamental lines of inequality, such as those connected with gender or ethnicity, could be defined nowadays (1991: 6). He also argued importantly that *"human self-actualisation, both on the level of the individual and collectively, emerges from the shadow of 'emancipatory politics'"* (1991: 9).

To sum up, this chapter has demonstrated how the extensions of juridical citizenship during the last few centuries have provided new space for the development of identity and how sociology has dealt with these phenomena. It has critically reviewed the current scholarship on citizenship in sociology and proposed an understanding of this complex phenomenon more in line with the current social realities of Western Europe. It has also presented the key mechanisms of identity formation, which operate within the spaces opened up by extensions of citizenship, and formulated the main research questions.

---

[88] By a 'subject' he means, after Alain Touraine (1993), *'the desire of being an individual, of creating a personal history, of giving meaning to the whole realm of experiences of individual life... The transformation of individuals into subjects results from the necessary combination of two affirmations: that of individuals against communities, and that of individuals against the market'*. He also defines ' subjects' as 'the collective social actor through which individuals reach holistic meaning in their experience' (Castells 2004: 10) and argues that 'they are built.... as a prolongation of communal resistance (Castells 2004: 16).

CHAPTER III - Muslims in the Belgian and British Multicultural Regime

Let no one be in any doubt – the rules of the game are changing. Coming to Britain is not a right. And even when people come here, staying here carries with it a duty.
Tony Blair (2005)

Multiculturaliteit heeft bij ons geleid tot multicriminaliteit.[89]
Filip Dewinter (2005)

The emergence of the Muslim populations in Belgium and Great Britain has seriously disrupted the ways of managing ethnic and religious diversity in the public space that existed in both countries before their arrival. To a greater or lesser extent, it has transformed their multicultural regimes[90]. Most crucially the settlement of large Muslim communities within their borders has led to tension in the existing relations between church and state and calls for revisions of the content of the categories of 'public' and 'private' in the historically developed distinction between the 'public' and 'private' spheres. As Talal Asad reminds us *"the so-called private domain is continuously structured and re-structured by political, economic and legal practices that supposedly belong to the public domain"* (2003: 260). Ever since Habermas (1989) highlighted the central importance of the public sphere for modern liberal society, numerous critics have pointed out that it systematically excludes various kinds of people or types of claims from serious consideration (e.g. Benhabib 1992, Calhoun 1992, Fraser 1992, Modood 2004: 247). One of the groups of people most commonly excluded from the liberal public sphere, apart from women and subjects without property, are members of religious minorities. As mentioned earlier, a secular state accepts religion in the public sphere only on its own conditions. The level of their exclusion, however, varies from country to country as in every society there is a different level of tolerance for the manifestations of religiosity in the public sphere and especially for the manifestations of religiosity of new religious groups.

---

[89] In Flemish – "In our country mulitculturalism has led to *muliti-criminality*".
[90] The term multicultural regime refers here to a specific form of management of cultural diversity to be found in a given society. On different meanings of the term 'multiculturalism' see, for example, Guttman 1992, Vertovec 1998, or Joppke and Morawska 2004.

This chapter, which explores the main issues related to Muslim presence in Belgium and Britain will also shed light on differences in their levels of tolerance for the manifestations of Islamic religiosity in the public sphere. These levels of tolerance are one of the aspects of the larger opportunity structures (Koopmans 1999: 101, 2004: 451) including both an institutional element (e.g. political systems, models of incorporation of immigrants, frameworks of church and state relations) and a discursive element (e.g. established notions of who and what is considered reasonable and legitimate) that will be outlined in this chapter. By providing background information about the issues concerning Islam in both countries, it aims to indicate some of the general factors and events that might have influenced the social representations of citizenship of young organised Muslims. Thus, it is intended as a bridge between the theoretical framework sketched earlier and the presentation of the research findings in the following chapters.

In line with the comparative framework of the research, it begins with a short description of the key similarities and differences between the Belgian and British multiculturalisms. Then, it proceeds to portray how both the analysed countries have acquired substantial Muslim populations, describes their current situation and socio-economic profiles, and briefly presents who were the main informants and how the data was collected. In the last parts it explores the development of the incorporation policies for immigrants, the accommodation of Islam within Church and State structures and the main debates around Islam in both countries in the last two decades.

3.1 MULTICULTURAL BELGIUM AND BRITAIN

At first glance Belgium, which is a young and by European standards, a relatively small country seems not to have very much in common with six times larger and possessing much longer national history Britain. Yet a closer inspection of the two cases reveals many intriguing similarities. From the point of view of this research, the most pertinent similarity has obviously to do with the significant growth over the last decades of the importance of Muslim voices in the public debates. These voices have often constituted a major challenge in both countries since they implied a profound revision of the Belgian and British Christian heritage deeply rooted in the state and political structures (Favell and Martiniello 1998: 181-182).

Apart from this element of convergence that is almost taken for granted, as one of the general observations behind the study, one may notice that both countries are not only multinational, but also polyethnic. In other words, they are made up of not only national minorities, *"arising from the incorporation of previously self-governing territorially concentrated cultures into a larger state"*, but also of ethnic minorities *"arising from individual and familial immigration"* (Kymlicka 1995).[91] Applying the aforementioned definitions to the case of Belgium, one may find within its borders such national groups as the Flemings, Walloons and germanophones, whereas the United Kingdom is comprised of the English, Welsh, Scots and Northern Irish. The largest ethnic minorities that have settled in the former following WWII are the Italians, Moroccans and Turks, while in the latter they are made up of Southern Asians and West Indians. For this reason John Rex talks about Britain and Belgium as countries which are 'doubly multicultural' (Rex 1998: 12). Their double multiculturality exposes particularly clearly the imperfections of the traditional models of the nation-state developed throughout 19th and 20th century. Such models implied inter alia a high level of ethnic and cultural homogeneity of the populations living within borders of a certain state and were based on the assumption that each nation should have its own state (Martiniello 1998: 5). Although they do not reflect the socio-cultural realities of the analysing countries Belgian and British governments found them very useful, inter alia, in legitimizing a strongly assimilationist undercurrent in their approach to ethnic minorities.

Another important element of the convergence between the two countries in which the two cases studies of this research are located is their colonial past. Both countries were colonial empires, even though the territories controlled by the Belgians could not in any way match those in the possession of the British. This feature is important since it enables one to better conceive of their approaches to ethno-cultural diversity. As Favell and Martiniello demonstrate, the colonial experience of managing cultural diversity had a strong influence on the policies developed by the two countries 'at home' with regards to the newly established ethnic and religious groups. While in

---

[91] While analysing the ethno-cultural diversity of Belgium and Britain the definitions of the terms 'national minority' and 'ethnic minority' proposed by Will Kymlicka (1995: 10-33) seem more less satisfactory (in the case of Belgium one cannot say though that the national minorities were previously self-governing entities), however it is important to mention that his framework was criticised inter alia for being too North American and inapt for unmodified European use – see for example Favell and Modood 2003.

Britain these policies have been very strongly marked by the 'peripheralisation of race relations' which is, in fact, a manifestation of the British colonial idea of indirect rule applied to the new context of immigration, in Belgium[92] they are characterized by the 'paternalistic management' which harks back to the style of the Belgian administration in Congo and in the protectorates of Rwanda and Burundi (Favell and Martiniello 1998: 181).[93]

Yet another element that Belgium and Britain have in common are kings/queens as heads of the state. The role of the crown is certainly far from being the same in the Kingdom of Belgium and the United Kingdom, however in both kingdoms the monarchs are very important symbols of the countries' unity and integrity.[94] Thus, the abolition of monarchial rule in both countries is widely perceived as a step that could lead to their disintegration and, as such, it is not very welcomed. For example, according to a recent poll in Britain only 18 per cent of the people showed support for the idea of abolition of the monarchy (*Ipsos-MORI poll quoted in Reid* 2006). In Belgium in 2002, the idea of the establishment of the republic found supporters among 15 per cent of Flemings, 12 per cent of Walloons and 20 per cent of Brusselers (Govaert 2002).

From the point of view of this study, of crucial importance is also such element of convergence of the two countries, as the porousness and openness of their national identities. Both the British identity, as well as, the Belgian one are quite plastic constructions, which leave people who are supposed to adhere to them, as a result of being born or simply living within their borders, relatively large room for identitarian manoeuvre. This lack of the precise boundaries of Britishness and Belgianness is, I believe, something that enables Muslims born in both countries to say relatively easily that they are British, British-Pakistanis, British-Bangladeshis or Belgians, Belgian-Moroccans etc. What makes them an attractive source of identity is also the fact that both of them are being shared among many national groups and none of these groups can claim exclusive ownership of them. On the other hand, the notions of Englishness and

---

[92] More recently, with the process of federalization elaborated below, these policies came into the area of competencies of the main Belgian communities, and not of the Federal Government.

[93] These policies will be elaborated below while exploring the accommodation of Muslim populations in both countries.

[94] This is especially the case of Belgium where the monarch holds a title of 'the King/Queen of the Belgians' and not the title of 'the King of Belgium'. Belgium is in fact the only example of popular monarchy that remains in operation today (Koninckx 2000).

Flemishness, for instance, are usually treated by the 'new' Britons and Belgians, as closed ethnicities rather than open nationalities and, as such, they tend to be rejected[95]. The Flemish novelist Kristien Hemmerechts argues interestingly that the charm of being Belgian is that *"it doesn't represent much, it's the negation of having nationality so to speak"* (1998). The same idea is put forward by Rene Henoumont who claims that Belgians cannot define their national identity precisely (1992). Neither can the Britons, as has been evidenced by the recent debates around the Britishness tests[96]. Thus, I would suggest that the identities of Belgium and Britain are to some extent in their absence.

The last element of convergence between the two countries that I find pertinent to this research is a strong tradition of working class mobilization and protest. In both countries the trade unions constitute a very important social and political force which, especially in the past, played a key role in the politics of the countries on the central as well as a local level. From the point of view of this book the most crucial fact about the labour unions[97] is that they played in the past and to some degree continue to play (especially in Belgium) an important role of political schools for migrant political leaders (Martiniello 1988, 1992) and civic schools for a wider population of migrant workers (Phalet and Krekels 1998: 191).[98] In Belgium, where in contrast to Britain, immigrants were not granted any political rights after their arrival, it was in the unions that the question of political participation and voting rights for foreigners was first discussed in the early 1960s (Martiniello 1998: 111). It was also largely through the unions that the members of the first generations acquired civic skills and participated in wider community life. This situation changed when in 1984 the law demanding at least three fifths of the founding members of a given association to have Belgian nationality was abolished and immigrants could set up their own associations (Jacobs and Swyngedouw 2006: 135).

---

[95] I shall demonstrate it on the examples from the empirical material in the following chapters.
[96] These are the tests of the knowledge of English language and life in the UK, which all the people who apply for the British citizenship would need to pass from April 2007.
[97] Labour unions are understood here as associations of wage earners for the purpose of maintaining or improving the conditions of their employment.
[98] Another institution that was fulfilling such a role to a smaller degree were the Consultative City Councils of Immigrants (Conseils Communaux Consultatifs des Immigrés – Stedelijke Migrantenraden) (Martiniello 1998: 111-113)

As far as the key elements of divergence are concerned, the two most important have to do with the nature of the cultural diversity in both countries and its impact on their administrative structures. Although both countries are multinational, only in Belgium does this multinationality translate into linguistic diversity. Whilst Britain does not have an official language, the predominant spoken language is English. Other languages such as Welsh, Scottish Gaelic, Scots and Irish are recognized as legitimate autochthonous languages under the European Charter for Regional and Minority Languages[99], and are only spoken by a minority of people in Wales, Scotland and Northern Ireland. Thus, despite the survival of these languages, linguistic unity is reality in Britain. English is so omnipresent that even one of the strongest regional nationalist parties, the Scottish National Party, campaigns in English.

On the contrary, in Belgium the linguistic divide is a rule. Each national group speaks its own language, while the only bilingual area is the region of Brussels. The official state languages of the country are Dutch, French and German. The first language, Dutch (often referred to also as Flemish) is spoken by the majority of people in the country (around 60 per cent) who live mainly in Flanders, the northern part of Belgium and to smaller degree in Brussels. French, which is the mother tongue of around 40 per cent of Belgians, is spoken in Wallonia and in the region of Brussels.[100] The third state language of the country, German is the mother tongue of less then 1 per cent of Belgians (around 70 000) who live in the eastern part of the country in the so-called East Cantons. Although the Belgian constitution states that the Flemish, Francophone and Germanophone groups are the fundamental cultural communities in the country, the Flemish-Francophone divide clearly constitutes the central political axis.

British and Belgian multinationality has been accommodated differently within their state boundaries. In Britain, calls for greater autonomy have been accommodated by the process of devolution[101] which was accelerated after the Labour Party came to power

---

[99] One more British regional language recognized under this Charter is Cornish, spoken by a tiny group of people in Cornwall, in the South-West of England.

[100] Here it is worth mentioning that according to the latest research only 19 per cent of Walloons are able to speak Dutch, while 59% of respondents from Flanders claimed to speak French. According to the same research 51 per cent of respondents from Brussels claimed to be bilingual (French-Dutch) (Ginsurgh and Weber 2006)

[101] Devolution is understood here as the statutory granting of powers from the central government of a state to government at national, regional or local level.

in 1997. This process differs from federalism in that the powers devolved may be temporary and ultimately reside in central government thus, the state remains, *de jure*, unitary (Leeke et al. 2003: 3). Furthermore, the UK system of devolution is asymmetric, in that there are different levels of devolved responsibilities and there is no common pattern. In spite of the asymmetries each national group, except the English, now have their own parliament or assembly. The Scottish Parliament, the National Assembly for Wales and the Northern Ireland Assembly were established in 1999[102]. At the moment there is no devolution in England since the government withdrew plans for regional English government after its proposals were heavily defeated in referenda held in different parts of England[103]. However, certain powers were devolved from the UK Government in London where in 1999 the Greater London Authority (hereafter GLA) was created. The GLA is unique in Britain form of citywide government with a directly elected mayor[104] and a separately elected Assembly. The major areas in which the GLA has responsibility for include transport, policing, fire and rescue, development and strategic planning.[105] Although today Scotland, Wales, and Northern Ireland each possess a legislature and government alongside that of the United Kingdom, there is no serious political crisis on the horizon that could threaten the integrity of the state.

While Britain in spite of the process of devolution remains a unitary state still governed largely from Westminster, in Belgium multinationality has led to profound transformations in the state structures in the last 40 years. In 1970 Belgium was formally a pure unitary state, however, the constitutional reforms of 1970, 1980 and 1988, which put the recognition of cultural-linguistic diversity to the foreground, gradually gave rise to a more diversified political system, containing two sub-national institutional levels, namely regions and communities. After the constitutional reforms of 1992-1993, Belgium was officially transformed into a federal state (Newman 1996).

---

[102] For more information on the powers of each of the bodies and devolution in Britain see for example Henig 2002, Pilkington 2002 or Hazel 2003.

[103] In November 2006, an ICM poll showed that 68% of the 869 people interviewed in England favoured an English Parliament, so it is possible that the government will return to its plans of devolving its powers in England (Telegraph 27.11.2006).

[104] Since 2000 (re-elected in 2004) the Mayor of London has been Ken Livingstone - by conservatives often called 'Red Ken' for his left-wing views.

[105] For more information about the GLA are available on http://www.london.gov.uk/

Figure 3.1 COMMUNITIES AND REGIONS CONSTITUTING THE FEDERAL STATE OF
BELGIUM

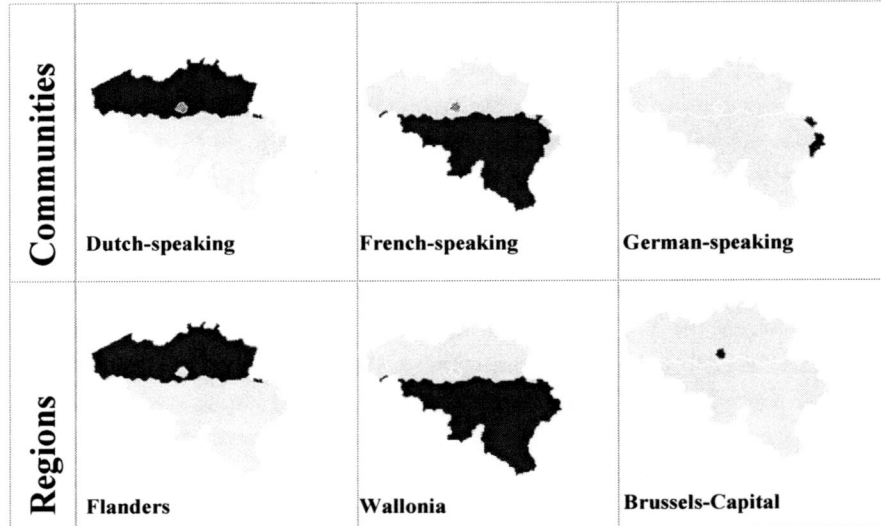

Communities	Dutch-speaking	French-speaking	German-speaking
Regions	Flanders	Wallonia	Brussels-Capital

As a result of this federalization by disaggregation the powers of the federal state,
which manages 60% of the country's public resources, were reduced to foreign policy,
national defence, public security, social protection, justice (including the official
recognition of religions discussed below), and the establishment of general economic
policy guidelines. Other powers were devolved to the regional (Flanders, Wallonia and
Brussels-Capital) and/or community federated entities (Dutch=Flemish speaking, French-
speaking and German-speaking – see the maps below). They embrace areas such as
regional development, the environment, housing, foreign trade, transport, employment
and vocational training, agricultural policy and scientific policy for the Flemish, Walloon
and Brussels Regions' Executives, and cultural policy, audio-visual media, education and
social action and assistance (including the integration of immigrants and their
descendants) in the case of the Flemish, French-speaking and German-speaking

100

Communities' Executives. Thus, in general the Regions have jurisdiction over the so-called 'space-bounded' matters, while the Communities have jurisdiction over the so-called 'person-related matters'.[106]

Furthermore, although, the Communities are not territorial entities, it is clearly delineated where they geographically have jurisdiction. In the Region of Brussels-Capital, geographically an enclave within the Flemish Region (also the capital of Flanders), powers are exercised not only by the Flemish, but also by the French Community. In practice, it means inter alia that although the French-speaking inhabitants of the city constitute an overwhelming majority (around 80 per cent)[107], Brussels remains an officially bilingual city and there are complex procedures which have developed over three decades of difficult negotiations to ensure this. Created nine years after the birth of Regions of Flanders and Wallonia (in 1989) the Brussels Capital Region has its parliament, to which 89 members (72 French-speaking, 17 Dutch-speaking) are elected on linguistically-divided lists (in order to be able to differentiate Flemish and francophones who are to decide over their own community matters), and government led by an officially linguistically neutral (in practice French-speaking) minister-president.[108]

Here it is also worth mentioning that, apart from the linguistic divide, which grew up in reaction to the domination of the French language, there are also two other important axes of social divisions in Belgium: denominational (Catholic vs. anticlerical, which resulted from the domination of Catholic pillar in the sphere of education, ethics and social security), and socio-economic (employers vs. workers, that emerged in response to the economic and legal domination of the employers). Furthermore, there are three major, regional political families or pillars (Christian-democrats, socialists and liberals) which historically coincided with the major types of segmentation. As a consequence of the 'language struggle' and the process of federalization, the pillars

---

[106] For more information on the powers of the Federal Government and different Regions and Communities see www.belgium.be
[107] According to a 2001 study by sociolinguist Rudi Janssens, 80% of the population of Brussels are more or less native French-speakers, 8.5% are native Dutch-speakers and 10.2% have both Dutch and French as a mother tongue (often mixed-language parents). The rest is made up of the allophones, who speak neither Dutch nor French (Janssens 2001).
[108] More information about the Parliament of the Region of Brussels-Capital isavailable on http://www.parlbruparl.irisnet.be whereas information about the Government of the Region can be found on http://www.bruxelles.irisnet.be . For more information about the history of the Region of Brussels-Capital and emergence of the Brussels identity see Govaert 1998.

which constituted the primordial social divide in Belgium split over the language issue that became the most significant divisive factor in the country. At the moment, the two major language groups have their own three pillars with a particularly strong Catholic pillar in Flanders (the Christian-democrats in power from 1958 until 1999) and the Socialist in Wallonia (Coorbayer 2002: 47-67)[109]. At the same time the notion of pillar (Dutch - *zuil*) has been replaced in recent literature by the one of 'political concerns' and sociological research has highlighted the emergence of signs of de-pillarisation (Dutch – *ontzuiling*) (Billiet 2006).

Finally, the last but not least general difference between the two countries that is pertinent to this book is that, while in Britain European commitment has always been problematic and national unity taken more less for granted, in Belgium the exact opposite is true, namely that national unity has been constantly debated (Dieckhoff 1996) and the European commitment treated as self-evident. For many Britons, in spite of the Eurotunnel and constantly growing mobility, for many Britons Europe continues to be 'something that very easily gets cut off by fog in the channel' – to paraphrase a famous old newspaper headline (Favell 2001: XIII). Thus, although the New Labour government is pushing the country towards closer cooperation with the European Union, a British society somewhat proud of its insularity is not particularly enthusiastic about governmental projects aimed at deepening British integration with the EU structures.[110] In Belgium, the topic which arouses similar or even higher levels of anxiety is that of a possible dissolution of the country. This was clearly visible, for example, during the recent affair around the popular RTBF (Belgian Francophone TV and Radio) programme 'Moi, Belgique', which on 13th December 2006 turned from a historical documentary into a fiction-documentary and 'informed' about the 'self-proclamation of independence by Flanders' and 'the break-up of Belgium'[111] (Lovens 2006). How problematic national

---

[109] In the political sphere in Wallonia the main three pillars are represented by CdH (Christian-democrats), PS (socialists) and MR (liberals) and in Flanders by CD&V (Christian-democrats), SP.a (socialists) and VLD (liberals).

[110] I am thinking here, for example, about the governmental plans of joining the Eurozone, which continue to receive very low public support. See the results of the Ipsos MORI surveys on this subject available on http://www.mori.com/europe/mori-euro-ref.shtml

[111] More information about this affaire can be found on the following website: http://fr.wikipedia.org/wiki/%C3%89mission_sp%C3%A9ciale_de_La_Une_du_13_d%C3%A9cembre_2006

unity in Belgium is has also been demonstrated by opinion polls. One of them, carried out by the Dedicated Research in 2005 showed, for instance, that only 31 per cent of Walloons, 26 per cent of Flemings and 21 per cent of Brusselers believed that Belgium would exist on maps of Europe in 50 years time (Le Soir 10.06.2005).

Summing up this sketch of the main points of convergence and divergence between Belgium and Britain and their multicultural regimes, one cannot overlook the fact that multiculturalism is never a single homogenous 'form of politics'. Although both countries are multicultural, and even doubly multicultural, they manage their cultural diversity differently. While in Britain multiculturalism refers to the existence of separate cultures among immigrants from relatively geographically dispersed region with sharply different cultures from the British, in Belgium the idea of the 'multicultural society', most commonly referred to as distinct national communities, is very reluctantly extended to as immigrant ethnic communities[112] (Rex 1998: 19, Favell and Martiniello 1998: 183). One of the reasons for this 'reluctance', which will be dealt with below, is that from the very beginning the debate about identity difference and the recognition of minority groups has been shaped in Belgium (especially in the North) by the most radical opponents of multiculturalism[113]. One of their most prominent representatives, for instance, famously declared that 'multiculturalism is leading to multi-criminality' (Dewinter 2005). This kind of authoritative arguments vis-à-vis ethnic and religious minorities, diffused widely by the opponents of multiculturalism, has strongly challenged the discourse and ideals of a society where difference is mutually enriching. Furthermore, I agree with Bousetta and Jacobs who have suggested that the underdevelopment of an overarching Belgian vision of multiculturalism is largely prevented by the multinational character of the country and the complex decision-making procedures devised to pacify the tensions between the two dominant communities[114]. As a consequence, when

---

[112] One of the exceptional moments when the notion of multiculturalism is referring to wider celebration of cultural diversity is, for instance, during the Zinneke parade organized bi-annually in Brussels. More information about the parade is available on www.zinneke.org
[113] The presence of the strong extreme-right 'racist' party in Belgium, Vlaams Belang, is in fact yet another point of divergence with Britain, where the British National Party is relatively weak and is not able to significantly influence the discourse on multiculturalism in the country. I shall return to this issue at the end of the chapter.
[114] The Belgian 'art of not debating' contentious issues is made of three main strategies: 'strategic underdefinition' (which will be shown below on the example of the government's definition of

103

consensus between Flemish and francophones is out of reach, non-decision becomes the most likely perspective, like for example in the case of Muslim veils at schools (Bousetta and Jacobs, 2006: 32-33). Before I elaborate on these points it is crucial to briefly outline how both countries have acquired substantial Muslim populations and provide some brief information about the target populations, areas and groups.

3.2 ESTABLISHMENT OF THE MUSLIM POPULATIONS

Initially, Belgium for more than one century from the time of its creation in 1830 was a country of emigration rather than immigration (Caestecker 2001). This situation changed in the 1920s when foreigners started to come to work in the rapidly developing mining and steel industries of the Walloon region and Limburg (Flanders). The two largest groups of immigrants consisted of Poles and Italians. According to the estimates of demographers until the Great Depression of the 1930s there were almost 170,000 foreign workers in the Belgian mines and factories amongst whom there were also numerous Muslims. The report of the Turkish Consulate in Antwerp from 1928 mentions the presence in Belgium of 3,303 Algerians, 1,291 Moroccans and 560 Tunisians (Bare 1992), while the report of the Federation of the Trade Unions of the Region of Charleroi from the same year talks about '*the Marabouts who go from one commune to another and have great influence on Muslim workers, (...) helping them practicing their religion in every detail*' (Report quoted in El Battiui at al. 2004: 4). That is why, some scholars argue that the presence of Muslims and Islam in Belgium is not really a new phenomenon, while at the same time admitting that the current 'visibility' of Islam in the country has its roots in more recent migratory influx (ibid).

As a result of the political changes after the Second World War some of the traditional areas of recruitment such as Poland became inaccessible. Initially the Belgian authorities thought that they would manage to meet the labour shortages by importing Italian workers. To this end they signed an agreement with the Italian government in 1946, promising to sell Italy a set amount of its coal production in exchange for Italian guest workers (Morelli 1992: 202). In the following years Italian immigration was the

---

'integration), 'salami technique' which slices policy domains as fine as possible, and an unwillingness to define ultimate policy goals (Jacobs and Swyngedouw 2002).

most important segment of the total immigration to Belgium and, between 1948 and 1958, on average 48.5 per cent of immigration to the country originated from Italy[115] (Grimeau 1993: 118). However, after the mining accidents in Quaregnon (February 1956), which caused the death of 7 Italian miners, and the even more disastrous one at Marcinelle (August 1956), in which 262 miners died, of whom 136 were Italian, this migratory influx fell dramatically. As a result, the Belgian government was forced to search for workers in other countries and signed adequate agreements with Spain (in November 1956) and Greece (in August 1957). A few years later it had become clear that even these agreements were not able to meet the labour shortages in Belgium and the government was forced to further expand its area of recruitment, starting to call for workers from outside Europe. In contrast to Great Britain though, it never opted for recruiting labourers from its former colony and protectorates i.e. Congo and Rwanda-Burundi[116]. Instead it gave preference to 'temporary' immigration from Morocco and Turkey, signing in 1964 appropriate bilateral agreements with both countries, and later from Tunisia (1969) and Algeria (1970).

Between 1962 and 1971 in total more than 544,000 foreigners came to Belgium, while 260,000 foreigners emigrated during the same period, resulting in a migration surplus of 284,000 foreigners (Martens 1976: 50). Morocco emerged as a country that would send the most people to live and work in Belgium by far. The economic conjuncture at that time was such that immigrant employment was no longer restricted to work in the mines but was available in many industrial sectors. As a consequence, Wallonia was less affected by this wave of immigration than Brussels and the Flemish cities of Gent and Antwerp. This new distribution of work in industry explains the high concentration of Moroccans and Turks in Brussels and large Flemish cities. Students of the migration flows point out also the differences in the form of recruitment and migration motives between the two main Muslim communities. While the Turkish emigration was more organized and essentially inspired by purely economic motivations, Moroccan migration, was less organized via official recruitment, and political and

---

[115] One of the outcomes of these migration flows is that until today the Italians (around 300 000) make up the largest ethnic minority in Belgium (Martiniello 1992, Perrin and Poulain 2002).
[116] According to Jacobs et al. Belgium did not opted for colonial labourers because she wanted to preserve a sufficient workforce for colonial exploitation in Africa (2004: 8).

cultural motives played a significant role in it (Surkyn & Reniers 1997, Lesthaeghe 2000). In both cases the immigrants came predominantly from rural areas. The Moroccan migration originated mainly from the Rif area[117] and a substantial part of this population were of Berber origin, whereas the majority of Turkish immigrants hail from the province of Afyon or bordering provinces.

According to the estimates of Albert Bastenier, the Muslim population of Belgium has grown from around 1,200 people in 1960, that is before the recruitment agreements with Morocco and Turkey were signed, to 65,000 in 1970 and around 200,000 in 1985 (Bastenier 1988: 133). Along with the establishment of the substantial Muslim population in the country the visibility of Islam also grew. One of the most important factors that influenced it, was the constructions and opening of Muslim places of worship. At the same time the establishment of mosques in Belgian and other European cities was a physical sign of a shift within migrants self-perception, from being sojourners to settlers. In Brussels, for example, the number of mosques has grown from 7 in the 1970s, 22 in the 1980s, 41 in the 1990s, 55 in 2000 to 77 in 2004 (see the table below).

Table 3.1 MOSQUES AND PRAYER HALLS IN BRUSSELS

Years	Moroccan	Turkish	Asian/Balkan	Other	Total
1970s	3	2	1	1	7
1980s	15	5	1	1	22
1990s	31	6	3	1	41
2000	34	12	8	1	55
2004	36	22	17	2	77

Source: (El Battiui et al. 2004: 14, Dassetto 2006a)

Due to an economic recession, Belgium in 1974, like many other Western European countries, imposed strict conditions on the entry of foreign labour but at the same time remained one of the most liberal countries in Europe with regards to the immigration of spouses and children. As a consequence, the flow of immigrants remained

---

[117] In all, over three-quarters of ethnic Moroccans in Belgium have their roots in Northern Morocco. Rif, and other Northern provinces of the country have always been oriented towards the Mediterranean world, and have had a long tradition of emigration (Surkyn and Reniers 1997).

almost as swift as before, with the difference that it now had a mostly female character. Here, it has to be stressed however that family reunification was promoted in Belgium, unlike in most European countries, as early as in the 1960s, due to the wishes of Walloon politicians to use immigration for demographic purposes[118] and in order to more successfully compete with neighbouring countries in trying to attract foreign workers. This type of immigration, but on a much smaller scale continues until this day in the form of marriage migration, as it is one of the only legal channels available for Turks and Moroccans to enter Belgium. According to a recent study, 57 per cent of marriages within the Muslim population in Belgium are marriages with one of the partners coming from abroad[119], whereas in the Netherlands this figure is estimated at around 75 per cent (Caestecker 2005). This type of marriages are most common within the Turkish community, while in the Moroccan community they are more popular among men than women (ibid). According to research carried out by Altay Manço, there are around 2000 people who come from Turkey every year to join their spouses in Belgium, which means that 60 per cent of the Turks who settle in the country every year come through marriage channel. Furthermore, he points out that 40 per cent of all the marriages amongst young Belgians of Turkish origin and 10 per cent of Belgians of Moroccan origin are arranged by their parents and that 25 and 15 per cent of the arranged marriages within the Turkish and Moroccan communities respectively are cousin marriages (Manço A. 2006).[120]

Apart from the constant, albeit minimal in comparison with pre-1973 migration, influx of Moroccans and Turks, Belgium like other European countries experienced an influx of refugees and asylum seekers from the end of 1980s amongst whom many were Muslims. This population, however, is very diverse and it is not possible to estimate how many of their members are Muslims, since often people coming from a certain country are not representatives of the (ethnic or religious) majority group but of persecuted or

---

[118] They were afraid that lower fertility rates in Walloon territories would result in the strengthening of the Flemish component in Belgium (Lewin 1997: 23).

[119] Mousaoui, who has studied these marriages within the Moroccan community, uses the terms 'endomixity' and 'endomixed marriages' to describe the endogamy across the nation-state boundaries (2006).

[120] Here is worth reminding that the dynamic growth of the Muslim population in the country (as well as in other European countries with the largest Muslim populations) is due to high fertility rates rather than to immigration.

discriminated minorities[121]. In 1996, for example, former-Yugoslavians accounted for almost a fourth of all asylum seekers, while the remainder originating from Eastern Europe and the former USSR, Africa (of which the Congolese constituted the largest group) and Asia (mainly from Turkey and Pakistan) (Jacobs et al. 2005: 8).

In the case of Great Britain, the emergence of the large Muslim communities in the country took place roughly at the same time. However the British contact with the Muslim world go much further back in time than the 20th century[122]. The British Empire, 'on which the sun was never set' because of its span across the globe, contained so many Muslims that the Lord Salisbury, the Victorian Prime Minister, used to say that "*Britain is the greatest Muslim power on earth*" (Masood 2006: 6). It was already at this time that the first small Muslim groups, consisting mostly of the Yemeni seamen, started to settle in the country's port cities (e.g. Liverpool and Cardiff). Although the first immigrants of South Asian origin, who today constitute almost three quarters of all adherents of Islam in Britain, started settling in a significant number in the country in the early 1940s, mass migration did not begin until the late 1950s.

The pioneer immigrants who arrived before or mainly during the Second World War were usually seamen and soldiers serving on British ships and in the army. They tended to postpone their return to their families in order to earn and save some money which they could take back home. In doing so, those seamen and soldiers became the first links in a 'chain migration' or the movement in which prospective migrants learn of opportunities, are provided with transportation and have initial accommodation and employment arranged by means of primary social relationships with previous migrants (Anwar 1979: 14). Without the financial help of the pioneer immigrants, their relatives back home would very often be unable to make a journey from the subcontinent to Britain. Thus, they played a crucial role in the establishment of a base for the Muslim communities in Britain; they were the bridgeheads of the mass influx which followed later. According to the estimations of Peach and Glebe, in the early 1950s when labour

---

[121] For example people arriving from Syria are often not the Muslims who make up 90 per cent of the population of the country but the faithful of the Syriac Orthodox Church.

[122] These contacts go back well into the Medieval period, and they came through learning and transfer of knowledge from the Middle East to Europe, often through the translation into Latin of Arabic scientific and medical manuscripts. Diplomacy and trade deepened these links and in 17th century, the universities of Cambridge and Oxford established chairs in Arabic. For more information about the impact of Islam on early modern Britain see Matar 1998.

migration from the South Asian subcontinent was in its early phases, the Muslim population of Britain was around 23,000. By 1961, there were about 82,000 Muslims in the country, rising to about 369,000 by 1971, some 553,000 by 1981, and about one million by 1991 (Peach and Glebe 1995). Along with the establishment of the substantial Muslim population the number of mosques in the country also grew. While in 1963 there were 13 mosques registered in Britain by 1973 this number had increased to 73 and a decade later there were 277 mosques. In 1985 according to Nielsen there were yet fifty more mosques (Nielsen 1992: 45).

The main 'pull' factor that stimulated this mass migration was similar to that in Belgium, namely a great demand for labour. Even though the Second World War was not waged directly on British soil, the country suffered enormously from it. The male population decreased hugely and some cities (e.g. Coventry) were turned into rubble after German bombing raids. Faced, therefore, with the massive task of reconstruction and acute labour shortages, the British government encouraged immigration, first from among European refugees displaced by the war, and then from Ireland and the Commonwealth. Before long, in some factories and industrial plants the overwhelming majority of workers were Asian (CRE 1996).

Ironically, the second major 'pull' factor which contributed greatly to the migration of South Asians to Britain was not supposed to be a 'pull' factor at all. On the contrary, the first Commonwealth Immigration Act introduced in 1962 was intended to discourage people from Commonwealth countries from migrating to Britain, rather than to encourage them to do so. The 'unintended effect' of the Immigration Act was, however, a significant increase in the number of South Asians entering Great Britain before it came into force in an effort to 'beat the ban' (Ballard 1994: 6). As Shaw points out, the very threat of the controls - which was widely publicised by travel agents in Pakistan and India - meant that some men who might otherwise not have migrated took up what seemed like a 'last chance' opportunity *(1994: 40)*. On the other hand, this closing of the gates of labour immigration generated an inflow of South Asians in increased numbers because of the already existing networks of migration - the above mentioned 'chains' of which soldiers and seamen were the first links. The voucher system which was briefly introduced under the 1962 Act (until the end of 1967) further strengthened the existing pattern of migration, that is the migration through chains of kinship, since those who already had jobs in Britain, had more chance of obtaining a voucher for their fellow kinsmen than people in Pakistan or India. Thus, the migration was largely limited to a few areas with long tradition of emigration such as Mirpur District in Azad Kashmir, Jhelum and Faisalabad Districts in Punjab, and Attock (then Campbellpur) District in the North West Frontier Province (Pakistan)[123], the Sylhet region in Bangladesh and Gujarat state in India. As a consequence of this kin-friend chain migration, the Muslim groups of South Asian origin that were emerging in Britain were, from the very beginning, tightly-knit ones.

Among the key 'push' factors that encouraged Muslims from South Asia to emigrate were high unemployment, poor quality of land, and the two great displacements of people: one in the scale of the subcontinent and the second on the regional scale. The first was caused by the partition of British India and the establishment of two separate countries: the secular republic of India with an overwhelming Hindu majority and Muslim West Pakistan and East Pakistan (from 1971 Bangladesh). This partition generated a huge number of displaced people who were looking for 'a new home'. As various surveys suggest, many of these people came to Britain, thereby becoming twice migrants (Anwar 1979: 21). The second displacement concerns the biggest South Asian group in Britain, Pakistanis, who were 'pushed' in great numbers to the decision of migration by the construction of one of the world's largest earth dams (Mangla Dam) in the area of the Mirpur district[124].

In the late 1950s and throughout the 1960s, many Turkish Cypriots, East African Asians and Muslims from Malaysia, Morocco and Yemen, decided to settle in Britain. The large entry of wives and children of the South Asian 'inter-continental commuters' was associated with the introduction of further restrictions on immigration (The Immigration Acts of 1968 and 1971). By the end of 1980s, most Muslim communities with exception of the Bangladeshi amongst whom the reunification of families started the latest, were made up of an almost equal percentage of men and women. As in other

---

[123] They were the most important recruiting districts for the (British) Indian Army and Navy (Khan 1977: 67)

[124] As noted earlier, this was a district with a long tradition of migration so many of the relocated people already had some relatives in Britain, and significant number of them used their compensation money to reunite with them.

European countries, the economic recession of the 1970s almost brought to a stop the economic migration from the Muslim world and marked the beginning of the influx of refugees and asylum seekers. The largest groups of Muslim refugees that have arrived in recent years to Britain are made up of Somalis, Bosnians and Afghans. Besides the Muslim refugees and highly skilled professionals, there is a constant inflow of Muslims from South Asia throughout the marriage channel.[125] Studies have suggested that up to 70 per cent of marriages in Britain's Pakistani and Bangladeshi communities are arranged with people from their country of origin. Furthermore the Fourth National Survey of Ethnic Minorities has found that the majority of these marriages (also among members of the second generations) were cousin marriages (Modood and Berthoud 1997: 319), which in practical terms means that members of such families are related to each other several times over by entirely different routes. This very high endogamy within extended family groups produces tightly knit families held together by multiple, overlapping consanguineal and affinal bonds (Ballard 1990: 231).

3.3 TARGET POPULATIONS

All studies that deal with Muslims inevitably have to define what they mean by this term. In this book, the category of a 'Muslim' is operated as one of the research questions, thus the following explanations aim only to provide the operational definition. Such a definition is necessary in order to avoid writing throughout the whole book 'Muslim' in inverted commas. This would seem appropriate in order not to essentialize the notion of Muslimness and in view of fact that for each Muslim adherence to Islam or being a 'Muslim' means different things. While for some Muslimness is mainly cultural, for others it is an attribute of ethnic identity which encompasses minimal involvement in religious rituals. Yet, for those who privilege the religious commitment, and on whom this study concentrated, this can take diverse expressions (e.g. mystic, missionary or militant). Before we shed light on the different subcategories of Muslimness, it is

---

[125] The British authorities seeking to restrict immigration through marriage introduced in 1980 the law of 'Primary Purpose Rule' under which, British citizens who married non-EU citizens had to prove that the marriage was not only a mere attempt to avoid immigration controls. This law was abandoned when New Labour came to power in 1997 which resulted in almost 50 per cent increase in admissions of foreign spouses and fiancé(e)s (Baldaccini 2003).

important to briefly describe an 'ideal type'[126] of Islamic identity which is a possible content of such an identity.[127]

In this ideal type definition that here is structured along the main lines of the 'official' understanding of Muslimness, being a Muslim would mean first of all to believe that Muhammad, son of Abd-Allah of Mecca, a merchant and former camel-driver, received divine revelations over a number of years from 610 onwards. It means to recite, at least once in one's lifetime, with sincere intention the simple Islamic creed, the *shahada* (Ar. الشهادة confession) which consists of two statements: 'There is no god but God' and 'Muhammad is the Messenger of God'. From this fundamental belief are derived further beliefs in (1) angels (Ar. *mala'ika* - particularly Gabriel, the Angel of Revelation), (2) the revealed Books (Ar. *kutub* - the Qur'an and the sacred books of Judeo-Christian revelation described in the Qur'an), (3) a series of prophets (Ar. *nabi*) or messengers (Ar. *rusul* - among whom figures of the Judeo-Christian tradition are particularly eminent), (4) the Last Day (Ar. *qiyama* - Day of Judgement) and (5) destiny (Ar. *qadar* – fate).

Secondly, if someone calls herself or himself a Muslim, s/he is supposed to face Mecca five times (or three times in Shiism) a day[128] to offer prayers (in Arabic *salawah* صلوة). The worshiper must be in a state of ritual purity accomplished by performing the ritual of ablution called '*wudu*'. The prayers can be performed alone or in congregation. Special importance is given to Friday midday prayers, which should be performed in congregation in the mosque, a rule which is mandatory for all Muslims male adults, while women may but need not go to the mosque. As the Fourth National Survey of Ethnic Minorities has shown in Great Britain, 65 per cent of Muslim males aged 16-34 claim to go to the mosque once a week. (Modood and Berthoud 1997). More recent quantitative research has shown that nearly half (49 per cent) of Muslim Britons professed that they pray five times a day, whilst 22 per cent pray at least one to three times a day (Mirza et al. 2007: 37). Quantitative research of a similar kind, carried out in Belgium between

---

[126] The concept is ideal in the Weberian sense when it removes itself from empirical reality to which can be compared or related.

[127] In shedding light on the content of the 'ideal type' of Islamic identity the differences between the Sunni and Shia Islam would be deliberately played down since they are not of significant importance to the drawing of this operational definition.

[128] Before sunrise, the second just after noon, the third in the later afternoon, the fourth immediately after sunset, and the fifth before retiring to bed

1994 and 1996, discovered that almost 90 per cent of men of Turkish origin and almost 75 per cent of men of Moroccan origin go to the mosque. This study also found that most practising Belgian Muslims affiliate with the 'mainstream' mosques and the number of believers, who go to mosques with so-called 'fundamentalist affiliations', does not exceed 15 per cent (Lesthaeghe 2000:147). A different study carried out in France observed that 35 per cent of the first generation and 14 per cent of the second generation practice daily prayer (Tribalat 1995).

The third pillar of Islam, and at the same time a third duty of every Muslim, is alms-giving to the poor (in Arabic *zakat* - زكاة). *Zakat*, which means 'purification' indicates that such a payment makes the rest of one's wealth religiously and legally pure. It should be no less than 2.5 per cent of a man's yearly income. With the establishment of modern secular states in most Muslim majority countries, *zakat* has been replaced by national taxation and welfare systems. Only a few countries, such as Saudi Arabia and Libya, have maintained official *zakat* systems along traditional lines. In Europe, like in most parts of the Islamic world, the payment of *zakat* by Muslims is a matter of voluntary charity dependent on individual conscience. The development in recent decades of Muslim relief and development organisation in Belgium and Britain (e.g. Islamic Relief) testifies that many Muslims in both countries follow this precept of Islam.

The fourth obligation for every Muslim is to fast (in Arabic *sawm* - صوم) during the month of Ramadan (ninth month of the Muslim lunar calendar). Fasting begins at daybreak and ends at sunset, and during the day eating, drinking, smoking and other worldly pleasures (e.g. sex) are forbidden. Any days during Ramadan on which the fast is broken should be made up as soon as possible during the following month, after the *Eid-ul-Fitr*, 'the feast of the breaking of the fast' which usually lasts for three days. Only the elderly, children, the incurably sick, menstruating, pregnant and breast-feeding women are exempted from it. Quantitative research shows that fasting is one of mostly widespread practices among members of the European Muslim populations (Maréchal et al. 2003: 17). As I have argued elsewhere, a high percentage of Muslims obeying the fast is connected, to some extent, to the high degree of social control in ethnic quarters inhabited by the followers of Islam (Pędziwiatr 2003).

The fifth pillar of the faith is the pilgrimage (in Arabic *hajj* - حج) to Mecca, prescribed for every Muslim once in a lifetime - "provided one can afford it" and provided a person has enough provisions to leave for his family in his absence (Welch 1997: 192). The *hajj* or the 'major' pilgrimage can be performed only during the Islamic month of Dhu al-Hijjah (literally 'Lord of the Pilgrimage') or more precisely on the eighth, ninth and the tenth of this month[129]. There are every year, around 25,000 British Muslims pilgrims who travel to Mecca for *hajj* and *umrah*[130]. To provide them with help and support, the UK Foreign and Commonwealth Office, in partnership with British Muslim organisations, has been sending a British Hajj Delegation to Mecca since 2000. An increase of people doing *hajj*, (as well as *umrah*) which has to do inter alia with the growing affluence of certain sectors of the Muslim population, is also observable in other European countries. In France, for instance, in only 2004 around 20,000 French Muslims traveled to Saudi Arabia for *hajj and umrah* (Le Monde 29.12.2004), whereas by the end of 2007 the number of French pilgrims in Mecca had almost doubled (Le Bars 2007).

Though the above described 'Five Pillars', which define the key elements of ritual practice for all Muslims, are the main signposts which indicate how to lead an Islamic lifestyle, the notion of being a Muslim is not limited to their obedience. Islam is commonly described as a legalistic religion. As such, one becomes a Muslim if s/he strives to live by God's word and the framework of law and rules known as the *shariah* (Ar. شريعة). The Islamic law divides all acts into five categories, those that are (1) obligatory; (2) recommended and customary; (3) neutral; (4) disapproved and discouraged; and (5) prohibited. While the 'Five Pillars' come within the first category, the major offences including, among others, drinking spirits, using intoxicants, disobeying one's parents or eating non-halal meat come within the last category. The same acts, however, can be placed by different schools of jurisprudence (*fiqh*) in different categories. For instance, more lenient legal schools, such as the Hanafi (*fiqh* of the majority of British Muslims) or Maliki (*fiqh* of the majority of Belgian Muslims), place in the second and fourth categories some practices, which a stricter school, such as the

---

[129] On the tenth day of this month the major Muslim feast, the Eid ul-Adha (Festival of the Sacrifice) is celebrated.
[130] *Umra* (Ar. عمرة) or the minor/lesser pilgrimage is a visit to Mecca performed by Muslims any time of the year. It is sometimes called the 'minor pilgrimage' or 'lesser pilgrimage', the *Hajj* being the 'major' pilgrimage.

114

Hanbali, regards as belonging to the first and fifth (Welch 1997: 198). The duties and obligations described above are only main traits of what it may mean to be a Muslim. They constitute an example of 'the box' which can be filled with further characteristics. To be a Muslim, as this book will demonstrate is not something given but above all a subjective process of the constructing of identity.

One can distinguish two major types of belonging to Islam: ethno-cultural and religious.[131] By an ethno-cultural Muslim I mean anyone born in an environment dominated by a Muslim tradition, belonging to a Muslim people, being of Muslim origin, with a name that belongs in a Muslim tradition and/or who identifies her/him self with, or considers her /him self to belong to this environment and tradition. It is a person who is socialized into, and has to some extent internalized, the Muslim cultural tradition – the Muslim *cognitive universe* (in Berger and Luckmann's sense, 1969) – and who has some Muslim cultural competence. This category of people are often described as 'sociological Muslims' (e.g. Maréchal et al. 2003). For them Islam is only a small part of the cultural environment in which they live since they have largely adopted the norms of conduct of secular European society. Whether they are agnostics, indifferent to religion or simply respectful of it, religious dogma means little to them and, apart from rites of passage, does not have a significant influence on their daily lives. While the ethno-cultural Muslims still largely follow Islamic ritual in life's rites of passage, they often rearrange or modernise their meaning. For example, the practice of circumcision continues but is rationalized not with religious obligation arguments but is justified as a sanitary custom and a practice which has an important symbolic meaning as it concerns the transmission of identity (Beishon, Modood & Virdee 1998).

Religious Muslims, on which this study concentrates, are people who profess specific beliefs, participate in religious services and other religious practices, personal piety and other elements of personal life style. There is obviously a significant diversity amongst the people who claim to be actively involved in the life of a religious community. Their belonging to the national Muslim populations and a larger *ummah* is differentiated according to many forms and practices, performed collectively and in

---

[131] For other typologies of Muslims in Europe see for example: Dassetto 1996: 124-140 or Maréchal et al. 2003: 8-11.

private. One may find amongst them Muslim mystics following the doctrine of a particular teacher (e.g. followers of Sufi orders) putting particular emphasis on the issues of spirituality, or those who adhere to a literal approach in the interpretation of sacred texts, proselytisers involved in social activities which mostly aim to bring Muslims back to Islam (e.g. followers of Tablighi Jama'at) and militants who engage in the Islamisation of not only Muslims but also of wider societies. The last group are often referred to as Islamists or political Muslims. As Sander points out, someone is a Muslim in the *political* sense if s/he has specific ideas about the place, role and function of religion (Islam) in society and claims that Islam in its essence or primarily is (ought to be) a political and social phenomenon (2003). It is this group of Muslims who are most actively engaged in the politics of Muslim identity and the reformulation of the concept of citizenship, therefore this book has paid particular attention to it. Some studies refer to religious Muslims who do not want to see their religion limited to only the private sphere and insist on its importance in the public sphere, as fundamentalists. This study tries to avoid using this category as not really adequate to the research of Islam and as one that has been heavily charged with very negative connotations. As Bejnin and Stork (1997) point out, the notion of fundamentalism is inescapably rooted in a specific Protestant experience whose principal theological premise is that the Bible is the true word of God and should be understood literally. In Islam, the belief that Qur'an is the literal word of God as revealed to his Prophet Muhammad through the intermediacy of the angel Gabriel is the core of the creed. There are discussions on which passages should be understood literally and which not, but the divine origin of the text has never been a topic of legitimate debate. Secondly the word 'fundamentalism' has very often been equated with 'radical Islam' and with a supposedly 'pure, unsullied, and authentic form of religion, cleansed of historical accretions, distortions, and modernist deviations' (ibid), and as such it has been understood as hostile to modernity.[132] In this form it represents a one-dimensional and simplistic view of religious movements that this research aims to challenge. Here it must be stressed however that the term 'Islamism' is not without drawbacks either. On the one hand, individuals labelled as Islamists often regard themselves as simply observant

---

[132] This is, in fact how many Islamist leaders present it, while in reality it is an effort to revitalize and re-Islamize modernity.

Muslims and oppose the use of the term. On the other hand, supporters of liberal movements within Islam[133] generally apply the term to distinguish themselves from groups and philosophies with which they do not identify. One important thing that needs to be said at this point is that Islamists are not a monolithic edifice but a very diverse group of people.

3.4 TARGET AREAS: MUSLIMS IN BRUSSELS AND LONDON IN THE WIDER CONTEXT

The study that seeks to explore the relationship between Islam and citizenship concentrates on the opinions of organised Muslims from two European cities: Brussels[134] and London[135]. As already mentioned, the choice of these two global cities[136] was not accidental. As organising centres of the new global economy (Giddens 2001: 690) with highly dichotomised occupational structures and as multicultural capitals[137] both cities are home to large and well organized Muslim populations that often experience serious levels of exclusion and disadvantage. The number of Muslims living in Brussels is estimated at around 162,000, while the diverse Muslim population of London amounts to 607 000 people.[138] In the first city Muslims make up around 16,5 per cent of its all inhabitants, while in London the figure is 8,5 per cent. The Muslim groups in both cities are part of larger national Muslim minorities that need to be at least shortly presented.

---

[133] By liberal movements within Islam I mean those which emphasize the autonomy of the individual in interpreting the Qur'an and Hadith and a more critical examination of religious texts together with traditional Islamic precedents; promotion of gender equality in all aspects, including ritual prayer and observance and an open view on modern culture in relation to customs, dress, and common practices; In addition to use of *Ijtihad*, the use of the Islamic concept of *fitrah*, or the natural sense of right and wrong, is advocated.

[134] In this book by 'Brussels' is meant nineteen autonomous municipalities, which together form the Region Brussels – Capital, and not only the municipality that contains the historical centre, officially named 'the city of Brussels' (in Dutch Brussel and in French Bruxelles).

[135] 'London' is understood here as administrative area of Greater London, which comprises 33 London boroughs.

[136] Some of the features of global cities are: highly dichotomised occupational structure, presence of denizens, multiculturalism, impact on the nature of the internal labour market (Cohen 1997).

[137] In contrast to London, Brussels, apart from being a multicultural city with almost 1/3 of its population being foreign inhabitants, it is also bi-national city.

[138] The estimation of the Muslim population of Brussels come from the recent article of Ural Manco (2004), whereas the figures for London come from the National Census (2001) www.statistics.gov.uk.

Table 3.2 MUSLIM POPULATIONS IN BRUSSELS AND LONDON

City	Muslim population of the city	Per cent of the whole population of the city
Brussels	162 000	16,5 %
London	607 000	8,5 %

3.4.1 MUSLIMS IN BELGIUM

The overall number of Muslims in Belgium is estimated at around 400 000 which is about 4 per cent of the total population of the country.[139] Similarly to other countries in the EU, the Muslim population in Belgium is very young. Almost 35 per cent of the Moroccans and Turks, who constitute the largest Muslim groups in the country, are below 18 years old, compared with 18 per cent of native Belgians. One of the consequences of this situation is that one-quarter of the inhabitants of Brussels who are under 20 years old are of 'Muslim origin'. Unsurprisingly, in 2002 in the region of Brussels the most popular names given to babies were Mohammed and Sarah (Bousetta and Maréchal 2003: 8).

The high fertility rates within the Moroccan and Turkish communities are the main reasons behind the continuous growth of the Muslim population in the country. In fact, the fertility rates amongst the Moroccan and Turkish women in Belgium are even higher than amongst women in Morocco and Turkey. For example, when in 1990 the total period fertility rate amongst the Turkish women in Belgium was 3.1, in Turkey it was 2.7. And when amongst the Moroccan women in Belgium this rate amounted to 4.0, in Morocco it was 3.3. At the same time, demographers have pointed out at the steady

---

[139] The fact that one may only provide the estimations of the number of Muslims in the country has to do with the Article 24 of the law of 4 July 1962 with regard to public statistics, (modified by the law of 1 August 1985) which stipulates that "In no case whatsoever can the investigations and statistical studies of the national institute for statistics be related to the private life, the political, philosophical or religious opinions or activities, race or ethnic origin". For more information about measuring ethnicity in Belgium see Jacobs & Rea 2005 and Jacobs et al. 2006. For more information about challenges of measuring the number of Muslims in Belgium and other countries of Western Europe see Pędziwiatr 2005: 46-47.

decline of fertility rates among women in Moroccan and Turkish communities and at the rise in age of marriage (Lesthaeghe 2000: 28-29).

In the country's multicultural Muslim community, the largest groups are made up of people of Moroccan (230,000) and Turkish origin (130,000)[140] (Manço 2004). While the Kurdish and Alevite communities (significant in Turkey) do not represent more than a few per cent of the migration which originated in Turkey, about 60 per cent of the intake from Morocco is of Berber origin (Lesthaeghe 2000:19). Members of the smaller groups come from Algeria (8,500), Tunisia (4,000) Bosnia-Herzegovina, Pakistan, Lebanon, Iran, Syria and Egypt. According to Maréchal, 113,842 people from the 'Muslim countries' acquired Belgium citizenship between 1985 and 1997. In addition, every year at least 8,000 Moroccans and 6,000 Turks receive Belgium citizenship. There are also 6,500 political refugees in the country from the Muslim world. The number of converts is between 3,000 and 15,000 (Maréchal 2002: 21).

The Muslim Voices project and Migration History and Social Mobility (hereafter MHSM) surveys have found out significant differences between two major Muslim groups in the country.[141] While the Turks still remain largely a very close-knit community and maintain many of their rural traditions (e.g. choosing spouses from one's parents' villages) the Moroccans appear to be far better integrated not only in the economic but also social, cultural and political sphere. For example, in contrast to the Turks where the majority resort to help from within the ethnic community in finding a job, only 35 per cent of Moroccans search for aid in finding work among other Moroccans. The representatives of the latter group also have a higher rate of mixed marriages with Belgians and a smaller percentage of home ownership in their country of origin. They master the country's languages better than the Turks and consequently they also do better in school. Part of the explanation of the better linguistic integration of Moroccans has to do with a history of orientation towards French as a colonial language and as a second language used for a long time in Moroccan secondary and higher

---

[140] The latest data suggest that there are almost 265,000 people of Moroccan and almost 160,000 of Turkish origin in Belgium. In this way the Moroccans are becoming the largest ethnic community in the country ahead of the Italians – around 262,000 (Hertogen 2007).
[141] These differences can be partially explained by different migratory patterns of the two groups elaborated in the following chapter.

education. Their much larger exposure to the Belgian media and press also plays a crucial role here (Glavanis 1999: 94, Lesthaeghe 2000: 19-21).

All groups of non-EU nationals are over-represented among the unemployed. Figures from the national employment agency show that, for instance in 2001 some 20 per cent of Turkish and 17 per cent of Moroccan workers in Belgium were benefit-entitled unemployed persons as compared to almost 10 of Belgian workers. Okkerse and Termote however proved that the actual rate of unemployment among these groups is much higher and can be even five times higher than amongst the autochthonous population (2004). Furthermore, while the average national unemployment rate at the end of 2004 was 7 per cent, the rate of unemployment among non-naturalised Turks and Moroccans was 38 per cent (La Libre Belgique 2004). According to one of my interviewees, who apart from being active in Muslim and wider civil society, is also a Muslim chaplain, around one third of all the prisoners in Belgium are Muslims (Hadijah).

One of the factors contributing to high levels of unemployment amongst Muslims in Belgium are the discriminatory practices at the labour market that will be discussed in more detail in the next chapter. Another important factor contributing to high rates of unemployment among the allochthons seem to be poor qualifications. The educational attainment of the first-generation Turkish and Moroccan immigrants is, by European standards, very low. Among the first-generation Turks, 33 per cent finished lower secondary and 53 per cent primary schools, whereas 14 per cent do not have any diploma. Among the first-generation of Moroccans, the situation looks even bleaker as almost 56 per cent of them do not have any diploma and 22,8 and 21,5 per cent finished secondary and primary schools respectively (Lesthaeghe 2000: 12). These figures significantly improve for the second generations, however both Belgian Turks and Belgian Moroccans are still a long way behind, for example, naturalized Italians and the national average. The large survey into the educational performance of second-generation immigrants (exclusively men) carried out between 1994 and 1996 has shown that 40 per cent of Moroccans and 41 per cent of Turks finish their education at the primary and lower secondary level (Neels and Stoop 2000: 289). Amongst the key factors contributing to the educational underachievement of these groups there are: low cultural capital, lifestyle elements hampering good school results and discrimination (Hermans 1992, Roosens 1998: 56-59).

The spatial distribution of Muslims across Belgium reflects the nature of the process of their immigration. For instance, Turkish participation in the initial guest worker programme was quickly turned into a chain migration system from very specific places. This resulted in moving substantial parts of the populations of villages and little towns from Turkey to Belgium. Furthermore, Turkish labour migration was more directed towards specific industries located all over the country. As a consequence Turks are quite poorly represented in the large urban agglomerations of Brussels (here they usually live in the municipalities of Schaerbeek or of Saint-Josse), Antwerp and Liege and make up many relatively small, homogenous communities spread over the country. The Moroccans, by contrast, are typically inhabitants of the three large agglomerations. In fact, 58 per cent of them live in Brussels alone, against 25 per cent of Turks. They can be also found, apart from Antwerp and Liege, in the province of Hainaut and the province of Limburg. The Moroccan communities are not only more heterogeneous in terms of area of origin, language (Arabic versus Berber) but also as far as socio-economic status and education are concerned (Lesthaeghe 2000: 25-26).

Although there is no precise data about the spatial distribution of Muslims in Brussels, as neither the question on ethnic nor religious belonging is part of the census, demographic studies show that more than 90 per cent of Turks and Moroccans living in Brussels are located in the inner city or as Eugeen Roosens has put it 'in the dilapidated quarters of Brussels' and exhibit very low mobility across the borders of the three-way spatial classification 'inner city – urban fringe – banlieu' (Eggerickx et al. 1999: 231). The table below, based on data from 1991 Census, presents the overview of the absolute numbers and proportion of Turks and Moroccans in different municipalities of Brussels.

121

Table 3.3 TURKS AND MOROCCANS IN THE REGION OF BRUSSELS-CAPITAL AND ITS
MUNICIPALITIES (CENSUS 1991)

Municipalities	Number of Turks	% in Region	% in municipality	Number of Moroccans	% in Region	% in municipality
Anderlecht	1,552	7.3%	1.8%	7,443	9.6%	8%
Oudergem	22	0.1%	0.07%	152	0.2%	0.5%
St-Agatha-B.	16	0.1%	0.08%	439	0.6%	2.4%
Brussel	2,606	12.3%	1.9%	18,126	23.4%	13.2%
Etterbeek	197	0.9%	0.5%	1,539	2.0%	4%
Evere	148	0.7%	0.5%	1,032	1.3%	3.5%
Vorst	108	0.5%	0.2%	4,949	6.4%	10.6%
Ganshoren	30	0.1%	0.1%	316	0.4%	1.5%
Elsene	267	1.3%	0.3%	3,082	4.0%	4.2%
Jette	115	0.5%	0.3%	998	1.3%	2.5%
Koekelberg	464	2.2%	2.9%	1,605	2.1%	9.9%
Molenbeek	1,420	6.7%	2%	14,083	18.2%	20.4%
Sint-Gillis	463	2.2%	1.08%	5,737	7.4%	13.4%
St-Joost	4,007	18.9%	18.7%	3,783	4.9%	17.7%
Schaarbeek	9,514	44.9%	9.2%	12,925	16.7%	12.5%
Ukkel	170	0.8%	0.2%	788	1.0%	1%
Watermaal-B.	10	0.04%	0.04%	58	0.1%	0.2%
St-Lam-Wol.	36	0.2%	0.07%	230	0.3%	0.5%
St-Piet-Wol.	37	0.2%	0.1%	124	0.2%	0.3%
Total	21,182	100%	2.22%	77,409	100%	8.11%

Source: Jacobs et al. 1999: 50.

One can also easily locate the major areas of the concentration of Muslims in the
city by looking at the results of the recent research on 'Mosques, Imams and the Teachers
of Islam in Belgium' commissioned by the Fondation Roi Baudouin. The research
showed that the highest number of mosques are to be found in Molenbeek-Saint-Jean (20
mosques), Schaerbeek (16), Bruxelles - historical centre (13), Anderlecht (11) and Saint-
Josse-tenc-Noode (7), while fewer ones can be found in Saint-Gilles (3), Ixelles (2),
Berchem-Sainte-Agathe (2), Koekelberg (1), Forest (1) and Evere (1)[142]. The Brussels'
municipalities with the highest number of mosques are those with the highest
concentrations of Muslim inhabitants. Out of all mosques in Brussels, 36 belong to the
people of Arab and Berber origin and 22 to the faithful of Turkish origin. The other
ethnic groups that have their mosques in Brussels are: ex-Yugoslavians (6), Pakistanis
(5), Albanians (4), Bangladeshis (2) and Black Africans (2) (El Battiui et al. 2004: 14).

---

[142] The total number of mosques in Brussels is 77 (in Wallonia 89 and in Flanders 162 - El Battiui et al
2004: 13)

Figure 3.2 MAP OF BRUSSELS [143]

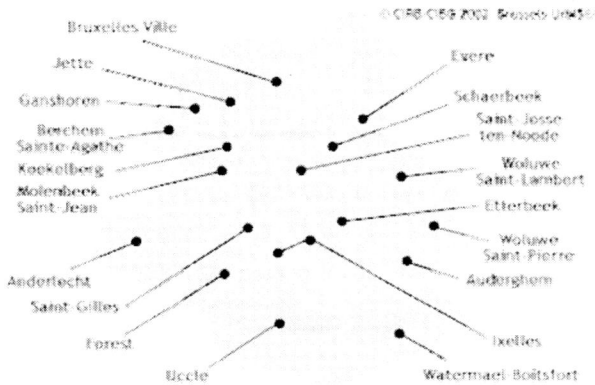

3.5.2 MUSLIMS IN BRITAIN

According to the Census 2001, which for the first time included the question on religious identity,[144] nearly 3 per cent of the population of the country, that is almost 1,6 million people, describe themselves as Muslims[145] (Office of National Statistics).[146] Islam in Britain has a visible South Asian character. The largest number of Muslims in Britain originate from Pakistan (658 000 of which, 54.5%, were born in the UK), Bangladesh (260 000 of which 46.6% were born in the UK) and India (136 000). All together Muslims of South Asian origin constitute almost three quarters of the adherents of Islam in Britain. There are also sizeable groups from Cyprus, Malaysia and the Arab countries. In the Census data, many of them are to be found within the category 'white' which accounts for 11,6 per cent of British Muslims. 6,7 per cent of Muslims in Britain are

---

[143] Map taken from http://www.rbc.irisnet.be/crisp/fr/presentation.htm
[144] The question, which in England and Wales was voluntary, was nevertheless answered by 92 per cent of people.
[145] Taking into account the immigration from the Muslim countries and especially the high fertility rate among members of the Muslim population one can estimate that in 2007 there are circa 1.8 million Muslims in Britain.
[146] If not stated otherwise the statistical information concerning Muslims in Britain come from Office for National Statistics http://www.statistics.gov.uk or General Register Office, Scotland http://www.gro-scotland.gov.uk

black and many of them come from such African countries as Somalia. The number of converts to Islam is estimated at about 10 000.

The Muslim population in Britain is very young. 33.8 per cent of Muslims are aged 0-15 years (national average is 20.2%) and 18.2% are aged 16-24 (national average is 10.9%). It also has fewer older people. However, at the other end, over 50 per cent of Muslims are under 25 years of age, compared with only 31 per cent of the national average. The fact that there are more Muslim children of school age than in other groups has implications for issues which are relevant to the education of the relatively large number of Muslim children in the areas of their concentrations. It is not uncommon in such cities like Birmingham, Leicester, Manchester or Bradford to find schools where 90 per cent of pupils are of South Asian origin.

Pakistanis and Bangladeshis are most likely to be unqualified. Nearly half of Bangladeshi men and women, and 27% of men and 40% of women of Pakistani origin have no qualifications. Low parental education levels, along with parental occupation, have been identified as key factors related to low achievement levels among Pakistani and Bangladeshi children (Anwar 1996: 47-48). In 2000, for instance, only 30 per cent of children of Pakistani and Bangladeshi origin in England and Wales gained five or more GCSEs at grades A-C, compared with 50 per cent in the population as a whole. However there are generally important differences in the achievement levels of boys and girls, with the former scoring on average 12 per cent lower than the latter. In the second largest British city, with the second largest Muslim population, Birmingham, Bangladeshi girls have actually overtaken white girls in terms of academic achievement (OSI 2005: 135-139).

Pakistani and Bangladeshi households in Britain are larger, 4.7 and 4.2 persons per household respectively, compared with the rest of the population (2.3 persons). Muslims in the country often live in joint and extended families. There are also fewer lone parent families among Muslims than in other groups. According to recent data, 15 per cent of Pakistani families are single parent families while the percentage for the white population amounted to 23 per cent and 54 per cent amongst the Black Caribbean.

Research has shown that when the economic situation deteriorates, the unemployment rate of minorities rises faster the rest of society (Modood and Berthoud

1997). In the UK, even in cities with a relatively small minority population, they account for a disproportionally large number of the unemployed. As the Labour Force Survey (Spring 2000) demonstrated, Bangladeshis and Pakistanis are two and a half times more likely than the white population to be unemployed and nearly three times more likely to be in low paid jobs. The proportion of young men from ethnic minorities without jobs is considerably higher than the average, even with the same levels of education and qualifications. The precarious economic situation of the Bangladeshi and Pakistani communities is also a result of the 70 per cent inactivity rate amongst females, who are looking after families and homes and do not enter the labour market.[147] (Kenway and Palmer 2007). Overall, the employment rate for Muslims in spring 2006 stood at 43.4 per cent and was the lowest of all religious groups. What is more, the employment rate gap between Muslims and the overall rate has risen in recent years from 29.9% to 31.3%. At the end of 2006 they had the highest inactivity rate amongst all religious groups (48.5%) and the highest unemployment rate (15.7%) (ENAR 2007: 13-14).

As in other European countries, Muslims in Britain are over-represented in the prison population. In 2002 almost 11 per cent of British prisoners (8 per cent of men and 3 per cent of women) were Muslims (compared to a national average of below 3 per cent). There were just over 1,000 Muslim prisoners in London at the end of September 2004, forming 16.9 per cent of the capital's prison population (GLA 2006: 90). The number of Muslims in prisons, mainly persons below 30 years of age, has risen dramatically in the last two decades. In 1991 there were only 731 Muslims in all British prisons. (Anwar & Baksh 2003: 38) At the same time Muslims are under-represented in the police, the judiciary, the civil service, the media and public appointments.

Muslims are not evenly distributed throughout the country. The active kinship and friendship networks and the process of chain migration have contributed to concentrations of Muslims in particular regions and cities. They are mostly found in the Greater London conurbation, and some other areas of the South-East, the Midlands, West Yorkshire and the South Lancashire conurbations. There is also a concentrated Muslim population in the central Clydeside conurbation in Scotland.

---

[147] In comparison the economic inactivity rate amongst 'White women' is about 25 per cent.

There are significant differences between the various Muslim communities in terms of settlement patterns. For example, while Pakistanis are more dispersed nationally, Bangladeshis are concentrated in large numbers in fewer areas, particularly in the East End of London in such districts as Tower Hamlets (71 000 - 36% of the population of the district are Muslims) and Newham (59 000 - 24%) which are also the districts with the highest proportion of the Muslim population in the country. Other large Muslim clusters are to be found in Birmingham (140 000 – 14 % of the total city population are Muslims) and Bradford (75 000 - 16 %).

There are at least two important differences between the national picture of the Muslim population and the London one. While outside the capital Muslims of South Asian origin outnumber those from other groups, in London there is almost an even split between Muslims from the Indian subcontinent (Pakistan, Bangladesh, India) and those from elsewhere.

Table 3.4 The areas with the highest concentration of Muslims in Britain

Area (City borough/City)	Number of Muslims	Per cent of the total population of the city borough/city
Tower Hamlets (London borough)	71389	36.4
Newham (London borough)	59293	24.3
Blackburn and Darwen UA	26674	19.4
Bradford	75188	16.1
Waltham Forest (London borough)	32902	15.1
Luton UA	26963	14.6
Birmingham	140033	14.3
Hackney (London borough)	27908	13.8
Pendle	11988	13.4
Slough UA	15897	13.4
Brent (London borough)	32290	12.3
Redbridge (London borough)	28487	11.9
Westminster (London borough)	21346	11.8
Camden (London borough)	22906	11.6
Haringey (London borough))	24371	11.3
Oldham	24039	11.1
Leicester UA	30885	11.0
Ealing (London borough)	31033	10.3
Kirklees	39312	10.1

Enfield (London borough)	26306	9.6
Rochdale	19248	9.4
Hounslow (London borough)	19378	9.1
Manchester	35806	9.1

Source: Office for National Statistics

The London's Muslims have roots in over 60 countries and speak more than 100 languages. The city's circa 300 mosques represent all kinds of *mazaahib* (schools of thoughts or religious jurisprudence) and the dozen or so Muslim bookshops give a good insight into the intellectual struggle for hearts and minds of especially young believers. Another important dissimilarity is that while in the Britain the largest Muslim group is made up of people of Pakistani origin, in London it is the Bangladeshis, constituting 24 per cent (143 000) of all Muslims in the city, who are the largest group[148].

Figure 3.3 MAP OF LONDON'S MUSLIM POPULATION[149]

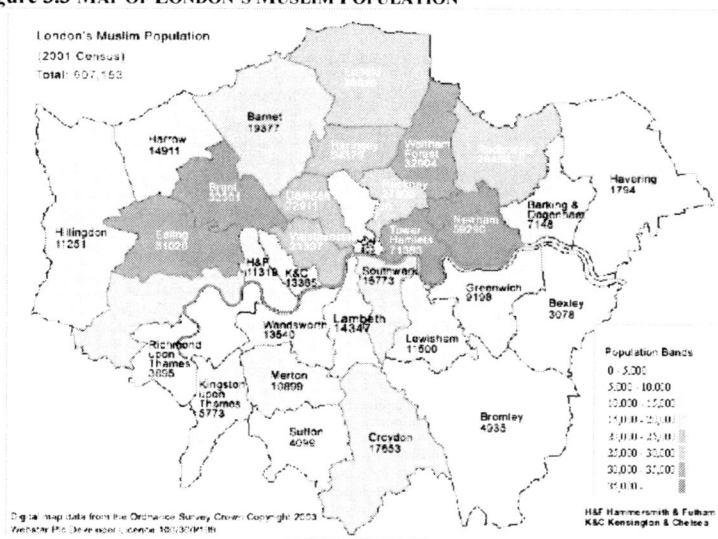

---

[148] Muslim of Pakistani origin are close behind 22 per cent (133 000). Data obtained from
http://www.salaam.co.uk/themeofthemonth/september03_index.php?l=2
[149] Map taken from http://data.webstar.co.uk

127

In line with the 'most different systems' design of comparative research, I have decided to choose Brussels and London as the geographical location of my study not only because of the structural similarities between the inner cities' Muslim populations in these two urban centres and the fact that in both of them one can observe the dynamic involvement of young Muslim in the debates about what it means to be a citizen and the rights and duties of Muslims as citizens, but also because of the differences between the two cities. The most important has to do with different approaches to citizenship[150]. While in Brussels, the dominant approach[151] to the issue of membership in a legally constituted political community follows the model of a social contract that emphasizes the social inclusion of individuals and individual rights in public sphere, in London it is the communal vision of citizenship that prevails. In the latter case, citizens are regarded not so much as autonomous individuals making private choices, but as members of specific communities, or social actors whose lives are intertwined and whose rights are recognized as part of group rights. This study shows the impact of these two models on subjective notions of citizenship among young European Muslims.

3.5 THE SELECTION OF KEY INFORMANTS

One of the main criteria that has been used to select respondents within the two national and urban centres was a generational one. As explained earlier, this study was interested in the perceptions of citizenship of young Muslims who were born in Europe or arrived to the analyzed countries in their childhood and posses not only legal citizenship rights but, above all, a range of forms of tacit knowledge, competences and taken-for-granted assumptions which allow them to engage in citizenship activities. Thus, the key

---

[150] Such elements of the cities' heterogeneity as their size, status within the state framework, presence or absence of a key political divide and a form of multiculturalism that one can observe within their boundaries were also taken into account.

[151] I use the term 'dominant approach' because this 'francophone approach' is not the only one that is in play in Brussels – see for example Jacobs 2004b. As the capital of Flanders, seat of the Flemish parliament and home to a significant Flemish population (around 10-15 per cent of Brusselers has Dutch-Flemish as their mother tongue) in Brussels one can observe also Flemish approach to citizenship that possesses many features of the British communal model.

informants of this study were men and women who described themselves as Muslims, had lived their formative years in Europe and were between 18 and 36 years old[152].

The second criterion which was used to draw the sample was an organizational one. It is very closely linked with the theoretical framework of study which emphasizes that the substance of sociological citizenship lies in participation in civil society. The interviews were carried out with organized Muslims, that is Brusselers and Londoners actively involved in the life of Muslim civil society. It was assumed that people engaged in the activities of the Muslim organizations would be characterized by a more reflective attitude towards religion and its role in the social life.[153] Apart from that it was taken into account that the organised Muslims have a significantly greater impact on the character of Islam in their respective countries than non-organised ones.

The third general criterion that was used to select key informants was a gender one. It was assumed that there might be significant differences in the way women and men mix religiosity and citizenship, hence interviews were carried out with both men and women regardless of the methodological difficulties it involved.[154] All these criteria were strictly obeyed when selecting the informants from within the organizations that in both cities were most actively engaged in addressing the issues of rights and duties of Muslims as citizens.

Before I specify the organizations which were the main reservoirs of informants of this study and explain this choice, it is important to broadly map out the Muslim non-profit sector within which I was operating. One of the ways of differentiating the organizations set up by Muslims in both countries in order to promote Islam is through the function they fulfil. In general one may identify five main types of organizations: mosques, grassroots membership organizations which deal with general needs as well as preservation and propagation of Islamic values (*dawah*), single-issue organizations (e.g. relief organizations, publishing groups), service organizations (e.g. Islamic centres and research bodies) and representative councils (e.g. federations and umbrella bodies)

---

[152] In Brussels 2 interviews were carried out with informants who were older than 36 years old but they perfectly fulfilled the other sampling conditions.

[153] As research into the voluntary sectors show being involved in non-profit organization implies an approach to society that emphasizes social change. This is also the view which was frequently expressed by the organized Muslims during the interviews.

[154] I address the issue of carrying out interviews with pious Muslim women below.

(Hussain 2003: 216). Here it is important to add that the aforementioned categories are not mutually exclusive and one organization may fulfil many functions at the same time.[155]

One can find all types of organizations in the analyzed cities. In spite of the impressive size of the Muslim associational sectors in Brussels and, even more so in London, they remain relatively weak. Their main weakness has to do with the scarcity of economic and human resources which they have at their disposal.[156] In contrast to Christian congregations, Muslim communities do not have real estate as a resource from which they can derive income. Their economically disadvantaged position has a direct influence on the condition of the civil society which they build. Apart from the fact that Muslim civil society is economically poor, it also suffers from shortages of human capital. The Muslim communities are made up of a majority of labourers with a rapidly growing but still relatively small elite. Similarly to the members of the working class, within the wider societies the propensity of Muslim labourers involved in civil society is rather weak. In consequence, a large proportion of Muslim civil society is run by a few dozen people who often appear on the committees of numerous organizations. Most of the work which the civil societies do happens on a voluntary basis and very few people are paid for their work. Most Muslim NGOs have either one paid post or none.[157]

In both analyzed cities one may observe Islamic organizational activity which can be divided, after Yasemin Soysal, into one which aims at creating alternative 'moral communities' that are foreign to the normative categories of European democracies, and those which try to use the dense network of associations to bring Muslim communities closer to the host society's public life, to encourage their civic participation, and thus foster cooperation and solidarity among citizenry (1997: 510). Furthermore, it is possible to think of three strategies in coping with minority status which are followed by

---

[155] For instance, a mosque can be at the same time a representative organisation (e.g. *Centre Islamique et Culturel de Belgique* before the creation of the Exécutif des Musulmans de Belgique – this case is elaborated in the following chapter)

[156] Although in both cities there are some signals of availability of structural financing to Muslim associations, these doors have until now generally remained closed.

[157] *The Muslim Council of Britain*, for example, employs only four people, while most of its members not only do not receive any money for their work for the organisation but often invest a large amount of their own money to be active in it. Its former Secretary General, Yousuf Bhailok, spent 50 000 pounds of his own money on activities related to the MCB while serving his 2 year term as its Secretary General (2001-2002). For more information about this organisation see Pędziwiatr 2007a.

organisations which treat Islam as a cultural resource in the construction of assertive Muslim identity: isolation from wider society, to prevent contamination from non-Muslims (the strategy advanced, for example, by the quietist transnational movement Tablighi Jama'at), strident resistance to western society (the strategy adopted, among others, by such salafi groups as the Hizb ut-Tahrir) and finally the strategy of engagement with wider society.

This research dealing with young organized Muslims in Brussels and London focuses mostly on individuals active in grassroots membership organisations, which follow the strategy of constructive engagement with local and national institutions and wider societies. However, some interviews were also carried out with members of groups that opt for other strategies (isolation or resistance to western society) in order to place the key material in a wider context. One of the main reasons why this research focuses on activists[158] from these kinds of organisations is that they play a crucial role in articulating the discourse on Islamic identity and citizenship within the secular context of Western European states. They constitute emerging new Muslim elites that try through various projects to contribute to the tackling of some of the issues faced by the European Muslim populations and thus at least partially solve the problem of collective uncertainty. In sociological literature, the groupings to which they belong are often called 'identity organisations'. This term refers to different types of associations and networks which use various kinds of social and political mobilization in order to promote specific identity.[159]

One of the key features of identity organisation from which the interviewees were selected is that they stress the need to make Islam more visible in the public sphere while at the same time seeking positive mutual interaction between things Western and things Islamic, including socio-political integration and self-integration (e.g. integrating aspects of one's thinking and behaviour which is Muslim and aspects of one's thinking and behaviour which is Western, so that there is no clear boundary or antagonism between the two). They are Islamist in a sense that they place Muslim identity at the centre of their

---

[158] By 'activists' of a certain organisation it is meant both formal and informal members who are not only passive consumers of its activities but those who have, to a larger or smaller extent, influence on the shape of this offer. This category is chosen, rather than the category of formal membership, because of the fluidity of the membership of Muslim organisations.

[159] These organisations were extensively studied mainly within the field of cultural studies and new social movements (Calhoun 1994).

activities and use the language of Islamic metaphors to think through their political destinies (Sayyid 1997: 17), however, they refuse to portray the situation of Muslims in Western Europe within the model of simplistic oppositions of *dar al-Islam* (the abode of Islam) and *dar al-harb* (the abode of war). In contrast to the Muslim revolutionaries and Salafis who often perpetuate this kind of vision, the vast majority of Muslim activists interviewed for this research promote various models of peaceful coexistence of Muslims with European societies.[160] They try to use Islam as a positive social capital in the interaction with wider society by taking pains to stress their strongly held religious identity. They neither want Belgian or British Muslims to close themselves in ethnic enclaves nor to assimilate with wider society. While stressing active participation in the wider society, they maintain that Islam has something distinctive to contribute to all spheres of social life and to understandings of justice, morality, etc. Thus they strive to convince non-Muslims that Islam is compatible with the values, norms and European legal systems and then propose cooperation which would confirm this coexistence.

In their work they concentrate mainly on the 'local issues' of Muslim communities such as 'identity crisis', educational underachievement, high crime rate, unemployment – to mention only a few areas - and try to establish partnerships with non-Muslim institutions. The global Islamic causes, such as the situations of Muslims in Palestine, Chechnya or Kashmir that are the main mobilisation themes of the Salafi-oriented groups, seem to play a much less important role in their agendas. Although we can find in their discourse elements of the rhetoric of victimhood and the usage of the negative mobilisation techniques, they do not make up their raison d'être.

An important feature of the organisations whose activists were interviewed in the course of the research is that the vast majority of their membership was born in Europe. They can be called second generation organisations not only because the majority of their membership is drawn from the offspring of Muslims immigrants who arrived in Belgium and Britain mainly in the 60s and 70s, but also because of the languages which they use. In contrast to first generation organisations, for whom the working languages are those of the countries of origin of the Muslim immigrants, the organisations on which we focus

---

[160] For example, *dar ash-shahada*, that is a "space of testimony", *dar-el aman* (abode of security) formulated as guideline for Muslim travellers and traders living temporally in the lands friendly to Islam, or *dar al-ahd* (abode of treaty) already introduced by ash-Shafi.

use mostly French (in Brussels) and English (in London). Although they continue to recruit their members within ethnic boundaries, they have been trying quite successfully to attract to their ranks Muslims from other ethnic backgrounds.

Yet another feature which clearly distinguishes them from the organisations of the first generation are their encouragement of Muslim women to get involved in the public sphere and to contribute to the welfare of Muslim communities and wider society. In all of the organisations analysed, women constitute a crucial part of the membership and play an extremely important role. This is also why they made up a significant part of the sample.

The Muslim organisations that possess the above sketched features and hence the ones which were the primary reservoirs of informants for this research are: the *Ligue Islamique Interculturelle de Belgique* (hereafter LIIB) and *Présence Musulmane* (hereafter PM) in Brussels, and *the Islamic Forum Europe* (hereafter IFE) and *the City Circle* (hereafter CC) in London.[161]

The first organisations in both cities, that is the LIIB and IFE, are structured around mosques in which the members of the first generation still have a significant authority. They are relatively progressive, in comparison with some other Muslim establishments in the countries, (one may, for instance, hear khutbas or sermons in them in French and English respectively and women are not discouraged from participation in religious and non-religious activities), but are rather conservative by Western standards. For example, during the conferences and seminars organised within their premises, the rules of purdah are strictly obeyed and women sit behind the men in separate rows (LIIB) or they are separated from men by a partition wall (IFE).[162] In the case of the PM and the CC, the mixing of men and women is taken for granted and viewed as absolutely 'normal'. For them the female sections developed by some Muslim organization (e.g. IEE) are not a sign of their progressiveness, but rather of their backwardness. They are neither attached to any mosques nor have any close links with the transnational religious movements. In contrast to the LIIB, which has such close links with the Ikhwan

---

[161] For detailed description of these organisations see Pędziwiatr 2008. Some of the projects run by these organisations will be analysed in depth in the next chapters.

[162] During the conferences organised or co-organised by the LIIB and the IFE outside of their premises, the rules of purdah were either not obeyed or they were obeyed loosely.

Muslimun, and the IFE, which has similar links with Jamaat-i Islami, the PM and CC like to emphasize their full organizational and intellectual independence. At the same time it is important to stress that the aforementioned and numerous other Muslim organisations only to a limited extent control the religious practice and a content of religious identities of their members and supporters. Many of my interviewees were for instance developing their religiosity while circulating between different organisations.

Although the aforementioned organisations are relatively young institutional beings, as almost all of them (with exception of the IFE) were set up within the last two decades, they nevertheless play an important role in the Muslim civil societies of the cities. Their position is especially strong when it comes to framing the discourse on citizenship among the Muslim populations in both cities. Because of their emphasis on the need to attain the 'fuller integration' of Muslims with their respective societies, they tend to enjoy good relations with the local authorities and hence play the role of religious brokers[163] not only within urban contexts but also within wider societies. The organisations from which the key informants were selected gather not only Muslims from the countries biggest ethnic communities but also from the smaller ones (e.g. converts). Although the informants were not selected through the ethnic criterion, the study made sure that the samples reflected the picture of the larger Muslim populations of Belgium and of Great Britain and that the respondents were mostly Belgians of Maghrebian origin and Britons of South Asian origin. In each city the author conducted more than 30 interviews out of which 50 (26 from London and 24 from Brussels) were selected for further analysis.[164] The major part of the data[165] was collected between April 2004 and April 2008.

Apart from interviews with the activists of the above mentioned organisations, the author also conducted interviews with members of other Muslim associations in order to place the key material more accurately within the wider spectrum of Muslim identity politics in both cities. Thus a small number of interviews were carried out with members of the *Federation of European Muslim Youth and Student Organisations (FEMYSO),*

---

[163] By a 'religious broker' I mean individuals and organisations that play a key role in the articulation of the identity narrative and discourse.

[164] More information about these interviewees are provided in the following chapters.

[165] Before starting its research in Belgium, the author worked as a researcher at the University of Bradford where he already began to gather material for this study.

Astrolabe, DéClik, Kawthar and L'Humanité Sans Frontiers in Brussels and activists of *the Federation of Student Islamic Organisations, Muslim Association of Britain, Islamic Society of Britain, Muslim Council of Britain* and *Hizb ut-Tahrir* in London.[166] In order to gather as rich data material as possible the author has used numerous data gathering procedures ranging from life history interviews, through semi-structured in-depth interviews and participant observation to the content analysis of the publications of the Muslim organisations and their members (if applicable). Moreover the author has consulted several members of his community of practice and community of discourse on the findings of this research.

3.6 INCORPORATION OF MUSLIM CITIZENS AND IMMIGRANTS

As described above, the Muslim populations from which I have drawn informants for this study emerged as a result of two different types of migration. In Britain the migration inflow was largely of a post-colonial character, whereas in Belgium it was a result of the bilateral agreements of the government with the states that had never been under the Belgian sphere of influence. The consequences of this difference are profound and multifaceted. On the one hand, in the former country Muslim immigrants on arrival were citizens[167] with equal rights to other inhabitants of Britain. In other words, from the moment they set foot on British soil, the doors of political and civic participation were widely open for them. As people who had obtained full political franchise, they could vote not only in local but also in national elections, and as research on the so-called 'Muslim vote'[168] shows they have been happily using these rights (Saggar 1998, Hussain 2006). Equally important, if not more important was the psychological dimension of the fact that Muslim immigrants were automatically incorporated into the national collectivity. It meant that from the time they appeared in British cities and factories, the autochthons had to start to get used to the thought that immigrants were 'here' to stay and

---

[166] For detailed information about each of these organisations see Appendix II. Some information about them one may find also in the next chapters.

[167] More precisely if they entered before the introduction of the Immigration Act of 1962 which cut off the right to access of British citizens of Commonwealth countries. In 1981 the British Nationality Act removed the right to automatic citizenship of those born in Britain to immigrant parents (this must now be applied for) (Vertovec 1996: 173).

[168] This vote traditionally went to Labour, at least until the decision of the Prime Minister Blair to take active part in the military operation in Iraq.

not just on a temporary basis, even though many of them might have envisaged a return to their homelands[169]. On the other hand, the autochthonous population in Belgium was not forced by the legal citizenship framework to think of the Muslim immigrants in any other way than as allochthons. Muslim immigrants on arrival in Belgium were merely guestworkers and, until recently, the only channel open for them to acquire political rights was to go through the procedure of naturalisation. One of the consequences of this fact is that they, and their children born in Belgium, were for a long time not included in the political collectivity and even at present, when the majority of them possess Belgian passports, they continue to be perceived by the wider public as foreigners.

The difference of the status between the Muslim immigrants in Britain and Belgium also explains one of the root causes behind the divergent approaches of the two countries to the issues of their social incorporation. Whereas the initial policies of integration in Britain adopted an assimilationist perspective, British nationality law (1948) and migration restrictive legislation (1962) soon paralleled with the integration policy based on the fight against racial discrimination (Favell 2001). As mentioned earlier, in Britain the key concept in the management of cultural diversity and social integration, understood as an equivalence of opportunity with the majority, has been the one of 'race relations'. It had developed in the situation in which it was widely believed that the only way of ensuring that the newly arrived citizens/immigrants had equality of opportunity and were not treated as second-class citizens, was to take some special measures. In other words, the category of 'race' was adopted when attempting to address the disadvantage of minority populations caused by discrimination. Not without importance in the choice of such a category were the events which took place in Britain at the end of the 1950s and abroad in the 1960s. The 'racial riots' which took place in Britain in 1958, in Notting Hill and Nottingham, crystallized the issue of migrant integration. The 'racialization' of the British policies in part reflected the fear of political elites that British 'race riots' might escalate to the crisis point of those experience in the United States in the 1960s. The consequence of this was that the policies which were about to be developed were more tailored to the fight with discrimination of the Afro-Caribbeans under the generic term 'black', than to fight with discrimination of migrants

---

[169] The role of the 'myth of return' among the first generation of Muslims was analysed in the first chapter.

from Indian sub-continent, that is the area of origin of the majority of Muslims in the country (Hiro 1991). Race relations politics has been extended to Indians, Pakistanis and Bangladeshis under the generic term 'Asian', even though this category has not been a very popular term of self-description among South-Asians (Bauman G. 1996).

The race relations industry developed through a series of Race Relations Acts, of 1965 (racial hatred and discrimination in public sphere), 1968 (employment, housing, public services) and 1976 (extension of the scope and introduction of the notion of indirect discrimination) (Bertossi 2003, Statham and Koopmans 2005). The 1976 Race Relations Act and subsequent legislation recognized the principle of 'racial equality' for individuals, and introduced measures for redress against discrimination on the basis of 'race, colour or national origins' and 'equal opportunities' especially in the labour market. In addition, the Race Relations Board which had been created in 1965 was replaced by the Community Relations Commission in 1968 and the Commission for Racial Equality (CRE) in 1976. Not only had the denomination changed (from Relations to Equality), but also the scope of action of the CRE was much more important than the former bodies.[170] Here it has to be noted that as I write, the race relations industry is in the process of yet another transformation as in February 2006 the Equality Act, establishing the Commission for Equality and Human Rights (CEHR) received Royal Assent. This new body, which came into being in October 2007, not only took over the responsibilities of the Commission for Racial Equality, but also those of the Disability Rights Commission (DRC) and Equal Opportunities Commission (EOC) and acquired new responsibilities to promote equality and tackle discrimination in relation to gender, gender reassignment, disability, sexual orientation, religion or belief, age, race and promote human rights, all in one organisation. From the point of view of the Muslim population in the country the most significant part of this new transformations is definitely the banning of discrimination in the provision of services on grounds of religion or belief.[171]

---

[170] Among the goals of this national race relations watchdog were notably to investigate discrimination in general and specific cases as well as in particular; to oblige people or institutions responsible for an act of discrimination to obtemperate; to assist juridical victims of discrimination; to develop codes of good practices; to advise the government on the evolution of the situation.
[171] More information about the CEHR is available on http://www.cehr.org.uk . The Equality Act 2006 is available on http://www.opsi.gov.uk/ACTS/acts2006/ukpga_20060003_en.pdf

Here, it needs to be also noted that in recent years one may observe the emergence of the elements of the 'faith relations industry' (Mcloughlin 2005: 55-58). The creation of this new 'industry' has been both shaped and itself influenced by Muslim identity politics. The most significant development in this direction was the foundation in October 2003 of the Faith Communities Unit, within the Home Office, which inter alia promoted 'community cohesion' through interfaith activities[172]. This Unit was strongly empowered by the introduction of the question about religious belonging into the census in 2001, and emergence of the new state-defined identity categories[173]. In 2006 it changed its name to the Cohesion and Faiths Unit and became part of the new Department for Communities and Local Government. On its web site one may read that *"faith communities are supported* (by the government – KP) *and their skills utilised in order to ensure that members of all faiths and none enjoy the same life opportunities".*[174] One of the most important events that has more recently pushed the 'faith relations industry' forward was the 7/7 bombing that will be discussed below.

The broad approach of equality in the context of ethno-cultural diversity was crystallised in 1966 in Britain by the Home Secretary, Roy Jenkins, for whom integration was *"not a flattening process of assimilation but equal opportunity accompanied by cultural diversity, in an atmosphere of mutual tolerance"* (Jenkins, 1966). Already at that time the three major goals of the British incorporation model were set: 1) equality of opportunity, which the institutions set up to deal with racial discrimination would achieve; 2) the acceptance of cultural diversity; and 3) the education of host people as well as immigrants in cultural tolerance (Rex 1998: 21). These general goals remain largely valid, not only for today's race relations industry in Britain, but were also successfully exported abroad and sometimes embraced uncritically, for example, by EU institutions (Bertossi 2003).

---

[172] Information about the interfaith activities supported by the government can be found on the web site of the Inter Faith Network for the UK www.interfaith.org.uk

[173] As Peter Skerry reminds us such state-defined identity categories have a profound impact not only on the state management of cultural diversity but also on individuals' conception of themselves. Like birth certificates and migration documents, the census is a crucial instrument in producing and maintaining ethnic, racial and, now with the inclusion of the religious category, also religious identities. In this way the census which enables us to understand the boundaries of certain nation, its strengths, weaknesses and the relationship of its part, can contribute also to maintaining these boundaries (2000:11).

[174] http://www.communities.gov.uk/index.asp?id=1503033

138

Malcolm Cross rightly describes the British approach to integration as an example of 'reactive multiculturalism' which, in contrast to the 'proactive multiculturalism' typical for such countries of immigration as Canada or Australia, "*is the generation of divergence by failing to deliver a promise of convergent opportunity or by actively fomenting inequality"* (1998: 90). Furthermore, this 'racial' form of social integration is a hybrid between assimilationism and cultural pluralism. It fully recognizes one form of cultural diversity - race - as the basis for requiring redress to the discrimination that prevents minorities from full access to social and political equality. At the same time, until recently it has downplayed other forms of cultural diversity, for instance, religious identification, by relegating them to the level of individual private concerns (Statham 1999: 604).

In the case of Belgium, the incorporation of Muslim immigrants meant first of all the change of their status of guestworkers or denizens to gaining at least partial political rights of the citizens. As mentioned above, the issue of granting immigrants voting rights had already been raised by the trade unions by the end of 1960s. It was then hotly debated in the 1970s and in the 1980s, when the Christian Democrat - Liberal government (1981-1987) openly refused to enfranchise the allochthonous population (Coenen and Lewit 1997, Jacobs 1999, 2001)[175]. The calls for the incorporation of immigrants into the national collectivity, by way of granting them voting rights and making them eligible to become candidates in local elections, were transformed into efforts at individual integration by means of naturalisation. The doors of the naturalisation of immigrants were gently opened up when the parliament voted in the so-called Gol Law[176], which had as its objectives: to limit the influx of illegal migrants, to repatriate certain immigrants, and to integrate the other immigrants by naturalisation (Rea 1997). From this moment the principle of jus soli, or the acquisition of nationality due to the place of birth, found a permanent place in the Belgian citizenship law and in the following years (1991, 1995, 1998, 2000) was progressively extended.[177] As a consequence of this softening of the

---

[175] The non-European immigrants were finally partially enfranchised in February 2004, following a heated political debate, which brought the government very close to a crisis. They could vote (but not to be candidates) for the first time during the local election in October 2006.

[176] Named after the Minister of Justice, Jean Gol, who was the author of the project.

[177] For more information about how the Belgian nationality law have extended the eligibility criteria see Rea 1997, 2004 or Bousetta et al. 2005.

rules of naturalisation, 434,814 foreigners, among whom 150,197 were allochthon Brusselers, became Belgian citizens between 1988 and 2002 (Rea 2004). This significant increase in the number of immigrants holding Belgian passports played in turn an important role in the electoral breakthrough of allochthon politicians in the local election in Brussels in 2000.[178]

Parallel to the advances in the political integration of immigrants were also developments within immigration policy and the social integration of immigrants. Until the late 1980s, the immigration policy focused mainly on controlling entry and settlement in the country, regulating access to the labour market and determining the conditions to be met for the acquisition of Belgian nationality. It was up to gatekeepers in the voluntary sector (e.g. trade unions and Catholic institutions) to assist foreign workers and their families in trying to 'fit into' Belgian society. However, there was for example no legal framework that would try to improve the immigrants incorporation by punishing open manifestations of racism and xenophobia. Such a framework came into existence in 1981 with the introduction of so-called the Moureaux Law (after Philippe Moureaux, then Minister of Justice), which banned discrimination on the grounds of race, colour, and ethnic and national origin. This initial legal anti-discriminatory framework was more recently strengthened by so-called Anti-Discrimination Act adopted in February 2003 (sometimes called Mahoux Law, after senator Philippe Mahoux) which banned discrimination on the grounds of various 'protected characteristics' i.e. sex, claimed race, colour, national origin, national or ethnic descent, sexual orientation, civil status, birth, wealth, age, religion or belief, current or future state of health, disability or physical characteristics[179]. This law applies to both direct and indirect discrimination and covers not only employer/employee relations, but also bans discrimination in the general provision of goods and services, in relations between government and civilians and in "any other public activity". In practice, however, the application of this anti-discrimination framework is limited by several deficiencies, in particular a lack of clarity and the difficulty of providing evidence of racially motivated acts in a criminal case (ENAR 2005, IFH 2002, 2006). Another problem seems to be the general lack of political

---

[178] During the 2000 elections in Brussels region only, 87 people of Muslim origin (77 of Moroccan and 10 of Turkish origin, including 23 women) became local councillors.

[179] This Act can be found in its entity in the *Moniteur Belge*, 12 February 2003.

will to fully empower the existing frameworks and implement them. As the research of Andrea Rea shows in Brussels region, for example, there is substantial funding for policies aimed at improving the social situation of economically disadvantaged groups and some funding for the promotion of culture and identity (available mainly from the Flemish Community Government - VGC), but the anti-discriminational policies are almost non-existent. This situation is thus, according to him, undermining the public policies of the local authorities, which have as their objective to improve social cohesion because they do not address one of the root causes of the their insecurity (Rea 2004). The existence of widespread discrimination of people of Moroccan and Turkish origin, not only in access to employment but also in housing and other sphere of social life, has been clearly demonstrated by sociological research.[180]

The study carried out in 1997 showed, for example, that the level of discrimination of migrants at all stages of the recruitment process on the labour market amounted in Brussels to 34,1 per cent (in Wallonia it was 27 per cent and in Flanders 39,3 per cent, DWTC 1997). This discrimination during the selection and recruitment process consisted specifically of a change in the recruitment procedure (supplementary requirements for migrants) or lies ('the recruitment has already taken place') or the imposition of different, less attractive, labour conditions, or the adoption of specific attitudes (distant, disapproving or paternalistic)[181] More recent study commissioned by the ORBEM or L'Office Régional Rruxellois de l'Emploi (Martens et al 2005), which is one of the most comprehensive since it includes not only elements of quantitative study but also of qualitative, confirms many of the findings of the older research (e.g. DWTC 1997, Arijn et al. 1998). At the quantitative level it found for instance that workers of Moroccan and Turkish origin (both, those who were naturalized and those who were not) were much more likely than representatives of other ethnic minorities (Italians, Greeks, etc) to work within specific sectors of the Brussels' labour market where the salaries are relatively low and the job insecurity high (e.g. cleaning, construction, foodservice and

---

[180] Here I shall point out the main findings of the research into discrimination on the labour market, while unequal treatment in other spheres of life will be elaborated in the following chapter.
[181] Different reports demonstrate also significant discrimination of the migrants and members of religious and ethnic minorities in other spheres of social life (EUMC 2004, 2005). More information about discrimination in housing and education in Brussels can be found in EUMC 2004 and EUMC 2005 reports, as well as, on the website on www.inrax.be and www.diversite.be

healthcare) and were almost completely absent in sectors of higher income and lower job precariousness (e.g. financial services, public services, post, telecommunication and IT). Thus, it confirmed the hypothesis of the ethnostratification of the local labour market which holds that the Brussels' market is divided into different ethnic layers with autochthonous Belgians and immigrants from the neighbouring countries (France, Luxemburg, UK, Germany and the Netherlands) at the top layers (highest income and highest job security), immigrants and Belgians originating from the Southern European countries (Italy, Greece, Spain and Portugal) at the middle layers (average income and middle-range job security), and immigrants and Belgians originating from Morocco, Turkey and sub-Saharan Africa at the low layers (low income and high job insecurity). (Ibid: 13-26) Furthermore, taking the longitudinal perspective, it showed that the ethnostratification is quite stable and that it is being reproduced in the generation of the Belgian-born children of Moroccan and Turkish immigrants. It also demonstrated that the possession of Belgian passport does not significantly improve the situation of Belgian Moroccans and Belgian Turks on the job market. In other words, it showed that contrary to the popular belief that unequal distribution of jobs between different social categories and members of ethnic minorities and discriminatory practices in the process of recruitment will disappear with the increasing number of people of Moroccan and Turkish origin going through naturalisation, such unequal distribution and discrimination persist. At the qualitative level, some of the most important findings of the research carried out by Albert Martens et al. are those which depict the wide range of discriminatory practices to be found in the local labour market. To the practices of unequal treatment identified by Arijn et al. 1998 the research team led by Albert Martens and Nouria Ouali, added inter alia the practices of setting up special uniform policies unacceptable for the persons searching for work by the employers, invoking the refusal of the clients, patients, etc. to be treated by the person of foreign origin, and using the strategy of 'discrimination by delegation' by asking the employment agencies to select only autochthonous Belgians (Fr. BBB – *Bleu Blanc Belge*). (Ibid: 82) Their research also showed that the victims of discrimination adopt numerous strategies of coping with inequalities in recruitment and selection, from the 'Westernisation' of names and surnames, through lowering their financial expectations and accepting jobs below their qualifications, to taking decisions about leaving the country. (Ibid: 81) Most importantly, from the point of view of this study, the research commissioned by the ORBEM confirms the widespread existence of discriminatory practices on the labour market. It found that 50 per cent of persons of foreign origin searching for employment (and participating in the research), were at least once victims of discriminatory treatment and that 27 per cent of the total number of 115 procedures of application for work encountered discriminatory reactions[182]. (Ibid: 30)

The development of Belgian integration policies only started at the turn of the 1980s and 1990s and was strongly influenced by two events, on the one hand, the first electoral successes of the extreme right party Vlaams Belang (then Vlaams Blok[183]), and on the other hand, the first city riots and fights between the police and the allochthon youth (Phalet and Kekels 1998). In the 9th of October 1988 local elections, Vlaams Blok, after having conducted an aggressive and openly xenophobic electoral campaign, obtained 3 per cent of votes in Flanders, and 18 per cent votes in the major city of Flanders, Antwerp.[184] Three years later in the general elections on 24 November 1991, often referred to as 'Black Sunday', the Vlaams Blok more than tripled its score from 1988 (Gijsels 1993). This was to a large extent a result of its politisation of immigration and skilful campaigning in which the traditional 'Other' (francophones) was replaced by a 'new Other', Muslims, whom the Vlaams Belang named Allah-thons (Ceuppens 2003) and called for their repatriation. After the Molenbeek and Forest Riots of 1991, in which for the first time the allochthon youth desperately searching for social recognition (Rea 2001), clashed with police, this task became relatively easy for Flemish extreme right.

The federal government, pressured by the sudden emergence of Vlaams Blok on the political scene, hastened decisions to fight more effectively against the process of social marginalization and to make naturalization easier. The wider policy framework was developed by a semi-official government body, attached to the administration of the Prime Minister, the Royal Commissariat for Migrant Policies (RCMP) set up in 1989. In

---

[182] At the same time, the authors of the research point out that the percentage of application procedures that met with discriminatory reaction goes up to 45, if it was possible to verify that two candidates - one of foreign origin and one 'autochthon' – apply for the same vacancy (Martens et al. 2005: 83).
[183] I shall return to the issue of the presence of the strong far right party in the Northern part of the country in section 3.8.
[184] For reasons behind the popularity of the Vlaams Belang in Antwerp see Swyngedouw 2000.

1993 this Commissariat was replaced by a permanent institution, Centre for Equal Opportunities and Fight against Racism (CEOFR[185]), which today together with the Movement against Racism, Antisemitism and Xenophobia (MRAX[186]), is one of the key organizations in the country providing assistance to victims of racial discrimination. Before the RCMP was dissolved it produced a monumental three-volume report in which the blueprint for what was to become the official Belgian approach to migrant affairs was outlined. Of particular importance is the Commissariat's definition of 'integration', seen on the one hand as the insertion of migrants into Belgian society according to three guiding principles: 1) 'assimilation where "public order" demands it; 2) consequent promotion of the best possible fitting in according to the orientating social principles which support the culture of the host country and which are related to "modernity", "emancipation" and "true pluralism" – as understood by a modern western state; 3) unambiguous respect for cultural diversity-as-mutual-enrichment in all other areas' and, on the other hand, as: 'promotion of structural involvement of minorities in activities and aims of the government' (definition quoted in Bloomaert 1998: 76-77). As one may easily detect this very broad definition, which was to become a pivotal concept for government policies on migrants and ethnic minorities, included both the formerly dominant assimilationist, French-style republican and class-based socialist interpretations of integration typical of Wallonia and the more identity-based, multicultural-friendly policy style found in Flanders (Ireland 2000). Moreover, the large interpretational space of the concept opened up the possibility of its legitimate usage in an oppressive, right-wing register focusing on law and order and unilateral adaptation, as well as in a soft, humanist left-wing register in which the values of minority protection and multiculturalism are invoked (Bloomaert 1998: 82). In other words, every party can freely choose to invoke from this definition what she wants; the francophones - emphasis on the 'social insertion' and the Flemings - respect for 'cultural diversity'.

Here it should be remembered that, after the federalization reforms, immigration policy is a competence of the federal government whereas integration policy is devolved as a competence of the different national communities (Favell and Martiniello 1998:

---

[185] More information about the Centre is available http://www.diversite.be
[186] More information about the Movement is available on http://www.mrax.be

144

185). Thus, every region has its own integration policy, while in Brussels, where both the Francophone and Flemish Communities exercise their powers, one may observe the existence of two integration policies, one based on the 'non-discrimination principle', in which cultural identity is neither supported nor penalized by public policy, and the other based on 'group-differentiated rights'. In practical terms it means that the Flemish (Community) government recognizes ethno-cultural minority groups and supports migrant self-organisations in Brussels, whereas the Francophone (Community) government has not been willing to recognize ethnic-cultural groups as specific entities in its policies towards allochthons and frames its policies in such a way that they are not specifically defined as target groups.[187] As Dirk Jacobs notices, the incorporation of immigrant (often francophone) self-organisations into Flemish policy networks is, at least partially, aimed at strengthening the sphere of influence of the Flemish community within the Region of Brussels-Capital (Jacobs 2004a: 55). This policy is obviously viewed by the francophones with suspicion who by denying the existence of ethnic minority groups, at least to some extent hope to downgrade the legitimacy of Flemish demands for group-differentiated rights and special representation (Jacobs 2004: 78-79). As for the immigrant associations, if they are able (and willing) to slightly 'Flemicise'[188], then they find the Flemish efforts highly interesting as they open for them new possibilities for funding and lobbying for them. As Favell and Martiniello have pointed out, they are able to 'go shopping' for funding and influence in either the Flemish or francophone community (1999). Thus, add Jacobs and Swyngedouw, the immigrant associations can strategically opt for different forms of collective mobilization – stressing either ethnic identity or neutral forms of social insertion (2002).

3.7 ISLAM WITHIN CHURCH-STATE RELATIONS

The incorporation of Muslims in Belgium and Britain also involves making space for Islam in the country's tradition of church and state relations, which determines the institutional framework within which representatives of Muslim interests and decision

---

[187] For more information about integration policies in Wallonia and Flanders see, for example, Rea 1993, Bloomaert 1998, Ireland 2000, Bousetta et al. 2005, or Gsir et al. 2005.
[188] To be eligible for funding an organisation has to be oriented towards emancipation, education and integration, has to function as a meeting point and fulfil a cultural function. Moreover, it has to operate using (also) the Dutch language - at least at the executive level (Bousetta 2005 et al.: 13).

makers interact. These traditions also to some extent determine how much room there is in a certain country for manifestations of Islamic religiosity in the public sphere. One can think of three general models of such relations: the strict church-state separation model in which religion and politics are seen as clearly distinct areas of human endeavour that should be kept in absolute separation from each other; the established church model, in which the state and the church form a partnership in advancing the cause of religion and the state; and the pluralist or structural pluralist model that sees religion not as a separate sphere with only limited relevance to the other spheres as the liberal strict separationists do, but as having bearing on all of life (Monsma and Soper 1997: 10-11, Pędziwiatr 2005: 34-36).[189] The second and third model most closely depict the relations between the church and the state in Britain and Belgium respectively. Before I move on to sketch the main features of these relations, it is important to note that all the traditions of church-state relations to be found in Europe have some elements in common. As Silvio Ferrari demonstrates, all of them are based on three underlying principles: firstly, the protection of the individual rights of religious freedom; secondly, the lack of competence of the state on religious matters and the independence of religious faith; and, thirdly the 'selective' collaboration between states and religious faiths (2003: 226-237).[190]

Starting from the presentation of the status of Islam in the British church-state framework, it is first worth remembering that the country has no written constitution so religious freedom cannot be guaranteed in this act, as it is the in the case of most EU countries (e.g. Belgium). The principle of religious freedom has thus been inscribed into special laws and international treaties to which the United Kingdom is a party. There is in fact in Britain not one, but two established churches, the Church of England (Anglican) and the Church of Scotland (Presbyterian), which both have a special relationship to the state[191]. I shall focus here, however, on describing the state-church relations in England, as this is the largest part of Britain and the area where the capital is located and where I carried out my fieldwork.

---

[189] Here it has to be stressed that these are theoretical constructs rather than real life models, and that no European country follows them in a pure form.
[190] Again these are only overarching principles and as it will be shown below in the case of Islam in Britain and Belgium they do not always hold.
[191] The Presbyterian Church of Scotland has been the established church in Scotland since 1707. The Church of Wales was disestablished in 1920 and became the Church in Wales, losing inter alia the possibility to have its bishops in the House of Lords as "Lords Spiritual" (Price 1990).

In contrast to the Netherlands or Sweden where the processes of secularization have profoundly transformed the state-church relations[192], in England the church has not lost its key powers and privileges and is still closely linked with the state in institutional terms. The monarch is the head of both state and church, and may neither be nor marry a Catholic. The King/Queen appoints the archbishops and diocesan bishops of the Church of England, from a list provided by the church, while the Prime Minister has an influence on the nomination of bishops.[193] At least 25 seats in the House of Lords, the upper chamber of Parliament, are given to the ecclesiastical hierarchy who reiterate the characterization of Britain as, first and foremost, Christian. All other churches and religions are excluded from both legal and symbolic connections between Church and State. The Act of Settlement 1701, the Marriage Acts 1946-1996 and the Prison Act 1952, in particular are widely felt to privilege Anglicans in England over other denominations and faiths. Also the law of blasphemy, which was crucial during the Rushdie affair[194], and the coronation oath exclude other religious groups. The latter, however, is supposed to change in the future as the HRH Prince Charles, strongly involved in interfaith initiatives, had announced that he wanted to be not 'Defender of the Faith'[195] (i.e. Anglicanism), but a 'Defender of Faith' (i.e. many faiths) (Modood 1997: 3). Thus, the future coronation ceremony is supposed to more accurately reflect the multi-religious social reality of contemporary Britain.

Despite this very close institutional connection with the state, neither Anglicanism nor other churches or religious communities receive any general financial assistance from the State, for example to pay their clergy. State finances absorb almost all of the costs of religious schools, which are very popular in Britain, as well as the numerous and very active religious non-profit service organizations. The most important effect of the existence of an established church, though, from the point of view of this research is, that it sustains the general assumption that religion has a public function to perform within civil society as a whole (Monsma and Soper 1997; Fetzer and Soper 2005: 25-61). As

[192] The Dutch state was until 1983 very closely linked with the Catholic and Protestant Churches, while Sweden till 2000 had an established church (Pędziwiatr 2005: 101 & 162).
[193] However, Gordon Brown intends to hand back to the Church the role of making the recommendation to the Queen on the appointment of the Church of England bishops, as part of a draft of constitutional reforms. (Grice 2007)
[194] The affair is discussed in more detail below and in the next subchapter.
[195] This is one of the official titles of the English monarchs.

Philip Lewis (2005) has rightly noted, this institutionalized public role of religion is something that apart from the full citizenship rights, had greatly enabled the expressions of Muslim identity in the public sphere. Furthermore, the research of Jyette Klausen showing that amongst the Muslim leaders from six European countries the British ones were the least likely to support church-state reform (2005), seeming to suggest that the British Muslim leadership is well aware of the 'opportunity spaces' for expressions of sacrum in the public sphere that have been sustained due to the existence of the established church.

Muslim organizations function in the country as legal entities under various legal categories (companies, associations or trusts which usually have charitable status) and there is no state intervention beyond that obliged by company or charitable law, which in most cases consists of the presentation of properly audited accounts. As charities they enjoy tax-exemptions and as religious non-profit organizations they receive state subsidies. For example, mosques and associations have become out contractors of the British state when it comes to caring for the elderly, teaching the languages of the parents' countries of origin or advising the young into employment. There are in the country around 1200 mosques and prayer halls but, similarly to other European countries, the purpose-built mosques make up only small percentage of all the Islamic places of worship in the country[196] (Peach 2000).

Religious education in Britain has had a multifaith character for more than 30 years. By law, state schools are required to offer religious education, the content of which is decided at the local level but, which reflects the fact that the principal religious traditions in the country are in the main Christian whilst taking account of the teaching and practices of the other principle religions represented in Britain. Such classes are obligatory although parents, if they so wish, can withdraw their children from them. Schools with a large Muslim student community may provide the opportunity to study Islam in their classes and hold collective prayers within the school buildings on Friday. Moreover, Muslim girls are allowed to wear Islamic headscarves as long as they are in

---

[196] According to the research carried out by Cari Peach the purpose-built ones make up 20 per cent of all mosques. These can be further divided into those with unadorned (9 per cent) and elaborate architecture (11 per cent). Converted churches, according to this estimation make up 9 per cent of total number of mosques (Peach 2000).

the school colours[197], and they may enjoy halal food in their canteens. The Qur'anic classes run in the mosque madrasas, are similarly to religious education in churches, synagogues or gurdwaras, not subsidized by the state. However, after many years of lobbying, the government has allocated funding for the first five Muslim schools.

There is no official Muslim representative organisation in the country, but instead a number of Muslim bodies have competed among themselves for influence in the corridors of power and claiming to represent the interests of British Muslims vis-à-vis the government. The latter has changed its views in terms of its preferred Muslim interlocutor and by tacitly supporting one or another organisation has influenced the landscape of Muslim representation in the country. While the Union of Muslim Organisations of UK & Ireland (UMO) was the first national umbrella organisation to be established in Britain (founded in 1970), it was the Muslim Council of Britain (created in 1997) which has managed so far to achieve the biggest successes in its lobbying of the government.[198] Before the attacks on London Transport Network on July 7th 2005, the position of the MCB as 'the voice of British Muslims' was so strong that it could not be challenged by any other organisation. After the attacks, the situation changed radically as the government tried to extend the array of Muslim leaders and organisations consulted. The MCB was accused of being inter alia 'too soft' on dealing with extremism within the Muslim communities has temporarily lost its privileged position in the corridors of power. Meanwhile the government has been tacitly supporting other newly created Muslim representative organizations such as the British Muslim Forum[199] (launched in March 2005) and the Sufi Muslim Council[200] (set up in July 2006).

In Belgium, as already signalled, the constitution guarantees freedom of worship (article 19), and demands that individual citizens must not be restricted in their religious choices and should be able to freely change their adherence (article 20). Furthermore, it

---

[197] The schools allow girls to choose between a standard uniform and a uniform of trousers and a tunic that has been specifically designed to accommodate the religious needs of Muslim girls. Other Muslim clothing such as, for example, jilbab (a full-length dress that covers all of the body except the face and the hands) has been banned as not conforming with the above mentioned uniform policy (Pędziwiatr 2006g)

[198] For more information about the Muslim representative organisations in Britain as well as about the details of the lobbying campaigns of the MCB, see Pędziwiatr 2007a.

[199] More information about this organisation representing mostly British Brelwis can be found on www.bmf-eu.com

[200] More information about this organisation representing mostly British Sufis from the Nakshbanija tarika can be found on www.sufimuslimcouncil.org

149

stipulates that the State has no right to concern itself with the appointment or designation of ministers of religion or to interfere in religious internal affairs (article 21), however it is obliged to pay the salaries and pensions of clergymen, and those of recognised secularist delegates (article 181).[201] These four constitutional articles constitute the institutional armature of the whole system. In a country which has inherited a Napoleonic legal system, there is a formal legal link between the state and church, or rather the 'churches'. In contrast to the French model of strict state-church separation, what has been at work historically in Belgium is a form of secularism grounded in the concept of the neutrality of the State vis-à-vis the internal organisation of religions. The State considers religion to be a part of the country's institutional framework and 'recognizes' religious groups which meet the needs of the population, or a sufficiently large portion of the population (Leman and Renaerts 1996: 165). Whereas the Parliament has jurisdiction over the granting of the status of 'officially recognised religion', the government or more precisely the Ministry of Justice, is responsible for supervising the procedure. Up till now the Government has accorded "recognized" status to six denominations: Roman Catholicism, Protestantism, Judaism, Anglicanism, Islam, and Orthodox Christianity. The seventh recognized 'religion' are the secular humanist groups represented by the Central Council of Non-Religious Philosophical Communities of Belgium.

Islam, as mentioned in the first chapter, was recognized and thus considered as one of the religions of Belgium in 1974, that is at the time where the vast majority of Muslims in the country were, in the light of law, not Belgians but foreign immigrants. It is much easier to understand 'the progressive' initiative of the Belgian authorities, if one looks at it against the background of the height of the oil crisis, which had devastating consequences for the economies of developed countries such as their. In other words, it is not a coincidence that the law of 19 July 1974 was voted in parallel to bilateral negations between Belgium and Saudi Arabia on oil contracts (Panafit 1999, Bussetta and Marechal 2003: 6). Here, however, it is important to note that the first projects of the recognition of Islam were already put forward from the end of the 1960s, when the state presented the Eastern Pavilon (from the World Exposition of 1897) to the Islamic community of

---

[201] One may read Belgian Constitution on http://www.fed-parl.be/constitution_uk.html

150

Belgium, represented by the Islamic and Cultural Centre (ICC)[202], an association controlled by the Embassies of Saudi Arabia and Morocco (Leman and Renaerts 1996: 166). Some authors also argue that recognition of Islam was determined by the need to find a solution to the problem of religious education for Muslim children at schools, while others speculate that the bill of recognition was passed in exchange for the closing of the gates of immigration (Blaise and Coorebyert 1997, Panafit 1997, 1999).

The recognition of Islam has opened up large funding opportunities for this religion and its followers, at least theoretically. The recognized religious communities according to law enjoy such privileges that other religious groups without official recognition are deprived of such as the right to religious instruction in public schools, the right to remuneration for the salaries of clergy, the right to provide chaplains in prisons, hospitals and reception centres, and the right to broadcasting time on public TV and radio. Moreover, the buildings which serve as places of worship are eligible for tax-exemptions and subsidies from local authorities to cover the cost of maintenance and renovation. The state subsidies to the recognized religious communities amount annualy to around 1.5 billion euros. 80 per cent of this money goes to the Catholic Church and 13 per cent to the humanists. The subsidies for each of the remaining religious communities do not exceed 0.6 per cent (Torrekens 2005). Such a distribution of state subsidies has been heavily criticized by members of the religious minorities, as one that no longer reflects the social and religious reality of the country. Although Islam has been officially recognized for more than three decades, this recognition is not fully effective as most of the aforementioned 'benefits' related to this status have yet to be implemented. A step forward in the direction of effective recognition was made in Wallonia on June 19th 2007 when the Walloon government officially recognised 43 mosques (out of 89 mosques in the region)[203] and inter alia promised to contribute financialy to their maintenance.[204] At the same time the federal government commited itself to pay the salaries of the imams in the recognized mosques (La Libre 20.06.2007).

---

[202] Until the establishment of the EMB this association has been a de facto representative of Muslims in Belgium. Its board of trustees is chaired by the ambassador of Saudi Arabia.
[203] The public were also informed that 5 mosques did not pass the screening of the Belgian Intelligence, however the reasons why these mosques were negatively verified by Sûreté de l'Etat (SE), were not communicated to the media.
[204] A handful of Brussels' and Flemish mosques were officially recognized in December 2007. More information about these recognitions is provided in the following chapter.

The only fully implemented privilege of a 'recognized religion' that Islam has benefited from is the right to religious education in public schools. The teaching of Islam was introduced to the school curricula in Belgium in 1978 and today there are more than 850 primary and secondary schools that organize courses of Islam for more than 30,000 pupils (Maréchal 2002). At the moment Muslim teachers are appointed by the authorities (and paid by them) on the recommendation of the Executive of Muslims of Belgium (EMB). Muslim pupils under the age of 17 can choose between the class of Islam and non-denominational ethics, whereas for those aged 17-18 such classes are voluntary.

Although there is no general ban on wearing hijabs or Muslim veils at school like in France, most schools in Wallonia and Brussels have in recent years banned them.[205] And thus, while in 2000 41 per cent of secondary schools under the authority of the French community did not allow to wear hijab, by late 2005, more than 70 per cent of these schools introduced such a ban through a change in the internal regulations (IHF 2006). In Brussels, for example, by late 2006 only 8 out of 111 secondary schools allowed Muslim girls to wear hijabs (Arripe 2005, Staszewski 2006). One of the most recent research into the issue of bans on hijab in Belgian schools found that more than 90 per cent of all francophone schools do not allow wearing of them (De Meyer quoted in Dorzée and De Mulenaere 2007). De Meyer found that the internal regulations of schools which introduced bans on headscarves (sometimes in the middle of the school year) generally lacked clarity and that they were, from the legal point of view, illegal (Ibid). One of the places where they can wear the hijab is the al-Ghazali Muslim school temporarily located in the Great Mosque in the Parc du Cinquantenaire. This is the only Muslim school which received some financial assistance from the French Community government (Leman and Renaerts 1996: 170, Caprioli 2005).[206]

One of the main reasons why Islam has not benefited from other privileges of the 'officially recognised religions' has to do with a lack of will amongst the decision makers to effectively implement the recognition of Islam. Another important factor that has contributed to the slowing down of the process of accommodating Islam within the

---

[205] This was possible after the governments of the French and Flemish community had granted public schools the right to ban the wearing of headscarves.
[206] The new Muslim school, Avicenna, which was opened by the Mosque al-Khalil in Molenbeek in September 2007 also applied for the state founding.

152

institutional structures of the country was the difficulty in establishing a representative body that would on the one hand fulfil the requirements of the state and, on the other hand, satisfy the needs and demands of the various Muslim groups that make up the Muslim population of Belgium. The process leading to the establishment of such a body was described by Felice Dasetto as 'turcification' (1997) of the policy characterised by no separation between church and state and direct interventions of the state in the affairs of Muslim communities. The main role of the Executive of Muslims of Belgium (*fr.* *Exécutif des Musulmans de Belgique)*, which came into existence in May 1999 after long and turbulent negotiations and elections[207], is to serve as the official interlocutor of the authorities on issues related to the practice of Islam in Belgium. Amongst the responsibilities of the Executive are: the organisation of religious education, training of imams and the appointments of Muslim chaplains in hospitals and prisons.

As demonstrated above, although in Belgium there has been considerable room for manifestations of Muslim religiosity in the public sphere officially (in some cases even more room than in Britain), this space has remained open largely only on paper due to a lack of enforcement mechanisms and an overarching debate on multiculturalism. In addition, in Brussels this room has been severely reduced by the strong influence of the religion-blind, republican approach to sacrum, which is quite hostile to religion in the public sphere.

3.8 THE MAIN DEBATES AROUND ISLAM IN BELGIUM AND BRITAIN

As I have argued at the beginning of this chapter the level of tolerance for the manifestations of Islamic religiosity in the public sphere depends not only on the institutional elements of the opportunity structures, but also on their discursive elements. In other words, how deeply the religiosity of Muslim Belgians and Britons is able to penetrate into the public sphere depends on both the frameworks of church and state relations, models of incorporations of immigrants, etc and the established notions of who and what is considered reasonable and legitimate. Here, however it must be stressed that the later notions have been under constant review. The limits of the discursive space for

---

[207] For more information about the process leading to the establishment of the EMB see for example Panafit 1999, Kanmaz 2002, Bousetta and Marechal 2003. The issues around the EMB will be elaborated yet in the following section and in the following chapter in the section 5.4.6.

the manifestation of religiosity in both countries analysed have been continuously re-negotiated in the public debates around Islam. Thus, before I point out key features of the faith-based citizenship as promoted by the Muslim leader almost equally popular among my Belgian and British interviewees, it is important to shed some light on the main debates around Islam in Belgium and Britain during which the notions of who and what is reasonable and legitimate have been defined and re-defined.

The debates around Islam in Belgium since the time when this religion gained a public visibility in 1974, have revolved around three major subjects: the representation of Muslims vis-à-vis the government, female veiling and religious radicalism.[208] The issue of who should speak with the government on behalf of the country's Muslims began to be discussed in Belgium even earlier than in many other European countries with more sizable Muslim populations. This was a direct consequence of the relatively early official recognition of Islam as one of the religions of Belgian citizens, which created a demand for a Muslim representative body. From the very beginning though, these discussions have been marked by many disagreements as to the role, goals and character of the Muslim representative body. There was no consensus over the shape of such an institution not only in the discussions between the state authorities and their Muslim interlocutors, but also amongst Muslim leaders and the members of the government themselves. In the absence of a representative body, the Belgian government attributed many prerogatives of such an institution to the Islamic and Cultural Centre (ICC), which *de facto* played such a role untill the end of the 1980s. As a result of a combination of national and international events[209], the powerful position of the ICC became increasingly criticised both from within the Muslim communities and also from the outside (Kanmaz 2002: 104) for a 'lack of representation'.

---

[208] There have clearly been many other themes around the Muslim presence in the country debated in the public sphere, however the goal here is to shortly elaborate only on those that have tended to reoccur most frequently.
[209] The Iranian revolution, war between Iran and Iraq, events in Lebanon were some of the highly influential international events that changed the mood of public opinion in the country, whereas the key national events included the increasing popularity of the far right, and closely linked with it, the development of the Belgian integration policies.

From the beginning of the 1990s there have been numerous efforts to form a body that would be 'truly representative'.[210] The religious (sectarian), ethnic and national diversity of the Muslim population in the country was one of the key obstacles in the formation of such an institution. Furthermore, the state had placed strict criteria for membership as it did not want any 'fundamentalists' in such a body and directly interfered in its shape (Hussain 2003: 239). When finally the institution which would satisfy the government and be acceptable to the Muslims was established in 1998/1999 it has endured crisis after crisis. The screening of the candidates to the EMB by the Intelligence service, insufficient funding to meet the wide range of goals and financial problems were only some of the issues that caused these problems. Although in 1998 it had been agreed that the next election to the Muslim Constituent Assembly and its Executive should be organized only in 2009, in July 2004 the government decided that an overhaul of the Muslim representative body was necessary and that it should take place four years earlier (in 2005). This controversial decision that was heavily criticized not only by the Muslim representatives but also by others (Nyman 2005) and resulted inter alia in very poor turnout during the elections and significant underrepresentation of persons of Moroccan origin (the biggest Muslim community in the country that largely boycotted the elections) within the renewed Muslim Constituent Assembly and the EMB.

In recent years the issue of the Muslim representative body is again being hotly debated in the public arena as a result of a new case in court of the mismanagement of state subsidies by the EMB.[211] At the beginning of February 2008 the Minister of Justice (Jo Vandeurzen) announced the delay of payment of the subsidy to the EMB caused by the lack of reliable information about the financial situation of the Executive. (HLN 01.02.2008) Three weeks later the court accused its President (Coskun Beyazgül) and two other members of the steering committee (Benjelloul Kissi and Atila Aydogdu) of "forgery and the use of forgeries and the misuse of the institution's property" (Le Soir and La Libre Belgique 26.02.2008). This information was followed by the resignation of Beyazgül from the post of the President of the EMB, the announcement of the Minister of Justice about the cancellation of the ministerial subsidy to the EMB and calls for a deep

---

[210] For more information about these efforts see, for example, Leman and Renaerts 1996, Panafit 1997, 1999 and Kanmaz 2002

[211] Similar case against the former leaders of the EMB was brought before the court in 2004.

reform of the Muslim representative body, its liquidation or the establishment of a new representative body (e.g. Muslim administrative council dealing only with the worldly matters of Islamic religious practice and uniting all the representatives of the recognized mosques[212]). Thus, not even after a decade of its existence, the EMB seems to be in the most profound crisis since its creation.

Another issue that has been hotly debated in Belgium, at least since the end of the 1980s, are Muslim headscarves. The outbreak of the so called Muslim headscarf affair (fr. *l'affaire du voile islamique*) in France in 1989, after three female students were suspended from school for refusing to remove their headscarves, marked the moment when also the Belgian public became increasingly interested in this topic. Since then it has been a permanent feature of the debates on Islam in the country. In these debates usually the use of headscarf in public schools and other public institutions is questioned with reference to the principle of the separation of church and state, and concerns are raised regarding the subjugation of women and the level of their integration with wider society. One of the results of the politization of Muslim headscarves has been a significant increase in the number of schools banning them. However, with the passage of time, hijabs have been increasingly unwelcome not only in Belgian schools but also in the labour market. This trend has apparently not managed to be reversed even by the highly publicized Naima Amzil affair, in which the owner of a seafood firm Rik Remmery (supported even by the King of Belgians, Albert II) did not give in to the demands of a group "New Free Flanders" to sack one of his employees (Naima Amzil) for wearing a hijab at work. The employment agency Randstad reported in October 2007 that 60% of workers in Belgium did not approve of wearing a headscarf or other any religious symbol to work, regarding it as inappropriate (Report quoted in Euro-Islam.info).

The level and nature of the antipathy towards Islamic veils in Belgium was recently assessed with quite high precision by the research into the perceptions of hijab amongst the autochthonous Belgians. The study, based on a representative sample showed that more than half of Belgians believed that wearing a hijab was against the

---

[212] More information about this proposal promoted by the organisation Vigiliance Musulmane one may find on its web site www.vigilancemusulmane.be or in Guttierez 2008. To find out about other proposals see www.wafin.be

dynamics of a modern society and should be banned in certain places, whereas one in three people in the country were bothered by women wearing headscarves in public places. Moreover, the research team headed by Vassilis Saroglou found that almost 20 per cent of Belgians were bothered by women in hijabs everywhere or regardless of the place in which they see them. One of the key factors behind this attitude of malevolence towards women wearing hijabs identified by the researchers was a subtle racism based not on race, but on the hatread of the nature of certain groups and a sense of cultural superiority. On the other hand, the intellectual and aesthetic openness, as well as the self-identification as citizen of the world and an adherence to universal values, were found to decrease negative attitudes towards hijab. The researchers of the Centre for Psychology of Religion at the Catholic University of Louvain-La-Neuve established also that almost 70 per cent of Belgians perceived the hijab as an indication of submission, 44.2 per cent believed that it is worn in order to mark the difference from the rest of the society and 30.8 per cent saw it as a symbol of 'anti-westerness' (Saroglou 2007).

Yet another subject that has been hotly debated in Belgium with relation to Islam is religious radicalism. From the mid 1980s, a key role in framing these debates, partially influenced by national and international events[213], have played into the hands of the far right parties: the francophone *Front Nationale de Belgique* and Flemish *Vlaams Blok*. The latter party was particularly successful in politicising the presence of Muslim allochtons and portraying them as dangerous religious extremists. For the leaders of the Vlaams Blok the Moroccan and Turkish, who settled down in Belgium, were not allochtons, but Allah-thons (Ceuppens 2003) who should not be integrated with Belgian society but 're-integrated' with the societies in their countries of origin. Such ideas, combined with calls for the secession of Flanders from Belgium, gave the party from the beginning of the 1990s a significant number of seats in the Belgian Chamber of Representatives. In order to prevent the Vlaams Blok from gaining power and to keep it out of the municipal, provincial, regional and national government coalitions, the other parties (Liberals, ChristianDemocrats, Socialists and Greens) have drawn up a '*cordon sanitaire*' (quarantine line) around it. Apart from that, the party in 2004 was condemned

---

[213] For instance, revolution in Iran, civil war in Lebanon, or more recently 9/11 and war in Afghanistan and Iraq.

by court for "repeated incitement to discrimination" and forced to start to function under a new name – *Vlaams Belang* (Flemish Interest). Although in the last general elections it lost one seat in the Chamber of Representatives, the total number of people who supported the party once again increased (see the table below).

Table 3.5 ELECTION RESULTS OF THE VLAAMS BLOK (VLAAMS BELANG) TO THE CHAMBER OF REPRESENTATIVES

Election year	Total number of votes on VB (in thousands)	% of overall vote	Number of seats
1978	76	1.4%	1
1981	66	1.8%	1
1985	85	1.4%	1
1987	116	1.9%	2
1991	405	6.6%	12
1995	476	7.8%	11
1999	613	9.8%	15
2003	761	11,5%	18
2007	800	11,9%	17

Clearly the portrayal of Muslims by the Vlaams Belang as radical extremists would not be so successful if there were no cases of violence commited in the name of Allah. In other words, not only the international but also the national context provided the proponents of this Islamophobic vision, portraying all Muslims as religious radicals, with numerous arguments. The sentence of Nizar Trabelsi to 10 years of imprisonment for plotting a suicide attack against the NATO air base at Kleine Brogel, the sentence of Tarek Maaroufi to six years in prison for his role in a Brussels-based fake passport ring that supplied Belgian passports to the men who assassinated former Afghan Northern Alliance commander Ahmed Shah Massoud, or the information about Muriel Degauque, a Belgian convert to Islam, who committed a suicide car bomb attack against a U.S. military convoy in Iraq, were only some of the events which have reinforced the

158

proponents of such a vision in their thinking and provided them with arguments to further promote the image of a Muslim terrorist.[214]

The issue of religious radicalism has also been one of the major topics of debate around Islam in Britain. As in Belgium, these debates have been to some extent shaped by the political far right. However, as I have already mentioned, the British National Party has been much less successful in moblising substantial political support for its Islamophobic ideas. In the 2005 UK general election, the party received only 0.7 per cent of votes, whereas two years later in the Welsh Assembly Election 2007 it came fifth in terms of votes and failed to win any seat in the Assembly. At present while the party has almost 50 local councilors around the country, it is being constantly marginalized by the main political parties and its influence in the localities is rather weak. Similarly to Vlaams Belang, it has relatively recently made anti-Muslimness one of the major tools of its propaganda machinery. On the web site of the party one may read that *"The BNP has moved on in recent years, casting off the leg-irons of conspiracy theories and the thinly veiled anti-Semitism which has held this party back for two decades. The real enemies of the British people are home grown Anglo-Saxon Celtic liberal-leftists ... and the Crescent Horde – the endless wave of Islamics who are flocking to our shores to bring our island nations into the embrace of their barbaric desert religion."* (BNP 2005) The party has called for inter alia the introduction of the 'no fly' policy for Muslims, or banning them from flying in and out of Britain, and for the 'end of the "islamification" of Great Britain' (BNP spokesman quoted in Taylor 2006).

However, the British discourse on multiculturalism has suffered its most serious blow in recent years not from the relatively weak and internally divided BNP, but from the Muslim radical preachers inciting hate towards *kafirs* (wrongly defined as all non-Muslims – Cesari 2004: 106) and from British citizens commiting violence in the name of Allah in Britain and elsewhere. It was the presence of such Muslim preachers in the

---

[214] Other events that have provided the propagators of the images of Muslim terrorists with arguments were, for example, the trial of the presumed Belgian members of GICM (*Grupe Islamiste Combattant Marocain*), and the arrest in Antwerp and Brussels a people linked to Rabei Osman El Sayed Ahmed (a main suspect in the Madrid bombings).

British capital as Abu Hamza al-Masri and Omar Bakri Mohammad, to name only the most notorious ones[215], which had gained London a pejorative sobriquet – Londonistan.

The first Muslim preacher is currently serving a seven-year prison sentence (from 2004, though the verdict was announced only in Februry 2006) for soliciting murder and inciting racial hatred. Before Abu Hamza al-Masri was placed in the high security Balmarsh prison, he used to be an imam of the Finsbury Park Mosque in North London. His fiery sermons and radicalism eventually led the Charity Commission that chose him to be an imam of the mosque in 1997 to strip him of the role six years later. This, however, did stop the leader of the group "Supporters of Shariah" from preaching and from publicly expressing support for al-Qaeda (Wiktorowicz 2005: 66-58). After his ejection from the mosque, he preached outside the gates until he was imprisoned on remand. Before this happened he had become a celebrity hate figure of the British tabloids. The Daily Mail, The Sun and other newspapers have frequently used excerpts of his speeches advocating violence to horrify their readers. The spokesman of the Muslim Council of Britan, Inayat Bungalawala, said about Al-Masri just before his imprisonment that *"This man has alienated the public from Muslims with his vile rants. British Muslims are growing impatient that he is still able to tarnish them with these remarks."* (Bungalawala quoted in Time Out 2005)

The second major charismatic Muslim preacher whose activism has significantly contributed to the portrayals of Muslims as radicals and their religion as a violent one was Omar Bakri. The founder of Al-Muhajiroun[216] (Ar. Emigrants) expelled from Saudi Arabia, settled in London in 1986. In contrast to Saudi Arabia, in Britain he was able to build the structures of the Hizb ut-Tahrir and organize high-profile events that drew the attention of the media without major obstacles. For example, in August 1995 in Trafalgar Square he called for Queen Elizabeth to convert to Islam and threatened that Muslims would not rest until "the black flag of Islam flies over Downing Street", while a few years earlier he declared that according to Islamic jurisprudence, Prime Minister John Major could be assassinated if he went to Saudi Arabia. His outlandish statements

---

[215] Other would be inter alia Abu Qatada al-Filistini, Anjem Choudary and Abu Izzadeen.
[216] The organisation was formally launched in 1983 in Mecca and was closely linked with the Hizb ut-Tahrir. In fact, Quintan Wiktorowicz claims that the name Al-Muhajiroun was just a cover name for the branch of HT. Omar Bakri was not allowed to set up an official HT branch in Saudi Arabia by the leaders of the organisation who did not want to test the official ban (2005: 7-8).

generated concern from the HT leaders and in 1996 he was forced to resign from the organisation. He, however, did not stop preaching and organizing controversial events.[217] Omar Bakri relaunched al-Muhajiroun and continued his activities under a new banner almost up until the moment of his departure to Lebanon in August 2005 following information that the government was planning to investigate certain Muslim clerics under treason laws.[218] He was banned from returning to Britain by the Home Secretary Charles Clarke, stating that Bakri's presence in Britain was "not conducive to the public good".[219] (Clarke quoted in BBC 2005).

Public debates on the subject of 'Muslim radicalism' have been instigated not only by the activism of the aforementioned (and other) radical Muslim clerics, but also following the news about the involvement of the British Muslims in violent actions in the country and abroad.[220] British Muslims have provided the public with numerous occasions to initiate such discussions. Before Mohammad Sidique Khan, Shehzad Tanweer, Germaine Lindsay and Hasib Hussain decided to strike against their own fellow citizens on July 7 2005, other young Muslims have embarked on the terrorist missions abroad. The first known British Muslim suicide bomber was Mohammed Bilal who, on Christmas Day 2000, rammed a vehicle packed with explosives into an Indian military post in Kashmir. Three years later 21-years old Londoner Asif Hanif detonated a suicide bomb in Mike's Place in Tel Aviv, killing three people. His 27-years old accomplice Omar Khan Sharif failed to detonate his bomb and was found dead in the sea a week after the attack. More recently, a few other individuals traveled from British cities to Iraq to carry out suicide attacks there against the forces of the coalition.[221] There were also a few British Muslims who either failed to carry out their deadly missions or their missions

---

[217] One of the most controversial events in the post-September 11 period organised by Omar Bakri was a conference entitled 'The Magnificient Nineteen'. The posters of the conference displayed the pictures of hijackers of the planes and a smiling Osama bin Laden with the excerpt from the Qur'an ' ... they were youth who believed in the Lord and We increased them in guidance'. (18:3) For more information about this event see Pędziwiatr 2003a.

[218] The official reason of his trip to Lebanon was a visit to his sick mother.

[219] For more information about Omar Bakri and his activism in Britain see Wiktorowicz 2005, Pędziwiatr 2003a, 2005, Husain 2007.

[220] In some cases the police investigators have managed to establish a close clausal relationship between the teachings of the aforementioned clerics and the acts of violence carried out by young British Muslims. The case of Asif Hanif and Omar Khan Sharif, who were students of Omar Bakri is one of the most evident (Pędziwiatr 2003a).

[221] The intelligence sources most commonly mention Idris Bazis from Manchester and Wail al-Dhaleai from Sheffield (McGrory & Hussain 2005).

were disrupted by the police, Richard Reid and Sajid Badat being just two of them. The first is serving a life sentence in the United States for attempting to ignite explosives in his shoe during an American Airlines flight from Paris to Miami in December 2004. The latter abandoned his plan to detonate a similar type of bomb in an aircraft, was sentenced to thirteen years in prison by a British court in 2005.

Although the subject of 'Muslim radicalism' in the post-July 7 period has been a dominant one, the public debates around Islam in Britain have not only concentrated on this issue. One of the topics that has been frequently discussed in Britain in relation to Muslim presence in the country is the subject of the limits of freedom of expression. Initially a wider public debate on this topic was triggered by Muslim protests over the publication of the book 'The Satanic Verses' by Salman Rushdie almost twenty years ago. The demands of some Muslims to ban a book that, in their view, abused the freedom of expression by trying to rewrite the life of Prophet Muhammad *"in an exceptionally abusive and obscene way"*[222] (Sardar 2005: 279) were not met and very quickly the protests started to escalate. In January 1989 Muslim groups in Bradford organized large demonstrations and book-burning, while a month later Ayatollah Khomeini issued a fatwa calling for the death of Salman Rushdie. Although the main issue surrounding 'The Satanic Verses' affair was freedom of expression, it was not the only one. Other issues which mobilized British Muslims surrounded the notion of blasphemy (what kinds of offences were included and, most importantly, which religions it covered) and whether offences to religious groups (e.g. incitement to hatred) were akin to offences relating to 'race' and ethnicity (Vertovec & Peach 1997: 8-7).

The protests against Salman Rushdie's novel and the reaction against them (see Modood 1992) played a crucial role in the creation of British Muslim identity politics. (Modood 2007: 136). However, they not only marked the watershed of Muslim collective engagement with the public sphere, but also the beginning of a specific portrayal of Muslims in the media which aimed to fit the existing stereotypes. More recently the issue of freedom of expeession, which was at the core of the Rushdie Affair, was hotly debated during the Danish cartoons affair and the controversy around Pope's Benedict XVI

---

[222] For more information about which elements of The Satanic Verses were for Muslims 'abusive and obscene' see Sardar and Davies 1990, Samad 1996 or Lewis 2002.

lecture at the University of Regensburg. Other issues that were brought up within the wider debates about Islam in Britain included inter alia, the wearing of the niqab or full veil covering the face, the provision of more state-funding for Muslim schools and the implementation by the government of the recommendations of the task group on tackling extremism (Home Office 2005).

In general, both in Belgium and Britain, Islam has been publicized mainly through the 'exceptional cases', that is all kinds of controversies around Islam and Muslims from the headscarves and The Satanic Verses affair to the more recent ones around the Danish cartoons and the Pope's speech in Regensburg. These affairs have become the forms of 'hermeneutical incidents' (Allievi 2001), which do not only have short term consequences, as examples of 'clashes of civilization', but also more durable ones, as they become stable points of reference in the subsequent interpretations of Muslims and Islam. Thus, these 'media events', as Dayan and Katz rightly point out, become in the collective memory equivalent of the historical monuments: a sort rhetorical instrument through which the social memory remembers itself (1992). The fact that this memory is usually made up of recollections of conflicts and clashes and, in general, of extraordinary events, does not prevent many people from applying it to 'ordinary' Muslims and 'non-sensational' Islam with predictable consequences.[223]

---

[223] As I am arguing elsewhere (Pędziwiatr 2008) the fact that Islam is publicized through 'exceptional cases' has to do with the philosophy of the media or some structural factors, rather than with deliberate attempts to demonize religion of Muslims.

CHAPTER IV - ISLAM AND CITIZENSHIP IN BRUSSELS

> *Je suis née en Belgique (...) ma langue maternelle est le français.*
> *J'ai du mal à m'exprimer en arabe ... Donc pour moi je ne me sens pas du tout*
> *étrangère. Pour certains oui ... le regard de l'autre ... j'ai des yeux noirs euh,*
> *je porte un voile... J'ai grandi ici et je mange comme les Belges euh, je suis belge.*
> *Mais de confession musulmane ...*
> (Naima)

"*I am of Moroccan origin, but I don't feel a foreigner. Even though for some of the people I am one, I do not feel at all a foreigner. (...)*" (Naima) – said one of my informants in Brussels. I heard similar voices from many other Belgian Muslims interviewed in the course of this research. Another argument that was put forward to me equally frequently in Belgium was the following one: "*We* (Muslims of 2nd and 3rd generation - KP) *have all the means to be full citizens, but we are not really.*" (Madiha) These opinions expressed by two young Muslim women touch upon some of the key issues that will be discussed in this chapter, exploring the depth, extent and content of subjective notions of citizenship of young organized Muslims, and some of the relationships between Islam and active social citizenship in Brussels. They particularly invoke the complexity of citizenship and its exclusionary nature. As Janoski and Gran have rightly observed, one of the features of citizenship is that it is "*an act of closure about a group of people it calls citizens*", in result of which "*some people are left out*" (2002: 35). Thus identity is a crucial aspect of citizenship that enables those who feel 'left out', like the aforementioned Belgian Muslims, to 'knock at the door of citizenship' (ibid) and to organize into social movements and interest groups so that they can participate as citizens in legal, political and social rights.

This chapter sheds light on the perceptions of citizenship of young organized Muslims in Brussels and provides some information about this 'knocking at the door of citizenship' in the Belgian context. It starts with a general description of the sample, pointing out the key socio-economic features of young Muslims interviewed in Brussels. Then it moves to explore how these people conceive of their Muslim and civic identities and how they frame their belonging. The explorations of the depth of citizenship of

165

young organized Muslims are followed by the analysis of the extent of their citizenship. This part of the chapter will focus on the elaboration of the resources for participation that are in the possession of the young Muslims and on how they account for activism in Muslim organizations and in the wider public sphere. The third part of this chapter is devoted to an assessment of the perception of civic rights by young Muslim Brusselers. The last part of the Belgian case study continues to explore the normative dimensions of lived citizenship of young Muslims by looking at their perceptions of the civic obligations and relationship between Muslim ethics and perceived requirements of citizenship.

4.1 MAIN FEATURES OF THE BELGIAN SAMPLE

As the core of this chapter constitute the views, opinions and narratives of twenty four members of the emerging new Muslim elite, with whom I had spent substantial amount between April 2004 and 2008, it is essential to begin with a brief sketch of the main features of this group people. The group consisted of ten men and fourteen women, all of whom wore foulard or headscarf. The overrepresentation of female informants in my Belgian sample is above all evidence of their significant presence amongst the organized Muslims in the city and of their relative openness to contact with the male, non-Muslim researcher[224]. With the exception of two female interviewees, of whom one was of Tunisian origin and the other one of Algerian origin, the rest of the young Muslims interviewed in the course of this research were of Moroccan origin. Similarly to the picture of the wider Moroccan population in the country, their parents or grandparents had most commonly immigrated to Belgium from the Northern provinces of Morocco. Consequently for many of them, especially those who still live with their parents (9 informants) the language which they often use at home is Berber, or more precisely *Riffi*, which is one of the Berber languages or *Tamazight* (Brett & Fentress 1997). The majority of them however speak French at home. Although numerous informants said that they spoke Arabic at home, many of them were quick to add that they did not really master

---

[224] At the same time, here it has to be stated that this study is not representative for the whole of Muslim civil society in Brussels so one should not draw conclusions like, for example, in all Muslim organisations in the city Muslim women play a crucial role or that all of them are willing to meet for a face-to-face interview with non-Muslim, male researcher.

this language and expressed the wish to improve their knowledge of it. Only three informants declared that they sometimes speak Dutch at home.

The majority of the members of the emerging new Muslim elite interviewed were married (13 people), while ten were single and one was officially engaged. One third of the informants were in their 30s while the rest were below 31 years old. Eleven informants were between 25 and 30 years old and five were below 25 years old. Most single interviewees lived with their parents, whereas those with their own families had moved out of their parents' houses. Seven married informants had children but the size of their family units could not in any way match that of their parents. While my interviewees had at most 3 children (2 people) they often originated from large extended families of seven and more children (one third of the respondents). Their fathers - in most cases unqualified workers - were usually the only breadwinners in the families as their mothers had never entered the job market. Three fourths of my informants were thus of working-class background and the parents of one fourth of them could be considered as representative of lower middle class and middle class[225]. Taking into account their class background and the fact that many of them have mothers and fathers who are allophones, most of them are extremely upwardly mobile as they are in the process of getting a university degree or have already acquired one. Almost all of the young Muslims that I interviewed had finished university or were in the process of completing their tertiary education and only two of them finished their education before university. Thus they constitute part of the new Muslim middle classes or *beurgeoisie*, to use the term popularized by Catherine Wihtol de Wenden and Rémy Leveau (2001). The majority of those who went to do their university diplomas were students of humanities and nine of them were students of natural sciences. The elaboration of the remaining characteristics of my Belgian informants is indicated in the table below and further analysis of the above mentioned features will be undertaken in the later sections of this chapter when I will move on to assess the depth and extent of the citizenship of young organized Muslims.

---

[225] The main parameter of the class position that is being used here has to do with the occupation of the parents. While the interviewees whose parents were in unskilled, usually low paid, manual occupations which I consider to be of working class background, those whose parents were semi-qualified or highly qualified workers I consider to have lower middle class and middle class origin.

Before I do so, however, it is important to account for what it meant for my informants to be a Muslim.

Table 4.1 Main features of the Belgian informants

Name	Sex and Age	Family Situation	Siblings	Accommodation	Language spoken at home	Origin	Education	Occupation	Occupation of the parents	Return the cou of origi
1. Masud	M28	Married	2b + 2s	Separate	Ar, Fr	Ma, (Br)	MA in IT	Engineer in IT sector	F-worker, M-housewife	Every 2 years
2. Kemal	M36	Single	4b + 3s	Separate	Ar, Fr	Ma, (Br)	Primary	Factory worker	F–worker, M-housewife	Last 7 y ago
3. Rashid	M27	Married	2b + 1s	Separate	Ar, Br, Fr	Ma, (Br)	MA in IT	Engineer in IT sector	F-worker, M-housewife	Rare
4. Khalil	M27	Married, 1 child	2b	Separate	Fr, Br, Dt	Ma, (Br)	MA in History	School teacher	F-worker, M-housewife	Rare
5. Jusuf	M39	Married	3s + 2b	Separate	Fr, Ar	Ma	MA in Philosophy and Rel.Studies	School teacher	F-worker, M-housewife	Rare
6. Murad	M34	Married	2b + 3s	Separate	Fr, Ar, Dt	Ma	Secondary, certificate CBAI of Multic.Anim	Unemployed	F-worker, M-housewife	Regula
7. Majd	M20	Single	4b + 3s	With mother	Fr, Ar	Ma	Towards BA in Chemistry	Student	F-worker, M-disabled	10-year last tim
8. Khasim	M26	Single	1b + 3s	With parents	Fr, Ar	Ma	MA in Physics	School teacher	F-disabled, M-housewife	Almost every y
9. Amjad	M38	Married, 3 children	2b + 2s	Separate	Ar, Fr	Ma	MA in Economics	School teacher	F-worker, M-housewife	Every y
10. Faisal	M33	Married	2b + 1 s	Separate	Ar, Fr	Ma	MA in Liter., DEA in History.	School teacher	F-worker, M-housewife	Regula
11. Nabihah	F28	Single	5s + 1b	Separate	Fr, Br, Ar	Ma, (Br)	BA in Social Work	NGO sector	F-ind. businessman, M-worker	Every 2 years
12. Hadijah	F35	Married	3s + 2b	Separate	Ar, Br	Ma, (Br)	BA in Economics	NGO sector	F-ind. businessman, M-housewife	6 times
13. Madiha	F22	Single	3s + 1b	With parents	Fr, Ar	Tn	BA in Pedagogy	Kindergarten assistant	F-worker, M-worker	Almost every y
14. Abida	F30	Single	6s + 1b	With parents or sister	Fr, Ar	Ma	BA in Dentistry	Unemployed	F-worker, M-housewife	Rare
15. Hafa	F27	Married, 1 child	5s + 3b	Separate	Fr, Ar	Ma	MA in Psychology	Shopkeeper	F-worker, M-	Every year

168

									housewife	
›. Falak	F23	Single	2s + 1b	With parents	Fr, Br	Ma (Br)	MA in Political St.	Student	F-q. worker, M-housewife	3 times
. Malak	F27	Single	3b	With parents	Ar	Ma	MA in Medical Biology	Researcher at the Laboratory	F-disabled, M-housewife	Every other year
. Rabab	F36	Married, 3 children	2b + 2 s	Separate	Ar, Fr	Ma	MA in English and Arab Literature	Manager in NGO	F-q. worker (died), M-pensioner	Regular, for children to keep the tradition
ꞏla	F33	Married, 2 children	7s + 1b	Separate	Ar, Fr	Ma	MA in Literature	Admin. Worker in NGO	F-worker, M-housewife	Regular, Whole family there
ꞏima	F23	Single	5s + 3b	With parents	Ar, Br, Fr	Ma, (Br)	BA in Dietetics	Dietician in Medical sector	F-worker, M -housewife	Rare
ꞏna	F23	Engaged	5s + 3b	With parents	Ar, Br, Fr	Ma, (Br)	BA in Social work	Student	F-worker, M-housewife	Rare
ꞏna	F30	Married, 2 children	2s	Separate	Fr, Ar, Dt	Ma	BA in Law	Unemployed	F- ind. businessman, M-housewife	Every 2 years
ꞏnah	F27	Single	6s + 1b	With parents	Fr, Ar, Br	Ma, (Br)	BA in Journalism	Student of Economics	F-worker, M-housewife	Rare
ꞏaysan	F30	Married, 1 child	1s + 3b	Separate	Fr	Alg	MA in Social Work	Student	F-worker, M-housewife	Rare

4.2 IDENTITY, ISLAM AND CITIZENSHIP

4.2.1 BEING A MUSLIM

One of the notions that was deliberately left 'semi-defined' in the earlier chapter was the one of 'a Muslim'. I did not provide a full definition of what it means to be a Muslim, arguing that such a definition would be essentialist and would inevitably reduce the wide spectrum of possible manifestations of Muslimness to be found in the social reality. It was assumed that for each person who describes himself/herself as a Muslim, to be a Muslim means something else. Thus, instead of defining what it means to be a Muslim, I have pointed out a number of attributes that are traditionally associated with the category of a follower of Islam and which could constitute a form of an ideal type of Muslim identity.

The findings of my research that concentrated on religious Muslims (which are in fact only one category of Muslims) substantiate the aformentioned assumption as each of my Belgian interviewees accounted differently for what it means to him or to her to be a Muslim. While some of the definitions of Muslimness of my informants stressed dogmatic and spiritual elements, other emphasized humanist and activist components. Often all these components were combined in one definition or in one narrative. Thus, instead of speaking about spiritual, humanist, activist and dogmatic young Muslims and building a forcibly reductionist typology, it seems more appropriate to speak about all these different 'ingredients', that is of spirituality, humanism, activism and Islamic dogma, present in their subjective notions of Islamic identity in larger or smaller quantities. The common feature of all the definitions of Muslim identity provided by my informants was that all of them were extremely elaborate and only exceptionally described the essence of Muslimness in a few sentences.

One of the elements that was particularly frequently evoked in the answers of my informants was the one of spirituality. Before I present some of their answers it is worth mentioning that there is no agreement among scholars on one meaning of the notion of spirituality and some of them even claim that *"we do not yet have the language or conceptual apparatus for refining our understanding of spirituality"* (McGuire quoted in Heelas & Woodhead 2005: 2). However most of them agree that some of the major features of spirituality are: experience, awareness, and appreciation of a 'transcendent dimension' to life beyond self; awareness of a connection with self and personal relationship with God/Spirit/Divinity/Nature; and an unfolding of life that calls for reflection and experience, including a sense of who one 'is' and how one knows. Robert Atchley, for example, defines spirituality as *"the capacity to experience the sacred directly"* and remarks that *"such experience can be cognitive, emotional, and/or motivational"* (2007). The sacred can be experienced within the framework of a given religion, as well as in opposition to a certain religion. In the case of the analysed group of people we are dealing with the spirituality in religion rather than spirituality as opposed to religion.

For many Belgian Muslims the various aforementioned dimensions of spirituality were at the core of their understanding of Muslimness. The most obvious one – reference to the divine/transcendental or belief in existence of God – was indicated by Lana, who in the following way contrasted her believing with the non-believing of her peers *"Well …*

today young people usually do not believe in God. I am happy that I do. I have still this belief ... this strong and sincere conviction. I am very happy that I still have it, because I could not continue to live without it". Belief in the existence of God is not only a feature of her personality that distinguishes her from other non-believing young people but also 'something' that, as she claims, provides her with an *'objective in life'* (Lana). Being a Muslim means for her both acquiring a socially recognizable identity and having a personal project in life. The same aspect of Muslimness was exhibited in the definition of Islamic identity by Murad who said that *"for me a Muslim is someone who believes in God ... the term non-believing Muslims doesn't make sense. Being atheist and Muslim is not possible"*. From this statement he went on to criticize organizations such as the Movement of Secular Muslims of France (Fr. *Mouvement des musulmans laïques de France* - MMLF) and French Council of Secular Muslims (Fr. *Conseil français des musulmans laïques* - CFML) recently created in France and representing secular Muslims[226], that for him are *'examples of intellectual frauds'*. In his opinion these bodies attract non-believing Muslims who *"know that the message of Islam is politically expanding and that it is selling very well in the media so they have decided to take the Muslim label just to attract the attention of the media and politicians"* (Murad). Several times during the interview he expressed discontent with the fact that 'non-believing Muslims' are claiming Muslim identity, which in his opinion should be reserved only for the believing Muslims.

Other interviewees who stressed the importance of spirituality in their definitions of Muslimness claimed that Islam is a religion which has greatly facilitated their personal self-development. This is particularly visible in the answers of two female informants, Anan who said that being a Muslim means *"... to be nourished by Islam and to blossom in this religion"* and of Falak for whom *"It is something that allows me to access the serenity and happiness (...) to personally develop to the maximum. It is something that is extremely powerful. (...) I have impression that to be a Muslim it means wearing rose tinted spectacles. It is something that allows to see things differently, to appreciate things differently. I am really happy that I have found the sense of my life in it ... very far from*

---

[226] A similar organisation has been recently created also in Germany. More information on the German Central Council of Ex-Muslims, can be found in Rashid 2007.

171

the caricatured images of suppressed women, closed in their homes and beaten by their husbands, brothers or fathers". Thus, the definitions of Muslimness of these young Belgian Muslim women have challenged not only the popular view, suggesting that adherence to Islam (as well as other religions) inhibits personal self-development, but also that it semi-automatically leads to reinforcement of the patriarchal structures in a society (Yuval-Davis 1992, Okin 1999).[227] Furthermore, through their definitions of Muslimness they seemed to appeal to the wider public for a more nuanced perception of Muslim women. Falak, in fact, did it explicitly when she said *"Once I've heard from the professor at the ULB - 'you are an atypical Muslim' (...) 'You are not like other Muslim women' – 'why'? 'Because you speak very good French, and so on and so forth...' But maybe it is not me who is not typical but it is your prejudices that speak through you? Go and see the reality – there are plenty of women like me"* (Falak).

Finally, several of the definitions of Muslimness of my interviewees who put emphasis on the spiritual dimension also had a strong missionary or *dawah (Ar. calling to Islam)* character. One such definition was Kemal's for whom being a Muslim meant first of all to be *"a carrier of the spirituality"*. The obligation of reminding people about God was also stressed by Jusuf, for whom being a Muslim meant above all *"to carry out a divine project"* or to promote Islam which for him was *"a divine project which God proposed to people so as they can adhere to it or not"*. Although put differently, with less emphasis on the spiritual dimension, the preaching element is also clearly visible in the following definition by Khalil, for whom the essence of Muslimness is in *"bearing witness to the faith and in presenting Islam to others, because if it is not Muslims who will be presenting Islam, who is going to do it?"*. All of the aforementioned informants who pointed out at the importance of *dawah* in their conception of Muslimness also insisted on the primacy of the principle of freedom of choice in embracing and renouncing Islam as well as in converting to another religion. As will be demonstrated below, most of my informants who were born into Muslim families argued that the fact that they were Muslims had very little to do with the fact that when they were born their

---

[227] In this regard I agree with Leyla Babes who has suggested that by tolerating the presence of women in the public sphere and encouraging the support which they provide for all forms of proselytism, Islamists have opened up the space to Muslim women claims, which contest the men's authority and their rigid conceptions of gender relations (2002: 237).

parents whispered *shahada* into their ears. Instead, they maintained that their 'being Muslim' was a result of a 'choice' which they had usually made in their adolescence.

Apart from elements of spirituality, the young Muslims' definitions of Muslimness bore also many marks of an all-embracing humanism. One such definition was given for instance by Madiha, for whom being a Muslim meant "... *to think more about others than about myself, not to be selfish, but to always take into account people who live side by side with me*". Similar point made Majd who argued that "*being a Muslim means being a model for others, so not only Muslims but also non-Muslims appreciate my way of being and my way of reacting*". Not only for him, but also for many other interviewees, the personal model that they strived to emulate was the prophet Mohammed.

A significant number of the conceptions of Islamic identity of Belgian Muslims were also characterized by a strong mark of activism. For numerous members of the new Muslim elite, social engagement was the key feature of a Muslim identity. Falak, for instance, argued that "*to be a Muslim does not mean just to rest among the Arabs, pursue the Qur'anic studies or a course on how to pray, but to participate actively in the life of the city, and to debate the societal problems such as drug abuse, criminality, etc*". For her 'a true Muslim' is someone who above all tries to resolve different societal problems or at least joins public debates on them. This point of view seemed to be shared also by another interviewee who pointed out that "*When you are reading the Qur'an, on several occasions it speaks about 'those who believe and do righteous deeds' .(...) So a Muslim is someone who takes action and participates. It is true that you can act on your own, but to participate, you need to participate with others.*" (Khalil). The main goal of the social engagement of Muslims is supposed to be the promotion of justice according to many of my interviewees. As one of them argued: "*For us, actually, justice is often a synonym of Islam. To do justice is to do Islamic work.*" (Kemal).[228]

Finally, a few of the young Muslims in Brussels, when asked about what was the meaning of Muslim identity to them, put an emphasis in their answers on the dogmatic elements. One of them was Murad, who argued that "*to be a Muslim, means to follow the*

---

[228] This kind of understanding of justice is very closely linked with Tariq Ramadan's conceptualization of jihad as the mobilization of all human forces and efforts to overcome injustices, poverty, illiteracy, delinquency or exclusion (Ramadan 2001: 68-69).

Islamic precepts, go to Mecca, pray, fast during the Ramadan ... It is like you pass your driving test and get a driving license. You must obey the driving rules. You need to stop at the red lights. If you don't do it you are going to have an accident". For him being a Muslim meant first of all to follow a 'religious road code'. One female interviewee, who also stressed the importance of Islamic dogma in her definition of Muslimness, pointed out that a follower of Islam is *"someone who tries to live according to the Islamic principles, who prays, observes Ramadan, etc."* (Hafa). The majority of the informants, however, tended to downplay elements of Islamic orthopraxy in their definitions of Muslim identity, and emphasized one or usually more of the above mentioned elements. Most of them also stressed that they 'became Muslims' at a certain moment, rather than simply 'were Muslims', and that their religious identities were dynamic and undergoing constant change. One may notice that for example in the following statement by the same interviewee which underlined the importance of Islamic dogma in a definition of Muslim identity *"I am still learning about Islam. I do not consider myself a good Muslim but simply a Muslim who constantly develops and searches, asks questions, who tries to translate the rationalist vision in the way that it is Islamic and that contextualizes Islam"* (Murad).

4.2.2 BECOMING A MUSLIM

As I have argued drawing a general theoretical framework, social identities in high modernity are reflexively made (Giddens 1991). It means that, apart from a very tiny group of people, who are still being born into certain roles and attached to them identities (e.g. heirs to throne), most people today have to undertake the risky task of constructing their own original identities. This also refers to young Muslims of the second and third generations born in Europe and to their religious identities. There are no longer uninterrupted transmissions of religious traditions between different generations or relatively straightforward re-appropriations of religious identities by children from their parents and this is also the case in Muslim families.

The findings of my research confirm one of the key points of the modernization theories in claiming that ready-made identities largely belong to the past and that we live in the world of do-it-yourself identities (e.g. Giddens 1991, Baumann 1995, Beck and

Beck Gernsheim 2002). Although all of my informants were born into Muslim families, and hence one could claim that they have inherited religious identities from their parents, most of them would not agree with such a suggestion. One may notice elements of disagreement with such an assumption in the following opinion of one of my interviewees: *"That is true, we may inherit it* (religion – KP) *when we are young, but at certain age everyone is getting more aware of the world and he or she can change religion to the one in which he/she feels best. So I think religion is really a personal choice now, certainly among many of the young Muslims."* (Madiha). She is not alone in admitting that she was a Muslim as a consequence of a personal choice that she has made. The same claim is also made by Kemal, who argues that being a Muslim *"It is a choice that I have made myself. It is a route as others that I have taken freely and consciously."* and Naima who confesses that *"My parents are not the parents that would give all the religion to their children. Islam is not a religion passed from a father to a son. It's a religion that pushes the individual to reflect and to go forward. We cannot copy the things that our parents have been doing. It isn't really the right way. I am not saying that this is an invention of religion, not at all, but rather ... it is a reflection. (...) If I got back to Islam, it is because I had reflected on it and made such a choice."*

At the same time young Muslim Brusselers do not negate the fact that they are not completely new to the religion which they have 'chosen'. They do acknowledge the fact that their parents have provided them with certain dispositions and religious knowledge. Many of my interviewees in a manner similar to Amjad, have pointed out that *"Islam has always been present in my house."* The acknowledgment of this Muslim habitus[229] can be noticed particularly clearly in the following utterance of Faisal: *"It has to be said that I was naturally bathed in the Muslim world ... through the parents' education. So they have passed something to us through the silence, through my mother, through the practice of things which can't be easily translated but which were present. And then*

---

[229] Religious habitus is understood here in line with Pierre Bourdieu's conceptualization: that is as specifically religious dimension of an individual agent's habitus that manifests itself most apparently, though not exclusively, in the religious field. He defined it himself as *"the principal generator of all thoughts, perceptions and actions consistent with the norms of a religious representation of the natural and supernatural worlds"* (Bourdieu 1971: 319) and as *"a lasting, generalized and transposable disposition to act and think in conformity with the principles of a (quasi) systematic view of the world and human existence."* (Bourdieu 1987: 124)

through my father (...) They have framed us well ... practically through the silence". The 'silent transmission of religion' evoked by Faisal grasps the essence of religious habitus or the cultural structures that exist in his and other second and third generation Maghrebians' bodies and minds, and the non-discursive knowledge about Islam that they possess very well and which might be said to 'go without saying' as it is acquired in the process of socialization in a Muslim family. It is usually through the silent observation of their parents praying and performing other religious rituals at home that my informants established their first contact with Islam. These first encounters were fortified later on in their lives when they were sent to Qur'anic schools in the local mosques and when they started to attend classes of Islam integrated in the Belgian schools' curricula.

While acknowledging the fact that some elements of their Muslim identities were inherited from their mothers and fathers, they have stressed very strongly that their parents have passed down to them only 'some religion', and not *"all the religion"*, as one of the interviewees has put it (Naima). By highlighting the incompleteness of the religious education received at home they usually implied that, on the one hand, the content of the religious message passed to them by their parents was in many ways unsatisfactory and that, on the other, they were provided with substantial room for manoeuvre with regards to the choice of a religion. Both these aspects are, for instance, present in the following account by Naima. *"I attended the Christian school. So, our parents gave me a choice. It was up to me to decide ..., but at the same time they privileged Islam and taught me its basis. So they prayed in front of me etc. But they didn't pass it down to me as an obligation, by saying 'you are obliged to do this' ... no, no, no. It was rather a form of orientation. So I am a Muslim, but why? What makes me a Muslim? From here I started to search my religion. In this way I could explore my religion and advance in it. And this I could do, not with the tools that I was provided with by my parents. Not at all. I had to learn these tools myself."* One of the tools she wished she had learnt from her parents, and which according to her would make her exploration of Islam easier, was the knowledge of Arabic. She pointed out that as quickly as, she discovered this weakness she signed up for an Arabic class at the university. Another informant criticized the "monolithic" nature of the parents' transmission of religious knowledge by saying that *"we were often told authoritatively: 'this is Islam'. But, in fact,*

Islam is much more richer than this; it is much more diverse than this. If we knew that, it would allow us to avoid many clashes." (Faisal). Amjad was yet another young Muslim Brusseler who talked openly about the deficiencies of his parents' religious transmission. He pointed out that *"although we were in contact with the religion, it was only a limited, traditional contact... neither my father nor my mother could read or write, so this was quite simplistic religious transmission."* However, similarly to other interviewees, he does not dismiss the efforts of his parents which were aimed at equipping him and his siblings with a religious base. On the contrary, one could hear from him many expressions of gratitude for these endeavours. The religious habitus, in line with Pierre Bourdieu's conception, provides Amjad and many other informants not only with certain 'frames' but serves as a basis for further adjustments, improvisations and corrections. This is because habitus, as Bourdieu and Wacquant have argued, is not the fate or extremely deterministic force that some people read into it, but it is always open to improvisation and creative modification in response to changing historical circumstances (1992: 133).

As demonstrated above, regardless of the level of exposure to Islam in their childhood, almost all of the interviewees claimed their present religious identities in terms of individual, voluntary appropriations. These young Muslim Belgians who stated that they "have chosen Islam", beyond some cultural heritage passed on or taken on, are thus part of a general movement which progressively imposes the figure of the 'convert' (along with that of the 'pilgrim' travelling the non-predetermined stages of his path of identification) as one of the central figures in the modern religious landscape (Hervieu-Léger 1999). Furthermore, by claiming to be Muslims 'by choice', rather than 'by inheritance', they are manifesting a fundamental postulate of religious modernity, which maintains that an 'authentic' or original religious identity can only be chosen and reflexively made. The focus of such a 'choice' or a 'conversion act' (be it "entering" or "returning" to religious faith) is that it acknowledges the personal commitment of the individual, autonomous believer. At the same time, it involves some reorganization of his/her life to follow the new norms upheld by a given community. In the case of Muslim women, for example, the moment of 'rediscovering' Islam is often followed by a decision to adopt an Islamic headscarf or hijab. One of my informants accounted for this moment

177

in the following way: *"When I was about 18 years old I made friends with peers who read the Qur'an, prayed and in this way I, in inverted commas, discovered my religion more profoundly ... I opened the Qur'an, started to read small booklets on how to pray (...) then naturally I put on a veil ... but I had to remove it for a year because apparently I was not ready to wear it. At this time there were not many women wearing veils, so it was perceived differently. I think it was more difficult than now, because many people were questioning it not only in the non-Muslim, but also in the Muslim community. I felt it as it was a heavy burden, even though my religiosity has never decreased. Then later, when I had constructed my spirituality I put it back"* (Sana). This testimony not only reveals a certain gradualism in the religious re-discovery of the young Belgian Muslim, but also demonstrates how the perception of the hijab within the Muslim community and in the wider society had influenced Sana to adopt the hijab, then to remove it, and finally to re-adopt it once again. There is no room here to elaborate on the issue of Muslim veiling at length, however, it should be noted that the hijab is not simply a symbol of female submission, as some people want to see it, but it is an extremely polysemic sign. As research from different European countries show (e.g. Watson 1994, Gaspard and Khosrokhavar 1995, Khosrokhavar 1997, Jacobson 1997, Babes 2002, Venel 2002, Fadil 2003), the Muslim headscarf fulfils numerous social functions. Farhad Khosrokhavar, for instance, demonstrates that young Muslim women, by adopting a hijab, can 'play' with their Muslim identity, settle their ambiguous relationship with both family and social environment, assert their identity as women by giving their fathers and brothers a fictive proof of submission while they are actually escaping from it or even reinventing the memory they lack in order to have access to self-esteem (Gaspard and Khosrokhavar 1995). Furthermore, Leila Babes, as well as Dounia Bouzar, observe that wearing an Islamic headscarf is viewed by certain Muslim women as a means through which they can be more effectively engaged in the public sphere (Babes 2002: 238, Bouzar 2005: 56-76). As I am going to demonstrate below, in the section devoted to the participatory dimension of citizenship, the last thesis can be also applied to most of the young Muslim women interviewed for this book. For the moment, however, it should suffice to say that Islam, like any other religion, is a toolbox, which is able to supply extremely diverse symbolic references.

Returning to the issue of choice in the construction of authentic religious identities it is worth remembering the words of Hervieu-Léger who, in his *Le pèlerin et le converti,* points out that religious re-discovery or conversion is a remarkably effective modality of self-construction in a world of plural identities, where there is no longer a central principle to organize individual and social experiences (1999). In such a world where traditions lose their hold and where daily life is increasingly reconstituted in terms of the dialectical interplay of the local and the global, there is a growing pressure on individuals to negotiate lifestyle choices among a diversity of options. All these conditions make the task of the reflexive construction of authentic identities a very difficult if not a risky one.[230] As I argued in the second chapter, the reflexive project of identity constitutes a particularly heavy burden for young Muslims, who often grow up in family conditions unfavourable for the development of successful 'do-it-yourself' biographies'. It should not be surprising then that sometimes efforts to build an authentic religious identity or personal searches for spirituality lead certain individuals to embrace non-dialogical exclusivist theologies. This risk, which I believe lies at the core of an understanding of Muslim, as well as other religious radicalisms in 21st century Europe, was also evoked by one of my informants who pointed out that *"We have more and more Muslims now that come to Islam through their own paths, and some of them become arrogant. They say: 'we know the truth, you don't know it'. To my understanding of Islam this stand is absolutely unacceptable. I am not in any way superior to Christians, Jews or members of any other religious group. I am simply a carrier of spirituality, of a belief, but it doesn't mean that I am superior to anyone without these features."* (Kemal). My interviewee, who compared himself to a *"... bee that takes a bit from wherever it goes",* after having frequented the meetings of the Salafi and Tablighi groups decided to embrace an open dialogical theology or the inclusivist theological perspective which implies a positive appreciation of other religions.[231] His case, however, confirms the fact that this is only one 'path to Islam' that is available today for the young Muslims in Brussels and although it is taken by the vast majority of them, it remains one from a wide

---

[230] Beck and Beck-Gernsheim talk about 'risk biographies', which can swiftly turn into 'breakdown biographies', if the wrong choice of career field is compounded by the downward spiral of private misfortune (2002: 3)

[231] For more information on inclusivist and exclusivist theological perspectives see, for example, Kubacki 2007.

variety of options. The existence of other options is well known inter alia due to media exposure of such cases as Muriel Degauque's, a convert to Islam who travelled with her partner Issam Goris (a Belgian of Moroccan origin), from the Rue de Mérode in the centre of Brussels to the city of Baquba, 50 km north of Baghdad, to strap explosives around her belt and detonate them in front of Iraqi policemen, killing five of them.[232]

4.2.3 LIMITS OF RELIGIOUS INDIVIDUALISATION

As I have mentioned in the opening chapter there is no agreement amongst students of European Islam as to the outcomes of the processes of religious individualization to be observed within Muslim populations. While some researchers argue that a growing number of religious 'pickers and choosers' in these populations is leading to a 'liberalization of European Islam' and emergence of 'critical Islam' (e.g. Mandaville 2001, Schifeur 2000), others claim that, in spite of individualization and the diversification of authority structures, the current situation is characterized by a relative stability of religious dogmas and that we are very far from 'liberal Islam' (e.g. Roy 1999, 2002, Wiktorowicz 2005). Without any ambition of providing decisive arguments in support of one or the other position in this academic debate (for which the character of this qualitative study does not anyway allow), but rather to assess the influence of modernity on the young Muslims' perceptions of the Islamic dogmas, this study asked members of the emerging new Muslim elite in Brussels about their opinion on the Islamic prohibition on Muslim women marrying non-Muslim men and on the prohibition of rejecting Islam.

As far as the first issue is concerned, the majority of the informants, both female and male, argued that a Muslim woman has the right to marry whoever she wants but at the same time they have stressed that, if she wants to be 'a good Muslim', she should try not to marry outside her religion. Their answers, in other words, tried to do the impossible, namely to reconcile the Islamic marriage requirements with the modern principle of freedom of choice of a life partner. One of such answers provided was Hadijah's, who argued that *"If a Muslim woman wants to marry a non-Muslim man, then*

---

[232] For more information about Salafi, Tablighi and Jihadi groups in Belgium see for instance Gringard 2006 or Verheyden 2006.

it's her personal choice, however it is against the global code of Islam". Similar argumentation was also used by Jusuf who asserted that *"As far as personal choice is concerned I fully respect it. A Muslim woman who marries a non-Muslim is still a Muslim. From the point of view of Muslim ethics though, Islam doesn't encourage and doesn't permit it."* Interestingly, however, most of the interviewees, who in a more or less implicit way confirmed the importance of this particular Islamic requirement, used non-religious reasoning to defend it. In other words my research seems to suggest that, even though certain Muslim dogmas are quite stable amongst the members of the emerging new Muslim elite in Brussels, it is not necessarily the religious legitimisation that keeps them intact. One of the most commonly quoted arguments in support of the religious prohibition for women to marry outside the Muslim community was a 'pragmatic' one - at least that is how the young Belgian Muslims viewed it. They argued that not only are marriages of Muslim women with non-Muslim men, but also relationships between Muslim men and non-Muslim women doomed to fail due to the partners' differences in worldview and life project. Furthermore, they claimed that it is much easier to take decisions in a non mixed-marriage, where both partners think to some extent along the same lines, than in the mixed one. The main points of this line of defence of the analyzed principle one may find in the following opinion of Majd who said: *"Me personally, I'd like to marry a Muslim woman because of my religious convictions. And because if both of us are Muslims we will have the same ideals and it will be easier for us to live together. In a mixed marriage there is a difference of mentality comparable to that, which one may find in a couple of a 19 year old with a 40 year old. Because of the difference in mentality it might not work. If my wife would say that I am crazy when she sees me praying, that is not going to work"*.

There was only one Muslim woman and one man in my Belgian sample who explicitly supported the analyzed principle and did not search for any justification to defend it. On the other hand, there were many male and female informants who spoke, if not in favour of the free choice of marriage partner, then at least in favour of wider debate on this issue. One of the female interviewees who had put the principle of free choice of marriage partner above the Islamic requirement was Hafa who said *"I know it is religiously forbidden* (to marry a non-Muslim – KP) *but I believe it is a personal choice*

181

after all. (...) The most important is that the partners understand each other." A male informant, Amjad, speaking in favour of the right for Muslim women to marry non-Muslims, stressed the relative nature of a religious prohibition by referring to the person of the second Caliph Umar ibn al-Khattab who also temporarily forbade Muslim men to marry outside the Muslim community. Al-Khattab introduced such measures when he noticed that 'exoticism' was pushing a growing number of Muslim men into the arms of Christian and Jewish women rather than into the arms of Muslim ones (Amjad). According to Amjad, who claimed to know many young Muslim women married with non-Muslims and living in perfect harmony and 'in respect of each other's spiritualities', this prohibition should be suspended. Yet another interviewee, Maysan, did not go so far as to call for the suspension of this prohibition but instead called for an opening up of debate on this issue. She pointed out that *"To some extent this debate is already open. For example the ECFR[233] has recently issued a fatwa saying that a woman who converted to Islam and is already married to a non-Muslim does not have to break up her marriage. The family life has in this case a priority. This is what I told to my friend who has exactly the same problem. She converted to Islam and she continues to live with her husband, whom she loves, and who does not want to hear the word 'islam."* (Maysan)

Numerous interviewees have also spoken strongly against the practices of forced marriages by arguing similarly to Falak that *"forced marriages have nothing to do with religion"* and that *"Islam encourages a woman to choose her husband."* They have also tried to contextualize the Muslim obligation that stipulates that a Muslim woman cannot marry without the consent of her guardian (usually her father). One of my informants pointed out, for example, that *"If she (a Muslim woman – KP) wants to marry someone (...) she needs to have her guardian with her to sign, but this is a bit like in the city hall where you also need to have witnesses. So her father (guardian - KP) says 'yes' or 'no' ... but he doesn't have the right to say 'no' like this. He can say 'no' only if he sees that the chosen man is really someone who is not good, who is violent etc. (...) The right of the guardian lies mainly in making the woman to reflect on the choice she made ..."* (Naima). In other words, this young Belgian Muslim argued that the role of a woman's guardian in

---

[233] ECFR stands for the European Council for Fatwa and Research set up in 1997 on the initiative of the Federation of Islamic Organisations in Europe and presided over by Yusuf al-Qaradawi. For more information about the organisation as well as about sheikh al-Qaradawi see Pędziwiatr 2006c.

contemporary Belgium is mainly an advisory one. Thus, similarly to a few other informants she has tried to translate the requirements of Islam into the conditions of life in the high modernity.

The answers of my informants to the question about their views on the prohibition of renouncing Islam went largely in the same directions. Almost all the Belgian Muslims interviewed in the course of this research spoke strongly in favour of the free choice of religion. They did it inter alia by stressing that faith is for them *'a purely private matter'* (Rashid) or by emphasizing that they view it as *"a matter of private choice"* (Malak). Khasim for instance argued that *"(...) if someone doesn't recognise himself any more in the Islamic principles and is not flourishing with them, then he can make the choice of leaving Islam and it is only his own problem ... no one can say anything"*. There have been many other voices similar to Khasim's one, which shows that in the case of this particular element of Muslim dogma, the vast majority of my informants subscribed to the key principle of religious modernity and against the Muslim prohibition of conversion to another religion.

From this short sketch of the influence of modernity on the important elements of the Muslim dogma one may draw two general conclusions. Firstly, that the processes of modernization are advancing in different areas with dissimilar swiftness and therefore in one area (e.g. prohibition of the Muslim conversion) they can make quite significant advances, whereas in another area (e.g. the prohibition of marrying outside the Muslim community for women) they are much less visible. And secondly, that in spite of the strong individualist component in the religious experience of Muslims in Europe, the content of this experience does not necessarily have to be individuating.

4.2.4 BEING A CITIZEN

Having discussed how the young Muslim Belgians conceive of their religious identities and having accounted for the main issues related to their Muslimness in the context of life in the highly reflexive society, it is time to elaborate on the identity dimension of the social representations of citizenship of my informants. As I have argued above, the young Muslims' perceptions of the citizenship are likely to have an influence not only on their understanding of their rights and obligations as citizens, but also on whether they participate in wider social life, and if so, in what form. This is one of the major reasons why this study asked young Muslim inhabitants of Brussels about their banal definition of citizenship.

It was established that, where civic rights are largely interpreted as negative freedoms and where references to citizenship in public debates are almost omnipresent (*"where everyone talks about citizenship"* (Murad), to use the words of one of the interviewees), members of the emerging new Muslim elite hold extremely elaborate and multidimensional definitions of citizenship. The elaborate nature of their definitions of citizenship is especially evident when compared with the same type of definitions of young Muslim Britons, explored in the following chapter. Thus this shows that for those analysed it is not only the terms 'citizen' and 'citizenship' that are meaningful but also the language of citizenship itself. Having meticulously analysed these definitions it was possible to distinguish four major ways in which the young Belgian Muslims talked about citizenship[234]. In other words, my informants have perceived citizenship in terms of one or usually more than one of the following models: the socially constructive model, the lack-of-recognition model, the effective identification model and last but not least, the contractual model. In what follows I explain what constitutes the essence of each of the models and present excerpts of the interviews with Muslim Brusselers to more clearly portray them.

It will start with the presentation of the socially constructive model because it was by far the most popular model of citizenship to be found amongst my interviewees in Brussels. The vast majority of my informants, both men and women, while speaking about what it means for them to be a citizen and about their representations of citizenship, used such vocabulary as 'being active', 'getting involved in the civil society', 'being sensitive to the societal problems', 'being of use to others', 'being up-to-date in what is happening in the country', and 'contributing to the society', which is emblematic of the constructive way of thinking about citizenship. The essence of the model analysed constitutes the taking of a constructive approach towards the society in which one lives. Many elements of such an approach may be noticed for instance in the definition of

---

[234] Here it has to be stressed that the actual, concrete narratives usually combine different models that are not mutually exclusive.

citizenship by Murad. According to him a citizen "... *it is someone who takes into account the fact that he lives in a certain state and who gets involved, as actively as possible, at the local and national level"*, whereas citizenship is "... *not simply voting every five years. This is just a joke of citizenship. The real citizenship is when someone takes actions when the principles of democracy are shaky, when there is discrimination, racism and when the political and economic worlds kidnap the society by, for example, introducing ultraliberal policies or promoting sectarian visions of politics. A citizen has to make himself heard in a peaceful and intelligent way, and eventually by taking an issue to court. By participating in the demonstrations, writing letters to the newspapers, creating lobby groups, etc."* Also the following definition of citizenship by Rashid bears many features of the constructive social approach "... *when I talk about citizenship, for me it isn't something for free. If my understanding of citizenship was to be taken into account while granting people Belgian citizenship there would not be many Belgians. For me, citizenship means something dynamic, active and not passive. Citizenship means engagement, active involvement in the society in which we are living."* For Rashid, who similarly to several of my interviewees only obtained a Belgian passport when he was 18-years old, citizenship is something that one has to strive for every day and should not be taken for granted. He is aware of the fact that not many people share such demanding views on citizenship and that is why he suggests that if his vision had been applied then not many people would hold Belgian citizenship. Yet another way of defining citizenship in the light of socially constructive model can be observed in the answer of Faisal, who pointed out that for him citizenship is above all "... *a platform which translates the society and which enables everyone to get involved in the society in its own way"*. This banal definition of citizenship is not only socially constructive, as it emphasizes the importance of engagement in the society, but also pluralistic, since it assumes that everyone is different and has an opportunity to contribute to society differently. Here it is worth mentioning that the understandings of citizenship of my interviewees are not just sets of abstract ideals, but ideals that are often lived by them in daily life as most of them have tried, sometimes very successfully, to put these ideals into practice. Murad has, for example, frequently written letters to newspapers and won a case in court for discriminatory treatment. Rashid has been actively involved in the development of recommendations aimed at countering discrimination in the labour market by the youth branch of the Confederation of Christian Trade Unions (Fr. *Confédération des Syndicats Chrétiens*), whereas Faisal has been active in numerous Muslim and non-Muslim organisations.

The subjective notions of citizenship of the members of the emerging new Muslim elite in Brussels, which bear many features of the socially constructive model of citizenship, emphasize also the importance of such prosaic civic actions as picking up litter or helping older people. The emphasis on the latter element can be seen for instance in the following statement of Nabihah: "(…) *I can't imagine that we are putting her* (grandmother – KP) in *to an old people's home. Just out of respect. And this is also a question of citizenship, to look after old people"*. Other aspects of constructive citizenship, which are often underestimated or overlooked in debates about citizenship, are referred to by Sana, who pointed out that for her citizenship means *"to try to get involved in the society through different actions and in every day life … through the small civic actions, such as sorting out litter, or (…) in education, trying to help your children flourish."* This kind of linking of ecological themes and parenting with citizenship, testifies to the wide and multidimensional understanding of citizenship by my informants. Their banal definitions of what it means to be a citizen, which exemplify the socially constructive model of citizenship, are also closely related with their understandings of 'good' citizenship that will be discussed below.

The second most popular model of citizenship that could be gleaned from the interviews with young Muslim Belgians was the lack-of-recognition one. Under this model citizenship means above all being genuinely recognized as a citizen and treated as a full citizen and not as a 'half-citizen' or 'second-class citizen'. The key argumentation that one may find in many answers exemplifying this model is that citizenship indicates being recognized and treated as full citizen, which is followed by the statement about the exclusionary nature of the citizenship in Belgium that 'leaves out' (Janoski & Gran 2002: 35) many of my interviewees. Those who felt particularly 'left out' in my Belgian sample and hence who have most commonly referred to this model of citizenship were women. One of them pointed out that citizenship means *"To be respected as a full citizen and not to be constantly confronted with the question of the veil … to be viewed as a true Belgian.*

186

Not to say that we are Belgians of foreign descent (Fr. *Belges d'origines* - KP), *but just Belgians. Not to constantly make the distinction between the indigenous Belgians* (Fr. *Belges des souches* - KP) *and Belgians of immigrant origin.* " (Hafa). According to Hafa, one of the major obstacles to the full recognition of Muslim women born in Belgium as Belgian citizens is the politisation of the Muslim veil and the discrimination they have faced if they decide to wear it.[235] According to her, as far as the larger Muslim population is concerned, an important obstacle is to be the discursive habit of referring to the offspring of Moroccan and Turkish immigrants (sometimes also to the children of other immigrants) as *Belges d'origine étrangère (Eng. Belgians of foreign extraction).* This descriptive tendency, according to many of my interviewees, divides Belgian citizens into a supposedly more trustworthy group of indigenous Belgians and the somewhat 'less equal' Belgians of immigrant origin, or as 'Belgians in the inverted commas', as one of the country's politicians called them.[236]

The problem of the lack of recognition of young Belgian Muslims as truly Belgian has been also signalled by other interviewees: Abida, another Muslim woman, pointed out that "*Even now some people do not consider us to be Belgians. In April I went to a training seminar on diversity and cohesion (...) with a Belgian speaker from the European Council. I asked him a question as a Belgian and he answered as if I was a Moroccan. And this I see as a problem. If I present myself as a Belgian I would like to be answered as a Belgian.* " Another of my female interviewees, whose subjective notion of citizenship also bore many features of the lack-of-recognition model, argued that "*the more religious beliefs we* (Belgian Muslims – KP) *have, the more difficulties we have to be recognized as citizens, especially in comparison with others who are also different, but do not manifest their religious convictions. I just want to be recognized as a citizen ... as anyone else who was born in this country, and not to be in an advantaged position in comparison with believers of other religions.* " (Madiha) She not only reiterates the lack-

---

[235] The cases of this discrimination will be explored below in the section devoted to the normative dimension of citizenship of my informants.
[236] I am thinking here about the Anne-Marie Lizin (Parti Socialist) who in the francophone News on 9th December 2005 referred in such a way to the two Belgians of immigrant descent (Mesut Sen – Belgian Turk and Moussa Zemmouri – Belgian Moroccan) detained till April 2005 in the Guantanamo Bay. The MRAX on 23rd December wrote an open letter to the socialist MP demanding explanations whether she used such a phrase because of the supposed actions of the two individuals or because they were of immigrant origin, to which it has never received a reply.

of-recognition thesis but also suggests that Belgian Muslims are not viewed as truly Belgian because they are reluctant to embrace the secularization which has deeply marked the post-war Belgian society.[237] The alleged *contradictio in adjecto*, of being a (practising) Muslim and being a Belgian, is according to Abida the main reason why Muslims are not being recognized as full citizens. This point of view seems to be shared also by Khalil who has pointed out that *"... the generations which were born here have no problems with considering themselves as Belgian citizens (...) admittedly, of Muslim faith, but also Belgian citizens. So, it is not contradictory ... these two things are absolutely compatible. It is necessary to put the things into the right order."* The call for a more inclusive citizenship, which is at the core of all Muslim demands for recognition and fairer treatment, may be noticed in the subjective notion of citizenship of Jusuf who argued *"I am a Belgian citizen because I was born in Belgium and I live here, this is my country, this is my culture, my society. But my society is plural and it has to accept me with my spiritual belonging, with Islam."*

The category of recognition in this model embraces a large field of potential demands that can be formulated with reference to the image of an 'ideal citizenship' (Marshal 1950: 29). The scope of the potential demands is set, on the one hand, by the iconic dimension of the social representation of citizenship or the actual image of citizenship, and on the other hand, by the symbolic dimension of the social representation of citizenship or the meaning of citizenship. The wider the gap between the meaning of citizenship or the official discourse on citizenship enshrining the principle of equality and the practise of citizenship, the more demands are framed with reference to citizenship. How large this field might be one can see, for example, in the following definition of citizenship by Majd. *"To be a citizen means to live in a community with everyone without discrimination. Certainly it is an ideal world that I have in front of my eyes but this is my goal."* This and other expectations that are being framed with reference to citizenship will be explored in more details in the latter part of this chapter devoted to the normative dimension of citizenship.

---

[237] For more information about the secularization processes in Belgium see, for example, Dobbelaere et al. 1978 or Voyé 1999.

The third model of citizenship that has been quite popular amongst both male and female members of the new Muslim brokers in Brussels, although not as popular as the aforementioned, is one of effective identification. The key feature of this model is that it puts special emphasis on the importance of identification with a given place, be it country, region or a city, and with everything that is related to this place. The subjective notions of citizenship (or elements of them) of the young Muslims that uphold to this model stress that citizenship means above all to feel part of the given community and to identify strongly with its history, culture, traditions, achievements in various disciplines, etc. Furthermore, the effective identification model, as a one which implies a sense of feeling comfortable, accepted and respected in a particular social or physical environment, visibly differs from the analyzed above lack-of-recognition model which is linked with a sense of uneasiness. This model is exemplified by such statements of my interviewees as, for instance: *"Citizenship means to be part of the society and to feel that one belongs to it. "* (Abida) or *"To be a citizen it means most importantly to consider oneself a member of the national community ... to really consider oneself Belgian. The future of this country is also your future in the sense that you cannot be not interested in the problems that are there, in Belgium (...) As a citizen one needs to be interested in everything that may contribute to a creation of more just and human society with equality of chances for everyone "* (Khalil).

But *"do we really feel Belgian? Are we truly concerned by what is happening in Belgium?"* – asked one of my female informants (Jannah) during a meeting of the young Muslim activists closely linked with the organization LIIB in mid December 2005, just after the riots in the French banlieues. These are also the questions that are often addressed by the media. I shall provide some more elaborate answers to them, with reference to the analysed group of people, after the presentation of the main models of perceptions of citizenship. For the moment it has to suffice to mention the opinions of two other informants who perceive citizenship along the main features of the effective identification model. For one of them, Majd, citizenship has meant *"... to live among people. I was born here. I know Belgium, its history, and if she has any problems I have to help her. Because this is a country that has accepted me with open arms (...) and for this I am thankful to it. "* According to him if one truly feels Belgian, s/he should not only

189

know its history but also be ready to make sacrifices if the country was endangered. The effective identification with the country in which one is living means for Majd also that one does not lead a life within its own ethnic and religious communities, but makes an effort to reach out to people from other ethnic and religious backgrounds. A similar point was also made by Masud who argued that *"To be a citizen means not to close yourself within your own community, but to cross its boundaries in order to show others that there are also Muslims in the society. Today Muslims are viewed as a minority, so they also act a minority. Being a citizen means to mix with others and to show them that there are also Muslims living in this society."* Like Majd, he suggests that too strong a reliance on one's own community is detrimental to effective civic identification. In this way both interviewees seem to reiterate the main arguments of the mainstream francophone discourse on communitarianism viewed as a form of ethnocentrism and self-concentration which, by putting the emphasis on the rights of minorities or collective rights, may endanger human rights (and all sorts of freedoms) understood as individual rights.

Finally, the last but not least model in terms of which some of the analysed Belgian Muslims understood citizenship was the contractual one. Interviewees, whose definitions fit into this model spoke about citizenship by referring to a set of rights and responsibilities, including voting rights, and to the laws and rules in the society. As such, this model proposes quite a minimalist vision of citizenship which is largely limited to the adaptation of the legal structures of the country. In my Belgian case study interviewees often referred to this model as the foundation or basis of citizenship and then proceeded to elaborate on their definitions with the elements of one or more of the aforementioned models. There were only two interviewees, Malak and Khasim, who upheld this thin vision of citizenship and did not enrich their conceptions of citizenship with reference to components that make up the essence of other models. For them being a citizen meant merely to respect certain principles and rules.

One of the interviewees who began her definition of citizenship with reference to the elements of this model to later on speak about other, features was Hafa who has pointed out that citizenship means *"to live in accordance with all the laws and rules of this society."* Another one was Khalil who argued that *"The first condition* (of citizenship

– KP) *it is really the adherence to the constitution. I would say that, if there are people who are not happy with the Belgian constitution, they simply shouldn't live in Belgium. (...) To be a citizen means to adhere to the constitution.... This is a sort of contract that you make with the country. Even when you are born here, you need to respect this contract. (...) I can't imagine that someone calls himself a citizen and takes from the Belgian constitution what he wants.*" The emphasis of Khalil on the importance of the adherence to constitution in citizenship recalls the wider European debates around the concept of constitutional patriotism influential in the development of the European Union (Lacroix 2002) and usually associated with the German philosopher Jürgen Habermas. According to the principle of constitutional patriotism, citizenship should rely on a shared sense of values inscribed in a constitution, rather than a common history or ethnic origin (Habermas 1992-3).

Here it has to be also remarked that while merely mentioning voting rights in the definition of citizenship as one of the rights of citizens (in the case of Belgium as one of the obligations of citizens) that fits within a model of contractual citizenship, then for example the following interpretation of this obligation by one of my interviewees goes far beyond a thin contractual model. "*Voting is also a civic action but more important is what one does before going to the polling station. Why do I vote, for whom, what is his/her programme. All these are the steps that one needs to take before going to vote. I think many people in Belgium do not take these civic steps before voting. But we are not citizens just because we go to vote. I think being a citizen is an accomplishment of all these actions taken before.*" (Rashid) For Rashid, voting is not an accomplishment of citizenship but rather a pretext for other civic actions that should be taken before going to the polling stations. As such his interpretation of the voting obligation (right) as part of the definition of what it means to be a citizen, locates him closer to the socially constructive, rather than to the contractual model of citizenship.

4.2.5 BEING BELGIAN

How do the members of the emerging new Muslim elites in Brussels frame their belonging? What levels of belonging are the most meaningful for them? Is it the transnational religious belonging, ummah with which they most strongly identify or

191

rather their belonging is framed with references to the national and regional/city belonging? Before elaborating on these issues it is worth remembering that, like all identities, the expressions of the belonging of my interviewees are dynamic and contextual and often vary depending on the conditions in which they are expressed. [238] This means, for example, that when being abroad some of my interviewees might feel very strongly Belgian, whereas arriving back in Belgium they might identify with other co-religionists rather than with other compatriots. Secondly, it has to be reminded that different (multiple) identities that people may hold do not have to be mutually exclusive and may actually include each other. For example, someone may feel equally strongly Belgian and Flemish,[239] Muslim and Brusseler.

My study shows that for the vast majority of the young Muslims analysed in Brussels, national identity was very meaningful. In other words, in a manner similar to the statement of Naima which opens this chapter, many of my interviewees (both female and male), have declared that they feel strongly attached to Belgium and wider Belgian society. One of the ways of phrasing this attachment was through critical opinions about the politics of integration and expressions of concern about the internal conflicts in the country. The following opinion of Khalil clearly depicts it: *"Now, they should stop talking about integration. We are no longer immigrants, but citizens. Now, honestly, when I see a television debate on the question relating to the Belgian society I'm truly interested in it. When they talk about the issue of BHV[240], or the linguistic tensions between the Flemings and francophones ... all these topics concern me as a citizen. That is why I say that my attachment is really on the level of the country – Belgium"*. Another

---

[238] These issues are explored at length in the section of the theoretical chapter dealing with the issue of identity in the high modernity.

[239] This was actually one of the conclusions of the research carried out by Jaak Billet et al. (2000) who found out that almost 45 per cent of Flemings felt as much Flemish as they did Belgian.

[240] BHV stands for Brussels-Halle-Vilvoorde, which is the biggest and the only bilingual electoral district in the country that encompasses both the officially bilingual Brussels-Capital Region, as well as, an officially unilingual Dutch-speaking area, Halle-Vilvoorde, around it. The contentious district was created at the early stages of the federalisation of the country (1961-1965) as a result of the strong lobbying of the Flemings who were afraid that the predominantly French-speaking city would continue growing uninterrupted into the surrounding Flemish countryside, and without respect for the Flemish nature of those places. Today the Flemish parties want to split the district in order stop the increasing francophonisation of the Flemish outskirts of Brussels which has been caused by the settlement of the growing number of the francophones in these areas. The francophones are radically opposed to the split of the BHV since it would mean a significant loss of substantial number of voters who would be deprived of the right of voting for the francophone parties. One of the most popular francophone politicians Elio di Rupo famously declared that the split of the BHV would mean the beginning of the end of Belgium (Pędziwiatr 2005c).

interviewee who claimed to be strongly attached to the place in which he was born was Amjad. He has argued that *"Belgianness is for me something non-negotiable. The fact that I was born to the parents who came to this country from abroad does not diminish my citizenship. I am Belgian in the full meaning of this term. To be a Belgian citizen means for me to do everything so as this country stays Belgium and does not become two separate entities which is now being debated."* Similarly to Khalil, his expressions of a sense of belonging to the national community are followed by statements about deep concern over the future of the country. That is also the reason why he argues later that *"To be a Belgian today means to act and to bring a little bit of this cement which used to exist once between the Walloons and the Flemings. I think we can be this cement. So being Belgian citizen means to strive to keep the integrity of Belgium."* (Amjad) Thus, in line with the provocative title of an article by Anne Morelli and Jean-Philippe Schreiber – 'Are the Immigrants the Last Belgians?' (1998) - he seems to suggest that people like him or the children of immigrants who settled in the country after the Second World War, are the 'last Belgians'. He believes that his duty is to act as a bridge between the Flemings and the Walloons. It is easier to understand these concerns if one takes into account the results of the surveys such as the one mentioned in the previous chapter, which indicated that almost 80 % of the inhabitants of Brussels in 2005 thought that Belgium as a country would not exist on the maps of Europe by 2055 (Le Soir 10.06.2005).[241]

There were also numerous young Muslim women in my sample for whom national belonging was extremely important. One of them was Falak who argued that: *"For me Belgium it is something untouchable, it is really my country, my soul and my life. 21st July, the day of the National Holiday we really celebrate at my home ... it is a family event, we go to watch fireworks together. (...) Oddly enough I could be even considered as one of the Belgian nationalists in the sense that for me the worst thing that can happen is the secession of Wallonia or Flanders. That is also why I carefully follow the news concerning, for example, the issue of BHV, and I am struck how little attention is paid to Belgium. And I often say to myself – watch out for Belgium! We have to keep*

---

[241] More on the possible future scenarios for Belgium see for instance Martiniello & Swyngedouw 1998 or Monette & Laporte 2007.

it." Here, once again the strong sense of belonging to the national community, manifested inter alia in the celebration of the National Holiday, is coupled with expressions of anxiety about the development of the federalization project.

But the expressions of attachment to Belgium of the members of the Brussels' rising new Muslim elite are not only limited to statements of concern about the future of the country. They include also many declarations of appreciation of different aspects of life in Belgium ranging from the quality of social services, through the rule of law, to achievements in sport. Nabihah for instance stated that *"Belgium is my country, I was born here. I did everything here. I like Belgium a lot ... The way how the social security is organized - it is one of the best in Europe. Also education... I feel good in Belgium. (...) It might be a small country but it is strong.".* Another interviewee drew a comparison between Belgium and Morocco: *"I am very proud of being Belgian because although it is a small country, it has found its own place in the world. It is a small country with great history. It is a country which has marked to some extent the world and which has given us the rights that in other places we* (Muslims – KP) *don't have. For example, as Muslims we have here more rights than in other countries. We have, for example, many social rights which other people even in European countries don't have. Here we can also speak openly. In Morocco we cannot speak openly. Here if something doesn't go well we can organise a demonstration. We cannot do this in Morocco....*" (Majd) He is not the only one to draw this kind of comparisons. Other interviewees who do so are Jannah, who stated that '*I believe that here in Belgium I live a better life as a woman, as a Muslim and as a citizen than I would have lived in Morocco."* and Kemal, who pointed out that *"here we have freedom of speech that one cannot find in Morocco."* Jusuf advances yet other reasons for which he feels 'at home' in Belgium. He has argued that *"I am not a nationalist, but I am proud of being Belgian in the sense that I think life in Belgium is good. Belgium does not prevent me from practising my faith - it is neither a dictatorial country, nor a totalitarian one. I am proud of living in this country, because my viewpoint and spirituality contribute to the development of the Belgian society. Belgium takes account of the Muslim presence as well as the Jewish presence and others. I am proud of the fact that the country takes into consideration my presence."* Thus, one of the things that he is proud of as a Belgian is that his country has formally recognized

194

Islam as one of the religions of the citizens of Belgium. Other interviewees have invoked such diverse reasons for which they feel proud of being Belgian as, for example: hospitality, cultural diversity, freedom, history of the Christian workers movement and its fight for social rights and cultural heritage, especially the one that can be seen in such cities as Brugge or Ghent. Many have also declared that they feel attached to their country for such prosaic reasons as achievements in sport. *"When Justine Henin wins Roland Garos I am very happy that our small country can shine abroad. Even when Belgian footballers play with Morocco I support Belgians."* - asserted Masud. However, not only my male interviewees were inclined to watch football matches and support the Red Devils (Fr. *Diables Rouges)* or the Belgian national football team. One of my female informants recalled that *"I think it was in 1998 during the Football World Cup, there was a match between Belgium and Morocco. At that time it was an existential question – who do you support? And although I am not a great fan of football I wholeheartedly supported Belgians."* (Falak). Thus, if there was a football equivalent of Norman Tebbit's cricket test[242] then many of my interviewees would have easily passed it.

Some of the young Muslims analysed felt that they did not have to account for their Belgianness because it was self-evident. Faisal invoked the following episode *"In Denmark I was asked whether I am a truly Belgian, and I said 'I don't know ... what does it mean for you to be truly Belgian?' I'm definitely more Belgian than Brel[243], ha, ha, ha ... so, yes, obviously I am Belgian. When I arrive at Brussels airport I know that I am at home."* Numerous other interviewees alike Faisal highlighted the vagueness of the notion of Belgianness to which they were supposed to adhere. Many of them realize that they are Belgians and how strongly they are attached to different aspects of life in Belgium when, for instance, they go outside the country. This situation was reported to me inter alia by Abida, who pointed out that *"when I go abroad after a week, two or three, I am getting homesick. I am starting to miss my country. And it is weird because I go to beautiful and sunny places and I shouldn't miss Belgium."* and Falak who stated *"When I had the*

---

[242] The conservative British politician Norman Tebbit in an interview with the *Los Angeles Times* referred to the test named after him in the following way: "A large proportion of Britain's Asian population fail to pass the cricket test. Which side do they cheer for? It's an interesting test. Are you still harking back to where you came from or where you are?" (quoted in Howe 2006)

[243] Jacques Brel - a famous Belgian French-speaking singer-songwriter - considered by many also to be a poet, given the quality and evocative power of his lyrics.

chance to go for holidays to Africa, Niger, last summer, I felt very happy when they called me and my friends a Belgian group. The same when we go to France, we are also called the Belgian team... ".

Not all the young Muslims analysed, however, paid so much attention to the national belonging and felt equally strongly Belgian as the aforementioned interviewees. There was also amongst them a small minority who were neither concerned about the future of Belgium nor about the ongoing political debates. One of them was, for instance, Hadijah who declare: *"I was born in Belgium thus I have Belgian nationality... Instead of saying the I am proud of being Belgian I would rather say that I do not mind being Belgian"* or Lana who said that *"I am much more proud of being a Muslim than of being a Belgian, because for me being Belgian it is just a nationality (...) it is just a simplistic attachment, it is the conditions in which I live here. I could also live somewhere else."* Yet another interviewee argued that *"I don't think one should be proud of being Belgian or whoever. I am just a Belgian. It doesn't bother me."* (Hafa) For these informants, the notion of Belgianness was devoid of any substantial content and was not one with which they would associate strong emotional feelings. They tended rather to give a priority to a transnational religious belonging (e.g. Lana) or other forms of belonging.

Significantly larger was the group of young Muslims, interviewed by the author who were critical about different aspects of the history of Belgium, the way of life and politics in the country. They not only deplored the Belgian colonial past and the more recent Marc Dutroux affair, but also spoke at length about all kinds of discriminatory practices that Muslims have been victims of in their view, which will be explored below. While pointing out various infamous elements of Belgian history, life and politics they simultaneously insisted that being critical of one's own country is one of the major tasks of a responsible citizen and that their criticism is only a sign that they care about Belgium.

4.2.6 BEING SUPRANATIONAL

As far as their relationship with the country of origin of their parents is concerned, half of my informants declared that they visit it quite regularly (four of whom have said to go to the Maghreb almost every year), whereas half claimed to have paid a visit to the parents' country of origin irregularly and less frequently than every 4 years. My study thus shows that the members of the emerging new Muslim elite do not necessarily choose the villages and cities of birth of their parents in Morocco (Tunisia and Algeria) as their preferred holiday destination and hence the relationships of the second and third generations with the countries of birth of their parents are becoming increasingly loose. Some of them go for holidays to other Muslim (particularly Turkey, Egypt, Lebanon or Syria) or non-Muslim countries and do not follow the example of their parents described by Abdelmalek Sayad as *atopos* or as those *"trapped in that 'mongrel' sector of social space betwixt and between social being and nonbeing"* (Sayad 1984, 1988). One who continues to cross the Straits of Gibraltar every year pointed out that these trips *"It is a principle established by our parents and I think it is important to give some logic to our presence here and not to disconnect with the country of origin. What we also have as a principle is the family link, so that is why it is fundamental to return. I have still a family in Morocco, uncles, aunties ... And my wife, she also has a lot of family there, so it is indispensable* (to pay visits to them - KP)." (Amjad) Thus, for Amjad these trips are important not only from a point of view of maintaining family contacts but also in order to better relate to his own condition in Belgium. Another interviewee Nabihah declared that *"Morocco, it is nice for holidays. I go there for holidays so I don't see the everyday life' part of Morocco. But I think it will be difficult for me to live there longer because I have a different mentality. I have a Belgian mentality which does not coexist easily with the mentality of the over there. I am very actively involved in various projects here and there I go only for holidays ... If I was involved in some projects connecting, for example, with the Moroccan trade unions. I would like to go there, at least to improve my language."* Here one may see that despite relatively frequent visits, the interviewee does not feel fully comfortable in the 'country of holidays' and cannot imagine a prolonged stay there unless this would involve being there in a professional capacity. The elements of transnational[244] identity which mark many of the narratives of belonging of my interviewees may be seen particularly clearly in the following statement of Malak *"When*

---

[244] Transnationalism, in the broad understanding of the term that is used here, embraces a variety of multifaceted social relations that are both embedded in and transcend two or more nation-states, cross-cutting sociopolitical, territorial, and cultural borders. For more information about transnationalism understood as one of the key aspects of the globalization processes, see for example Vertovec and Cohen 1999, Vertovec 2001 or Remennick 2007.

we stay here for too long, at a certain moment, at least me, I feel a lack of my roots, of my traditions. So at certain moments I feel like leaving for Morocco ... also to see my family... the place where my parents lived, where, I used to spend all my holidays... But on the other hand, when we stay too long time there we have also (feeling of – KP) lack of the other side, our roots here." The recent developments in technology and telecommunications infrastructures have enabled Malak and millions of others persons who feel affinity with particular areas on the globe while living in other places to be 'here' and 'there' at the same time or to spend some time 'here' and a little bit of time 'there'. Although students of globalization argue that, in the era of Internet and transcontinental flights, geographical distance between certain places has lost its meaning, I believe that the relative geographical proximity of Morocco and hence the relatively low cost of travel between Belgium and Morocco[245], plays an important role in the vitality of these connections.[246]

In order to revitalise the Moroccan (or wider Maghrebian) elements of one's identity or to go back to its ethnic roots, the children of immigrants do not necessarily have to cross the Straits of Gibraltar, but can also do so by delving into the rich Moroccan social and cultural life in Belgium. There have been also some efforts to accommodate the transnational elements of identities of young Belgian Moroccans and to inscribe them into the country's history by a few schools in Brussels, which have, for instance, organised study trips to the cemetery of Chastre (close to Gembloux) where 185 Moroccan, 161 Algerian and 5 Tunisian infantry who lost their lives while fighting with the Germans during the Second World War were buried (Devillers 2007).[247]

As far as supranational European identity is concerned, quantitative research shows that the Region of Brussels encompasses the highest percentage of Belgians who identify with Europe. According to research carried out by Billiet et al. 30 per cent of Brusselers identified first and foremost with territorial entities larger than Belgium (Europe or the world), whereas in Flanders this is only 12 per cent people (2000). The

---

[245] With the low cost airlines (e.g. JetairFly, Jet4you) one may travel to Morocco from Belgium and back for as little as 150 Euros.

[246] This is particularly clear in comparison with the situation of people of Pakistani or Bangladeshi origin living in Britain that will be explored in the next chapter.

[247] This episode of the history has been portrayed in the film 'La couleur du sacrifice' by Murad Boucif (2006). More information about the film can be found on http://www.lacouleurdusacrifice.com

fact that the most important institutions of the European Union have their headquarters in Brussels has clearly had an influence on this. However, the presence of the European Commission and the European Parliament in Brussels does not necessarily influence the identification of the young Muslims brokers who live in the city. Although some sympathized with the European project and strongly identified with Europe, like Jannah who said that *"I am very happy that I was born not only in the capital of Belgium but also in the capital of Europe"*, for the majority of them it was not a particularly meaningful identity. One may see it clearly, for instance, in the following statement by Masud *"I am European in theory but in practice I do not really know what it means"*. Thus, my study shows that the young Belgian Muslims living in the heart of Europe were largely devoid of strong supranational European identity.

The identity transgressing the national boundaries that appealed to many of my interviewees was the diasporic[248] religious one. Many of the young Belgian Muslims felt fairly strongly attached to the worldwide Muslim community. The actual level of attachment towards an imagined ummah varied from person to person. Falak, for instance, pointed out that *"the fact that I am a part of the worldwide Muslim community is as important, as my belonging to the Belgian nation."*, whereas Rashid argued that *"As a Muslim I feel to be part of the community of faith. It is not important where I live, in Mars, Jupiter, in another galaxy, because my spiritual identity is always with me."* Kemal advanced yet another hierarchy of attachments when he argued that *"Among my priorities at the first place is my family. Then I concentrate a lot at the local level which is a level at which I can act and improve things. Then there is also a international dimension. For example, I feel obliged to do my best to further the Palestinian cause. One thing does not exclude the other."* In his understanding the most important part of belonging was the one to the family, then to the locality and only thirdly to the ummah. The following understanding of the link between the Belgian Muslims and the ummah provided by Jusuf probably most accurately captured the attitude of the majority of the members of the emerging new Muslim elite in Brussels towards the worldwide Muslim community. He said that *"(...) Ummah concerns me at the level of my faith. This is the*

---

[248] As Vertovec and Cohen point out such type of identity is often constituted negatively by experiences of discrimination and exclusion, and positively with a historical heritage (e.g. Islamic civilization) or with contemporary world cultural or political forces such as, for example, Islam (1999: XVIII).

community of faith. (...) Ummah for me, it is something utopian. It exists for me only at the symbolic level of the faith. Speaking about ummah as something real is utopian, because we are of different cultures, different realities and different developments. We have similar spiritual sensibility, because we share the same faith. My brothers in Palestine, Iraq, Chechnya, Morocco, ... are my brothers in faith. I have a spiritual link with them, but my brothers in humanity, who live in my city, my region, have the same rights to me as anyone else, because I live the same reality as they do." The majority of my interviewees responded in a similar fashion by invoking the importance of the identification with other 'brothers and sisters in faith', or with ummah, were at the same time stressing deep bonds linking them with their neighbors and compatriots.

4.2.7 BEING A BRUSSELER

As I have argued above, the fact that the vast majority of my interviewees feel strongly attached to the country in which they were born, does not exclude also the significance of other forms of identity. My research has found that for the interviewed members of the rising new Muslim elite it was not only national identity that was meaningful but also the local. Thus, while the thesis of Hassan Bousetta about the weak local identity amongst the people of Moroccan descent living in Brussels might be accurate when applied to the whole community (Bousetta in Kuyssche 2004), it does not hold for the young Belgian Muslims brokers. The latter are actually characterised by fairly strong local identity. One may detect it in such statements of my interviewees as for instance the following ones by Masud "*I feel Belgian (...) More specifically I feel attached to Brussels, because I am a Brusseler. I was born here, I have family here, my friends, my history and places that I know.*", by Hafa "*I love Brussels. I like its noise, its liveliness, rapidity... I like the countryside, but only in Brussels I feel at home. And apart from it is a capital of Europe, so it is a place of convergence of many things.*" or by Jannah "*I fully understand my sister who lives now in the Netherlands and who told me that if her husband wasn't great she would have never left Brussels. She regrets leaving it a lot. In Brussels there are enormous possibilities for anyone who has got some courage.*" While some of my interviewees argued that they were strongly attached to their city simply because they were born in Brussels, they had their families and friends there and spent their almost entire life in this urban discursive space, others pointed out various elements of this space that have a particularly strong appeal for them. The aforementioned noise, liveliness, rapidity and wide range of possibilities were only some of the reasons for which my interviewees felt strongly attached to their city. Many of them also highly valued Brussels' cultural diversity and the fact that one may find people in the city from all over the world. This multicultural character of Brussels is, according to Hafa, not only a feature which distinguishes the Belgian capital from other cities of the country, but also a reason for which racism is less widespread in Brussels than in other more culturally homogenous areas of the country.

Among the other aspects of life in Brussels which were important to my interviewees was also the proximity of other coreligionists. This aspect was inter alia brought up by Khalil who argued that "*moving a little bit out of the city centre, where it is calm, would be nice, but I think it is important to have a place where we* (Muslims – KP) *can meet ... social places where those who share the same values could find each other. One may develop spiritually in the solitude, but the practice must be also undertaken in a group. For example, the Friday prayer should be done with other believers and not individually.*' Taking into account a fact that almost all of Brussels' 77 mosques are located in the areas of high concentration of Muslims, that is the central areas of the city, means that Khalil, as well as many other practising Muslims who could afford better housing outside the city centre, might be reluctant to move out to the suburbs. This issue was also raised by Amjad who pointed out that in the suburbs "*we feel that there is comfort of calmness, but there is also something missing, that is the proximity of God. This proximity, we can obviously create in our houses, but the fact of going to a mosque, of meeting other people that we know or don't know, we can't. This feeling of being part of the community of belief who gathers for one reason, to pray to God... it is one of the elements which constitute an added value of the centre of Brussels in comparison with other more secluded areas*".

The young Muslims interviewed expressed attachment not only to certain religious and non-religious features of life in Brussels but also to specific elements of the visibly static urban space. The most commonly mentioned element of this space was the main city's square or Grand Place. Murad for instance said that "*The Grand Place is very important to me. Between the age 15 and 20, I was at the Grand Place almost every day. And some of my friends were even joking by saying 'you are married with the Grand Place'... ha, ha, ha...* (interviewee laughing – KP) *I think this square is really magnificent. It is one of the most beautiful squares in the world. (...) I remember a few years ago there was an ice ring on the Grand Place. With the Christmas tree, crèche, special lights there was some real magic in it".* Later on he explains that he adores everything what is related to the religious and festive elements, whether they are Muslim or non-Muslim. The way he refers to Christmas decorations on the main city's square substantiates this claim. The Grand Place and the area around it is also an important landmark and hence a crucial point of reference for Falak, who admitted that *"I often walk in the historic city centre nearby Grand Place, with my rucksack on my back and I am happy that I belong to this city. I find it one of the most beautiful cities. Particularly the Grand Place, which is really my favourite area in town."* Yet other elements of the city's static space which have been important to my interviewees are: the districts in which they live, or used to live, schools which they used to frequent, youth centres and mosques.

For most of my interviewees, Brussels was not simply the city of their birth, but a symbolic space and a repository of enjoyable, as well as, sometimes painful memories. How diverse elements can this symbolic space encompass one may see for instance in the answer of Murad who has said that *"For me Brussels it is a very charming city... it is Jacques Brel, les marionettes* (puppets – KP) *and Sporting Anderlecht[249]."* Another interviewee has argued that *"I am strongly attached to Brussels because I was born in Brussels... and I am part of its history and evolution. When I go through the quartiers where I used to grow up, my heart starts to beat faster. It is the souvenirs, the anchorages, sometimes the places which re-call the pain. And then I have also my points of orientation, my habits... yes I am a real Brusseler. I can't imagine now to live far away from Brussels... I feel good here."* (Faisal) In this example, one can see clearly the complexity of the attachment of the young Muslims interviewed for this book with Brussels. They do not discard the sometimes painful memories of growing up and living in Brussels, but juxtapose them with the positive and neutral memories and, in most

---

[249] One of the major Brussels' football clubs.

cases, express opinions, which testify to a fairly strong local identity, such as, for instance, *'I cannot imagine living in another place'* (Naima). For some of my interviewees this strong attachment to Brussels is something that they perceive as absolutely natural and which does not need any further explanation. Khasim, for example, claimed that *"We cannot be not-attached* (to Brussels – KP) *when we were born here"*, whereas Madiha has said that *"I think it is always like this that people are most strongly attached to the places where they were born and where they grew up"*. The fact of having the city's map imprinted into their minds, or at least having numerous 'points of orientation' in the static urban space was also an important factor for which my interviewees felt 'at home' in Brussels, and talk about themselves as Brusselers with certain pride.

As mentioned earlier, the notion of 'a Brusseler' (Dutch – *'Brusselaar'*) has been traditionally reserved for the autochthonous inhabitants of Brussels speaking a particular mixture of Flemish and French. I have decided to use it with reference to my Belgian interviewees, first of all because of the depicted above elements of the fairly strong local identity that I could identify in their narratives on belonging. Secondly, I refer to them as Brusselers because some of them used the Dutch word *'Brusselaar'* when describing themselves as inhabitants of Brussels. In this way they seemed to suggest that they were also deeply rooted in the Brussels' context and that no one group could claim monopoly to autochthony.

Before I move on to analyse the participatory dimension of citizenship of the young Muslim Brusselers, it is important to point out that according to sociological research there is a strong relationship between the localised sense of citizenship and active citizenship. My research confirms the hypothesis of Stürmer and Kampmeier (2003) in particular, who suggested that community identification plays a crucial role in community volunteerism and local participation. In my opinion the strong emotional attachment of the members of the emerging new Muslim elite to the place in which they are living, with its rich social tissue, has a significant influence on their involvement in society. In other words if they did not feel so strongly attached to Brussels, as well as Belgium. I do not think they would get involved in the different projects depicted below. At the same time my research shows that even though the young Muslims analysed do not always consider local issues as more important than the national or international one, they know that it is mainly at the local level that they can 'make a difference' and hence concentrate on it. As one of my interviewees pointed out '*If I want things to improve, it is first of all in the place where I am, because I know my locality and its problems, so consequently I can improve things more in the place where I am than in other places. If I can improve things elsewhere it is good too, but first of all, I need to do it in my surrounding.*' (Madiha) Not only Madiha but also other interviewees argued that, through being active in the Muslim organisation and in the wider public sphere, they wanted to cater for the needs of all the people and not only Muslims. The focus on local projects seems to be above all a result of pragmatism.

4.3 PARTICIPATION, ISLAM AND CITIZENSHIP

Having analysed the depth of citizenship of the young Muslims in Brussels it is time to shed some light on the extent of the participatory dimension of their citizenship. The main objectives of this section are thus: firstly, to elaborate on the circumstances in which members of the rising new Muslim elite have become active in Muslim organisations and through them in the wider public sphere; secondly, to assess the key resources which have enabled them to move beyond the formal to the more substantive forms of citizenship; thirdly, to indicate the major reasons for which they are active and lastly to account for what they perceive to be the most important results of this activism.

Before I move on to the assessment of the empirical material, it is worth recalling a point concerning the unique relationship between identity and social participation from the second chapter that is particularly pertinent here, namely that to act as a citizen requires first a sense of agency, the belief that one can act; and that acting as a citizen, especially collectively, in turn fosters that sense of agency (Lister 1997: 38). To put it differently, it is important to bear in mind that to participate actively in a society one needs to, first of all, feel like doing so, or feel a desire of being a 'subject', which Alain Touraine defines as the desire to create a personal history and of giving meaning to the whole realm of experiences of individual life (1993). This desire is, in turn, strengthened when one takes active part in societal projects and is given the opportunity to achieve fuller self-actualisation, not only on the level of the individual but also collectively.

Taking into account the importance of identity in social participation, it seems necessary to begin the assessment of the extent of the citizenship of young Muslim Brusselers from the issue of agency and its relationship with religious rediscovery.

4.3.1 MUSLIM IDENTITY AND AGENCY

The careful analysis of the empirical material, which consisted of the extensive histories of involvement of the young Muslims in the given Muslim organisations and in the wider Muslim and non-Muslim civil societies, shows that there is a very strong positive correlation between their re-appropriation of religious identities and their sense of agency. The vast majority of my interviewees, as I am going to demonstrate below, claimed to begin to be actively involved in society when they rediscovered their religion. Only a few informants argued that they had always been involved in collective projects. Even these interviewees, however, pointed out that their 'spirituality' pushed them to get involved with civil society and to serve people more actively. One of them, Maysan, for instance argued that *"the heart of my involvement is God ... but it is also a question of personality. If I didn't believe in God, which I find now difficult even to imagine, I would still serve people. Because I began to serve people before I was a believer. I always wanted to serve people... that is why I studied social work (...) When I discovered my religion I got involved more, because this is the heart of Islam. The best man is the one that serves people. So my faith completed my will to serve people."*

In the case of the majority of my interviewees, the involvement in Muslim and wider civil society was directly linked with their rediscovery of their religious identity. This one may see particularly clearly in the following accounts of my informants. Hafa, for example, said *"When I learnt about my religion I became more self-confident about it, and got more active."*, whereas Masud pointed out that *"As a consequence of my personal exploration I realized that as a Muslim it is important to be active and to help my neighbours and community. The thought to get involved in the activities of the Muslim organization or associations was growing in me gradually. I decided to get actively involved in the activities of the Muslim association in order to help people and to bring something positive to the society in which I live."* For the majority religious rediscovery, which proves to be an extremely effective modality of self-construction in a world of plural identities, marks the beginning of a more dynamic involvement not only into the life of the Muslim community but also larger society. Thus in their case the self-confidence resulting from the fact that they have found their own paths to meaningful personal identities is closely linked with both intensified involvement in the activities of the given Muslim organisations and wider civil society. The re-appropriations of Muslim identities seem to have an empowering influence on them. While the religious rediscovery or 'conversion' is an important source of the self-actualisation on the level of the individual, the activism within the Muslim and wider civil society leads to self-actualisation on the level of the society.

The process of the reappropriation of the religion of their parents by my interviewees, which as I have shown above is closely linked with their increased sense of agency, consists of two major and largely parallel processes: the positivisation of Islam and the intellectualisation of Islam. The first process is mostly about 'reversing of the stigma' (Sayad 1991: 254-255) associated with Islam, and constructing of the form of 'positive Islam' defined by Leila Babès as a *contre-image* to the negative image of Islam presented by the media and maintained by certain segments of the public opinion (Babès 1997: 11). In the group of young French Muslims analysed by the author of '*L'islam positif*', the process of their positivisation of Islam was greatly facilitated by the 'seduction' of the Catholic Church and in particular by its promotion of such values as tolerance, willingness to mobilise for God, sincerity and charity (1997: 74). In my interviews with Belgian as well as British Muslims I did not observe any explicit references to the impact of the teachings of the Church on the process of positivisation of Islam by my interviewees, however some of the young Muslim Brusselers spoke about the assistance of the Church in the early attempts of the Muslim self-organisation (e.g. Murad and Nabihah). A more general process that has significantly influenced the creation of the *contre-image* to the negative image of Islam was the one of intellectualisation of Islam, that can be understood as the acquisition by my interviewees of the extensive knowledge about Islam and their spiritual development resulting mainly from the self-study of Islamic sources, all kinds of materials on Islam (books, booklets, tapes, cds etc) and attendance of conferences, seminars and courses given by Muslim preachers. This process takes place mainly outside a family circle since parents, as I argued earlier, are usually not capable of passing 'all the religion' on to their offspring and often are not even able to equip them with an understanding of classical Arabic, the sacred language of Islam, without which the acquisition of Islamic knowledge is considerably slower.

The clear elements of the process of positivisation of Islam can be found, for instance, in the following account of Murad: *"My religious development started from the rejection of Islam and transformed into the appreciation of it. The fact that at the beginning I had a negative perception of Islam was linked mostly to the behaviour of certain Muslims, who interpret Islam in a violent, radical, or harmful way that I could see either around me or on the telly. My attitude to it progressed gradually from the time when I was around 18 years old, when I started to be interested in Islam (...) A decisive moment was when I realized that there is a significant difference between the universal message of Islam, and what certain Muslims are doing"*. According to Murad *"If one tries to scratch beneath a little bit he can identify two positions. One rather positivist, which will allow you to relativise, contextualise and to go further and to live Islam in a positive way, and which offers some solutions to certain problems. And another one, which wants you to focus on certain ambiguous, and harsh passages in Qur'an. One shouldn't forget that Qur'an is a text that is addressed to people and people have their bright side and the dark side."* For him positivisation meant above all the ability to re-interpret Islam in such a way that it is compatible with life in the modern society. In his view, Islam was not a totalizing power or an overarching framework that was able to provide answers to all possible questions but only a key to solving some problems. Although many of the analysed Muslims would agree with the points made by Murad, it is worth stressing that this is only one of the possible interpretations of a 'positive way of living Islam'. Each of the interviewees understood this 'positive way of living Islam' differently. While some stressed, similarly to Murad, the importance of being able to contextualise Islamic sources within the realities of life in the 21st century Europe, others emphasised the ethical and humanist dimensions of Islam whilst some argued that living Islam positively means to be empowered by the religion to work for the community and society.

As for the evidence of the intellectualisation process in Murad's religious biography, it can be found, for instance, in the following excerpt. *"When I was at school I didn't pay much attention to Islam. I was in denial of Islam. Later I undertook my own research. I've read a lot of books, participated in numerous conferences and constructed my own opinion about Islam. From the age of 21/22 I started to perceive Islam as something more positive, than negative. I continued to learn about it ... "*. The personal research mentioned by my informant is nothing else but the process of search for knowledge about Islam that is not limited to the sources available, such as mass media in the wide understanding of the term encompassing also electronic media (e.g. Internet), but which require more effort. As in the case of many other interviewees, it seems that Murad's faith becomes stronger as he learns about his religion. Thus, in line with the point made by Françoise Champion that (religious) knowledge validates believers' faith (1996), knowledge about Islam seems to confirm and strengthen faith of my interviewees. In some cases, as I am going to show below, it also enables them to gain more self-pride and become more assertive.

Rashid is another interviewee whose account of the religious development not only bears numerous marks of the process of positivisation but also parallel with it, process of intellectualisation. He asserted that *'When I was younger I had an inferiority complex with regards to my religion. I did everything I could to hide it. I didn't want others to know that I believe in God and practice religion. I felt ashamed of being a Muslim. As the time passed and I was becoming 15, 16, 17 years old I read many books on Islam ... started to enjoy them and this complex faded away. I became more proud of who I was. I had the inferiority complex, which also mixed with the crisis of adolescence, during the period between 8 and 15 years old. But afterwards, when I learnt about my religion I became proud of it and this complex disappeared. I wasn't any more ashamed of my religion and the fact that I believe in God and have a faith."* Rashid also claimed that, as he gradually freed himself from the stereotypical ideas about Islam, or as called them *"prejudices against my religion"*, he not only became more emancipated but also asserted his place in the society more courageously. In the course of the process of intellectualisation he also learned about the religious diversity of Muslim population that he was not aware of. He said that *"when I arrived in Brussels* (from another Belgian city in which he was born – KP) *I met with some other young Muslims who asked me what tendency I was following. I didn't understand what tendencies they were talking about. So they told me, 'Sunni, Shia, Hanbali, Maliki... etc'. I answered: 'I am of no tendency... I am simply a Muslim'. So I found out that in Brussels there are several tendencies and school of jurisprudence – something that my father didn't teach me about. He simply taught me to be a Muslim, to believe in God and the Prophet and the Qur'an."*

My interviewees gained their knowledge about Islam not only from written sources and by attending seminars of various Islamic preachers but also from the various multimedia materials produced by these preachers. One who was particularly well equipped in all kinds of multimedia resources on Islam was Kemal. He said that *"I knew that I was a Muslim, but I was disconnected from the knowledge about Islam, I didn't know anything about it. And one day I listened to the tape on Islam and it has touched me directly into my heart (...) I didn't receive any proper Qur'anique education, translation of the life of the Prophet etc. I didn't have any clue about these things. So when I started to listen to the tapes they touched me a lot. Now I am very rich in all sorts of audiovisual material on Islam. So I have learnt a lot from teachers of all tendencies."*

I could trace the elements of the positivisation and intellectualisation processes not only in the religious biographies of my male interviewees but also female ones. One of them was Falak who argued that *"We all pass through the age of 14-16 years old when we start to ask ourselves existential questions: Who am I? What is morality? Does God exist? etc. I was attending a very secular school, where I could often hear that God is dead, God doesn't exist ... na na niii, na na naaa...I passed through this phase of doubt. I rejected completely religion. But at the same time, I remember I signed up, for example, for the course on Buddhism. Because deeply inside I searched for something, I wanted to live some spirituality, but didn't know which one. And later, I think I can say honestly and without hesitation that the seminar of Tariq Ramadan which was organized here* (on the campus of the Université Libre de Bruxelles - KP) *enabled me to answer a lot of the existential questions that I was asking myself. He demonstrated to me that we can be Muslims, citizens, Europeans who live fully their religion and Belgian and European citizenships. This was a shocking revelation because at that time this kind of discourse (idea), which now is fairly common, was quite rare. Being Muslims and citizens at the same time was considered as something incompatible. I think, through this conference, which has greatly affected me and raised my awareness I became also more eager to actively participate in the society.*" From this extensive account of Falak, the transition from the moment when she rejected Islam to the moment when she re-embraced it, one may learn inter alia that the process of rediscovery of Islam by the young Muslims born outside *Dar al-Islam,* does not necessarily have to be a gradual one, but can also be fairly swift and marked by certain 'fateful moments', that can be understood after Giddens as transition points which have major implications not just for the circumstances of an individual's future conduct, but for self identity (1991: 142-143). For Falak, such a fateful moment was the encounter with the Muslim preacher Tariq Ramadan, especially popular among the younger generation of practicing European Muslims (particularly those from the rising middle classes). The ideas promoted by the grandson of the founder of the Muslim Brotherhood appealed so strongly to this student of political science that she not only decided to assert her Muslimness in everyday life more firmly, but also to get involved more dynamically in the Muslim and the wider civil society.

Falak was not the only member of the emerging new Muslim elite in Brussels whose re-appropriation of Muslim identity has been strongly influenced by a charismatic Muslim leader or leaders. Many other interviewees underscored the importance in their personal spiritual journeys of such encounters, especially with the European-born Muslim leaders who speak fluent French and are able to meaningfully refer in their speeches and writings to the problems faced by young Muslim in everyday life, such as unemployment, discriminatory treatment, the crisis of identity etc. One of interviewees who did so was, for instance, Masud who said that '*I used to be a Muslim who didn't care about religion. I discovered Islam through the participation in several seminars given by such intellectuals as Tariq Ramadan, Hassan Iquioussen and others. I have become more and more interested in my religion. As a result of my personal searches I became more religious than my parents who were not really able to assist me in this spiritual search.*' For some of my Belgian interviewees, the religious significant others were also their school teachers of Islam. Majd, for instance, argued that '*These two men* (his professors of Islam at the primary and secondary school) *knew very well the society in which they have been living as both of them were born here. As the school teachers of Islam they knew the problems of the youth and they knew how to speak to the young in contrast with the ulema of the Saudi Arabia. The latter ones know how to interpret the Qur'an, but they interpret it in accordance to a different context than the one that we have here.'*

Some older interviewees also mentioned the classical ulama who had migrated from the Muslim world to carry out *dawah* among the Muslim populations in Europe in this context. One of the most commonly mentioned by them was the Egyptian-educated Muslim leader of the first generation, Sadek Charaf (1936 – 1993), who lived and preached in Belgium for almost twenty years[250].

Among the significant others who also had considerable influence on the rediscovery of Islam by my interviewees were their peers, friends and siblings. This was for instance the case of Sana who asserted that *"When I was about 18 years old I made friends with peers who read the Qur'an, prayed and in this way I, in inverted commas, discovered my religion more profoundly ... ",* or Jannah who spoke at length about the impact of her older sisters on her decision to firmly affirm her religious identity since they got involved in the Muslim civil society before her. One may find it easier to understand the extent of the impact of their siblings on their religious rediscovery and then on the decision to join certain Muslim association or organisation if one bears in mind that most of my interviewees have more than one brother and a sister and one third of them come from large extended families of seven and more children.

Finally, one of my informants claimed that no one had influenced her decision to assert her Muslimness and that it was a 'semi-natural' decision. Hadijah argued that *"Like all the youth I did not care much about religion until my 18th birthday . Then at age of 18-19 years I felt a need to return to my religious roots. So I started to read books about Islam, got interested in it and from this moment I started once again to practise it. There was no particular person or event that would influence my way of thinking about religion, but frankly it was a faith itself that lived inside me and at a certain moment externalized itself".* The period of 'externalization' of the Islamic identity by my interviewees, whether it was instigated by some fateful moments or rather had more gradual and as Hadijah would claim 'natural' course, was often characterized by

---

[250] For more information about Sadek Charaf see http://www.islam-belgique.com/articles1.cfm?articleID=3 (accessed 20th May 2007)

intensive questioning of all kinds of principles and certain dynamism. This was captured well by Faisal who pointed out that "(...) *my rediscovery of the spirituality was also as a result of the crisis of spirituality, of all sorts of questioning ... because it is very complicated, we are plunged into the universe which makes us doubt, which puts many things into question. We live the transitory phase between the first generation and the future generations, and then we begin to understand that we have become a kind of a relief group. So they* (e.g. journalists – KP) *ask us because it is much easier for them from the linguistic point of view... So we have gone with difficulties through this passage between the transmission* (of religion – KP) *by silence to the obligation of almost automatically becoming actors"*. Not only for Faisal, but also for many other interviewees, the period of religious rediscovery was a very tense one and, at the same time, positively dynamising and mobilizing. I believe the process of becoming religious brokers was possible to a large extent also due to the specific resources that they have in their possession that will be analysed in the following section.

4.3.2 RESOURCES FOR PARTICIPATION

As I have argued in the chapter II, one of the key differences between the legal understanding of the notion of citizenship and sociological one is that the latter not only takes into account whether certain groups of people are granted citizenship rights or not, but also looks into the resources that allow the practice of these rights. This is also the issue that is addressed here. The resources that allow the new Muslim religious brokers to choose between different courses of action and to move beyond the formal to more substantive forms of citizenship are assessed with the help of the Civic Voluntarism Model and the notion of habitus. Both the model and the notion were elaborated in the earlier part of the book, so here it should just suffice to remind the reader that, while the first one claims inter alia that there is a close link between people's level of involvement in voluntary activities and their level of reserves of time, money and civic skills, the second puts emphasis on the acquisition of certain dispositions in the process of socialization. These dispositions function on the practical level as categories of perception and assessment as well as being the organizing principles of action.

Having analysed the responses of my informants to the question about the time dedicated to the voluntary activism, I have found out that almost all of them devoted at least a few hours per week to such activism. The most engaged ones found it even difficult to answer the question, since for them involvement became almost an integral part of their lives and they did not see it as something separate any more. One such interviewee was Kemal who said that "*90 per cent of all my free time I devote to voluntary activity. In fact it is like a normal job... Obviously when I say that it is a job I do not mean a salary, but the sacrifice.*" Another was Jannah who claimed that she does not count the time that she devotes to voluntary work. Some of my interviewees treat activism in the associational sphere as their favourite hobby. This was a point made by Majd who said that "*I easily spend up to 20 hours per week doing various things related to my associational involvement. For me it is not a lot. I would like to do more. For me it is a kind of hobby, something that I like to do a lot.*" Other young Muslim activists claimed that involvement in the Muslim and wider civil society is a way of being for them, a lifestyle that requires them to act consistently in all aspects of daily life and thus implies living in accordance with one's ideals. The involvement practised by many of them corresponds to what can be called a 'search for ethical consistency', which aims to give meaning to the values they hold as individuals and as a group. It is a form of imperative or an obligation, rather than a hobby. One of the persons, who viewed it in this way was Naima, who argued that '*Our religion forbids us from doing nothing all day long. So you have to be active as much as possible, you have to try to help people in the best way you can. And this is what I try to do.*'

In general, their time engagement varies depending on the period of the year. If they are working on some bigger project then it usually requires more time from them. One such project are the large conferences frequently organized by Muslim organisations that will be discussed in more detail below. While Hafa, for instance, said that "*when we were organising the conference on Muslim women, or summer camp it required a lot of time*", Hadijah remarked that "*It* (her involvement – KP) *can be four hours per week, as*

213

well as, twelve hours per week. It really depends. And this is apart of my work as a
Muslim chaplain."[251]

My interviewees were able to invest considerable amounts of time running various associational projects (not only Muslim ones) as some of them were still studying, working part-time or searching for work and they did not have many family obligations. But even those who were full time employees or young fathers and mothers (seven interviewees) found spare time to invest in voluntary activity. On the other hand, the lack of surplus free time was also a reason why some of the Muslim activists interviewed had to temporarily withdraw or limit their work for the Muslim and wider civil society. Lana, for instance, pointed out *"Now, when I am coming to the end of my studies, preparing my dissertation, I have less time for it* (voluntary work – KP). *There are also other things that came into play which result in the fact that now I get involve less. But when I see my friends in the field* (associational sphere – KP) *I am jealous, I want to do so many things and I keep telling myself, quicker, quicker ... finish your work ... so as I could go back to the field".* Falak was another interviewee who had to temporarily limit her involvement for the similar reasons. She said that *"Earlier almost every day I was doing something for one or another association. This year I have withdrawn from many activities because it is my last year of studies and I want to concentrate on my thesis and exams – this is also some sort of personal engagement. Now I have one or two meetings per week".*

Full-time, part-time employment and unemployment benefits are also the main supplies of another important resource that people involved in the work of the Muslim organisations need, namely money. Thirteen of my interviewees were full-time employees at the time when this research was carried out, whereas six had part time jobs and five were receiving unemployment benefit. If they were not able to find the necessary financial means within Muslim organisations (usually in the case of Belgium possessing rather scarce financial resources[252]) to run a project or able to pay for it from their own

---

[251] Here it is worth mentioning that the latter, work she does for the moment also *pro bono*, since the issue of payments for the Muslim chaplains has not been regulated yet. It is one of the pending issues of the EMB.

[252] This has to do inter alia with the fact that, in spite of the formal recognition of Islam already in 1974, until today the issue of subsidies for the mosques and Muslim organisations has not been fully resolved. The lack of financial resources within the Muslim civil sector significantly hampers its activities. By 2006

pockets, then they tried to search for external funding. This task, in a city with the prevailing religion-blind approach to sacrum in the public sphere, is definitely not easy. However, some of my interviewees involved in the project called *Projection-Débat (Screening-Debate)*, which will be elaborated below, followed this strategy and managed to receive a grant of 4.500 Euros from the King Baudouin Foundation for buying material for the screenings (among others things DVD-player and camcorder).

The lack of financial resources like the lack of surplus free time, was also the reason why some of my interviewees decided to temporarily withdraw from voluntary work. This was the case for Hafa, who did some administrative work for the *Ligue Islamique Interculturelle de Belgique.* She pointed out that '*All the work that I was doing was voluntary. They didn't have any financial means. One can do this for a short time but not all the time. Without salary you cannot go far. That is why I was forced to quit the LIIB.*'

As I have mentioned earlier, the sociological understanding of citizenship takes into account not only formal rights, but also the key tools that enable people to exercise their rights, such as speaking and writing skills, a basic working knowledge of the social and political systems, skills in accessing and processing information, interpreting political talks etc. These 'tools' are part of the civic skills which the generation of European Muslims who lived their formative years outside Europe often lack. The Muslims who were born or grew up in Europe on the other hand, even if they do not manage to gain substantial amounts of cultural capital in the form of institutionalised cultural capital, are much richer than their parents in the embodied cultural capital or general knowledge about how European societies function, acquired during the process of socialization[253]. The members of the new Muslim elite emerging in Brussels and analysed in this book, possess in fact not only substantial amounts of embodied cultural capital, but also the institutional form of it, as almost all of them (with exception of two persons) have a university degree or are in the process of getting one. Moreover, three of them have been pursuing doctoral studies in social sciences which means that in the near future their positions as religious brokers may only become stronger.

---

in Brussels only two local councils (Molenbeek-Saint-Jean, Saint-Josse-ten-Noode) voted a law opening the channels for some symbolic subsidies for Muslim places of worship.

[253] For the definitions of the terms institutional and embodied cultural capital see chapter 1.

As I have mentioned at the beginning of this chapter, the possession of this institutional form of cultural capital is a feature that most clearly distinguishes them not only from their parents, who often do not possess any capital of this kind, but also from many other children of Muslim parents in Belgium who finished their education at the secondary level. Thus, one may see that the rising new Muslim elite analysed are, to a large extent, also an educational elite. Here it is worth noting that, as the vast majority of my interviewees come from the families of unskilled workers with no academic tradition, the acquisition of institutional cultural capital by them has rarely been an easy process In most cases it required a lot of hardship and sacrifice from them as their parents encouraged them, in their own ways, to achieve better educational results and thus to aspire to higher social status. The following account of one my interviewees clearly depicts this hardship: *'I was enjoying myself up to my 12 birthday. I was spending a lot of time on the street and hanging out with friends. Then my father called me and asked if I enjoyed myself. I thought he was asking about that day so I immediately answered 'yes'. But then he repeated the question in a slightly different way. He asked if I enjoyed myself enough during these 12 years. I was a little bit surprised by the question but I said again: 'Yes I did enjoy myself'. Then he said: 'it is good, because from today on you will not go out any more'. So the next three years I felt as I was in a prison. I was looking through the window how others were playing and enjoying themselves while I was staying in the house. But these years were necessary, because then when I was 16, 17 years old I didn't want to go out any more. I was studying, doing my homework, reading books and leaving the house only when my mother asked me to go to do shopping. Later I found out that I was the only person from my housing estate who went and finished university.'* (Rashid)

University is undoubtedly one of the important places where my interviewees have acquired the civic skills necessary to move from the formal to more substantive forms of citizenship but it is not the only one. Several respondents implied that it was also the contingency of the everyday environment of family life that led them to get involved in voluntary activity. Majd remarked, for instance, that *'My mother was active in the female self-help organisation. It was initially her and a relative of the family who pushed me from the very early age to get involve in helping others.'*, whereas Jannah argued that *"My mother has been always helping people so for me being active is a*

216

natural thing". Yet other interviewees, who indicated the importance of their family environments in their early pre-voluntary preparation, were Hadijah who said that *"From very early age I worked with other people* (helping out her father with his small business – KP). *So for me being active in the associative sector was a continuation of my earlier work."* and Nabihah, who asserted that *"If someone played a role in pushing me into voluntary activism it was my mother who is quite a combative person. She is not active but she has a great sense of altruism, openness to others. She is a person with a lot of positive energy despite the difficulties of life. I think it is largely from her that I have learnt to be assertive and open to others"*.

If not parents themselves, then often the respondents' siblings played an important role in their first involvements in the voluntary work for Muslim communities. Their older brothers and sisters, who got involved first with Muslim organisations, were often considered as role models. One of my interviewees claimed that in her involvement with the Muslim and larger civil society a crucial role was played not only by her older sisters, but also by the fact that she had very young brother who could not play a role of 'older brother – protector' and thus maintain social control over his sisters and restrain her (and her sisters) voluntary involvement (Jannah). Akin to the religious rediscovery, it is important to take into account the size of the families of my interviews to better understand their mobilisational power. The findings of my research confirm the crucial role of families not only as a source of civic skills and voluntary preparation, but also as the basis for recruitment, elaborated in the sociological literature on social capital by Portes (1998), Whitley (1999), Lowndess (2000) and Fevre (2000), to name only some of the studies. They uphold the view adopted by Whitley (1999), who suggests that community voluntarism requires a pre-existing level of cooperation and trust between individuals before they enter group life, and prove the importance of informal networks in mobilizing people to become active in the community. My research also shows that, in the analysis of community involvement, elements nurtured within families such as personality of the individual, their sense of satisfaction with life, a sense of individual morality and social identities arising out of 'imaginary communities' should not be ignored.

217

Moreover, the in-depth interviews demonstrate that, apart from the environment of the family, it is the wider social milieu that played a key role in informing the young Muslim Brusselers' political consciousness. The socialization of the people interviewed in the atmosphere of ethnic/religious mobilization has crucially conditioned their sense of organized action. Some of the events that have significantly contributed to rising the temperature of this atmosphere were the hijab affair in France and its echoes in Belgium and the riots in different parts of the town (e.g. Forest and Saint Gilles in May 1991, Molenbeek in April 1995, Anderlecht in November 1997), which were in most cases a consequence of the deterioration of the relation between the Police and the youth caused by the death of an adolescent of foreign origin (Rea 2001).

4.3.3 REASONS FOR 'BEING ACTIVE'

Having accounted for the major resources that enable members of the new Muslim elite in Brussels to move from formal to more substantive forms of citizenship and mentioning some of the contexts in which they were nurtured, it is time to demonstrate by means of a few examples how they use these resources in community activism. At the same time, I shall elaborate on some of the direct motivations that have pushed the analysed group of people to voluntary work. The possession of essential resources for active involvement in the public sphere does not explain why the people analysed bother to get involved as volunteers in Muslim and wider civil society or, as one of my interviewees put it, '*to make their mayonnaise*'(Kemal). What follows is a presentation of the major reasons for which the analysed people are being active in the Muslim and wider civil society, accompanied by the depiction of some of the activities of the organisations analysed.

One of the most common reasons referred to by the members of the Belgian new Muslim elite for activism was a general desire to improve the situation of Muslims, as well as, other members of the society that may need help. This motivation is in line not only with their perception of citizenship as mainly a constructive project, but also with their understanding of Muslimness. While one of my informants, for example, argued that '*The goal of being active is to improve my surrounding, as well as, to develop myself*' (Majd), another said that '*Islam pushes Muslims to believe in God and to do good... to do good for both the Muslim community, as well as wider society*' (Khalil).

218

This motivation was also widespread among my female interviewees, one of whom claimed that *'It is necessary to get involved in the society because it really needs us... to do projects, to do many things. We cannot stay isolated in our corner, because if we do, we won't evolve... there are plenty of people who need our help'* (Lana).

One of the activities of the Muslim civil society that goes in line with the aforementioned desires of the young activists are the educational projects - mentoring and educational assistance - developed by the LIIB. They are carried out along with Arabic courses for children and women and strictly religious courses of Islamic sciences that are provided by many Muslim organisations in Europe. Every year dozens of children profit from free private lessons given by the LIIB volunteers. People involved in these projects, who are aware of the educational underachievement of pupils from Muslim families, try to consolidate their knowledge in key national curriculum subjects (e.g. Maths, French), and to motivate them to strive for excellence in all they undertake. Thus by helping children to do better in schools, the volunteers try to improve their educational competences and in the future their prospects at the labour market. As one of the respondents pointed out *'If the young Muslims do not have the same educational competencies as others, they are already handicapped and they do not integrate in the same way. They integrate negatively in comparison with those who integrate positively.'* (Rashid)

The young Muslims activists accounted differently for the poor performance of Muslim children (particularly boys) at schools.[254] While some of them were highlighted the inappropriate educational methods used by the parents, others put most of the blame on structural inequalities and discrimination. Rashid, for example, noticed that *'in Brussels in general the boys are brought up in a much more laissez-faire manner than the girls. You can go out, but girls have to stay at home'*. This *'education of the heart'*, as he called it, is according to him the main reason why Muslim boys achieve lower educational results than the girls. Other reasons frequently stated by the respondents to explain the educational underachievement of Muslim children included: the underresourcing of schools attended by Muslim children, discouragement of Muslim

---

[254] For more information about the educational underachievement of Muslim children and some lines of its explanations developed in the Belgian literature see chapter III.

pupils by the professors to pursue further studies and orienting them to vocational training colleges, as well as, open discrimination of the Muslim girls in the form of the hijab ban.[255] These factors led some of the respondents to support the creation of Muslim schools. *'I don't think Muslim schools would contribute to the ghettoisation of Muslims. We are anyway in the process of ghettoisation of Muslims by, for example, introducing ban on headscarves that excludes Muslim girls from state schools.'* – argued one of them (Masud). [256]

The willingness to improve the performance of Muslim children at schools was not the only factor that drove the activists of the LIIB to get involved in the educational projects. Almost all the persons interviewed talked also about a strong desire to share their life experiences and personal successes with others. They were very well aware of the fact that not all those who come from similar social milieus were able to finish universities. In other words, one may notice in their narratives many features to suggest that they know that they are a minority, or an elite group within the population of young Muslims in Brussels. Some of them said that they treated involvement in the above mentioned projects as a way of giving back to the country since it has provided them with an education (e.g. Nabihah, Majd). Others, similarly to Madiha and Karim, argued that their aim was to share their life experiences, both positive and negative, with the Muslim youth, so as it could learn from their mistakes and be better equipped to *'overcome the crisis of identity'* (Madiha) and to *'avoid getting disconnected from the proper life'* (Kemal).

As I have argued above, my interviewees did not perceive their activism as a vehicle for the improvement of the situation of only Muslims, but also of a wider society. Their statements substantiate, for example, involvement of some of them (especially women), the activists of the PM, as well as, the LIIB, in the initiative aimed at feeding Brussels' homeless or SDF[257]. The project was launched by some of them during the month of Ramadan in 2002 and aimed at providing homeless people living in and around the Gare du Midi with food over four successive Sundays. This one off initiative to share

---

[255] The widespread, especially in francophone Belgium, banning of headscarf at schools is discussed at length in the chapter III.
[256] The issue of Muslim schools in Belgium will be discussed in more detail in the following section devoted to the explorations of the interviewees' claims framed within the citizenship discourse.
[257] SDF - (fr. Les sans domicile fixe) - people of no fixed abode.

with strangers the happiness of eating a meal after the whole day of fasting resulted later in the foundation of an association named Humanité Sans Frontière (HSF). Today the HSF, created in October 2002, prepares meals for around 120 homeless people every Sunday, not only during the month of Ramadan, and closely cooperates with such humanitarian organisations as, for example, Opération Thermos. In contrast to many other associations of this type, the HSF distributes food to the homeless not only during the winter time, but during the whole year. Every Sunday its volunteers, both Muslims and non-Muslims, distribute meals prepared in the kitchen of the Belgian branch of Islamic Relief amongst the inhabitants of two centres for homeless. As one of my interviewees who is dynamically involved in the work of the HSF stressed: *'We work with everyone and for everyone. Amongst the people that we are feeding only one-forth are Muslims'* (Malak).[258]

Many of the young Muslim Brusselers understood the improvement of the situation of Muslims in the society also in terms of self-education or increasing ones knowledge about Islam and the society in which they are living. Their desire sums up adequately the following confession by Khalil *'you know, you always got the urge to learn a little bit more about Islam'*. The people grouped in the association Présence Musulmane have been fulfilling this desire inter alia by organising, independently and with collaboration of other Muslim and non-Muslim organisations, conferences and seminars on topics dealing either explicitly or implicitly with Islam. In March 2004, for instance, the association organised a conference in the European Parliament entitled 'Muslim Feminism: from Paradox to Reality' with Saïda Kada, Christine Delphy, Fabienne Brion and Tariq Ramadan amongst the speakers. Almost a year latter (in February 2005) Muslim speakers from different European countries were invited by the PM to Brussels to debate the issue of Islamophobia, and in November 2005 the founder of the PM was back in Brussels to discuss with the priests (Jacques Willemart and Andre Tihon) and the rabbi (Albert Guigui) the role of religion in the public sphere during the PM conference entitled 'Public Sphere, Private Sphere – what frontier?'[259]. On average

---

[258] For more information about the HSF and the involvement of the young Muslim Brusselers in it see Pędziwiatr 2006b.
[259] These are only some of the conferences and seminars organised recently by the PM in Brussels.

221

the conferences organized by the PM are attended by around 500 people.[260] Some of them had only been organized by the members of the PM after overcoming numerous barriers and difficulties. One of the people behind the organisation of the conference on Muslim Feminism pointed out, for instance, that *'Yet a day before the conference the authorities of the European Parliament wanted to cancel it because they perceived it as an example of legitimization of Islamism. In addition, the Green Party was putting pressure on its MEP, Alima Boumediene Thiery, who was helping us to organize the conference, to withdraw from the initiative. (...) We knew that the realization of our idea will not be easy and that Alima is going to have many problems. She told us that we shouldn't worry and that she was taking everything on her'* (Maysan). The more difficulties the activists of the PM had to overcome in the realization of a given project, the bigger was their satisfaction after the realization of it.[261]

Self-education, which according to some of my interviewees should result in turning young Muslims into more active and critical citizens, has also been a key goal of the already mentioned project *Projection-Débat*, run initially in the premises of the LIIB. Its leaders wanted people who take part in it to be *'(...) not only consumers of information but actors who after consuming a massage take actions'* (Kemal, Rashid) The project consists of weekly screenings of films on topics ranging from the riots in the French suburbs, through unemployment, to the relations between parents and children in Muslim families, followed by a debate with an invited guest speaker. The guest speakers usually come from within the Muslim community (among the people invited to the event were for example a federal MP - Mohammed Boukourna (Parti Socialiste) and an independent journalist – Mohsin Mouedden (Radio EL WAFA)). Although the majority of the topics discussed during the Friday meetings attended by around 30 people are directly related to the problems faced by Muslims in the country, they are not only limited to them. The people, who lead the project try to cover subject areas of responsible citizenship as widely understood as possible and would happily see more non-Muslim specialists with whom the issues could be discussed. Their position in this matter sums up

---

[260] This figure, however, sometimes is much higher. For example, the conference of the PM organised in the midst of the Danish cartoons controversy (February 2006) gathered around 1000 people.
[261] More information about this particular event organised by the activists of the PM can be found Pędziwiatr 2006b and in the conference report Présence Musulmane 2007.

the following opinion of Majd '*A lot of Muslims think that we should only learn from the imams and only from other Muslims. This is wrong! We need to learn from all people who have some expertise.*'

The opinion mentioned above was not necessarily shared by the entire leadership of the LIIB. This is one of the reasons, apart from the complaints of some of the first generation leaders about the free mixing of women and men during the debates, that in time, the project which grew out of screenings of lectures of Hassan Iquioussen, Tariq Ramadan, Yacob Mahi and other Muslim preachers before the Friday prayers, started to move out of the LIIB. Since January 2005 the project leaders decided to organise the screening-debates in a nearby Youth Centre rather than in the LIIB, as they had hitherto been doing for several months. They claimed that in the new venue they were not only more independent, but also that non-Muslims who attended the projections from time to time could feel more at ease in the Youth Centre, than in the LIIB. At the same time, they have not broken relations with the leadership of the LIIB who sometimes come to the Friday meetings.

In the aforementioned move of the project *Projection-Débat* from the premises of the LIIB to the nearby Youth Centre, one may trace many elements of the desire of 'autonomisation' described by Leila Babès, with regard to young French Muslims. Similarly to the French Muslims, my informants active in the project *Projection-Débat* seemed to distance themselves from the space viewed as 'entirely Islamic', to a more neutral ground where they could debate issues, such as religion, with more freedom (Babès 1997: 133). Their strategy also bears some features of the post-Ikhwanism or independent Islamism described by Anne-Sofie Roald (2001: 56). Although they acknowledge the authority of some of the first generation leaders, they often are very critical about the opinions of these leaders and do not act unreflexively upon their recommendations. This also applies to the religious sources. For many of them the Qur'an, as well as, the Hadith are more sets of important principles, rather than collections of precise instructions how to lead a life in a given social context. In other words, they tend to make a distinction between the historical aspect of some precise instructions to be found in the holy book of Islam and the traditions relating to the words and deeds of Muhammad, on the one hand, and universalism of the general principles they include, on the other.

Another important reason behind the activism of my informants in the associational sphere has been the wish to counter at least some of the stereotypes associated with Islam and to rework the public image of their religion. My interviews with young Muslim Brusselers confirm the results of the earlier research signalling Muslims' disillusion with media coverage of Islam and anxiety related to the growing anti-Muslim sentiment (e.g. Maréchal et al 2003: 318). They also show that, at least among the members of this group, there is quite a strong sense of agency and the feeling of power to be able to rework negative images of Islam. In fact, the growing anti-Muslim sentiment and stigmatization of Islam seem to empower the activists to be more actively engaged in public debates and to make their voice heard. The elements of this empowerment can be noticed, for example, in the following account of Khalil '(...) *the image of Islam as presented by the media is not a rosy one. If I put myself in the shoes of someone who isn't a Muslim and who only learns about Islam from the media, who doesn't read anything, then it is true that I can instantly lump together Islam with violence and intolerance (...) Muslims have to be there* (in the public sphere – KP) *to falsify these images and to show what is a real face of Islam.'* and of Jannah '*I have been active in various kind of associations, Muslim and non-Muslim, always for the same reason, namely to show others the most true image of my religion, as well as, my culture. Because for me religion is an integral part of my culture, that is the culture of my parents.'* In the latter one can see that it is not only the biased portrayal of Islam, but also of the Moroccan culture that is pushing this particular informant to activism in Muslim and non-Muslim organizations. Taking into account the fact that she is very strongly influenced by the thought of Tariq Ramadan, one could argue that, at least in her case, the critique of Ramadan's scholarship as one that promotes a cultureless vision of Islam or Islam without room for ethnic distinctiveness advanced, for instance, by Dyab Abou Jahjah (2004) does not hold.

An important aspect of the efforts of the young Muslim Brusselers to counter the stereotypical images of Islam in their country is also their wish to make the Muslim presence in the country more 'banal' and more 'taken for granted'. Part of this 'banalisation' would be according to some of them a move towards making Islam part of internal rather than external politics. This desire was particularly clearly expressed by Amjad who argued that *'We should help the generation of our parents to construct a truly unequivocal discourse (...) to make Islam not an issue of the politics of immigration, and hence a peripheral one, but part of the internal affairs. So we want ... we campaign for the end of this political logic which perceives Islam as something foreign because it has come from abroad'*. In his perception, shared also by some other informants, the Belgian authorities, in spite of the formal recognition of Islam as one of the religions of the Belgian citizens more than 30 years ago, have not yet come to terms with this fact.[262] For another interviewee, this moment of the 'banalisation' of the Muslim presence in the country will be achieved only when the society acknowledges that the voices of religious Muslims can also add some value to social debates. That is why she said that *'I am participating in various lectures, conferences and seminars. Almost every week I participate in one. I try to demonstrate during these events that there are also Muslim voices in these debates. There are Muslim opinions on such issues as, for example, the Bolkenstain Directive[263] and the European Constitution'* (Falak).

Many of my female interviewees also said that, through their activism in the Muslim and wider civil society, they wanted to fight the stereotype of a Muslim woman as oppressed, dependent on their husbands, fathers and brothers and completely absent in the public sphere. One of them was Sana, who said that by telling her non-Muslim neighbours about different projects, in which she was involved, she managed to convince them that *"Muslim women are not just sheep which blindly follow their husbands"*. Another woman for whom this was a key motivation in her Islamic volunteering was Maysan who said *"At times, I go to the meetings where Muslim women are not expected and take active part in them. People are often astonished by what I am saying and tell me that they didn't realize that Muslim women have rights"*.

My study shows that the members of the emerging new Muslim elite are able to work the stigmatization of Islam to their advantage. Thus, the experience of going

---

[262] This issue will be discussed in the following subchapter.
[263] The EU Directive named after Frits Bolkestein (Dutch Commissioner) on services in the internal market aimed at enabling a company from a given member-state to recruit workers in other EU countries using the law of its home country.

'through the eye of the needle of the other' (Hall 1991: 21) does not weaken their agency and willingness to engage with the Muslim civil society but, on the contrary, strengthens it. By reversing the feelings of shame into dignity and self-esteem, the stigma of adhering to a religion commonly associated by the general public with violence and viewed as primitive, irrational and barbaric (EUMC 2006), becomes a source of empowerment and a symbol of positive identity affirmation; in a manner similar to the Black nationalism movement, where the slogans such as 'Black is beautiful', 'Black power' and 'up your mighty race' have been used to denote feelings of self-respect, the celebrating one's heritage and being proud of one's personal worth amongst African Americans (especially of sub-Saharan African origin). I believe it is important to view this 'empowerment-through-stigmatisation' in the larger context of the recent politisation of Islam, which has created discursive opportunities for this kind of empowerment by increasing demand for knowledge about Islam and Muslim populations in Europe and elsewhere. Some of this demand is being met by a growing number of scholars studying various kinds of processes within the European and other Muslim populations. There is, however, not only a continuous demand for expert knowledge of Muslim populations but also for the opinions of all types of community representatives, ranging from the internationally acknowledged Muslim leaders, through self-proclaimed religious leaders to ordinary believers or Muslim monsieurs and madames tout-le-monde. This is a niche which many Muslims active in all kinds of Islamic organisations have been tapping into. My interviews with young Muslims in Belgium show that they are fully aware of this demand and consciously take advantage of the opportunities it creates. Moreover, my research proves that some of them know their advantages over the first generation of community representatives educated abroad in responding to this demand very well, of which language fluency is one of the most important ones. This is demonstrated in the following assertion by Faisal: '*We live in the transitory phase between the first generation and the future generations, and we begin to understand that we have become a kind of a relief group. So they* (e.g. journalists – KP) *ask us because it is much easier for them from the linguistic point of view... '.*

Other reasons for being active in the associational sphere less frequently evoked by my interviewees[264] were a desire to meet other like-minded people and the wish to fulfil religious and civic obligations and thus be consistent with their values. Some also said that the main reason for being active was the ability to fulfil oneself. Khalil for example argued that *'When you believe in God, practice your religion etc.... at certain moment you want to participate and contribute to an association, why not a Muslim one. To in some way realise yourself... So you decide to get involved and then you are part of it.'*

Summing up this section, it is worth stressing that most of the interviewees claimed to be active in the Muslim and wider associational sphere for not one but many of the aforementioned reasons. There was no visible gender differentiation in the reasons for activism advanced by my interviewees, however women seemed to stress more in their answers the need for precise actions to achieve certain objectives, while men spoke in more abstract terms. The women's, as well as, men's answers seemed thus to be in line with the character of their activism: in the case of women, of a much more precise nature, often responding to some clear deficiencies and characterised by high efficiency, whereas in the case of men of a more widespread nature, often characterised by a great deal of theorizing and developing the discourse but with somewhat weaker real-life applications or practical dimension.

4.3.4 BENEFITS FROM PARTICIPATION

As I have argued above, the stigmatization of Islam seems to have an empowering effect on the group of people analysed and seems to increase their capacity to make choices and to transform those choices into desired actions[265]. In this last section of the subchapter devoted to explorations of the relations between Islam and the participatory dimension of citizenship, I shall look more closely into how activism in the Muslim civil society has been empowering the young Muslim Brusselers. I will do so mainly by assessing my interviewees' perceptions of the benefits from being active in the associational field.

---

[264] Here it is worth stressing that fewer references to these motives for activism does not necessarily mean that they were treated by the interviewees as less important.
[265] I have borrowed this general understanding of empowerment from the World Bank reports. See www.worldbank.org/empowerment

Having carefully analysed these perceptions, I found that the activism has been empowered the young Muslims most by opening up new channels of intellectual and spiritual development for them. The vast majority claimed that through being active in the Muslim organisations they were able to learn new things not only about their religion, and thus significantly improve their understanding of Islam, but also about the society in which they were living. My interviewees could learn about wider societal issues in the environment of the Muslim civil society inter alia through participation in the debates and conferences with various representatives of the wider society (e.g. politicians, journalists who were not necessarily Muslim), organized by their associations. Numerous sessions of the project Screening-Debate had such a character, as well as, for example a conference on *'Muslim Women of Belgium: work, family and leisure'* organized by the LIIB in cooperation with the Confédération des Syndicats Chrétiens during the International Women's Day in 2005. One of the active participants of the Screening-Debate sessions said, for instance, that *"I benefit from the activism in the sense that I understand things better. We've invited* (to the sessions – KP) *ex-prisoners, street workers, policemen and politicians... This has allowed me to better understand certain things. You have some understanding of the things but it is only partial. The activities enabled me to enrich myself with the experience others."* (Rashid)

However, the main type of knowledge which my interviewees have acquired through participation in the activities of Muslim organisations, is the religious one. As I have argued earlier, the active participation of the young Muslims in the conferences, seminars, debates and other activities of the Muslim organisations plays an important role in the wider process of intellectualisation of Islam by the young European Muslims. Some features of this process can be found, for example, in the account of Yusuf, who said that *"The activism in the Muslim civil society has allowed me to rethink my position and question certain things in Islam as I was learning by listening to others and by finding out my weak points and where I was missing something. In this way I could improve my education and my discourse."* Another of my interviewees argued that because he could stay in contact through his associational activism with such people as Tarik Ramadan, Yacob Mahi and Hassan Iquioussen, it allowed him *"to say intelligent in the society in which the stupidity sometimes becomes the main postulate."* (Amjad)

By being involved in Muslim civil society, the young Muslims analysed have not only had an opportunity to learn about their religion and the wider society but also to develop communication, management and leadership skills. These are also the skills which they latter use plentifully while asserting themselves as new religious brokers and when actively exercising their civic rights. The following account of Falak shows how successful certain Muslim organisations are in teaching their members these skills. *"It is very enriching when one gets involved in the Muslim associational sphere. In terms of professional training I have learnt a lot of management and communication skills, for example, to lead meeting, no to be afraid of raising voice in front of the large audiences,. It has helped me a lot. In the past I was not able to speak in front of my class and now I often speak in front 500 people. "* (Falak) If the organisations are not teaching young activists all these skills at once they are able to develop at least some of them. This was the case of Lana who said that *"In the associational field I learnt that you must have you project well structured before launching it. You must thoroughly study it, reflect on its objectives, means and ways of implementing it. "*

In order to be successful religious brokers the members of the new Muslim elite need to possess not only certain knowledge and skills, but also need to have a rich social network. My research shows that the Muslim organisations in which they are active also significantly enhances their capacities in this matter since they function as quite effective vehicles of generating social capital. The main type of social capital which they generate is a bonding one that reinforces exclusive interactions, homogeneity (Putnam 2000: 22) and, in the analysed case, Muslim identity. This type of social capital constitutes a kind of sociological superglue (ibid: 23). In practice, it manifests itself in the fact that most friends that members of the emerging new Muslim elite make, through various religious meetings and projects, are Muslims. It is not uncommon that young Muslims also find their future husbands and wives through activism in Muslim civil society. In some way, conferences, seminars and other events organised by Muslim organisations also play a role of matchmaking sessions. This observation, made on the basis of participation in numerous events of the analysed organisations seems to confirm one of the interviewees of Nathalie Kakpo who said of the conferences of Tariq Ramadan in the small French town of Moligny close to the Swiss border that *'Some guys come to the conferences to search for future wives. They think that women who come here are good, that they are correct'* (Salima quoted in Kakpo 2007: 43).

In some cases the exclusive social capital which my interviewees acquire through their activism is not only limited to the Muslim community in Belgium but transgresses national frontiers. One of the persons who acquired the transnational bonding capital through her involvement in the Muslim civil society was Jannah, who argued that *"Muslim organisation is like a great present. As a result of my involvement in the Muslim organisation, now when I go to London I know many people there and I feel safe. Because I know that there are people who are ready to help me."*

However, the involvement of my interviewees in the Muslim civil society results not only in generating the bonding social capital, but also enables the accumulation of the bridging social capital. The latter capital was conceptualised by Robert Putnam as one that reinforces inclusive interactions, horizontal trust and reciprocal connections between people from different walks of life. As such it can generate broader identities and reciprocity and acts as a kind of sociological WD-40 (Putnam 2000: 22-23). My interviewees could also accumulate such capital through their involvement in the Muslim civil society, as some friends that they made via this activism were from outside of the Muslim community. For example, the organisation by the LIIB (in cooperation with CSC) of the conference on *'Muslim Women of Belgium: work, family and leisure'* in 2005 gave the young Muslim women the opportunity to not only take active part in the wider societal debates of which they have usually been only the subject, but also allowed them to establish contacts with non-Muslim individuals and institutions participating in the conference. One of the interviewees actively involved in the preparation of the conference said that '(...) *organising the conference was interesting because we tried to identify people from different cultures and environments. This was very ambitious but I think we were quite successful. With some of the people and institutions that we co-operated, we keep in touch until today.'* (Abida) The young Muslims women active in the PM were able to accumulate the same kind of capital, for instance, in the course of preparation of the already mentioned conference on Muslim Feminism in the European Parliament in March 2004. The considerable potential for generating bridging social capital is also possessed by the sessions of the project Screening-Debate, as its organisers tried to invite to the debates guest speakers and participants from outside the Muslim community.

Finally, the last but not least major benefit from the activism in the Muslim civil society evoked by many of my interviewees was personal satisfaction. One of the interviewees who felt in this way about the outcomes of her volunteering in the associational sphere was Abida. She said that *"The involvement in the sessions* (of the project Screening-Debate – KP) *gives me above all a lot of satisfaction, particularly when people say that they have learnt something new. Even if it is just the first time that they spoke through the microphone. I'm happy that I could influence people in a positive way."* Similar feelings about her involvement in the Muslim civil society were shared by Maysan who asserted that *"(...) spreading the real message of Islam, message of peace, partnership... This gives me great satisfaction".* At times the satisfaction from being involved in the different projects of Muslim organisations was felt by my interviewees as a sense of 'being in the right place and doing the right things'. This was for instance the feeling of Hafa, involved in some of the educational projects of the LIIB, who said *"It was important for me. I was happy when our projects were running well. I felt that I was doing what I should be doing ... ".*

In general, the involvement in different associational projects gave my interviewees a feeling of being valued and needed, which in a city with very high unemployment, especially amongst the Muslim communities, is of crucial importance. Moreover it allowed many of them *'to remain coherent with themselves'* (Amjad) and with their beliefs. My results in this matter tend to substantiate the claim of Tariq Modood who pointed out that from their faith and collective solidarity, Muslims gain self-pride and oppositional energy (Modood 2006: 48). This is the pride and energy which they use plentifully when claiming various rights within the country's institutional citizenship framework. In the following subchapter I shall analyse some of these claims, together with my interviewees' banal notions of citizenship rights.

4.4 ISLAM AND CITIZENSHIP RIGHTS

Citizenship has been often described as a 'contextualised concept' (Siim 2000: 1). This means, inter alia, that various groups (e.g. women, ethnic, religious and sexual minorities) experience exclusionary citizenship practices and fight for full inclusion from the vantage point of specific, differentiated cultures and practices of citizenship as they are consolidated in the areas in which they live. This also applies to the group of young Muslims analysed who, in spite of being born in the country and holding the same passports as other Belgians, often do not feel that they are treated in the same manner as other citizens of Belgium. As I have shown in the first part of this chapter, the lack-of-recognition model of citizenship, pointing out at certain deficiencies in the supposedly equal distribution of citizenship, is one of the most popular among the new Muslim brokers in Brussels. This section of the empirical chapter will further explore the exclusionary aspects of the citizenship, as it is lived and understood by my Belgian interviewees, and shed some light on the part of the normative dimension of citizenship which opens up the space for different claims-making. In particular it will focus on the analysis of the field between the hegemonic form of citizenship rights and the young Muslim Brusselers' understanding of rights or between their perceptions of what citizenship rights are and what they should be. As I have argued earlier, the wider the gap between the official discourse on citizenship upholding the principle of equality and the actual practice of it, the more claims are formulated with reference to the 'ideal citizenship' (Marshall 1950: 29).

4.4.1 BANAL DEFINITIONS OF CITIZENSHIP RIGHTS

Before I shed light on the aspects of the citizenship that do not live up to the expectations of my interviewees, it is first worth looking at their overall understanding of the citizenship rights. My interviews with the young Muslims in Brussels have shown that they had a fairly well developed understanding of what their citizenship rights are or to what they are entitled to as citizens of Belgium. Their subjective definitions of the citizenship rights were very rich and not only included elements of civil and political rights, but also social and, to a lesser extent, cultural rights. One may notice these elements, for instance, in the following statement of one of my interviewees who said, *"We have the same rights as other citizens. The right to free expression and movement, to association, to justice and equal opportunities, to education and employment ..., as well as, the right to be myself."* (Faisal) The right to be different from others - in Faisal's words 'to be myself' - as one of the citizenship rights, was also stressed by other interviewees. One of them, Nabihah, for example, pointed out that among the rights that she had, were besides *'(...) the rights concerning employment, housing, political representation and the right to the human dignity"* also *"the right to be recognized in the way I am, with my principles and values"*. At the same time, the vast majority of my informants stressed that they saw their rights as similar to the rights of other citizens. Yusuf, for instance, argued that *"I do not ask for any special rights. I don't ask for anything special because I am a Muslim. I want only the Constitution to be respected and applied equally to all citizens regardless of their faith, colour of skin and personal convictions. I ask only for the same egalitarian treatment of all citizens. I don't ask for a privileged position."* Exactly the same point was made by Majd who said that *"I see my rights as absolutely equal to the rights of any other Belgian"*.

Apart from stressing the egalitarianism of citizenship rights, many of my interviewees emphasized that the rights should not be conceived in abstraction, but in relation to the obligations. Thus, they argued that citizenship rights always go hand in hand with citizenship obligations. One of these interviewees was Murad who pointed out *'There are rights because there are obligations and vice versa"*. Another one said that *'I see my rights through the obligations that I have... It is important to learn to read these rights. As long as we fulfil our obligations as citizens, we cannot be striped of our rights."* (Amjad) In his as well as Murad's understanding, citizenship is a two-sided, reciprocal membership which involves both rights in a given community and responsibilities towards it.

Furthermore, citizenship rights were understood by the majority of my informants not in the passive form, that is as the rights handed down from above by the state (see e.g. Bendix 1964), but as the rights that must be achieved through some effort, even if they are formally granted. One may see this, for example, in the opinion of Amjad who pointed out that although generally the citizenship rights are ascribed to citizens, sometimes "*we* (people of the second and third generation - KP) *have to insist a little bit more than older citizens so as our rights are fully respected*". His view about the need to make an effort in order to profit from the supposedly ascribed citizenship rights was shared by many other interviewees. According to Khalil, for instance, "*the rights are snatched... they are not going to fall on you out of the sky. If you have a right to something, it is up to you make a move and snatch it.*" The same point was also made by Murad who claimed that "*one needs to fight everyday to have his or her citizenship rights*". I believe this way of understanding the rights of a citizen by my interviewees had partially to do with the specific situation of inconsistency between the wide juridical framework and much narrower path of its application that will be discussed in more detail further in this section.

In general, as it could be expected, the young Muslim brokers were characterised by and large by strong civic identities and also possessed a substantial knowledge of their citizenship rights. This knowledge, coupled with some resources as presented in the former section, enabled them to assert their position in the forefront of the Muslim identity politics in the city. As I am going to demonstrate below, this politics has been powered not by the claims for exceptional rights, or dissociative demands that call for something substantively 'new', but largely for the acculturative demands or calls for parity of rights and equality with other groups.

The key argument that I could trace in the interviews with almost all of my Belgian informants was that, although they might officially have the same rights as other citizens, the application of these rights looks radically different. The disillusionment with the existence of the discrepancy between the rights, as they are stated in the major legal acts and the way how they are executed in the social reality, can be seen in the following statement of Naima who said that "*We have citizenship rights, but unfortunately certain people abolish them, ... they don't want us to have them. We have all the rights here in Belgium... Something that I like a lot about Belgium is that we live here in a democratic society, which is not that common in the world. But - and here I insist on 'but' - some people do not recognize our right*s". In many ways, similar argumentation can also be found in the account of Madiha. She stated, that "*Officially we have the same rights but they are not respected. A lot of things must change so as we can really feel citizens. One* *has to be recognised as a citizen in the same way as others, regardless of one's religious, ethnic or other characteristics."* The gap between the letter of the law which constitutes the backbone of citizenship rights internalized by my interviewees and the empirical reality of these rights was also pointed out by my male informants. Majd argued that *"In general we have the same rights as other citizens, but there are people who do not respect them."*, whereas Masud said *"It is clear that Muslim citizens in Belgium do not have the same rights as other citizens."*

How do the rights of my interviewees, and also to some extent those of other members of the Muslim communities in the country, differ from the rights of other, non-Muslim citizens? In what way the rights of the former group are inferior to the rights of the latter group? What are the major areas in which the young Muslim Belgians saw their citizenship rights as not being fully respected? Before I explore these questions it is important first to shed more light on the issue of recognition and the phenomena which at first may seem contradictory, that is on the one hand, the desire of my informants to be included in a wider society, and considered to be 'the same', and on the other hand, their wish to preserve their religious distinctiveness and be noticeable as 'different'.

4.4.2 RIGHT TO SAMENESS AND RIGHT TO DIFFERENCE

The vast majority of those interviewed pointed out that they felt themselves to be Belgians of a second class inter alia because they were not fully recognized as citizens of the country. The dominant feature of the narratives of the young Muslim Belgians was a strong desire to fully participate in the life of society, or 'to be like other Belgians'. This craving for the right to participate in the sameness, or for being included in the more flexible and open conception of 'us', can be seen particularly clearly in the numerous statements of my interviewees criticizing the discursive habit of referring to the offspring of Moroccan and Turkish immigrants (that is to them) as 'Belgians of foreign descent' (Fr. *Belges d'origine étrangère)*. One of my interviewees who strongly disagreed with this habit was Amjad. He argued that *"We need to stop constantly using the notions of Belgians of foreign descent and autochthonous Belgians, because this only slow downs the process of intellectual reaching out to the others. Each time someone says 'Yes, but you are of Moroccan or Turkish origin' the barrier in the approach to the other is being* erected. *We need to stop it... Today we are full citizens and we need to discuss all the things on the equal footing."* In the view of Amjad, and many other members of the emerging new Muslim elite, the discursive practice of differentiating between Belgians who have lived in the country for generations and those whose parents settled after the Second World War, only served the purpose of legitimising the unfair treatment of the latter group. According to my interviewees, this practice belittles their status as full citizens of Belgium and thus exposes them to all kinds of discriminatory treatment that will be discussed below.

Another common way of emphasizing by my informants that the situation has changed since their parents arrived to the country and that now they should be fully embraced in the category of 'Belgians', was the open disagreement with the application of the concept of integration in relation to children of immigrants who were born in Europe. One of the interviewees who dismissed the concept of integration and judged it as inadequate to deal with the situation of young Moroccan Belgians, Turkish Belgians and other Belgian-born children of immigrants was Khalil. He argued that *"Now, the young generations consider themselves as fully Belgians ... We are fed up when we are being lectured about the integration. They are speaking about the integration to the people who were born here, ha, ha* (laughing – KP) *or to the people whose parents were already born here in Belgium and who speak better French than Arabic... speaking about the integration in such a context really doesn't make sense."* In their views politicians and other opinion leaders who talk about integrating young Belgian Moroccans and Turks with the wider society do not mean social insertion, but acculturation and assimilation. Rashid, for instance, stated *"I have nothing against the social integration. It means to know the language of the country, to know its culture, have an employment – these are some of the key means enabling social integration. I agree with them. But if one needs to integrate in the sense of assimilation, forgetting about their parent's culture and religion, then I do not agree."* Most of my interviewees shared Rashid's point of view and expressed concerns about the usage of the category of integration by political actors as a magical remedy to all the problems of the poor city quarters and as a vehicle for improvement of the situation of the offspring of Moroccan and Turkish immigrants in the educational, economic and other spheres of social life. Although the voters of the political party that calls for the 'reintegration of the Muslim immigrants with their own communities back home' (one of the postulates of the Party of the Flemish Interest or Vlaams Belang) constitute only a small minority in Brussels[266], the politisation and reformulation of the concept of integration by the party leaders also played a role in the aversion of my interviewees to it.[267]

Other important ways of claiming the right to the sameness by my interviewees were their frequent assertions of the strong attachment not only to the national identity, heritage and the places in which they lived but also to many other aspects of life in Belgium. They spoke at length, and often with disappointment, about the instances when their strong positive feelings towards the country and the place in which they were born were questioned or not treated seriously. One of the persons who expressed a profound sadness resulting from such a situation, and thus very firmly called for inclusion into the more flexible and hybridized notion of Belgianness, was Falak. She recounted the following story introducing it as an 'anecdote': *"Once I was walking in the city centre, approaching the Grande Place and an old SDF standing at the corner of the street started to shout to me – 'Miss, Miss' – I said 'yes?' and then he said – 'to Mecca it is that way' ha, ha, ha ...* (laughing but with sorrow in the voice – KP) *(...) Then he said 'return to your place'. 'But here is my place, Sir!' 'How many times I need to say it! My home is here!'... For me, who feels profoundly Brusselian, I sometimes have a feeling that we will never be accepted. And, thus we sometimes have the feeling of not being accepted. For example, with all this debate about the Muslim headscarf... I am a little bit saddened, excuse-me. I am going to cry...* (she cries – KP)".

As I have mentioned earlier, the young Muslim Belgians were not only claiming the right to the sameness (the 'right to Belgianness'), and wanted their presence in the midst of the Belgian society to be banalised or 'taken for granted', but also they demanded the right to maintain their religious identity (the 'right to Muslimness') and wanted this difference to be recognized. In many cases they expressed the desire to have a right to the difference at the personal level, not necessarily linked with any social

---

[266] During the last federal elections on 10th June 2007 less than 10 per cent of the inhabitants of the electoral district of Brussels-Halle-Vilvoorde voted for Vlaams Belang.

[267] On the Vlaams Belang political presence and strategies in Brussels see Jacobs 2000, whereas on the reformulations of the concept of integration in Belgium see Blommaert 1997 and 1998.

group. A good example of a such a claim can be found in the following statement of Abida " *I want the right to be different from others, which does not exist. We live in the society where people are quasi-cloned, not different from each other. I want to have this right not necessarily as a Muslim. I want to have the right to be different while at same time respecting the rights of others.*" However, the claim for the right to the difference was not only limited to the private sphere, but it also extended to the public sphere and linked more directly with the Muslim population of Belgium and Islam, as one of the recognized religions of Belgian citizens. It included, inter alia, such claims, that will be analysed below, as a demand to recognize the right of the Muslim women to wear hijabs at schools, at work and in other public spaces, the right of Muslim pupils to be provided with halal food at school and to have their own state-funded Muslim schools, the right to state subsidies for the construction and maintenance of mosques, payments of salaries to imams, etc. The country's framework of the State-Church relations, as outlined in the previous chapter, provides considerable room for the implementation of the Muslim citizens' right to the difference and assertion of Islam in the public sphere. However, due to different reasons, they have only partially managed to take advantage of the opportunities it offers.

To fully understand what it means to have its difference recognized, it is worth recalling what recognition from the theoretical point of view means. It should not be thought of as something that is given once and for all, but as a continuous process that takes place on three major levels: cognitive, normative and practical. Cognitive recognition refers to the problem of perception. The difference has to be perceived since, as Werner Schiffauer rightly notices, nobody wants to be recognized for the wrong reasons (1999: 2). At this level, the young Muslim Belgians, as well as other believers of Islam in the country, have nothing to complain about. As I have just demonstrated, their difference is often noticed by others even contrary to their will but the problems arise when we move to the next levels. Recognition in its normative dimension assumes that the difference is, if not appreciated, at least positively valued. At this level, recognition is conceived as the opposition of devaluation and discrimination. Thirdly, at the practical level, recognition means that some action is taken and that it does not remain just a 'lip service' (Schiffauer 1999: 3). As I am going to show below the situation of Muslims and

Islam in Belgium is at present quite far from the moment when one could talk about the normative and practical recognition.

4.4.3 CONTESTED EQUALITY OF RIGHTS IN EDUCATION

One of the areas in which many of my interviewees saw their citizenship rights as not being fully respected was that of education. Although in theory citizenship guarantees all citizens free access to a quality education, in practice this access has been strictly limited inter alia by the decisions of some school authorities to not accept applications from pupils whose parents are immigrants or of immigrant origin. This issue has been brought up, for instance, by Rashid, who argued that *"Discrimination starts already at school. The director of the school cannot refuse to admit a kid just because his parents are immigrants. The discriminations starts at school, then goes to the job market and to housing"*. The practice of rejecting the applications of children of immigrant origin by schools of good reputation, along with such a major factor as the spatial concentration of Muslims in certain city quarters, results in the existence of schools where more than 50 per cent of pupils are of a migrant background or 'concentration schools', as they are called by the researchers (e.g. Vanhoren et at. 1995), or 'dustbin schools' (Fr. écoles poubelles) and 'ghetto schools' (Fr. écoles ghettos), as they were frequently depicted by my interviewees. The sociological research has shown that attending such schools has a negative effect on the school careers of the second-generation children (e.g. Roosens 1995, Hermans 1995, Timmerman 1999a). Their pupils are more likely to repeat a year and tend to end up in vocational training, finishing their education at the secondary level.[268] While most autochthonous pupils opt for general secondary education (ASO), and a smaller number for technical secondary schools with few in the vocational training (BSO), the Muslim children are over-represented in BSO and TSO offering poor

---

[268] Education is one of the areas that was devolved during the constitutional reforms (see chapter III) so there is no one homogenous Belgian educational system. However, both Flemish and Francophone systems have many similar features. In both systems, children generally start going to pre-school when they are two and a half years old. Compulsory education begins at the age of six. After primary school, at the age of twelve, children move on to two 'orientation' years in secondary school. At the age of fourteen, they have to choose between vocational training (BSO – *Beroeps Secundair Onderwijs* - in Dutch, or ESP - *Enseignement Secondaire Professionnel* – in French), technical training (TSO – *Technisch Secundair Onderwijs* – in Dutch, or EST - *Enseignement Secondaire Technique* – in French) and general secondary education (ASO – *Algemeen Secundair onderwijs* - in Dutch, or ESG - *L'Enseignement Secondaire Général* – in French).

employment prospects.[269] Thus BSO schools, and to a smaller extent TSO schools, in major urban areas are usually concentration secondary schools.

My interviewees, who (with exception of two people) possessed a university diploma or were in the process of obtaining one, represent the minority of Belgian Muslims who were successful at school. According to studies carried out by Hermans (1995) and Timmerman (1999a) that explicitly searched for factors that contribute to the education success of the second-generation Moroccans and Turks, one major factor was the avoidance of the concentration schools.[270] They found that the parents of the successful Muslim students deliberately chose a primary school with as few pupils of immigrant background as possible. Children who avoided concentration schools were usually well prepared for the orientation years and therefore more likely to move on to general secondary education (ASO), preparing for the university. The usage of this strategy could also be detected among the parents of some of my interviewees. The following account of one of my interviewees confirms the results of the earlier research. *"I did my first three years of the school in the place where 99 per cent of pupils were Muslim and where there was only one girl with the name Helen. This was not normal. (...) I changed the school because my father who was very vigilant found that the school that I was frequenting could not provide me with maximum of opportunities for the future. So I changed the school and started to go to one of the best schools in Brussels which aims at preparing pupils for the university. There were few Muhammads and Fadilas and many Helens."* (Falak)

The strategy used by the father of Falak might be successful only in the situation when the authorities of the schools with good reputation allow the admission of children of immigrant origin. In the Flemish community a special law (Decreee of Equal Chances in Education) was passed in June 2002 (implemented from January 2003) in order to, inter alia, guarantee parents the right to enrol their children in schools of their own choice. In the French Community, the schools of which were attended by all my

---

[269] For more information about the level of the educational underachievement of Muslim children see the socio-economic profile of the Muslim population in Belgium in the chapter III.

[270] Apart from that their studies stress the role of the parents in determining the degrees of success of their children. Hermans (1994) puts great emphasis on discipline, guidance and encouragement on the part of the parents, whereas Timmerman (1999a) points out at the crucial role of mothers in stimulating their daughters.

interviewees and by the vast majority Muslims in Brussels, such a law was voted after long parliamentary debate and many protests only in February 2007, and is supposed to be operational from September 2008. It stipulates, inter alia, that schools are obliged to enrol pupils on a first-come, first-served basis and are not allowed to reject the application of a pupil unless they have already reached their maximum capacity.

One of my interviewees did not have a vigilant father who could guide him through his educational choices, and moved - as he claimed – 'by mistake', from a prestigious school to a concentration school. He accounted in the following way for the differences between the two schools: '*The school that I went to was seriously under-resourced in comparison with the one from Uccle. In Uccle everyone had its own educational material with its own key, everyone had its own box, jacket and other things. Everyone was responsible for them. This was one of the ways in which we were thought responsibility. In my new school there was a constant lack of everything... In addition, many professors treated us as imbeciles and were deliberately orienting pupils to the professional schools. Many of my friends were, for instance, good at maths and physics but did not do that well at chemistry, and because of this they screwed up*". *(Majd)*

In the account of Majd one may notice two other major claims of unfair treatment in education that I could hear from my informants. The first is a claim of being treated unfairly in comparison with other Belgian pupils by frequenting schools that are under-resourced. This in fact, was also one of the major reasons for which the francophone green party (Ecolo) was criticizing the law that is supposed to guarantee parents the right to inscribe their children to the francophone school of their choice and thus promote social mixing. One of the representatives of the Party Yves Reinkin, for example, dismissed the claims about the promotion of social mixing by the new law of the Minister Marie Arena and argued that the government of the French community should rather invest more money in the concentration schools.[271]

The second claim of Majd is of a more serious nature and concerns the discrimination of Muslim pupils by teachers who orient them towards vocational training instead of encouraging them to go to schools which prepare them for the university. The

---

[271] See the article 'Décret inscription adopté' in Enseignons.be on
http://www.enseignons.be/actualites/pedagogique/index.php/2007/02/28/184-decret-inscription-vote

existence of this kind of non-institutional form of discrimination is substantiated, for example, by the EUMC report on Migrants, Minorities and Education (2004: 53-56). The report shows that low expectations from the side of teachers seriously deter some ethnic minority pupils from doing well.[272] The low expectations and sometimes even prejudice, apart from biased test results, have been named as the key factors in the wrongful assignment of pupils to appropriate classes. The existing research shows that Muslim pupils in Belgium are not only more commonly refereed to vocation training, but also that they are over-represented in special education schools created to provide education for pupils with a disability or severe learning and cognitive difficulties. The aforementioned EUMC report demonstrates that the problem of 'excessive' referral of children of immigrant origin to special education is particularly noticeable in the French community where the share of 'foreign pupils' is about 12 per cent in the primary and secondary schools and over 18 per cent in special education (2004: 28).

Yet another form of discrimination faced by Muslim pupils at school should be signalled here, and frequently mentioned by my interviewees, is the exclusion from schools for cultural reasons. I am thinking here in particular about the situations when the introduction of bans on headscarves in given schools (sometimes even in the middle of the school year) forced Muslim girls who wear them on a daily basis (and who do not want to take them off at school) to move to other educational institutions where hijabs are allowed.[273] This issue, which is a prime example of religious discrimination, extends also to other spheres of social life and in particular to the labour market, therefore it will be elaborated below in more detail.

Some of my interviewees also complained about the Eurocentrism of the school curricula, and in particular that they are silent about the great achievements of the Muslim civilization and its crucial influence, through Muslim Spain, on the European Renaissance. Majd, for instance, argued that *"We never study about Muslim civilisation. We never learn about the great Muslim inventors who have invented numerous things...*

---

[272] Here it has to be recalled that the educational underperformance of Muslim pupils is a result of many factors and not merely of institutional and non-institutional discrimination. Some of the key factors that influence it are: the socio-economic status of the parents, parental education and aspiration, the age of school entry and participation in pre-school programmes. What the Belgian authorities have been doing in order to tackle some of these issues may be discovered, for example, in Rea 2002 or Nicaise et al 2003.

[273] The schools that still allow Muslim girls to wear hijab (apart from Islamic schools) are usually the concentration schools of bad reputation.

We never learn that at certain time the world of Islam was so powerful that the West was afraid of it.", whereas Rashid pointed out that *"At school there was nothing about the importance of the Muslim civilization in the construction of European civilisation. Until today this legacy is silenced in the Belgian history books. I would have had smaller inferiority complex if this contribution acknowledged and was part of the history books."*

Before moving on to explore another sector in which many of my interviewees saw their citizenship rights as not being fully respected, namely the economy, it is worth pointing out the specific context of education system in Brussels and its direct link with labour market. The francophone schools in Brussels most commonly attended by Muslim pupils have clearly favoured a 'uniform' system of education, in accordance with France's Third Republic, discrediting social and cultural differences and not paying too much attention to pupils' knowledge of Dutch language (Raedt 2004: 22). One of the major reasons for this has been ongoing struggle for power between the francophones and the Flemings and the fears of the former about the 'cultural expansionism' of the latter[274]. Knowledge of Dutch, however, in Brussels is often essential. Applicants seeking non-menial jobs in this bilingual city are usually required to be fluent in the two main official languages, whereas fluency in English comes often as a third condition. The francophone schools have been severely failing Muslim, as well as other children, by not preparing them sufficiently enough from the linguistic point of view, for the future professional life in the officially bilingual city. In general the educational system has reproduced the structure of social inequalities and contributed significantly to exclusion from within (Fr. L'exclusion de l'intérieur - Bourdieu and Champagne 1993).

4.4.4 CONTESTED EQUALITY OF RIGHTS IN ACCESS TO EMPLOYMENT

The labour market was one of the major areas in which my interviewees felt 'second class citizens' and in which they felt that their rights to equal opportunities and fair treatment seriously lacked content. The vast majority of my interviewees shared the view of Rashid, quoted at the beginning of this section, that *"Discrimination starts at school,*

---

[274] According to some francophone inhabitants of Brussels, the Flemish community has created bilingual schools in the city not so much in order to give immigrant children a Flemish cultural base, but in order to turn them into the future constituents of the Flemish political parties (Raedt 2004: 22). Here it is worth noting that the other side is also accusing the francophone of cultural expansionism inter alia by francophonisation of traditionally Flemish areas neighbouring Brussels.

then goes to the job market (...)" and argued that the moment when they are most harshly made aware of the fact that the possession of the Belgian passport does not guarantee equality is when they want to enter labour market and start to apply for jobs. As one of my interviewees pointed out *"In the light of the law every citizen is equal, however, if someone goes to the job interview he/she may find that it is not necessarily the case."* (Abida) The same problem was also invoked by Majd who stated that *"We as Arabs, as on one singer sings, we are given jobs as long as the employer doesn't see our face. When only a candidate shows up for the interview he/she is immediately dismissed. This is a real discrimination and racism."* Yet another interviewee argued that because of the existence of the discriminatory practices *"Many Muslim men and particularly Muslim women do not even have the possibility to go to a job interview."* (Murad) Furthermore, the young Muslim Brusselers made a distinction between racial discrimination in the labour market, which in their view mostly affects Muslim men, and religious discrimination which most frequently affects women.

While a few of my interviewees felt disempowered by the discrimination in the labour market and preferred, for example, to take employment with a lower salary and job security in order to avoid discriminatory treatment, most of them declared themselves to be unafraid of discrimination. Some of them were also involved in various activities aiming at combating the phenomenon of the differentiated treatment of individuals on the labour market on the basis of their (real or perceived) racial, ethnic, religious, gender and other differences. One of them was Rashid who stated that *"I am member of the youth branch of the CSC (Confédération des Syndicats Chrétiens - KP) where I am part of the group that deals with the problems of discrimination at labour market. (...) It has been almost two year since we proposed to different political parties the idea of anonymous CV. Some people say that it doesn't solve the problem but puts if forward. I think differently. I believe it removes the first barrier, and gives the people who are dismissed instantly because of their Muslim names, at least a chance to have an experience of a job interview, so people can learn how to sell themselves. Now people do not even have this experience."* A similar view about this particular measure to fight discrimination was offered by another actively involved in anti-discrimination initiatives. Nabihah argued that *"there is not only religious discrimination but also gender, age, disability, etc. In most cases the applications of the 'not suitable candidates' are thrown into bin. The anonymous CV will allow these people at least to defend their letter of motivation and their CV."*

The opinions of my interviewees about the widespread discrimination of Muslims in the labour market confirm numerous sociological studies (e.g. Martens 1990, Beauchesne 1994, DWTC 1997, Arrijn et al. 1998, Martens et al. 2005) which were elaborated at length in the earlier chapter. One of the important findings of the recent large study into the phenomenon of discrimination of people of foreign origin on the labour market carried out by Martens et al. (2005) was that both male and female representatives of the ethnic minorities, both highly as well as poorly qualified, face unequal treatment in access to employment. At the same time, the researchers pointed out that it is the highly qualified women from the minority communities that are particularly frequently victims of discriminatory treatment (Ibid: 83).

From the point of view of this book it is important to ask why is it Muslim women face more discrimination in the labour market and - as my interviewees claimed - mainly of the religious type? I believe the answer to this question lies mainly in the attitudes of the Belgian society towards such a visible sign of adherence to Islam as hijab or Muslim headscarf. As one of my interviewees pointed out *"The issue of wearing hijab is significant one because it shows the uneasiness of the coexistence of the different points of view, cultures and civilisations. Unfortunately, there is an apprehension of Islam and Muslims in the society. Many people perceive a woman wearing hijab as an enslaved one and think that freeing her from her hijab would also give her more freedom. The best way to do it, they think, is to ban wearing hijab and in particular to ban it in schools."* (Jusuf) The apprehension of the visible sign of belonging to the Islamic community was already observed in European societies by researchers in the 1990s. At the end of the 1990s they coined the term hijabophobia in order to describe the antipathy towards headscarves for Muslim women to be found not only in the country with the largest Muslim population in the Western Europe (France) but also in other European countries (Glavanis 1999: 20). As I have shown in the earlier chapter one may observe in Belgium a growing 'public concern' about hijabs, or hijabophobia which results inter alia in the increasing number of schools that are introducing bans on 'all religious signs'- but in practice - on hijabs. This growing antipathy towards Islamic veils, especially in the francophone Belgium, has been significantly influenced by the French debates on hijab[275]. Many of my interviewees pointed out that especially in this case, one may see a fulfilment of the popular saying that holds that 'When it rains in France, it drizzles in Belgium.'[276] The calls of some of the Belgian politicians[277] to follow the example of France in its treatment of hijab in schools clearly substantiate this observation.

The findings of the recent research into the social representations of hijab amongst the Belgian society (Saroglou 2007), elaborated in the earlier chapter, confirmed earlier studies arguing that we have in many European countries (including Belgium) *"a broad misunderstanding of headscarves and their symbolic nature'* (Glavanis 1999: 20). They also confirmed the observations of my interviewees about the predominantly negative perceptions of hijab in the society and, stemming from them, a certain intolerance towards women wearing Islamic veils.

The negative effects of the hijabophobia in Brussels are particularly visible on the local labour market. Many of my female interviewees spoke at length about the discriminatory treatment which they had experienced while applying for jobs because they wore hijabs. One of them was, for instance, Madiha who said that *"It has been a year and a half that I have been searching for work, and each time when I am invited for the interview I am asked if I am going to continue to wear my veil."* She does not want to remove the veil because she believes that working with children in the crèche (posts for which she applies) does not require it, and thus she keeps looking for a full-time employment where she would be allowed to wear it. Another interviewee who encountered this specific type of discrimination while trying to find a job that would be in line with her professional and academic profile was Hafa. She asserted that *"I was several times told that I suited perfectly to the vacancy but in order to get it I had to*

---

[275] I am thinking here in particular about the introduction of the general ban on the conspicuous religious symbols in French schools (from September 2004), which was one of the recommendations of the Stasi report, that is a report drafted by the special investigative committee headed by Bernard Stasi, then ombudsman of France (*médiateur de la République*) which examined how the principle of *laïcité* should apply in practice.

[276] Probably it would be more appropriate to say that 'when in rains in France then it drizzles in Wallonia and Brussels'.

[277] I think in particular about the opinions of the senators Anne-Marie Lizin (PS), Alain Destexhe (MR) and the Interior Minister Patrick Dewael (VLD) in favour of the general ban on hijabs expressed in Belgian press in January 2004.

remove my hijab. These were the vacancies in my domain, namely psychology. And I refused (to remove hijab - KP), because I need to work with my hijab. It is just me, they have to accept it. This was for the position of therapist at the CPAS (Centre Public Aid Sociale) and in the NPO (Non-Profit Organisation - Fr. ASBL - Association Sans But Lucratif - KP) in the central district of the town. These were the two cases when I was told openly during the job interview that this is an obstacle in my recruitment."

One may successfully apply to the cases of my female interviewees and other young Muslim women intending to find employment with their hijabs in Brussels the hypothesis formulated by Fabienne Brion and Ural Manço in 1998. They pointed out that "the more strongly one's Muslim identity is proclaimed, the greater the exclusion from the labour market" (Brion & Manço 1998). This hypothesis is also confirmed in the findings of the research into the situation of the Muslim women wearing hijab on the local labour market carried out by Nadia Ben Mohammed. The researcher of the Free University of Brussels found inter alia that the negative perception of hijabs (and Islam in general) among the employers, both in the public, as well as, in the private sector, contributed to the delegitimization of Muslim women's choices to wear the hijab and meant in practical terms the exclusion of the women wearing Islamic veils from certain posts. Moreover, she observed that while the employers of the public sector usually invoked the principle of neutrality and respect of other religious convictions in the public sphere in their discriminatory treatment of women wearing hijabs, the employers in the private sector invoked the rule of profitability, which implies undertaking actions that would please their clients (Ben Mohammed 2001: 6). The end result of the antipathy towards Islamic veils amongst employers in both the public and private sector is the exclusion of Muslim women wearing them from the labour market. Ben Mohammed aptly points out also that, apart from the de facto exclusion of Muslim women in hijabs from the labour market (by employers), one may observe also their self-exclusion by the Muslim women themselves. The second type of exclusion functions in line with the mechanism described by Leon Festinger in his theory of cognitive dissonance (1957). Muslim women wearing hijabs, envisaging the future rejection of the employers to offer them an employment and thus being confronted with failure and uncomfortable tension (cognitive dissonance), prefer not to apply for jobs or at least for certain kinds of jobs.

247

(Ben Mohammed 2001: 9) In many individual cases one may actually observe the combination of the two exclusions. This is true, for example, in the aforementioned case of Hafa, who was told openly two times during the job interview that either she could either remove her hijab or she would not be employed. She said that *"I have been faced so many times with this question of hijab while searching for job in my field that I have decided to stop applying for these kind of jobs. I am thinking rather about continuing my studies and becoming more independent and not being obliged to explain my boss why I am wearing hijab. This is one of my projects - to work as an independent therapist."* In her case, self-exclusion (the decision to not apply for jobs that fit her current professional profile) is supposed to only have a temporary character, however in many other cases of women interviewed by Nadia Ben Mohammed it has more a permanent character and manifests itself, inter alia in resignation, lack of professional ambitions and low self-esteem. (Ibid: 7)

Although the researcher of the ULB focused mainly on the discrimination of Muslim women on the labour market as a result of widespread antipathy towards Muslim headscarves in her study, she did not oversee also other potential sources of their unequal treatment. She did so, in particular, by pointing out that women wearing Islamic veils are triply vulnerable in the context of the Belgian labour market: firstly, as persons of immigrant origin; secondly, as women; and thirdly as Muslims (Ibid: 3). In the wider context of Belgian society, one of my interviewees claimed that Muslim women are doubly discriminated; within their own ethnic communities, where they try to challenge the traditional male domination and within wider society, where apart from patriarchy they also have to face xenophobia and Islamophobia (Maysan).

4.4.5 CONTESTED EQUALITY OF RIGHTS IN CRIMINAL JUSTICE, HOUSING AND SOCIALISING

Apart from facing unequal treatment in the sphere of education and access to employment, some of the members of the emerging new Muslim elite also claimed that they did not feel they were considered full citizens of Belgium when they observed how other Muslims, or people of foreign origin in general, are treated in the criminal justice system. Many of my interviewees were very critical about the portrayal of youths of foreign origin by the media and opinion leaders as potentially criminal elements. Some of them argued that this portrayal played a significant role in the process by which certain behaviour patterns of the youth and their members are transformed respectively into crime and criminals. One of my interviewees Murad, for example, deplored *"the criminalization of the youth of foreign origin by the Minister of Justice"* in the years of 1999-2003 (Marc Verwilghen) who commissioned a report aimed at finding out whether youths with immigrant background are more delinquent than the autochthonous youth.[278] According to Murad, *"one may easily compare the Minister's initiative with the vision of Adolf Hitler who tried and managed to convince people that having Roma or Jewish origin is conducive to crime"*. In his view, one should rather pose the question about the 'overcriminalization' of the youth of foreign origin, rather than about its 'overcriminality'. The same concerns, although on a different level, were also brought up by Faisal, who argued that *"Muslim citizens are bounded by the same law, but how this low is being interpreted and how the human factor is being involved in it, is another thing. One may just look into the statistics to see that when the court announces a verdict all kinds of 'face features offences' (Fr. délits de faciès) are involved in it. The judges are, for example, much more severe with regards to certain profiles of people rather than to others. The law is the same for all, but its application varies"*.

Similarly to the aforementioned issues raised by my interviewees, that is unequal treatment in access to education and employment, also in this field existing research substantiates their claims. The study by De Valkeneer demonstrates, for example, that the practice of racial and ethnic profiling is widely used by police in Brussels. It establishes that persons of foreign origin (especially young people) are stopped and questioned by the police much more often than the autochthon Belgians, even when there are no clear grounds for doing so (e.g. a crime has been committed in the vicinity or a general spot check of identity cards) (De Valkeneer quoted in Rea 2002). Another researcher argues that the police in its proactive work is much more preoccupied with surveying people identified as potential delinquents and verifying if they are not wanted, than with questioning persons actually committing offences (Francis 2000).

Persons of a foreign origin are not only overrepresented in the prison population, as I already demonstrated in the third chapter, but they are also overrepresented amongst

---

[278] More information about this highly controversial initiative one may find for example in Brion et al. 2000

the people kept in custody, especially in relation to drug cases. The study of De Pauw, shows that if persons of Moroccan origin and autochthonous Belgians are involved in similar drug cases, 62.9 per cent of people from the former group and only 42.9 per cent from the latter are placed in custody. This difference is especially high for those between 20 to 24 years of age. (De Pauw quoted in Rea 2002) At the same time, people of foreign origin are less likely to benefit from alternative measures to detention. Probably most importantly, the existing research shows that the prison sentences of the people of immigrant origin for such offences, as for example, theft, fraud or breaking the law on drugs, are twice as long as the sentences of autochthonous Belgians. (Brion 2000: 225-227) Thus, without denying the offences committed by the youth of foreign origin, numerous studies confirm their unequal treatment at all stages of the criminal justice system, from the moment of questioning by the police till the announcement of the verdict.

The two last, but by no means least areas in which some of my interviewees saw their citizenship rights as not being fully respected, were housing and socialising. One of the persons who invoked the discrimination of Muslims in access to housing was Khalil. He stated that "*if you have an Arab head, I tell you, it is ten times more difficult to find an apartment in Brussels.*" Although he might have somewhat exaggerated the scale of the phenomenon it is definitely present. In the following account the same interviewee demonstrates one of the ways in which it manifests itself: "*A friend of mine was looking for an apartment with his wife and fixed an appointment with the landlady to see one. When they came, the landlady opened the door and started to shout 'oh my God!!!' - she was that afraid of seeing him and his wife in hijab in front of her door. They had to go away without seeing the apartment.*" (Khalil) The EUMC report on migrants, minorities and housing (2005), as well as many other Belgian studies, confirm the existence of the discriminatory treatment of persons of immigrant origin on the housing market. From 4 to 5 per cent of complaints about discrimination addressed to the Centre for Equal Opportunities and Fight against Racism (CEOFR), between the years 1997 and 2002 were about discrimination in the field of housing. These complaints were mostly from people of Moroccan and Turkish origin. A limited discrimination test carried out by

250

CEOFR in collaboration with ALARM[279] found that 58 per cent of callers with a 'foreign sounding name' or foreign accent were told that the property was not available (EUMC 2006: 55).

Finally, the discrimination in socializing was mainly invoked by my male informants who had more freedom to participate in the socializing activities of wider society. They spoke about their deep disappointment when they learnt that the negative freedom opened for them the possibilities of taking part in the social life of the host society was restrained by the lack of positive liberty or possibilities; in this case, places where they could actually make use of their negative liberty. This element may be noticed for instance in the following account of Murad: *"When I was young I couldn't go to a discotheque. Each time when I wanted to go out on Saturday or Sunday, whether it was here or in Flanders, I was denied. At the beginning you learn that you are not welcome and then you don't go there any more and spend the evening in the quartier. (...) I was denied the right to enter the clubs either because 'it was a private club', and it was really funny to see the selection that the bouncers made, or simply, I was told to' get lost'. (...) One day there were three of us. I was about 23 years old. One friend of mine was of Turkish origin but with white complexion, and the other was of Austrian origin, We decided to go to a club in the centre of Brussels. The first friend entered without problems, as well as the second. When I opened the door the bouncer said that 'In this place people can only enter in pairs and not in triples'. My friends went furious. Not me. I was used to it."*

4.4.6 CONTESTED EQUALITY OF THE TREATMENT OF ISLAM

The members of the rising new Muslim elite in Brussels claimed that their citizenship rights missed some content not only because of the existence of widespread unequal treatment of Muslims in education, employment, criminal justice and other areas but also because of the unfair treatment – in their opinion - of their religion, which since 1974 has been officially one of the religions of Belgian citizens. As I have argued in the earlier chapter, in spite of the fact that Islam was recognized by the state more than thirty years

---

[279] Action pour logement accessible aux réfugiés à Molenbeek (Action for accessible housing for refugees in Molenbeek).

ago, it has still not fully benefited from its status of a recognized faith. This situation led many of my interviewees to feel as second-class citizens whose rights are not being taken seriously into account. They argued similarly to Masud that *"there hasn't been equality among the recognized faiths"*.

One of the major areas in which they saw the differences between the treatment of Islam and other religions recognized by the State was a right for subsidies from local authorities to cover the cost of construction, maintenance and renovation of the places of worship. Rashid, for instance, pointed out that *"although Islam was recognized in 1974, nothing changed. It means that it still the believers themselves who have to set up a place to do the prayers. Almost all the mosques in Brussels are the product of the goodwill of believers. It is them who gave the money to construct mosques. Belgian state is neutral vis-à-vis religious matters, but it is supposed to finance the places of worship of recognized faiths and the Muslim places of worship are not financed."* Another interviewee who also brought this issue up was Khalil. He stated that *"it is the believers who finance the mosques. This happens in the situation when normally Belgian state gives us the right to have a subsidy. This is the way how Belgian system is organized. Now the reality is that there is no state founding and mosques sometimes get into debt. I don't find this normal. We often have to pray in the mosques that are far from being mosques... in the adopted warehouses, basements, etc. I personally don't find them worthy of Islam".* As I have mentioned in the earlier chapter it is only now, as I write, that the local governments have been taking the first steps in order to financially support mosques. While the Wallonian government recognised the first 43 mosques (on June 18th 2007) roughly on the same basis as other places of worship, the integration minister of the Flemish region indicated in January 2005 that mosques will be required to meet special conditions that do not apply to other religious communities, in order to be approved for public founding, such as using the Dutch language except for when reciting the sacred scriptures and showing tolerance for women and homosexuals (HRWF 2005).[280] In Brussels the first five mosques were officially recognized on the 13th December 2007.[281]

---

[280] The first six mosques were officially recognized in Flanders on 22nd December 2007. From that moment they receive state subsidies and their imams get their wages from state funds. However they only qualify if

While mentioning the issue of lack of support for mosques my interviewees also invoked the subject of funding for imams. The state, by law, remunerates the salaries of clergy who are employed by recognized religious communities. However, to the disappointment of many of my interviewees, the salaries of imams have so far not been covered. Similarly to the issue of recognition of mosques this situation is also in the process of changing. Already, at the end of 2004, the federal parliament approved funding of close to 5 million Euros to cover the salaries of imams working in about 100 mosques (Expatica 2004). These funds are supposed to be allocated to the mosques approved by the regional authorities, which are in charge of the control of places of worship.

The members of the emerging new Muslim elite also pointed out at the lack of equal treatment of Islam in the country's burial policy. Rashid, for instance argued *"All the faith groups have their own burial sections, so Muslims born in Belgium should also be given their sections at the cemeteries."* Until recently, it was generally not an issue, because most deceased Muslims were transported back to their countries of origin for burial, but this situation has been changing with younger generations of Muslims. The designation of Muslim sections at the cemeteries, similarly to construction of purpose-built mosques, had for my interviewees not only a practical importance but also a symbolic one. These sections, to some extent even more than mosques, are strong signs of the Muslim presence on Belgium's territory. That is also one of the major reasons for which the request of their creation has aroused a great deal of opposition not only in Belgium but also in other European countries (see Allievi 2003b: 356-358).

Among other issues that were mentioned by my interviewees less frequently in the context of unequal treatment of Islam as a recognized faith, were inter alia the right to have state-paid chaplains in prisons and hospitals, the right to their own programmes on TV and radio and provision for halal food in schools. In general the position of most of them on these issues was similar to that of Rashid who pointed out that *"Although recognition of the faith at the general level was very good, at the practical level there*

they can show that they are 'integrated' and can speak Dutch fluently. The names and addresses of the recognized mosques can be found on the following website of the EMB.
[281] The names and addresses of the recognized mosques can be found on the following website of the EMB.

have been yet a lot of inequalities in comparison with other faith groups. When we will have the same rights as other faith groups then it will be good."

The second crucial part of the complaints about the unfair treatment of Islam as a recognized religion related to the creation and functioning of the Executive of Muslims of Belgium (EMB) or the official interlocutor of the authorities on issues related to the practice of Islam in Belgium. Many of my informants expressed resentment that the government has unduly sought to influence the composition of the Muslim Executive by screening the candidates endorsed by the Muslim Constituent Assembly by the Belgian State Security Services before approving them. One may see the elements of this resentment, for instance, in the following statement by Jusuf *"Religion of Islam is the only faith community, which goes through the process of elections. The problem is not the fact that there are elections, but the interference of the state in this process and in the internal affairs of the religion. Here, I see a clear example of unequal treatment with regards to Islam (...) It would be much better if the state allowed the community to organize itself with all its tendencies - secular, orthodox, and progressive - and to chose itself the representatives. Instead the state took precautions against 'religious fundamentalists' and produced a law of screening, which targets directly Muslims... and this is something I cannot agree with. Recognising and financing religions is good, because in reality it is the citizens who finance religions by paying taxes, but to interfere in the internal affairs of the religions is unconstitutional and unacceptable."* Another informant who was very critical about the state involvement in the shaping of the composition of the Muslim representative body was Khalil. He argued that *"Muslim representation is an object of differentiated treatment. The state demands Muslims elected to the EMB to go through the screening and then it attaches to certain individuals who do not pass through it the label of fundamentalists. But it doesn't define what it means by this term. What shocks me is that sometimes people who are known in the community for their discourse of openness are named fundamentalists. This is truly sad... And then what criteria are used to exclude them* (from the EMB- KP)? *... What type of Muslims we want (in the EMB- KP)? For me a fundamentalist it is someone who does not accept the diversity of views and wants to impose his/her vision of things on everybody. You can find fundamentalists not only amongst Muslims, but also, for example, amongst*

254

the secularists who want to impose their own way of thinking about others. It is also fundamentalism." Yet another interviewee was asking why the numerous conditions imposed on Muslim representative body are not applicable to other religious communities. Hadijah argued that there are also many people who have radical ideas in other religious communities. *"Is the Belgian state going to request from the Catholics or Jews to exclude such persons from their representative bodies? Obviously not."* – she asserted

It was clear for my informants that the government has interfered in the composition of the Muslim Executive because it feared that Muslims with radical views may gain influence in it. The government's views in this matter were partially influenced by such events as, for example, terrorist attacks committed in the name of Islam (e.g. 9/11) and by the information provided by Belgian Intelligence. In its 2001 report the Belgian Permanent Committee of the Control of Intelligence Services (known as 'Comité R') claimed, for example, that the Muslim Executive and other Muslim organizations have links with 'foreign extremist movements' (Report quoted in Nyman 2005). The fact that this report was heavily criticized for its poor methodology and lack of objectivity by researchers in the field (Dassetto and Maréchal 2002) had apparently very little impact on its reception. As a result the direct involvement of the state in the shaping the composition of the EMB its relations with Muslim Executive have been strained ever since the institution was created.

Finally, my interviewees also invoked the differentiated treatment of Islam in comparison with other recognized religions while referring to the more recent episode of the deterioration of relations between the government and the Muslim Executive, which started with the introduction of the law in July 2004 stating the necessity for organising new elections within the Muslim population to fully renew the membership of the Muslim Constituent Assembly and its Executive. This imposition of new elections on the Muslim community, in spite of the earlier agreement that the EMB's mandate would terminate at the end of 2008, was perceived by some of my interviewees as yet another example of direct interference of the state in the religious affairs, or as Felice Dassetto called it, the 'turcification of Islam' (Dassetto 1997). This was also one of the reasons why elections organized in March 2005 for the renewal of the EMB were largely boycotted by the Moroccan population of Belgium.[282]

4.4.7 KEY DEMANDS – ACCULTURATIVE OR DISSOCIATIVE ?

In the second chapter I have argued that one may divide the demands made by Muslims in Europe into two categories: claims which call for parity of rights or equality with other faith groups who have been granted special treatment in the past, and claims which call for rights that are not in the possession of other religious groups in the country. The first type of claims I have called after Statham et al. (2005) acculturative demands, since they are formulated within the frame of the state's ways of managing cultural diversity, whereas the second type of claims I have called dissociative demands, since if realized they set the specific group apart from all other groups.

Having applied the aforementioned conceptual grid to the claims made by the interviewed members of the new Muslim elite emerging in Brussels, one may see that almost all of their demands are of the first type, namely acculturative ones. In other words, while demanding from the state, for example, not to intervene directly in the internal affairs of the religious community, to the pay salaries of imams and provide financial support to mosques, they do not ask for some special treatment for Muslims which will disassociate them from other groups, but for the egalitarian treatment. The key demands which they formulate are calls for parity and not for some special rights. This idea was probably most clearly captured by Rashid who said that *"What we demand is to apply the acquis of the other faith groups also to us. Nothing more, but also nothing less."* In fact, my research shows that in some cases they do ask even for less than they are entitled to. In other words, they do not necessarily want the full application of the benefits of other religious communities to themselves. This one may see particularly clearly with regards to the issue of Muslim schools.

Muslims, similarly to other recognized religious communities, have the right to establish private schools that are eligible for state funding.[283] So far, there has been only

---

[282] For more information about the EMB and the last election see, for instance, http://www.suffrage-universel.be/be/beminu.htm, http://www.vigilancemusulmane.be/ , or http://www.embnet.be

one Muslim primary school in Brussels that receives state-funding. The school al-Ghazali was opened in September 1989, following the two Brussels communes' refusal to arrange for a course on Islam in their public primary schools (Shadid & van Koningsveld, 1995: 123). When asked about their views on the Muslim schools, the vast majority of my interviewees were not enthusiastic about the idea of the creation of more Islamic schools. At the same time, the interviewees who were for the creation of such schools provided only negative reasons for their establishment such as the bad reputation of the state schools frequented by Muslim children and the exclusion of girls wearing hijabs. The first issue was brought up by Masud who said "*I am for the Muslim schools, because we are going anyway to ghettoized schools*", whereas the second one by Jusuf who argued that "*The reality pushes certain parents to send their daughters to Islamic schools because they wear hijabs. There are more and more Muslims who think about sending their kids to Islamic schools. If the schools have a pluralist profile, this might be a good idea ...*".

The predominant reasons for which my interviewees were against the creation of more Muslim schools in Belgium was the fear that such schools may only further marginalize Muslims in society and set them aside from the wider society. The gist of this fear can be discerned, for instance, in the following assertion of Falak: "*Personally I am against Muslim schools, even though in Belgium every religious community can set up its schools, so there are Jewish, Catholic and other religious schools. I am against such schools because I am for the ethnically and religiously-diverse schools. Someone who goes to the Muslim primary school will find himself/herself completely lost among the non-Muslims in the secondary school. So it would be counterproductive to open such schools. A school is supposed to prepare people to live in a diverse society. It is only a diversified school that can achieve that.*" One of my male informants who shared many points with Falak in this matter was Kemal who said "*I am against religious schools. I think it is important to grow up with others different than us. I, for example, grew up with Andre, Jacqueline... and thus we have this psychology of diversity. But If we grow up only among other Mohammads and Fadilas, and yet if the professors come from abroad,*

---

[283] Information about the Jewish, Catholic, Protestant and other religious schools of the recognized faith communities can be fund, for example, in *Agenda Interculturel* no. 238 (2005)

it is going to end up with disaster. I know some young people who use to go to the Muslim primary school situated in the Islamic Centre. When I talk to them I notice that they are not self-critical and a little bit out of touch with reality. For them, for example, when a boy kisses a girl at the corner of the street it is shocking. For me it is not shocking. They do whatever they want. It is their choice. "

In general the negative views of most of my informants about Muslim schools were coherent with their criticism of the concentration schools which many of them attended. They opposed the idea of creation of Muslim schools, perceiving them as only a deterioration of the marginalization of Muslim children symbolized by the concentration schools. This one may see for instance in the following statement by Majd *"I am against these kinds of schools. In my opinion the way forward is not by setting up Muslim schools but by improving the existing schools, their staff, equipment and by having more diversity at school. On the whole there is very little mixing at school. Most of the Muslims live in the centre of Brussels and in other areas there are very few of them."* Their opinions on this issue also showed that they have a very strong attachment to the cultural diversity in which they live on the daily bases. One of my interviewees argued, for instance, that *"I wouldn't like my daughter to go to the Islamic school. School is like a small society. I would like her to profit from the diversity of the society in which she is leaving. If I wanted to send her to a Muslim school I would move to Iran or Saudi Arabia."* (Maysan) At the same time even those members of the Muslim elite who were very strongly opposed the idea of creation of more Muslim schools defended the right of the existing schools to receive state funding.

To sum up, I think the members of the rising new Muslim elite are not asking for all the elements of acquis of other religious groups, because they above all want to participate in the sameness, hoping that with time they will be able to find more room for themselves in the Belgian conception of 'us' and redefine it from within. Such a new, more flexible and open conception of 'us', which will allow Muslims to more easily assert some elements of difference is inter alia thanks to their efforts *in status nascendi.* However, taking into account only the complexity of the country, achieving it in some concrete form will probably take yet some time.

4.5 ISLAM AND CITIZENSHIP OBLIGATIONS

In the last section of this chapter I intend to continue to shed light on the normative dimension of lived citizenship of the young Muslim Brusselers, but this time I shall look into their perceptions of citizenship obligations. This dimension of citizenship, as I have argued in the second chapter, was particularly weakly developed in the theory of citizenship by T.H. Marshal, who referred to it is as 'a Dunkirk spirit that cannot be a permanent feature of any civilization' (1992: 46), and strongly emphasized especially by the civic republican writers[284] (e.g. Oldfield 1990, Habermas 1998). The latter writers stressed the importance of the duties of citizenship inter alia in the maintenance of social order and social cohesion by developing various models of a 'good citizenship', which enumerate the features of a 'good citizen'. Although usually less elaborate, such models of a good citizenship were also held by most members of politically organized communities, including my interviewees. In what follows, I am going to inter alia concentrate on the members' of the new Muslim elite in Brussels understandings of what it means to be a good citizen. Before I elaborate on the features of a good and bad citizen as viewed by my informants, I shall first assess their subjective notions of citizenship obligations and their views on the relations between the obligations of the citizenship and the demands of faith.

4.5.1 BANAL DEFINITIONS OF CITIZENSHIP OBLIGATIONS

In a manner similar to the subjective notions of citizenship rights, the banal definition of citizenship obligations of my interviewees were fairly sophisticated and pointed out at the complexity of the individual and collective responsibilities resulting from the membership in the political community. Moreover, for the young Muslims interviewed the obligations of the citizenship were natural consequence of possessing citizenship rights.

---

[284] Here, however, it has to be stressed that the civic republican writers do not have a monopoly on this subject. One of the models to which I am going to refer in the later part of this section and which I mentioned in the theoretical chapter was defined by the liberal thinker William Galston (1991).

Amongst the most commonly stressed elements of the obligations of a citizen by my interviewees was a duty to fight with all forms of injustice and discrimination. Maysan, for instance, said that *"The most important obligation is to denounce all forms of discrimination... To fight, to be to be recognized as a full citizen and not a citizen of second zone."* The same point was made also by Murad when he argued that *"The workers in the 19ᵗʰ century needed to fight for their rights, although they were indigenous Belgians and Christians. Our societies are constructed in such a way that marginalized groups will always need to fight for their rights. The workers had to fight for decades to achieve the minimum. Now Muslims in Brussels who have been living here since 1964 have to also fight to acquire the same rights. Even if the situation is different I think one can make such comparisons. The duty is still the same - to get involved and to fight against the injustices and discrimination."* Clearly, this understanding of the obligations of the citizenship of my interviewees is directly linked with their lived citizenship and in particular with their individual experiences of unequal treatment analyzed above against the background of the sociological research on these issues. It subscribes also very strongly to the notion of 'social jihad', whose promoter, Tariq Ramadan, defines it as mobilizing all human forces and directing all efforts in order to overcome such adversities as social injustices, poverty, illiteracy, delinquency or exclusion (Ramadan 2001: 66-69). This notion of jihad, which will be elaborated in more detail in concluding chapter, fits within the wider concept of greater jihad, which means the 'struggle to improve one's self and/or society', as opposed to the narrower, but much more widely popularized notion of lesser jihad, which refers to fighting with the enemies of Islam through the external and usually physical effort (Halliday 1995, Esposito 2002).

While the struggle against discrimination and social exclusion as one of the key obligations of a citizen should be carried out, according to my interviewees, mainly in the localities, they do not forget about the wider contexts in which these phenomena exist. The emphasis on this wider context, which is also a clear example of the transgression of religious and ethnic loyalties beyond the national boundaries, one may see for instance in the following statement by Khalil. *"We know how catastrophic the conditions in which live Palestinian people are. We see the abuses of the basic rights of this population by the Israeli government. These kinds of injustices also need to be denounced and it is not only the Muslims that have to do it."* At the same time another interviewee argued that while fighting for justice one needs to stay impartial as far as it possible. He asserted that *"... if a Jew is attacked, Muslims have to fight with the injustice done to him as if he was a Muslim. Unfortunately everyone in their communities makes a distinction; the Jews speak for the Jews, Muslims for the Muslims, etc. I find this sad."* (Murad)

Another obligation of a citizen that was mentioned by several of my interviewees was a duty to respect others and to live in harmony with everyone. In the background of their definitions of this obligation, as something taken for granted, was often a respect of the existing legal framework. These features one may find for instance in the definition of citizenship obligation of Abida, who said that *'There are many obligations but probably the most important one is, to do everything what one can, in order to live with others in peace... Generally one needs to always remember about others and that one's freedoms end, where the freedoms of the other start."* Or in the following definition of citizen's obligation of Naima *"My obligation as a citizen, is to live with others in mutual respect. However, I stress, it has to be a process in two directions. If I respect others, the others have to also respect me."* One of my informants went even further and claimed that a key obligation of a citizen is *'to do everything in order to improve intercommunity relations in Belgium."* (Majd)

As could be expected from a group of people who are actively involved in different initiatives of the Muslim and wider civil society, another important obligation of citizenship frequently mentioned by my informants was a duty to take an active part not only in the political processes, but also in the major social debates. As I have mentioned earlier, the obligatory voting functions in Belgium (just like in such countries as, for instance, Luxemburg, Greece and Cyprus) should not be generally treated as a civic obligation (because it is imposed by the state[285]), but rather as a civil obligation.[286] However, as Morris Janowitz rightly points out *"A compulsory act does not have to be performed mechanically and without critical concern for its justice and relevance. In fact, because it is compulsory, the citizen has a special obligation to be concerned about its social and political content and consequence."* (1980: 5) The point made by Janowitz,

---

[285] People who abstain from voting can be sanctioned with a fine and recidivists may be subject to disenfranchising.
[286] For elaboration of the difference between the two see chapter two.

who tries to rescue the elements of scholarship of Marshall dealing with citizens obligations, support the findings of my research, which indicate an appreciation of the fact that voting is obligatory amongst my Belgian interviewees and their understanding of voting in much wider sense, than merely casting a ballot. Most of my interviewees who referred to voting as an important citizenship obligation also spoke about numerous other steps (such as studying the programmes of the political parties, profiles of the candidates, their stand on different issues) before going to the polling station or posting a vote.

Apart from being involved in the political processes one needs to, according to for example Falak, try to take some interest in the wider social debates and if possible join them. She pointed out that citizenship obligations include *"Certain political participation, as well as, participation in the social fora and public debates."* For Nabihah and some other interviewees, the citizenship obligation of active participation in the life of the society rather meant involvement in the projects of the civil society aiming the whole society. She argued that *"An obligation of citizen is to be useful. We have not received all this richness in the form of education to waste it. Our work should profit not only Muslims but also others."* One of the specific uses of the knowledge of the Belgian society possessed by the members of the rising new Muslim elite that another interviewee saw was its transmission to those who are lacking it. Murad argued that *"all those Muslims who think that they have fewer rights than others should learn to fight for these rights with the arms of democracy, with words spoken and written.(...) We have a very good democratic system, even if it is not perfect. It gives people the means to express themselves. Unfortunately many young people do not know what is democracy, don't know how it works, and don't have the means to use it. That is why they go and burn cars.* (Referring to the riots in the French banlieues – KP) *We have to teach them to use the arms of democracy."*

Yet another obligation of a citizen, according to some of my interviewees, is to be loyal to one's country, which is some form of patriotism.[287] One of them, Amjad said, for instance, that *"It has become quite popular in recent years to suspect the loyalties of the Muslims living in the country. People often suggest that Muslims are claiming to be*

---

[287] By patriotism I mean here the loyalty to the state as different from the loyalty to the nation (nationalism). More on this distinction see Connor 2007.

attached to Belgium only now, when they are a minority, but when they become a majority they will stop doing so. For me this citizenship obligation is actually non-negotiable. If tomorrow a Muslim state attacks Belgium I am going to be in the first row fighting to defend it. Obviously it is quite abstract, but I feel very strongly about it". In indicating the importance of loyalty to one's country as one of the obligations of citizenship, my interviewees were consistent with the declared strong attachment to Belgium. This obligation on the more concrete level translated into a common concern amongst them about the fate of Belgium. They understood defence of the country in terms of maintaining its oneness and opposing efforts to further devolve the powers of the federal government[288]. They often repeated that they do not recognize themselves neither in the Walloon nor in the Flemish dimensions.

Finally, a minority of my interviewees perceived citizenship obligations as fulfilment of such civil duties imposed by the state as voting (in the case of Belgium), being in waged employment, paying taxes, sending children to school till certain age, and obeying the law and the Constitution. Some of the informants who viewed responsibilities of a citizen in such a way tried to give them a deeper meaning. One of them was Jusuf whose definition of obligations of citizenship included apart from the elements of the civil duties also reference to moral duties. He said that *"I think my most important obligation is to be an honest citizen, that means someone who cares about the future of this country, who goes to vote, who pays the taxes, respects the law... At the same time, it means to be someone who favours the good, justice and the truth. These are also my moral obligation that spring up from my spirituality."* It is this relationship between the obligations of citizenship and the demands of the faith that needs further elaboration and that will be discussed in more details below.

4.5.2 BETWEEN THE OBLIGATIONS OF CITIZENSHIP AND THE DEMANDS OF THE FAITH
As I have demonstrated in the second chapter, the relationships between citizenship and a religion may take radically different directions. On the one hand, religious beliefs and loyalties of citizens may be the basis for a state's unity, fundaments of its social cohesion

---

[288] These kind of reforms are actually one of the key elements of the political programme of the biggest party in the country - the winner of the elections in June 2007 - CDV-NVA.

and key factors behind a peaceful coexistence of its diverse communities. On the other hand, religions may build communal bonds that do not coincide with those linking the citizens of the given state and thus threaten the basis of its unity, deepen social divisions and in some cases even lead to outbursts of violence. One of the crucial factors determining which direction these relationships take, is one of the compatibility or incompatibility of the obligations of citizenship with the demands of the faith and vice versa. This is also a reason for which I have asked the members of the emerging new Muslim elite in Brussels about their perceptions of these relationships.

The vast majority of my interviewees believed that there are no incompatibilities between the demands of citizenship and those of Islam. They argued that the obligations of the faith and those of citizenship are either identical or complementary. Rashid, for example, claimed that *"There is no incompatibility between civic and religious duties. Many religious duties, such as for instance, trying to improve the society or respecting others, are also civic duties. My religion demands from me to be a value added to the society... to offer something to the society, something good, to improve its condition and the condition of its citizens. Not only Muslims but everyone. If a Jewish neighbour that I know isn't well I have to help him. He is my neighbour, he is a human being, he lives side by side with me, and therefore I have to help him. The same applies to the agnostics, atheists and others. There is no favouring. The Prophet of Islam, Peace Be Upon Him, said 'Help your brother in humanity - Muslim as well as non-Muslim - who is just or unjust'. And then his companions asked him, but how could we help someone who is unjust. And the Prophet said 'Make him to stop doing injustice. Help him to end his injustice'. So this pushes me to help everyone."* Thus, he linked civic duties with the universalistic massage of Islam. Another interviewee who played down the demands of Islam that may come into conflict with those of the citizenship was Jusuf. He said that *"I have been thinking about this question for many years and I have not found any incompatibilities between being a practising Muslim and being a Belgian citizen. It doesn't create any problems. On the contrary Islam always dictates the sense of the responsibility ... it expects from Muslims to accomplish their duties before claiming their rights."* Yet, later on he added *"There might be things that pose problem, but they just need to be properly discussed and almost always some practical solution can be found."*

Before I point out some of these 'problematic areas' noticed by other interviewees it is worth quoting the opinions of yet two more interviewees who defended the thesis about the complementary nature of Islamic and civic duties. One of them was Jannah who argued that *"It is my religion that tells me to go and vote, that orders me to respect other people and help them, that expects me to be just and honest in the professional work I do. But it is the citizenship that constitutes the context in which I can implement these things."* Another informant who saw the relationships between the religious and civic demands as complementary was Amjad. He claimed that citizenship is in need of the spiritual dimension because if it lacks this dimension it may degenerate. For instance, the civic obligation of being honest, in his opinion, if it is enforced by religious ethics, has more chance of remaining a meaningful obligation. He argued that, if there was more religious ethics in the local politics in Wallonia then the region could be spared from such financial and corruption scandals as those around racing track in Spa-Francorchamps[289] and the management of social housing in Charleroi[290].

Not all my interviewees believed, though, that civic and religious obligations always go hand in hand or that they always reinforce each other. One of the areas in which some of them saw them to be incompatible was the context in which the civic obligation to educate oneself was enforced, and more precisely the consequences of the bans on hijab introduced in the vast majority of francophone schools in recent years (De Meyer 2007). This issue was brought up inter alia by Sana who argued that *"From the Muslim point of view, I know that I can do what I want in the Belgian society, but from the citizenship point of view there are constraints. The citizenship demands from me not to follow all my religious precepts. In education, one needs to remove the veil in order to go to school, so Belgium does not take into account the beliefs and practices of members of the Muslim community."* In her view the demand of the faith requiring from a Muslim women to wear the headscarf[291] should not be contradicted by national legislation. The

---

[289] Despite the critical opinions of experts, the Walloon government signed an expensive contract aimed at keeping the Formula One Grand Prix in Francorchamps.

[290] The leading members of the Socialist Party in the city of Charleroi (including the Major of the city) were accused of corruption in the management of social housing company 'La Caroloregienne'.

[291] In fact, different Mazhabs (school of religious jurisprudence) interpret the Qur'anic instruction requiring from women to *'reveal of their beauty only what normally shows and draw their veils over their bosoms'* (Sura 24.30-31) in different ways. The Qur'an enjoins modesty in dress and behaviour for both women and men, but it does not require either to wear veils (Welch 1997: 199-200).

current situation according to her and some other interviewees may only result in the fact that Belgian Muslim women will feel less Belgian.

The second area, in which according to my interviewees one could observe a potential conflict between the obligation of the citizenship and the demands of the faith, is that of the economy. One of the key demands of citizenship in this domain is to possess a full-time employment. This obligation may be difficult to fulfil, according to some of my interviewees, if a certain believer wants to strictly obey the prayer requirements. One of these interviewees, Kemal, argued that *'By and large, there are no incompatibilities between the Islamic obligations and those of the citizenship, however it requires some adaptations. For example, we are supposed to pray 5 times a day. If at work I can't do it, I pray in the evening at home. It is not a problem for me. There are a lot of instances where we can adapt and not to touch the sensitivity of others. I don't mind that I can't pray at work. Anyway, I can see positive development in the place where I work. In the past, each year for New Year's Eve we were given as presents bottles of alcohol. For three years now we haven't received alcohol but other things.'* Yet another interviewee accounted for the potential conflict between the citizen's obligation to work and an Islamic requirement to go on pilgrimage or to perform *hajj*, at least once in your lifetime. He claimed that *"Generally there are no clashes* (between obligations of citizenship and those of the faith - KP), *however sometimes they may happen. For example, if I decide to go on the pilgrimage and leave my teaching obligations behind. Some Muslim teachers have the courage to say to their employers that they leave for hajj, others go on the basis of falsified medical tests. So they go to encounter God on the basis of the treason of their engagements as citizens. "* (Faisal) My interviewee disapproved of fulfilling the religious requirement in such a way that it is to the detriment of citizen obligations

4.5.3 IMAGE OF A GOOD CITIZEN

As suggested above, all people living in the politically organised communities possess more or less elaborate definitions of what it means to be a good citizen. In the last part of this chapter I intend to shed light on the young Muslim Belgians' conceptions of a good citizen. In order to provide as complete picture of their social representations of a good citizen as possible, I assessed these representations in a twofold manner. Firstly, by asking them directly about the features of a good and bad citizen and secondly (after the question about the features of a good and bad citizen was already answered), by presenting them with a list of 'the virtues of responsible citizenship' from the model of William Galston (1991), introduced in the chapter II, and asking them to choose the most important 'virtues' and explain their choice. That is also the order in which I intend to proceed in this section.

Having carefully analysed the images of a good citizen of my interviewees, I have found that one of their prevailing features was the emphasis on the respect for others. My interviewees claimed that this general obligation of citizenship is instrumental so as citizens of the given country could live together in harmony. For some it meant a largely passive obedience of the legal framework of the country by its citizens. This was for example the perception of Khalil who said that "*a good citizen it is someone who adheres totally to the Constitution and the legal framework of the country*" and to a smaller extent by Hafa who claimed that "*a good citizen it is someone who feels good in his skin and who is faithful to himself while at the same time obeying the rules of the country. It means to be clear with the state and with himself.*" For the majority, however, it assumed a more active form of respect and meant similarly to Nabihah and Malak "*to be on good terms with its environment, its neighbours, family, friends and colleagues.*" (Nabihah) or '*to be just with everyone and to be tolerant of Muslims as well as non-Muslims.*" (Malak). This active, and sometimes even militant, form of respect one may also see in the following definition of a good citizen by Maysan for whom it meant "*To above all respect the law of the country. But if the country's law is racist you need to fight to change it.*" By stressing the importance of a respect for others, my interviewees meant also recognition for themselves as citizens of the country. This mutual character of respect invoked by my interviewees one may see particularly clearly in the following statement by Naima: "*The most important thing really is to respect the other. If we respect the other, we can advance a lot. If we respect the other we will be more open to him/her and at least some of the prejudices will disappear.*" As one can see the 'respect for others' was in the statement of Naima phrased as 'respect for the other'.

The second prevailing feature of the social representations of a good citizen of my interviewees was their emphasis on the constructive elements of citizenship. Thus, their social representations were closely linked with the most popular model of citizenship amongst them, that is the socially constructive one, elaborated in the first section of this chapter. One may notice the stress on the constructive elements of citizenship, for example, in the following conception of a good citizen of Kemal who argued that *"It is someone who contributes to the society and is not only a consumer of the state services. It is someone who gives back to the country for the fact that it has provided him with education, job, etc. It is someone who acts."* In some definitions, as for instance the following one, this stress on the constructive character is mixed with the emphasis on the identification with the country: *"Good citizen it is someone who gets involved, and contributes to the country so as it could develop and s/he with it."* (Sana) In other conceptions of my interviewees it is the identification with the local level that is pointed out. One may see it in the assertion of Nabihah who argued that *"Good citizenship means also to care about your town, city borough. You should try to get involved on this level in the social as well as political sphere and express your opinion, your point of view. Not only when you are unhappy with certain things but also when you are happy with them."* Another interviewee stressed that the constructive engagement that characterises a good citizen requires the tools to participate. He argued that *"The good citizen who does not possess these tools should try to acquire them by studying, reading, and in general educating oneself, and only then claim things when they need to be claimed. One needs to claim them in a democratic way, intelligent way, not by burning cars or attacking someone violently."* (Murad) Yet another interviewee, in her definition of a good citizen, pointed out the problem of resources in constructive civic engagement. She said that *"I would like very much to have greater opportunity to influence the new laws, to pass my ideas, to be part of the political party. This is for me an ideal of a good accomplished and involved citizen. But for all this, one needs to have time."* (Lana) Finally, one interviewee who emphasised the constructivism of a good citizen argued that *"a person who gets involved in the society in the light of the values that drive him or her, must sometimes stand in opposition to its own religious and ethnic community in pursuit of his or her vision."* (Faisal)

Among other elements that made up part of the images of a good citizen of my informants the most frequently mentioned ones were honesty, helpfulness, love of justice, industriousness and being a goal-oriented.

Interestingly, a bad citizen in the eyes of my interviewees was not someone who breaks the law or does not obey the Constitution, but above all someone who stays indifferent and passive. In other words a bad citizen was defined almost wholly by the members of the new Muslim elite emerging in Brussels in terms of a failure to make a positive contribution to the society. Murad, for instance argued that *"The bad citizens are those who are not aware of what it means citizenship - who think that they are good citizens simply by casting their vote. Today this is not enough. It is necessary to participate slightly more, simply because you are in a democratic space that gives you an opportunity to do so. You should take advantage of the fact that you are part of the 20 per cent of the world population who has a possibility to claim things democratically."* In many ways similar argumentation used Rashid who said *"A bad citizen it is someone who watches soap operas all week, then goes to vote on Sunday and returns back to the couch to watch soap operas"* and Khalil who argued that *"that is above all indifference that defines a bad citizen. It is someone who is neither interested in the political nor in the social issues of the country in which he lives."*

As mentioned earlier, in order to more fully assess my interviewees' conceptions of a good citizen I asked them to choose from the list of 'virtues of the responsible citizenship'[292] (Galston 1991: 221) the virtues which they find most important and to explain their choice. From amongst the twelve virtues, the one that was chosen most frequently by the young Belgian Muslims, both women and men, was the general virtue of law-abidingness. Most of the explanations of my interviewees who chose this virtue highlighted the necessity of having a legal frame accepted by all the citizens in order for people to live together in harmony. The most important points raised by the interviewees explaining the choice of this virtue were mentioned by Jusuf who said that *"The law-*

---

[292] The list included such 'general virtues' as courage, law-abidingness and loyalty; 'social virtues' such as independence , open-mindedness; 'economic virtues' that constitute of work ethic, capacity to delay self-gratification and adaptability to economic and technological change; 'political virtues' which translate into capacity to discern and respect the rights of others, willingness to demand only what can be paid for, the ability to evaluate the performance of those in office, willingness to engage in public discourse (Galston 1991: 221-4) and a category of 'other' for other possible virtues.

abidingness is crucial, because we need a framework, or the limits to be able to live together, and we absolutely need to respect them, in the interest of everyone. " The choice of this virtue by my interviewees as the most important one is in line with their vision of a good citizenship, as described above, with its emphasis on the respect for others enforced by the Constitution.

The second most commonly chosen virtue of responsible citizenship was the social virtue of 'independence'. The importance of independence was emphasised particularly strongly by my male interviewees. The explanations of the interviewees who believed that this is one of the most important features of a good/responsible citizen indicated a broad understanding of the term of independence. While some spoke about the political and economic independence – for instance, Murad who argued that *"it enables democrats to retain credibility"* – others invoked a much wider understanding of the term. Jusuf, for example, claimed that *"intellectual, financial and political independence - also from foreign political powers – is vital for a good citizen."* Once again, it is easier to comprehend the prioritization of this virtue by my interviewees if one takes into account the aforementioned findings of this research with regards to the issues of religious identity (in particular the phenomenon of the religious individualisation) and participation (in particular the phenomenon of post-ikhwanizm or organisational autononomisation).

The virtue of courage described by Galston as a 'general one', the virtue of open-mindedness described by him as 'social one', and the capacity to discern and respect the rights of others described by him as 'political virtue', were the third most commonly chosen virtues by my informants. These young Belgian Muslims who invoked the importance of the virtue of courage in their conceptions of a good citizen usually argued that it is instrumental in addressing the problems in the society and in improving it. One of the interviewees who believed that courage is an important feature of a good citizenship pointed out that *"Someone needs courage in order to address the problems of injustice that some people face in our society. One needs courage to say it and to fight for change of this situation."* (Majd) This feature was more strongly emphasised by my male interviewees than by the female ones.

270

The possession of the virtue of open-mindedness as a key feature of a good citizen was particularly strongly emphasised by my female interviewees. One of them Sana argued that *"for a more harmonious life in the multicultural society, the open-mindedness is absolutely essential"*, whereas another one, Hosna said that *"to be open-minded means above all to be able to listen to others and to be able to understand others' point of views"*. One of the male interviewees who pointed out the importance of open-mindedness in his conception of a good citizenship said that *"one needs to have an open mind, in order not to fall into some sect"*. (Majd)

The capacity to discern and respect the rights of others, classified by Galston as one of the major 'political virtues' of responsible citizenship, was yet another virtue commonly chosen by both men and women in my sample. One of my male interviewees who stressed the importance of this virtue argued that a good citizen it is someone *"who is not egoistic or egocentric, but someone who feels responsible for others. I have to always measure my interests and collective interests."* (Jusuf) The female interviewee, Nabihah, pointed out the mutual character of this virtue by saying that *"the struggle for the rights of others result also in it that people fight for our rights. This also means to respect another person as he or she is, even if this person is not at your level, not to crash someone."*

Finally, the last of the virtues of a responsible citizen that were particularly meaningful to my interviewees were a willingness to engage in public discourse and loyalty. Both of the virtues were especially favoured by my female interviewees. One of them who stressed the importance of the willingness to engage in public discourse argued that *"although I belong to a certain minority, I think it is very important that the voice of this minority is heard in the wider public debates. Without a constructive engagement in these debates our voice will never be heard and things will never improve."* (Sana) One of my male interviewees who believed that this virtue is crucial for any good citizen pointed out some of its limits by saying that *"My ideas and my vision of things need to be confronted with other visions and ideas, and what is going to emerge will be a mix of them. Today's problem, however, is that the collective platform allows only to emerge some ideas. A good thing would be if all these ideas, heritages, and civic potentials were taken into account."* (Faisal) Loyalty was understood by the interviewees who believed

271

that it should be a feature of a good citizen largely in the traditional way - that is as a form of attachment to the country/state.

CHAPTER V - ISLAM AND CITIZENSHIP IN LONDON

Although I wasn't born here - I came when I was about four years old - I can relate to this country much more, than to Bangladesh, where I was born. I struggle to speak Bengali. With my wife I speak English. Only with my mother I speak Bengali. So I consider myself as a citizen of this country. I don't see any contradictions between my Islamic faith, my Islamic identity and being a British citizen.
(Abdel)

Even though the vast majority of the members of the emerging new Muslim elite in Britain do not see, similarly to the aforementioned interviewee, any contradiction between their religious belonging and the national one, the polls show that only a minority of the general public is ready to believe these declarations. According to, for instance, the Gallup poll from April 2007 carried out on the representative sample of 500 Muslims and 1200 members of the wider population, nearly three-quarters of the Muslims said they felt 'loyal to the United Kingdom'. However, just 45 per cent of the wider population said '*Muslims living in the UK were loyal to the nation*' (Survey quoted in BBC 2007).[293] The events of 7 July 2005 clearly played a significant role in the emergence of this wide gap between the self-perception of national belonging amongst the British Muslims and the perception of their national belonging among the wider society. In contemporary Britain, as Yahya Birt rightly points out, "*it has become commonplace to suspect the loyalties of the country's Muslims*" (2006: 6). In the post 7/7 reality British Muslims are regularly asked to deny their alleged sympathies for terrorism, while their feelings of Islamic solidarity are thought to equal at best indifference or at worst hostility to patriotism.

---

[293] The same survey has shown that Muslims were more likely that the general public to express confidence in the police (78% to 69%), national government (64% to 36%), the justice system (67% to 55%) and elections (73% to 60%). The survey has also found that Muslims were more likely to take a positive view of living side-by-side with people of different races and religions. 35 per cent of the general public preferred living in a neighbourhood made up mostly of people who shared their religious or ethnic background in comparison with 25 per cent of Muslims (Gallup report quoted in BBC 2007).

The discrepancy between the way in which British-Muslims view their loyalty[294] and the way their loyalty is viewed by other citizens of the country is one of the issues that will be discussed in more detail in this chapter exploring the social representations of citizenship of the members of the new British Muslim elite. The structure of this chapter is similar to the previous one. It first of all, depicts the main socio-economic features of the group of young Muslims interviewed in London and then, it moves on to shed light on the religious and civic identities of the young British Muslims. After exploring the depth of the citizenship of my informants it looks more closely at the participatory dimension of their citizenship and in particular at the resources and motivations for activism within the Muslim organisations and wider public sphere, and perceived benefits from it. Finally, the last two sections of the chapter focus on the normative dimensions of lived citizenship of the young Muslim Londoners. They explore in particular the interviewees' perceptions of the civic rights and obligations.

5.1 MAIN FEATURES OF THE BRITISH SAMPLE

In the course of the fieldwork in the British capital I interviewed sixteen men and ten women, of which one was not wearing a hijab. The vast majority of my informants, similarly to the larger picture of the Muslim population in the country, were of South Asian origin. Fourteen of them came from the Bangladeshi community that constitutes the largest Muslim community in London, eight of them were from the Pakistani community, which is the largest Muslim community in the country[295] and one person was of Indian origin. The remaining three interviewees were of North African (two) and South African origin (one). Almost all of the interviewees claimed to speak at home apart from English, the languages of their parents, that is in the case of the interviewees of Bangladeshi origin, Bengali or Bangla, the interviewees of Pakistani origin, Urdu and Punjabi, the interviewee of Indian origin, Gujarati and Urdu (with a wife from Pakistan) and the interviewee of Tunisian origin, Arabic and French. Many of them, however, like

---

[294] The aforementioned Gallup research asked about the loyalty with relation to the nation, however it is important to remember that loyalty can be conceived in much broader way. Such understanding of loyalty proposes, for example, Piotr Sztompka who defines it as *"an obligation to refrain from breaching the trust that others have bestowed upon us and to fulfil duties taken upon ourselves by accepting somebody's trust"* (1999: 5) or Jack Barbalet for whom *"loyalty ... is a feeling of the viability of the arrangement of elements in which cooperation takes place."* (1996: 80)

[295] See the detailed profiles of the Muslim populations of London and Great Britain in the chapter three.

Abdel quoted at the beginning of this chapter, claimed to 'struggle to speak' these languages as their fluency in them has been weakening with every generation. Besides, the usage of the 'parents languages', three of my interviewees of South Asian origin claimed to speak Arabic at home, which they had learnt either during the extended study stays in the Arab countries of the Middle East (e.g. Jordan and Egypt) or studied them in Europe.[296] The actual number, however, of the interviewees who claimed to be able to speak Arabic amounted to seven.

The majority of the interviewed members of the emerging new Muslim elite in London were single (14 people), eleven were married and one was officially engaged. Seven of my informants were between 31 and 36 years of age, ten were between 25 and 30 years old and nine were between 18 and 24 years of age. The minority of the informants did not live with their parents (11 people), whereas the majority of them (especially those who did not set up their families yet) were living under the same roof with their parents, brothers and sisters, and sometimes other members of the family (15 people). The families to which my British interviewees were born were somewhat smaller that those of my Belgian interviewees. While, for example one third of my Belgian informants had seven siblings, in Britain only two of my informants came from such large families. The rest came also from extended families[297] but not as large family units. Six of my informants had between 5 and 6 brothers and sisters and ten had 3 to 4 siblings. The structure of the families of the remaining interviewees who had either up to two siblings (6 people) or no brothers and sisters at all (2 people), reflected the wider family structure of the British society. The family units set up by my informants were also similar to those of the wider society and not to the families to which they were born

---

[296] For example one of my interviewees learnt Arabic in The European Institute of Human Sciences in Wales – (more information about the Institute can be found on http://www.eihs.org.uk), while other two in the similar type of institution in France.

[297] Here it has to be noted that although such factors as, for example, the design of the typical British house aimed for a nuclear family unit, changed the structure of the tradition South Asian families, this structure survived in the broader sense. If the majority of British Muslim households are physically nuclear most of them have close relatives living nearby. Thus although the extended family does not live under the roof of one house it often lives under 'the roof ' of the same street or the city borough (Ballard 1994: 45, Anwar 1998: 99-101, Modood 1997: 98).

into. Three of my interviewees, who were married, did not have any children, four of them had only 1 child, one of them had 2 children and three of them had 3 children.[298]

One of the factors that could have an influence on the smaller sizes of the family units to which my British interviewees were born, in comparison with those of my Belgian interviewees, was a somewhat higher social position of the families of my British interviewees. While in Belgium only one fourth of the parents of my interviewees could be considered as representatives of lower middle class and middle class, in my British sample more than half of the interviewees (15 people) were of such a social background. In other words, the fathers of my British informants were twice more likely than those of the Belgian informants to be independent businessman, engineers, physicians, teachers, etc. It was also more common among my British interviewees (mainly among those who were not of working-class background) that their mothers also entered the job market and worked inter alia as classroom assistants, community workers and teachers.

By and large, the interviewed young Muslim Londoners were upwardly mobile, as all of them were either in the process of obtaining a university degree (9 people) or already possessed one. The majority of those, who already obtained a university degree or were in the process of getting one, were students of humanities (16 people), and ten of them were students of natural sciences. The elaboration of the remaining characteristics of my British sample indicated in the table below and further analysis of the aforementioned features is undertaken in the latter sections of this chapter.

Table 5.1 MAIN FEATURES OF THE BRITISH INFORMANTS

Name	Sex and Age	Family situation	Siblings	Accommodation	Language spoken at home[299]	Origin	Education	Occupation	Occupation of the parents	Returns to the country origin
1. Dirar	M23	Single	2 s + 2 b	With mother	Eng, Bengali	Bd	MA in Pharmacy	Student	F-worker (died), M-housewife	Regular
2. Razin	M20	Single	4 s	With parents	Eng, Bengali	Bd	BA in Economics	Student	F-teacher, M-	3 times

---

[298] It is worth reminding that it is a picture of the family structure of my interviewees at the time when the research was carried out and not the final shape of it.

[299] The languages spoken at home are presented in the order of importance in which the interviewees spoke about them.

									classroom assistant	
ur	M30	Married, 1 child	2 b + 2 s	With extended family	Eng, Bengali	Bd	BA in Politics	School teacher	F-worker, M-housewife	Rare
az	M35	Married, 3 children	3 b + 2 s	Separate	Eng, Bengali	Bd	BA in Social Work	Youth animator	F-worker, M-worker	Every 4/5 years
	M30	Married, 1 child	2 b + 2 s	Separate	Eng, Bengali, Arabic	Bd	MA in Oriental Studies	PhD student and businessm an	F-worker (died), M-housewife	Rare
n	M25	Single	1 b + 2 s	With parents	Eng, Bengali	Bd	MA in Politics	Youth animator	F-cook (died), M-housewife	Rare
	M23	Single	1 b	With mother	Eng, Bengali	Bd	BA in Islamic Studies	Student at EIHS in Wales	F-worker (died), M-housewife	Rare
o	M20	Single	2 b + 2 s	With parents	Eng, Bengali	Bd	BA in Arabic	Student at SOAS	F-doctor, M-teacher	2 times
	M24	Single	4 b + 4 s	With parents	Eng, Bengali	Bd	BA in Law	Student	F-worker, M-worker	2 times
	M29	Married, 1 child	2 b + 2 s	Separate,	Eng, Urdu	Pk	MA in Economics	Forensic Accountan t	F- teacher, M-community worker	Every 3 years
	M31	Single	1 s	With family	Eng, Urdu	Pk	BA in IT	Businessm an	F-businessma n, M-physiothera pist	Regularly
	M34	Single	None	Separate	Eng	Eg-Ng	MA in Economics	Consultant	F-engineer, M-housewife	Rare
	M30	Married	2 s	Separate	Eng, Urdu	Pk	BA in IT	Business Consultant	F-engineer, M-housewife	20 years ago
z	M22	Single	2 s + 1 b	With parents	Eng, Urdu, Arabic	Pk	MA in IT	Student	F-engineer, M-housewife	Rarely
an	M30	Married, 2 children	3 b	Separate	Eng	Bd	MA in Law	Lawyer	F-butcher (died), M-housewife	Never visited
	M29	Married, 3 children	3 b + 2 s	Separate	Eng, Gujarati, Urdu	In	MA in IT	IT consultant	F-shopkeeper, M-housewife	Never in India, family in South Afr.
	F21	Single	3 s + 1 b	With parents	Eng, Bengali	Bd	BA in Medicine	Student	F-teacher, M-classroom	3 times

# Name										
									assistant	
18. Rushd	F33	Married, 3 children	4 s + 4 b	Separate	Bengali	Bd	BA in Chemistry PGCE	Consultancy and parenting courses	F-imam, M-housewife	Regularl
19. Rasha	F28	Married	4 s + 5 b	Separate	Eng, Bengali	Bd	MA in Politics	Manager	F-businessman, M-housewife	Every 2/ years
20. Jada	F28	Engaged	2 s + 4 b	With parents	Eng, Bengali	Bd	MA in Biomedical Sciences	Manager at Community Centre	F and M – carers of a disabled son	Once
21. Afnan	F31	Married, 1 child	1 s + 5 b	Separate	Eng, Urdu	Pk	MA in Economics	Teacher	F-engineer (died), M-housewife	Once or twice
22. Samar	F22	Single	None	With parents	Eng, Urdu	Pk	MA in Law	NHS manager	F-engineer, M-lawyer	Every other yea
23. Shahd	F32	Married	1 s	Separate	Eng	Za	MA in Psychology	NHS therapist	F-engineer, M-housewife	None
24. Rana	F34	Single	2 s + 1 b	With parents	Eng, Urdu, Punjabi	Pk	PhD in Psychology	Family therapist	F-businessman (died), M-housewife	Every other yea
25. Yumn	F27	Single	3s + 2b	With parents	Eng, Arabic, French	Tn	MA in Astrophysics	Student	F-teacher, M – housewife	None
26. Nadira	F22	Single	2 b	With parents	Eng, Urdu, Arabic	Pk	MA in Medicine	Student	F-engineer, M-housewife	Rarely

5.2 IDENTITY, ISLAM AND CITIZENSHIP

5.2.1 BEING A MUSLIM

Before exploring the issue of civic identity of the members of the emerging new Muslim elite in London it is essential to first shed some light on different dimensions of their religious identities. As I have argued in the earlier chapter, this study did not provide in its conceptual section a full definition of what it means to be a Muslim in order to inter alia leave the room to the young European Muslims to answer this question in their own words. Similarly to the young Belgian Muslims, my interviewees in London gave very elaborate answers while accounting for their understandings of Muslimness. The definitions of Muslimness of the young Muslim Londoners, alike those of the young

Muslim Belgians, were characterised by weaker or stronger emphasis on one or more of the following elements: spirituality, activism, humanism and the Islamic dogma.

The element that was probably most strongly stressed by, both the female and male interviewees was the one of spirituality[300]. For many of them one of the major features of being a Muslim was the possession of a feeling of 'being connected' with the divine or the sacrum. The emphasis on this 'connection' one may observe, for instance, in the following definition of Rana who said that being a Muslim *"means, first and foremost, to have connection with Allah and it means - I guess – that this connection with Allah is fostered through particular text and practices, and ways of being that provide you with a certain kind of landscapes. So my sense of who I am and the things that form the day-to-day life are Muslim practices, but all these things come second to connection with God or Allah."* This connection with the divine takes also in the perceptions of young Muslim Londoners other forms. One of them is a feeling of being in the constant presence of the divine like in the radical empiricist vision of the world developed by the popular Irish philosopher of 18th century, George Berkeley, which links the existence of the material world with the existence of God by suggesting that the world exists only because God is constantly observing it. The elements of such radical empiricism one may observe in the vision of being a Muslim of Shabaz who said that *"Being a Muslim means everything to me. That is the reason why I live, reason why I get up in the morning... Because I sincerely believe that the blood that goes through my veins now, when I woke up in the morning, and during these eight hours of sleeping when my heart was beating and I wasn't thinking about anything, someone was doing it. I believe all the things I have, were provided by God ... I feel I should be grateful to him and follow him. That is also the reason why I am here speaking to you. It is also a way of worshiping my Lord and pleasing him".* Another informant who also argued that a crucial part of Muslimness is the constant worship of God was Mumtaz. He argued that *"As a Muslim I have been sent down to this world for a purpose and I feel the most important thing is worshiping one Creator. That worship is very comprehensive and includes things like how you deal with your parents, how you deal with your wife, how you deal with the society. So when you see me walking around I am constantly in the state of worship. I am constantly in the*

---

[300] For explanation of notion of spirituality as used in the book see chapter IV.

mood of submitting into my Creator. I'm not gonna do anything bad, although I am tempted from time to time. But I am always in the mindset that I'm worshiping my Creator who knows what I'm doing... ". As one may deduce from the aforementioned assertion, Mumtaz's understanding of worship is quite broad. Akram was another informant who stressed in his definition of Muslimness the importance of being constantly aware of the presence of God. He argued that *"To be a Muslim for me means to have God in the forefront of your mind. To be aware of Allah (PBUH) not only when I am praying but all the time. But Allah (PBUH) is not God who created the universe and removed himself from it. That he (PBUH) is all watching, all seeing and he will take me into account for my deeds at the day of judgment. "*

Finally, some of the young Muslim Londoners invoked also in their definitions of Muslimness stressing the spiritual ingredients, the significance of submitting to the 'divine order'. This understanding of Islam comes from the very name of the religion, for the Arabic word *al-islam* (Ar. الإسلام) means 'surrender' as well as the peace that issues from this surrender to God. (Nasr 2002: 8).[301] Both these elements were emphasised by my informants: the first one, particularly strongly by men, whereas the latter one by women. Adel was one of my male informants who pointed out that *"to have faith is to submit to God. Whatever God says I do, whatever God forbids me from doing I don't do. So having the faith, being a Muslim determines my whole life. As God says in the Qur'an, we were created first and foremost to serve God in this life in order to attain/obtain the best hereafter, paradise."* On the other hand, Rasha argued that Islam helps her *"to place herself in relation to God and to be happy internally",* whereas another female interviewee, Nadira, said that being a Muslim *"it is about leading your life in a particular way, which brings you happiness. Knowing that this is the right way, you are very happy, you get inner peace by living in this particular way, and by being a Muslim. "*

In contrast to the Belgian interviewees, the young Muslim Londoners did not mention explicitly in their definitions of what it means to be a Muslim the need to carry out *dawah* (Ar. calling to Islam).[302] This does not mean, though, as I am going show

---

[301] Here it is worth mentioning that word describing an adherent of Islam, that is a 'muslim' (Ar. مسلم , feminine 'muslimah', Ar. مسلمة) literally means "one who submits to God".

[302] Some of them did it implicitly, like for instance quoted below Maha who said that the obligation of Muslim should be *'(...) to seek knowledge to practice religion fully and then teach others how to do it ".*

below, that in their activism they have not been referring to the necessity to call to other Muslims as well as non-Muslims to embrace Islam, or specific kind of Islam.

Alike the definitions of Muslimness of the members of the new Muslim elite in Brussels, those of the young British Muslims bore also many marks of all-embracing humanism. One may see them for instance in the following definition of Afnan who said that *"to be a Muslim to me ultimately means to be a good person. And it is to be somebody who is of use to others, making a positive contribution in some way. Somebody who is polite, friendly, tolerant, understanding, inclusive and who knows how to relate to the people around him/her – that is for me what a Muslim is."* or in the definition of Samar who argued that *"It means to be a good person and to remember that we'll be held accountable for the actions we do and hence we have to be good in this world and good to the people around us ... because we'll be judged on that."* At the same time morality derived not only by Samar but also by many other of the interviewed young Londoners from religious grounds locates them somewhat far away from the classically understood religious humanists.[303]

It is not only the conceptions of Muslimness of my female interviewees that were characterized by strong emphasis on the importance of being a 'good human being', but also the definitions of the interviewed men. One of them, for example, argued that *"Being a Muslim means a lot of things. It means compassion, humbleness ... in religious terms it means to believe in one God and its Messenger. It is about following his example and realizing that your presence in this world is just a short part of the long journey, and that you have to do good in this world. (...) Being a Muslim is not what is going on in the media or what happened on 7/7* (the terrorist attacks in London on 7th July 2005 – KP). *I would define my religion as something very positive. Something that has to offer the whole community. It is about charity, not allowing your neighbour to starve etc."* (Kadir) Another one stated that being an adherent of Islam it means *"at the end of the day treating others the way you'd want to be treated yourself, at this kind of basic human level. It's what I think makes us Muslims ... because Islam comes from peace and submission. Once someone understands this core message, everything else falls into the*

---

[303] The latter term usually describes believers of a certain religion who do not necessarily hold their religion to be a source for their moral values derived rather from humane morality.

right place. " (Razin)   The last, but not least interviewee whose definition had strong humanist character as it tried to play down the differences between various religions and emphasised the significance of being a good person was Fadi. He argued that *"If we go beyond mechanics - not drinking alcohol, praying in the Mosque, etc.- then I think being a Muslim is not different to being part of any religion, whether it is Hindu, Christian, Jewish. In any religion, if you take the mechanics away,(...) then the key point is to be a better person and to strive to please God. "*

As one could expect from the young people actively involved in various projects of the Muslim and wider civil society, their conceptions of Muslimness were also strongly marked by the sense of necessity of active involvement in the society. One can detect this for instance in the following definition of Dirar who said that *"I think to be a Muslim, we need to maintain our Islam and the articles of faith on the one side, and at the same time whichever society we are living in, as Muslims we need to positively contribute to the development of those societies, and that is what I feel to be a Muslim is all about. We need to act so as people can see that a Muslim in Britain is not someone who is here to kill people, or to destroy the country, but someone, who is helping in a development of the country. Someone who is helping in the service of the people and helping in the advancement of the society. "* Clearly, the aforementioned definition of Muslimness has been strongly influenced by the events of 7 July 2005 and 21 July 2005[304] shortly after which this interview was conducted. However, most of my interviewees were referring to the necessity of contributing to the society in their conceptions of what it means to be a Muslim without the references to the events from July 2005. Their own involvement in the Muslim and wider civil society which predated these events could be one of the possible explanations for that. Mazin was one of the interviewees who pointed out at the importance of activism in his conception of Muslimness without the references the bombings and attempted bombings. He said that *"Islam to me means making a positive difference. It means to make a contribution to the society that you live in. To be a Muslim, it means that whatever society you are living in,*

---

[304] On 21 July 2005 (two weeks after the 7 July bombings) four attempted bomb attacks disrupted part of London's public transport system. On 11 July 2007 the four attempted bombers Muktar Ibrahim, Yassin Omar, Ramzi Mohammed and Hussein Osman were found guilty of conspiracy to murder and sentenced to jail for a minimum of 40 years. For more information on the attempted bomb attacks see, for example, Campbell 2007.

you will make a contribution. " (Mazin) In order to give his claim more legitimacy Mazin referred to the Holy Book of Islam by saying that *"One of the most beautiful ayat* (Ar. verses - KP) *in the Qur'an are those which say 'we have made you into nations and tribes so you may know one another, but the best of you on the side of Allah is who is best in deeds*[305] *and that's the measure of society."* (Mazin) Other interviews who emphasised the significance of the activism in their definition of what it means to be a Muslim were Akram and Mansur. While the first one argued that *"being a Muslim means that you have to try and do as much as you can in terms of gaining good actions through the service to your community"*, the latter one said that *"I see myself as belonging to the global ummah, and locally to the Muslim community here, so for me it means being involved, being out there, knowing what is happening, being practically involved with people, not giving just lip service, not just looking at narrow definition of Muslimness"*. According to Akram and Mansur, as well as many other British interviewees, the major part of their activism should take place within the boundaries of community defined if not in religious than in ethnic terms. Some interviewees though held a much wider understanding of community which was embracing the whole society.

Like my Belgian informants, some of the members of the new Muslim elite in London stressed also in their definitions of Muslimness the importance of struggle for justice, which is obviously strongly linked with the analysed above active societal involvement. One of them was Afnan who said that *"I took my small daughter to the peace vigil at the Trafalgar Square*[306] *and we went to many other marches. We have done so much stuff together. Mainly because I want her to grow up with the sense of justice that Islam has. I want her to understand that if something is wrong you can do something fighting that wrong in the right way. And if there is something right, you have to believe that this is the right thing and to stand up for it "*.

Finally, some of my interviewees put an emphasis in their definitions of Muslimness on the dogmatic elements, such as for example Islamic orthopraxy. Maha, for instance, claimed that in order to be a Muslim one needs to strictly follow the precepts

---

[305] These verses in the translation of Qur'an by Mohammed Marmaduke Pickthall go as follow: *"O mankind! Lo! We have created you male and female, and have made you nations and tribes that ye may know one another. Lo! the noblest of you, in the sight of Allah, is the best in conduct. Lo! Allah is Knower, Aware."* (Qur'an 49: 13)
[306] She refers to the vigil held a week after 7/7 in commemoration of all who died during the bombing .

of Islam or 'to live by Islam'. She said that *"There are people with Muslim names who would consider themselves Muslims but who do not live by Islam. So to me a true Muslim is somebody that lives by Islam, who follows the Prophet, tries to seek knowledge to practice religion fully and then teaches others how to do it".* Another female interviewee whose understanding of Muslimness was largely limited to the orthopraxic elements was Yumn who argued that being a Muslim involves *"certain beliefs, ways of thinking about God and paths of creation, also certain obligations, how do you interact with this world, certain principles to guide your life".* Also, the following part of the Mansur's conception of being a Muslim stressed these elements *"Initially it is a personal thing. As a Muslim, I believe in the Qur'an, in the Prophet Muhammad and follow the pillars of Islam."* As many other members of the Muslim elite in London he later on mentioned several other elements that in his view were features of a Muslim which all in all constituted an elaborate definition of Muslimness.

5.2.2 BECOMING A MUSLIM

Although my British informants stressed less strongly than my Belgian interviewees that they were Muslims by choice and believers *in statu nascendi,* and not fully formed adherents of Islam who 'quasi naturally' inherited the faith in Allah from their parents, the elements of religious individualisation were also clearly visible amongst the members of the new Muslims elite in London. One may notice them, for example, in the following statement of Marwan who said that *"Intellectually it is not good enough that my parents, forefathers were Muslims ... I had to be convinced, otherwise I would choose to abandon Muslim life and follow the life which many Westerners live. So it was this intellectual thinking process that led me to the conclusion that there is God."* He decided to embrace religion of his parents only after a long period of questioning religious traditions that they have passed to him and most notably the belief in the existence of God. Similar features of re-appropriation of Islam one may observe in the religious biographies of many other young Muslim Londoners. One of the informants who spoke about a long personal journey to the religion of her parents was Afnan. She claimed that she started to think more seriously about Islam only after the death of her father at the age 19, while before she was mostly 'questioning everything that was going on around her'. This event, which also in the case of some other interviewees (e.g. Rana, Akram) marked an important turning point in their perception of Islam, was also a moment, from which she gradually began to return to Islam. She stressed the importance of the larger social context in her re-discovery of Islam – *"It happened when I was at university and met a lot of Muslims. Before university I didn't really have friends who would be practicing their faith really"* - and yet, at the same time, she claimed that *"I have never felt pressured to become a practicing Muslim. Quite the opposite, people saying 'don't change, you do not need to, everything is fine, God will still be happy with you'. At that time it wasn't popular, as it is now, ha, ha, ha ...* (laughing –KP) *to be a practicing Muslim. 'Why do you make life difficult for yourself?' But I think when you feel obliged within yourself you can't fight that. You have to follow what your heart is telling you to do and you have to be strong enough in your belief so as you can explain others your transformation in the best way."* While for Marwan re-embracing the religion of the parents was mostly an intellectual process, in the case of Afnan it was largely a spiritual quest. She claimed to choose to believe in Allah after a great deal of thinking about it, but essentially as a response to the 'call of her heart'. In general my female interviewees were much more likely than the male ones to stress the importance of the quest for spirituality in their religious re-discoveries. This does not mean though that none of my male interviewees claimed to be attracted to Islam by its 'spiritual massage'. One of them was, for instance, Fadi who said that *"I started praying very late. I didn't believe in anything until my 19-20 birthday and then I started to look at life and think that there is more to life than partying, girls, cars and stuff like that. I started to look more into religion and especially into the spiritual side of it."* He was also one of a few British informants whose re-discovery of Islam went through the denial of any affiliation with Muslims in the earlier part of his life. Not only to his personal religious biography, but also to many other members of the interviewed young Muslim Londoners, one could apply the following statement of one of the informants of Leila Babes who said *"Islam was the religion of my parents, but over the last years it has become mine"* (1997: 75). Similarly to the informants of the French researcher, for many of my interviewees religion became a very attractive fabric for building an authentic social identity while the act of re-appropriation of Islam itself, that

285

could be viewed as a form of conversion[307], proved to be a very effective modality of self-construction in the world of do-it-yourself identities. Constructing an original or authentic social identity, which as I have argued in the second chapter is a reflexive project imposed on every individual by the forces of modernity, is definitely not an easy task in the city of more than seven million inhabitants. It seems that 'being true to oneself', to use the words of Charles Taylor (1992: 78) requires in such a global city like London some extra reflexivity. This might be also one of the reasons why some radical Muslim movements (e.g. Al-Muahjiroun[308]) have developed especially strong social bases in London, which gained the British capital a pejorative sobriquet – Londonistan[309]. In the latter part of this chapter dealing with the participatory dimension of citizenship of the new Muslim elite in London I shall return to the issue of the fateful moments during which my interviewees decided to embrace anew, more fully or just in a different way, religion of their parents, whereas now it is important to elaborate on the inherited part of their re-discovered or 'chosen' religious identities.

As much as the religious identities of my British interviewees are chosen or constructed by them during longer or shorter periods of religious explorations, they are also largely inherited from their parents. All my British interviewees, including those who strongly emphasized the individualized character of their belief in Allah, acknowledged as a fact that the religiosity of their parents had also stronger or weaker impact on their own perception and practice of Islam. Almost all of the young Muslim Londoners came from practising Muslim families. The religious habitus was thus imprinted into their minds and bodies from a very early age. The degree of religiosity of their families and hence strength of cultural structures or religious habitus, however, varied. In the family lives of some of my interviewees, Islam was present but did not occupy a central place. This was, for example, the case of Afnan who pointed out that

---

[307] For an overview of phenomenon of conversion to Islam in the European context see Allievi 1999.
[308] Al-Muhajiroun is a defunct Khawarij (historically first radical dissent group in Islam which combined rigorous puritanism and religious fundamentalism with an exclusivist egalitarianism – Esposito 1998: 43-45) organization set up in Great Britain in 1986 (originally set up in March 1983 in Mecca, Saudi Arabia) by notorious Muslim leader Omar Bakri. For more information about the group dissolved in October 2004 see Pędziwiatr 2003a or Wiktorowicz 2005.
[309] The term which was originally coined by the French counter-terrorism agents refers to the presence of the number of exiled Islamist groups that especially in the 1980s and 1990s established political headquarters in the city. More recently it has been popularized by conservative British journalist Melanie Philips who published a book entitled '*Londonistan: How Britain is creating a terror state within*' (2006).

"My parents were not really practising Muslims. Islam didn't feature in their lives. For most we used to go to Eid service as a family. And somebody within a family would lead a special prayer. But there was nothing regular and consistent about it. They believed in hereafter in terms of a paradise and hell. All these things were familiar, but there was nothing really done specifically that you could say that it is a consistent path." or of Shahd who asserted that "My parents are largely secularized but they always had a sense of godliness or faith in higher power. We grew up largely secular with some sense of God." In the case of the majority of families of the young Muslim Londoners Islam played much more important role. Most of them claimed 'to be brought up with religion'. Rana, for example, asserted that "Religious practices were part of day-to-day life in my family and it was an important part of my upbringing and something that I highly value. When I went to university I guess I moved away from it and I started questioning things more because I lived away from home ... I started to engage less in the practices of it but I never would describe myself as an atheist. I always had a connection and a sense that there is something other than the material things." In some of the other interviewees' biographies one may observe features of even stronger religious habitus inculcation. Among the interviewees who claimed that religious practice occupied a central part in their family life was, for instance, Kadir who said that "I come from a religious family. During the upbringing I always fasted and prayed." and Dirar who asserted that "My father was someone who always encouraged us to religious learning and education - something that I particularly enjoyed mainly because he did it in a very nice way. Thus, he in a way encouraged us." Yet another interviewee who emphasised the importance the family life in her perception of Islam was Rasha who claimed that "My family is a practicing Muslim family so I have been brought up as a practicing Muslim and all of my brothers and sisters are practicing." In my opinion the members of the new Muslim elite in London whose parents paid particular attention to the transmission of the religion to their children were particularly strongly predisposed by their religious habitus to embrace religion of their parents.

At the same time one needs to remember that religious habitus which prepared my interviewees to the re-discovery of Islam was not only limited to influence of the family circles but went beyond them. The Muslim habitus beyond the family context had a particularly strong influence on my interviewees who lived in the city quarters described by Felice Dassetto as Muslimtowns. One of such areas is definitely that borough of Tower Hamlets in which grew up many of my informants and which has the highest concentration of Muslims in the country[310]. The call to prayer (Ar. أذان - adhan) broadcast from the minaret of the East London Mosque, numerous shops closed for Iftar[311] during the month of Ramadan and requests not to enter shops with food or drink during the month of Ramadan are only some of the elements of the wider Muslim habitus generating thoughts, perceptions and actions consistent with the Islamic orthodoxy, in which grew up many of my interviewees. A crucial part of this wider habitus within which the central religious beliefs and values are articulated and hence validated and reinforced make up also mosques visited by my informants from the very early age. One of the young British Muslims even said that *"Ever since we were young the masjid* (mosque in Arabic - KP) *was like a second home. We used to go to it for the classes* (Qur'anic classes - KP) *and for other activities, especially during the fast days* (during the month of Ramadan – KP*). It's always been like a family place. I was always going to mosque for the activities and to help out with the activities. It's been like this ever since I can remember."* (Maha) Clearly her becoming a Muslim has more to do with adding to her religious belief and/or practice some personal tint rather than re-discovering Islam anew.

Alike in Belgium, the re-embracing of Islam by young Muslim women was usually followed by their decision to start to wear hijab and some re-organisation of the current life. That is how one of my interviewees accounted for the circumstances in which she decided to put on hijab: *"I was putting headscarf when going to the Qur'anic class and putting it off after the class. When I was 15, 16 years old, many people around me were suddenly becoming practicing. People that I knew, who had boyfriends and girlfriends and were quite wild according to our definition, were turning to religion. And there I was who was never doing things like that and I thought 'oh, gosh they are better than me'. Anyway I wished them all the best, and still continued to be myself, which is jeans, jumpers, and a bit of praying. Then at the university I was sitting at my biochemistry lesson and I remember my lecturer saying that 'if one amino acid changes*

---

[310] More than 36 per cent of the inhabitants of this district are Muslims. For more information about the spatial distribution of Muslims in the capital and in the whole country see chapter three.
[311] *Iftar* (Ar. افطار), refers to the evening meal for breaking the daily fast during the month of Ramadan.

in the DNA structure, the child will be severely disabled'. (...) And then something clicked inside me ... 'gosh, Allah is there and it is my duty to worship him'. And then I slowly started to go to the prayer room, read the leaflets that were there, and then adopted hijab more consistently.'' (Jada) As I have argued in the third chapter, a Muslim headscarf in Britain is not only integrated into the school uniforms, but even into the Police uniforms and as such it is quite widely tolerated and less questioned in the public sphere. In contrast to Belgian Muslims women, female adherents of Islam in Britain putting on headscarves are thus facing significantly weaker social ostracism from the part of the wider society. This, however, does not mean that the adoption of hijab by young Muslim women passes completely unnoticed especially by their non-Muslim friends and colleagues. As the following account of Afnan suggests, the first reactions of her social circle to the decision of taking up hijab were very reserved: *"When I put on the headscarf I had a lot of people coming over to me asking – 'oh, did you convert?' because they thought I was a Hindu, for some reason, ha, ha...* (laughing - KP). *I think my name wasn't particularly Muslim and I didn't dress particularly Muslim even though I didn't wear short skirts. But people just assumed I wasn't a Muslim. (...) People who were friends took a step back because they didn't know how to be with me any more. It was a hard time because I think they thought they can't joke in front of me any more, they couldn't swear etc. Although I was still the same person people didn't know how to relate to me any more. It was interesting to see that just one outer change meant all these different sort of perceptions being placed on me without me being able to defend myself.''* Similarly to my Belgian female interviewees and in spite of much more tolerant general approach to hijabs of the wider British society, many of the young Muslim women in London putting on headscarves faced, especially in the initial period, some form of social ostracism.

5.2.3 LIMITS OF RELIGIOUS INDIVIDUALIZATION

As I have argued in the first chapter, although most students of the Muslim populations in Europe agree with the observation that these populations are characterised by a growing religious individualisation, there is no agreement among the researchers on the consequences of this individualisation (Peter 2006). Some of them argue that these processes are leading towards the liberalisation of the Islamic orthodoxy and development of more critical Islam (e.g. Schiffauer 2000, Mandaville 2004), whereas others put forward an opposing hypothesis claiming that individualization is leading towards stabilisation of the religious dogmas (e.g. Roy 1999, 2002, Wiktorowicz 2005). The recent research on Muslims in Britain commissioned by the conservative think tank Policy Exchange, for instance, tends to support the arguments advanced by the latter group of researchers (Mirza et al. 2007). One of the general conclusions drawn by Mirza et al. holds that there is a growing religiosity amongst the younger generation of Muslims and that they feel they have less in common with non-Muslims than do their parents (ibid: 5). The researchers of the Policy Exchange draw such conclusion inter alia on the basis of the respondents answers to the questions testing their attitudes to different aspects of shariah law. Amongst these questions there are ones that inquire about the young Muslims' attitudes to marrying outside the Muslim community by Muslim women and to apostasy, which I also asked members of the new Muslim elite in London. Before I elaborate on the views of my interviewees on these issues and thus attempt to sketch the limits of their religious individualization, it is worth presenting shortly major findings of the quantitative study of Policy Exchange in this area.[312]

In the study of Mirza et al. 56 to 55 per cent of the respondents who were between 16 and 34 years old agreed with the statement that 'a Muslim women may not marry a non-Muslim', whereas in the group of 45 years old and older respondents 40 to 42 per cent agreed with this statement. As far as the issue of apostasy is concerned, 36 to 37 per cent of the young cohort (between 16 and 34 years old) agreed with the statement that 'Muslim conversion is forbidden and punishable by death', while only 19 per cent of the older respondents (45 years of and older) agreed with this statement (ibid: 47). The younger respondents of the Policy Exchange study were also less likely to accept the reinterpretation of shariah law to reflect modern ideas about human rights, equality for women and tolerance of religious conversion (ibid: 48). In general the authors observed

---

[312] The study commissioned by the Policy Exchange was carried out between July 2006 and January 2007. During this period the polling company, Populus, conducted a quantitative survey of 1003 Muslims in the UK, through telephone and internet questionnaires, whereas researchers asked further questions to 1025 people from general public and conducted 40 semi-structured interviews. More on the methodology of the Policy Exchange study see Mirza et al. 2007: 19.

that the younger age groups tended to agree with the dogmatic interpretation, whereas the older age groups were more likely to disagree.

Similarly to the findings of Mirza et al. many of my British interviewees, both women and men (alike the Belgian interviewees) insisted on the importance of the maintenance of the Islamic principle limiting the choice of a future husband for Muslim women only to the men of the Islamic creed. Some of them did not try to search for any explanations why this principle should be maintained but in the same way as Jada just stated that *"I agree with this ban. It is stipulated in the shariah and I think it should stay as it is"*. Others referred to arguments of the Islamic orthodoxy in support of the principle. One of them was, for instance, Marwan who claimed that *"This question of marrying non-Muslim for a Muslim women is not an appropriate one. Muslim women are not allowed to marry non-Muslim men for many reasons... First a Muslim woman would need to answer who her God is. If she wants to obey her Lord, the responsibilities and duties her Lord gives then she obeys this principle. As Muslims we believe that marriage is a contract and that contract is defined by the Creator... man has responsibilities and woman has responsibilities. It is not an issue of women being discriminated."* Alike the young Belgian Muslims, many of my interviewees in London used the argument of the incompatibility of the religiously mixed couples and claimed that relationships of such couples are deemed to failure. One of them was, for example, Rushd who said that *"I am part of the New Muslims project where we have a lot of mixed couples and a lot of them try to maintain their marriage to a non-Muslim partner, and they find it very difficult because of the struggle over the faith in children's upbringing. It often becomes such a big struggle that they cannot cope with it. So in the majority of the times it doesn't work."*

At the same time some of my interviewees who supported the idea of free choice of a marriage partner for Muslim women used the arguments of the social reality of mixed marriages and their personal knowledge of such marriages to legitimate their position. Afnan, for instance, claimed that *"The question of a choice of future husband is a tough one. To my knowledge it is not acceptable but at the end of the day I think it is their* (Muslim women's – KP) *choice. I can't say whether this is right or wrong. My brother married a French girl and they get on very well. She is still Catholic and my brother is Muslim and it works for them. Had it been the other way round, I think it would work also well."* The most common answers, however, that I could hear from half of my informants who tended to disagree with the limitations of the choice of a future husband imposed by Islam on Muslim women were the following ones expressed by Shabaz - *'Woman should be allowed to do in this matter what she wants"* - and by Rana - *"I don't have problems with it but I know that I have very unconventional views about it"*. The young Muslims like Rana and other interviewees who spoke in support of the free choice of marriage partner are in minority in the light of the findings of Mirza et al. 2007 although their views are not really unconventional since they find substantial support in the Muslim communities[313] and within a wider society. Similarly to the Belgian Muslims my British informants also spoke against the practice of forced marriages.[314]

As for the issue of apostasy, the views of the young Muslim Londoners were largely in line with the values inseparably linked with modernity. In other words, almost all of the young British Muslims spoke in favour of the right to a free choice of religion. At the same time many of them stressed that they were aware of the fact that their stand might not be necessarily upheld by all the ulema (Ar. علماء Muslim scholars). The ambiguity of this situation is for instant apparent in the following statement of Rushd: *"Apostasy is forbidden and yet, at the same time, there is no compulsion in faith. If someone doesn't want to be a Muslim I cannot force him to be one. In the Islamic country the things may look differently."* Other interviewees chose to dismiss the Islamic ban on conversions and stressed the message of Islam on non-compulsion. One of them was Adel who emphasised that no-one should be forced to adhere to a certain religion or to embrace one. He argued that *"Islam allows someone to leave religion if he or she does not feel like being a Muslim. One of the principles of Islam is that there is no compulsion or coercion in faith. You cannot also coerce a person to become a Muslim. Our duty is to convey the message and teach the message."* Yet another interviewee Fadi claimed that *"People have the right to do what they want. They will be accounted for at the end of the day, because this is the whole point of religion."*

---

[313] In the study commissioned by the Policy Exchange more than half of the Muslims between 45 and 54 years old did not agree with the statement that 'a Muslim woman may not marry a non-Muslim' (Mirza et al. 2007: 47).
[314] According to the special Forced Marriage Unit in the Foreign and Commonwealth Office there are around 250 cases of such marriages a year. More information about these cases can be found on http://www.fco.gov.uk (accessed 01.08.2007).

In general, my research shows that the young Muslim Londoners only partially embraced the values inseparably linked with modernity and if they did, they often embraced them 'on Muslim terms' (e.g. the aforementioned opinion of Adel). Thus, it supports these students of the Muslim population in Europe, who claim that the individualization of religious beliefs does not necessarily need to result in questioning the key religious dogmas (e.g. Maréchal 2003: 13-17 or Göle 2003: 814). Moreover, my findings prove an existence of a dynamic translation of the realities of life in 21st century Europe into Muslim terms. Parallel to this Islamisation of modernity is a process of modernisation of Islam and adaptation of Islamic practices into the social realities of contemporary Britain (Europe) that will be explored in more details in the following chapter. Both aforementioned processes are accompanied by the process of re-drawing of the distinction between the 'central' belief elements and the 'peripheral' one.

5.2.4 BEING A CITIZEN

Having discussed how the young Muslim Londoners conceive of their religious identities and having elaborated on some aspects of the individualisation of these identities, it is time to explore the depth of their citizenship or the identity dimension of their social representations of citizenship. As I have argued in the preface to this book the way in which my interviewees understand citizenship is likely to have impact not only on how they view their civic rights and duties or on the content of their citizenship, but also the extent of their citizenship, that is on the form and intensity of their participation in the social life. That is also the major reasons for which I asked the young Muslim Londoners about their personal definitions of citizenship.

As I have signalled in the earlier chapter the definitions of citizenship of my British interviewees were somewhat less elaborate than those of the young Belgian Muslims and the thin contractual vision of citizenship had many more supporters than in Brussels. I believe this has to do at least partially with the fact that citizenship for much of the twentieth century has not been often debated in Britain, unlike in Belgium. As Pattie et al. notice the term 'citizen' was until recently viewed even as inappropriate in Britain since the British were more likely to be described in the mainstream discourse as dutiful and respectful subjects rather than engaged citizens (2004: XV). Although this situation has radically changed in recent years with the government ministers preoccupied with civic renewal agenda as a mean of raising participation, reducing crime and promoting voluntary activity (Blunkett 2001, 2003) and with the introduction of citizenship studies into the schools curriculum as a compulsory subject (Crick 2002), the idea of being a citizen and of citizenship has apparently not been yet fully internalized by the inhabitants of Britain, including British Muslims. However, for most of the young Muslim Londoners both the concept of a citizen and of citizenship were quite meaningful.

Like the Belgian interviewees, the young Muslim Londoners have most commonly defined citizenship in line with the socially constructive model of citizenship. However, their second, third and fourth most popular models of citizenship were different than those to which subscribed the definitions of the young Belgian Muslims. Let us first look more closely into their definitions of citizenship that espouse the socially constructive model. Many of the features of this model, build on the idea that citizens should constructively engage with the society, one may find in the following definition of Sajid who said that *"Citizenship is how you focus yourself in this world. The problem is with people who say 'don't get involved with dunya'.[315] These people do not understand the purpose of Islam, which is for this world, not for the next world. God will look after the next world. There is no challenge in the next world. It is this world that matters. Citizenship is part of that. You know, you need to live somewhere. The question is how best you can contribute to the place in which you have chosen to live in."* The contribution to the local and wider society was also the key element of the definition of citizenship of Mumtaz who compared his own understanding of citizenship with the one of the member of the Hizb ut-Tahrir[316] that he knew. He said that *"I believe if I live here, if I am part of this society, I need to contribute to it. I should care if, for instance, the hospitals or schools are being run properly. If they are not I should try to intervene. I said to an HT* (Hizb ut-Tahrir – KP) *member - 'your daughter is going to the same school as mine. Shouldn't you then be concerned about the facilities in the school?'. I am, and that is why I am involved. I want to see the facilities, I want to see computers, culturally*

---

[315] In Islamic terminology the word *dunya* (Ar. دنيا) means 'this world' - and its earthly concerns and possessions - as opposed to more spiritual realms, or the hereafter.
[316] For more information about this Muslim organisation see chapter three and the appendix II.

sensitive curriculum, whereas my friends from HT would come up with the strange argument – 'we are waiting for Islamic state'. I find this argument very shallow. There is a lot of poverty in the world; I have a responsibility for that. My brothers from the HT would wait for the Islamic state to solve it. They want to collect zakat[317] after the foundation of such state. I give my zakat now because by the time it happens millions of people would die." Another subjective definition of citizenship that bears numerous marks of the socially constructive vision was the one of Razin, who linked the concept of citizenship with the one of Muslimness[318], by claiming that *"Being a citizen is actually not much different to being a good Muslim. Living in this country makes you a citizen, by merit or by right - at the end of the day you have to pay your taxes, to fulfil your civil duties... So these are the things that you have to do. But I think people generally don't engage more than that. For me citizenship is a kind of giving something back because we always benefit unknowingly... we don't realize perhaps how fortunate we are to have the education that we do, how fortunate we are to go to schools, universities, to get the jobs and these kind of things. I think to be a citizen you need to appreciate that, trying to give something back to the system, and trying to improve the system if there are failings in it."* In Razin's opinion there is much more depth in the concept of citizenship than *"having a National Insurance number, paying taxes, having a house and a car etc."* He disagreed with the very thin vision of citizenship which in his view characterises *'the majority's conception of citizenship'* and argued that an essence of citizenship was *"Trying to make change and trying to make things better for the society that you are living it."* Shabaz was another interviewee whose subjective notion of citizenship subscribed into the socially constructive model and who similarly to Razin made a direct link between being a Muslim and being a citizen. He argued that *"being a citizen means almost the same things as being a Muslim, because to be sincere as a Muslim, to follow God, one would need to be an active citizen who wants to stand up for justice and fight for people's rights. It means trying to remove things like binge drinking, huge crime, racism, etc. You*

---

[317] For detailed description of the third pillar of Islam see chapter three.

[318] Juxtaposing the concept of citizenship together with the one of Muslimness, which was very common amongst the members of the emerging new Muslim elites in both analysed cities is one of the key features of the devout Muslim citizenship discussed in more details in a chapter IV.

know ... we are living in the world of problems, so my outlook is to try to make the world a better place. Being citizen is part of that. It goes hand in hand with my faith."

The wish to 'make the world a better place' - to use the poetics of Razin - was not only the key feature of the definitions of citizenship of many of my male informants but also of the female ones. Roxana, who described herself as *"a constructive and interactive citizen"*, said, for instance, that *"Citizenship means above all to be very active in terms of being part of the society and being up-to-date what is happening."* Another Muslim woman interviewed in London claimed that *"Being a citizen means to be someone who contributes to the society that you are living in and the state that you are living in. It means also to be honest, just and kind and to have compassion."* (Rana) She was not the only one to place the general values such as honesty, justice, kindness and compassion at the heart of the conception of citizenship. Many other interviewees who espoused the socially constructive model of citizenship did so, and thus they were significantly widening and deepening their subjective notions of citizenship. Alike in the Belgian case study, many of the definitions of citizenship of the young Muslim Londoners which exemplified the socially constructive model of citizenship were also linked with their conceptions of 'good citizenship' that will be explored in the last sections of this chapter.

The significant number of the members of the rising new Muslim elite in London understood citizenship in terms of the effective identification model of citizenship, which emphasises the importance of identification with a given place, be it country, region, city or a city borough, and with everything that is related to this place.[319] As I have argued in the earlier chapter, this model implies the feeling of 'being at ease' (especially in social and cultural terms) in a particular social environment, and being accepted and respected this environment. One of the subjective notions of citizenship that subscribes into this model is the one of Afnan who argued that *"to be a citizens it means to feel that you belong to the community that you live within, Muslims and non-Muslims. To feel that their problems are also your problems, that you do not exclude yourself from issues that arise within that society and again being able to make contribution not for the king or queen, but for the people that you live among."* The features of the effective

---

[319] Different levels of this identification are explored in more details in the following sections of this chapter.

296

identification model of citizenship are also clearly visible in the definition of Khalil which included some multiculturalist elements. For him being a citizen meant *"to be part of the community while at the same time maintaining your cultural and religious identity. Respecting that you are within the community where there are different religious or cultural identities. (...)."* And then he quickly added *"I am very comfortable being British Muslim. I love being in the UK. I think we have many more rights here than in any other countries."* (Khalil) Similarly to his statement the following opinion of Abdel,[320] which makes part of his subjective definition of citizenship, subscribes into the model of effective identification: *"Although I wasn't born here - I came when I was about four years old - I can relate to this country much more, than to Bangladesh, where I was born. (...)"* Part of the definition of citizenship of Mumtaz who juxtaposed his own perception of citizenship with the ideas about it promoted by the Hizb ut-Tahrir, was also stressing the importance of strong identification with the wider social environment and its elements. He argued that apart from trying to contribute to the society, *"being a citizen means that I am part of this society. I live and work, and members of my family live and work here, so we are part of it* (British society – KP)*... unlike members Hizb ut-Tahrir who do not feel part of the British society although they live and work here. They use the hospitals and all other facilities when they need them... and then they say: 'we are not part of it'. I find this argument strange."* Yet another young Muslim Londoner interviewed in the course of the research argued that being a citizen means not only to identify with certain place, but also to follow its culture. Here Adel however clarified that not all the elements of the British culture are worth following, but only those which were earlier Islamised. He said that *"It is maybe a trivial example but in the Middle East men wear certain clothes, right... so their culture is there, but our culture is to wear shirt and trousers, so we wear them. As Tariq Ramadan said at the recent conference[321], British culture has good and bad things, but we take the good things. Islam adopts the good things from the cultures of different people, you see."* Other interviewees whose notions of citizenship espoused the model of effective identification did not argue that being a citizen involves following the culture of certain country previously Islamised, but rather

---

[320] Quoted in its integrity already in the opening of this chapter.
[321] The interviewee refers here to the conference entitled 'Islam - The Middle Path' organized by Da'watul Islam in the Regents Park Mosque in London on 24th July 2005.

insisted on the broadly understood identification with the wider society. Yumn pointed out, for instance, that for her *"To be a citizen means to have a sense of belonging to the society, to appreciate its principles and law, (...) to feel a sense of responsibility towards the society in which one is living"*, whereas Akram argued that citizenship means that *"I live here, I see my future here, and I know that I have to contribute to making my future in this country fair, just and stable future."* There were no visible gender differences in espousal of this model of citizenship by my interviewees. Like the former model it was equally often supported by the male, as well as, the female informants.

The next model in terms of which my interviewees understood citizenship was a contractual one. As I have argued in the former chapter this model is characterised by largely legalist and minimalist perception of citizenship. The fact that it was almost as widespread among the young British Muslims as the earlier one, that is the model of effective identification, explains why the subjective notions of citizenship of the Muslim Londoners were somewhat less elaborate than those of the Muslim Belgians. While the conception of citizenship of the latter group, analysed in chapter five, were beginning from the contractual model and then enriched with elements of other models, the subjective notions of my British interviewees were often limited only to the minimalist vision. One of the examples of such conception was the definition of citizenship of Marwan who asserted *"I deal with the nationality law as a specialist, but I have yet to see what it means to be a citizen, rather then basically obedience to the law of the country."* Another British interviewee who perceived citizenship within such minimalist framework was Sadik, who said that *"As a citizen I have rights, responsibilities and duties like everyone else and I have no problem with that."*

The thin contractual vision of citizenship was also espoused by some of my female interviewees. One of them, Samar argued that *"you can be recognized as a citizen just by living in certain places and certain time. It doesn't mean anything else than being a person in the society. Being a Muslim, on the other hand, encompasses a lot more than being a citizen. Being a Muslim brings a lot more responsibilities with it."* For another one, Maha, citizenship was mainly about being *"A member of a society or a community who lives by the laws of the society and is able to use freely the rights that the community withstands."* Yet another young Muslim woman interviewed in the course of this research

298

said bluntly *"I don't know how to define citizenship. To be a law-abiding citizen? I guess respecting the rules of the country."* (Nadira)

In contrast to Belgium the lack-of-recognition model of citizenship which in the Belgian capital was particularly strongly embraced by the young Muslim women, was rarely espoused by the young Muslim Londoners. Some features of this model one may notice for instance in the following statement of Rasha: *"Now, the way how Islam and Muslims are being misrepresented in the media - you do feel quite upset. Generally, I am quite happy to see myself as a citizen, the issue is if others will accept me or not."* According to her, although most Muslims are in the light of law citizens of Britain, in the current post-9/11 and even more so the post-7/7 climate, they are often not perceived by others as full citizens of Britain. Such opinions were nevertheless not very widespread amongst my British interviewees most of whom did not perceive citizenship in line with this model. This, however, as I am going to demonstrate in the latter part of this chapter, does not mean that all my interviewees thought that they were recognized and treated as full citizens.

5.2.5 BEING BRITISH

"It is mark of self-confidence: the English have not spent a great deal of time defining themselves because they haven't needed to" (Paxman 1999: 23). The interviewed young Muslims born or socialized in Britain (and to some extent also other Muslims in Britain) are in the less comfortable situation than the English described by Jeremy Paxman, the popular author and BBC journalist, since from the very early age they had to work out in what proportions they are British, Muslim and Asians – to mention only three major points of reference most of them had to take into account. To some extent they were then well prepared when I approached them and asked about the different ingredients of their identities which were most meaningful for them. Before I elaborate on the answers with which they came up, it is worth reminding that like all identities, the expressions of belongingness of my informants are relatively dynamic and contextual, and may vary depending on the conditions in which they are expressed.[322]

---

[322] For elaboration on the identities in the high modernity see chapter two.

Contrary to the popular perceptions of the Muslims' feelings of attachments (or rather non-attachment) to Britain and the British nation amongst wider the population (Gallup report quoted in BBC 2007), my study shows that for the majority of the young Muslim religious brokers in London national identity was quite meaningful. Many of them similarly to Abdel, whose statement opens this chapter, said to relate to Britain much more than to the countries of their parents. One of my interviewees who felt deeply attached to Britain and had no objection to call himself British was Dirar, who alike Abdel spent the first years of his life (in his case six years) in Bangladesh. He argued *"I don't see another place for me. This is my home, this is my country. There is no other country for me. My parents brought me from another part of the world, but I'm alien to that part of the world. I don't know the land, I don't know the context and I don't know the people there."* Another interviewee who shared strong feelings of belonging to the British nation was Shabaz. He said *"Yeah definitely I feel British. I was born here. Here I have my friends. The way I think, analytical thinking is from here. All these means a lot to me."* Similar opinions I could detect among my female informants. One of them, Afnan, asserted: *"I feel British, in the sense that, this is my home, this is where I belong to, how I think, what I stand for. And it is tough, if people do not see me like that because these are the values I do stand for. Being British does not necessarily mean to go to the pub on Friday night (...). I think you can be British and still be a Muslim quite easily. I have never had any problem with that. We have spoken about the identity clashes so much, in so many seminars, interviews and to me, it is straightforward: I am Muslim and I am British and I am happy to be both otherwise I would not be here."* She, alike most of my interviewees had no difficulty with the hyphenated or multiple identities. At the same time she expressed anxiety about the possible denial of recognition of her multiply identities by the wider society, which is reminiscent of the elaborated above lack-of-recognition model of citizenship. This real or imagined denial to embrace in the category of Britishness other ways of 'being British' was also the reason for which many of the respondents of Tariq Modood found it difficult to call themselves 'British'. According to him, some of the British-born Asians and Caribbeans do not call themselves 'British' because they feel that the majority of white people do not accept them as such on the grounds of their race or cultural background: through hurtful 'jokes', harassment, discrimination, etc (Modood 2001: 74).

Most of my interviewees, however, who make up the emerging new Muslim elite asserted their Britishness quite firmly. Many of them took the fact that they are British for granted and did not think about it in their daily life. Alike some of my Belgian informants, many of them said that they had realized how strongly attached they were to different aspects of life in their country only when they left it. This was, for instance the case of Kadir, who pointed out that *"When we go back home to our ancestral countries like India or Pakistan we discover how important is Britain for us and we will be flying the flag. But in the UK no one sees that we are happy, because we are British. There is no question there."* or the case of Fadi, who said *"If I go to Saudi Arabia, I say that I am British and I hold up my passport. First thing I do. Then I get ripped off by the locals ... hahaha* (laughing - KP). *Everywhere I have been I am British. I have been to Jordan, Dubai, America, all over Europe. Everywhere I am British."* Another interviewee, Yumn even defined her Britishness in relation to the situation of travel outside the country. She argued that *"It is something that you feel when you go somewhere else, abroad, and when you come back you feel more at home; you feel that you appreciate things about it. You feel comfortable to be yourself in that place."* Yet another informant, Sajid claimed to be so deeply attached to Britain that he finds it very hard to leave the country and stay abroad for longer periods. He said *"I get a headache when I am supposed to go overseas. And it is enough that I go for a week and I get homesick."* He, however, did not associate it with his strong feelings of belonging to Britain but argued that *"It is a matter of human condition."* This interviewee, as well as, many others found it difficult to go away from Britain also because this country accommodates many (if not most) members of their families so leaving the country is often synonymous with stretching the vital family ties.[323]

The notion of Britishness that emerges from my interviews with the young Muslim Londoners is the one that is largely unreflexive and the one, which my informants claim to possess almost 'by default', or as a 'natural' consequence of the fact

---

[323] I shall elaborate more exhaustively on this point in the next section devoted to supranational dimension of the identities of my interviewees.

that they were born or grew up in the country. This is particularly clearly visible in the following statement of Fadi, who said *"I was born here, so I don't see it* (Britishness – KP) *as something extraordinary, I am British. I have always been. I didn't come here and struggle for years to get British citizenship. To me being British is what I am. It is not something that I had to learn to do. I was born and bread here, so I don't really care much for going and seeing the House of Parliament or whatever. To me Britain is more than the history. It evolves and I am part of the growth and the evolution of Britain. If I went to Pakistan, I am sure I would be a complete stranger and they would see me a mile off. To me being British is just who I am, the way I talk, the way I queue, the way I drive."* Similar understanding of Britishness as the general sum of experiences of life in the country one may find in my interview with Mazin who argued that *"For me to be British, I wouldn't say it is by default, but it has come through my life experiences. I went to public school* (private school – KP)... *old school tie, old boy network, I went through all that. It is a very nasty experience I am sorry to say. I faced a lot of racism when I was growing up. But this is a cream this society produces and it has changed me in some ways, in many ways it hasn't changed me. At the same time I have seen the discipline of the public school, I have seen the institution's work, how sport is emphasized, how you learn about competition - all this kind of influence that came into my life and then at the end of that you have to define who are you, why did you go through these experiences."* Mazin claimed that he took the best things out of the Britishness that had shaped him when he was growing up and now he was able - also thanks to the Muslim civil society - to use some of his experiences to contribute to the wider society.

The most common understanding of British identity among my interviewees was the subjective one. For most of the young Muslim Londoners 'being British' meant above all to 'feel British' or to identify with widely understood notion of Britishness. One may notice the elements of such understanding of the British identity, for instance, in the following statement of Adel who said *"I am a British. I don't feel Bangladeshi. I eat Bengali food yeah, but I eat British food too. I speak Bengali that is true, but I speak better English than Bengali. I can't speak properly Bengali. I speak better Arabic than Bengali because I studied it. Does it mean that I am more Arab than Bengali? You see. Does being British mean to eat fish and chips? Or wear a tie? I don't know what it means*

302

to be British. (...) I just feel myself as British. I visited Bangladesh, I visited the Middle East. I didn't feel there at home." Another informant whose understanding of the British identity was in many ways similar to the Adel's one was Nadira's who argued "I have been up and down in England, that should make me British. I don't know what it is, but I just feel it." Also the understanding of the British identity by Rushd has many marks of the subjective identity. She stated "Yes, I am British because I have been living for all my life in Britain. I feel attached to this country because I know that this is a place, where I can get along. I know how things work, and I have a part in it. I do love where I live." The porousness and openness of the British identity, elaborated in the chapter three, which enables newcomers to relatively easily embrace it, made it also difficult for my interviewees (as for many other inhabitants of the country) to enlist some concrete constitutive elements of it. Thus the most important elements of this identity that emerged from my interviews were the knowledge of the place and feelings of being part of it.

Some of my interviewees were not, however, comfortable with the idea of British being anything more than a legal title. One of them was, for example, Razin who stated "I am British and I always think of British as a kind of result of the fact that I was born in Britain. I wouldn't say I am English, because English has a stronger attachment to the race and ethnicity, so that is hard to do. But British - the fact that you were born in Britain or you went through the process of naturalization – yes." Britishness, in his understanding, was mainly a legal citizenship resulting from the birth in the country where there is jus soli, (such birthright citizenship was in operation in Britain till 1983) or from successful naturalization. He made also an important point about the English identity as being strongly linked with the racial category of whites and viewed as closed ethnicity. This opinion was also shared by many other young Muslim Londoners interviewed in the course of this research. Two of them were Nadira, who said "English, it would be someone white. They are English. British is anyone. English is some whose roots and ancestry is in England." and Samar who stated "I am British. I never say English. English for me is White Caucasian. I can be British-Muslim or British-Pakistani." Such perceptions of the category of English amongst the members of other ethnic and religious minorities in the country prove also other studies (e.g. Modood & Berthoud 1997).

303

Finally, there was also a small minority amongst my informants who with the strong local accents said that they were neither attached towards their localities nor to Britain, and claimed to feel uncomfortable calling themselves British. One of them was Jamil who stated that *"I have certain nostalgia towards the places I have lived in and the places I have seen. Not doubt about that. But if you asked me if tomorrow there was an Islamic caliphate what would you feel more attached towards the caliphate, or this state* (Britain – KP), *I would go for the first option. Probably every Muslim who believes in the notion of Islamic caliphate would love to live in the state that reflects our value system. In no way negating the feelings and nostalgia we have towards various issues within the UK."* Another interviewee who shared the same viewpoint with Jamil, while not sharing his 'nostalgia' to certain aspects of Britishness, was Marwan. He argued that instead of feeling attached to the country *"I feel attached to my ideas, because the place where I live is not a place where I chose to live. I need to live in some country. I was born here yeah, I was born British. It doesn't mean anything more than the fact I live in the country and I obey the law of the country, and contribute as Muslim as much as I can. I have some sense of belonging and sense of responsibility, but I don't know what it means to be attached. Yes, my upbringing, my childhood was in this country, but you can't be attached to soil, bricks and mortars. You have to be attached to the community, I feel attached to certain sections of this society."* The sections of the wider society to which Marwan felt mostly attached and with whom he strongly identified were the Muslim sections of the British society.

The vast majority of my informants, who in contrast to the aforementioned interviewees, did not feel uncomfortable calling themselves British, British-Muslims, British-Pakistanis etc. expressed not only a general attachment to Britain, but also to numerous aspects of life in the country. One of the most frequently mentioned aspect of life in Britain that was highly appreciated by my interviewees was the cultural diversity. Samar, for instance said *"I feel I am a British citizen and I have attachments towards the country. I like the fact that it has so much diversity and that it values good people. There is room for people of different cultures, faiths, backgrounds and viewpoints to share the same say, and to be recognized on the basis of how they contribute rather than on the basis of anything else. (...)"* Akram was another interviewee who identified multiculturalism as one of the key aspect of Britishness and declared to deeply value it. He argued that *"A wonderful thing of being British is that it is not one set in stone culture. Britain is a multicultural society that is proud of its diversity and hence I can have an opinion which is different yet partly part of the space which defines Britishness, which is huge. And it facilitates many, many members of different ideas and inclinations to be British."*

Yet a different aspect of life in Britain, closely linked with multiculturalism, was deeply appreciated by my interviewees was high level of tolerance for otherness and open-mindedness. The appreciation of these elements one may notice, for example, in the following statement of Jada who said *"What I like about Britain is that you can do what you want to do and people would not really look down on you, or look at you differently... Is like the other day I saw a lady walking down and she had practically all her face and ears pierced, her hair was a bit here and a bit there, but nobody really looked at her twice saying "Oh my God! This is so weird!' People just walked by and she was allowed to do, what she wanted to do, whereas in Bangladesh or maybe in other countries, you won't be allowed to do certain things, if you do not fit into the rules whatever the rules of that country are."* Afnan was another female interviewee for whom these values were crucial. She stated *"I cherish open-mindedness in Britain. You will always find people, who are open-minded and understanding of what it is to be from a different race or a different culture. To be respected as an individual and not to be judged suspicious because of the color of me skin or the background that I come from."* Yet another informant, Fadi, for whom the essence of Britishness was tolerance for others, said about the British society that *"It is very open, very adopting. It is not perfect but I think the great thing about it is that I can sit with Hindus, Christians, Jews, atheists, x, y, z, and I have no issues with them. If I sit in Pakistan with an Indian maybe someone would have an issue. If I sit with a Palestinian in Israel someone would have an issue.... In Britain there is no problem, you sit down, you talk your problems through. It is the best place to resolve issues. That is what I cherish about Britain."* Even my informant Jamil who did not feel British asserted that *"There is something about the British people which is great and that the government is now changing. The feeling of tolerance which for many decades has been a positive force in this society. This toleration for one another is a great virtue. And unfortunately these ideas are now being suppressed by the government.*" His complaints about the changing political climate eroding the tolerance of the British society were however not widely supported by other interviewees. On the contrary, some of my informants argued that in spite of the terrorist attack perpetrated by young Muslims on 7th July 2005, the British society was still largely tolerant. One of them was Thaqib said "*I feel proud of being British, for example, in a moment like some time ago when I was standing at the London United Vigil at Trafalgar Square*[324]. *I was proud that there were so many people there who stood with me and they did not blame me for what happened on 7/7.*"

Moreover, many of my interviewees claimed to be proud of various kinds of freedom that they possess as citizens of Britain, while at the same time comparing them with freedoms in other parts of the globe. Afnan, for instance, stated "*I am happy of the freedoms that we have and which are denied elsewhere in the world, such as, freedom of speech, freedom to lobby, to campaign, to education, freedom to develop as a person. I think that is quite a big thing.*" Another female interviewee, Rana touched upon similar issues when she argued "*I value democratic system that works in the sense that there are regular elections which by and large are fair and you can vote. There are all these things you cannot take for granted because they do not exist everywhere else. I value the education system with all the opportunities that it gives you as a person.*" As individuals whom education often enabled emancipation, these informants clearly knew the value of it. However, the opportunities opened up by acquisition of the institutional cultural capital were more widely appreciated by my informants. One of my male interviewees who mentioned the significance of it was Shabaz. He said "*I enjoy the importance this country gives to education, to trying to find out the truth about the world, progress in research. These are great qualities. This place provides avenues for people to be honest. So also the trade unions, newspapers to some extent are trying to convey different opinions on certain issues.*" Another interviewee Mansur engaged in comparison of the political freedoms in Britain and in the countries of the Middle East drawing on his own experiences. He said "*I was in Jordan as a student, and the political freedoms there and*

---

[324] He refers to the vigil organized on 12th July 2007 by the Major of London Office with the Trades Union Congress and representatives of London's different faiths and communities.

306

here is day and night different. Even though Jordan is a safe heaven of the Middle East, where you can speak loudly and clearly, and express your feelings, but even then there are restrictions. Here, I have the freedom to say whatever I want."

There were also numerous interviewees who while explaining their attachment to Britain pointed out the importance of positive liberties in the form of social rights, the welfare state and various opportunities. Sajid, for instance, stated *"I am proud that we have National Health Service, which on the whole works ..."* Another interviewee, Rasha, argued that *"If you want to do something you can do it, you just need to work hard. I think we are here very well resourced in that way. There are so many things you can get involved with, in the Muslim community, as well as, in the wider community."* The same appreciation of the existence of various opportunities for social involvement, as well as personal advancement and strong believe in meritocracy, I could trace also in the interviews with other young Muslim Londoners.[325] One of them, Mansur, for instance, argued that *"I am part of the society which is advancing technology, which has a high level of education and which has a bright future. I am proud to be part of that. I am proud that as a teacher I can make changes in people's lives in school and at colleges. I am proud that I have the opportunity and the chance to go and to make those differences. In other place I probably would not have that chance. In Saudi Arabia I won't have that chance. I am Saudi or I am nobody."*

The young Muslim Londoners claimed to be happy to be British also for numerous more 'mundane reasons'. Kadir, for example, said that for him such a crucial element of the everyday life in Britain was food. He explained that *"It is not the British food that I cherish so much but the way Britons welcome so many different cultures within the society in food. You can go anywhere in London and you will always find an incredible variety of food."* Another interviewee to some extent in the same vein argued that *"I identify with fish and chips. Really! I loved this funny ad after the Olympics bid saying 'yes, we have lousy food, but we won the Olympics*[326]*' – I can identify with that."* (Shahd) For a different informant, Mazin, such a key element of Britishness that he

---

[325] Here it is worth mentioning that many of these features of Britishness to which my informants were so strongly attached are also features of modernity. In other words 'being British' in their case is to a large extent synonymous with 'being modern'.
[326] She refers to the wining bid of London over Paris (54-50) for the Summer Olympic Games 2012 announced on 6th July 2005 that is a day before the tragic terrorist attacks.

particularly cherished was the British sense of humour. He said *"One of the most important things to me, and that might be a minute point ... I love the British sense of humour. I think it is so clever. I think it is the most sophisticated in the world and it is generally funny. The satire lightens the moods. I know the British go a little bit over the top when it comes to comedy and satire. I went the other day to a business meeting, but unfortunately everyone was joking about everything. This is a British trait and sometimes it irritates the Americans and Europeans. We don't joke at funerals... at least until the coffin is in the grave ... hahaha* (laughing- KP*). This whole thing also breeds tolerance because we can laugh about ourselves and we can laugh about things and this is essentially saying 'don't take life so seriously'. It is very important part of living together (...). British sense of humour is a great contribution to the world."* Yet, some other interviewees argued that such 'minute points' – to use the words of Mazin – or reasons for which they feel attached to the country are British achievements in sport. Akram, for example said *"I am an England fan, I was very disappointed that we have lost in the recent cricket match so easily."* Another male interviewee Mumtaz asserted *"I'm a passionate football follower. When Britain plays with Pakistan I support Britain. The Bangladesh is crap ... hahaha (Laughing – KP), but if they play against Britain I support both teams. I'm not a cricket fan but when Bangladesh played with Pakistan I would go and have a laugh."* Also some of my female informants cherished this aspect of Britishness. One of them was Jaheda who said *"I support England in football matches and I am screaming and shouting. Sincerely I am cheering for English and British football players."* Thus, one may conclude that if the Norman Tebbit's cricket test extended also to football then most of my interviewees would pass it or semi-pass it (e.g. Mumtaz cheering at the same time for both Bangladeshi and English teams).[327]

The members of the emerging new Muslim elite were, at the same time, very critical about some other aspects of British history, current affairs and politics. As far as the historical aspects are concerned they were particularly critical about the British colonialism and its legacy. As for the current affairs issues, one of the elements which

---

[327] Here it is worth mentioning that during the FIFA World Cap 2006 not only the inhabitants of the predominantly White districts of London were flying English flags, but I could also see many young British Asians in the Tower Hamlets and other Muslimtowns of London driving with the flags attached to their cars and flying them out of their windows. For more information about British Asians and football see Burdsey 2006.

especially deeply annoyed them was the country's foreign policy and in particular the British involvement in the war in Iraq. Almost all of the interviewees declared to be profoundly disappointed with the decision of the government to join the USA-led 'Coalition of the Willing' and then after the invasion of Iraq to become one of the major occupying forces (apart from the Americans and in much smaller degree Poles) in the country. Sajid for instance said *"I am not proud of the things which are not good like our foreign policy. We do not have to blindly follow America. After all, once we were an empire."* Another interviewee Mansur argued that *"Not only as a student of politics but above all as a citizen of this country I don't agree, for example, with the British Iraqi policy and Palestinian policy."* Yet some other interviewees complained about the ethnic and racial profiling by the Police, stop-and-search policy and the new anti-terrorist measures. All these issues will be explored in greater detail below, in the section of this chapter devoted to the analysis of the content of my interviewees' subjective notions of citizenship.

5.2.6 BEING SUPRANATIONAL

The young Muslim Londoners interviewed in the course of this research had much looser relations with the countries of origin of their parents than my Belgian interviewees. While half of the members of the latter group declared to visit the countries of their parents regularly, in my British sample only seven interviewees said to pay visits to their families or members of larger *biraderi*[328] in Bangladesh and Pakistan regularly and not less frequently than every three years. The remaining nineteen young Muslim Londoners travelled to South Asia and Africa less frequently than every four years or they have visited the countries in which they or their parents were born sporadically (up to three times) or they have never visited them (four informants). One of the few informants who did keep a dynamic contact with the country of origin of her parents and regularly flew to South Asian was Rasha. She explained that *"I have this very strong connection to my parents' country, because my parents made sure that we learnt Bengali. We've spent a*

---

[328] *Biraderi* is an extended kinship group defined through male lineage, of close and more distant relatives, who tend to be of the same caste status. These groups pay key social role (and sometimes also other roles - e.g. political) among the first generation of immigrants. For more information about the Biraderi and its significance amongst the South Asian Muslims see for example Ballard 1994, Lewis 2002 or Akhtar 2003.

year or so at the age of eight in Bangladesh. I had teachers there. I am quite unusual in the local area in the sense that most of the people have a lot of family here, whereas we don't. We've got most of our family back in Bangladesh. " Another informant who paid a regular visits to Bangladesh was a student of pharmacy Dirar, for whom it was more the case of keeping in touch with his own country of origin than with parents' country of origin. He stated that *"I was born in Bangladesh and came to Britain at the age of six, so I've managed to get a good understanding of the society and the context of Bangladesh from young-child's perspective. I have some of that baggage with me, which I feel kind of proud of sometimes, to have a sense of who I was and who I am at this moment. "* By and large, the numerous family and *biraderi* members back on the Asian subcontinent and the efforts of the parents to keep the contact alive with them were the most commonly mentioned reasons for regular travels to South Asia by those interviewees who were inter-continental travellers flying to Pakistan or Bangladesh at least every three years.

Conversely, having most of the family members in Britain was one of the major reasons why majority of my interviewees paid only sporadic visits to Pakistan and Bangladesh. The argument of geographical distance and hence of high cost of such a travel was also mentioned by some interviewees. Besides many of them claimed that they were not very much attached to the parents' countries that would make them to visit these countries more often. One of them was, for example, Jada who argued that *"I have been to Bangladesh only once and I didn't like it and didn't enjoyed it... because the feeling which I had was 'this is not home'. I wouldn't like to settle down there. Some of my friends say: 'I am going back home', but I wouldn't use this phrase. Bangladesh is not a home to me. This* (Britain – KP) *is home to me. I feel very British. I am attached to everything here.... "*

Another interviewee who felt like Jada about the parents' country of origin, was Nadira. She said *"I would not want to live in Pakistan, cos the mentality of people over there is different. I remember when we were on holidays. They were really lovely, but I am not just like that. I have a different character (...) I couldn't live in Pakistan. There is a difference of humour, different entertainment... the ways they lead their lives. The only reason I am attached to Pakistan is because I love my family and they still live there. If all my family moved to Britain, Pakistan wouldn't mean much to me at all. "* Yet, some other interviewees claimed not to look forward to visits to South Asia because many elements of the Asian life (apart from families and friends from the same ethnic group) they had at reach in their city boroughs. The institutional completeness (Brenton 1964) or the existence of the wide range of ethnic and religious services (including inter alia various shops with ethnic products, restaurants, mosques, ethnic and religious radio-stations, associations, etc.) in the areas where they lived was in the case of many informants sufficiently fulfilling their need of contact with Asian culture and traditions, or with their ethnic 'roots' as on the interviewees (Rana) called them.

There were also some informants, who were in two minds about their attitudes to the parents' countries of origin and those countries' cultural heritage. On the one hand, they wanted to keep the contact with these countries and their heritage through, for instance, learning their languages and, on the other hand, in the situation of choice between improving their knowledge of Arabic and improving their understanding of Urdu, Punjabi, Pashto, Bangla or other languages of the parents' country/area of origin, in most of the cases they were choosing learning Arabic[329]. One of such interviewees was Maha who stated *"I hate the thought of losing my heritage and I want to have that back. (...) I am personally losing my mother tongue and is saddens me. I'd like to keep that. I didn't learn it at school. Now it is more common* (that pupils learn the 'ethnic languages' at schools – KP), *also Arabic. On the other hand, if I had to choose between Arabic and Bengali, I would choose Arabic, because I'm in the process of learning Arabic. It is more of a priority to be able to understand my religion. That is what I am trying also to teach children at the summer school* (organized by her Muslim association – KP). *Try to learn Arabic because translations never do justice to the Arabic. Bengali you can always learn, later on. But, I know it is already getting late."*

At the same way as the members of the emerging new Muslim elite in London prioritized the acquisition of the knowledge of Arabic over the improvement of their knowledge of languages of the ethnic communities which they were part of, they also prioritized the belonging to the worldwide Muslim community over the belonging to the

---

[329] These tensions between the diasporic orientations towards a South Asian aesthetic diaspora and the Muslim diaspora are explored in depth by Pnina Werber in her book on 'Imagined Diasporas Among Manchester Muslims' (2002).

Bangladeshi, Pakistani or other ethnic diasporas.[330] In other words, their sense of relationship, empathy and solidarity with other co-religionists in other countries of the world was significantly stronger that their sense of relationship with co-ethnic members in different parts of the globe. One may detect this strong sense of connection with Muslims in other parts of the world or the diasporic religious identity, for example, in the following statement of Afnan: *"I have a feeling and a need to be part of the ummah, because wherever you go as a Muslim if you see other Muslims and you greet them 'as-salaam', you are immediately connected, you immediately have something in common. What is happening in Iraq, in Afghanistan and all these faces…. I do feel for that, because I feel like there are people of my faith and I will continue to do what I can for them."* The same strong features of the Islamic diasporic identity constituted inter alia by identification with Islam as contemporary world cultural and political force one may observe in the opinion of yet another female interviewee, Maha, who said *"Subconsciously, you know you are part of the ummah, because there are Muslims all over the world, and everybody feels part of the ummah. You always see news about Muslims suffering, so you always feel the ache and the pains of the Muslim people and you keep them in your prayers… you keep them in your mind and try to help ummah"*. As Pnina Werbner notices in her "Imagined Diasporas …" the Pakistanis (I think it equally applies to the Bangladeshis) in Britain have redefined themselves not only as conventional diaspora focused on a national homeland, but also as a Muslim diaspora[331] (2002: 12). I believe the emergence of the new generations of British Pakistanis and British Bangladeshis who similarly to my interviewees do not feel very attached to the parents' countries of origin played a crucial role in this latter redefinition. Thus, the

---

[330] By a diaspora (Gr. *Speiro* – to sow, *dia* – over) I mean after Marienstras (1989) a group based on a degree of national, or cultural, or linguistic awareness of a relationship, territorially discontinuous, with a group settled elsewhere. Generally a diaspora can be understood as a social form (concerned with the extent and nature of social political and economic relationship), as type of consciousness (involving aspects of collective memory) and as a mode of cultural reproduction (relating to the global flow of cultural objects, images and meanings). More on the notion of diaspora and different types of diasporas see Cohen 1997.

[331] Here it is worth mentioning that there is no agreement among the students of diasporas if this notion can be applied to religious communities. Robert Cohen for example points out that universal religions cannot become diasporas because they are philosophically grounded in a transcendence of space and time (1997: 188-189). On the other hand, John R. Hinnells argues that the terms 'migrants' and 'religion in migration' are unsatisfactory and proposes a term 'diaspora religion' for religion of any people who have a sense of living away from the land of the religion or away from 'the old country' (1997: 686). More information on this academic debate one may find in Vertovec 2004.

invention of Muslim diaspora among the British South Asians resulted from the fact that the British-born members of these communities were not able to reconnect with other co-ethnic members in other parts of the globe as meaningfully as their parents and from refocusing of their attention from the Asian subcontinent to the Islamic peripheries and the Muslim communities often persecuted and displaced beyond the Islamic heartland. Hence they have rediscovered their connection to Palestine, Bosnia, Chechnya, Kashmir and even Uzbekistan. How effectively some of them have been exploring these newly rediscovered connections one may see, for example, in the following opinion of Jamil who said *"On the top of the list there must be the ummah, no doubt about it. Not only because of the religious obligations but also because of the political dimension, because today there is immense opportunity available to us in the West to speak on behalf of our wider ummah, which actually the ummah has not been able to project. So the Muslims in Andijan did not have the possibility to contact the media, as we had here and convey what took place in Andijan.*[332] *"* They are able to extensively explore these newly rediscovered connections inter alia due to recent advances in the communications technology. Thus, the cyber ummah or the Islamic interconnectivity on the Internet enables them to more effectively enact the imagined global ummah.[333]

In contrast to most of the members of the emerging New Muslim elite in Brussels, who tended to think about the ummah in more symbolic terms, many of my British interviewees spoke about the worldwide Muslim community as there were no differences, antagonisms and sometimes bloody conflicts between various Muslim groups living in different parts of the globe (e.g. an ongoing conflict between Shi'a and Sunni Muslims in Iraq, Pakistan or Lebanon). For many of my British interviewees, unlike the young Belgian Muslims, the ummah existed not only at the symbolic level of the faith, but also as almost real community. This community was enacted by the British Muslims' sense of solidarity and empathy with Muslim victims of the armed conflicts in different parts of the world (especially Palestine, Iraq, Afghanistan and Kashmir) whose images have been

---

[332] He refers to the Andijan massacre which occurred when Uzbek Interior Ministry and National Security Service troops fired into a crowd of protesters in Andijan, Uzbekistan on 13 May 2005. The official death toll of 187 people is being disputed.

[333] For illuminating exploration of the relations between the historical ummah and the idea of ummah, on the one hand, and the cyber ummah, on the other, see Cooke and Lawrence 2005.

circulating not only in the channels of global media but also in the local media[334]. Thus, I tend to agree with Pnina Werbner, who suggests that the global myth of the transnational Islamic community, is a central feature of the new British-Muslim self-understanding. (Ibid)

Yet, a different type of supranational identity such as European identity had very few supporters amongst my British interviewees. The only interviewee who felt strongly about it was Akram who asserted that *"I see myself as European. I think it is very important that Britain has joined the EU. We should be part of Europe and an active part of Europe. Rather than being at the peripheries of Europe, and having things being dictated to us. I think we should be part of the European Force. I do not agree with the Conservative euro-sceptical policy at this level."* For the vast majority of my interviewees the European identity was not a meaningful identity to which they would feel attached. However, by not identifying with the European project they do not necessarily distinguish themselves from the wider British public. As I have argued in the third chapter, Britons have very ambiguous stand towards Europe. They see themselves "with Europe but not of it" - to use the words of Winston Churchill. The attitudes of the young British Muslims towards Europe are largely within this national climate. As the researcher of the Islamic Foundation, Dilwar Hussain aptly pointed out *"Muslims in this country would follow this pattern of thinking* (very ambivalent stand towards Europe – KP) *in one way or another. They do not really have connections with Muslims in France or Germany. They still talk about going to Europe, if they are going to France or to Germany. (...) I think they have weaker sense of European identity than Muslims in other European countries because of the national British climate. It is very typical of any other British or English person in terms of their attitude towards Europe. Muslims would have the same concerns about the Euro, being 'ruled by Brussels', and things like that. All sorts of stereotypical things which come off when a British person is asked about his or her attitude towards Europe, Muslims would also resound."* (Hussain quoted in Pędziwiatr 2006d)

---

[334] The British military presence in such places like Iraq and Afghanistan has clearly contributed to the high frequency of appearance of images of 'Muslim victims' in the British media which strengthens the Muslim groups for whom the victimization is the major mobilization strategy.

5.2.7 BEING A LONDONER

As I have argued above the multidimensionality of social identities means that one might be strongly attached to the national community as well as to the religious one, and these two attachments do not have to be mutually exclusive. This was for instance the case of many of my Belgian interviewees. In the case of my British informants most of them emphasised that they felt firstly Muslims and Londoners, and only then British. Thus, it seems that for most of the members of the emerging new Muslim elite in London, the diasporic religious and local identities were even more meaningful than the national identity. One of these informants was, for example, Kadir who said *"I feel first Londoner and then British. It is very different being in London because it is such a mix, such a rich culture and each culture enriches the whole London. That shows who we are. I think it is this mix that I feel most strongly attached to. I think this is why the Muslim communities come in here and they feel very much at home."* Another interviewee who stressed that his attachment to London was even stronger than his attachment to the whole country was Fadi. He argued *"I'm a Londoner more than I am British actually. I'm very proud of being a Londoner and if I go for instance to Manchester or Birmingham, or anywhere else in the country, I am very specifically seen as a Londoner."* In other words, he suggested that his local identity was also very easily deciphered by inhabitants of other big cities in the country. Yet, another interviewee, Dirar, emphasized the importance of the relationships that linked him with the city for his own self-understanding by saying *"I am attached to the whole of the UK if not Britain itself. Most strongly to London. I am a Londoner. It is the best place to be."* The same very strong sense of the local identity I could find among my female informants. One of them Yumn argued, for example, *"Because I lived mostly in London I feel mostly attached to London. It is very vibrant, diverse and open. My sense of belonging is more to London that to Britain. I am attached to the diversity of people that live here, who all come from different backgrounds, but they all feel the same sense of belonging to London."* Yet another young Muslim woman, Afnan, interviewed in the course of the research asserted *"I don't think I could call home anywhere other than London now. This is my home. This is my city. I think I could travel abroad and I could probably live temporarily elsewhere, but I think I would always return to London. So I would consider this my home, my children's home and children*

children's home. This is where I am, this is where I belong and I think I wouldn't fit in anywhere, and I wouldn't be happy anywhere else." She was not the only informant who emphasized her strong emotional attachment to the capital of Britain and who called it 'my home' or 'my city'. These phrases were also used by many other young Muslim Londoners. One of them was Sajid who stated *"Of course I feel attached to London. I have no other place. When London was bombed* (on 7/7 – KP) *I thought – 'how dare anyone could hit the city'. This is my city. This is my people. Even when looking from religious perspective: look at the areas bombed. Edgware Road and Aldgate East are respectively the Arab quarter and Bengali quarter. They* (the suicide bombers – KP) *were going out to kill Muslims. Regardless how you look at it of course you belong here. Our heart is here."*

The strong local identity of my interviewees had also its visible sub-local dimensions. One of such sub-local identities that emerged particularly clearly from my interviewees with the young Muslims in London was the identity of an East Londoner. Most of my interviewees who lived in such boroughs of East London as Tower Hamlets, Newham, Hackney and Waltham Forrest (which are also the areas of the highest concentration of Muslims in the city[335]) very strongly identified with these places. They spoke about themselves as East Londoners, East Enders[336] and sometimes as Cockneys[337]. One of them was for example Akram who asserted *"I feel very strongly a Londoner. I am an East Londoner even more than Londoner. I am a Cockney even more than that ... hahaha* (laughing – KP). *I feel to be a part of East London."* He also explained what made this part of London so special that he was so deeply identifying with it, in the following way: *"There is an identity in East London. This place has always been a home of people who have migrated from their countries. This is the place where*

---

[335] Please see the table with the areas of the highest concentration of Muslims in the country in the chapter three.

[336] The term refers to the inhabitants of today's borough of Tower Hamlets and the southern part of Hackney. Traditionally the East End has contained some of the poorest areas of London. This area throughout the history has absorbed numerous waves of immigrants who have each added a new dimension to its culture and history. Most notably it absorbed the French Protestant Huguenots in the 17th century, the Irish in the 18th century and Ashkenazi Jews fleeing pogroms in Eastern Europe towards the end of the 19th century. From the beginning of 1960 it has been a major settling area for the Bangladeshis arriving to Britain.

[337] The term "cockney" refers to working-class inhabitants of East London, and the slang used by these people. A "true" Cockney is often said to be someone born within earshot of the Bow Bells, i.e. the bells of St Mary-le-Bow church in Cheapside in the City of London. On the cockney slang see Hughes 1979.

they have made themselves *financially stable and then they spread their wings. But with me, I wouldn't feel comfortable living outside East London, because this is the place where things are happening, this is where you get the vibrancy of London as a city."* Another interviewee, Rasha, said *"I am very much attached to the local area, East London because I would think very hard before moving out. I like being here, I like people, I know my way around very well."* Yet another interviewee who also argued that his bond with this particular part of London was so strong that he would not like to move out from it was Mansur. He stated *"I can't live outside Tower Hamlets. I've been to Manchester - I didn't like it. I've been to Bradford - I didn't like it. Oldham - didn't like it. I have to live in Tower Hamlets. I can't live outside the East End. I grew up here. I like it much more than anywhere else."* Maha who did move out from the East End accounted for her feelings about this decision of her parents with whom she lived in the following way: *"I was very attached, that is why I was sad to move. We moved last year, but I am always back in the area for my studies. I am very attached to this place, to East London. Above all I feel Tower Hamletser, hahaha* (laughing – KP)."

One of the major reasons for which my interviewees felt deeply attached to London, or some parts of the capital like, for example, the East End, was their cultural diversity. Mazin for instance argued that *"For me London is the best place in the world to be. (...) Everyone gets something in London. It is such a wonderful place. There are people from all nationalities. Here on the Edgware Road you have some Arab influences... you get shawarma, shishas etc. If you go to Golders Green you will have the Jewish influence. In Stoke Newington Road you will have Turkish influence. If you go to Brick Lane there is Bengali influence and different foods. Everyone really gets on in London."* And then he added *"I can't say we live in an integrated society but I don't think you have to integrate in order to enjoy the contributions that other people make."* Another interviewee for whom the multiculturalism of London was one of the major reasons for identification was Dirar. He claimed that *"All the multis that you can get basically, we've got in London ... hahaha* (laughing – KP). *Multi-race, multi-culture, multi-religion... everything is multi here. It is good to be part of it. These are the things that I appreciate most about London."* The same point was made by Razin who said *"I wouldn't like to live anywhere else than in London. I am attached to London and mainly*

*to its people. This is the main reason why I feel happy to identify myself as a Londoner...
because of the people here and the fact that 300 languages are spoken in London[338], the
multicultural dimension. "* The extremely high level of cultural diversity that my
interviewees were so fond of in London was recently termed by Steven Vertovec as
'super-diversity'. By introducing a new term into the vocabulary of social science
Vertovec wants to underline that the level and kind of cultural complexity that one may
find in London (as well as in other super-diverse cities of Europe) surpasses anything that
European countries have previously experienced (2006).

The important reason for which the young Muslims strongly identified with
London was also the level of tolerance and acceptance of otherness that they felt was
particularly high in their city. One can trace elements of it for instance in the opinion of
Fadi who argued *"Being a Londoner means also being multicultural, being accepted by
anyone for who you are and what you are, and accepting others. In London you can meet
every religion, every thinking, whatever it is and we get on. I've sat side by side with
friends who were Israeli, some of them were in the army, and if I see them, or bump into
them I would say 'how are you doing?' Honestly, I have many friends like that, because
we are in London, and I went to college with them. That's what the great thing about
London is - that you can be totally different and yet you talk. "* This tolerance was tested
particularly thoroughly after the terrorist attacks on 7th July 2005 and the unsuccessful
attacks two weeks later. Nevertheless, according to most of my interviewees, it managed
to pass this test successfully. Their argumentation was in a similar vein to Razin who said
that *"After the 7th July attacks literally nothing happened in London. There were
obviously some fringe elements who did a few things, like throwing stones at windows of
mosques etc. but it didn't really go much more than that. Up north it maybe did... like the
guy who was killed in Nottingham.[339] In London where the attacks took place things went
normal. London has gone on with its life and I think that is quite good."*

---

[338] The figure of 300 languages spoken in London mentioned by my interviewee comes originally from a
survey of no less than 896,743 London schoolchildren concerning which language(s) they speak at home
(Baker and Mohieldeen quoted in Vertovec 2006).

[339] He is referring to the religiously motivated murder of Kamal Butt from Pakistan outside a corner shop in
Nottingham three days after the 7 July bombings.

A significant number of my interviewees also saw London as a city of many opportunities, where everyone's sense of agency could be efficiently channelled. One of the interviewees who probably emphasized the existence of a wide range of career options and opportunities for community involvement for the inhabitants of London the most strongly, was Fadi. He argued that *"The great thing about London is that it allows you all the freedom, more than anywhere else in the world, to be the best that you can be. In work and in social activities. In work because if you want to earn one million pounds – no problem. Whatever you want is here. From a social perspective, one day I can be sitting in my house and another day I can be helping organizing the biggest demonstration this country has ever seen in its history with people from Hollywood, celebrities, American politicians like Jesse Jackson.*[340] *One day I am sitting doing something and the next day I am in front of two million people on stage with Jesse Jackson, Tim Robins, you know, huge people, Ken Livingstone, big MPs (*Members of Parliament – KP*), lords. That what London allows me to do. The sky is the limit."* Not only Fadi, but also other interviewees - as upwardly mobile people - strongly believed in meritocracy and perceived British society, contrary to some studies in social mobility (e.g. Goldthorpe and Payne 1986), as a generally open society.[341]

Like the young Belgian Muslims, my interviewees in London also highly appreciated such aspects of life in the British capital as the proximity of other coreligionists and the existence of the well-developed religious institutional structures. One of them, for instance, argued that *"The diversity of London is personified in East London. There is a strong Muslim community here which is a bonus for me as well. I like a lot being near to the East London Mosque and the Muslim community here."* (Akram) Other interviewees claimed that they liked their city boroughs for the presence not only of mosques and other Muslims but also such elements of the religious institutional structure like local Ramadan Radio – a station broadcasting during the month of Ramadan – Qur'anic schools, Muslim bookshops etc. The Fourth National Survey has

---

[340] The interviewee is referring to the demonstration against the war in Iraq that took place in London on 15th February 2003. According to the organizers, two million people took part in the demonstration although police put the figure at 750,000.

[341] In that sense they seemed to support the claim of Peter Saunders (1996), heavily criticized by other researchers of social mobility (see Giddens 2001: 303), that Britain is a true meritocracy because rewards go naturally to those who are best able to 'perform' and achieve.

found that the majority of members of ethnic minorities preferred to live alongside others from their own ethnic group for reasons of social support and shared linguistic, cultural and religious traditions. (Modood and Berthoud 1997: 221) My interviews with the young Muslim Londoners largely supported these findings. They also demonstrated that my informants were aware of the fact that by living in social spaces where Islamic beliefs were widely shared their religious identity was reinforced. One of the elements that contributed significantly to this reinforcement of religious identities was the high level of social control in the Muslimtowns of London, that made it very difficult, for example, for a Muslim person to publicly violate the rules of fasting during the month of Ramadan or for a Muslim woman to meet in the public place in person with a man who was visibly not a member of her family. The social control of the latter type may be detected for instance in the following statement of one of my female interviewees who said, *"I could meet up with you* (the author – KP) *on the street in Tower Hamlets, but I choose not to. Not because of what I think other people would say, because really they can't give a damn, but I just choose not to. Not to offend others."* (Jada)

The young Muslim Londoners were also attached in their localities to non-religious elements of the static space with parks and their former schools being the ones that were most commonly mentioned. Rana, for instance, stated *"The geography is important ... Certain places in London are very important to me, like for example Regents Park, the South Bank Centre. Those kind of places where I have had interesting experiences. For me they are also part of London, because they are part of my memory and the sense of who I am."*, whereas Maha argued that *"The building of my primary school is a key spot in my mental map, because my primary school days were the best. Everyone says that their schools, teachers, experience were the best and wherever you are your memories can't be taken away from you and obviously your attachment goes with it."*

Last, but not least, numerous young Londoners interviewed in the course of the research said they were strongly attached to the whole city or its particular boroughs because of their own involvement in different projects of the local Muslim civil society and sometimes also wider civil society. While strongly identifying with the global Muslim ummah, as I have argued above, most of them were at the same time deeply convinced that the local arena was the most promising place for involvement in terms of potential results. One of my female interviewees argued that "*Locality is the most important to me, because that is where I am involved mostly....*" (Rushd), Another male interviewee said "*I am very attached to my local area, to what is happening locally, because I have more ability to make a positive change in the locality...*". (Akram) Many other interviewees shared their points of view and were involved in numerous projects of Muslim and the wider civil society that will be discussed in more detail in the following section.

5.3 PARTICIPATION, ISLAM AND CITIZENSHIP

Having explored the depth of citizenship of the young Muslim Londoners, I shall now move on to the analysis of the participatory dimension of their citizenship. I will firstly elaborate on the circumstances in which my interviewees became active in the Muslim organisations and in the wider public sphere. Subsequently the major resources that enabled them to move from formal to more substantive forms of citizenship will be assessed. Thirdly, I shall shed light in this section on the reasons for which they are active before finally elaborating on what my interviewees saw as the most important outcomes of their activism.

5.3.1 MUSLIM IDENTITY AND AGENCY

A few decades ago it was widely believed that the religious figure was destined to disappear from the political horizon in Europe. It was largely perceived as a pre-political subject, a residue of an incomplete modernization with no recognition for agency in modern politics. As Nilufer Göle rightly points out, the intellectual conceptions and historical horizon of progress have denied agency to religion in general, but even more so to Islam. (2003: 812) Today Islamism, in its broadest sense, expresses a mode of social and political agency. Contrary to the modernist narratives that have assumed the death of religion, it is the assertion of religious difference that is shaping Islamic agency. By asserting their religious identities, many of the young Muslim Londoners interviewed in the course of this research, similarly to the young Belgian Muslims described in the earlier chapter, found new strength not only to engage more actively with their coreligionists, but also with their compatriots. In other words my research shows that the moment of re-appropriation of religious identities by the members of the emerging new Muslim elite is positively correlated with the beginning of their dynamic involvement within Muslim and wider civil society. It seems that the re-discovery of religion of their parents in a new form enables many of them to more firmly ascertain their position in the society.

One may notice the aforementioned relationship, for instance, in the following statement of Akram who claimed that *"My religion has made me more active as a citizen, as a participant and member of this society. It has empowered me to work more for the benefit of the people of this country."* Another male informant, Fadi, argued that *"If I wasn't working with my Muslim organisation, I wouldn't be doing anything for the society. I think I would be just earning money and spending it. I think by working with my organisation I got involved more with social activities. Other members of my family are traditional. They earn money and spend it – that's it. And then you die."* He suggested that it was religious rediscovery that made him realize that there was more to life than materialism and consumption. Similar dissatisfaction with the consumerist lifestyle and a strong sense of agency grounded in Islam can also be found in the following opinion of Sajid who said that *"If I do what I do, it's because at the end of the day I believe I would face God on the day of judgement and I'll have to explain him exactly what I have been doing for 80 or 90 years. And I want to say more than just that I grew up, got a job... It is very good, I'm not knocking people. But if God has given you more abilities, then you have more responsibilities."* His sense of agency was more specifically grounded in the sense of accountability to God for the days passed on the earth and for the special qualities he was equipped with, whether he made use of them or not. One may also notice in the opinion of Sajid an idea that was frequently evoked by the members of the emerging new Muslim elite, namely that those who have the appropriate qualities or resources are somehow obliged to take action and tackle certain societal problems.[342]

Not only my male interviewees, but also the female ones felt a strong desire to create their personal histories after rediscovering Islam and wanted to engage more dynamically with their respective local communities and wider society. One of them,

---

[342] These resources will be analysed in detail in the following section.

Nadira, pointed out for example that *"I was quite passive before. I didn't care much about the societal issues. I would go about my own things. But after I joined the Muslim organisation I realized I got to really contribute to the society. What are you doing here? – I asked myself. You got to make some difference, you got to really contribute to the society... make some positive thing."* Another informant, Rana, said *"I think my turn to Islam made me a better person in a lot of ways. I think this also carries over in the work that I do with non-Muslims and wider society too. It has made me question ethics a lot more than I would have done otherwise or that I did before. It has given me an experience of living in different worlds, living in different kinds of communities and I think that gives you a better perspective, which actually is really valuable because you can imagine different realities, and the value of different realities, rather than just one way of being."* She not only claimed that re-embracing Islam had empowered her personally but also that it enriched her worldview and enabled her to see things with a higher degree of complexity. Another different female interviewee who also strongly emphasized the importance of her Muslim identity on the way how she interacted with wider society was Yumn. She asserted that *"As a Muslim I feel Islam has an influence on every part of your life, because Islam is comprehensive. It is not just about prayer it is about how you live your whole life, how you interact with other people. It encourages sense of social responsibility, carrying about the society and others around you, and doing something for the society. There is always a feeling that whatever I do, Islam has an influence on that."*

However, not all of the members of my British sample understood Islam as 'comprehensively' as Yumn and felt that it had overarching influence on their ways of being, like some other aforementioned interviewees. A female interviewee, Shahd, said, for instance, *"I think religion adds value enormously to who I am. It is a guidance, reminder and helps me to check myself. But I like to think that the values which I have and which are behind my actions aren't religious values. They are general values and human values."* Also some others acknowledged that their sense of agency was not solely driven by religious convictions but had sprung from other sources that will be discussed below.

Now, it is worth pointing out some elements of the two major, largely parallel processes that characterised the re-appropriations by my interviewees of the religion of their parents. The first process, which I call after Leila Babès (1997) the one of positivisation, manifests itself in the construction of a form of positive Islam that contrasts with the image of Islam maintained by a considerable part of the wider society. It is essentially a process of reversing the images of a violent, intolerant and backward religion that are attached to Islam by some sectors of European societies, and turning such a self-constructed form of a 'positive Islam' into a source of dignity and self-esteem.

In contrast to my Belgian informants, the young Muslim Londoners interviewed in the course of this research rarely spoke about their personal journeys to Islam in terms of a transition from a rejection of Islam (e.g. Murad and Rashid in Brussels) to the re-appropriation of the faith of their parents. The process of positivisation of Islam in their case progressed rather from a relatively neutral to a positive attitude towards the religion. Moreover, my interviews showed quite low levels of internalisation of the negative social representations of Islam by the members of the new Muslim elite in London.[343] Many of the young Muslim Londoners said that they progressed from the stage when they paid not much attention to Islam, to the stage of starting to get some interest in it, learning about it and beginning to appreciate it. This was, for instance, the case of Thaqib who claimed that *"I was like other kids. I had no interest in religion. Towards the end of my college years I became more interested in the Islamic work. That is why I also decided to learn Arabic at SOAS* (School of Oriental and African Studies – KP). *I wanted to have a better understanding of the Qur'an, more than anything else."* or the case of Shabaz who said *"I got interested in religion quite late, coming up to eighteen/nineteen. Before then not really. I wasn't religious at all. Before eighteen I wasn't doing any prayers. I have a family, I would say more Muslim by name. We were not religious at all."*

The young Muslim Londoners, as they re-embraced the religion of their parents, not only developed a positive image of Islam as a contemporary social force, but also as a historical one. One may clearly see this form of positivisation in the following statement of Dirar *"In history we have seen that Muslims in whatever context they were, they*

---

[343] In my opinion, one fruitful way of explaining this would be by referring to the substantial religious habitus of my interviewees assessed above in the section 'Becoming a Muslim'.

always were on the positive side of the contribution to the society. So when they came to Spain, they didn't destroy it, but rather developed it into a rich civilization and even today the richness of the civilization is there and if you go, you would see amazing architectural designs Muslims have left (...) ". Furthermore, a few of my interviewees, in the process of re-embracing Islam, were both developing a positive perception of their religion and constructing a quasi-idealist vision of Islam. According to this vision, their religion was not only a superior system of beliefs, in comparison with those offered by other faiths, but also a blueprint for the organisation of the social and political life. This viewpoint aptly summarised an inscription on their t-shirts saying 'Not East, not West, Islam is the Best'.

The second process working in parallel to the positivisation of Islam is its intellectualisation, which is a direct result of the acquisition by my interviewees of substantial knowledge about Islam. They have acquired this knowledge not only through the institutional channels, that is for instance by attending Qur'anic schools and Islamic seminars, but also through semi-institutional ones (e.g. attendance of conferences organised by Muslim organisations, talks given by Muslim leaders and debates with Muslim scholars) and self-study of all forms of materials on Islam available in their local Islamic bookshop, public library or on the Internet. Similarly, to my Belgian informants, many of the young Muslim Londoners learnt about their religion not through the institutional channels, but through self-study. Thus, their 'personal journey to Islam', to use the expression mentioned by numerous interviewees, also had its individualised educational dimension. They are part of an increasing number of Muslims who are reading the Qur'an with their own eyes, looking for answers to the complex realities and exigencies of the modern world. Before I quote some excerpts of the interviews which depict the process of intellectualisation, it is important to remind the reader that their 'journey to religion' or the appropriation of knowledge about Islam takes place in the situation of open competition and contest over both the interpretation of religious symbols and control of the institutions, formal and informal, that produce and sustain them.[344] As Hefner rightly points out, the contemporary pluralization and fragmentation

---

[344] I shall elaborate more on this situation of destabilization of religious hierarchies caused inter alia by the development of the electronic mass media in following chapter.

325

of Muslim authority amounts to a participatory revolution and to a democratization of the religious sphere (2001: 4). The analysed group of emerging new Muslim elite which significantly benefits from these new conditions is to some extent also their outcome.

One of my interviewees in London whose religious biography was marked by clear features of the intellectualisation of Islam, was Afnan. She asserted that "*At the university, I realized that I call myself a Muslim, but it is only a name, because I don't pray, I don't really do anything that would be significant of me being a Muslim, but it is only because I was born a Muslim. I started to look into it, did a lot of reading, studying, spoke to a lot of people and I think definitely by the second year of the university I'd taken on a different understanding of who I was as a person, and from there I started developing and forming an understanding of who I am, how to relate to the environment around me. (...) I remember thinking – 'I have to stop sitting on the fence now. I know all this information, I've got to do something with it.*" Her testimony demonstrates a transition from the time when she almost unreflexively identified with the religion of her parents, to the moment when she had acquired new knowledge about Islam and felt obliged to act upon it. In her opinion, the knowledge about Islam that she acquired significantly strengthened her faith. She also acknowledged that it pushed her to take some concrete action that would validate her claim to the full membership of the Muslim community. It was noteworthy she said that "*It is quite interesting to learn* (about Islam – KP), *but it is scary to make that change" (Afnan).* One of the actions that she took in order to confirm to her new understanding of being a Muslim was the adoption of the hijab analysed in the earlier part of this chapter. Another interviewee whose re-appropriation of religion of his parents bears numerous features of the intellectualisation process was Adel. He stated that "*I was born a Muslim, I was born to a Muslim family. But I became truly interested in religion only when I finished my secondary education. At that time I started to read books about Islam and attending conferences, seminars, talks, lessons, courses on Islam. I took my learning experience from there and afterwards I went abroad and became a full time student of Islam. All in all, it has been about seven years that I am learning about Islam. I spent two years learning Arabic and shariah at the university in Jordan.*" In the case of Adel, interest in Islam in the early stages of his education and the self-study of religion promoted by his parents resulted in the decision to study religion at the academic level in the Muslim college. When Adel completes this degree, he would be able to become an imam, chaplain or teacher of Islam.

Like in Belgium, the intellectualisation process also involved some efforts of my interviewees to learn the holy language of Qur'an. One of the young British Muslims who has made a special effort to learn Arabic was Shabaz, who said *"I always thought that learning Arabic would be good. When I was doing the rituals like prayer and so on, it was done in Arabic and a lot of things I was saying I was repeating in English, because it was very important to me to understand what I was saying and benefit from it. This was one of the reasons why I went to the Muslim college in France. Many of the things in Islam are in Arabic and in order to benefit from them you need to know it. For example, during the Ramadan there is a Tarawih prayer - the whole Qur'an is being recited during the 30 days - which last for an hour and you do not have a clue what is being said because you are reciting the Qur'an in Arabic. So these are the benefits of understanding straight away. I realized how important it was* (to know Arabic - KP) *when I came back. I could try to understand what we believe are the words of God, Qur'an (...) try to understand its meaning directly and to feel the impact directly. That is something that I managed to feel only after learning Arabic."* Shabaz was one of the three interviewees of South Asian origin who decided to dedicate at least a year of their lives to learning Arabic. They spoke at length, not only about the spiritual benefits of having a minimum understanding of Arabic or 'having a tool due to which they could understand their faith better' (Thaqib), but also mentioned the numerous non-religious advantages of knowing Arabic such as: having access to literature, feeling at home in ¼ of the world and feeling at ease with Arabs.

Finally, it is worth remembering that the analysed process of intellectualisation has not been merely limited to the second and third generation, but is also observable among the first generation. At times, the intellectualisation process amongst the first generation has even been stimulated by the re-embracing of Islam by the young British Muslims. This clearly depicts the following opinion of Shabaz who said: *"Now my parents started realizing, as they were getting older, the importance of the question 'where will we go?'. They always had a connection with Islam, but to be honest with you, they didn't know much about their faith. When I started to develop more my understanding of Islam, I had books, booklets and other material so they were picked up sometimes. We might have discussed a few things and then their understanding increased and then they came to like it... something which makes sense to them, something they understand and they thought they want to live by it."* In this case, the religious re-discovery of the son also led to the change in the attitudes of the parents to Islam.

As I have already mentioned in the earlier part of this chapter, the re-discovery of Islam by my interviewees took place either over an extended period of time and had a gradual character or was marked by fairly swift transformations initiated by certain 'fateful moments' (Giddens 1991: 142-143). One such critical transition point was the death of a member of a family. This was, for instance, the 'fateful moment' of Rana, who pointed out that *"after my father's death I started finding out more* (about Islam – KP) *and I guess building my own relationship to it, rather than through received or inherited ideas... and that has been much more interesting because it has been developing my own relationship with Allah and really discovering the beauty of my religion."*

Another turning point, after which some of my interviewees decided to embrace anew, more fully or just in a different way the religion of their parents, was marked by their encounters with some significant others. Such significant others were not only certain charismatic Muslim leaders whose discourse appealed particularly strongly to my informants, but sometimes also encounters with 'ordinary Muslims' – their friends, colleagues or siblings – whose practice of religion or opinions about it struck a chord with my interviewees' understanding of Islam. One Muslim leader whose discourse was particularly well received by my British informants was that of the American Sufi, Hamza Yusuf.[345] Interestingly, this representative of traditional Islam was not only popular among the members of the organisations with some Sufi sympathies, but also amongst some members of the organisations that are generally very critical about traditional Islam. The following opinion of Jada shows that the preferred religious authority of the leadership of a certain organisation (here IFE - Islamic Forum Europe) is not necessarily identical with that of their members. She pointed out *"Sufism within the*

---

[345] Hamza Yusuf is an American scholar of traditional Islam, who has been tirelessly promoting Islamic ethics and spiritual Islam. (e.g. Yusuf 2004) For more information about this influential (particularly in the English-speaking world) Islamic scholar see for example O'Sullivan 2001, Q-News 2003, Birt 2006 or check the unofficial website devoted to him and his work http://sheikhhamza.com

IFE is perceived badly. But, I am looking into people like Hamza Yusuf and others like him and according to my understanding they are very balanced. They are not telling you to give up your prayers, and to become some freak, but they are telling you to take the hadith and to read it ... having good character and good morals, and things like that." She also asserted, *"Going to the meetings of Sufi circle filled a spiritual vacuum in me"* (Jada). Tariq Ramadan, was another Muslim leader that had a considerable influence on my interviewees. One of them, young Muslim woman, for instance, stated, *"In terms of figureheads, one of the persons who inspire me a lot is Tariq Ramadan. I've got to say that he is the one who makes me think..."*. (Afnan) Another interviewee, who spoke highly about the grandson of Hassan al-Bana and claimed that this Muslim leader had significant influence on him, was Adel. He said, *"What I like about his discourse is the emphasis on the self-criticism rather than blaming others for our downfall... always be analytical whatever we say. We as Muslims, we need to know our force in order to go forward. He also rightly stresses the difference between Islam and culture and that cultural practices such, for example, forced marriages cannot and shouldn't be legitimized by Islam."*

Apart from the two aforementioned Muslim leaders to whom the vast majority of my respondents referred to as the key figures of religious authority, the young Londoners also mentioned other Muslim intellectuals, leaders and ulema (both living and deceased). Amongst them were Abdul Hakim Murad, Ziauddin Sardar, Abdullah bin-Beya, Yusuf al-Qaradawi, Maulana Maududi and Hassan al-Banna. Most of the young British Muslims also claimed to have more than one leader, who had a significant influence on their understanding of Islam. Many of them argued in the same vein as Sajid who said, *"There are number of scholars one reads, understands, values and knows from... so I would not point to one individual. And it is good that one doesn't. I don't think anyone should be a student of one sheikh. There is a concept in Islamic tradition called taqlid, which means to blindly follow your sheikh. But why would God give you a brain, if you were not supposed to use it?!"* Thus, not only Said but also many other interviewees were strong supporters of *ijtihad*, which in the general terms can be understood as independent thought or interpretation of religious text.[346]

As I have mentioned earlier, the re-discovery of Islam by some of my interviewees was not that much a result of influence of one or another Muslim leader, but rather an outcome of interactions with devout peers, friends or siblings who had rediscovered Islam before them. Probably the most telling in this regard is the account of Shabaz who said *"All happened when my brother, who is 2 years older than me and who studied at the university, came home one day and said to me 'you have to pray!' .... I got really annoyed that he is telling me what I have to do, especially as a big brother. I said: 'you can't tell me what I am supposed to do'. (...) I think he got attracted to the Islamic society, he liked it and then he tried to order some people at home like me to change me. Since then what happened was, he told me to pray and I was really annoyed and angry but decided to do it because he was bigger than me. I just did it. And I asked him 'why do you tell me to do it?'. I was finding out why I have to pray. So, I started reading books and finding out and from there I started finding out more about what is Islam."*

Finally, yet importantly, a crucial role in the re-discovery of Islam by many of the interviewees was also played by well developed institutional structures. The young Muslim Londoners self-consciously embraced Islam not only at home, under the influence of their parents and siblings, but also in the wider social space, in which different Muslim organisations and associations play a prominent role. The religious institutional structures which, as I have argued above, were one of the reasons for which my interviewees liked to live in areas of high concentration of Muslims in the city, or 'Muslimtowns' as they are called by Felice Dassetto (1996: 283), also played a significant role in the re-discovery of religion by my interviewees. Some of my interviewees came into contact with Muslim associations as early as primary school[347]. However, most of them decided to join them only when they went to college or to the university. One of my interviewees, for instance, recalled that *"They* (Muslim associations and their members - KP) *were around ... but as a young person I was kind of*

---

[346] The concept of *ijtihad (Arabic* اجتهاد *)* will be discussed in more detail in the following chapter while elaborating on the new Muslim leadership.

[347] At this level they usually try to make the young Muslims acquainted with Islam through games and plays. For insider's detail account of how they do it see Husain 2007: 32-34.

running away from them ... hahaha (laughing - KP). *I wanted to pray and wanted to fast, but I was young and there were lots of other opportunities out there for me, like drugs, girls, nightlife, sports and all other things this society has to offer."* (Mumtaz) He spoke at length about the 'difficult circumstances' in which he took the decision to join the Muslim association and declared that only after he had made such a decision did he felt 'spiritually comfortable'. Yet, some other interviewees argued that they tried to keep away from the Muslim societies at their colleges and universities because they were dominated by members of Hizb ut-Tahrir (e.g. Jada and Afnan).

The accounts of many of them resembled the following by Akram who said, *"At college I met some of the brothers that were leading the Islamic Society. They introduced the college environment to us and invited us to programmes. Sometimes I would go, sometimes I wouldn't. They also invited us to the prayers... And through there I got involved."* In general, my research demonstrated that the relatively well developed religious institutional structures in London played a significant role in the re-discovery of Islam by young Muslims and in their mobilisation to activism for the Muslim and wider community.

Finally, it is also important to point out the time frame within which my interviewees rediscovered the religion of their parents and joined the Muslim organisations. As in Belgium, this generally happened in my interviewees' middle and late adolescence. Hence, if we live in the age of 'do-it-yourself biographies' (Beck and Beck-Gernsheim 2002), as I have argued in the second chapter, then the period of adolescence is particularly marked by many moments when one has to decide whom to become and how to direct its own biography. It is a period of heightened reflexivity when the questions such as 'who am I?' and 'who shall I become?' become particularly pertinent. It should not be surprising then that my interviewees most commonly experienced the aforementioned turning points in their biographies during this period.

5.3.2 RESOURCES FOR PARTICIPATION

Before I account for the key motives that drove the young Muslim Londoners interviewed in the course of this research into activism in religious organisations and the wider public sphere, I shall briefly present the main resources or the essential means that allow them to chose between different courses of action and to move beyond the formal to more substantive forms of citizenship. As I have argued in the second chapter, the sociological understanding of citizenship goes beyond the narrow legal conception of the term. In contrast to the latter conception, the sociological understanding of the phenomenon looks not only into the formal possession of citizenship rights by certain people, but also into whether they possess resources which enable them to exercise these rights. As numerous sociological studies show (e.g. Verba et al. 1995, Pattie et al. 2003) the more resources people have, the more active they are in the public sphere.

One of the key resources which positively influences the social activism of people is a surplus of unstructured time. Any social activism is time consuming and therefore people who do voluntary work need to possess a surplus of free time that they are ready to devote to certain activity. My British interviewees, in a similar manner to the Belgian ones, devoted at least a few hours per week to associational activism. Some of the most actively involved ones devoted so much time to this activism that it became the main essence of their lives. One such person was Razin who stated *"It is difficult to say* (how much time I devote to the activism - KP) *because you are obviously living it and it is your life."* Another interviewee who spoke in the same vein was Afnan who said *"It is internal part of my life. I do not see it as something separate any more. I devote all my free time to voluntary activism."* This is also a reason why not only Razin and Afnan, but also numerous other interviewees, found it difficult to specify how much time they devote to the associational activism. Furthermore, some of my interviewees, albeit a minority, found it even difficult to think about their involvement in the Muslim civil society and wider civil society in terms of an investment of their free time. One of them was Akram who claimed, *"The understanding that I have is that all my life should be dedicated for Allah. I don't compartmentalize my time. This is for Muslim organisation, this is for the local community, this I for my family.... Every single action you do is for the sake of Allah, so me sitting here with you, me visiting families at homes, visiting the sick, me helping an old lady with her shopping is all part of my work for Allah."*

While some of my British interviewees spoke about their activism in the Muslim and wider civil society in terms of fulfilling an obligation, others spoke about it as their favourite hobby. However, in both cases one could observe clear elements of a search for ethical consistency, giving meaning to deeply held values acquired in the process of socialization. This search for ethical consistency was emphasized particularly strongly by those who viewed their activism as a fulfilment of religious obligations. The activism of those interviewees who claimed that it was their favourite pastime also had an ethical dimension, although it was not a straightforward but more a latent one.

Similarly to my Belgian interviewees, the time engagement of the young Londoners in the Muslim and wider civil society varied depending on the time of year. One of the periods of the year during which they were devoting some extra time to associational activity was the period of summer holidays. As Rushd explained *"I tend to do something every day, so roughly on the day to day basis 3-4 hours. This is just structured time if you think about the attended meeting etc. Summer holidays is one of the times of particular intensity because we have major events taking place at that time".* Another period of higher intensity of voluntary work of my interviewees was the time of Ramadan when, for example, a number of the young Muslim Londoners living in the vicinity of the East London Mosque got involved in Muslim Community Radio[348]. Many of my interviewees were also more actively involved in associational activism after the terrorist attacks in the USA in September 2001 and in London in July and August 2007. This was partially related to the higher demand of the media for Muslim spokespersons. However, even in the less controversial moments and sometimes even while being away from London, some of my interviewees kept investing substantial amounts of their free time in voluntary work for their local organisation or community. One of them was Adel who stated, *"Even when I am in Wales I am involved in the activities of my Muslim organisation* (in London – KP) *through phone and the Internet. During the holidays it is a full time job and while I am away a part time one."*

The young Muslim Londoners interviewed for this research were able to invest considerable amounts of their time into activism in the Muslim and wider civil society because more then one-third of them were students and some of those who already completed their studies were self-employed or worked only on a part-time basis. More

---

[348] Muslim Community Radio, broadcasting during the month of Ramadan from the East London Mosque, is one of many local Ramadan Radios spread around the whole country (e.g. Birmingham, Glasgow, Luton – see http://www.radioramadhan.com). More information about this joint initiative of the London Muslim Centre and the Islamic Forum Europe can be found on http://www.merlive.net/programmes.htm.

than two-thirds of them had not started a family yet and hence did not have many family obligations to limit their free time. However, even those who had children and were full-time employees were able to devote at least a few hours per week to associational activism. One of them, Afnan, was able to find spare time while she was full-time employee and even more so when on maternity leave. She said, *"There is always stuff going on. People need you for seminars, conferences, mentoring projects, TV stations are calling you and want your opinion as a Muslim women, etc. So I have always been involved in lots of things. It is part of my life. Since I am on maternity leave I am more flexible. I am juggling my baby, but at the same time I am able to make many things."*

As in the Belgian case, the lack of a surplus of free time was one of the reasons why some of the interviewed young Londoners had to temporarily limit their involvement in Muslim and wider civil society. Those informants who were students usually limited their associational involvement during examination periods, whereas those who were full-time employees withdrew from social activism during intensive moments before certain deadlines in their jobs or while leaving abroad for work. One of the interviewees who had to limit his social activism due to work-related circumstances from time to time was, for instance, Fadi. He claimed to be unable to devote a great deal of time to associational activism recently because he was away, travelling to different parts of the world as a manager of one of the biggest British companies.

On the one hand, full-time employment sometimes impinged on my interviewees' activism in the public sphere, like in the case of Fadi, but on the other hand, it also provided them with another key resource necessary in social activism, that is money. One needs to possess some financial resources while doing voluntary work - not only because such work is rarely remunerated, but also because it often requires from the persons working *pro bono* an investment of their own financial resources. The majority of my British interviewees, as full-time employees (in some cases of very profitable companies), did not feel financially restrained from being active in the Muslim and the wider civil society. On the contrary, their financial stability pushed them to more dynamic involvement in different activities which they would have probably never done had their financial situation been different. This feeling of financial security can be detected, for example, in the following statement of Sajid who said, *"In our organisation a lot of people are reasonably well to do, they have good jobs, reasonable salaries and in time their salaries will get better because they are in the best firms."* Thus, clearly some of the members of the emerging new Muslim elite in London have enough financial resources that they do not have to think about their economic situation while doing voluntary work. What is more, some of my interviewees felt so financially secure that they were also willing to invest their own financial resources in this activism. As one of my interviewees declared, *"In our organisation people are prepared to put their hands into the pockets, and give some of their savings into the organization. So we are in a very strong position, because we can go to people and literally say - we want to run a project for you and we will bring the volunteers and the money"* (Mazin).

In contrast to my Belgian informants, many of my interviewees (especially those living in the East London), who did not have as high financial security as some of the aforementioned ones, were able to find financial resources to run a certain project either in Muslim organisations (which tended to be in better financial situation than their Belgian counterparts) or via local authorities (which were much more favourably disposed to local religious organisations than their Belgian counterparts). In this sense, London seemed to be much better resourced than Brussels. Although Islam is not recognised as a religion of the citizens of the country, as in Belgium, the authorities and especially local authorities often viewed Muslim organisations as partners and cooperate with them while tackling numerous issues of social life such as, for example, educational underachievement amongst the Muslim schools, gang conflicts, drug addiction etc.[349]

In order to get involved in voluntary activism one needs, apart from a surplus of free time and some financial resources, various civic skills. Verba et al. point out that those who possess the requisite organizational and communications capacities, or civic skills, find it less daunting to get involved. Moreover, they demonstrate that when inputs of time and money are coupled to civic skills, then people become not only more likely to participate but also more likely to be effective when they do (Verba et al. 1995: 271). The young British Muslim interviewed in the course of this research were also quite rich in this type of resource. As persons, who were either born in Britain or who arrived in the country in early childhood, they had acquired an in-depth knowledge of the mechanisms

---

[349] I shall elaborate on these projects in detail in the following section.

through which this society works and had learnt during the process of socialisation numerous civic skills, such as for example, speaking and writing skills, and the skill to interpret political talk. The members of the emerging new Muslim elite in London possessed not only substantial amounts of the embodied cultural capital, but also the institutional form of it[350], as all of them already had a university degree (and often from the most prestigious establishments such as Oxbridge or University College, London) or were in the process of obtaining one. There were also amongst my interviewees two persons who were pursuing PhD studies in Humanities and one already holding a PhD. I could trace numerous features of a feeling of superiority over other less educated members of the Muslim population or the feelings of being a Muslim elite not only amongst those interviewees who finished the best British universities or those who had the highest academic qualifications, but also amongst those who had lower academic qualifications or finished less prestigious universities. It is easier to comprehend this feeling of educational superiority amongst some of my interviewees while remembering about the larger picture of relatively weak education results of Muslim pupils and students elaborated in third chapter. One of the informants who manifested a strong self-awareness of being the elite was, for instance, Sajid, who stated that, *"Intelligent Muslims have such an important part to play that they cannot just sit and do nothing, otherwise we will be dominated by the nutcases we have out there"*. He argued that members of the Muslim elite whom he called 'intelligent Muslims' must be particularly proactive at present so as their voice would be louder than the voice of more radical groups within the Muslim population which easily catch the attention of the sensationalist media.

As people, who came from the families of relatively higher social status than the families of my Belgian interviewees, the young Muslim Londoners interviewed in the course of this research spoke little about the hardship of acquiring institutional cultural capital. In contrast to some of my Belgian interviewees, the educational path of the majority of them was quite straightforward and did not involve moments of particular

---

[350] Both terms, embodied and institutional cultural capital used in the sense given to them by Pierre Bourdieu (1986) were defined in the chapter 1.

hardship. In the majority of cases, their families provided them with the conditions conducive to achieving good educational results.

The young British Muslims acquired the civic skills necessary for the effective exercise of the citizenship rights not only through the educational system but also at home. Numerous informants implied that it was the contingency of everyday family life which taught them the essential civic skills and pushed them to associational activism. Kadir noticed, for example, that *"My parents have always been involved with community in terms of helping charity causes. At the moment when my mother retired she does only community work. ... So I think that has played a role as well in my activism."*, whereas Sajid asserted that *"I come from a family who is quite concerned about what is going on. My father was always involved in community work. He had that passion for community work and it seems he has passed it also to me."* Also many of my female interviewees argued that the 'passion for community work', to use Sajid's expression, was passed on to them at home. One of them was Rasha who argued that she had been active in the Muslim and wider civil society due to her 'family background'. She recalled, *"My mother has always been active in various local activities. She actually organized one of the first activities for young women, so we became involved naturally. At that time there was no organizational structure. She used to having girls' club where the Muslim girls would get together and do things and only then the ELM* (East London Mosque – KP) *took over the responsibilities."* For her, being active in the Muslim organisation and in the wider civil society was 'a natural thing' or something taken for granted. She had observed her parents actively engaging in the life of the local community and wider society since she was very young and she began to do the same very early in her life. Similar memories were held also by Rushd who said, *"When I was young I saw my parents organizing a lot of meetings in our house. Because the mosque wasn't here, a lot of the gatherings used to happen in people's houses and local community centres. So I used to watch the meetings taking place, people taking notes. So these initial skills and observations are taking place in my parents house and then slowly as we were growing up the value that we are responsible for our actions and that we are responsible for those around was very much given to us by my parents."*

All the aforementioned opinions show how important the role of habitus *or* 'the durably installed generative principle of regulated improvisations ... [which produces] practices' (Bourdieu 1997a: 78) was in the involvement of my interviewees into voluntary activism. They also demonstrate that many of the members of the emerging new Muslim elites in London were very well 'trained' from the early age to become community activists and in some cases eventually community leaders. They were also appropriately equipped in order to become such leaders. Taking into account some of the life histories of the members of the emerging new Muslim elite, one may conclude that their level of pre-voluntaristic preparation, acquired within the family environment, was so advanced that they almost could not escape from getting involved in voluntary activities and that they became involved in the Muslim and wider civil society almost 'by default'. Thus, I believe that many of the members of the emerging new Muslim elite in London interviewed for this book could be called 'activists by default'. Within their family environments, they had not only learned numerous civic skills, but they were also often recruited, if not by their parents then by their siblings, to one or another organisation or association. My findings in this matter stay in line with the sociological literature on social capital, which demonstrates that families are both key institutions of pre-voluntaristic preparation, and yet an important basis of recruitment (e.g. Portes 1998, Whitley 1999 and Lowndess 2000).

Moreover, my interviews with the young Muslim activists demonstrate that, apart from the environment of the family, it was also the wider social milieu that played a crucial role in informing the young Muslim Londoners' political consciousness. The socialization of my interviewees in the atmosphere of ethnic/religious mobilization has crucially conditioned their sense of organized action. Some of the most significant events that had contributed to raising the temperature of this atmosphere were the Rushdie affair[351], the Balkan war, the conflict in Kashmir, the war in Chechnya and more recently the anti-war movement.[352] The importance of some of these events on the atmosphere of

---

[351] For more information about this first major case of the political mobilization of Muslims in Britain see chapter four.

[352] One of the most important moments in the history of this movement (in which organizations such as for instance Muslim Association of Britain played a crucial role) was organization of one of the largest demonstration ever seen in Britain (between 750,000 and 2,000,000 people according to different sources) against the imminent invasion of Iraq on 15 February, 2003. More information about the movement and its

ethnic/religious mobilization and indirectly on the personal biographies of my interviewees one may observe, for example, in the following opinion of Sajid who stated, *"I grew up during the 1980s, which was a very ideologically driven time. Cold war, Islamic Revolution, Afghanistan... Then when I went to the university, Bosnia started, which is a thing that annoyed a lot of Muslims and non-Muslims as well. And the feelings ... 'what is the West doing about that?' 'Why is it not doing anything apart from standing by?' 'Is it because they are Muslims?' So, there was a kind of anger there. These kind of things made me more interested."* Similar accounts were heard from other interviewees and may be read in the autobiographical books written by second generation Muslims (e.g. Husain 2007). The extensive media coverage of different conflicts from around the world, in which people of Muslim faith were a part, was one of the factors that helped the local leaders to politicize Islam and to construct strong diasporic identities among the young British Muslims explored in the earlier section of this chapter. These diasporic identities constructed within the environment of dynamic diasporic politics were particularly strong amongst my interviewees from East London. The mobilization around the religious identity in this part of London has recently brought up some significant political results. It is in this part of city where during the 2005 general elections the only representative from the Respect Party (founded on January 2004 in the midst of anti-war protests[353]), George Galloway, was elected to the Parliament.

5.3.3 REASONS FOR 'BEING ACTIVE'

Having accounted for the main resources that enable the young Muslim Londoners to turn the idea of devout citizenship into practice and mentioning some of the contexts within which they were nurtured, it is time to point out the key motivations behind the activism of the members of the emerging new Muslim elite. As I have already mentioned, the possession of resources for active involvement in the public sphere does not explain

---

successes in mobilisation of Muslims as well as non-Muslims can be found on www.stopwar.org.uk and in Murray and German 2005.

[353] The Respect Party in which the two main players are the Socialist Workers Party and the Muslim Association of Britain has sometimes been derided as the coalition of 'Trotskyists and Taliban'. Only six months after its creation in June 2004 the Party got 1,5 per cent of the vote in the European election - more than the Scottish National Party (1,4 per cent) and (Welsh) Plaid Cymru (1.0 per cent). For more information about the Party and wider anti-war movement known as Stop the War Coalition (STWC) see, for example, Yaqoob 2003, German 2003, Murray and German 2005 or Birth 2008.

why people decide to get involved in the activities of the Muslim organisations and act as religious brokers in the public sphere - or 'to get their hands dirty' as one of my respondents (Sajid) put it. In this section, I shall elaborate on the main reasons of this activism as seen by the young Muslim Londoners and at the same time shed light on some of the projects within the Muslim and wider civil society in which my interviewees had been involved as active players.

One of the major motivations behind the involvement of my interviewees in Muslim and wider civil society was a desire to improve the situation of the Muslim community[354]. This desire was voiced by Rana, who said about her involvement in the Muslim organisations that it is *"a way of connecting and contributing to my community."* She also argued, *"I have to make a contribution particularly in the Muslim community because I see so many difficulties and issues that are there."* Another interviewee who saw numerous issues within the Muslim community and got involved in the Muslim civil society in order to tackle them was Rushd. She explained that for her, involvement in the Muslim organisation is *"a way of channelling my energy and my intellectual ability to use that for the betterment of the community"*. She viewed her involvement in the Muslim organisation largely in the utilitarian way and said, *"I don't see it as something running my life dictating to me what I need to do, but rather as a way of utilizing my abilities. (...) I find that doing things on your own is less efficient. Your single voice isn't heard as much as the collective voice... I feel that the organisation gives us this collective voice, facility to do certain things"*. Most of my interviewees, like Rana and Rushd, wished above all 'to make a difference' and wanted to do something about the numerous problems faced be Muslims in the country, from a lack of social integration, through discrimination to underachievement in education. It is the last issue that was taken particularly seriously by the leadership of the two major organisations from which I drew majority of my informants. Hence, in both organisations (the City Circle – CC and the Islamic Forum Europe – IFE) educational projects were at the top of the priority lists.

---

[354] I am using the concept of community in the singular rather than in the plural because that is the way my interviewees spoke about it. At the same time it is worth remembering that from the sociological point of view there is no one homogenous Muslim community in Britain (as well as in other European countries) but Muslim communities.

For example, among several projects carried out by the CC, college mentoring, Saturday school and Jannah Club, occupy the most important places. The main goal of the first educational project, run by circa 25 members of the CC, is to show students from one of the colleges in the London borough of Tower Hamlets, which is one of the poorest areas in the country, that there is *"another life that they may aspire to"* (Samar). Mentoring essentially involved providing students with career guidance, role models, as well as with practical skills such as filling out job applications and teaching them interview techniques. Another educational project, the Saturday School, seeks to provide a supplementary education to students' aged between 8-19 years. Around 1000 children benefited from the help of 90 teachers-volunteers by the end of 2005. The main goal of the project is to consolidate students' knowledge in National Curriculum subjects (maths, English and science) and to motivate them to strive for excellence in all they undertake. The last educational initiative undertaken by the CC, the Jannah Club, has a more religious dimension as it aims to provide children (3-11 years old) with an integrated approach to the study of the Qur'an and the Arabic language.[355]

All of the projects mentioned above had, according to people who run them, the same objective, that is *"to create a balanced and sensible individual (...) the focus is on Muslim kids doing well at schools, because only then they can get better jobs and aspire in life, performance and so on. "* (Kadir). All of them also sprang from the same negative assessment of the current situation of Muslims in the country and in particular from an analysis showing the poor performance of Muslim children at schools. This main motivation behind the educational projects run by the CC is evident, for example, in the following statement of Sajid: *"Intellectually we are backward, economically we are backward. Look where all indicators are. Muslims have to learn so much!"*

As I mentioned earlier, the IFE has also tried, albeit through different means, to improve the educational performance of Muslim pupils. To this end it has run a scheme called Improving School Attendance in Partnership since 2002 (hereafter ISAP). The ISAP, funded by the local city council and run from the East London Mosque by the members of the IFE, is an example of a faith-based approach to improving the attendance and performance of children of Bangladeshi origin at schools in the borough of Tower

---

[355] For more information about the projects, see www.thecitycircle.com

341

Hamlets.[356] Here, it is worth mentioning that the schools in the borough have registered some of the worst rates of attendance in the country. Within the scheme, a representative from the Mosque (sometimes together with an imam) visits families to explain not only the legal obligation but also the importance of attendance in moral and social terms. Apart from this, the youngsters are given incentives to attend including certificates, pens and T-shirts and, as a result of this scheme, twelve primary schools in Tower Hamlets involved in the ISAP have registered a five to ten per cent increase in attendance.[357]

The goal to improve the educational performance of Muslim children has also been behind the efforts of some of the leadership of the IFE to create a Muslim school. Such a school, for boys only, was created in the East London Mosque in January 2005. As one may read in the school brochures, its intention is to 'contribute towards producing a new generation of scholars (alims) and leaders (da'ees[358]) who will become good citizens, guide their communities and make a significant contribution to contemporary British society.' The London East Academy offers a curriculum that includes National Curriculum subjects and Islamic sciences with a special emphasis on Arabic language. The school, maintained from the fees of the parents, passed positively the Ofsted (Office for Standards in Education, Children's Services and Skills) evaluation in the same year when it was created (see Ofsted 2005).

Apart from the willingness to improve the performance and attendance of Muslim children at schools, numerous interviewees talked also about a strong desire to share their personal successes with others. Thus, their desire to work towards the betterment of the Muslim community has been strongly grounded in their belief that they have something special to offer the community. This conviction and a sense of being an elite one may see clearly for instance in the following statement of Sajid: *"If we have made it,* (achieved personal success - KP) *we need to try to transfer these skills back to the community and help others below us to get there as well."* One may see it also in the opinion of another member of the CC who asserted that, *"The primary reason why I am with this*

---

[356] The same faith-based approach is used also by a scheme aimed at fighting with drug-addiction within the Bangladeshi community and run by the activist of the IFE and independent workers. For more information about Nafas, which has been much more successful in fighting with the drug-addiction within the Bangladeshi community than state run agencies see http://www.nafas.org/

[357] For more information about the ISAP see http://news.bbc.co.uk/2/hi/uk_news/england/2318949.stm

[358] In some documents the LEA uses a term 'leaders' and in other Arabic term da'ees (داع) ,meaning a person who invites people to understand Islam - a preacher or a missionary.

organisation is that I wanted to give back to the society. It is simple philosophy – you have privileged life – what can you give back?" (Mazin). According to Mazin, the economically privileged situation in which he grew up obliges him to assist others who grow up in less stimulating conditions. A financially secure upbringing and a good education also made Samar, one of the managers of the educational projects, to feel that she had some advantages in life over other members of the Muslim population and that she should try to help others who were less privileged. Numerous interviewees active in the IFE structures also spoke in the same vein. One of the activists of the organisation explained to me, for instance, that "What I have been able to get from this society and community, I want to give back to the community and society. The only way I can give it back is by staying in this community and sharing the qualities that you have gained over the years and this I feel I can do by my engagement with the community, involvement in the community services and the activities that we are doing. I think that is the main point." (Dirar) In contrast to the activists of the CC they, however, did not stress, while explaining their desire 'to give back to the community and society', that they came from families with relatively higher positions in the social stratification (when it was applicable) than other members of the Muslim population. Instead, they put emphasis on the importance of hard work and common effort in achieving success.

Here, it is also worth mentioning that while some of my interviewees spoke about their decision to 'give back to the community' in terms of their personal choice and desire, others rather used such terms as 'a duty' or 'an obligation'. Jamil who said that "I see this work (activism in the Muslim organisation - KP) as an obligation, which Islam has laid down." was one of the interviewees from the latter group. Another person who viewed activism in the Muslim and wider civil society as a duty was Jada. She asserted that "To me involvement in the organisation is a result of an obligation to give services to my local community... I see it as a duty."

The young Muslim Londoners also argued, albeit less often than my interviewees in Brussels, that they got involved in the projects of the Muslim and wider society in order to do something not only for their own community but also for the whole society. Afnan for example said that "(...) ultimately the aim of being active in the Muslim organisation is to work within a society that you are living in the best possible way and to

343

make a positive contribution to it". Another interviewee, a student pharmacist from a different organisational structure declared, *"I love serving people. Every individual I can bring a smile to gives me a lot of satisfaction, it gives me a lot of reward, and community work does that."* (Dirar) Moreover he stated that, *"I like to work with two groups of people: the very young and the very old, because these are the two groups of people that the most need help. My pharmacy work allows me to engage with the elderly people, people who are distressed and ill, whereas my involvement in the Muslim organisation enables me to work with the young people."*

The motivations of Afnan, Dirar and other interviewees to contribute through their involvement in the Muslim organisation to both their own religious community and wider society were also reflected in the projects of the analysed organisations. One of the projects of the CC which has crossed the boundaries of the Muslim community is Feeding London Homeless. For several years now, members of the CC have been collecting money and then supplying dinners to one or more London's homeless peoples' hostels with a mix of people from various backgrounds, races and religion. For example, during the Ramadan of 2003 alone, the CC distributed over 2700 meals to homeless hostels. As with other projects, one of the most important stimuli that pushes them to do so has its roots in religion. In this particular case they refer, for example, to verses in the sura *Al-Insan* (ar. Man) which say: *"We feed you for the sake of Allah alone: no reward do we desire from you, nor thanks"* (76: 8-9).[359]

The leadership of the IFE has been also actively involved in various projects aimed at improving the situation of all the inhabitants of London, not only Muslims. Probably one of the most significant schemes in which they have been active for many years is the East London Community Organisation (TELCO)[360]. The organisation, coordinated by the Citizen Organising Foundation (COF),[361] was created almost a decade ago and today brings together over 35 faith groups, schools, student organisations, union branches and charities across 5 East London boroughs. The faith groups have played a particularly important role in TELCO. According to the Director of COF, it has to do

---

[359] For more information about this project see http://www.thecitycircle.com/projectfeeding.php
[360] More recently, after the creation of similar organisations to TELCO in other parts of London, TELCO became a part of the wider network called London Citizens.
[361] For more information about the COF see http://www.cof.org.uk/

with the fact that *"The civil society in Britain is pretty dead apart from faith institutions and to some extent trade unions. Other kinds of institutions are largely evaporating"* (interview with Neil Jameson, 24th October 2004). TELCO has been very successful, for example, in putting pressure on the local authorities and companies to increase the minimum wage up to 'living standards'[362], lobbying for the one-off regularisation of the undocumented migrants or "shadow people"[363] as they are referred to in the COF literature, or calling for more affordable housing in London.[364] Numerous members of the IFE have been actively involved in all the aforementioned projects. The Director of the COF, while asked about the cooperation with the East London Islamists said that, *"We work mostly with people who are very moderate, increasingly comfortable British Muslims who have put their roots here. Many of them were born here and know that the Islamic state is not realistic and if you ask them privately they do not particularly want it. They like the freedom and the respect for democracy. The groups which are exclusive would not join us, because the criteria for joining are: commitment to democracy, an open and free society, justice, dignity, and self-respect. (...) The politics we teach is 'I will work with You, if you work with me. The fundamentalist groups will not agree with this model."* (interview with Neil Jameson).

Another reason for which many of my interviewees said they got involved in the Muslim organisation was desire to gain more information about their religion as well as society as a whole. The religious character of this aspiration was expressed, for instance, by Akram who claimed that, *"Since the moment of my rediscovery of Islam I had this desire to learn more about Islam and to apply it in my life. And as I have been endeavouring to do this, I have been more active with my Muslim organisation, because in my opinion I can practice my Islam better and more comprehensively with the movement or with the group. "*, whereas its more general character was uttered by Shahd who explained that, through activism in the Muslim organisation *"I want to be reflecting and changing. I want to be able to be knowledgeable about things, because today to be a Muslim is also to be kept informed. I think my organisation is a good vehicle to do that. "*

---

[362] See the details of the living wage campaign on http://www.livingwage.org.uk/
[363] For more information about this campaign see http://www.strangersintocitizens.org.uk/index.html
[364] Thanks to the lobbying of TELCO, the East London Mosque has also managed to achieve its own goals. One of the most important ones was purchasing of the land on 27th November 1999 for the extensions of the mosque and building London Muslim Centre. For more information see Malik 2000.

The activists of the IFE have been able to satisfy this desire inter alia through the regular seminar organised by the organisation in the East London Mosque called *Halaqah* (in Arabic 'circle', can also be understood as 'a study circle'). The majority of these seminars have been devoted to the study of some religious issues (e.g. understanding of the Shariah on 10-12 August 2007), however societal and political themes are also discussed. For instance, the theme of the *Halaqah* on 5th May 2007 was 'Bosnia in the Post Conflict Era – Prospects and Challenges' and the presentation was given by Bosnian alim Ahmet Alibasic.[365]

In the CC it is the Friday sessions that play a role of a study circle. The aim of the weekly gatherings is inter alia to act as a forum of debate and discussion on the issues concerning the Muslim population in the country. Although the vast majority of speakers and listeners at these sessions are Muslims, it is not uncommon to find among the panellists, as well as the audience, people of non-Muslim faith. For example, one of the gatherings after the 7 July bombing devoted to 'the criminal distortion of the Islamic texts'[366] was filmed by the BBC programme Panorama, while two weeks later Roger Mosey, BBC Head of Television News, was under a storm of questions from the audience trying to explain how BBC works and 'how it sees the world'[367]. In recent years, and in particular after the 9/11 and 7/7 terrorist attacks, the CC Friday sessions have started to play not only a role of important intra-community debate forum, but have also attracted the attention of broadsheet newspapers, referring to the opinions expressed during these sessions. (e.g. Bunting 2005, Sardar 2005a, Masood 2005 or Pędziwiatr 2005b) They have begun to influence the larger discourse on Islam in the country and in wider Europe. Thus, ironically, the organisation that does not make any claim to represent the Muslim population in the country or to speak on its behalf, in contrast to, for example, the Muslim Council of Britain or British Muslim Forum, has played a

---

[365] The list of the events from the last months can be found on
http://www.islamicforumeurope.com/live/ife.php?doc=events
[366] For more information about this particular session of the CC see:
http://www.thecitycircle.com/events_full_text2.php?id=350
[367]For more information about this particular session of the CC see:
http://www.thecitycircle.com/events_full_text2.php?id=351 The full list of topics and descriptions of debates (with sometimes downloadable audio/video files of a given debate) can be consulted on
http://www.thecitycircle.com/pastevents.php

significant role in shaping the debate on the possible causes and results of the terrorist attacks in London.

My interviews with young Muslim Londoners have confirmed the results of earlier research signalling Muslims' disillusion with the media coverage of Islam and anxiety related to the growing anti-Muslim sentiment (e.g. Poole 2002, Maréchal et al 2003). Hence, another important reason for which many of them claimed to start to be active in the Muslim and wider civil society was grounded in this disillusion. A significant number of both male and female interviewees claimed to be active in the associational sphere in order to clarify the misconceptions about Islam and its believers. One of them was, for instance, Adel who said that, *"It is a duty of every Muslim to falsify all the misconceptions about Islam and doing it in a collective manner is better than doing it on your own."* A female interviewee, Yumn, claimed that, *"Even if it wasn't the primary thing why I got involved. I think it is quite important to explain to people our stand on different issues and also try to clarify the misconceptions that some are trying to spread."* Many other female interviewees argued that they want to fight not only the stereotypes of Muslims in general, but more particularly with the simplified images of Muslim women. One of them was Rushd, according to whom *"A lot of people have misconceptions about Islam, particularly about Muslim women and I feel that it is our duty to erase some of that, eradicate some of these misconceptions."*

My study has also shown that among the core members of the emerging new Muslim elite there is a very strong sense of agency and a feeling of power to be able, with organisational resources, to fight effectively the stereotypical images of Islam. This one may notice in the opinion of Abdel who in the following manner accounted for the reporting of his organisation after the 7/7 bombing: *"We got about 300 media agencies coming to the mosque in the last days... I could not do this on my own. Because there were people behind, we could accommodate them. I think we had an impact on the reporting. It has been very sensitive, mature, balanced, as oppose to the previous one, when it was often inflammatory."* As I have already mentioned, growing anti-Muslim sentiment is one of the factors that significantly empowers young Muslim religious brokers to be more actively engaged in public discourse and to make their voice heard. According to Shahd 'becoming public' about things that until recently Muslims

347

considered 'private' is necessary, since "... *you can't expect people to understand you if you are not willing to engage at that* (public – KP) *level.*". The same, very strong conviction about the uniqueness of the current situation and a need for action was expressed by Sajid who asserted: *"intelligent Muslims have such an important part to play that they cannot just sit and do nothing, otherwise we will be dominated by the nutcases we have out there"*. This statement also clearly demonstrates how self-confident some of the members of the emerging Muslim elite are about its own qualities and hints of the fierce intra-elite fight for 'symbolic capital' or recognition.

Finally yet importantly, the reason for which numerous young Londoners said they joined Muslim organisations was a desire to meet like-minded people and stay in touch with them. As I am going to show below, various gatherings organised by the analysed Muslim associations serve as very effective vehicles of social networking. In the case of one of the analysed organisation (the City Circle), the desire 'to get to know other Muslim professionals' has actually been one of the root causes behind the setting up of the organisation. It is evident for instance in the following account of one of its founding members: *'Initially it was more like people getting together for a bit of a lecture, but really to go out afterwards for curry. Because nobody knew anybody. In London it is difficult to connect with people cos it is such a huge city, whereas in the smaller cities you can get to know people fairly easily'* (Afnan). As one may find from the description of the first sessions of the CC, some of the people who were behind its inception were new to London and the establishment of the organisation was also for them a means through which they could enrich their social capital.[368]

Summing up this section it is worth mentioning that most of the interviewees mentioned not one but many reasons for getting involved in the Muslim and wider civil society. In other words, their decisions were influenced by numerous factors at once and not by a single issue. I did not observe any significant differences in the explanations of community activism between male and female interviewees. However, similarly to Belgium, my female interviewees in London were often involved in very precise projects, whereas the activity of men was more widespread.

---

[368] This point will be elaborated in more detail in the next section.

5.3.4 BENEFITS FROM PARTICIPATION

In the last part of this section, devoted to the analysis of the participatory dimensions of citizenship of the young Muslim Londoners, I shall elaborate on how they have accounted for the benefits from being active in Muslim and wider civil society. As I have already mentioned, the stigmatisation of Islam seems to have empowering effect on the members of the emerging Muslim elite. In what follows I shall shed light on how young Muslim Londoners have been taking advantage of this situation and how community activism has increased their capacity to make choices and to transform those choices into desired actions and outcomes.

One of the major benefits from the participation in the civil society was according to my interviewees the possibility of spiritual and intellectual self-development. The vast majority of the members of the emerging new Muslim elite in London claimed that through being active in the Muslim and other organisations[369], they were able to learn new things, and thus significantly improve their understanding of Islam and also of the society in which they were living. The organization by the analysed associations of regular seminars and debates with various representatives of the society (politicians, journalists etc) who are not necessarily Muslim, is one of the occasions during which young Muslims can learn within the context of the Muslim civil society about the wider societal issues. One of my female interviewees said for example *"Of course I benefit from being involved in the Muslim civil society. It furthers my knowledge of Islam, of human beings, of the times that we are living in ..."* (Rana). Another female interviewee active in the different associational structures claimed that *"Organisation for me is a mean to self-development."* (Rushd). While some of my informants said they generally benefit from being active in the Muslim and wider civil society, others stressed that they benefited mostly spiritually. Akram belonged to the latter group for instance, observing that, *"While I am serving the community I am also helping myself spiritually because I believe that if you are to develop yourself as a spiritual person, you should be at the service of the people that live around you."*

---

[369] Including inter alia local ethnic organisations (e.g. Blentham Green Bengali Association), political parties (e.g. Labour Party or Respect Party very popular in East London), ecological organisations (e.g. Greenpeace) and specific target organisations (e.g. Citizen Organising Foundation)

Another benefit from activism that was noticed by the young Muslim Londoners has been the development of their social capital. For example, the City Circle's weekly gatherings not only contribute to enriching the debates on Islam in the country and provide many of its participants with intellectual and spiritual nourishment, but constitute also an important meeting-place for likeminded people. Thus, these weekly debates/seminars should be considered as very important vehicles for the generating of social capital or bases of social networking among young Muslim professionals in the global city. The fact that today the core members of the CC have numerous best friends among other members of the organisation[370] means that it has very efficiently fulfilled its role as a base of social networking. Although the main outcome of this networking is building the bonding social capital, as the majority of friends that members of the CC make through the meetings and projects are Muslims, it allows also to build bridging social capital (particularly at the institutional level) as the CC is closely cooperating with a number of non-Muslim bodies.

I believe one may understand why the CC as well as the IFE has become a successful vehicle in generating social capital among the practising young Muslims only if one is aware of the meagre social lives some of the British Muslims have. This phenomenon was described very clearly by one of my informants who noticed that, "*if you are not married, Islam can be a lonely place, because you don't necessarily want to do something that is wrong, so you say to yourself - I'd rather not go out.*" (Mazin). In his opinion one of the issues with Islam, when it is taught in Britain, is a strong emphasis on what to do and what not to do, or things that are *halal* and *haram*, and the fact that it produces a substantial unexplained '*grey area in between'*. Furthermore, he observed that practising Muslims, who are not sure of what is allowed and what isn't, tend to stay away from that 'grey area' that encompasses a great deal of social life. And even if they know what is allowed and they do not want to limit themselves to bowling, they need likeminded people to do that with and places where they could meet such people. The CC

---

[370] The research has found that some of the members of the CC have not only made very good friends among the people involved in the CC projects and frequenting its Friday sessions, but met in the organisation their future wives and husbands.

and the IFE have clearly provided both male and female young Muslim professionals[371] with these avenues, and therefore they have managed to attract many young people.

The CC and IFE have not only been making the religion of Islam a 'less lonely place' for practising Muslim singles by filling the 'grey area' in between things that are *halal* and *haram*, but are also contributing to building an alternative to drinking culture, that is the most popular way of socializing among young Britons. Obedience of the Islamic prohibition of drinking alcohol entails *"refusal of commensality"* and *"rejection of social intercourse"* to use the terms of Mary Douglas (1970: 40), and, in practice, means exclusion from a very important part of British culture. Practising Muslims are thus forced to search for other means of socialising, other aspects of the country's culture, that would comply with Islamic instructions. The desire to create a viable alternative to drinking culture has, in fact, been one of the most commonly advanced explanations by the informants linked with the CC for setting up the association. It is clear for instance in the following account of one of its members: *"While I was doing my work I kind of always felt as you was wearing a straight jacket because I did not participate in pub culture and the rest of it – I was not interested in it. So I very strongly felt the need of finding a halal alternative, where we Muslims could hang out and chill out without being concerned about alcohol and all these issues."* (Sajid) Although the CC has not solved the problem of halal ways of socializing for all concerned young Muslim Londoners, it has definitely provided some of them with an important substitute to the mainstream ways of hanging out and chilling out.

Closely related to the provision of the halal ways of socializing is also another benefit from being active in the Muslim and wider society, which was named by my Belgian interviewees as 'avoidance of getting disconnected from the proper life'. One of the young Muslim Londoners interviewed in the course of the research spoke about it in the following way: *"Since joining* (the Muslim organisation – KP) *these were one of the best years of my life really... Kept me engaged, kept me out of trouble. I also helped others to keep out of trouble and kept others engaged. In that time we have developed a*

---

[371] Apart from the aforementioned avenues for development of social capital, both the CC and the IFE have been running nurseries for pre-school children, which provide young mothers with opportunity to meet and network. More information about the CC nursery can be found on http://www.thecitycircle.com and on the IFE one on http://www.islamicforumeurope.com/live/ife.php?doc=rainbow

lot of interesting projects that I felt were long lasting and fulfilling." (Mumtaz) There were also other young Muslim men in my sample who believed that involvement in a Muslim civil society has spared them, for example, from such forms of crime which frequently affected the second and third generation of Muslims such as drug trafficking, theft or violence against the person. As in Brussels, some of my interviewees talked about their involvement in the Muslim organisation and in a wider public sphere as a way of leading a life of 'a good Muslim'. They often suggested that sticking to their organisations or more importantly 'holding fast' to Islam, allowed them to keep away from juvenile delinquency and other phenomena traditionally associated with the 'difficult youth' and to attain greater self-realisation in life. Thus, my research confirms the point made by Göle who noticed that Islam provides young European Muslims with ethical guidance for conduct in their daily life and offers a personal basis to construct themselves as 'moral citizens' (2004: 820).

In order to be successful religious brokers, members of the emerging new Muslim elite in London need to possess not only some social capital and knowledge about their religion and other coreligionists, but also certain communication, management and leadership skills. My interviews with the young Muslim Londoners show that one of the places where they significantly improve these skills are their respective organisations. Thaqib, for example, claimed that, *"The involvement into Islamic work has given me more skills as a person. I've acquired some leadership and management skills."* Another interviewee, arguing in the same manner, asserted that, *"By my engagement with the community I have developed a lot of qualities that I feel I would not be able to gain If I had not participated in the organization. You put a lot young people, my age, in a public platform of two-three thousand people and they would not be able to get a word out of their mouth, let alone articulate an argument. From a very young age, 17, I was put to speak to the big forums of people, student, sometimes intellectuals. These are the communication skills that I have developed."* (Dirar) He also said that he had found these particular skills very useful at work when he was required to make a presentation. He declared in a very self-contented way that *"some of the managers in my job are fascinated by the way I am able to articulate my arguments."* Yet another interviewee, Rushd, stressed that the numerous skills that young Muslims develop within the associational sphere are passed on to them by other colleagues. Thus, she viewed community activism as a sort of sphere of exchange of skills. She pointed out that *"There is always people below you - in terms of those who have just joined - and you can train them, so you are carrying out your skills. And there is people above you who is looking on to see how they can better your skills."* (Rushd)

The last but not least major benefit from activism in the Muslim organisation evoked by most of the young Muslim Londoners was personal satisfaction. One of my informants who mentioned it while speaking about her activism in the Muslim civil society was Afnan. She said that, *"this volunteering gives me great sense of self satisfaction because you feel you have done something good. I don't think I would do it otherwise."* Jada, who is active in different associational structures, spoke about her involvement to some extent in the same way. She asserted that, *"I benefit from the activism in the Muslim organisation in terms of getting the satisfaction that we have achieved something or we have done something successful. Just say, for example, Muslim Community Radio* (run from the ELM during the month of Ramadan – KP). *I heard many times from people saying: 'we really loved listening to your show'. So, that is like a mental satisfaction to me. I know yeah, they have enjoyed it and that it was not boring. I did something worthwhile... I mean, instead of just sitting at home and staring at the ceiling. So, I get that satisfaction (...)"*. In addition, my male interviewees evoked personal satisfaction as one of the major benefits they get from their volunteering. Fadi for instance argued that, *"You can get power out of it* (activism – KP) *and you can get satisfaction out of it. Whether it is a Muslim cause or a Christian cause, when you help people, you get satisfaction out of it, that you don't get out of doing a job. I do it to get a personal satisfaction."*, whereas Dirar remarked that *"Obviously I benefit from it personally not materially. I don't get any money from it. My main benefit is personal satisfaction. (...) I think it is the biggest reward you can get, more then money or anything."*

To sum up, the involvement of young Muslim Londoners in the Muslim and wider civil society enabled them not only to rediscover their own authenticity and sense of being someone, but at the same provided them with the equipment necessary to move from the formal to more substantive forms of citizenship. In other words, it gave them

353

both the oppositional energy inscribed in self-pride (Modood 2006: 48) and the tools, which are essential for the constructive channelling of this energy. While moving to substantive forms of citizenship, members of the emerging new Muslim elite in London have been calling for different citizenship rights more assertively, which will be discussed in the following subchapter.

5.4 ISLAM AND CITIZENSHIP RIGHTS

Having elaborated on the depth and extent of the lived citizenship of the young Muslim Londoners, I intend to focus on the content of this citizenship in the remaining two subchapters. In the first, I shall shed light on how the organised Muslims view their rights as citizens and in the following on how they perceive their citizenship obligations. As I have already mentioned, citizenship, like identity, is contextual and different individuals and groups living in diverse conditions experience it and conceive it in a different manner. While most of the citizens of the country tend to feel embraced by its all-inclusiveness, some citizens do not necessarily feel fully included in the country's citizenship framework. In contrast to Belgium, I did not hear many Muslim voices in London pointing out the exclusionary aspects of citizenship. This is also a reason for which the lack-of-recognition model of citizenship, as I have argued above, did not have many supporters amongst my interviewees. This does not mean, however, that there is no gap between the hegemonic form of citizenship rights and the young Muslim Londoners' understanding of these rights, or between their perceptions of what are the citizenship rights in a given time and what should be these rights. As I am going to demonstrate below, although relatively narrow, such a discrepancy exists and it opens up room for different claims-making. Before I tackle this issue and answer how the rights of the Muslims citizens in the eyes of my interviewees differ from the rights of other citizens, it is important, though, to shed some light on the overall understanding of citizenship rights by the members of the rising new Muslim elite.

5.4.1 BANAL DEFINITIONS OF CITIZENSHIP RIGHTS

As with my interviewees in Belgium, the young Muslim Londoners had substantial understanding of what they are entitled to as citizens of Great Britain. First, their subjective notions of citizenship rights consisted of numerous references to civil rights. Many of my interviewees, while defining their rights, spoke extensively about freedom of speech, conscience and association, the right to equal treatment, the right to hold property etc. One of them was for instance Akram who pointed out that, *"I have a right to follow my religion, I have a right to make friends whoever I want to make friends with. I have a right to speak about the injustices around the world. As a British citizen all these rights are protected for me and I am proud of that because I know that many Muslims in the Muslims countries do not have these rights."* Another interviewee who emphasized civil rights elements in his definition of citizenship was Fadi who observed that, *"I know that if police stops me and calls me black bastard I can get them done for that. If I was in Saudi Arabia, and this would happen to me I don't think I could do much. My father lived in Saudi Arabia. He hated it. He was discriminated against because he was an Asian."*

The young Londoners also defined their citizenship rights in terms of political rights such as, for example, active and passive electoral right, which developed historically along with the strengthening of Parliamentary democracies. Not only my male interviewees, but also interviewed Muslim women, referred to political rights when explaining their understanding of citizenship rights. One of them was, for instance Yumn who said that, *"I think it is important to have your right to participate in different aspects of society, in politics etc."* Also within the subjective notion of citizenship rights of Rana were such elements belonging to the political rights as *"a right to vote, right to influence the government and to have a representation within this society."*

The social rights were relatively rarely part of the subjective notions of citizenship rights of my British interviewees. Some of the few interviewees who referred to them were Shahd, who spoke about the right to access to health care and social care, Sajid who talked about the right to earn a living, and Akram who mentioned *"the right to the services and facilities of this country"* and *"a right to live here in security"*. By security Akram meant, however, not only economic protection but security extending to other spheres of life.

Finally yet importantly, numerous definitions of citizenship rights of my informants also included elements of cultural rights understood as a right to be taken under the citizenship canopy and yet stay culturally different. This right was inter alia expressed by Mansur, who stated that, "*My rights are defined by unwritten constitution, as we call various conventions. But leaving the textual things aside, I have my right to be who I am (...) As long as it doesn't offend others and interfere with their lives, I have a right to be who I want to be*". One may also notice elements of these rights in the following explanation of Rana: "*It is hard to be equal and be different, so then I feel like, I guess, I have a duty to keep pushing that debate to allow to be different and being equal. I feel I have those rights and those rights give me the sense of empowerment to challenge anybody, whoever they are Muslims or non-Muslims, and I know the ethos of the place and what it stands for. In that sense, I feel like I am an equal citizen as anybody else, but my day-to-day experiences may not make me feel like I belong to the same extent... because of that constant questioning of your ways, and who you are, and this realization of awareness that you are different.*" She claimed that she could use this otherness to distance herself from other citizens but she, similarly to many other young Muslim Londoners interviewed for this research, decided to use it in an opposite manner. She stated that "*I use that otherness to say that we need to engage even more. I am trying to use it for this purpose, but sometimes I am tired of it too.*" (Rana) Her aforementioned utterance shows that even the most strongly motivated Muslim activists who tried to engage with wider society and show other British citizens that they are not so much different from them, experience moments of resignation. During such moments they temporarily cease to believe that they will ever be recognized as full citizens of the country and begin to think that their calls for the right to the sameness, while maintaining some right to the difference, will never by answered positively. This, at first sight a contradictory demand to be considered 'the same' and at the same time 'as different', will be explored in more detail below.

Before I tackle the issue of the right to sameness and the to difference in the British context, it is worth mentioning that, as in Brussels, the vast majority of my interviewees in London stressed that they view their rights as similar to the rights of other citizens of the country. They spoke in the same way as Abdel, who claimed "*I see my rights as anyone else's. I don't want special treatment for myself because I am a Muslim. That would be wrong. I don't believe in positive discrimination. I believe the rights I have should be the same as anyone else's. At the same time the government must realize that*

Muslims have their sensitivities, so when you are dealing with them, there needs to be a discussion." It is these sensitivities that are often, according to Abdel, wrongly perceived as calls for special rights.

While speaking about their citizenship rights, most of the interviewees stressed that they should not be conceived in abstraction, but always in relation to the obligations. One such interviewee was Razin who said that "*There are two sides of the coin. One is rights and the other one is responsibilities. Because we have rights, the freedoms that we enjoy, freedom of free speech, freedom of this and that, there are also responsibilities. It is ok to say that you have rights, but it is important to recognize that we have also responsibilities that come with being a citizen.*" Also other informants, both male and female, insisted that speaking about citizenship rights without citizenship obligations was not very fruitful.

In line with the constructive model of citizenship, that was by far the most popular model amongst my British and Belgian interviewees, many of the young Muslim Londoners perceived citizenship rights not only as rights that are handed down from above by the state, but also as a result of the grass-root processes, some struggles and claims-making.

The view that Muslims have to fight for their rights using non-violent means was expressed inter alia by Sajid, Marwan and Shabaz. Yet another interviewee Kadir, argued that '*because Muslims kept very quite, haven't really engaged for a long while – it is only recently that they started engaging – that some of their rights have been lost ... Because they haven't stood up and said 'I am not happy with this, I am not happy with that'. It is only now. It is a little bit late admittedly, that they would come and say 'I am happy with this rule, I am not happy with that rule'.* Furthermore, Rasha argued that because many Muslims did not have to fight for their rights, but were granted them automatically, then some of them now did not know what their rights were and how to use them.

5.4.2 RIGHT TO SAMENESS AND RIGHT TO DIFFERENCE

In contrast to the situation in Brussels, the young Muslim Londoners found it much easier to assert their belonging to the national community. In other words, the members of the emerging new Muslim elite in London have been much more successful in exercising their right the sameness as well as their right to the difference. I believe this is conditioned by two major factors: firstly, the difference in the legal citizenship status of the vast majority of Muslims in Britain in comparison with that of Muslims in Belgium, and secondly the multicultural and anti-racist policies that have been in place in Britain for more than three decades now.[372]

In my opinion, the young Muslim Londoners find it easier to call themselves British because in the majority of the cases already their parents (and sometimes already their grandparents) had British passports. Thus, unlike the young Belgian Muslims (whose families sometimes might have been living in Europe the same period), they are not the first generation of Muslims in the country who have almost automatically received legal citizenship, but the second or third generation. As I argued at the beginning of the second chapter, all social identities (including civic identity) are 'a matter of ascription': by individuals/groups of themselves and of individuals/groups by other people and groups (Jenkins 1996: 98), which means that it is not enough that my informants felt British, but they had to be perceived as British also by other members of the society. The sense of belonging, crucial to citizenship, comes through mutual recognition and respect. As Bikhu Parekh reminds us, members of society have to 'feel both that they belong to a common political community and that it belongs to them and one cannot belong to a community unless it also accepts one as its valued member' (Parekh 1999: 449). The British society had to get accustomed to the presence of significant number of citizens of Muslim faith from as early as the 1950s, thus it had enough time for mental adjustment. The crucial factor which was elaborated in the third chapter was that these newcomers were, from the moment of arrival in Britain, not allochtons but citizens with full political franchise. Thus, the legal citizenship framework forced the autochthonous Britons to think about Muslim immigrants as about 'us' and not as about 'them', and enabled the latter to some extent 'feel British'.

A similarly important force that was pushing the autochthonous Britons to view their newly arrived neighbours from the former colonial territories as equal citizens (or at that time rather as British subjects) were the multiculturalist and anti-racist policies that

---

[372] Apart from these two conditions, the degree to which my interviewees were able to make use of their citizenship rights was obviously determined by their personal trajectories and in particular by their reserves of educational, cultural and financial capital.

were put in place already in 1960s (e.g. Race Relation Acts of 1965 and 1968). These policies, empowered by the creation of the Commission for Racial Equality in 1976, have aimed to promote cultural tolerance in a country that was becoming not only increasingly multiracial, multinational and multiethnic, but also multireligious. At the time when the first policies were being drawn up, religious diversity did not seem to be important, hence the main emphasis was put on racial differences. At present, as I have argued in the third chapter, the race relation industry that was a direct result of these policies has been under major reconstruction. This is related inter alia to the fact that some of the major dividing lines in the society (e.g. racial differences) lost their importance, while at the same time new division lines have emerged. One o such new division line that has appeared recently is religion - hence the emergence of elements of the faith relations industry that is supposed to redress the balance between different faith communities (McLoughlin 2005: 55-58).

In spite of the aforementioned conditions and special measures taken by the British authorities in order to ensure that all the citizens are treated equally and that they live in the tolerant and inclusive society, some of my interviewees claimed that they did not feel fully embraced in this society and the category of Britishness. One of the interviewees who expressed a desire for greater equality and called for a more open category of 'us' was Rana. She argued that although racism in its straightforward manifestations had been fought quite successfully and, to some extent, it had been eradicated, it still existed at more subtle level. She pointed out that such racism did not manifest itself in the hostile way but, for example, *"in a constant questioning about things like the fact that you don't drink* (alcohol – KP)*, your loyalty to your family or connection with your family. It is at that level - the stuff that you do, or the values you hold. They are seen as surprising, different from the norm, or you need to justify and explain them. (...) That makes you constantly aware of your difference and it can be quite hard doing this all the time. I think a lot of the times it is easier to hide those things rather than show them who you are as a person in day-to-day life"*. Her strategy to blend into the wider society by hiding some of the 'surprising' elements of her personality has also been popular among other young British Muslims. For many people who may not have as rich cultural capital as some of my interviewees this might actually be the only way of proving that 'they are like others', or that they are British.

An important way of claiming the right to sameness by the young Muslim Londoners has also been their frequent expressions of strong attachment to the national identity and its various elements. As I have demonstrated above, in the section devoted to the analysis of the depth of citizenship of my interviewees, for the vast majority of them being British was extremely meaningful. They not only a express general attachment to Britain, but also to numerous more mundane aspects of life in the country. Similarly, to the Belgian interviewees they were also very irritated by any suggestions that they were not part and parcel of the British society.

At the same time, as it is clear from the aforementioned opinion of Rana, the young Muslim Londoners wanted their presence to be not only banalised, or taken for granted, but also to be recognized.[373] They claimed not only the right to the sameness (Britishness), but also to difference. At the personal level, the latter right has usually been expressed in terms of 'being true to oneself', 'being authentic' and being original. These themes, as I have shown in the second chapter are typical for all the searches of identity in the high modernity, when the individual is forced to reflexively construct his or her own biography. At the societal level, this right has usually been understood as the recognition of some group rights. In the case of my interviewees, for whom the religious component of their identity is one of the most important ones (if not the most important one), Islam is the major source of authenticity and originality on the basis of which they construct their biographies. It should not be then surprising that they also want some recognition of this major source of originality of their identities in the public sphere. In what follows, I shall analyse some of the major calls for the recognition of the right to differences at the societal level, which included inter alia claims to: more state-founded Muslim schools, prayer facilities in the state schools, more room for Islam and Islamic civilisation in the school curricula together with the calls for the right to the sameness. As it should become clear, most of these claims are formulated within the existing state and

---

[373] The oscillation between these two desires is according to Jean Leca a major feature of the 'contestatory citizenship' (1986).

church relations framework depicted in chapter three, and with reference to the ideal of equality inscribed in the notion of citizenship.

Before I depict some of the areas where my interviewees saw their citizenship rights as not being fully applied, it is necessary to mention that there was no agreement among them whether Muslims in the country are being treated equally in comparison with other British citizens or not. The diversity of opinions was particularly clear with regards to the issue of discrimination and its causes. The vast majority of the interviewees believed that in spite of the formal recognition as citizens and numerous anti-discrimination measures, they as well as other people of Muslim faith were not treated equally. Thaqib, for instance, observed that *"It seems everyone has the same rights but sometimes the spotlight and media is on us. I think Muslim community is more exploited than others, which does not necessarily take away your rights, but you are treated in somehow different manner than other communities."* Other interviewees spoke in less general terms and pointed out at various inequalities in different areas of social life such education, criminal justice or access to employment that will be explored below. While some of them put the blame for these inequalities on mainstream society, others referred to global mechanisms or to Muslims themselves. One of interviewees who saw the reasons for the inequalities experienced by British Muslims in the more global situation and the behaviour of some coreligionists was for example Sajid. He argued that *"Muslims have equal rights, but they need to exercise them. It is unfortunate at the moment, because of the global situation, Muslims have no choice of theirs. They have become a new chosen enemy after communists. Islam is a new bogeyman. So the cause is that Muslims feel the pain greater than others. So, for example, when the bombs exploded in London (*on 7 July 2005 – KP), *Muslims were also affected* (there were also people of Muslim faith who died and were wounded in the attacks – KP). *And we also feel the backlash. So we are attacked from both sides. It is simply not fair. The terrorist kill us and there are also racist who want to kill us. It is uniquely sad situation the Muslims find themselves in. And they are not in control of anything. There is feeling of hopelessness. It is a loose-loose situation. People are killed and those who were left behind suffer."*

Some of the interviewees believed that the non-Muslim majority does not have a monopoly on the unequal treatment of the Muslim minority. They pointed out that, to

361

some extent, the perception of the wider society as racist is a Muslim invention. One of the interviewees who made such a point was Rana who said "*I think technically Muslims have the same rights as other citizens. The country is quite good in terms of its diversity policies, but on the practical level there are still barriers and some of them are imposed by mainstream society because I do think we still live in a racist society. On the other hand, some of those barriers are self-imposed by Muslims feeling that they cannot engage with non-Muslims and the outside world.*" Another Muslim Londoner who spoke in the same manner was Samar. She claimed that, "*Some of the Muslims are vulnerable. On the whole they have the same rights, but I think there are instances where they have higher unemployment. I think it is a mixture of social factors not just that they are treated unequally. I think some of the reasons for them not being on the same playing field are of their own creation.*"

Finally, a few my interviewees believed that Britain has been very successful in managing its cultural diversity and there is not much to complain about. One them was Fadi who said, "*People can't discriminate on me, because of my colour, my religion. If I go to a job, no one would say: 'you are brown - get lost'. No one would say: 'why are you going for an hour on Friday to pray? - get lost'. My work has actually a prayer room. Most big organizations have prayer rooms. I can say I don't want to eat certain meat. In my current company they actually provide also halal food. What more I can ask for?*". Yet another interviewee who saw the future of the Muslim population optimistically was Jada. She quite controversially put the blame for the unequal treatment of Muslims solely on them by arguing that, "*If you go around acting like a victim, you will be treated like a victim. Muslims for far too long have been going around saying that we are victims, that is why they have been treated unequally!*"

5.4.3 CONTESTED EQUALITY OF RIGHTS IN EDUCATION

Education was one of the areas in which some of my informants saw their citizenship rights as not being fully respected. As I have already mentioned, citizenship in theory guarantees all citizens access to quality education. Some of my interviewees did not fully profit from this right, firstly because of the decision of their parents to send them to specific schools that did not necessarily provide such high standard education. While in the case of Brussels - where a director of a francophone school could without explanation refuse to admit a pupil of an immigrant origin - one could talk about the situation of forced segregation, in the case of London (and in other cities of the country) one has to do rather with the situation of self-segregation. Muslim parents, at least in theory, have a right to place their children in the school of their choice and the school directors cannot dismiss their applications.[374] Research, however, shows that very few parents profit from this right and that the level of ethnic segregation in schools is even higher than such segregation in local neighbourhoods, and that ethnic segregation is particularly high for pupils of Pakistani and Bangladeshi origin (Burgess and Wilson 2004).

Although of crucial importance, segregation was not the only problem that my interviewees saw in education. While academic studies usually give the explanations of the low levels of academic achievement amongst Muslim students in terms of poverty, social deprivation and language difficulties, some of the young Muslim Londoners also spoke about the obstacles to their full achievement of potential that related to their experiences as members of the ethnic and religious minority. Rana was one of a few interviewees who declared that she had had experiences of racism at school. In my opinion, the fact that she, as well as other informants, mentioned this issue only briefly means that these experiences did not constitute insurmountable difficulties in their overall education. This seems to confirm the fact also that all of them possessed a university degree or were in the process of obtaining one and were above all an emerging new Muslim educational elite.

Apart from the prevalence of ethnic and religious prejudices that, according to some research, crucially influences the educational achievement of Muslim students and lead to their weak performances (OSI 2005, GLA 2006), these levels of achievement are a result of a number of different factors. Among the most significant it is possible to mention, for instance, the lack of Muslim role models in schools and the low expectations that some teachers have of Muslim students. Moreover, it is worth remembering that most Muslim children in Britain, in contrast with Belgium, attend mosque schools or other supplementary schools outside normal school hours in order to receive an education

---

[374] About the school choice and ethnic segregation in Britain see an excellent report commissioned by the Runnymede Trust (Weekens-Bernard 2007).

in Islamic beliefs and practices. This places an additional burden on Muslim children, in terms of both time and intellectual effort, which may also negatively influence their overall educational performance.

Some of my interviewees also complained about the Eurocentrism of the school curricula that *"Teach mostly about the achievements of the European civilization without a broader contextualization of the facts."* (Maha) According to Tufyal Choudhury, who coordinated a large scale study on Muslims in Britain financed by the Open Study Institute, the school curricula in the country could much more effectively encourage cross-cultural understanding if they would undertake two major shifts. First of all, they should change in such a way to give the studied material a more global focus, whereby European and Christian culture is contextualised in terms of world civilisation. Secondly, the curricula should, in his opinion, include more references to the Muslim contribution to European learning and culture, particularly in the fields of art, literature, mathematics, geometry, science, history, philosophy, astronomy and medicine. (OSI 2005: 105). While the first suggestion of the report struck a chord with the aforementioned opinion of Maha, the latter one was in line with the complaint of some of my informants (e.g. Dirar) that the school curriculum did not provide them any information about Muslim role models. For Dirar such a role model about whom he wished he had learnt more at school was, for instance, Salahuddin Al-Ayyubi (known also as Saladin). He argued that *"Under the Christian rule Jews did not have total freedom in the Holy Land. When Salahuddin Al-Ayyubi conquered the place he declared religious freedom for all, and gave security to those who wanted to remain in the country in the vicinity of the holy places".* [375]

Yet, another aspect of the educational system that did not live up to the civic expectations of some of my interviewees was the Muslim representation within the governing boards of the schools. As one of my interviewees, Kadir said *"We don't have all the rights we should do. Taking the schools for example, there should be more representation of the Muslim schools. There should more Muslim governors".* The issue of Muslim schools will be discussed in detail below, whereas here I would like focus on

---

[375] The study carried out by the team led by Choudhury also found that many Muslim parents would appreciate the option for their children to study Arabic in school, and also for them to receive a form of Religious Education that gave them more opportunities to enrich their understanding of their own faith as well as studying others. (OSI 2005: 105)

the second issue. This is an issue which was widely elaborated on in the OSI report (2005). Its authors noted that greater participation by Muslims in all aspects of the education system is central to ensuring that educational policy is sensitive to their needs. However, the numbers of Muslim teachers and governors in schools are very low, and drop-out rates for Muslims on teacher training courses are higher than average. (OSI 2005: 106) For example, in Newham, (the London borough next to Tower Hamlets[376]) 25 per cent of all children are Muslim (Pakistani and Bangladeshi) and only two per cent of school governors are from these communities. This under-representation is typical in cities across the country where there are significant Muslim populations, even in schools where Muslim pupils make up 70 to 90 per cent of the school population. As the report on Muslims in London points out, school governors have an important role to play in educational institutions by influencing what happens in the school. They can initiate measures that may resolve or make progress towards dealing with many issues. (GLA 2006: 46) My interviewees mentioned this problem, knowing how significant power the school governors have.

The issues such as wearing hijab at school, the provision of halal food, or the provision of the prayer facilities are generally regulated quite well in Britain, which is probably the reason why none of my informants in London raised them.[377]

5.4.4 CONTESTED EQUALITY OF RIGHTS IN ACCESS TO EMPLOYMENT

Another area in which many of my interviewees saw their citizenship rights as not being equal to the rights of other citizens was the labour market. As I have demonstrated in the third chapter, Muslims constitute one of the most marginalised and disadvantaged faith groups in Britain. According to the socio-economic analysis by the Office for National Statistics of the religious dimension of the 2001 Census, Muslims, in comparison with other faith groups, had for example the highest rates of unemployment. Of young people aged 16-24, 17.5 per cent of Muslims are unemployed, compared to 7.9 per of Christians and 7.4 per cent of Hindus. As in Belgium, Muslims also tend to be over concentrated in

---

[376] See the map of London in the chapter three.
[377] For more information about these regulations see chapter four. On regulations concerning various aspects of religious practice at the state schools in Britain see MCB report 'Meeting the Needs of Muslim Pupils in the State Schools' (MCB 2007).

certain sectors of the economy: 40 per cent of Muslim men in employment were working in the distribution, hotel and restaurant industry, compared with 17 per cent of Christian men. Moreover, 40 per cent of Muslims are in the lowest occupation groups, compared to 30 per cent of Christians. Muslim men are among the least likely to be in managerial or professional jobs and the most likely to be in low-skilled jobs (OSI 2005: 16).

Such situation of Muslims on the labour market is to some extent related with the fact that as a faith group they have relatively poor educational qualification. This factor, however, does not fully explain according to my interviewees the fact that Muslims are the most deprived faith group in Britain. Several members of the emerging new Muslim elite in London suggested that this deprivation is to some extent also a result of discriminatory treatment of Muslims on the job market. Razin, for instance, said that, *"Theoretically we are equal citizens, but practically not necessarily. Freedom from discrimination is in theory ok, but in practice it is difficult to police or to maintain it, especially on the job market. Figures published recently by the Muslim Weekly show that in general 87 per cent of the graduates find jobs and in the Muslim community 76 per cent. So it is 11 per cent less graduating Muslims who would get jobs. Now, whether that is something that has to do with the Muslim community or it is discrimination? I think it is a bit of both. I think there are evident examples when Muslims are not treated as equitably as other members of the society."* Another interviewee who argued that the discrimination in access to employment seriously infringed the citizenship rights of Muslims was Rasha. In her opinion, this discrimination was particularly difficult when people were restricted in their professional careers. She said *"Some members of my family have had quite bad experiences when they have been referred, in the long way, to wrong faces, or they had bad references because they were Muslims. So I know a lot of cases. They are neither major not minor. My brother in law, for example, is a doctor, ophthalmologist, but it is very difficult for him to get jobs. Middle range is quite ok, but after certain level it becomes very hard. To break up to the management level is very hard."*

The existence of ethnic and religious discrimination in access to employment is also confirmed by numerous studies. In 2004 the BBC, for instance, conducted a survey in which fictitious applications were made for jobs using applicants with the same qualifications and work experience, but different names. Researchers found that the white candidates – with the names John Andrews and Jenny Hughes were successful in getting interviews 23 per cent of the time while the black African applicants - Abu Olasemi and Yinka Olatunde - had a 13 per cent success rate. For Fatima Khan and Nasser Hanif, the candidates with Muslim names, the success rate was just 9 per cent (BBC 2004). The European Union Monitoring and Advocacy Program (hereafter EUMAP), in its report on the situation of Muslims in the UK from 2002, argues that Muslims experience penalties in employment through discrimination around their faith and often ethnicity. The 'Muslim penalty' is described by the EUMAP as a combination of factors including negative stereotypes, prejudice, ignorance and hatred, which result in Muslims experiencing disadvantage in the labour market (OSI 2002). Religious discrimination has been reported as being slightly more likely to occur in the private sector than the public sector and discrimination tends to occur rather in practices than in policies. Unfair treatment usually occurs around uniform and dress codes, time off for religious holidays, lack of understanding of religious customs and career progression (GLA 2006). Another recent study, commissioned by the Joseph Rowntree Foundation, found inter alia that male ethnic minorities in managerial and professional jobs would earn up to a quarter less than their white counterparts. Its authors also argued that labour market discrimination is deep-rooted, widespread and persistent and called for the introduction of more interventionist, anti-discrimination policies in the workplace (Clark and Drinkwater 2007).

Apart from the aforementioned general difficulties in accessing the labour market (statement of Razin) and progressing (Rasha) some of my interviewees accounted for some specific difficulties faced by Muslims in the workplace which according to them infringe on their civil rights. One such frequently mentioned difficulty was the access to prayer facilities. Rushd, for instance, argued that *"To have full citizenship rights means to be able to practice your faith and also to have the facilities if you want to pray five times a day. Working people often find it difficult to find a prayer space and a lot of hardship is given to have these breaks because in the winter we have to pray quite close to the afternoon."* Another interviewee working in the school said that, *"A lot of people say 'leave religion behind when you enter the work place or school'. I have had this said to me many times."* (Afnan) At the same time some of the interviewees pointed out that since the introduction of the new law forbidding discrimination on religious grounds in employment, the provision of goods, services, and facilities,[378] and as a result of more intense lobbying by the Muslim organisations,[379] the situation of believers of Islam in the job market has somewhat improved.

As in Belgium, some of the difficulties that people of Muslim faith encounter on the job market more specifically affect women in hijabs, as those carrying visible markers of being Muslim. In spite of the fact that Britain has promoted policies of tolerance and diversity, allowing female Muslim pupils and students to wear hijabs at schools, colleges and universities, and accommodating the hijab in many work places,[380] it has not been fully immune to hijabophobia. One of my female interviewees who wears a headscarf and has experienced this phenomenon was Rushd. She said *"I have been to a job interview for a teaching post in the girls only school, where they* (the representatives of the school authorities – KP) *have openly said looking at my hijab that I was not the example they wanted for their students."* Later on she added that the situation in Britain in this respect was anyway much better than in other European countries and declared: *"I wouldn't like to have a situation in Britain similar to this in France where wearing the hijab is forbidden."*[381] Another female interviewee Afnan said *"If you are a Muslim and wear the hijab you put all these negative perceptions upon you and you can get only to a certain level within the company. And it is important that we* (Muslim women wearing the headscarves – KP) *will continue to allow people to see that we can wear hijabs and be effective workers. There are a lot of professions where it is still quite difficult. Even though you are getting more people now. So generally there is a lot of work to do."*

---

[378] For more information about this piece of legislation see chapter III.

[379] The MCB has for instance organised in 2003 numerous seminars instructing community leaders and organisations about the introduction of the Employment Equality Regulations making it unlawful to discriminate against workers because of their religion, which come into force from 2nd December 2003.

[380] For example, the female Muslims officers working in the Metropolitan Police Service can wear the hijab on duty.

[381] Here it is important to clarify that there is no general ban on Islamic headscarves in France, but the so called 'Stasi law' (from the Commission on secularism led by Bernard Stasi) banned them ("ostentatious religious signs"), since September 2004 in French schools.

Moreover, she argued that Muslim women faced double discrimination based on the grounds of gender and religious adherence.[382]

5.4.5 CONTESTED EQUALITY OF RIGHTS IN CRIMINAL JUSTICE

Confidence in the criminal justice system is central to a sense of belonging and inclusion in society and yet some of the young Muslim Londoners interviewed for this book expressed doubts about this system. More precisely, they saw their citizenship rights as not being fully respected when it comes to policing and criminal justice. One of the issues that raised particularly often by them was that of excessive, in their view, anti-terrorist measures introduced in the aftermath of the September 11 terrorist attack[383] and the disproportionate use of the stop and search with regards to their coreligionists. Akram was one of my interviewees who complained about the latter issue. He declared that, *"Every citizen has the right to free movement in this country. However, the Black community had been stopped and searched disproportionately often in comparison to the white community. And the Black community has campaigned and worked tirelessly with the Police authority to eliminate this problem and the Muslim community and Asian community must also engage in trying to eliminate this problem. I don't believe in collective responsibility."* His last sentence, indicating that he perceives this policy to be a direct result of the illegal actions of some individuals from within the Muslim population that have been involved, is particularly significant. This perception of stop and search was also shared by some other young Muslim Londoners. The research carried out by ICM for the Guardian (16 March 2004) showed that the disproportionate increase in the stop and search of civilians was a major cause for concern among Muslim

---

[382] This observation of Afnan was actually one of the major findings of the research of Marie Parker-Jenkins and her collaborators in analysing the career destinations of Muslim women in this country (1999). Another study picked up on the way in which stereotypes about Muslim women impact on the lives of these women. Its author Claire Dwyer notices that gendered, class and racialised explanations reinforce dominant representations of young Muslim women as both oppressed and powerless, stereotypes that impinge directly on the lives of Muslim women (Dwyer 2000). Other studies show that Muslim women wearing visible markers of religious identity are frequent targets of racist attacks especially after such major blows to intercommunity relations as those resulting from the terrorist attack which took place on 11th September 2001 (in the USA), 11th March 2004 (in Spain) and 7th July 2005 (in Britain) to mention only the most important ones (OSI 2005, ENAR 2007).
[383] I am thinking here about the Anti-terrorism, Crime and Security Act 2001 which amended the Crime and Disorder Act 1998 to include provisions for religiously aggravated crimes and the Prevention of Terrorism Act 2005 which replaced the immigration provisions of the Anti-terrorism, Crime and Security Act 2001, introducing inter alia a system of control orders designed to disrupt and prevent terrorist activity.

communities. The poll reported that over two thirds of Muslims feel that the anti-terrorist laws are being used unfairly against Muslim communities. Moreover the Metropolitan Police Authority (MPA) Stop and Search Scrutiny found that Asian and Muslim communities perceived the increase in stop and search of people to be related to faith, the 9/11 attacks and the subsequent 'war on terror' (MPA quoted GLA 2006). The increase in the use of the Terrorism Act powers appears to substantiate this perception and has spread a sense of fear amongst some Muslims. This is for instance clearly visible in the following statement by Afnan, which could equally come from the pages of 'The Trial' by Franz Kafka: *"They* (the representatives of the security forces – KP) *are allowed to come into your home, detain you and not actually tell you the evidence against you. You could be implicated just because Muslim community is a big community and at the same time it is also a small community. You feel quite scarred that somehow you could known someone involved in something in which you are not, just because you are in the public sphere."*

One of the controversial measures, which the government planned to introduce under the Anti-Terrorist Act after the July 7 bombings, was the ban on Hizb ut-Tahrir, the pan-Islamist vanguard political party, which calls for the creation of a unitary Islamic state or caliphate, which has been very active in Britain.[384] This measure was widely discussed in the media and amongst my interviewees. Most of them, although they did not endorse the ideas promoted by the organisation and were sometimes very critical about it, were at the same time against such a ban. Samar for instance argued that *"I don't think the new legislation banning some groups is really needed. They may preach things that are not appropriate but I feel there must be a better way of dealing with them that what they plan to do."* Another interview in the same spirit declared that *"I don't think they should be banned. There were always radical philosophies: socialist, communist and other. Banning them would be very counter-productive. If there is no public airing of things then it becomes more intense and much more secret, and they would get much more support as an oppressed group."* Probably most clearly the position of many of the

---

[384] The calls for the ban of the organisation were repeated by the leader of the Conservative Party more recently (in June 2007) after the foiled attacks in London and Glasgow airport. This intention, initially phrased by Tony Blair, has not been realized. After two reviews since 2005, the government has decided that for the moment there is insufficient evidence to ban the group.

interviewed young Muslim Londoners captured Afnan who said *"I don't think HT should be banned on the basis that there is a free speech and people should be allowed to say whatever they want. But, on the other hand, I would quite like them to be banned because it would help our cause* (hahaha – laughing - KP). *It is almost like the BNP* (British National Party – KP) *of the Muslim population. If you don't give them too much attention, and you don't let them feel too self-important, nobody will pay any attention to them. When they are banned they get whole attention, and say that they are banned because they are Muslim. My personal opinion is – there will be no skin off me nose if they are banned, but I think it is a wrong thing to do."*

The interviewees who felt that Muslims in the country were not equal in comparison to other citizens in the face of the criminal justice system also complained about the lack of Muslim representation in the Police. In their opinion, both the criminal justice system and policing would improve if this number were higher. There are no definitive figures on the number of Muslim staff in the Metropolitan Police Service but the Association of Muslim Police estimates that there are between 275 and 400 Muslim police officers in London. The Metropolitan Police Commissioner estimated that London needs another 2,000 Muslim police officers for the Metropolitan Police Service to be representative (GLA 2006).

Unlike my Belgian interviewees, the young Muslim Londoners did not see any significant differences in their citizenship rights and the rights of other citizens in access to housing and in socializing. As I have shown above, there exist different barriers for Muslims in access, for instance to socialising, however these obstacles result rather from the decision of the British adherents of Islam not to lead a social life similar to non-Muslim compatriots than from the widespread openly discriminatory attitude of the latter.

5.4.6 CONTESTED EQUALITY OF TREATMENT OF ISLAM

A few members of the emerging new Muslim elite in London argued that their citizenship rights also lacked some content when it comes to the fair treatment of their religion in comparison with other religions present in the country. The two issues, which they raised most frequently, concerned the existing law on blasphemy and the access to the state-funding for religious schools.

The first issue is directly linked with the Satanic Verses affair and elaborated in detail in chapter three, was mentioned for instance by Yumn. This young Muslim woman pointed out that *"According to the law we have the same rights apart from the blasphemy clause."* In my opinion, the fact that only a few young Muslim Londoners mentioned this issue, which played a key role in the beginning of the public mobilisation of British Muslims, demonstrates that today the public assertiveness of the believers of Islam in the country stems from different challenges. The disagreement with the discriminatory treatment of Muslims and Islamophobia in different spheres of social life, opposition to the military intervention in Iraq and Afghanistan and the condemnation of violence committed in the name of Islam are only some of the themes which preoccupied the minds of my interviewees.

A few of the young Muslim Londoners also complained about the non-equitable treatment of Islam, in comparison with other faiths in the country, in the access to funds allocated by the state to religious schools. One of them, Rasha, argued that, *"Not having state-founded Muslim schools in the situation when other faith groups have them is a clear sign of unequal treatment."* She also claimed that, *"there are problems with building Muslim schools. I think that it is being held back a lot."*

The research shows that only some 20 000 out of 371 000 Muslim children aged five to 16 attend schools maintained by Muslim charitable trusts (OSI 2005). There are about 130 such schools in the country, of which 37 are located in London. (GLA 2006: 45) Parents and the community provide the funding for the majority of these schools. As I have already mentioned in the third chapter, today only 5 of them receive state aid[385]. The first state-aided Muslim school, Islamia Primary, was founded in 1983 by the pop singer Cat Stevens who converted to Islam and changed his name to Yusuf Islam. After several refusals, the school won state support in 1998. Established in 1992, the Association of Muslim Schools (AMS), supports individuals and institutions developing full-time schooling for Muslim children. As with the best schools of any faith, the best of Britain's Muslim schools are popular with parents because they shine in academic league tables and because they offer an environment for children which accommodates their faith,

---

[385] By contrast, 99 per cent of Britain's 7,000 state-funded faith schools are Anglican or Catholic. For comparison, in 2001, there were 33,000 Jewish children of school age who were entitled to 13,000 places in state-maintained Jewish schools (Masood 2006: 30).

morality and ethics. I shall return to the issue of Muslim schools below, while discussing the character of the demands voiced by the members of the emerging new Muslim elite in London.

5.4.7 KEY DEMANDS – ACCULTURATIVE OR DISSOCIATIVE?

It is possible to divide the claims made by Muslims, such as those analysed above, into two major categories: on the one hand, claims which call for parity with other religious groups who have acquired some special rights in the course of the history; and, on the other hand, requests for rights which are not yet in the possession of any other group. After applying this conceptual grid, elaborated in detail in the second chapter, to the claims made by my British interviewees one may observe that like the young Belgian Muslims, the members of the emerging new Muslim elite in London formulated mainly acculturative demands rather than dissociative ones. At the same time their repertoire of claims is somewhat smaller than the Belgian one presented in the earlier chapter, which has to do, inter alia, with the fact that many of the potential claims of the British Muslims have been already accommodated within the countries multicultural regime. The right to the provision of halal food at schools and hospitals, the right to wear the hijab at schools and colleges or in many workplaces and some other rights for which Belgian Muslims have been calling for several years, are taken for granted by many British Muslims. However, the most important acculturative claim - to be perceived by other citizens as full members of society - has yet in many cases to be met, in a manner similar to Belgium.

The young British Muslims interviewed in the course of the research, like the young Muslim Brusselers, did not even ask for some of the rights to which they are entitled as British citizens. This is well portrayed by their attitudes to the religious schools. As I have mentioned above, only a few of the interviewees brought up the issue of the fact that state aid to the Muslim schools is much smaller that such aid allocated to other faith communities. At the same time, the vast majority of my informants did not view it as an issue. What is more, many of them were not only unconcerned about the lack of the state funding for Muslim schools, but were opposed to the whole idea of creation of Muslim schools. One of the major reasons for which the large proportion of the young Muslim Londoners were against the Muslim school was a widespread conviction that such schools stood in opposition to the idea of a multicultural society, viewed above all as an open society, without segregation. One of the interviewees who shared this belief was, for instance, Shabaz who said *"I think it is important to let your children go out and to know where they are living. Keeping them in the environment where there are only Muslims, maybe they will not know how to react with non-Muslims."* Another likeminded individual was Rana. She asserted that, *"Personally I am not an advocate of Muslim schools because I think if you go to the Muslim school and then you need to integrate with the wider society, later it is much harder."*

Apart from the arguments that Muslim schools are not conducive to a multicultural society, some of my informants also doubted the quality of such an education. In the following statement of Afnan one may detect both arguments: *"They (Muslim schools – KP) are always under-resourced. Their teachers are not properly qualified because they don't have the money. I do not think they are the best for allowing the individuals to integrate into the multicultural society. At the end of the day they will have to integrate into the wider society. If they stay in their own little niche it is difficult for them to be able to relate to that and work within that. We are part of the wider society."*

One of the major arguments that was used by the minority of my informants who supported the idea of the creation of Muslim schools was that such schools would enable the formation of Muslim individuals, confident in their faith, who would be better equipped for their encounters with modernity. One of the interviews who made this point particularly strongly was Rasha. She argued that, *"Muslim schools should be encouraged because when people are made to give up their own culture, they become more confused, and that is where you get the confusion and people who don't know who they are. If people are more grounded, then they are confidently able to interact with the wider society in a positive way and I think we need more of that."* According to a few of my informants who thought along these lines, the transmission of Islamic beliefs and values which in the supplementary school is only partial should be prioritized and it is possible to do so only within the framework of a Muslim school.

374

Some of my interviewees also supported the idea of the creation of Muslim schools because they believed that state-schools had not been able to cater for the needs of the Muslim pupils. One of them, Rushd - who had her own children in such school - said that in *"In the state school little things, day to day events become a struggle"* and that *" (...) my children were not happy, I wasn't happy and eventually I had to withdraw them into the Islamic school where their total outlook has changed. Their personalities, confidence, everything has changed and I don't believe in the fact that if you put your children into the Islamic schools they become ghettoised, they become internal,... all that is not true. It depends on the school and the management. The school to which I have sent my children really changed them. They are much, much happier and academically they are doing very well."*

Finally, like many of the young Belgian Muslims, some of the young Muslim Londoners gave negative reasons for the establishment of the religious schools. One of them was an inhabitant of the London borough of Tower Hamlets, Thaqib, who asserted, *"I don't think we should have too many Muslim schools in this country, however in some kind of areas, like here, it is necessary, because of the large amount of Muslims. It will not close the community because it is already a largely Muslim area, anyway."*

To conclude, many of the young British Muslim did not demand all the rights to which they are entitled as citizens of the country, fearing that this may isolate them from other members of society. On the other hand, a small but very vocal part of my sample did not fear self-isolation and much more courageously and assertively than the young Belgian Muslims depicted in the earlier chapter, demanded the elements of acquis of other religious groups. The country's framework of management of ethnic, cultural and religious diversity or multicultural regime provided them with substantial room for manoeuvre. At the same time, almost all of the interviewed young Muslim Londoners expressed concerns about the future of this framework and the relatively open and flexible notion of Britishness which were seriously shaken on July 7 2005 by the acts of violence committed in the name of Allah. As I am going to show in the following section, many of them viewed with opposition the religious radicalism that may lead to such actions and worked towards harmonious relations with other communities as a key citizenship obligation.

5.5 ISLAM AND CITIZENSHIP OBLIGATIONS

The last section of this chapter will be devoted, as the earlier one, to the normative dimension of lived citizenship of the young Muslim Londoners. It will move on, however, from an examination of the subjective notions of citizenship rights of my British interviewees, to an analysis of their perceptions of citizenship obligations. As I have noted above in the former section, many of my interviewees, while speaking about the citizenship rights, also raised the issue of civic responsibility, arguing that 'this is the other side of the coin' (Razin), which should never be forgotten. And yet some other informants, similarly to Kadir, claimed that *"We have never really been asked about obligations of citizenship. Until recently it would be just answered by who we are."*

The issue of citizenship obligations as a forgotten one, has not only been rediscovered by some of my interviewees and other British citizens but also by the theory of citizenship. As I have mentioned in the chapter II, this dimension of the Marshallian theory of citizenship has been rather underdeveloped. The last section of this chapter aims to contribute humbly to these reflections by shedding light on the ordinary perceptions of citizenship obligations by the young Muslim Londoners. It will also elaborate on how the members of the emerging new Muslim elite in London view the relations between the obligations of citizenship and the demands of the faith and what according to them means to be a good/bad citizen.

5.5.1 BANAL DEFINITIONS OF CITIZENSHIP OBLIGATION

While the subjective notions of citizenship rights of the young British Muslims were as complex as the same definitions of my Belgian informants, their perceptions of the citizenship obligations, although quite well developed, lacked somewhat the sophistication and depth of the definitions of the young Muslim Brusselers. One of the reasons for that might lie in the much less omnipresent discourse on citizenship and the responsibilities of citizenship in the British public debates.[386] Similarly to the young Belgian Muslims, however, the young Muslim Londoners pointed out many of the complexities of the individual and collective duties resulting from the membership in the political community.

---

[386] Please see the section on 'Being a citizen' of this chapter for an elaboration of the issue.

As could be expected from a group of people, who are actively involved in different initiatives of the Muslim and wider civil society aimed at the improvement of the living conditions in their localities and nation-wide, the most commonly stressed elements of the obligations of a citizen was a duty 'to work for the betterment of the society'. This duty was emphasised equally strongly by my female as well as my male interviewees. One of the female interviewees, Samar, said for example that *"The obligation of a citizen is to contribute to the society: to do something meaningful. Not only make a difference to my life but to make a difference to lives of others."* Another female interviewee, Afnan argued that a key citizenship obligation is *"To do everything what I can, within the system that I live in, for the betterment of all people."* Mazin was one of many male informants who stressed the importance of the duty of working for the betterment of the society and its impartial character. He argued that a major responsibility of a citizen is *"to make a positive contribution to this society, to make it better. There are many things wrong with this society, as well as, with other societies. We have to decide if we want to be part of the problem or part of the solution."* He later on explained that being part of the solution meant for him many things: *"not only being proactive, knowing your neighbour, doing something good, but above all working hard in job whatever job you are given"* (Mazin). He recalled *"I remember the words of Mohammed Ali who was once asked: 'if you were not a boxer, what would you have been?' His answer was 'Whatever I'd have been, I'd have been the best at that job'. And that what is all about being a citizen. You have to be the best you can with what God has given you."*

Not only Mazin but also other interviewees conceived the work for the betterment of the society as a form of 'common good' shaped through deliberation over the particular interests of every member of the society. This understanding fits very neatly with the communitarian vision of citizenship, which holds inter alia that the individual can only realize her or his interests and identity through deliberation over the 'common good', and that the individual liberty is maximized through public service and the prioritization of the 'common good' over the pursuit of individual interests (Jones & Gaventa 2002: 3-4).

The emphasis on the work for the betterment of the whole society, marking the numerous subjective definitions of citizenship obligations of my interviewees, is also in line with the most popular model of citizenship amongst the members of the emerging new Muslim elite in London (as well as in Brussels), namely the socially constructive one. At the same time, very few of my British informants spoke about fighting all forms of injustice as an important citizenship obligation. In contrast to my Belgian interviewees, for whom social jihad was the most important citizenship obligation, my British interviewees relatively rarely referred to fighting injustices locally and globally as an important civic duty. One of the possible explanations of the lack of these references would probably lie in their lived citizenship, which was not very strongly marked by the personal experiences of unequal treatment.

Another major obligation of a citizen, according to my British interviewees was a duty to strive to 'maintain harmony with other communities and citizens of the country'. In their view, 'maintaining harmony with others' meant also paying special attention to self-accountability and self-responsibility. This idea was well captured by the editor of the Q-News[387], one of the oldest Muslim magazines in the country, who argued in the recent issue of the magazine that, *"Our faith instructs us to hold ourselves to account, before holding others to account."* (Alam 2003) Many of my British interviewees were aware of the fact that harmony in the society is preconditioned by the existence of substantial room for self-criticism within different communities, enabling their members to address certain problems first within their own groups and only then to look for the external culprits or external factors that might have contributed to these problems. The explanations of the possible reasons that might have led to the July 7th bombing provided by my interviews suggest that within the Muslim population in Britain there is sufficient space for self-criticism. My interviewees, before speaking about 'the dodgy foreign policy'[388] and, in particular, about the influence of the active involvement of the British army in military operations in Iraq on the radicalisation of young British Muslims, referred to many problems within the Muslim population. The crisis of religious leadership, the shortcomings of Islamic scholarship, the communication barrier between parents who grew up on the Asian subcontinent and children born in Britain, the crisis of

---

[387] More information about the Q-News one may find on www.q-news.com or in Pędziwiatr 2005: 91.
[388] This term 'dodgy foreign policy' as the major culprit of the 7/7 was originally used by Salma Yaqoob, vice-chair of Respect and chair of Birmingham Stop the War Coalition. She famously declared that 'Shoddy theology does not exist without a dodgy foreign policy" (Yaqoob 2005).

identity and lack of Muslim role models were some of the most frequently mentioned ones.[389]

Many of my interviewees believed that their citizenship obligation to maintain harmony in the society also involved addressing some of the aforementioned problems within the Muslim community. Kadir, for example, spoke at length about tackling 'the problem with imported imams who cannot provide any spiritual guidance without being able to understand people's mind first', whereas Sajid made the following point about the shortcomings of the scholarship of some popular Muslim scholars: *"The view of Yusuf al-Qaradawi on suicidal bombings is not acceptable. 'Is the suicidal bombing permissible by Islam?' – the answer is 'no'. There cannot be any 'ifs' or 'buts'. Because these people give wishy-washy answers then people are confused. On the issue of wife beating: 'can men beat women?' – the answer again is 'no'. The answer shouldn't be 'no, however there are certain circumstances in which ...'. The are no special circumstances. There are no 'howevers'. This has been a failure of Islamic Muslim scholarship and this is one of the key problems we need to resolve".*

At the same time, other interviewees spoke about the importance of maintaining harmony in the society, within the context of discussion about the citizenship obligations, without explicit reference to the situation of their own religious community. Instead they referred general or common profits of such harmonious relationships. Rushd, for instance, asserted that *"I have to maintain the harmony in the society that I live in.... that I don't do anything that would create chaos. I have to try to maintain the safety and well-being of my community and society regardless who it is. I am not just looking after Muslims, my non-Muslim neighbours are as important as the Muslim one."* Yet another interviewee who in a somewhat similar way saw citizenship as his key responsibility was Akram. He believed that one of the key duties of a citizen is *"to ensure the safety and security and that there is tolerance in your society. It is an appreciation of the difference of each other, the tolerance of that difference, and commonality among those people who are different. Working for the same goals and working for the same ends."* The respect for others and for otherness had, according to numerous young Muslim Londoners, a

---

[389] These arguments are explored at length in Pędziwiatr 2005b. Many of these points were integrated in the report of the Governmental task force entitled 'Working Together to Prevent Extremism' (Home Office 2005).

crucial everyday-life dimension. This dimension was particularly stressed by my female interviews. One of them, Samar, argued that a major duty of a citizen is *"To be considered of other people. Taking interests in welfare of other people"*, whereas Jada pointed out the importance of *"Not showing anger in public, being polite and being courteous. "*

Numerous young British Muslims understood the citizenship obligations as civil duties - that is obligations enforced by the state, rather than as duties imposed by the society or civic obligations. This highly legalistic perception of the responsibilities of a citizen characterized, for example, the understanding of Adel who believed that *"The most important citizenship obligation is to uphold the law and not to break it. To work with other people and not to act against the law of this country. "* Another interviewee whose subjective notion of citizenship obligation was largely limited to the enumeration civil duties was Abdel. He said that, *"My obligations as a citizen are similar to obligations of other citizens. First and foremost, I have to follow the law and respect it. Then, I have to pay the taxes, send my children to school etc. "* This understanding of the citizenship obligation was especially common among my male interviews. One of the few female interviewees who upheld this relatively 'thin' vision of citizenship obligations was Maha who argued that their essence is *"Not to break the law. Respect the environment and people's property, Don't commit crime and don't vandalise .... general things like that, that a lot of people don't respect nowadays."*

Moreover, some of my interviewees also mentioned voting as an important duty of a citizen. While in Belgium voting is obligatory and an example of a civil duty, in Britain it should rather be considered a civic one. Razin, who argued that 'voting is crucial to keeps the country running' was one of the informants who considered it an important civic obligation. Other interviewees spoke more generally about a civic duty to be active politically and socially. Amongst them there was a considerable number of women. Rasha, for instance, argued that *"Holding politicians to account is one of the key responsibilities, especially in the situation when people, in general, are less and less interested in politics. "* whereas Yumn asserted that *"The most important duty of a citizen is to participate in different fields including the political field".*

Finally, some of the subjective notions of citizenship obligations of my interviewees bore many features of patriotism understood here after Walker Connor (2007), as loyalty to the state. One may detect, for instance, in the definition of key duties of a citizen by Sajid who said that *"It means that you have to act in the best interest of the country. You cannot have only selfish interests. You have to think what is best for the country, wider community and society"*. It is also clear in the statements of Akram, who said that *"My obligation as a citizen is not to work contrary to the security and safety of my country"*, and Abdel, who argued *'It is our duty to represent this country wherever we go, for its values, for its goodness"*.

As will be explained below, some of the aforementioned key elements of the subjective notions of citizenship obligations of my interviewees are very closely linked with their models of good citizenship. Before I shed light on these models, however, it is worth exploring the young Muslim Londoners' perceptions of the relations between the obligations of citizenship and the demands of faith.

5.5.2 BETWEEN THE OBLIGATIONS OF CITIZENSHIP AND THE DEMANDS OF THE FAITH

As I have argued in the second chapter, a religion in various social contexts interacts with citizenship in different ways. It may either act as a powerful uniting force, that constitutes the basis of a country's social cohesion, or as a dividing force, which significantly deepens country's social divides. The compatibility or incompatibility of the demands of the faith and obligations of citizenship is one of the crucial factors which determines the impact of religion on citizenship. This was also the main rationale behind asking the young Muslim Londoners about their perceptions of these issues.

As in Brussels, the vast majority of my informants thought there were no incompatibilities between the duties imposed on them as citizens by the society and the state and the requirements of their religion. On the contrary, many of them believed that faith enabled them to fulfil their citizenship obligations more completely. Thaqib, for instance argued that *"Religious and civic obligations are not incompatible. They have to go together because as a religious person truth should be more important to you than anything else. And if you can provide that to the civic life or political life that's a lot."* In his view, honesty or truthfulness, which should be the major feature of a character of a religious person, could provide some extra value not only to the social, but also to political life. He also suggested that only religion can breathe a new spirit into these dimensions of public life. Another interviewee, who in the somewhat similar way believed that religion could only strengthen citizenship and that it could do so by supplying it with an extra spiritual dimension and force, was Shabaz. He argued that *"Faith gives meaning to citizenship, because it is a part of my faith to be a citizen and to do the duties of citizenship. The most important obligation is to obey the law and order of the country. There is no law that tells you that you need to help people in danger. There is no law that says that I cannot lie to people, so there is something that my faith keeps in too"*. Yumn was one of my female informants who was strongly convinced that the only relationship that one may observe between the demands of the faith and the obligations of citizenship is that of complementation. She asserted, *"I've never felt myself that there is any contradiction. As I said Islam is not just a theoretical thing. It is about being Muslim wherever you are, and part of that is obeying the law, implanting the principles of justice, cooperation, which are very compatible with the obligations of a citizen. It should in principle only strengthen these obligations."* Another British Muslim woman interviewed for this book who saw the faith as a factor consolidating her citizenship obligations was Rana. According to her, *"Those things* (religious and citizenship obligations – KP) *are incomparable. The answer every time is gonna be your allegiance to Allah, to your faith. But that doesn't mean I have less of allegiance to the place I am in because if that relationship with God makes me understand his creation better, then it should make me a better citizen wherever I live because I should have that respect within me."*

Among the young Muslim Londoners who believed that the demands of the faith are compatible with those of the citizenship, but who did not necessarily argue that they mutually strengthen one another were inter alia Afnan and Razin. The first interviewee stated that, *"I have never been asked to do something that would go against my faith. I can't see why the civic responsibilities would compete with who I am"*. (Afnan) She did not see any areas in which there might have been a conflict between the civic and religious responsibilities. In the view of the second interviewee, there was not even a common platform on which they might have clashed. Razin asserted *"I don't think there is an incompatibility between my obligation as the citizen and the believer. The civic duties that you have are the practical things that you do, while religious ones made up the content of ethics and the way you want to live your life."*

Not all the interviewees shared the opinion of the aforementioned informants. Some believed that the conflicts between the demands of the faith and responsibilities of the citizenship were not completely unthinkable. Among those interviewees who spoke about the prospective incompatibilities between the two types of duties was Maha. She said that *"Generally I do not see many disagreements between what my faith demands from me and what my citizenship asks for, unless someone tells me take my hijab off. In such a case I would fight it."* Sporadic incompatibilities between the requirements of the faith and those of the citizenship, which however can be relatively easily solved, were also seen by Nadira. She argued that *"If, for example, there was a particular law about something that was contradictory to my belief, then I would follow my belief. But, apart from insignificant incompatibilities there would never be anything like this. You may dislike certain things, but no one is going to put a gun to your head and say you must do this. I mean they might be doing things that you are not happy about, (...) but my rights are not infringed upon."*

Furthermore, a few of my interviewees argued that, in some aspects, there might exist serious disagreements between the demands of the faith and the obligations of citizenship. One such 'problematic area', where according to some of my interviewees existed such disagreements, was politics or more precisely some policies of the state. Many of the young British Muslims stressed that they might be required to be loyal to the state, but not to be lenient towards the controversial policies of the state. Shabaz, for instance, claimed that *"As a citizen it is my duty to speak out if there is something that I don't agree with that the government is doing. Being a citizen and being a loyal one it is my duty to speak out, if I feel that something that they are doing is not right."* Another interviewee, Rasha, asserted *"In my personal life I have never seen any contradictions between my religion and citizenship, apart from when we* (British Muslims – KP) *disagree with what the government is doing, but then I have ways of expressing that within the system."* In her opinion, as well as that of Shabaz, the obligations of citizenship also include support for the policies of the state. Both of them, however, stressed that if these policies are not in line with their religious consciousness then they have full rights to speak about it and disapprove of such policies in a peaceful and democratic manner.

Yet another area of potential conflict between the demands of the faith and obligations of citizenship was, according to one of my interviewees, education and more precisely the content of sex education as it is taught in the British non-religious schools. This interviewee said *"From my perspective there is one thing which is problematic. I was teaching science in the secondary school and I felt that the way sex education is thought wasn't doing justice to the diversity that we have. I am not for free mixing and relations before marriage so when you are teaching that, it affected me and the way I dealt with it. I talked with the head of the department about that. I told her: 'look at the ills in the society related with such teaching: teenage pregnancy, single parents, etc.'"* (Rushd) She explained that recently she was able to persuade her superiors that the teaching of sexual education, as it is designed in the school curriculum – in Rushd's perception part of her civic obligations – is against her religious views and the requirements of the faith. She also stated with a contented smile that as a result of these discussions she was able to slightly modify the teaching material so it embraced some of her cultural and religious sensitivities.

Finally one of my interviewees questioned the whole division between the religious and civic duties. According to Marwan such a division is meaningless from the point of view of Islam in the way how he perceived it. He stated *"All our duties come from Islam. We do not compartmentalize different aspects. You are a human being, you don't compartmentalize different aspects of yourself and likewise we don't compartmentalize duties."*

5.5.3 IMAGE OF A GOOD CITIZEN
The last section of this chapter explores the young Muslim Londoners' conceptions of a good citizen. As with the young Muslim Belgians, my British interviewees were first asked about the features of a good/bad citizen and only then a list of 'the virtues of responsible citizenship' developed by William Galston (1991)[390] was presented to them, and they were asked to choose the most important ones and explain their choices.

---

[390] For elaboration of this list see the second chapter.

Having meticulously analysed the social representations of a good citizen of the young Muslim Londoners, I have found that one of the prevailing features of these representations was the emphasis on the care for the widely understood environment in which one is living. At the same time, the environment was conceived by my interviewees not only as the social and political one, but also as the natural environment. This crucial feature of good citizenship was put probably most concisely by Rana who said that, *"a good citizen it is someone who cares about the place in which he or she is living."* This care, according to some of the young Muslim Londoners should be beginning already from themselves and their family houses. One of my interviewees noticed, for instance, that *"Looking after yourself is a very important part of being a good citizen. I don't think citizenship is waving the flag or singing the national anthem. Part of it is also to look after yourself and to rise a good family, Family is very important part of being a citizen, because families create communities and communities make the country. And families are better for children than single parents. The children that you bring up today and teach ethical values will ultimately go and be the citizens of tomorrow. If you set an example of getting drunk and sleeping around I think the next generation will be worse."* (Fadi)

From the smallest social units, the focus of 'caring citizens' should, according to my informants, expand to the larger social groups, communities and the whole society. Many of the young Muslim Londoners argued that a good citizen has to primarily care about his or her neighbours and their localities. One of them, Kadir, claimed that a good citizen *"It is someone who is taking into account his neighbour. Somebody who wants the same for his neighbour as he has. Someone who gives some of his money to charity. Someone who says good words to its neighbours."* He also added that *"It is important that Muslims start to engage locally, because we have our problems in the UK and we are probably best suited to deal with them. It does not mean ignoring the advice of others, but that we need to focus here and not somewhere else. Once we start locally then we can move to national or even global level."* The emphasis on helping neighbours and focusing on the localities were also found in numerous interviewees with the young Muslim women. Afnan, for instance, stated that *"Good citizenship is about being good to others and about improving the society and environment around you in the best possible* way, whatever that might be: being involved in recycling, helping your neighbour etc. From small things to the big things." Another, female interviewee Nadira argued that "As a citizen you have to be concerned about your environment, from picking up your litter and things like that, to dealing with people. You should care about this land just as much as you care about your own house."

Furthermore, numerous interviewees, whose social representations of a good citizen stressed the importance of caring about the wider environment, also mentioned law-abidingness an important feature of the 'caring citizen'. This feature of a good citizenship which also transpired to be the most commonly chosen virtue from Galston's list of 'the virtuous of responsible citizenship' (in Brussels, as well as, in London), was often mentioned only briefly as it was an element taken for granted. One of the interviewees who referred to it in such a way was Rasha, who said that "a good citizen is not only someone who is law-abiding, but someone who cares about the whole society." and then elaborated on examples of such behaviour.

Similarly to the young Belgian Muslims, my interviewees in London also pointed out many proactive features that should characterize a good citizen. In their view, such a citizen has to above all constructively engage in the society.

This constructive approach that should be emblematic of good citizenship one may notice, for example, in the definition of Mansur who said that "A good citizen it is someone who sees the problems within the society and goes out there to help to resolve them. Somebody who is concerned, involved and active." Yet another interviewee who stressed these elements, Abdel, argued that "A good citizen it is somebody who works towards the betterment of the society, works actively in promoting dialog and developing this society and its future generations." In the same spirit, Mumtaz, working as a youth worker, claimed that "If I can help a young person who is vulnerable to become a good citizen, a good person, that is my contribution, because that person could have been very destructive." Some of the major diving forces behind such constructive citizenship should be, according my interviewees, a desire for fairness and justice. One may notice the emphasis on them, for example, in the following definition of Kadir, who argued that "A good citizen it is someone who feels the pain when he sees wrongdoing globally or locally. Someone who thinks that there should be justice and fairness in this world. But at *the same time it is someone who is realistic and knows from where to start. There is no use getting upset and saying that the world is a mess. You have to start somewhere changing it and locality is the best place to do so."*

Amongst the other elements that made up part of the images of a good citizen of the young Muslim Londoners, the most frequently mentioned ones were truthfulness, honesty and perseverance in pursuing its goals.

As it could be expected, the key feature of a bad citizen, according to my British interviewees, was the lack of interest in pursuing common goals or lack of interest in caring for the wider environment that characterized a good citizen. The concentration on achieving personal goals without caring about the wider community and society was for many of my informants the most significant feature of a bad citizen. At the same time they were aware of the fact that individualism, with its emphasis on striving for personal goals, is one of the major principles of the society in which they live. That is why instead of suggesting a thorough reconsideration of this principle, they rather called for striking an appropriate balance between the pursuit of individual and collective goals. One of the interviewees who advanced this strategy was, for instance, Yumn who stated that *"Being a bad citizen means to be individualistic and to think only about your own interests and your own rights (...) One has to also think about its own obligations towards society and towards other people."* On the other hand, interestingly, one of my interviewees claimed that not caring enough about your own health is also a feature of bad citizenship. Fadi pointed out that *"If you don't look after your health, your body then there is an element of bad citizenship in it, because you are relying on the state."*

As I mentioned earlier, from Galston's (1991) twelve 'virtues of responsible citizenship' the one which was most frequently chosen by the Muslim Londoners, both women and men, was the general virtue of law-abidingness. This virtue was even more popular among my British interviewees than among the Belgian ones. Most commonly, the young Muslim Londoners argued that the possession of such virtue amongst citizens is indispensable for the existence and survival of every society. Rasha, for example, stated that *"Law-abidingness is crucial because If you don't have law and order then you are going to have a chaotic society"*. Yet another interviewee said that he chose law-abidingness first of all *"because without law you don't have a society"* (Shabaz). At the

387

same time, many of my informants stressed that one has to be vigilant about the content of the existing laws. Shahd, for example, pointed out that "*If you say law-abidingness then you need to ask what is the law. Are we living in the Orwellian state, where to inform on your neighbour is seen as law-abiding? Good and bad are shifting.*" Yet a different interviewee asserted that "*I am not one of this people who would say 'I am British to the end.' I wouldn't be British till I die, because if Britain tomorrow becomes a Nazi state, I would give up my passport. (...) I could be also the I am not Muslim to the death, because I could tomorrow decide that Hinduism is better for me. I don't think anything is fixed.*" (Fadi)

The next most commonly chosen virtues of responsible citizenship were the general virtue of courage and the social virtue of open-mindedness. While the first virtue was particularly popular amongst the male interviewees, my female informants most commonly mentioned the latter. Those young Muslim Londoners who chose the virtue of courage as the second most important virtue of responsible citizenship pointed out its importance in any process of claims-making. One of them stated in explaining his choice that "*In the democratic system as we have here, if something is wrong you have the right to change it by peaceful means. In order to do so I think you need courage to protest peacefully. When you see that something is wrong, then within a system you have to be brave enough to say 'this is wrong' and 'I don't agree with that'*". (Kadir) Another interviewee in the same manner asserted that "*One needs to have the courage to engage with those people in power and to strive to change policies over the period of time.*" (Afnan). Those informants who chose open-mindedness as the second most important virtue of responsible citizenship argued, on the other hand, this virtue is absolutely necessary in the society so as its members are "*able to listen to each other and are able to understand each other*" (Maha). Yet another interviewee declared that "*I chose open-mindedness, because I think it is very important to be able to accept the difference in the society*". (Shabaz)

The capacity of discerning and respecting the rights of others described by Galston (1991) as one of the key political virtues was the third most commonly chosen virtue of responsible citizenship by my British interviewees. It was equally frequently mentioned as the third most important virtue by both my female and male informants.

One of my female informants argued that this is a crucial virtue *"because you have to be not only responsible for yourself but also those around you."* (Afnan), whereas another stated *"citizens need to possess this virtue because they need to be able to live together and work collectively on the task."* (Rana) Furthermore, Shabaz, one of my male informants who chose this virtue, argued that *"capacity to discern and respect the rights of others is linked with open-mindedness. We live in the world where people have different interests, but we have common values. We share more similarities than differences. Respecting each other differences is absolutely necessary."* His view was also shared by Fadi who stated that *"respect for others is part of law-abidingness and it leads to harmony"*.

Finally, the last but not least virtue of a responsible citizen that was particularly meaningful to my interviewees in London was the virtue of loyalty. Similarly to Brussels, this general virtue was particularly popular among my female informants. Probably most elaborately, the choice of this virtue was explained by Rana who stated that *"I put down loyalty but I don't mean blind loyalty. Loyalty in the sense that you care about something or you are connected to it. But then for me also ultimate loyalty is when you have the courage to question things that you don't think are right things or that are damaging."* As one may notice the notion of loyalty proposed by Rana is quite broad one. A narrower understanding of loyalty was proposed by one of my male interviewees who chose loyalty as key virtue of a responsible citizen. He explained that he mentioned loyalty because *"we need to respect the country that looks after us. I have no respect for people who criticize the UK so much that they are abusing the hospitality. It is our country. I get very angry when people complain about the UK in general and I get very protective. I think this is inbred."* (Kadir)

CONCLUSION

The best way to be close to God is to claim your rights as a citizen.

Tariq Ramadan (2006a)

The outgoing Secretary General of the Muslim Council of Britain, one of the country's organisations which strive to represent British Muslims vis-à-vis the government[391], announced during his valedictory speech on 4 June 2006 that 'the age of the politics of Muslim identity is over', and called for Muslims to engage more actively in non-Muslim civil society (Sacranie 2006). The sociological research on Islam in Europe shows, however, that the age of Muslim identity politics is far from yet over and that some Islamic organizations continue to take the 'Muslim power' approach (Modood 2003), mainly nourished by despair at the victimization of Muslims in different places of the globe, to attract new followers[392]. At the same time, and here the former Secretary General of the MCB has a point, one may observe a growing trend amongst the Muslim organizations to move from a politics of identity, which is preoccupied with difference and otherness, towards a politics of identity that increasingly emphasizes also elements of sameness. An analogous observation is made also by one of the editors of "European Islam: Challenges for Public Policy and Society", Amel Boubekeur, who points out that 'the cultural and religious otherness' is no longer the privileged means of expressing contestation by the political Islam in Europe (2007: 40). In practice it means, inter alia, an increasing co-operation between Muslim organisations and wider civil society in tackling different social issues (drug addiction, homelessness, family violence, etc.). In my opinion this major change in the public mobilization of Islam in Europe, already signalled in the first chapter, is not so much related to the recent pressures on European Muslims to prove their loyalty and attachment to the their societies, but is above all a result of the re-definitions of the notion of citizenship, and of the fact that the largest Muslim

---

[391] For more information about this and other Muslim organisations in Britain claiming to represent 'the country's Muslims' vis-à-vis the government see Pędziwiatr 2007a.

[392] One such organisation is, for instance, Hizb ut-Tahrir. For more information about the organisation see Taj-Farouki 2003, Wiktorowicz 2005, Karagiannis & McCauley 2006.

communities in Europe are constituted today of a majority of people who are born and bred Europeans. As I have shown in the two earlier chapters the vast majority of the members of the emerging new Muslim elite in Brussels and London stressed very strongly their profound attachment to their countries and cities (sometimes even city boroughs). They were also genuinely concerned not only about the fate of their coreligionists, but also other compatriots.

My objective in this concluding chapter is twofold. First of all, I intend to sum up the major findings from the case studies, exploring the various dimensions of the active social citizenship of the young Muslims in the urban/national setting within which they are generally perceived as individuals (Brussels/Belgium) and in the place where they are usually viewed as members of religious, ethnic or other social groups (London/Britain). While doing so I shall highlight the key similarities and differences in the perception and practice of citizenship by the young Muslims in these two localities. Secondly, using data from my fieldwork, I am going to explore one of the major changes in the public mobilisation of Islam in Europe, namely a move from the politics of Muslim identity to the politics of Muslim citizenship.

6.1 ISLAM AND ACTIVE SOCIAL CITIZENSHIP IN BRUSSELS AND LONDON

Before recapitulating the major findings of the study with regards to citizenship and its complex interactions with the religion of my informants, it is important to briefly recall the key features of their religious identities. The research began only with a tentative definition of what it means to be a Muslim and operated the category of 'a Muslim' as one of the research questions, in order not to essentialise the identity, which in the social reality manifests itself in the multitude of forms. This proved to be an appropriate strategy since one of the major features of the religious identities of my informants turned out to be their strong personal character. Both the young Muslims in Belgium and in Britain stressed that, for them, being a Muslim was not (or not only) something which they had inherited from their parents, but a consequence of long personal journeys to the religion of their parents. The subjectivity of the process of building religious identities was emphasised particularly strongly by my Belgian interviewees. Although numerous young Muslim Londoners argued that they had rediscovered Islam either in their colleges or universities, the Belgian informants did it more frequently and in a more elaborative way. It was most commonly the members of the latter group who claimed that they had chosen to believe in Islam and that if they did not feel good with it, they would have converted to a different religion. Clearly for the members of the emerging new Muslim elite in Brussels, as well as in London, Islam proved to be a very effective modality of self-construction in the world of do-it-yourself identities (Beck and Beck-Gernsheim 2002: 3).

As far as the female aspect of the construction of the religious identity is concerned in both cities, the re-embracement of Islam by young Muslim women was usually associated with their decision to start to wear a hijab. Hence, putting on headscarves in the case of most of them seemed to be not the result of the imposition of the will of their family members on them, but rather an outcome of their personal decisions.[393] In both localities the young Muslim women who decided to wear hijab faced some form of social ostracism. However, while in Britain hijabs have been incorporated into school uniforms and other professional uniforms thus meaning that this ostracism tends to fade with the passage of time, in Belgium it seems to be increasing. One of the factors that has been contributing to the latter situation is the institutionalization of this ostracism in the form of internal school bans on wearing the Islamic headscarves.[394]

The second major feature of the religious identities of the interviewed young Belgian and British Muslims was their diversity. As I have shown above, the definitions of the Muslimness of my informants contained various degrees of spiritual, humanist, activist and dogmatic ingredients. In the case of every interviewee these ingredients were mixed in dissimilar ways and in diverse proportions. While some informants put emphasis in their definition of what it means to be a Muslim on spiritual elements, others stressed different components. There were no significant differences between the voices from the two cities in terms of which elements were more strongly emphasised and which were stressed less often. In both localities, the spiritual elements seemed to be stressed particularly strongly, while the dogmatic ones were least popular.

---

[393] At least my interviewees claimed that the changes in the way they dressed resulted from their personal decisions. Clearly these decisions have been influenced by numerous other factors (among which the family pressure and the peer pressure possibly play some role) however explorations of these factors was not the goal of this study.

[394] This factor has been elaborated more thoroughly in chapters four and five.

393

At the same time, the aforementioned diversity of the definitions of Muslimness resulting from the individualization of religious beliefs did not necessarily lead to plurality of interpretations of Islamic dogmas. As my research has shown, in both urban and national settings some of the key religious dogmas remain fairly stable. Thus, in spite of the strong individualist components in the religious experience of young Muslim Brusselers and Londoners, the content of this experience is not individuating. This I have shown, for example, while assessing the attitudes of the young European Muslims to the Islamic prohibition of marrying outside the religious community for Muslim women. My results in this matter tend to support these students of the Muslim populations in Europe who argue that the individualization of religious beliefs does not need to result in questioning of the key religious dogmas (e.g. Göle 2003, Maréchal et al. 2003).

Having recalled the major findings of the research with regard to the religious identities of the young organised Muslims in Brussels and London, it is time to point out the key similarities and differences in their perception and practice of citizenship. As in the empirical chapters I shall first discuss the identity dimension of their citizenship and then the participatory and normative dimensions. First of all it is important to recall that for both analysed groups citizenship was a meaningful concept and particularly so for the young Muslims in Brussels. In both localities my interviewees most commonly defined citizenship in line with the socially constructive model of citizenship. Among those who perceived citizenship in such a way there was a group of 'constructive citizens', and a much smaller group of 'indebted citizens'. The first, larger group consisted of the interviewees who invoked numerous values (religious and non-religious) that were supposed to be the key generator of their active engagement in the society, whereas the members of the latter group pointed out in their definitions of citizenship the necessity of 'giving back' to the state, society, community, etc., for the services and benefits that they have used or enjoyed. The indebted citizens' vision of citizenship generally invoked a more focused duty and hence conjured up the conventional notion of citizenship (institutionally oriented), while the vision of constructive citizens which advocated wider category of civic obligations indicated post-conventional citizenship.

The next most popular models of citizenship which the young Belgian and British Muslims espoused in their social representations varied. While in Brussels, the members of the emerging new Muslim elite often regarded citizenship within the lack-of-recognition model, in London they viewed it rather in terms of the effective identification model. Moreover, the contractual model of citizenship was much more popular amongst young Muslim Londoners than amongst my interviewees from Brussels. If one was to draw a scale of different models of citizenship, on the one end of it, there would be the socially constructive model, as an example of the thick, maximalist citizenship and, on the other end of it, there would be contractual model, as an example of the thin, minimalist citizenship. The effective identification and lack-of-recognition models would be placed in the middle of such a scale.

Figure 6.1 SCALE OF THE DIFFERENT MODELS OF CITIZENSHIP

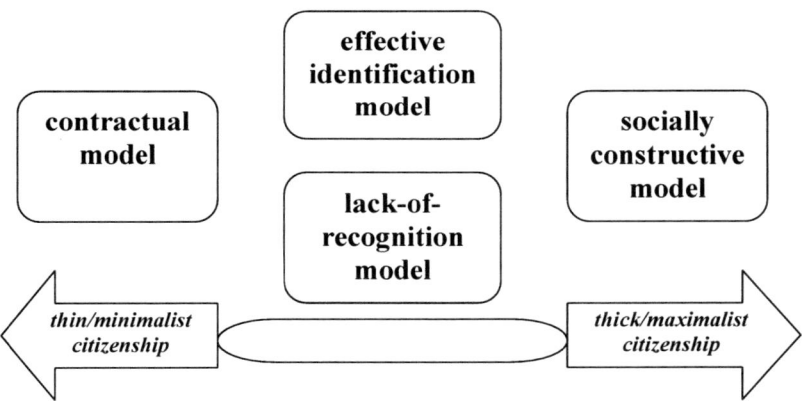

In the empirical chapters I have explored some of the possible causes behind the popularity of different models in the two localities. Here, it is important to recall that, in spite of these differences, most members of the emerging new Muslim elites in the two cities said they were very strongly attached to their national identities. Some of the elements of these identities to which they felt particularly strong attachment were: cultural diversity, various freedoms (especially freedom of religious practice and freedom of speech) and the quality of social services. However, sometimes they were also attached to such mundane elements of Belgianness and Britishness as food or elements of the physical environment. Both my interviewees in Brussels, as well as those in London frequently mentioned that they felt deeply Belgian and British respectively, but not necessarily in a stereotypical way. Their understanding of these two identities went beyond conventional schemes and aimed to redefine the categories of Belgianness and Britishness in such a way, so as they become even more inclusive. Moreover, many of my informants in Belgium demonstrated attachment to the national identity by expressing concerns about the future of the country endangered by the communitarian conflict with the francophones, on the one side, and the Flemings on the other.

Apart from expressions of deep attachment to their national identities most of my informants felt very strongly about their local environments. In London, for example, many of my interviewees said that they felt firstly Muslims and Londoners and only then British. As I have argued in the earlier chapters, this plurality of belongings (that do not have to be mutually exclusive) is possible due to the multidimensionality of social identities. The strong local identity of my British (and to lesser degree Belgian) interviewees was thus inscribed in their confident feelings of belonging to the wider national community. The strong sense of belonging to local communities (or sub-local ones - in the case of some British informants), sustained inter alia by the in-depth knowledge of the given locality, was also one of the key elements in legitimizing their authority in the local contexts. Similarly to national identities, the local identities of my informants were not only marked by the sense of attachment to certain aspects of life in Brussels and London, but also to elements of the visible static urban space such as local mosques, school buildings, parks, etc.

The social identities of my informants also had their visible supranational dimension. While their links with the countries of origin of their parents seemed to be weakening, the supranational religious identity has been gaining popularity. To put it differently, the sense of relationship, empathy and solidarity amongst my interviewees with other co-religionists in other countries of the world was significantly stronger than their sense of relationship with co-ethnic members in the countries of origin of their parents or in other parts of the globe. The creation of the supranational Islamic diasporic identity or the Muslim diaspora (Werbner 2002) was particularly advanced amongst my British informants. It was amongst the young Muslim Londoners that the notion of ummah as a geo-political reality or as Dar al-Islam was particularly popular. They were much more likely to perceive ummah as a form of religious and political authority and not only as a community united by common beliefs, ethics and morality.[395] The latter, theological and ethical understanding of ummah prevailed amongst most of my Belgian interviewees. The young Muslim interviewed in the Belgian capital, frequently described as the heart of Europe, were also more likely than Muslim Londoners to think about themselves as Europeans. In both groups, though, this form of supranational identity had very few supporters.

Moving the comparison of the lived citizenship of the young Muslims in London and that of the young Muslims in Brussels from the dimension of identity to the one of participation, it is necessary to stress that in both localities one of the most important stimuli for active involvement in the social life of their ethnic/religious communities and in the public sphere of wider society was the rediscovery of the religion of their parents. With the rediscovery of Islam, usually taking place in middle and late adolescence, progressing through the processes of positivisation and the intellectualisation of the religion of their parents, my interviewees not only seemed to gain a new energy for activism within their ethnic and religious communities, but also more firmly ascertained their position within the Belgian and British societies. Thus, by subjecting themselves to Islam they have not only become much more assertive religious subjects, but also societal subjects. In other words, subjecting themselves to the religious authority did not deprive them of their agency, but on the contrary, stimulated it positively. Islam, in their case, did not constitute a barrier for interactions with non-Muslim Belgians and Britons, but the opposite of it: it encouraged and facilitated such interactions. The fact of adhering to religion commonly associated by non-Muslim Europeans after September 11th 2001, March 11th 2004 and July 7th 2005 terrorist attacks with violence and bloodshed appeared as stimulating and mobilizing factor for my informants' agency. Their practice of Islam enabled them to generate both bonding and bridging social capital. As a result of this

---

[395] For elaboration of the three major dimensions of the concept of ummah: theological, ethical and geopolitical see Babès (1997: 166-170).

practice, their web of relationships within the ethnic and religious communities had significantly enlarged in a manner similar to their web of relationships outside of these communities.

While the majority of my informants claimed that their social activism was strongly influenced by their religious rediscovery, some of them were socialized from the very early age to become community activists and (in some cases) eventually community leaders. I encountered many young Muslims who received a substantial pre-voluntary preparation within the family environment in London. In the case of some of them this pre-voluntary preparation was so advanced that they almost could not escape from getting involved in voluntary activities and they became involved in the Muslim and wider civil society almost 'by default'. This phenomenon of 'activists by default' has also been facilitated in London by the relatively dense network of Muslim organisations and associations which have been recruiting members from the very early age.[396] In Brussels these institutional structures are much scarcer and thus some of the 'activists by default' may easily slip through the Muslim institutional net and become active in the wider civil society.[397]

In both cities analysed, as it could be expected, the members of the emerging new Muslim elite possessed substantial resources that allowed them to choose between different courses of action and to move beyond the formal to more substantive forms of citizenship. My interviewees' participatory form of citizenship was enabled inter alia by the fact that they had at their disposal such key resources as time, financial means and civic skills. The degree of possession of the first two resources varied significantly amongst the interviewees. Some of them had substantial financial resources but not much time for voluntary activism, whereas others had surplus of unstructured time and scarce financial means. In this matter their resources appeared to be complementary to one another. As far as the third resource is concerned, its possession was spread amongst the British and Belgian interviewees more evenly. The members of the emerging new Muslim elite in Brussels and London were characterized, in particular, by having

---

[396] For more information about some of the key organisations and associations within this institutional structure see chapter III. For an insider's perspective on early phases of mobilization and recruitment see Husain 2007.
[397] For instance, many young Belgian Moroccans are active in the youth branch of the Confederation of Christian Trade Unions - CSC.

substantial amounts of embodied and institutional cultural capital, and hence they constituted above all an educated elite.

They employed these resources to achieve a wide range of communal and societal goals from the improvement of the situation of the Muslim communities in the country, and in particular educational results of Muslim youth, to the improvement of the society as a whole. They have also made use of them in order to achieve such individual objectives as intellectual and religious self-development, the acquisition of the new social capital and gaining satisfaction, to mention only the major ones. At the organizational level, the aforementioned resources of my interviewees were used, above all, to further Muslim demands for equal citizenship rights and for more room for the Muslim heritage and values in the British and Belgian public spheres. The exact content of these demands was analysed in the separate sections of the empirical chapters dealing with the normative dimension of the lived citizenship of the young Muslim Londoners and Brusselers, thus here, I intend only to recall the major similarities and differences between the calls for these rights in the two analysed capitals.

One of the key features of the calls for less exclusionary citizenship rights was that they implied not only the right to be different, but even more so (especially in Brussels) the right to be the same. The young Muslims in both cities demanded inter alia more equal treatment in access to quality education and employment.[398] They also contested the supposed equality of rights in criminal justice and the 'equal' treatment of their religion within the country's framework of church and state relations. In Brussels, where the problems faced by members of the Muslim communities in different spheres of life were more numerous than those faced by Muslims in London, the calls for the right to the sameness were voiced particularly frequently. Although many of the Muslim Brusselers argued that their only demand is the application of the *acquis* of the other faith groups to their co-religionists, in some cases (e.g. the right to state-founded faith schools) they did not even ask for parity of rights. The same phenomenon was present, though less often observed, in London. The British interviewees were, in general, more successful in exercising their right to sameness and their right to difference within the country's notion of citizenship. The anti-racism policies that have been developed for more than three

---

[398] In addition in Brussels they spoke also about the unequal treatment in access to housing and socializing.

decades and the fact that most of my interviewees' parents or grandparents came to the country from the territories of the former British colonies played a very important role in it.

Another common feature of the understanding of citizenship rights by my interviewees in Brussels and London was that these rights are rarely handed down by the state, and more often one needs to fight for them. This was particularlly the understanding of the citizenship rights of the young Muslims from Brussels. They were aware of the fact that the only way for them to become recognized as full citizens of the country was to put some pressure on the authorities and the societies that can provide them with such recognition. Moreover, many of my British interviewees argued that, if someone did not fight for his or her rights but was granted them automatically, then such a person was likely not to know her or his rights and the way how they should be exercised.

Yet another common feature of the understanding of citizenship rights by the young Belgian and British Muslims was the emphasis on the fact that these rights should not be thought in abstraction, but always in relation to civic duties. In their view, speaking about the civic rights without mentioning 'the other side of the coin' (Razin, London) was one-sided and not very fruitful. While speaking about civic rights, the members of the emerging new Muslim elite in London, for instance, very often brought up the issue of the fight with religious extremism and framed it as one of their key civic duties. Clearly the events of July 7th 2005 had a significant impact on this.

In general, the concept of citizenship obligations, like that of citizenship rights, was highly meaningful to the interviewed young Belgian and British Muslims. This dimension of citizenship was particularly strongly emphasised by my Belgian interviewees, whose subjective notions of citizenship obligations were somewhat more elaborate than those of my British informants. One of the major obligations of citizenship according to the young Muslims in Brussels was the duty to fight with injustice and all forms of discrimination. This understanding of the key obligation of a citizen was closely related to the lived citizenship of many of my Belgian interviewees. In Britain, on the other hand, this aspect of the obligations of a citizen was relatively rarely mentioned and instead my British interviewees stressed the importance of a duty to strive to live in harmony with other citizens around them. In both localities though, in line with the socially constructive model of citizenship equally popular in the two countries, my interviewees argued that an important obligation of a citizen is to contribute to the society in whatever form one is able to do so, and to be 'part of the solution', rather than 'part of the problem'.

Moreover, in the British as well as the Belgian capital, the vast majority of the members of the emerging new Muslim elites did not see any major incompatibilities between the obligations of citizenship and the demands of their faith. On the contrary, numerous young Muslims in Brussels and London argued that their religious convictions pushed them to fulfil their citizenship obligations with greater attention. Many of them saw religious and civic demands as complementary and claimed that religion strengthened their citizenship. Some of them aptly pointed out that civic obligations could not be enforced by the state thus they needed other underpinnings. Religious ethics often provides such support and makes these obligations more meaningful. One of the areas, in which some of my Belgian interviewees saw incompatibility (or prospective incompatibility) between the civic and religious obligations, was the educational sector. According to these interviewees the obligation to pursue an education should not be conditioned by the removal of hijab at school. In their opinion the increasingly popular prohibition to wear Islamic headscarf at school, viewed by some as a religious obligation, has created such an incompatibility. Also some of the British interviewees saw the prospective clash between the demands of their religion and obligations of citizenship in the area of education, but not in the formal conditions of following it, but rather in its content (particularly sex education). More often though they pointed out that British foreign policy could be a prospective source of such incompatibilities. They asserted that their support for the controversial policies of the state (especially military operations in Iraq and Afghanistan) should not be taken for granted.

Both my interviewees in Brussels and London held fairly sophisticated conceptions of a good citizen. Some of the major features of such a citizen, according to my Belgian subjects, were respectfulness to others, as well as, to the legal framework of the country, constructive involvement in the society and honesty. My British interviewees, on the other hand, pointed out such features of a good citizen as caring for the widely understood environment, law-abidingness and constructive engagement in the society. Interestingly, in both localities a bad citizen in the eyes of my interviewees was above all someone who lacks interest in pursuing common societal goals and who stays indifferent and passive, and not someone who does not obey the law.

Figure 6.2 THE MOST IMPORTANT VIRTUES OF RESPONSIBLE CITIZENSHIP ACCORDING TO YOUNG MUSLIMS IN BRUSSELS AND LONDON.

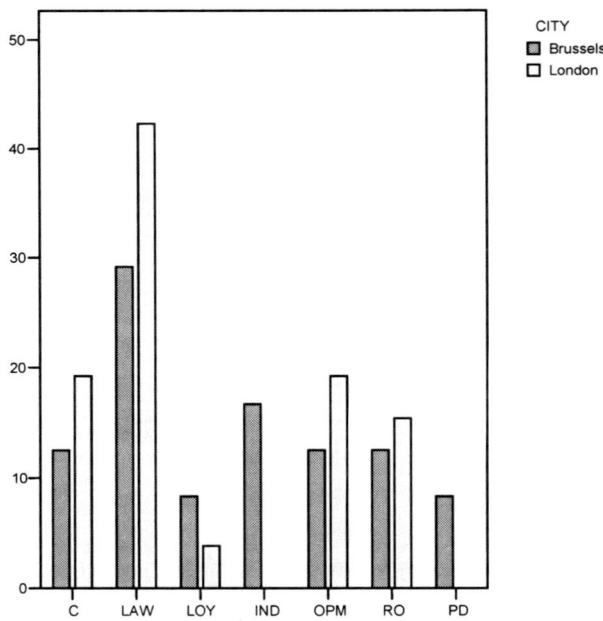

The legalistic perspective, however, was taking hold when my interviewees were asked to choose from the list of different 'virtues of responsible citizenship' (Galston 1991). Both in Brussels and London the most commonly chosen virtue of 'responsible citizenship' was the general virtue of law-abidingness. This virtue was particularly strongly stressed by my British interviewees. The next most popular virtues of responsible citizenship amongst the young Belgian and British Muslims varied. While in Brussels my interviewees chose the social virtue of independence, the British interviewees opted rather for the general virtues of courage and the social virtue of open-mindedness. The third most commonly chosen virtue of responsible citizenship by my informants in London was the capacity to discern and respect the rights of others. Apart from this virtue, my informants in Belgium chose as the third most important virtue, courage and open-mindedness. Finally, while the young Muslims in London highlighted loyalty as the fourth most important virtue of responsible citizenship, my interviewees in Brussels added to loyalty a willingness to engage in public discourse (see the bar chart above).[399]

6.2 MUSLIM CIVICNESS AND UNCOMPROMISING MUSLIMNESS

Having reviewed the major similarities and differences between the perception and practice of citizenship by the young Muslims in Brussels and London, it is time to elaborate on the background of one the most significant shifts in the mobilisation of Islam in Europe clearly visible in the research material, that is a move from politics of Muslim identity to the politics of Muslim citizenship. As I have argued in the first chapter, this move has been closely linked with the development of a civic consciousness among certain segments of the Muslim populations in Europe (Bousetta and Jacobs 2006: 32-33) and a construction of a new type of identity – 'Muslim civicness'. This is a form of identity, which prevailed amongst my interviewees both in Brussels and in London. It has been emerging from the shadows of 'emancipatory politics', (Giddens 1991: 9) mixing elements of Muslimness with those of active citizenship. It is, in fact, an outcome of the specific configuration of the relations between inclusive Muslimness and citizenship. Much less popular, although also noticeable amongst a few of my interviewees, was an identity which places itself at the other end of the continuum from citizenship to Muslimness, namely 'uncompromising Muslimness'. In this form of identity Muslimness

---

[399] C in the bar chart in figure 7.2 stands for 'courage', LAW for 'law-abidingness', LOY for 'loyalty', IND for 'independence', OPM for 'open-mindedness', RO for 'the capacity to discern and respect the rights of others, and PD for 'willingness to engage in public discourse'.

is largely exclusive since, while the later type of identity bears many features of resistance identity, described by Castells (2004: 9) as a *"form of collective resistance against the dominant identity"*, the former has numerous features of 'project identity' defined by the author of 'The Power of Identity' as *"a situation when social actors, on the basis of whatever cultural materials are available to them, build a new identity that redefines their position in their society, by so doing seek the transformation of overall social structure"* (ibid). The remaining part of this section will be devoted to an exploration of the major features of these identities and their manifestations in the different dimensions of citizenship of my interviewees.

The first and foremost feature of Muslim civicness, an identity that characterized the vast majority of young Muslim Brusselers and Londoners interviewed for this book, is that it supports national narratives fairly strongly. Its support for national projects is not only limited to the emphasis of the importance of identification with other compatriots, but also stresses the significance of the emotional attachment to the country in which one is living, its territory and various elements of the national culture, including national ceremonies and rituals. Thus it quite firmly upholds national identities and, in manner akin to traditional accounts on citizenship (e.g. Marshall 1950 or Brubaker 1988), it links citizenship with a nation.

This feature of Muslim civicness is probably most clearly portrayed in the statement of one of my interviewees from Brussels who said *"I am a practising Muslim and a practising Belgian."* (Khalil). For this interviewee, as well as many others, the religious and the national identity did not contradict each other but, on the contrary, they were mutually reinforcing. That is also why many of them liked to say, as Kadir did, that *"I am very comfortable being British and Muslim."* In their view, the two identities largely overlapped and consequently some of them strongly opposed more rigid definitions of secularism which excluded religion from citizenship. One of them was Hadijah who stated that *'you cannot cut someone in the middle and say that this part belongs to the citizenship and that to religion. Muslimness and citizenship are inseparable entities'*. In general, they proposed viewing the two 'entities' as functioning in harmony with each other and opted for a pluralistic definition of identity, which assumed the possibility of possessing multiple and hybrid identities. If they did distinguish between the two identities, like Rashid who pointed out that *'spiritual identity is vertical and the civic one is horizontal,'* they did so only to stress that they closely and positively interact with each other. [400]

Moreover, the support for the national narratives that characterised most of my interviewees in Brussels and London also meant their strong emotional attachment to their countries and localities. The significant support for the effective identification model of citizenship amongst my British and Belgian interviewees was one example of such an attachment. Also the numerous statements of my Belgian and British interviewees explored in chapters five and six testified to their strong identification with their countries, cities and sometimes even city boroughs. Here, however, it is important to note that when my interviewees stressed that they should be viewed as part and parcel of British and Belgian societies, they subscribed not to the unitary concept of a nation[401], which does not leave a room for particular identities, but to the pluralistic definition of this term that takes into account the existence of such identities within a larger 'imagined community' (Anderson 1991). The latter understanding of a nation one may notice, for instance, in the statement of Yusuf who said that *"I am a Belgian citizen because I was born in Belgium and I live here, this is my country, this is my culture, my society. But my society is plural and it has to accept me with my spiritual belonging, with Islam."* Also my British interviewees stressed that they felt part of the national community as long as this community was ready to accept and not undermine their difference. The porous nature of the boundaries of the Belgian and British national identities explored in chapter four clearly helped my interviewees to claim 'being the same' and yet 'being different'.

Furthermore, by supporting national narratives, the members of the emerging Muslim elites did not cease to identify with their co-religionists in other parts of the world. As I have shown above the sense of empathy and solidarity with Muslims living in other parts of the world was particularly strong amongst British Muslims. The majority of my interviewees perceived the worldwide ummah as the community united by the common beliefs, ethics and morality, rather than as a form of political and religious authority. For them identification with other believers of Islam in the world did not

---

[400] Similar argumentation and distinctions may be found in Ramadan's 'To Be a European Muslim' (1999: 153-198) Below I shall elaborate in more detail on some major intellectual sources of Muslim civicness.
[401] For more information about the concept of a nation conceived in this way see Brubaker 1988.

exclude the identification with other compatriots. In their opinion these two identifications were not mutually exclusive and it was perfectly possible to be attached to the religious and national community at the same time.

A minority of my interviewees constructing an identity bearing many features of a resistance identity, or uncompromising Muslimness, took a radically different stand in this matter. For these interviewees the ummah was not an imagined community but a 'semi-real' community and a geo-political reality, with which identification could be only exclusive. In their opinion one could not be at the same time attached to the national entity and to the worldwide ummah or to its compatriots and to 'brothers and sisters in faith', and one had to make a choice between the national and religious allegiance. Thus, while the Muslim civicness promoted inclusive Muslimness, the members of the Muslim communities developing uncompromising Muslimness were characterised by exclusive religious views. One of the interviewees promoting these views argued, for example, that "*Our primary allegiance is to our ummah, and secondly to the Muslim community here and to the problems this community faces (...).*" (Jamil) The identity of Jamil and other interviewees who shared his ideas was exterritorial in the sense that it did not have any clear geographical boundaries. Their situation could be described as 'being in, but not of the country', in contrast with the interviewees engaged in the creation of Muslim civicness who were 'in and of the country'.

Another significant feature of uncompromising Muslimness is that it does not support national narratives and largely disregards national projects. If it takes national identities into account, it does so only in order to stress their secondary role, in comparison with the overarching religious identity or Muslimness. The subordination of the national identity to the religious may be observed, for instance, in the following statement of Raihan who said that "*I am a British Muslim, but only because the sentence 'British Muslim' is grammatically more correct than 'Muslim British'.*" Some of the believers more actively involved in the development of this identity did not even like to mention that they hold national passports. The interviewees contributing to the construction of uncompromising Muslimness also often lacked emotional attachment to the country in which they were living and various elements of the national culture. One of them Lana argued, for instance, that "*I am much more proud of being a Muslim than of being a Belgian, because for me being Belgian it is just a nationality (...) it is just a simplistic attachment, it is the conditions in which I live here. I could also live somewhere else.*" For her, similarly to some interviewees in Britain, national belonging was artificial and not worthy of strong emotional feelings. Such feelings were supposed to be reserved, in her opinion, for only supranational religious belonging. Paraphrasing the expression of another young Belgian Muslim (Khalil) one could say about the Belgian/British Muslims who hold similar views to Lana that they are 'practising Muslims', but not necessarily 'practising Belgians/Britons'.

At the level of citizenship participation, people, who would not mind calling themselves practising Muslims and practising Belgians/Britons, were characterized above all by social activism, which was not limited to their own religious group, but which transgressed Muslim symbolic boundaries and aimed at all the members of society. The empirical chapters portrayed some of the projects undertaken by the members of the emerging new Muslim elites in Brussels and London, which clearly went beyond the traditional *dawah* and engaged creatively with wider society. Raising money for hostels for the homeless in London, joining the campaign for the 'living wage' and feeding Brussels' homeless are only some of the projects analysed above that portray how Muslim civicness manifests itself in practical terms. The young Muslims involved in these kind of projects were also happy volunteering for non-Muslims NGOs such as, for instance, Amnesty International, Greenpeace or Citizens Organising Foundation. For many of them it was not important whether it was 'an Islamic cause', but above all they wanted to be sure that it was 'a just cause'. They were willing to lobby not only for Muslim causes, but also for non-Muslim ones. This impartiality was, for example, stressed by Murad who said "*... if a Jew is attacked, Muslims have to fight with the injustice done to him as if he was a Muslim (...).*" The interviewees willing to engage in the fight for non-Muslim causes were also more likely than others to talk about the non-Muslim issues that should be fought for. If they spoke about injustice in the world they did not concentrate only on Muslims in such places as, for instance, Palestine, Chechnya or Uzbekistan, but saw the problem of injustice much more globally and not limited only to their co-religionists.

On the other hand, the young Muslims whose major identification was with the ummah were reluctant to get involved with wider civil society. Their social activism was generally confined to the frontiers of the Muslim community in the country and abroad. The people involved in the construction of the uncompromising Muslimness, in line with their disregard for national identities, also disapproved of participation in mainstream politics, viewing it as an act of giving recognition to national projects. On the whole, they concentrated on lobbying for Muslim causes without paying attention to non-Muslim issues. This type of lobbying, mainly nourished by despair at the victimisation and humiliation of Muslims in places such as Palestine, Kashmir and Chechnya, has been termed by Tariq Modood a 'Muslim power' approach (2003: 109). As it is possible to guess, the social capital which they have gained as a result of such lobbying is mainly bonding one (Putnam 2000: 22). It reinforces their exclusive interactions with other brothers and sisters in faith and the homogeneity of the group to which they belong.

As far as the content of the demands of Muslims involved in the creation of uncompromising Muslimness is concerned, its major feature was an emphasis on the right to difference. The Muslim believers, who constructed such a resistance identity wanted above all to be seen as different and used every opportunity in order to stress their 'otherness'. They did so, for example, by assertively calling for the rights gained by other religious groups in the course of history to be applied to them also. While the young Muslims in Brussels and London involved in the creation of the opposite identity, namely Muslim civicness, were ready to resign from some elements of the *acquis* of other religious groups (e.g. right to the state-funded religious schools), they were not willing to do so. It is also not uncommon that the believers who developed an uncompromising Muslimness called for exceptional group rights.

On the other hand, the Muslim civicness at the level of citizenship rights manifests itself above all in the strong emphasis on the right to sameness. As I have shown in the empirical chapters, the vast majority of the members of the emerging new Muslim elites stressed that they would like to participate more fully in sameness and to be included in the more flexible and open conception of 'us'. While maintaining their religious identity, they wished to be recognised as citizens equal to others. They wanted their presence in the midst of the Belgian and British society to be banalised, or 'taken for granted'. They believed that the banalisation of their religious otherness might provide them with enough room to manifest their religiosity more openly and at the same time be active citizens. If they called for the right to difference, they framed such requests very carefully so as not to set themselves aside from the wider society. By and large, however, their requests had the character of the acculturative demands rather than dissociative ones.

One of the major features of Muslim civicness at the level of citizenship obligations is that it puts emphasis on the importance of caring for all members of society regardless of their religious allegiance, or on having obligations vis-à-vis all the citizens without distinction of creed. In other words, it stresses that in everyday activities one should not only care about his or her co-religionists, family or kin, but also about other members of the society. Numerous young Muslims interviewed in the course of the research developed their Muslim civicness by, for instance, pointing out that they had obligations not only towards members of their own religious community, but also towards other members of society, and by asserting that the latter obligations were as equally important as the former. Nabihah in Brussels, for example, argued that "(…) *Our work should profit not only Muslims but also others.*", whereas Samar from London said that "*The obligation of a citizen is to contribute to the society: to do something meaningful. Not only make a difference to my life, but to make a difference to lives of others.*"

The opinion of Thaqib from London that "*Being a good Muslims and a good citizen is synonymous*" highlights yet another significant feature of Muslim civicness, namely that this identity perceives the demands of the faith and those of citizenship as highly compatible. Most of my interviewees in Brussels and London believed that if these demands were at times not compatible, then such sporadic incompatibilities were easily solved.. Moreover, many of them also argued that their religious convictions pushed them to fulfil citizenship obligations with greater attention and that religion made citizenship obligations more meaningful to them. The gist of this idea was captured by Khalil who spoke of Islam as "*an engine of citizenship*". In his view, which was widely shared by my interviewees in Brussels, as well as in London, it was religion which gave a deep meaning to such rudimentary civil/civic duty as, for instance, casting a ballot. It also underpinned numerous more abstract civic obligations such as, for example, honesty, helpfulness, truthfulness, love of justice, industriousness, etc., which unlike the civil obligations cannot be enforced by the law.

On the other hand, the uncompromising Muslimness position views the obligation of citizenship and those of the faith as highly incompatible. It also perceives prospective clashes between the two as not easily solvable. Some of the adherents of this type of identity do not even want to recognize that there might be citizenship obligations which are different from the demands of the faith, attributing all obligations to Islam. One of them was Marwan who asserted *"All our duties come from Islam."* If the adherents of the uncompromising Muslimness distinguish between the two types of obligations, then they usually stress that the religious duties take a lead. In line with this idea, Muslims also involved in construction of the uncompromising Muslimness prioritize the obligations towards the Islamic ummah. In other words, the obligations towards the brothers and sisters in faith dominate over the obligations towards non-Muslims.

To sum up, the major features of the Muslim civicness, which was the prevailing identity amongst the vast majority of the interviewed members of the emerging Muslim elites in Brussels and London, were: support for national projects, activism beyond Muslim symbolic boundaries, emphasis on the right to sameness and stress on the obligations vis-à-vis all the citizens regardless of their religious adherence. The views about citizenship and religion espoused with this project identity may, in my opinion, constitute a firm basis for building a successful Muslim civil society.

On the other hand, the key features of the uncompromising Muslimness that characterised only a tiny minority of the interviewed members of the new Muslim elites in Belgium and Britain were: dismissal of national projects, activism largely within Muslim symbolic boundaries, emphasis on the right to difference and prioritisation of the obligations towards Muslim ummah. (See the table below) The views on citizenship and religion associated with this identity constitute in my opinion a rather weak basis for a successful Muslim civil society.

Table 6.1 KEY FEATURES OF THE MUSLIM CIVICNESS AND UNCOMPROMISING
MUSLIMNESS

anifestations in fferent dimensions of tizenship	MUSLIM CIVICNESS	UNCOMPOROMISING MUSLIMNESS
tizenship identity epth of citizenship)	- Support for national projects	- Dismissal of national projects
	(e.g. stressing importance of identification with other compatriots and elements of the national culture and heritage)	(e.g. stressing importance of identification with 'brothers and sisters in faith' or Muslim ummah)
tizenship participation xtent of citizenship)	- Activism beyond the Muslim symbolic boundaries	- Activism largely within Muslim symbolic boundaries
	(e.g. willingness to engage for non-Muslim causes)	(e.g. unwillingness to engage for non-Muslim causes)
tizenship rights ontent of citizenship)	- Emphasis on the right to the sameness	- Emphasis on the right to the difference
	(e.g. readiness to resign from the right to parity, acculturative demands)	(e.g. unwillingness to resign from the right to parity, dissociative demands)
tizenship obligations ontent of citizenship)	- Emphasis on the obligations vis-à-vis all the citizens without distinction of creed	- Prioritisation of the obligations towards Muslim ummah
	(high degree of compatibility between the obligations of citizenship and demands of the faith)	(low degree of compatibility between the obligations of citizenship and demands of the faith)

411

6.3 MUSLIM CIVICNESS AS A PROJECT IDENTITY

Having pointed out the most significant features of Muslim civicness and contrasting it with uncompromising Muslimness, it is time to shed more light on the former identity that is being developed by numerous young Muslims in Europe and which was particularly popular amongst my interviewees. The popularisation of this identity has been one of the major factors contributing to the significant shift in the mobilisation of Islam in Europe from the politics of Muslim identity to the politics of Muslim citizenship. As I have argued earlier, the Muslim civicness bears many traits of the 'project identity' understood here after Castells as 'a situation when social actors, on the basis of whatever cultural materials are available to them, build a new identity that redefines their position in their society, by so doing seek the transformation of overall social structure' (2004: 9). The Muslim civicness redefines the social position of Muslims engaged in its development and transforms social structures mainly by challenging the traditional public-private sphere divide (e.g. the popular understanding of the role of religion in the public life) and by calling for the transformation of the existing power structures between the 'established' and the 'outsiders' (Elias & Scotson 1965).

According to the dominant narrative, the public sphere is not a privileged domain of religion, and especially so, if it is a religion of a relatively newly established minority group.[402] As Talal Asad reminds us, religious practice and belief are highly welcomed (since without the idea of religion the concept of the secular cannot do) but mainly in the private sphere or in the space where they cannot threaten political stability and the liberties of a 'free-thinking' citizen (2003). By asserting the importance of Islam not only in the private sphere but also in the public one, my interviewees clearly transgress the boundaries drawn by modern liberal states. By the very fact of mobilizing politically along religious lines they de-centre a fundamental public-private distinction of a modern liberal state, which sees religion as a matter of personal concern rather than public. At the same time they do not call for the total abolition of this distinction, like some more radical believers, but for its rebalancing. They seek a gradual transformation of the

---

[402] It is not without importance which religious group strives for more room in the public sphere. Some newly set up Christian evangelical communities find it much easier to claim such a space than, for example, Muslim groups. The former ones are, in fact, re-claiming it, while the latter one claiming it the first time in the history of the analysed countries.

existing structures, rather than revolutionary change. By emphasizing the importance of religion not only in the private domain but also outside of it, they also suggest that political secularism is not religiously neutral and, as such, it should not be taken for granted. As numerous feminist scholars have shown (e.g. Benhabib 1992, Fraser 1992, Lister 1997 and Voet 1998) the assumption that difference must be privatized works as a 'gag-rule' to exclude matters of concern to marginalized and subordinated groups (such as, for instance, women) who want erstwhile private gender relations to be the subject of collective deliberation and reform. Thus, what would earlier be called 'private' matters have become the basis of the struggle for equality.

By extension, *toute proportion gardée*, the same might be said of the religious practice of European Muslims. Their political integration in terms of equality inevitably involves challenging the existing boundaries of the public realm. As Tariq Modood aptly notices, such integration essentially flows from the process of discursive engagement, as marginal groups begin to confidently assert themselves in the public space, and others begin to argue with and reach some agreement with them (2004: 247). The focus of this process of discursive engagement is on participation in a discursive public space, while equality becomes defined as inclusion within a political community, not in terms of accepting the rules of the existing polity and its hallowed public-private boundaries, but rather in terms of some redefinition of the existing rules and boundaries. In this respect the advances achieved, for instance, by feminism (with its slogan 'the personal is the political') have acted as benchmarks for subsequent groups who have introduced new categories of identity into politics such as Muslims.

The meaningful engagement of young European Muslims in a discursive public space has above all been possible due to their possession of substantial cultural capital. The embodied and institutional cultural capital has enabled members of the emerging new Muslim elites in Brussels and London to choose between different courses of action and to move beyond the formal to participatory forms of citizenship. In other words, substantial cultural resources have allowed them to enact their citizenship status or to take up a role of citizen and engage with it creatively from within their religious tradition. These resources have allowed them to become subjects without distancing themselves from one of the major sources of authenticity that they have at their disposal, namely their religion. Their sense of agency, or the belief that they can act, has been visibly strengthened by the possessed cultural capital. Acting as a citizen, especially collectively, as Ruth Lister rightly notices, in turn fosters such sense of agency (1997: 38).

The form which they could enact, that is legal citizenship, is also of crucial importance. The role of a citizen enabled them to present themselves as equal and, to some extent, similar to others around them and thus, provided them with a significant tool to challenge the 'established', and try to at least minimally shake their domination in the discursive public sphere. As Elias and Scotson (1965) demonstrate in their study of 'Winston Parva' in East Midlands of England, this domination is not easily shakeable since the communal feelings of belonging and ownership, membership of important community roles, integration into informal (and formal) local networks and local knowledge, and many other resources give established groups the upper hand in the 'relations of definition' between themselves and newer groups. All of these power resources also enable the established to make their evaluations stick and, as the practice shows, these evaluations are rarely favourable to those who are 'less established'. This is because established groups tend to generate 'group charisma', or a sense of their own superiority as a group, based on a 'minority of the best' as part of their social and self-identity. Their self-image tends to be based on evaluations rooted in the best aspects of the group whilst ignoring other elements that might contaminate such an image and, as such, it forms an important aspect of the group's internal solidarity and sense of community. This 'rosy' self-image of the established is sustained through the vital mechanisms of communal 'gossip' and everyday conversation. Established groups produce 'praise-gossip'[403] when discussing their own group, but use 'blame-gossip'[404] to describe other groups, which they do not consider as 'one of theirs' or 'established enough' (ibid).

The European Muslims viewed by many 'established' Europeans as outsiders are often targets of stigmatizing labels. Their relative lack of substantial power resources (as a whole group), leaves them vulnerable to the gossip and stigmatization of more powerful

---

[403] 'Praise-gossip' means that the best elements perceived by the established group form the basis for discussion and evaluation whilst negative elements are not openly discussed.

[404] 'Blame-gossip' is exactly the reverse, as outsider groups are discussed and assessed in terms of what are considered to be their worst elements.

414

groups. Over time, some of them come to accept and take on the stigmatized form of identity created for them by the 'established'. They come to see their own group as inferior and see themselves as inferior people, idealizing and imitating the established's behavioural codes, manners and so on in order to raise their valuation of themselves. This, according to Elias and Scotson reduces their power chances even further by reinforcing claims to the superiority of the established. Furthermore, the generational transmission of stereotypes ensures that 'outsiders' are continually reminded of their interior status (ibid).

The aforementioned scenario, however, does not take into account the fact that 'outsiders' with the passage of time also start (faster or slower[405]) to acquire some power resources and are not deemed to accept forever stigmatising labels. This is clear, for instance, when comparing the situation of the black people in America after the Second World War and at present, when Barack Obama resides in the White House. The example of African-Americans who, more than half a century ago, started to actively challenge their negative stereotypes and create their own positive evaluations (e.g. 'black is beautiful')[406] also demonstrates that the outsiders-established relations are not easily erasable and are often part of the long-term process of social change over many generations. Moreover, these long-term processes are subject to a reversal of present trends, rather than being simply linear pathways which once embarked upon become somehow inevitable.

In the analysed cases of Muslims in Belgium and Britain one may also observe a process of a narrowing of the gap between their own and the established's power. At the same time many of the established continue to view their Muslim compatriots born in Europe as outsiders. The members of the emerging new Muslim elites possess some power resources that allow them to at least partially reduce the scale of the 'blame-gossip' generated by the established. Those who are developing Muslim civicness have learnt to reject the stigmatising labels of the established without rejecting the whole

---

[405] This largely depends on the structure of a given society. One may expect that in a society with high social mobility such a process should be relatively fast. The state and to a lesser extent supranational bodies (e.g. European Commission, United Nations) act as important mediators in the relations between the 'established' and the 'outsiders'.
[406] The shifting balance of power between white and black groups in America is clearly explored, with the usage of the established-outsiders framework, by Dunning 2004. For an analysis of the civil rights movements from the social movements' perspective see McAdam et al. 1996 or McAdam 1999.

system created and largely run by them.[407] This seems to be an efficient strategy for redefining their position in societies, which is a key goal of the project identities. Armed with legal citizenship, substantial civic skills and other resources, they are beginning to quite successfully 'break into the bounded Britain and Belgium'.[408] They are beginning to achieve some success not only in contesting the hegemonic constructions of the cultural and religious boundaries of the British and Belgian nations, but also in opposing elements of the 'blame gossip' generated by the established. The first task they accomplish, for instance, by demonstrating their in-depth knowledge of Belgian and British society and profound affection to their respective countries, whereas the second one, by writing to local and national newspapers or appearing in TV and Radio programmes and correcting some of the fairly widespread derogatory images of Muslims and Islam.[409]

In conclusion, however, it must be stressed that the relative success achieved by Muslim groups in shaking the domination of the 'established' in the discursive public sphere and re-balancing the relations between themselves and non-Muslim Belgians and Britons are not definite and irreversible. On the contrary, these achievements can be erased fairly easily and the significant gap between the power chances of the 'outsiders' and the 'established' can be re-created. This was particularly noticeable after the terrorist attacks committed in the name of Allah on 11 September 2001 (USA), 11 March 2004 (Spain) and 7 July 2005 (Britain).[410] The attacks marked the point when one could clearly observe an increase in the 'blame gossip' trying to force as many people of Muslim faith as possible to accept 'group disgrace'. At the same time, after the attacks it was possible to see numerous symptoms of a reversal of the process leading to the more equal balance of power between the established and outsiders. Interestingly, these temporary reversals in the processes of power re-balancing seemed not to discourage members of the Muslim

---

[407] Those who develop uncompromising Muslimness, on the other hand, tend to reject not only the stigmatizing evaluations, but also the whole system within which they are generated.
[408] This expression I have borrowed from Sean McLoughlin (1997) analyzing how representations of belonging of the Muslim in Bradford challenge the hegemonic constructions of the racial, cultural and religious boundaries of Britain.
[409] How widespread such images are in Belgium and Britain may be gleaned from, for example, Allen and Nielsen 2002 or EUMC 2006.
[410] One could add to these list of 'turning points' in the relations between Muslims and non-Muslims in the West the religiously motivated murder of Theo van Gogh on the streets of Amsterdam on 2 November 2004. Although of much smaller scale, this event had a tremendous impact on the collective memory of not only the Dutch, but all Europeans.

communities already involved in the public sphere from even more active involvement. As I have shown above, the members of the emerging new Muslim elites were particularly successful in turning the stigma associated with their religion into a source of empowerment or 'group charisma' rather than 'group disgrace'. It is important to stress that the channel of 'empowerment-through-stigmatisation' analysed in the earlier chapters is only open for those members of the Muslim communities who possess the necessary tools to deal with the stigma resulting, for instance, from the traumatic events. This also proves the phenomenon of the double capacity of cultural traumas observed by numerous scholars (Sztompka 2002, Alexander et al. 2004), which in spite of their immediate negative, painful consequences, show their positive, functional potential as forces of social becoming.[411] On the whole, my interviewees possessed the necessary resources to turn the stigmas, such as those resulting from the aforementioned traumatic events, to their advantage. Those who were engaged in developing Muslim civicness even in the most unfavourable circumstances took pains to stress a strongly held religious belief and used Islamic practice in order to interact more effectively with the rest of society. The late Ottavia Schmidt di Friedberg described such attitudes, which characterised also some of her interviewees, as 'riding the tiger' (2002: 89). In my opinion this metaphor aptly captures not only the risks involved in maintaining such an attitude, but also the difficulty in using one of the major emerging global symbols of contestation of the West (i.e. Islam) to interact with the members of European (Western) societies.

6.4 THE MODERNIZATION OF ISLAM AND THE ISLAMIZATION OF MODERNITY

The project identity developed by the vast majority of the members interviewed of the emerging Muslim elites places itself in the midst of two larger processes setting a wider spectrum of relations between Islam and modernity: the modernization of Islam and

---

[411] According to Sztompka the 'constructiveness' or 'destructiveness' of such an ambivalent social phenomenon as trauma depends on four major factors: the strength of initiating traumatogenic change, the gap between old and new cultural syndrome, the size of the traumatized groups, the scope of individual resources (education, connections, rootedness, financial capital), and the openness of the channels of mobility, which allow individuals to escape the traumatized groups or social positions and liberate themselves from trauma (2004: 194).

Islamization of modernity. While the first process aims to transform Islam so that it becomes relevant to modern social and political life, and thus acquire characteristics considered typical of modernity (Martinelli 2004: 5), the latter rather aims to transform modernity so that it becomes 'Islamically acceptable' or more in line with the 'correct' form of Islamic practices (Asad 1993: 210). The majority of my interviewees, who presented themselves as modern, subjects clearly sympathised more with the former process than with the latter, although some features of the Islamisation of modernity were also detectable in their answers. Before I demonstrate it by means of a few examples it is crucial to first point out the key features of the two processes in question.

One of the key features that characterises both processes is a postulate that the gate of *ijtihad* (independent interpretation, reasoning), which was formally closed in the Sunni tradition after the formation of the major Islamic schools of law in the 9th century, must be reopened. In both processes *ijtihad* is viewed as a duty of each generation of Muslims to give fresh interpretations and applications to the principles of the Qur'an, whereas the lack of such a fresh interpretation, that represents the Islamic tradition of imitation or *taqlid,* is perceived as the main cause for the stagnation of Muslim societies. Here, however, the similarities end because while those who promote the modernization of Islam see *ijtihad* as a method with which Muslims could transform their religion so that it becomes more relevant to modern life, the supporters of the Islamization of modernity advocate rather its usage for the purpose of the re-introduction of traditional Islamic structures and institutions.

Furthermore the supporters of the adaptation of Islamic practices into the social realities of contemporary Europe generally hold positive valuations of different dimensions of modernity. They appreciate not only the negative and positive freedoms guaranteed by liberal democracies (a part of political modernity), but also the vast commercialization of goods and services in a tendentially global market (a part of economic modernity) and relatively open and tolerant culturally diverse societies based on individual autonomy (a part of socio-cultural modernity). By and large, they accept the modern conditions as given and try to adapt Islamic practices to these conditions.

On the other hand, the supporters of the adaptation of modernity to Islam tend to have rather negative valuations of different dimensions of modernity. They perceive modern conditions not as given, but as changeable and want their religion to actively shape these conditions. In their opinion, modernity has to become more Islamic or it requires some 'Islamic lifting'. At times if such a 'correction' is not feasible, then they try to at least translate given modern conditions into Muslim terms so that they appear 'Islamic'. This kind of 'pseudo-Islamization' is supposed to inter alia confirm the relevance of certain Islamic practices in the contemporary conditions.

It is important to recall that both processes, which remain in constant interaction with each other, have a long history. As Michael Watt aptly points out, Islam possesses a long tradition of reform – *islah* (Ar. اصلاح) and revival - *tajdid* (Ar. تجديد), which is as much rooted within its own tradition, as it is a response to Westernization in its various forms (1999: 88). Thus, while Muslim reformism (from the 19ᵗʰ century onwards) emerged as a consequence of the direct encounter with Western modernity, it is important not to forget that Islam has been 'in dialogue' with changing conditions of life for a much longer period and more precisely since the time of the prophet Muhammad. Down through the ages, the ulema, sufi masters and charismatic preachers undertook the renewal of the community in times of weakness and decline, responding to the apparent gap between the Islamic ideal and realities of Muslim life. Also most revivalist movements[412] in the 18ᵗʰ and 19ᵗʰ century were primarily motivated internally[413] (Esposito 1992: 49-50).

The reform and revival influenced by pervasive external factors was undertaken in the Muslim world during the 19ᵗʰ and 20ᵗʰ century. They were the consequence of direct and intensive interactions of Islam with Western modernity which started with arrival of European colonialism to its shores. Thus, the direct encounter of Islam with Western modernity was from the very beginning deeply marked by the challenge of European colonialism and intensified by the threat posed by the wave of Christian

---

[412] By such movements I mean the Mahdi (1848-1845) in Sudan, the Sanusi (1787 – 1859) in Libya, the Wahhabi (1703-1792) in Saudi Arabia, the Fulani (1754-1817) in Nigeria, the Faraidiyyah of Hajji Shariati Allah (1764-1840) in Bengal and the movement of Ahmad Brelwi (1786-1831) in India, to name the most important ones.
[413] In other words they responded to a decline whose root cause was identified as being within the Islamic world. The major ideological elements of their program were belief that Islam was the solution and return to the Qur'an and the Sunnah was the method, and belief that a Muslim community should be governed by shariah and all who resisted is should be considered the enemies of God.

419

missionary activity, which came with the colonizers.[414] This encounter has resulted in a whole range of responses from rejection and confrontation to admiration and imitation, which are explored exhaustively elsewhere (e.g. Donohue and Esposito 1982, Lapidus 1988, Zubaida 1993, Esposito 1998, Burgat 2003). One of these responses, Islamic modernism, was developed originally by Jamal al-Din al-Afghani (1839-1897) and his disciple Muhammad Abduh (1849-1905)[415] and constituted the watershed of the analysed processes of modernization of Islam and Islamisation of modernity. The views on modernity of the aforementioned thinkers in many ways resembled those of the members of the emerging Muslim elites in Europe. Most importantly, just as the approach of Muslims modernists from the 19th and 20th century to different aspects of modernity was highly ambiguous, the attitudes of contemporary young Muslim Britons and Belgians were so too.

On the one hand, most of them embraced the key elements of political, economic and socio-cultural modernity. They, for example, highly appreciated the negative and positive freedoms guaranteed by liberal democracies (a part of political modernity) in which they happened to live. Rashid from Brussels stated that *"I am proud of my country that allows me to express myself... to say things that do not work without being afraid of being tortured, charged or whatever."* Similar opinions were also expressed by many of my male and female interviewees in London. Abdel, for instance, argued that *"You can learn more about Islam here in London than in Muslim countries, because of the political freedoms we have. There are a lot of things that people don't know about. Here you can openly talk about them."*, while another Muslim Londoner said *"I am proud of my country and in particular of its law, which upholds justice and fairness"* (Adel). Due to the aforementioned freedoms, one of my female interviewees in Brussels (Jannah) claimed to live in Belgium *"(...) a better life as a woman, as a Muslim and as a citizen than I would have lived in Morocco".*

They also accepted the vast commercialization of goods and services in a tendentially global market, which is part of economic modernity. As professionals

---

[414] As Esposito notices *"the double threat of colonialism was that of the crown and the cross"* (1992: 52).
[415] Other representatives of this largely intellectual movement that preached the need and acceptability of a selective synthesis of Islam and modern thought were Muhammad Iqbal, Allal al-Fasi, Abd al-Aziz al-Thalabi, Abd al-Hamid ibn Badis and Sayyid Ahmad Khan (See, for instance, Donohue and Esposito 1982, Lapidus 1988 and Esposito 1992).

working in the large international companies, some of them were in fact part of this globalising market. They were also aware of the fact that Muslims would need to adapt to these economic conditions in order to survive as a distinctive religious community. This was probably put most bluntly by Sajid who said *"(...) Muslims need to show greater humility. Intellectually we are backward, economically we are backward. Look where all indicators are. Muslims have to learn so much!"*

Finally, by and large most of the young Muslim Belgians and Britons also agreed with the key precept of socio-cultural modernity, namely that society is based on individual autonomy. This was particularly clear when they spoke about the freedom to choose one's religion.[416] Khasim from Brussels, for instance, argued that *"(...) if someone doesn't recognise himself any more in the Islamic principles and is not flourishing with them, then he can make the choice of leaving Islam and it is only his own problem ... no one can say anything"*. Similar views were also expressed in London where one of my interviewees claimed that *"People have the right to do what they want. They will be accounted for at the end of the day, because this is the whole point of religion (...). "* In the view of Fadi, shared by many other interviewees, people have the right to convert from one religion to another and they cannot be prevented by any ban on conversion. Such an attitude also assumed respect for other religious and cultural identities crucial for the peaceful coexistence of different communities in highly diverse societies. This tolerance for otherness was particularly praised by Sajid who stated that *"Let's face it, British society is much more tolerant than Saudi Arabian, or Pakistani. That is why Muslims are queuing in front of the British embassy in Jeddah ... they want to get to the better world!"* All in all most of my interviewees in Belgium and Britain presented themselves as modern persons.

On the other hand, they strongly questioned the secularist vision of the public sphere freed from religious practices and manifestations, and largely upheld the Islamic principle of limiting the choice of a future husband for Muslim women to only men of the Islamic creed. The Islamic practice limited only to the private sphere did not, in their eyes, adhere to the spirit of Islam and as such was seen as unattractive. After Desmond Tutu, who famously said that *"Our God does not permit us to dwell in a kind of spiritual*

---

[416] This issue is explored in depth in chapter IV and V.

ghetto, cut off from the real life out there... our faith is not something we put on, like our Sunday best, only for Sundays. It is for every day" (Tutu quoted in Richards 2003), my interviewees strongly believed that religion has an important role to play in the public sphere and cannot, indeed should not, be limited only to the private domain.

The agreement with the religious principle which prohibits Muslim women from marrying men of different faiths was another instance elaborated in earlier chapters which clearly set many members of the new Muslim elites against the features of modernity. Thus, Muslim civicness that is being developed by most of them situates itself in the midst of the processes of modernization of Islam and Islamization of modernity. It is a Janus-like creation. In many aspects it advocates the modernization of Muslim religion, whereas, in some, an Islamization of modernity.[417]

On the more general level the project identity mixing elements of Islamic tradition and modernity questions the popular perception of Islam as a religion set against the forces of modernity. This kind of image of Islam that wants to play an active role in the society and politics is proposed, for example, by al-Azmeh. He described Islamism as utopian, ahistorical and protofascist (1993: 93). A similar static, reactive, anti-modern and angry picture of political Islam is drawn by many other scholars (cited in Lubeck 1995: 3). In my opinion, such models of relations between Islam and modernity in which they are set against each other are simplistic and overlook the vast array of interactions that actually take place between them. This book has demonstrated some of them and has shown that Islamic tradition can be modernised and that modernity can be Islamicly traditionalised.

A great deal in today's Islamism is new and modern, while the groups engaged in advancing it are far from being homogenous. Islamism is modern not only because it provides a reasoned discourse about a number of topics relevant to life in highly individualised European societies (social cohesiveness, representative government, gender relations, etc.), but also because it constructively engages with many issues of modern societies. This contemporary Islamism that emphasizes inter alia plurality in place of singular authoritative voice, historicity rather than fixed scriptures, and the future

---

[417] An interesting elaboration on the two processes in the context of Muslim communities/organisations in France may be found in Bouzar 2005: 75-90.

instead of the past, Bayat proposes to call 'post-Islamism' (2005). As a project, post-Islamism, in a manner akin to the project identity of Muslim civicness, strives to marry Islam with individual choice and freedom, with democracy and modernity. Clearly, for the tangible results of these endeavours time is needed to discern their impact.

Future research should not only try to assess the efficiency of the post-Islamist endeavors aimed at deconstructing the traditional Islamist discourses, but also analyze the spread and popularity of post-Islamist ideas. In order to do so it would have to make greater use of the quantitative methods. It should also enlarge the unit of analysis and look into relations between Islam and citizenship in other European cities and countries with substantial Muslim populations. Such an enlargement of the unit of analysis would be, for example, important to answer the question of how far we can generalise about the shift from the politics of Muslim identity to the politics of Muslim citizenship detected in the research. It would also enable to verify some other observations made in this study.

Another way of making further progress in the area would be to look more closely into the formation of different Muslim elites that try to represent their coreligionists in the corridors of power and to assess their relations with the elites within the national majorities and other minority elites. This study has only touched upon these issues since its main interest lay in the explorations of the relations between religion and citizenship. Further analysis of the relations between different Muslim elites and between Muslim and non-Muslim elites could, however, bring many fruits and enable us to better understand the populations in question and the transformations within them.

6.5 WHAT LIES AHEAD?

This book aimed to uncover what it means to be a practising Muslim and a full member of Belgian and British society or what it means to be a Muslim citizen in Belgium and Britain. While answering this question it strived not only to shed light on the different dimensions of citizenship of young European Muslims but also to explore relations between their religious and civic identities. However, there was also a more general question, which lay behind this study, namely 'what does it mean today to belong to society?' As I stated in the second chapter, this was one the major questions which framed the wider philosophical background of the study since, in spite of the

423

reformulations of the meanings of the main components of citizenship, it did not lose its validity. In the context of this research it is of key importance because it highlights the issue of social integration and the building of a cohesive society that are very often discussed in relation to the presence of substantial Muslim communities in Europe.[418] The dominant narrative often puts the blame on a lack of social cohesion in certain areas solely on their most visible inhabitants who happen to be Muslims. However, as Beck and Beck-Gernsheim (2002) remind us, Western European societies are poorly integrated not only as a result of their increasing cultural diversity, but even more so, as result of the processes of individualisation. According to Bauman, individualization spells trouble for citizenship and citizenship-based politics because the concerns and preoccupations of individuals qua individuals fill the public space, claiming to be its only legitimate occupants and elbowing out everything else from public discourse (2002: XIX). He goes even further by calling the individual 'the worst enemy of the citizen' (ibid). What are the possibilities of the reintegration of such highly individualised societies and increasing their social cohesion? There are not many.

One of them is integration through values, which was the driving force of classical sociology from its founding fathers to Parsons. Beck and Beck-Gernsheim call this integration through a 'transcendental consensus' (2002: 17). At the same time they point out that in contemporary multicultural societies this option has been losing its popularity since the diversification of cultural perceptions and connections people have to make for themselves eat away at the very foundations on which value communities can feed and constantly renew themselves (ibid). However, if this channel of re-integration has been losing popularity among wider populations, it seemed to be very popular amongst my interviewees, many of whom stressed the compatibility of Muslim values with those of the societies in which they lived.

Another possibility of the re-integration of western societies advanced in public debates is integration through expanding prosperity. Supporters of this option believe that the enhancement of social cohesion of a highly individualised society is possible through integration on joint material interests. Their assumption, which is highly disputable, is

---

[418] For elaboration of the degrees of cultural, identity, social and structural integration of Muslims in Europe see Pędziwiatr 2005: 197-204. On Muslims and social cohesion see the latest report by Hiranthi Jayaweera and Tufyal Choudhury (2008).

that material interests and institutional dependence (consumption, labour market, the welfare state) are sufficient to create cohesion. As Beck and Beck-Gernsheim aptly notice, the supporters of this option tend to confuse the problem with the solution while making a virtue out of the necessity of disintegrating groups and group allegiances (2002: 18).

The third proposition of integration, through a revival of national consciousness in contrast to the former, found some supporters among my interviewees (especially in Brussels). As I have argued in the fourth chapter, the strong emphasis on the national identity made by some of my informants in the Belgian capital has to be understood, at least partially, by the situation of the crisis of national identity and the Flemish-francophone rivalry. With globalization and the mobilisation of ethnic identities (not only in Belgium but also in Britain and in other countries) the national integration is also losing ground. Apart from that, this type of integration tends to generate polarization which often leads to encapsulations against 'aliens'. Thus, a given society that employs this type of integration strategy becomes more cohesive, but frequently at the cost of turning back the wheels of social modernisation.

Finally, the last type of integration is the one that, on the one hand, adopts the conditions of life in high modernity and, on the other hand, successfully mobilizes and motivates people for the challenges present at the centre of their lives (unemployment, destruction of nature etc.). This alternative type of integration, which brings individuals together around shared local, regional, national or global concerns, is possible according to Beck and Beck-Gernsheim only if no attempt is made to arrest and push back the breakout of individuals and if people make a conscious use of this situation and try to forge new, politically open, creative forms of bonds and alliance (ibid). After René König they interestingly argue that post-traditional societies threatening the cohesion of this civilization can only become integrated, if at all, through the experiment of their self-interpretation, self-observation, self-opening, self-discovery, indeed, self-invention (2002: 19).

I believe the aforementioned self-invention is crucial not only for the future re-integration of the analysed societies but also for the fuller integration of the analysed group of people (Muslims) within wider societies. The project identity developed by the emerging Muslim elites can be seen as such an attempt at self-invention. Will it enable the Belgian and British Muslims to break into the bounded Belgium and Britain and to more fully integrate with their societies? All one can say now is that it is a phenomenon *in statu nascendi* and it is impossible to predict its future development. However, one may be certain that it will have a significant impact on the situation of Muslims in Europe.

In February 2008 the cover of the Time Magazine (vol. 171, no. 6) featured the faces of several members of the European Muslim elite (some of them were in fact faces of my interviewees) with the title 'Europe's Muslim Success Story'. Today this 'success story' is shared only by a small proportion of the European Muslims and members of their communities, while the majority experiences serious levels of exclusion and disadvantage. The improvement of the situation of the Muslim communities in Europe will depend not only on the effective struggle against at least some of the forms of exclusion and disadvantage faced by the members of these communities, but also on the results of the Muslims' efforts to re-invent and position themselves as citizens and full members of the European polities. The latter objective is particularly difficult to attain. Before European Muslims achieve this goal they will need to work tirelessly to reconstruct popular images, assumptions and representations of their religion and their communities within wider societies. The members of the analyzed new Muslim elites have been already doing so and will surely not rest until they achieve some tangible results.

BIBLIOGRAPHY

Abbas, T. (2005). *Muslims in Britain after 7/7: the problem of the few*. Retrieved on 14th December from http://www.opendemocracy.net/conflict-terrorism/muslims_3120.jsp

Abenchikar, D. (1993). *L'islam des Maroxellois*. Bruxelles: CBAI.

Ahmed, A.S. (2003). *Islam Under Siege*. Cambridge: Polity Press.

Ahmed, S.T. (2003, 23-26 April). *Young Muslims and Muslim Media in Britain*. Paper presented at the New Media, Technology and Everyday Life in Europe Conference, LSE, London.

Ainlay, S., Becker, G., Colleman. (1986). *The Dilemma of Difference: A Multidisciplinary View of Stigma*. New York: Plenum Press.

Alam, F. (2003, December). Editorial. *Q-News*.

Al-Azmeh, A. (1993). *Islams and Modernities*. London: Verso.

Alexander, C. (2000). *The Asian Gang: Ethnicity, Identity, Masculinity*. London: Berg Publishers.

Alexander, J. C., Eyerman, R., Giesen, B., Smelser, N.J., Sztompka, P. (2004). *Cultural Trauma and Collective Identity*. California: University of California Press.

Allen, C., Nielsen, J. (2002). *Summary Report on Islamophobia in the EU after 11 September 2001*. Vienna: EMUC

Allievi, S. (1999) *Les Convertis à l'Islam. Les Nouveaux Musulmans d'Europe*. Paris: L'Harmattan

Allievi, S. (2001). *Islam in the Public Space: Social Networks, Media and Neo-Communities*. Papered presented during the Second Mediterranean Social and Political Research Meeting, Florence, March 21-22.

Allievi, S. (2003). Islam in the Public Space: Social Networks, Media and Neo-Communities. In S. Allievi, Nielsen (Ed.), *Muslim Networks and Transnational Communities in and Across Europe*. Leiden and Boston: Brill.

Allievi, S. (2003a, 25-26 April). Multiculturalism in Europe. Paper presented at the conference on *Muslims in Europe post 9/11*, Oxford, St. Anthony's College.

Allievi, S. (2003b). Relations and Negotiations: Issues and Debates on Islam. In B. Maréchal, Allievi, S., Dassetto, F., Nielsen, J. (Ed.), *Muslims in the Enlarged Europe*. Leiden: Brill.

Allievi, S. (2007). Western Europe and its Islam. *International Sociology*, 22(2), 197-200.

Ally, M.M., (1979). *The growth and organisation of the Muslim community in Britain*. Birmingham: Centre for the Study of Islam and Christian-Muslim Relations, Selly Oak College.

Akhtar, S. (1989). *Be careful with Mohammed: the Salman Rushdie affair*. London: Bellew Publication

Akhtar, N. (2003, 26 August). *Pakistan Clans 'Abusing' British Politics*, from http://news.bbc.co.uk/2/hi/uk_news/magazine/3181851.stm

Ameli, S. R. (2002). *Globalization, Americanization and British Muslim Identity*. London: Islamic College For Advanced Studies Press.

Ameli, S. R., Merali, A. (2004). *Dual Citizenship: British, Islamic or Both? - Obligation, Recognition, Respect and Belonging*: Islamic Human Rights Commission.

Amiraux, V. (2001). *Acteurs de l'islam entre Allemagne et Turquie. Parcours militants et experiences religieuses*. Paris: L'Harmattan.

Anderson, B. (1991). *Imagined Communities. Reflections on the Origins and Spread of Nationalism*. London: Verso.

Andrews, A. Y. (1993). Jammat-t-Islami in the United Kingdom. In B. Barot (Ed.), *Religion and Ethnicity: Minorities and Social change in the Metropolis*.

Anwar, M. (1979) *The Myth of Return: Pakistanis in Britain*. London: Heinemann

Anwar, M. (1988). Muslim community and the issues in education. In B. O'Keffe (Ed.), *Schools for Tomorrow. Building Walls or Building Bridges*. London: Falmer Press.

Anwar, M. (1996). *British Pakistanis: Demographic, Social and Economic Position*. CRER University of Warwick.

Anwar, M. (1998). *Between cultures: continuity and change in the lives of young Asians*. London, Routledge.

Anwar, M., Bakhsh, Q. (2003). *British Muslims and State Policies*: Centre for Research and Ethnic Relations, University of Warwick.

Apel, K.-O. (1993). How to ground a universalistic ethics of co-responsibility for the effects of collective actions and activities. *Philosophica, 52*(2), 9-29.

Appadurai, A. (1997). *Modernity at Large: Cultural Dimensions of Globalization*. Minneapolis: University of Minnesota Press.

Appelt, E., Jarosch, M. (Ed.). (2000). *Combating Racial Discrimination: Affirmative Action as a Model for Europe*. Oxford: Berg.

Appleby, S. (2000). *The Ambivalence of the Sacred: Religion, Violence, and Reconciliation*. New York: Rowman & Littlefield Publishers,.

Arkoun, M. (1994). *Rethinking Islam: common question, uncommon answers*. Oxford: Westview Press.

Arrijn, P., Feld, S., Nayer, A. (1998). *Discrimination in access to employment on grounds of foreign origin: the case of Belgium*. Geneva: ILO.

Arripe, A. (2005). *Voiler et dévoiler*, Louvain-la-Neuve: Presses Universitaires de Louvain.

Asad, T. (1993). *Genealogies of Religion*. Baltimore: John Hopkins University Press.

Asad, T. (2003). *Formations of the Secular: Christianity, Islam, Modernity*. Stanford: Stanford University Press.

Atchley, R.C. (2007). Spirituality, Religion, and Aging. In Ritzer, G. (Ed.), *Blackwell Encyclopedia of Sociology*. Blackwell Publishing.

AVID (2002). *Rekrutering in Nederland voor de Jihad: van incident naar trend*. Den Haag: Ministerie van Binnenlandse Zaken en Koninkrijkrelaties.

AVID (2004) *Van dawa tot jihad. De diverse dreigingen van de radicale islam tegen de democratische rechtsorde*, Ministerie van Binnenlandse Zaken en Koninkrijksrelaties.

Babès, L. (1997). *L'islam positive*. Paris: Les Editions de L'Atelier.

Babès, L. (2002). Feminisme, islamisme, modernité. In I. T. Leonetti (Ed.), *Les femmes et l'Islam: Entre modernité et intégrisme*. Paris: L'Harmattan.

Baldaccini, A. (2003). United Kingdom. In J. Niessen, Schibel, Y., Magoni, R. (Ed.), *EU and US approaches to the management of immigration*. Brussels: MigPolGroup.

Balibar, E. (2001). *Nous, citoyens d'Europe? Les frontières, l'État, le peuple*. Paris: La Découverte.

Ballard, R. (1990). Migration and Kinship: the differential effect of marriage rules on the processes of Punjabi migration to Britain. In: Clark C., Peach C. Vertovec S. *South Asian Overseas*. Cambridge University Press

Ballard, R. (ed) (1994). *Desh Pardesh - The South Asian Presence in Britain*. London: Hurst & Company,

Banaszak-Karpińska, E. (1998). *Tożsamość jako kategoria badawcza w badanich nad jednostką i społeczeństwem*. Wrocław, Acta Universitatis Wratislaviensis no. 2060

Barbalet, J. M. (1996). Social Emotions: Confidence, Trust and Loyalty. *The International Journal of Sociology and Social Policy, 16*(9/10), 75-96.

Barth, F. (1969). Ethnic groups and boundaries – the social organization of culture difference. Oslo: Universitetsforlaget

Basch, L., Glick-Schiller, N., Szanton-Blanc, C. (1994). *Nations Unbound: Transnational Projects, Postcolonial Predicaments, and Deterritorialized Nation-States*. Basel: Gordon and Breach.

428

Bastanier, A. (1998). The Importance of the Religious Factor in the 'Ethnic Consciousness' of Moroccan Immigrants in Belgium. In M. Martiniello (Ed.), *Multicultural policies and the state: a comparison of two European societies.* Oxford: Oxford University Press.

Bauman, G. (1996). *Contesting cultures: Discourses of identity in multi-ethnic London.* Cambridge University Press

Bauman, Z. (1995). Modernity and Ambivalence. Cambridge: Polity Press.

Bauman, Z. (1995a). Life in Fragments. Essays in Postmodern Morality. Oxford: Blackwell.

Bauman, Z. (1999). *In Search of Politics.* Cambridge: Polity.

Bayat, A. (2005). What is Post-Islamism? *ISIM Newsletter, 16*(Autumn), 5.

Bazeley, P. (2007). *Qualitative data analysis with NVivo.* London: Sage.

BBC. (2002, 11 October). *Mosque cuts truancy levels,* from http://news.bbc.co.uk/2/hi/uk_news/england/2318949.stm

BBC. (2004, 12 July). *Shocking racism in jobs market,* from http://news.bbc.co.uk/1/hi/business/3885213.stm

BBC. (2005, 9 August). *Cleric Bakri 'will return' to UK,* from http://news.bbc.co.uk/2/hi/uk_news/politics/4133150.stm#

BBC. (2007, 15 April). *UK Muslims 'more loyal than most',* from http://news.bbc.co.uk/2/hi/uk_news/6557003.stm

Beauchesne, M.-N. (1994). La discrimination des travailleurs d'origine étrangère : Quelles pratiques en entreprises. *Critique Régionale*(21-22).

Beck, U. (1992). *The Risk Society.* London: Sage.

Beck, U. & E. Beck-Gernsheim (2002). *Individualization. Institutionalized Individualism and its Social and Political Consequences.* London-Thousand Oaks-New Delhi: Sage Publications.

Beck, U. (2001). *The Brave New World of Work.* Cambridge: Polity Press.

Beinin, J., Stork, J. (1997). *Political Islam: Essays from Middle East Report.* New York: Tauris.

Beishon, S., Modood, T., Virdee, S. (1998). *Ethnic Minority Families.* London: Policy Studies Institute.

Bellah, R., Madsen, R., Sullivan, W.M, Swindler, A., Tipton, S.M. (1986). *Habits of the Heart.* New York: Harper & Row.

Bendix, R. (1964). *Nation-Building and Citizenship.* New York: Wiley.

Benhabib, S. (1992). *Situating the Self.* Cambridge: Polity.

Ben Mohammed, N. (2000). Les droits polyethniques. : L'exemple des femmes musulmanes voilées d'origine maghrébine sur le marché de l'emploi. In: Rea, A. and Mohammed, N. *Politique multiculturelle et modes de citoyenneté à Bruxelles. Bruxelles: ULB.*

Ben Mohamed, N. (2001). La discrimination raciale à l'embauche des jeunes filles musulmanes voilées, *Travail-emploi-formation,* octobre.

Bergeaud-Blackler, F. (2004). Social definitions of halal quality: the case of Maghrebi Muslims in France. In M. Harvey, McMeekin, A., Warde, A. (Ed.), *The qualities of food. Alternative theories and empirical questions.* (pp. 94-107). Manchaster: Manchaster University Press.

Bergeaud-Blackler, F. (2007). New challenges for Islamic ritual slaughtering: a European perspective. *Journal of Ethnic and Migration Studies, 33*(6).

Berger, P.L. (1969). The Social Reality of Religion. London: Faber & Faber.

Berger, P. L., Luckmann, T. (1967). The Social Construction of Reality: A Treatise in the Sociology of Knowledge. London: Anchor.

Berman, P. (2003). *Terror and Liberalism.* New York: W.W. Norton & Company.

Berns McGown, R. (1999). *Muslims in the Diaspora: The Somali Communities of London and Toronto.* Toronto: Toronto University Press.

Bertossi, C. (2003). Negotiating the Boundaries of Equality in Europe. *The Good Society, 12*(2), 33-39.

Bianchini, F., Bloomfield, J. (2001). Cultural Citizenship and Urban Governance in Western Europe. In N. Stevenson (Ed.), *Culture and Citizenship*. London: Sage.

Billiet, J. (2006). Verzuiling en ontzuiling in België. In E. Witte, Meyne, A. (Ed.), *De geschiedenis van België na 1945*. Antwerpen: Standaard Uitgeverij.

Billet, J., Doutrelepont, R., Vandekeere, M. (2000). Types van sociale identiteiten in België: convergenties en divergenties. In K. Dobbelaere, Elchardus, M. Kerkhofs, J. Voye, L., Bawin-Legros, B. (Ed.), *Verloren zekerheid. De Belgen en hun waarden, overtuigingen en houdingen*. Tielt: Lannoo.

Billig, M. (1997). *Banal Nationalism*. London: Sage Publications.

Birt, Y. (2006). Between Nation and Ummah: Muslim Loyalty in a Globalizing World. *Islam21, 40*, 6-11.

Birt, Y. (2008). Islamophobia in the Construction of British Muslim Identity Politics. In P, E. Hopkins, Gale, R. (Ed.), *Muslims in Britain: Race, Place and Identities*. Edinburgh: Edinburgh University Press.

Blair, T. (2005). *Press conference briefing*. Retrieved 25.03.2008, from http://www.number10.gov.uk/output/Page8041.asp

Blaise, P., De Coorebyter, V. (1993). L'islam et l'Etat Belge. *Res Publica, 35*(1), 23-38.

Blaise, P., De Coorebyter, V. (1997). La reconnaissance et la représentation de l'Islam. In R. Lewin (Ed.), *La Belgique et ses immigrés*, . Bruxelles: De BOeck.

Blommaert, J. (1997). The slow shift in orthodoxy: (re)formulations of 'integration' in Belgium. *Pragmatics. Special issue on conflict and violence in pragmatic research, 7*(4).

Blommaert, J. (1998). Integration Policies and the Politics of Integration in Belgium. In M. Martiniello (Ed.), *Multicultural Policies and the State: A Comparison of Two European Societies*. Utrecht: ERCOMER.

Blunkett, D. (2001). *Politics and Progress*. London: Politicos.

Blunkett, D. (2003). *Civic Renewal: A New Agenda. CSV Edith Kahn Memorial Lecture*.: Home Office.

BNP. (2005). *Nationalism and Israel*, from http://www.bnp.org.uk/news_detail.php?newsId=1057

Boender, W. (2002). Religious freedom and the neutrality of the state. The position of Islam in the European Union. *ISIM Newsletter, 7*, 37.

Bonne, K., Verbeke, W. (2006). Muslim consumer's attitude towards meat consumption in Belgium: insights from a means-end chain approach. *Anthropology of Food, 5*(April).

Boubekeur, A. (2007). Political Islam in Europe. In S. Amghar, Boubekeur, A., Emerson, M. (Ed.), *European Islam: Challanges for Public Policy and Society*. Brussels: CEPS.

Bourdieu, P. (1971). Intellectual field and creative project. In: M. F. D. Young (ed.), *Knowledge and Control: New Directions for the Sociology of Education*. London: Collier MacMillan.

Bourdieu, P. (1977). *Outline of a theory of practice*. Cambridge: Cambridge University Press.

Bourdieu, P. (1986). The Forms of Capital. In J. Richardson (ed.), *Handbook of theory and research for the sociology of education* (pp. 241-258). New York: Greenwood Press.

Bourdieu, P. (1987). Legitimation and structured interest in Weber's sociology of religion. In: Whimster, S., Lash, S. (Eds.), *Max Weber, Rationality, and Modernity*. London: Allen and Urwin. 119–136.

Bourdieu, P. (1990). *The Logic of Practice*. Cambridge: Polity Press.

Bourdieu, P. ed. (1993). *La misère du monde*. Paris: Seuil.

Bourdieu, P., Champagne, P. (1993) Les exclus de l'intérieur. In Bourdieu P. (ed.), *La misère du monde*. Paris: Le Seuil.

Bourdieu, P. Wacquant, L.J.D. (1992). *An Invitation to Reflexive Sociology*. Polity Press

Bourdieu, P., Wacquant, L. (2000). The organic ethnologist of Algerian migration. *Ethnography, 1*(2), 173-182.

Bousetta, H. (1997). Citizenship and political participation in France and the Netherlands. *New Community, 23*(2), 215-231.

Bousetta, H. (2000). Institutional theories of immigrant ethnic mobilization: relevance and limitations. *Journal of Ethnics and Migration research* 26(2): 229-245.

Bousetta, H. (2000a). *Immigration, Post-immigration Politics and the Political Mobilisation of Ethnic Minorities. A Comparative Case-Study of Moroccans in Four European Cities. Brussels:* IPSoM, unpublished doctoral dissertation.

Bousetta, H., Jacobs, D., Kagné, B., Martiniello, M., Rea, A., Swyngedouw, M., Nys, M. (1999). *Multicultural Policies and Modes of Citizenship in Belgium: The Cases of Antwerp, Liege and Brussels:* UNESCO-program Management of Social Transformations (MOST).

Bousetta H., and Maréchal B. (2003). *L'Islam et les musulmans en Belgique : Enjeux locaux et cadres de reflexion globaux,* Bruxelles: Fondation Roi Baudouin.

Bousetta, H., Gsir, S., Jacobs, D. (2005). *Active Civic Participation of Immigrants in Belgium:* European research project Politis.

Bousetta, H., Jacobs, D. (2006). Multiculturalism, citizenship and Islam in problematic encounters in Belgium. In M. e. al (Ed.), *Multiculturalism, Muslims and Citizenship: A European Approach.* London: Routledge.

Bouzar, D. (2005). *Monsieur Islam n'existe pas.* Paris: Hachette Littérature.

Brett, M., Fentress, E. (1997). *The Berbers (The Peoples of Africa):* Blackwell Publishing Limited.

Brenton, R. (1964) Institutional Completeness of Ethnic Communities and the Personal Relations of Immigrants. *American Journal of Sociology,* vol.70 no.2, 193-205.

Brion, F., Manço, U. (1998). *Exclusion and the job market. An empirical approach to Muslim women's situation in Belgium.* Brussels: Study commissioned by the European Commission.

Brion, F., Rea, A., Schaut, C., Tixhon, A. (coord.). (2000). *Mon délit ? Mon origine. Criminalité et criminalisation de l'immigration.* Bruxelles: De Boeck.

Brubaker, R. (1988). Citoyennetè, identitè francaise et principe d'exclusion. In C. Withol de Wenden (Ed.), *La citoyennetè.* Paris: Edilig/Fondation Diderot.

Brubaker, R. (1990). Immigration, citizenship and the nation-state in France and Germany. *International Sociology, 5*(4), 379-407.

Bruce, R., Oneal, J., Cox, M. (2000). Clash of Civilizations, or Realism and Liberalism Déjà Vu? Some Evidence. *Journal of Peace Research, 37*(5), 583-608.

Bujis, F.J. (2002). *Democratie en Terreur. De Uitdaging van het Islamitisch Extremisme.* Amsterdam: SWP.

Bujis, F.J., Rath, J. (2002). *Muslims in Europe: The State for Research.* New York City: Russell Sage Foundation.

Bunt, G. (2000). *Virtually Islamic: Computer-mediated Communication and Cyber Islamic Environments.* Cardiff: University of Wales Press.

Bunting, M. (2005, 14 July). The heavy mob will get us nowhere. *The Guardian.*

Burdsey, D. (2006). Football. In N. Ali, Kalra, V.S., Sayyid, S., ed. (Ed.), *A Postcolonial People: South Asians in Britain* (pp. 108-109). London: Hurst & Company.

Burgat, F. (2003). *Face to Face with Political Islam.* London: I.B.Tauris.

Burgess, S., Wilson, D. (2004). *Ethnic mix: how segregated are English Schools?* Bristol: Centre for Market and Public Organisation.

Caeiro, A. (2003). Adjusting Islamic Law to Migration. *ISIM Newsletter 12,* pp. 26-27.

Caeiro, A. (2005). The Muslim Leaders of the French Representative Body: Religious Authorities or Political Actors? In: McLoughlin, S. and Césari, J. (eds) *European Muslims and the Secular State.* London: Ashgate.

Caestecker, F. (2001). Migratiecontrole in Europa in de 19de eeuw. In Art, J., Francois, L. (Ed.) *Docendo discimus* (pp.241-256). Gent: Academia Pres.

Caestecker, F. (Ed.). (2005). *Huwelijksmigratie, eenzaak voor de overheid?* Leuven: Acco.

Calhoun, C., ed. (1992). *Habermas and the Public Sphere*. Cambridge, MA: MIT Press.

Calhoun. C. (1994). *Social Theory and the Politics of Identity*. New York: New York University.

Calhoun, C. (2000). *Social Theory and the Public Sphere*. In: Turner, B., S., ed. The Blackwell Companion to Social Theory, Oxford, Blackwell.

Campbell, D. (2007, July 12). 21/7 bomb plotters sentenced to life. *The Guardian*.

Caprioli, N. (2005). Moison, mosquee, ecole. *Agenda Interculturel*(238).

Casanova, J. (1994). *Public Religions in the Modern World*. Chicago: Chicago University Press.

Casanova, J. (2001). Civil society and religion: retrospective reflections on Catholicism and prospective reflections on Islam. *Social Research, 68*(4), 1041-1080.

Castells, M. (1997, 2004). *The Power of Identity*. Oxford: Blackwell.

Castles, S. (1994). Democracy and Multicultural Citizenship. Australian Debates and their Relevance for Western-Europe. In: R. Bauböck, *From Aliens to Citizens*, Aldershot: Avebury.

Castles, S., Davidson, A. (2000). Citizenship and Migration: Globalization and the Politics of Belonging. New York: Routledge.

Cesari, J. (1994). *Etre Musulman En France*. Paris/Aix-en-Provence: Karthala/Iremam.

Cesari, J. (2003). Muslim Minorities in the West: The Silent Revolution. In J. Esposito, Burgat, F. (Ed.), *Modernizing Islam: Religion in the Public Sphere in the Middle East and in Europe*: Rutgers University Press.

Cesari, J. (2004). *When Islam and Democracy meet: Muslims in Europe and in the United States*. New York: Palgrave.

Cesari, J. (2005). Mosque Conflicts in European Cities: Introduction. *Journal of Ethnic and Migration Studies, 31*(6), 1015-1024.

Ceuppens, B. (2003). Allah-thons, Hassidim, Punks…: Autochthony discourse in Flanders. In B. H. Saunders, D. (Ed.), *Whiter Multiculturalism'? A politics of dissensus* (pp. 167-184). Leuven: Leuven University Press.

Champion, F. (1996). Croire en l'incroyable: les nouvelles religiosites mystiques-esoteriques. In L. Babès (Ed.), *Les nouvelles manières de croire. Judaïsme, christianisme, islam, nouvelles religiosités*. Paris: Éditions de l'Atelier.

Christians, L. L. (1996). L' intégration religieuse en droit belge. *L'agenda interculturel, Religions dans l'Etat*, 13-17.

Clark, K., Drinkwater. (2007). *Ethnic Minorities in the Labour Market*. London: Joseph Rowntree Foundation.

Clarke, P. B. (1994). *Citizenship*. London: Pluto Press.

CLRAE (1992) Europe 1990-2000: multiculturalism in the city. The integration of immigrants, Consejo de Europa, *Estudios y Textos*, núm. 25, Estrasburgo.

Coenen, M. T., and Lewin, R. (Ed.). (1997). *La Belgique et ses immigres - Les politiques monquees*. Bruxelles: DeBoeck Universite.

Cohen, R. (1997). *Global Diasporas - An Introduction*. London: UCL Press.

Cohen, S. (1972). *Folk Devils and Moral Panics. The Creation of Mods and Rockers*. New York: St. Martin's Press.

Connor, W. (2007). Nation-State. In B. Ritzer (Ed.), *Blackwell Encyclopedia of Sociology*. London: Blackwell Publishing.

Constant, F. (1998). *La citoyenneté*, CLEFS, Paris.

Cooke, M., Lawrence B.B. (Ed.). (2005). *Muslim Networks from Hajj to Hip Hop*: University of North Carolina Press.

Coolsaet, R. (2005). *Al-Qaeda: The Myth. The Root Causes of International Terrorism And How To Tackle Them*. Ghent: Academia Press,.

Coorebyter, V. (2002). *La citoyenneté*. Bruxelles: CRISP.

432

Cox, J. L. (2003). Religion without God: Methodological Agnosticism *and the Future of Religious Studies*, from www.thehibberttrust.org.uk/ documents/hibbert_lecture_2003.pdf

CRE (1996). *Ethnic Minorities in Britain*. London: Commission for Racial Equality.

CRE. (1989). *Law, Blasphemy and the Multi-Faith Society. Report of a Seminar*. London: Commission for Racial Equality.

CRE. (2003). *Richard Commission Evidence Session*, from http://www.richardcommission.gov.uk/content/printpage.asp?ID=/content/evidence/writt en/cre/supplementary/am-briefing-e.asp

Creswell, J. W. (1998, 1999). *Qualitative inquiry and research design: Choosing among five alternatives*. Thousand Oaks, CA: Sage.

Crick, B. (2002). Education for citizenship: the Citizenship Order. *Parliamentary Affairs, 55*(3), 488-504.

Cross, M. (1988). Multiculturalism and the state: a British paradox. In M. Martiniello (Ed.), *Multicultural policies and the state: a comparison of two European societies*. Utrecht: ERCOMER.

Crossley, N. (2001). Citizenship, Intersubjectivity and the Lifeworld. In N. Stevenson (Ed.), *Culture and Citizenship*. London: Sage.

Dassetto, F. (1988). *Le Tabligh en Belgique: diffuser l'islam sur le traces du Prophete*. SYBIDI Papers 2. Louvain-la-Neuve/Bruxelles: Academia et SYBIDI.

Dassetto, F. (1996). *La construction de l'Islam européen: Approche socio-anthropologique*. Paris: Harmattan.

Dassetto, F. (1997). Islam en Belgique et en Europe: facettes et questions. In F. Dassetto, Allievi, S. (Ed.), *Facettes de l'islam belge*. Louvain-la-Neuve: Bruylant-Academia.

Dassetto, F. (2001). *Migration, societes et politiques: Belgique, Europe et les nouveaux defis*. Louvain-la-Neuve: Academia-Bruylant.

Dassetto, F. (2003). After September 11th: Radical Islamic Politics and European Islam. In B. Maréchal, Allievi, S., Dassetto, F., Nielsen, J. (Ed.), *Muslims in the Enlarged Europe*. Leiden: Brill.

Dassetto, F. (2004). *Islams du nouveau siècle*. Bruxelles: Labor.

Dassetto, F. (2005). *La rencontre complexe : Occidents et islams*. Bruxelles: Academia Bruylant.

Dassetto, F. (2006). Islams locaux et globalisation islamique: elements pour questionnement theorique. *Recherches sociologiques et anthropologiques, 37*(2), 3-18.

Dassetto, F. (2006a). L'islam en Belgique. *Public lecture held in the* Facultés universitaires Saint-Louis, Bruxelles, 05.12.2006.

Dassetto, F. (2007). Islam belge et bruxellois : état des connaissances. In P. Delwit, Rea, A., Swyngedouw, M. (Ed.), *Bruxelles : ville ouverte. Immigration et diversité culturelle au coeur de l'Europe*. Paris: Harmattan.

Dassetto, F., Bastanier, A. (1984). *L'islam transplanté*. Anvers: Editions EPO.

Dassetto, F., Bastanier, A. (1987). *Enseignants et enseignements de l'Islam au sein de l'école officielle en Belgique*. Louvains-La-Neuve: CIACO.

Dassetto, F., Bastanier, A. (1993). *Immigration et epace public: La controverse de l'intégration*. Paris: L'Harmattan.

Dassetto, F., Allievi, S. (Ed.). (1997). *Facettes de l'Islam belge*. Louvain-la-Neuve: Bruylant-Academia.

Dassetto, F., Hennart M.N.,. (1997). Rite sacrificiel dans la ville de consommation> pratiques et signification de l'Aid el Kebir: quelques aspect. In F. Dassetto, Allievi, S. (Ed.), *Facettes de l'islam belge*. Bruxelles.

Dassetto, F., Maréchal, B. (2002, 27 June). L'islam vu par le comité R. *La Libre Belgique*.

Dassetto, F., Nielsen, J. (2003). Conclusions. In B. Maréchal, Allievi, S., Dassetto, F., Nielsen, J. (Ed.), *Muslims in the Enlarged Europe* (pp. 531 - 542). Leiden - Boston: Brill.

Dassetto, F., Bastanier, A. (1993). *Immigration et epace public: La controverse de l'intégration.* Paris: L'Harmattan.

Dassetto, F. (1997). Islam en Belgique et en Europe: facettes et questions. In F. Dassetto, Allievi, S. (Ed.), *Facettes de l'islam belge.* Louvain-la-Neuve: Bruylant-Academia.

Davie, G. (1994). *Religion in Britain since 1945 – Believing Without Belonging.* Oxford, Blackwell Publishers

Dayan, D., & Katz, E. (1992). *Media events: The live broadcasting of history.* Cambridge, MA: Harvard University Press.

Delanty, G. (2000). *Citizenship in a Global Age: Society, Culture, Politics.* Buckingham/Philadelphia: Open University Press.

Delanty, G. (2002). Two Conceptions of Cultural Citizenship: A Review of Recent Literature on Culture and Citizenship. *The Global Review of Ethnopolitics, 1*(1), 60-66.

Delanty, G. (2003). Citizenship as a learning process: disciplinary citizenship versus cultural citizenship. *International Journal of Lifelong Education, 22*(6), 597-605.

Denzin, N. K., & Lincoln, Y. S. (2003). *Handbook of qualitative research.* Thousand Oaks, CA: Sage.

Denscombe, M. (2000, 2003). *The good research guide: for small-scale social research projects.* Buckingham: Open University Press.

Dépelteau, F. (2006). Review of the Radical Islam Rising: Muslim Extremism in the West by Quintan Wiktorowicz. *Canadian Journal of Sociology Online, March-April.*

Devillers, S. (04.04.2007). Le sacrifice des tirailleurs africains. *La Libre Belgique,* p. 36.

Dewinter, F. (2005, 16.06.2005). Interview with Philip Dewinter. *Metro.*

De Meyer, V. (2007, 23 June). Ces règlements scolaires à peine voilés. *Le Soir,* pp. 2-3.

Dieckhoff, A. (Ed.). (1996). *Belgique: La Force de la Désunion.* Bruxelles: Editions complexe.

Dittrich, M. (2003). *What Perspectives for Islam and Muslims in Europe.* Brussels: European Policy Centre.

Dobbelaere, K., Billet, J., Creyf, R. (1978). Secularization and Pillarization: A Social Approach. *Review of the Social Sciences of Religion, 2.*

Doise, W. (1984). Social Representations, Inter-group Experiments and Levels of Analysis. In: Farr, R.M., Moscovici, S. (Eds) Social Representations. Cambridge: Cambridge University Press.

Donohue, J. J., Esposito, J.L. (1982). *Islam in Transition: Muslim Perspectives.* New York: Oxford University Press.

Doomernik, J. (1991). *Turkse Moskeen en Maatschappelijke Participatie. De Institutionalisering van de Turkse islam in Nederland en de Duitse Bondsrepubliek.* Nederlandse Geografische Studies 129. Amsterdam.

Douglas, M. (1970). *Natural Symbols: Explorations in Cosmology.* New York: Pantheon Books.

Dorzée, H., De Mulenaere, M. (2007, 23 June). Ces règlements scolaires à peine voilés. *Le Soir.*

Duchesne, S. (1997). *Citoyenneté à la française.* Paris: Presse de Science Po.

Duchesne, S. (2003). French Representations of Citizenship and Immigrants: The Political Dimension of The Civic Link. *Immigrants and Minorities, 22*(2-3), 262-279.

Dunning, E. (2004). Aspects of the Figurational Dynamics of Racial Stratification: A Conceptual Discussion and Developmental Analysis of Black-White Relations in the United States. In S. Loyal, Quilley, S., (Ed.), *The Sociology of Norbert Elias.* Cambridge: Cambridge University Press.

Durkheim, E. (1915, 2001). *The Elementary Forms of Religious Life.* Oxford: Oxford University Press.

Durkheim, E. (1957). *Professional Ethics and Civic Morals.* London: Routledge

Durkheim, E., (1953). Individual and collective representations. In Durkheim, E., *Sociology and Philosophy.* London: Cohen & West Ltd.

Duveen, G.(2001). Introduction: the Power of Ideas. In G. Duveen (Ed). *Social representation: Studies in social psychology*, London: Polity Press.

DWTC. (1997). *Etnische discriminatie bij de aanwerving: belgische deelname aan het internationaal vergelijkend onderzoek van het Internationaal Arbeidsbureau.* Brussels: Federale Diensten Voor Wetenschappelijke, Technische en Culturele Aangelegenheden - DWTC.

Dwyer, C. (2000). Negotiating diasporic identities: young British South Asian Muslim women. *Women's studies international forum, 23*(4), 475-486.

Eade, J. (1989). *The Politics of Community, the Bangladeshis in East London.* Aldershot: Ashgate.

Eade, J. (1997). *Living the Global City: Globalization and local processes.* London: Routledge.

Eade, J. (2002). *Placing London: from Imperial Capital to Global City.* Oxford: Berghahn Books.

Eade, J. (2004). Rather than making upset. In J. Eade, Jahjah, D.A., Sasen, S. (Ed.), *Identities on the Move.* London: British Council.

Eade, J., Garbin, D. (2002). Changing Narratives of Violence, Struggle and Resistance: Bangladeshis and the Competition for Resources in the Global City. *Oxford Development Studies, 30*(2).

Eaton, R. M. (1993). *The rise of Islam and the Bengal frontier, 1204–1760.* New Delhi: Oxford University Press.

Eder, J. (1993). *New Politics of Class.* London: Sage.

Edmunds, J. Turner, B. S. (eds) (2002) *Generational Consciousness, Narrative and Politics.* Lanham: Rowman & Littlefield.

Eggerickx, T., Kesteloot, C., Poulain, M., Roesems T., Vandenbroecke, H. (Ed.). (1999). *De allochtone bevolking in België.* Brussels: NIVS & DWTC.

Eickelman, D., F., Piscatori J. (1996). *Muslim Politics.* New York: Princeton University Press.

El Asri, F. (2006). Different Ways around the World: The Achievement of singer Sami Yusuf. In V. Martensen (Ed.), *Religion and Society Crossdisciplinary European Perspectives* (pp. 141-154). Aarhus: University of Aarhus.

El Battiui, M., Nahavandi, F., Kanmaz, M. (2004). *Mosquée, imams et professeurs de religion islamique en Belgique: état de la question et enjeux.* Bruxelles: Fondation Roi Baudouin.

Elias, N., Scotson, J.L. (1965). *The Established and the Outsiders.* London: Frank Cass & Co.Ltd.

ENAR. (2006). *Repondre au racism en Belgique.* Brussels: ENAR.

ENAR. (2007). *Racism in the United Kingdom - Shadow Report 2006.* Brussels: ENAR.

Entzinger, H. (2000) The dynamics of integration policies: a multidimensional model in Koopmans, R. and Statham, P. (eds.) *Challenging Immigration and Ethnic Relations Politics.* Oxford: Oxford University Press. 97-118

Entzinger, H. (2003). Les jeunes musulmans d'un Rotterdam pluriculturel: une vision "maigre " de la citoyenneté. In Wieviorka (Ed.), *L'Avenir de l'islam en France et en Europe.* Paris: Balland.

Esposito, J. (1992). *The Islamic threat: Myth or reality?* Oxford: Oxford University Press.

Esposito, J. (2000). *Islam and Civil Society:* RCS Working Papers. European University Institute.

Esposito, J. (2002). *Unholy war. Terrorism in the name of Islam.* Oxford: Oxford University Press.

Esposito, J., Burgat, F. (2003). *Modernizing Islam: Religion in the Public Sphere in the Middle East and in Europe: Rutgers University Press.* London: Hurst and Company.

Es-Saidi, M. (2007). Filles voilées à l'école: les cibles faciles. *Journal du Mardi.*

EUMC. (2004). *Migrants, Minorities and Education: Exclusion, discrimination and anti-discrimination.* Report available online on: http://eumc.eu.int/eumc/material/pub/comparativestudy/CS-Education-en.pdf

EUMC. (2005). *Migrants, Minorities and Housing: exclusion, discrimination and anti-discrimination*. Report available online on:
http://eumc.eu.int/eumc/material/pub/comparativestudy/CS-Education-en.pdf
EUMC. (2006). *Muslims in the European Union: Discrimination and Islamophobia*. Report available online on:
http://eumc.europa.eu/eumc/material/pub/muslim/Manifestations_EN.pdf
Expatica. (2004, 16 December). State to Pay Imams. *Expatica*.
Fadil, N. (2003). Muslim Girls in Belgium: Individual Freedom through Religion? *ISIM Newsletter*(13), 18-19.
Falk, R. (1994). The making of global citizenship. In B. Steenbergen van (Ed.), *The Conditions of Citizenship*. London: Sage.
Favell, A. (2001). *Philosophies of Integration: Immigration and the Idea of Citizenship in France and Britain*. London: Palgrave.
Favell, A., Martiniello, M. (1998). Convergence and divergence between Belgian and British multiculturalism. In Marco Martiniello (ed). *Multicultual Policies and the State*. Utecht: ERCOMER
Favell, A., Martiniello, M. (1999). *Multi-national, multi-cultural and multi-levelled Brussels: national and ethnic politics in the `Capital of Europe'*. WPTC-99-04
http://www.transcomm.ox.ac.uk
Favell, A., Modood, T. (2003). The Philosophy of Multiculturalism: The Theory and Practice of Applied Political Theories. In Alan Finlayson, ed., *Contemporary Political Philosophy: A Reader and a Guide*. Edinburgh: Edinburgh University Press. pp. 484–95.
Feagin, J.R. (1991). *A case for the case study*. Chapel Hill (N.C.): University of North Carolina Press.
Fennema, M., Tillie, J.N. (1999). Political participation and political trust in a multicultural democracy. Civic communities and ethnic networks in Amsterdam. *Journal of Ethnic and Migration Studies, 25*(4), 703-726.
Ferrari (2003). The State and Legal Systems with Regard to Islam. W: Maréchal, B.; Allievi, S.; Dassetto, F.; Nielsen, J. (red.) *Muslims in the Enlarged Europe. Religion and Society*, Leiden/Boston: Brill
Ferrari, S., Bradney,. (2000). *Islam and European Legal Systems*. Darthmouth: Ashgate.
Festinger, L. (1957). *A Theory of Cognitive Dissonance*. Stanford: Stanford University Press.
Fetzer, J. L., Soper, J.Ch. (2005). *Muslims and the State in Britain, France, and Germany*. Cambridge: Cambridge University Press.
Fevre, R. (2000). Socializing Social Capital: Identity, the Transition to Work, and Economic Development. In: Baron, I., Field, J. & T Schuller (eds.), *Social Capital – Critical Perspectives*. Oxford: Clarendon, Oxford, pp. 94-110.
Fletcher, R. (1998). *Moorish Spain*. London: Phoenix Giant.
Francis, V. (2000). L'etraner, objet de toutes les attentions: etude des pratiques de ciblage policier. In F. Brion et al. (Ed.), *Mon delit? Mon origine*. Bruxelles: De Boeck.
Fraser, N. (1992). Rethinking the Public Sphere. In C. Calhoun (Ed.), *Habermas and the Public Sphere*. Cambridge: MIT Press
Frégosi, F. (2000). Les contours discoursifs d'une religiosité citoyenne : laïcité et identité islamique chez Tariq Ramadan. In F. Dassetto (Ed.), *Paroles d'islam: individus, sociétés et discours dans l'islam européen contemporain*. Paris: Maisonneuve-Larose.
Foblets, M. C. (1996). *Familles-Islam-Europe. Le Droit Confronté au Changement*. Paris: L'Harmattan.
Fourest, C. (2004). *Frère Tariq*. Paris: Grasset.
Gale, R., Naylor,. (2002). Religion, planning and the city: The spatial politics of ethnic minority expression in British cities and towns. *Ethnicities, 2*(3), 387-409.

Galston, W. (1991). *Liberal Purposes: Goods, Virtues and Duties in the Liberal State.* Cambridge: Cambridge University Press.

Garbin, D. (2005, 17 June 2005). *Bangladeshi diaspora in the UK: socio-cultural dynamics, religious trends and transnational politics.* Paper presented at the European Human Rights Conference on Bangladesh. School of Oriental & African Studies, University of London.

Gaspard, F., Khosrokhavar, F. (1995). *Le foulard et la République,* . Paris: La Découverte.

Geaves, R. (1995). *Muslims in Leeds.* Community Religions Project, University of Leeds

Geertz, C. (1966). Religion as a Cultural System. in Banton M. (ed) *Anthropological Approaches to the Study of Religion.*London: Tavistock.

Geertz, C. (1968). *Islam Observed - Religious Developments in Morocco and Indonesia.* New Haven: Yale University Press.

Geisser, V. (2003). *La nouvelle islamophobie.* Paris: La Découverte

Geisser, V., Kelfaoui, S. (1998). Tabous et enjeux autour de l'ethnicité maghrébine dans le système politique français. *Revue Européenne des Migrations Internationales, 14*(2), 19-32.

Gellner, E. (1968). A Pendulum Swing Theory of Islam. *Annales Marocaines de Sociologie, 1,* 5-14.

Gellner, E. (1996). *Conditions of Liberty.* London: Cambridge University Press.

German, L. (2003). Ant-War Movement. In F. Reza (Ed.), *Anti-Imperialism: a guide for the movement.* London: Bookmark.

Giddens, A. (1991). *Modernity and Self-Identity: Self and Society in the Late Modern Age.* Cambridge: Polity Press.

Giddens, A. (2000). *Runaway World: How Globalization is Reshaping our Lives.* New York: Routledge.

Giddens, A.,Birdsall, K., (2001). *Sociology.* Cambridge: Polity Press

GLA. (2006). *Muslims in London.* London: GLA-Greater London Authority.

Glynn, S. (2002). Bengali Muslims: the new East End radicals? *Ethnic and Racial Studies, 25*(6), 969-988.

Goffman, E. (1963). *Stigmata: Notes on the Management of Spoiled Identity.* Pelican Book

Gibbs, G. R. (2002). *Qualitative Data Analysis: Explorations with NVivo.* Buckingham: Open University Press.

Gijsels, H. (1993). *Le Vlaams Blok.* Bruxelles: Editions Luc Pire.

Gilliat-Ray, S. (2006). Educating the Ulama: Centres of Islamic religious training in Britain. *Islam and Christian-Muslim Relations, 17*(1).

Gilroy, P., Grossberg, L., McRobbie, A. (Ed.). (2000). *Without Guarantees: In Honour of Stuart Hall:* Verso.

Ginbsurgh, V., Weber, S. (2006). La dynamique des langues en Belgique. *Regards Économiques - IRES-UCL, 42,* 1-10.

GLA. (2006). *Muslims in London.* London: GLA-Greater London Authority.

Glavanis, P. M. (1999). *'Muslim Voices' in the European Union: The Stranger Within. Community, Identity and Employment,* Final Report, Brussels: European Commission. Targeted Socio-Economic Research (TSER) SOE1-CT96-3024.

Glynn, S. (2002). Bengali Muslims: the new East End radicals? *Ethnic and Racial Studies, 25*(6), 969-988.

Greeley, A.M. (1972). *The Denominational Society.* Glenview: Scott Foresman

Grimeau, J.-P. (1993). De immigratiegolven en de spreiding van vreemdelingen in België. In Morelli, A. (ed.), *Geschiedenis van het eigen volk. De vreemdeling in België van de prehistorie tot nu.* Leuven: Kritak, 115-125.

Grignard, A. (1997). L'islam radical en Belgique a travers la litterature de propagande. In F. Dassetto, Allievi, S. (Ed.), *Facettes de l'islam belge*. Louvain-la-Neuve: Bruylant-Academia.

Grignard, A. (2006). L'islamisme radical en Belgique, entre nationalisme et globalisation : une vision policière. *Studia diplomatica, 60*, 127-132.

Goffman, E. (1959). *The Presentation of Self in Everyday Life*. London: Penguin

Goffman, E. (1963). *Stigma: Notes on the Management of Spoiled Identity*. New Jersey: Prentice-Hall.

Göle, N. (2002). Islam in Public: New Visibilities and New Imaginaries. *Public Culture, 14*(1), 173-190.

Göle, N. (2002a). Close encounters: Islam, modernity and violence. In C. Calhoun, Price, P., Timmer, A. (Ed.), *Understanding September 11*. New York: New Press.

Göle, N. (2003). The Voluntary Adoption of Islamic Stigma Symbol. *Social Research, 70*(3).

Göle, N. (2004). Islam in Europe. *Index on Censorship, 33*(4), 110-116.

Göle, N. (2006). Islam, European Public Space and Civility. In K. Michalski (Ed.), *Conditions of European Solidarity*. Budapest: Central European University Press.

Goldthorpe, J. H., Payne, C. (1986). Trends in intergenerational class mobility in England and Wales 1972 -1983. *Sociology, 20*.

Govaert, S. (1998). A Brussels Identity? A Speculative Interpretation. In K. Deprez, Vos, L. (Ed.), *Nationalism in Belgium: Shifting Identities 1780-1995*. London: MacMillan Press LTD.

Govaert, S. (2002). Frémissements républicains dans l'opinion belge. *Le Monde Diplomatique, 10*(16998), 18-19.

Grice, A. (2007, 22 June). Blair will become a Catholic. *The Independent*.

Gsir, S., Martiniello, M., Meireman, K., Wets, J. (2005). *Belgium: Current Immigration Debates in Europe: A Publication of the European Migration Dialogue*.

Gunsteren van, H. (1978). Notes on a Theory of Citizenship. In P. Birnbaum, Lively, J., Parry, G. (Ed.), *Democracy, Consensus, and Social Contract*. London: Sage.

Gupta, A., Ferguson, J. (Ed.). (1997). *Culture, Power, Place: Explorations in Critical Anthropology*. Durham: Duke University Press.

Guttman, A. (1992). Introduction. In Taylor, C. (Ed) *Multiculturalism: Examining the Politics of Recognition*. Princeton: Princeton University Press. 3-24

Habermas, J. (1962, 1989). *The Structural Transformation of the Public Sphere: An Inquiry Into a Category of Bourgeois Society*. Cambridge: Cambridge University Press.

Habermas, J. (1992-3). Citizenship and National Identity: Some Reflections on the Future of Europe. *Praxis International, 12*(1), 1-19.

Habermas, J. (1998). The European nation-state: on the past and future sovereignty and citizenship. *Public Culture, 10*(2), 397-416.

Haenni. (2005). *L'Islam de marché : L'autre révolution conservatrice*. Paris: Broché.

Hall, S. (1991). Old and New Identities: Old and New Ethnicities. In A. D. King (Ed.), *Culture, Globalization and the World-System: Contemporary Conditions for the Representation of Identity*. Basingstoke: Macmillan.

Halliday, F. (1995). *Islam and the Myth of Confrontation: Religion and Politics in the Middle East*. London: I. B. Tauris.

Hamel, I. (2007). *La vérité sur Tariq Ramadan : Sa famille, ses réseaux, sa stratégie*. Paris: Favre Sa.

Hammar, T. (1990). *Democracy and the Nation State: Aliens, Denizens and Citizens in a World of International Migration*. Avenbury: Aldershot.

Hausby, E. (2006). Islamic House Purchase Loans in Britain. *ISIM Newsletter, 17*, 28.

Hazell, R. (Ed.). (2003). *The state of the nations 2003: the third year of devolution in the United Kingdom.*: Imprint Academic.

438

Heater, D. (1999). *What is Citizenship?* Cambridge: Polity Press.

Heckmann, F. (1994). Nation, nation-state and policy towards ethnic minorities. In B. Lewis, Schnapper, D. (Ed.), *Muslims in Europe*. London: Pinter.

Heelas, P. (1996). Introduction. Detraditionalization and its rivals. In P. Heelas, Lash, S., Morris, P. (Ed.), *Detraditionalization*. Cambridge: Blackwell.

Heelas, P., Woodhead, L. (2005) *The Spiritual Revolution. Why Religion is Giving Way to Spirituality*. Oxford: Blackwell Publishing.

Hefner, R. (2001). Public Islam and the Problem of Democratization. *Sociology of Religion, 62*(4).

Heitmeyer, W. (2001). Lack of Recognition: The Socially Destructive Consequences of New Capitalism. In A. Herskamp van, Musschenga, A.W. (Ed.), *Many Faces of individualism*. Leuven: Peeters.

Hemmerechts, K. (1998). Belgique/België. In Pickels, A., Sojcher, J., *La Belgique toujours grande et belle*. Brussels: Complexe.

Henig, S. (Ed.). (2002). *Modernising Britain: central, devolved, federal?* London: Federal Trust.

Hennart, M-N., Dassetto, F., (1997) Rite sacrificiel dans la ville de consommation. Pratiques et signification de l'Aïd el Kebir : quelques aspects. In: Dassetto, F., *Facettes de l'islam belge*. Louvain-la-Neuve: Bruylant. 201-209.

Henoumont, R. (1992) *Au bonheur des Belges! Histoire d'une identite*. Monaco: Editions du Rocher.

Hermans, P. (1994). Opgroeien als Marokkaan in Brussel. Een atropologisch onderzoek over de evolutie de leefwereld en inpassing van Marokkaanse jongeren. *Cultuur en Migratie*.

Hermans, P. (1995). Moroccan Immigrants and School Success. *International Journal of Educational Research, 1*.

Hervieu-Léger, D. (1999). *Le pèlerin et le converti. La religion en mouvement*. Paris: Flammarion.

Hinnells, J. (1997). *A New Handbook of Living Religions*. London: Penguin Books.

Hiro, D. (1989) *Black British, White British*. London: Grafton Books.

Hitchinson, F. (1978). *De islam in België : een sociologische problemstelling*. Leuven: KULeuven Faculteit sociale en politieke wetenschappen.

Hollenbach, D. (2002). *The Common Good and Christian Ethics*: Cambridge University Press.

Hollway, W., Jefferson, T. (2000). *Doing qualitative research differently: free association, narrative and the interview method*. London: Sage.

Holston, J. (Ed.). (1999). *Cities and Citizenship*. Durham: NC: Duke University Press.

Home Office. (2005). *Working Together to Prevent Extremism*. London.

Hopkins, PE. (2006) Youthful Muslim masculinities: gender and generational relations. *Transactions of the Institute of British Geographers*, 31(3), 337-352.

Howard, M. (2005, 17 August). Talk about the British dream. *The Guardian*.

Howe, D. (2006). Tebbit's loyalty test is dead. *New Statesman*.

HRWF. (2005, 14 February). Public Financing of Islam More Restrictive Than That of Other Religions in the Flanders'.

Hubert, C. (1999). Intégration, nationalité, citoyenneté : les stratégies d'action au sein de l'immigration aujourd'hui en Belgique. *Recherches sociologiques, 1*, 131-138.

Hughes, A. (1979). *English Accents and Dialects: An Introduction to Social and Regional Varities of British English*. London: University Park Press.

Huntington, S. P. (1998). *The Clash of Civilizations and the Remaking of World Order*. New York: Simon & Schuster.

Husain, E. (2007). *The Islamist*. London: Penguin.

Husband, C. (1994). The Political Context of Muslim Communities. In B. Lewis, Schnapper, D. (Ed.), *Muslims in Europe*. London: Pinter.

Hussain, D. (2003). The Holy Grail of Muslims in Western Europe: Representation and their relationship with the state. In J. Esposito, Burgat, F. (Ed.), *Modernizing Islam: Religion in the Public Sphere in the Middle East and in Europe: Rutgers University Press*. London: Hurst and Company.

Hussain, D. (2004). British Muslim Identity. In S. Seddon, Hussain, D., Malik, N. (Ed.), *British Muslims Between Assimilation and Segregation*. Leicester: Islamic Foundation.

Hussain, D. (2006). Brytyjscy muzułmanie 9/11 i 7/7. In K. Pędziwiatr, Górak-Sosnowska, K., Kubicki, P. (Ed.), *Islam i obywatelskość w Europie*. Warszawa: Elipsa.

Husson, J. F. (2000). Le financement public des cultes, de la laïcité et des cours philosophiques. *Courrier hebdomadaire du CRISP, 1703-1704*, 90.

Husson, J. F. (2006). *Pour une formation des imams en Belgique: points de reference en Belgique et en Europe*. Bruxelles: Fondation Roi Baudouin.

IHF. (2006). *Belgium*: International Helsinki Federation.

Ireland, P. (2000). Reaping What They Sow: Institutions and Immigrant Political Participation in Western Europe. In R. Koopmans, Statham, P. (Ed.), *Challenging Immigration and Ethnic Relations Politics: Comparative European Perspectives*. New York: Oxford University Press.

Isin, E. F., Wood, P.K. (1999). *Citizenship and Identity*. London: Sage.

Isin, E. F., Turner, B.S. (Ed.). (2002). *Handbook of Citizenship Studies*. London: Sage.

Jacobs, D. (2001). Immigrants in a Multinational Political Sphere: The Case of Brussels. (pp. 107-122) In Rogers, A. & Tillie, J. (eds.), *Multicultural Policies and Modes of Citizenship in European Cities*, Aldershot: Ashgate.

Jacobs, D. (2004). The Limits of Multicultural Citizenship In a Bipolar Setting: Brussels' case. In R. Maier (Ed.), *Citizenship and identity*: Shaker Publisher.

Jacobs, D. (2004a). The challenge of minority representation in Brussels. In Aubarell, G., Nicolau Coll A. & Ros, A. (eds.) *Immigració i qüestió nacional. Minories subestatals i immigració a Europa*. Barcelona: Editorial Mediterrània.

Jacobs, D., Nys, M., Rea, A., Swyngedouw, M. (1999). *Multicultural Policies and Modes of Citizenship in Belgium*. Brussels: The Region of Brussels-Capital.

Jacobs, D., Martiniello, M. & Rea, A. (2002). Changing patterns of political participation of citizens of immigrant origin in the Brussels Capital Region: The October 2000 Elections. *Journal of International Migration and Integration / Revue de l'intégration et de la migration internationale*, 3 (2): 201-221.

Jacobs, D., Swyngedouw, M. (2002). The Extreme-Right and Enfranchisement of Immigrants: Main Issues in the Public Debate on Integration in Belgium. *Journal of International Migration and Integration / Revue de l'intégration et de la migration internationale*, 3 (3-4): 329-344.

Jacobs, D., Phalet, K. & Swyngedouw, M. (2004). Associational Membership and Political Involvement Among Ethnic Minority Groups in Brussels. *Journal of Ethnic and Migration Studies*, vol 30 (3), 543-559.

Jacobs, D., Rea, A. (2005). Construction et importation des classements ethniques. Allochtones et immigrés aux Pays-Bas et en Belgique. *Revue Européenne des Migrations Internationales*, 21 (2): 35-59.

Jacobs, D. & Swyngedouw, M. (2006). La vie associative marocaine et turque dans la Région de Bruxelles-Capitale. (pp.135-158) In Khader, B., Martiniello, M., Rea, A. & Timmerman, C. (eds.) *Penser l'immigration et l'intégration autrement. Une initiative belge inter-universitaire*, Bruxelles: Bruylant.

Jacobson, D. (1996). *Rights Across Borders: Immigration and the Decline of Citizenship*. Baltimore: Johns Hopkins University.

Jacobson, J. (1997a). *Islam in Transition: Religion and Identity among British Pakistani Youth*. London, Routledge.

440

Jacobson, J. (1997b). Religion and Ethnicity: dual and alternative sources of identity among young British Pakistanis. *Ethnic and Racial Studies*, vol. 20, no. 2

Jahjah, D.,A. (2004). Interview with the leader of the Arab European League available on Open Democracy www.opendemocracy.net

Janoski, T., Gran, B. (2002). Political Citizenship: Foundations of Rights. In E. F. Isin, Turner, B.S. (Ed.), *Handbook of Citizenship Studies* (pp. 13-52). London: SAGE Publications Ltd.

Janowitz, M. (1980). Observations on the Sociology of Citizenship: Obligations and Rights. *Social Forces, 59*(1), 1-24.

Jayaweera, H., Choudhury, T. (2008). *Immigration, Faith and Cohesion*. London: Joseph Rowntree Foundation.

Jenkins, R. (1996). *Social Identity*, London: Routledge.

Janssens, R. (2001). Taalgebruik in Brussel. Taalverhoudingen, taalverschuivingen en taalidentiteit in een meertalige stad: Brussels VUBPRESS.

Jarymowicz, M. and Szustrowa, T. (1980) *Poczucie własnej tożsamości- żródła, funkcje regulacyjne*. Warszawa, KIW

Jenkins, R. (1996). *Social Identity*. London: Routledge

Johnston, P. (2006, 25.08.2006). Islam poses a threat to the West, say 53pc in poll. *The Daily Telegraph*.

Joly, D. (1988). Making a place for Islam in British society. Muslims in Birmingham. In T. Gerholm, Lithman, Y.G. (Ed.), *The New Islamic Presence in Western Europe*. London: Mansell.

Joly, D., Imtiaz, K. (2002). Muslims and citizenship in the United Kingdom. In R. Leveau, Withol de Wenden, C., Mohsen-Finan, K. (Ed.), *New European Identity and Citizenship*. Aldershot: Ashgate.

Jones, E., Gaventa, J. (2002). *Concepts of Citizenship: A Review*. Brighton: Institute of Development Studies.

Joppke, C., Morawska, E. (2004). *Towards Assimilation and Citizenship*. London: Macmillan.

Juergensmeyer, M. (2003). *Terror in the Mind of God: The Global Rise of Religious Violence*. California: University of California Press.

Kakpo, N. (2007). *L'islam, en recours pour les jeunes*. Paris: Sciences Po Les Presses.

Kanmaz, M. (2002). The Recognition and Institutionalization of Islam in Belgium. *The Muslim World, 92*.

Kenway, P., Palmer, G. (2007). *Poverty among ethnic groups. How and why does it differ?* York: Joseph Rowntree Foundation.

Kepel, G. (1994). *A L'Ouest d'Allah*. Paris: Editions du Seuil.

Kepel, G. (2002). *Jihad. The trial of political Islam*. London: Tauris.

Karagiannis, E., & McCauley, C. (2006). Hizb ut-Tahrir al-Islami: Evaluating the threat posed by a radical Islamic group that remains nonviolent. *Terrorism and Political Violence, 18*(2), 315-334.

Khan, V.S. (1977). The Pakistanis: Mirpuri Villagers at Home and in Bradford. In: J.L. Watson (ed.) *Between Two Cultures*. Basil Blackwell, Oxford.

Khosrokhavar, F. (1997). *L'Islam des jeunes*. Paris: Flammarion.

King, G., Keohane, R.O., Verba, S. (1994). *Designing social inquiry : scientific inference in qualitative research*. Princeton: Princeton University Press.

King, J. (1994). *Three Asian Associations in Britain*: ESRC University of Warwick.

Klausen, J. (2005). *The Islamic Challenge: Politics and Religion in Western Europe*. New York: Oxford University Press.

Klooseterman, R. J., van der Leun J., Rath, J. (1998). Across the Border: Economic Opportunities, Social Capital and Informal Businesses Activities of Immigrants. *Journal of Ethnic and Migration Studies, 24*, 239-258.

Knott and Koher (1993). Religious identity among young Muslims women in Bradford. *New Community* 19(4).

Kohnen, F., Maréchal, B., (1997). L'idée de liberté et d'individu chez jeunes filles musulmanes. Une approche socio-anthropologique sur le territoire bruxellois. In Dassetto, F. Allievi, S. *Facettes de l'Islam belge*. Louvain-la-Neuve: Bruylant-Academia.

Kołakowski, L. (1981). *Main Currents of Marxism: Its Rise, Growth and Dissolution*: Oxford University Press.

Koopmans, R. (1999). Political. Opportunity. Structure. Some Splitting to Balance the Lumping. *Sociological Forum, 14*(1).

Koopmans, R., Statham, P. (2000). *Challenging Immigration and Ethnic Relations Politics: Comparative European Perspectives*. Oxford: Oxford University Press.

Koopmans, R. (2004). Migrant mobilisation and political opportunities: variation among German cities and a comparison with the United Kingdom and the Netherlands. *Journal of Ethnic and Migration Studies, 30*, 449-470.

Kubacki, Z. (2007). The Question of Salvation and Faith-based Radicalism. (pp. 131-137) In C. Timmerman, Hutsebaut, D., Mels, S., Nonneman, W., Van Herck, W. (Ed.), *Faith-Based Radicalism: Christianity, Islam and Judaism between Constructive Activism and Destructive Fanaticism*. Brussels: P.I.E. Peter Lang.

Kubiak, H. (1982). *The Polish National Catholic Church In The United States of America From 1897 to 1980*. Kraków: PWN/Uniwersytet Jagielloński.

Kuisma, M. (2001, 28-30th June). *Globalisation and Citizenship – The Impossible Equation?* Paper presented at the MultiLevel Governance – Interdisciplinary Perspectives, Sheffield.

Kuyssche, N. (21.10.2004). L'exception maroxelloise. *La Tribune de Bruxelles*.

Kymlicka, W. (1995). *Multicultural Citizenship*. Oxford: Oxford University Press.

Lacroix, J. (2002). For a European constitutional patriotism. *Political Studies, 50*(5), 944-958.

La Libre Belgique (2007, 21 May). Les Marocains dépassent les Italiens. *La Libre Belgique*.

Lambert, P.-Y. (1999). *La participation politique des allochtones en Belgique - Historique et situation bruxelloise*. Louvain-la-Neuve: Academia-Bruylant.

Lapidus, I. M. (1975). The separation of state and religion in the development of early Islamic society. *International Journal of Middle East Studies, 6*(4), 363-385.

Lapidus, I. M. (1988). *History of Islamic Societies*. Cambridge: CUP.

Lash, S. (1994). Reflexivity and its doubles: structure, aesthetics, community. In U. Beck, Giddens, A. and Lash, S. (Ed.), *Reflexive modernization. Politics, tradition and aesthetics in the modern social order*. Cambridge: Polity Press.

Lash, S. (1999). *Another Modernity, A Different Rationality*. Oxford: Blackwell.

Lathion, S. (2003). *Musulmans d'Europe: l'émergence d'une identité citoyenne*. Paris: L'Harmattan.

Leach, E. (1976). *Culture and Communication: the logic by which symbols are connected*. Cambridge: Cambridge University Press

Le Bars, S. (2007, 19 December). Jeune, cadre sup' et pèlerin à La Mecque. *Le Monde*.

Leca, J. (1986). Individualisme et citoyenneté. In P. Birnbaum (Ed.), *Sur l'indyvidualisme* (pp. 159-212). Paris: Presses de la FNSP.

Leca, J. (1992). Questions on Citizenship. In C. Mouffe (Ed.), *Dimensions of Radical Democracy*. London: Verso.

Leeke, M., Sear, Ch., Gay, O. (2003). An introduction to devolution in the UK. *Research Paper of the Library of House of Commons, 3*(84).

Leman, J., Renaerts, M. (1996) Dialogues at different institutional levels among authorities and Muslims in Belgium. In Shadid, W.A., Van Koningsveld, P. S. (Ed.) *Muslims in the Margin: Political Responses to the Presence of Islam in Western Europe*. Kampen: Kok Pharos. 164-181.

Laporte, C. (2008). L'Eglise ne fait plus recette. *La Libre*. 9th July.

Le Soir (2004). *L'Europe de bonne foi*. 10th December.

Lesthaeghe, R. (Ed.). (2000). *Communities and generations: Turkish and Moroccan populations in Belgium*. Bruxelles: NIDI/CBGS Pubications.

Leveau, R., Mohsen-Finan, K. and Withol de Wenden K. ed. (2002) *New European Identity and Citizenship*. London: Ashgate.

Lesthaeghe, R. (Ed.). (2000). *Communities and generations: Turkish and Moroccan populations in Belgium*. Bruxelles: NIDI/CBGS Publications.

Lewin, K. (1947). Group decision and social change. In: T.M. Newcomb and E.L. Hartley, Editors, *Reading in social psychology*. New York: Holt.

Lewin, K. (1948). *Resolving Social Conflicts: Selected Papers on Group Dynamics*. New York: Harper.

Lewin, R. (1997). *La Belgique et ses immigrés*. Bruxelles: De Boeck.

Lewis, P. (1994, 2002). *Islamic Britain*. London: I B Tauris & Co Ltd.

Lewis, P. (2005). Muslims in Europe: Managing Multiple Identities and Learning Shared Citizenship. *Political Theology, 6*(3).

Lewis, P. (2006). Only connect: can the ulema address the crisis in the transmission of Islam to a new generation of South Asians in Britain? *Contemporary South Asia, 15*(2), 165 - 180.

Lister, R. (1997). *Citizenship: Feminist Perspectives*. London: Macmillan.

Lister, R., Smith, N., Middleton, S., Cox, L. (2002). *Negotiating Transitions to Citizenship*. Loughborough: CRSP, University of Loughborough.

Lister, R., Smith, N., Middleton, S., Cox, L. (2003). Young People Talk about Citizenship: Empirical Perspectives on Theoretical and Political Debates. *Citizenship Studies, 7*(2), 235-253.

Lister, R., Smith, N., Middleton, S., Cox, L. (2005). Young people talking about citizenship in Britain. In N. Kabeer (Ed.), *Inclusive Citizenship*. London: Zed Books. Lovens 2006

Lijphart, A. ed. (1971) *World politics : the writings of theorists and practitioners, classical and modern*. Boston (Mass.): Allyn and Bacon.

Loobuyck, P. (2007). *The Position of Religious Arguments in Political Decision-Making: the discussion in contemporary political philosophy*. Paper presented at the Religion in Post-Secular Age: Public or Private?, Budapest 1-2 February.

Lowndess, V. (2000). Women and Social Capital: A Comment on Hall's Social Capital in Britain. *European Journal of Political Science* 30: 533-540

Lubeck, P. (1995). *Globalization and the Islamist Movement*. Unpublished paper, Department of Sociology, Santa Cruz: University Of California.

Luhmann, N. (1995). *Social Systems*. Stanford: Stanford University Press.

Mach, Z. (1993). *Symbols, Conflict and Identity*. Albany: SUNY.

Malik, M. (2003). Accommodating Muslims in Europe: Opportunities for Minority Fiqh. *ISIM Newsletter, 13*.

Malik, N. (2000). *The East London Mosque - Organising in Action*. London: The Citizen Organising Foundation.

Malik, N. (2004). 'Friends, Romans, Countrymen?' In S. Seddon (Ed.), *'British Muslims Between Assimilation and Segregation'*. Leicester: Islamic Foundation.

Manço, A. (2006). Arret sur les niveux de lecture. *Agenda Interculturel, 245*.

Manço, U. (2000). *Voix et voies musulmanes de Belgique*. Bruxelles: Publications des Facultés Universitaires Saint-Louis.

Manço, U. (2001). Populations musulmanes de Belgique et la stratification du marche du travail. *Revue Quebec*.

Manço, U. (2004). Musulmans et islam en Belgique, in *La Lettre de D'un Monde à l'Autre*, no. 7, Juin

Manço, A., Manço, U. (2000). Religiosité et rapport à l'intégration de jeunes hommes issus de l'immigration. In Manço, U., *Voix et voies musulmanes de Belgique*. Bruxelles: Publications des Facultés universitaires Saint-Louis. 167-188

Manço, U., & Kanmaz, M. (2005). From Conflict to Co-operation Between Muslims and Local Authorities in a Brussels Borough: Schaerbeek. *Journal of Ethnic and Migration Studies, 31*, 1105-1123.

Mandaville, P. (2001). Reimagining Islam in Diaspora: The Politics of Mediated Community. *International Communication Gazette, 63*(2-3), 169-186.

Mandaville, P. (2003). What does Progressive Islam look like? *ISIM Newsletter, 12*, 34-35.

Mandaville, P. (2004). *Transnational Muslim Politics: Reimaging the Umma*. New York: Routledge.

Mann, M. (1987). The Ruling Class Strategy and Citizenship. *Sociology, 21*, 339-354.

Maréchal, B. coord. *(2002) L'islam et les musulmans dans l'Europe élargie: radoscopie*. Louvain-La-Neuve: Academia Bruylant.

Maréchal, B. (2006). Les Frères Musulmans européens, ou la construction des processus locaux et globaux. *Recherches sociologique et anthropologiques, 37*(2), 19-34.

Maréchal, B. (2008). *The Strength of the Brothers – Roots and discourses of the Muslim Brotherhood in Europe*. Leiden: Brill.

Maréchal, B., Allievi, S., Dassetto, F., Nielsen, J. (Ed.). (2003). *Muslims in the Enlarged Europe*. Leiden - Boston: Brill.

Marienstras, R. (1989). On the Notion of Diaspora. In G. Chaliand (Ed.), *Minority Peoples in the Age of Nation-States*. London: Pluto.

Marshal T.H (1950, 1992). *Citizenship and Social Class*. Cambridge: Cambridge University Press.

Martens, A. (1976). *Les immigrés: flux et reflux d'une main-d'oeuvre d'appoint: la politique belge de l'immigration de 1945 à 1970*. Louvain-La-Neuve: EVO.

Martens, A. (1990). L'insertion des immigrés dans l'emploi. In A. Bastanier, Dassetto, F. (Ed.), *Immigration et nouveaux pluralismes*. Bruxelles: De Boeck.

Martens, A. (2005). Ethnostratification du marche de l'eploi. *Agenda interculturel*. No 236, Octobre.

Martens, A., Vertommen, S., Verhoeven, H., Ouali, N., Dryon, Ph. (2005). *Discriminations des personnes d'origine étrangère sur le marché du travail de la Région de Bruxelles-Capitale*. Bruxelles: ORBEM.

Martinelli, A. (2004). *Global Modernisation: Rethinking the Project of Modernity*. London: Sage.

Martiniello, M. (1988). Elites, leadership et pouvoir dans les communautes ethniques d'origine immigrée. *Sybidi Papers n° 1*. Louvain-la-Neuve: Academia

Martiniello, M. (1992). *Leadership et pouvoir dans les communautés d'origine immigrée*. Paris: CIEMI: L'Harmattan.

Martiniello, M. (Ed.). (1998). *Multicultural policies and the state: a comparison of two European societies*. Oxford: Oxford University Press.

Martiniello, M. (2001). *La citoyenneté à l'aube du 21ᵉ siecle*. Bruxelles: Fondation Roi Baudouin.

Martiniello, M., Swyngedouw, M. (Ed.). (1998). *O ù va la Belgique? Les soubresauts d'une petite démocratie européenne*. Paris: L'Harmattan.

Marzec, J. (1998). *The Role of the Polish Roman Catholic Church in the Polish Community of the UK - A Study in Ethnic Identity and Religion*. Community Religion Projects, The University of Leeds.

Masood, E. (2005, August). A Muslim Journey. *Prospect*.

Masood, E. (2006). *British Muslims: Media Guide*. London: British Council.

Matthews, R., Tlemsani, I. (2004). Islamic Banking and Mortgage Markets in the UK. In B. Shanmugam, Perumal, V. and Hanuum Ridzwa, A. (Ed.), *Islamic Banking: An International Perspective*: University Putra Malaysia Press.

McAdam, D. (1999). *Political Process and the Development of Black Insurgency, 1930-1970*. Chicago: University of Chicago Press.

McAdam, D., McCarthy, J. D., Zald, M.N. (1996). *Comparative Perspectives on Social Movements: Political Opportunities, Mobilizing Structures, and Cultural Framings*. Cambridge: CUP.

MCB. (2007). *Meeting the Needs of Muslim Pupils in State Schools*. London: Muslim Council of Britain.

McConnell, M. W. (2000). Believers as Equal Citizens. In N. L. Rosenblum (Ed.), *Obligations of Citizenship and Demands of Faith: Religious Accommodation in Pluralist Democracies* (pp. 90-110). Princeton: Princeton University Press.

McCutcheon, Russell T., ed. (1999). *The Insider/Outsider Problem in the Study of Religion*. London and New York: Cassell.

McGrory, D., Hussain, Z. (2005, 14 July). New wave of British terrorists are taught at schools, not in the mountains. *The Times*.

McKinnon, C., Hampsher-Monk, Iain. (Ed.). (2000). *The Demands of Citizenship*. London/New York: Continuum.

McLoughlin, S. (1997). *'Breaking in to bounded Britain': discrepant representations of belonging and Muslims in Bradford*. Unpublished PhD, University of Manchester, Manchester.

McLoughlin, S. (2005). The State, New Muslim Leaderships and Islam as a Resource for Public Engagement in Britain. In J. Cesari, Mcloughlin, S. (Ed.), *European Muslims and the Secular State*. London: Ashgate.

Mead, G. H. (1967). *Mind, Self and Society from the Standpoint of a Social Behaviorist*. Chicago: Chicago University Press.

Mirza, M., Senthilkumaran, A., Ja'far, Z. (2007). *Living Apart Together: British Muslims and the paradox of multiculturalism*: Policy Exchange.

Modood, T. (1992). *Not Easy Being British: Colour, Culture and Citizenship*. London: Runnymede Trust/Trentham Books.

Modood, T. (Ed.). (1997). *Church, State & Religious Minorities*. London: Policy Studies Institute.

Modood, T. (2000). Anti-Essentialism, Multiculturalism, and the 'Recognition' of Religious Groups. In W. Kymlicka, Norman, W. (Ed.), *Citizenship in Diverse Societies*. Oxford: Oxford University Press.

Modood, T. (2001). British Asian Identities: Something Old, Something Borrowed, Something New. In D. Morley, Robins, K. (Ed.), *British Cultural Studies* (pp. 67-78). Oxford: OUP.

Modood, T. (2003). Muslim and the Politics of Difference. In S. Spencer (Ed.), *The Politics of Migration: Managing Opportunity, Conflict and Change*. London: Blackwell Publishing.

Modood, T. (2004). Multiculturalism, Muslims and the British State. In S. J. Sutcliffe (Ed.), *Religion: Empirical Studies*: Ashgate.

Modood, T. (2006). British Muslims and the Politics of Muliticulturalism. In: Modood, T., Triandafyllidou, A., Zapata-Borrero, R. (Ed.). (2006). *Multiculturalism, Muslims and Citizenship: a European Approach*. London: Routledge.

Modood, T. (2007). *Multiculturalism: A Civic Idea*. London: Polity.

Modood, T., Berthoud, R. (1997). *Ethnic Minorities in Britain - Diversity and Disadvantage*. London: Policy Studies Institute.

Modood, T., Triandafyllidou, A., Zapata-Borrero, R. (Ed.). (2006). *Multiculturalism, Muslims and Citizenship: a European Approach*. London: Routledge.

Mohr, I. (2002). Self-positioning and Islamic instruction in Germany. *ISIM Newsletter, 9*(29).

Mohr, I. (2002a). Islamic Instruction in Austria and Germany. *CEMOTI*, N° 33

Mohsen-Finan, K. (2002). Promoting A Faith-based Citizenship: The Case of Tariq Ramadan. In R. Leveau, Withol de Wenden, C., Mohsen-Finan, K. (Ed.), *New European Identity and Citizenship*. London: Ashgate.

Mol, H. (1976). *Identity and the Sacred*. Oxford: Basil Blackwell.

Monette, P.-Y., Laporte, Ch.,. (2007). *Belgique - ou vas-tu?* Bruxelles: Mardaga.

Monsma, S., Sopper, J.Ch. (1997). *The Challenge of Pluralism. Church and State in Five Democracies*. New York: Rowman & Littlefield.

Montanari, I. (2001). Modernization, Globalization and the Welfare State: A Comparative Analysis of Old and New Convergence of Social Insurance Since 1930, *British Journal of Sociology* 52(3): 469-494

Morelli, A., Schreiber, J-P.,. (1995). Are the Immigrants the Last Belgians? In K. Deprez, Vos, L. (Ed.), *Nationanalism in Belgium: Shifting Identities*. New York: St. Martin's Press.

Mouffe, C. (Ed.). (1992). *Dimensions of Radical Democracy*. London: Verso.

Mousaoui, J. (Ed.). (2006). *Mariages endomixtes marocains. Du chant des sirènes aux alliances éclatées*. Paris: l'Harmattan.

Murray, A., German, L. (2005). *Stop the War: The Story of Britain's Biggest Mass Movement*. London: Bookmarks.

Neels, K. (2000). Education and the transition to employment: young Turkish and Moroccan adults in Belgium. In R. Lesthaeghe (Ed.), *Communities and Generations: Turkish and Moroccan populations in Belgium*. Brussels: VUB University Press.

Neels, K., Stoop, R. (2000). Reassessing the ethnic gap: employment of younger Turks and Moroccans in Belgium. In R. Lesthaeghe (Ed.), *Communities and Generations: Turkish and Moroccan Populations in Belgium*. Brussels: VUB University Press.

Newman, S. (1996). *Ethnoregional Conflict in Democracies: Mostly Ballots, Rarely Bullets*. Westport: Greenwood Press. Nicaise, I., Groenez, S., Vleminckx, K., Demeuse, M., Berghman, J. (2003). *The Belgian National Action Plan for Social Inclusion 2001-2003: a preliminary evaluation*. Leuven: KULeuven.

Nielsen, J. S. (1979). *Forms and problems of legal recognition for Muslims in Europe*. Birmingham: Centre for the Study of Islam and Christian-Muslim Relations.

Nielsen, J. S. (1984). *Muslim settlement in Britain*. Birmingham: Centre for the Study of Islam and Christian-Muslim Relations.

Nielsen, J. (1992, 2004). *Muslim in Western Europe*. Edinburgh: Edinburgh University Press

Nielsen, J. S., Dassetto, F. (2003). Conclusions. In B. Maréchal, Allievi, S., Dassetto, F., Nielsen, J. (Ed.), *Muslims in the Enlarged Europe*. Leiden - Bostonm: Brill.

Nussbaum, M.C. (1994). Patriotism and Cosmopolitanism. *Boston Review* 19(5) 3–34

Nyman, A.-S. (2005). *Intolerance and Discrimination against Muslims in the EU*: Report of International Helsinki Federation.

Office for National Statistics, www.statistics.gov.uk

Okin, S., M. (1999). *Is Multiculturalism Bad for Women?* In: Is Multiculturalism Bad for Women? Susan Moller Okin with Respondents, red. J. Cohen et. al., Princeton, New Jersey: Princeton University Press.

Okkerse, L., Termote, A. (2004). Singularité des étrangers sur le marché de l'emploi: à propos des travailleurs allochtones en Belgique. *Etudes statistiques, 111.*

Oldfield, M. (1990). *Citizenship and Community: Civic Republicanism and the Modern Ideology*. London: Routledge.

Ortmans, J. (1996). *La place de l'islam dans la construction identitaire chez les jeunes issus de l'immigration maghrébine*. Louvain-la-neuve, UCL, Mémoire de licence en sociologie.

OSI. (2002). *Monitoring Minority Protection in the EU: The Situation of Muslims in the UK*. Budapest: Open Society Institute.

OSI. (2005). *Muslims in the UK: Policies for the Engaged Citizens*. Budapest: Open Society Institute.

446

O'Sullivan, J. (2001, 8 October). 'If you hate the west, emigrate to a Muslim country'. *The Guardian*.
Ouali, N. (2000). Affirmation de soi et sécularisation des identités musulmanes. In: Manço, U. *Voix et voies musulmanes de Belgique*. Bruxelles: Publications des facultés universitaires saint-Louis: pp. 189-194.
Pakulski, J. (1997). Cultural Citizenship. *Citizenship Studies, 1*, 73-86.
Panafit, L. (1997). Les problematique de l'institutionalisation de l'islam en Belgique (1965-1996). In F. Dassetto, Allievi, S. (Ed.), *Facettes de l'islam belge*. Louvain-La-Neuve: Academia-Bruylant.
Panafit, L. (1999). *Quand le droit écrit l'Islam. L'intégration juridique de l'Islam en Belgique*. Bruxelles: Bruylant.
Panafit, L. (2003). Ethnicité et citoyenneté dans l'espace public belge. In R. Leveau, Withol de Wenden, C., Mohsen-Finan, K. (Ed.), *De la citoyenneté locale*. Paris: IFRI.
Parekh, B. (1997). Religion and Public Life. In T. Modood (Ed.), *Church, State and Religious Minorities*. London: PSI.
Parekh, B. (2005). British Commitments. *Prospect Magazine, 114*(September).
Parekh, B. (2006). Europe, liberalism and the 'Muslim question'. In T. Modood, Triandafyllidou, A., Zapata-Borrero, R. (Ed.), *Multiculturalism, Muslims and Citizenship: a European Approach*. London: Routledge.
Parker-Jenkins, M., Haw, K. F., Irving, B.A., Khan, S. (1999). Double Discrimination: An Examination of the Career Destinations of Muslim Women in Britain. *Advancing Women in Leadership, 2*(1).
Parrin, N., Poulain, M. (2002). *Italiens de Belgique: Analyses socio-démographiques et analyse des appartenances*: Academia Bruylant.
Pauly, R. J. (2004). *Islam in Europe: integration or marginalization?* Aldershot: Ashgate.
Pattie, C., Seyd, P., Whiteley, P. (2004). *Citizenship in Britain. Values, Participation and Democracy*: Oxford University Press.
Paxman, J. (1999). *The English: Portrait of a People*. London: Penguin Books Ltd.
Peach, C. (2000). *Plural Societies - Multi Cultural Cities*. Working Paper no. 12, School of Geography, University of Oxford.
Peach, C., Glebe, G. (1995). Muslim Minorities in Western Europe. *Journal of Ethnic and Racial Studies* 18(1), 26–45.
Peach, C., Vertovec, S. ed. (1997). *Islam in Europe - the Politics of Religion and Community*. University of Warwick.
Pedersen, L. (1999). *Newer Islamic Movements in Western Europe*. Aldershot: Ashgate.
Pędziwiatr, K. (2003). Islam amongst the Pakistanis in Britain: the Interrelationship Between Ethnicity and Religion. In M. Marczewska-Rytko (Ed.), *Religion in a Changing Europe: Between Pluralism and Fundamentalism*. Lublin: Marie Curie-Sklodowska University Press.
Pędziwiatr, K. (2003a, 11 September). Nielojalni poddani królowej.*(Disloyal Subjects of the Queen) Rzeczpospolita*.
Pędziwiatr, K. (2004). Umiarkowany reformator, czy podstępny ekstremista, (Moderate Reformist or Sneaky Extremist), *Rzeczpospolita*, September 16.
Pędziwiatr, K. (2005). *Od islamu imigrantów do islamu obywateli: Muzułmanie w krajach Europy Zachodniej, (From Islam of Immigrants to Islam of Citizens: Muslims in the Countries of Western Europe)*. Kraków: Nomos.
Pędziwiatr, K. (2005b, 8 August). Islam przeciw bombom (Islam Against the Bombs). *Gazeta Wyborcza*.
Pędziwiatr, K. (2005c). Kraj, którego nie będzie? *Polskie Radio*.
Pędziwiatr, K. (2006). New Muslim Elites in the City. *ISIM Newsletter, 18*(Autumn), 24-25.
Pędziwiatr, K. (2006a). Mahomet, i żarty na bok. *Polish Radio*.

Pędziwiatr, K. (2006b). Religijny wymiar wolności i społecznego zaangażowania wsród młodych muzułmanek w Belgii i Wielkiej Brytanii. In K. Leszczyńska, Kościańska, A. (Ed.), *Kobiety i religie*. Kraków: Nomos.

Pędziwiatr, K. (2006c, 10 January). Szejk globalny. *Polish Radio*.

Pędziwiatr, K. (2006d). *What Muslims Want from Europe?*, from http://www.arabia.pl/english/content/view/39/16/

Pędziwiatr, K. (2006e, 09 May). Islam po europejsku. *Rzeczpospolita - Dodatek 'Półksiężyc nad Europa'*.

Pędziwiatr, K. (2006f, 09 May). Konflikt o chusty. *Rzeczpospolita - Dodatek 'Półksiężyc nad Europa'*.

Pędziwiatr, K. (2006g). Muzułmański radykalizm w Europie: główne tropy badawcze oraz cechy radykalnego dyskursu muzułmańskiego. *Bliski Wschód: społeczeństwa - polityka - tradycje, 3*(3). 47-64

Pędziwiatr, K. (2007). Muslims in Europe: Demography and Organizations. In Y. Samad, Kasturi, S. (Ed.), *Islam in the European Union*: Oxford University Press.

Pędziwiatr, K. (2007a). Creating New Discursive Arenas and Influencing the Policies of the State: Case of the Muslim Council of Britain. *Social Compass, 54*(1).

Pędziwiatr, K. (2007b). Public Mobilisation of Islam in Europe. Possible Outcomes of the Activism within Student Islamic Societies. In C. Timmerman, Hutsebaut, D., Mels, S., Nonneman, W., Van Herck, W. (Ed.), *Faith-Based Radicalism: Christianity, Islam and Judaism between Constructive Activism and Destructive Fanaticism*. Brussels: P.I.E. Peter Lang.

Pędziwiatr, K. (2007c). Religion and Active Social Citizenship Amongst Professional Muslim Londoners. *Journal of Moving Communities, 7*(1), 3-22.

Pędziwiatr, K. (2008). *Publicising, Secularizing and Integrating Islam in Europe*. Paper presented at the Religion and Democracy in Contemporary Europe, Jerusalem.

Pędziwiatr, K., Górak-Sosnowska, K., Kubicki, P. (Ed.). (2006). *Islam i obywatelskosc w Europie (Islam and Citizenship in Europe)*. Warszawa: Elipsa.

Pędziwiatr, K. (2007a). Creating New Discursive Arenas and Influencing the Policies of the State: Case of the Muslim Council of Britain. *Social Compass, 54*(1).

Perrin, N., Poulain, M. (2002) Italiens de Belgique. Analyses socio-démographiques et analyse des appartenances. Sybidi Papers, 28, Louvain-la-Neuve: Academia.

Peter, F. (2006). Individualization and Religious Authority in Western European Islam. *Muslim World, 96*(4).

Peter, F., & Arigita, E. (2006). A special issue: Authorizing Islam in Europe: Introduction. *Muslim World, 96*(4), 537-542.

Pfaff, S., & Gill, A. J. (2006). Will a million Muslims march? Muslim interest organizations and political integration in Europe. *Comparative Political Studies, 39*(7), 803-828.

Phalet, K., Krekels, B. (1998). Immigration et Intégration. In: Martiniello, M., Swyngedouw, M. (éd.), *Où Va la Belgique? Les Soubresauts d'une Petite Démocratie Européenne*. Paris: L'Harmattan.

Phalet, K., Orkeny, A. (Ed.). (2001). *Ethnic Minorities and Inter-Ethnic Relations in Context: A Dutch-Hungarian Comparison*. Aldershot: Ashgate.

Phalet, K., Swyngedouw, M. (2001). Les représentations sociales de la citoyenneté et de la nationalité : une comparaison entre immigrés turcs et marocains et Belges peu scolarisés à Bruxelles. *Revue Internationale de Politique Comparée*.

Phalet, K., Swyngedouw, M. (2002). National identities and representations of citizenship: A comparison of Turks, Moroccans and working-class Belgians in Brussels. *Ethnicities, 2*(1), 5-30.

Phalet, K., ter Wal, J., van Praag, C. (2004). *Moslim in Nederland. Een onderzoek naar de religieuze betrokkenheid van Turken en Marokkanen. Samenvatting.*: Den Haag: SCP-Ercomer.

Philips, M. (2006). *Londonistan: How Britain is Creating a Terror State Within.* London: Gibson Square Books Ltd.

Pietrzyk, D. (2001). Civil Society - Conceptual History From Hobbes To Marx, *Marie Curie Working Paper.* Penglais: University of Wales.

Pilkington, C. (2002). *Devolution in Britain Today:* Manchester University Press.

Piscatori, J. (2000). *Islam, Islamists and the Electoral Principle in the Middle East.* Leiden: ISIM.

Pocock, J. G. A. (1992). The Ideal of Citizenship since Classical Times. *Queen's Quarterly, 99,* 33-55.

Portes, A. (1998). The *Two Meanings of Social Capital,* Sociological Forum, Volume 15, Issue 1, Mar 2000, Pages 1 – 12

Portillo, M. (2005, 17 July). Multiculturalism has failed but tolerance can save us. *The Times.*

Poole, E. (2002). *Reporting Islam: Media Representations of British Muslims.* London: Tauris.

Poulter, S. M. (1986). *English law and ethnic minority customs.* London: Butterworth.

Présence Musulmane. (2007). *Musulmanes féministes: du paradoxe à la réalité.* Bruxelles: Présence Musulmane.

Price, D. T. W. (1990). *A History of the Church in Wales in the Twentieth Century:* Church in Wales Publications.

Purdam, K. (1996). Settler Political Participation: Muslim Local Councillors. In W. A. R. Shadid, van Koningsveld, P.S. (Ed.), *Political participation and identities of Muslims in non-Muslim states.* Kampen: Kok Pharos.

Putnam, R. (2000). *Bowling Alone: The Collapse and revival of American Community.* London: Simon & Schuster.

Qur'an - in the translation of Mohammed Marmaduke Pickthall available on http://www.sacred-texts.com/isl/pick/index.htm

Radcliffe, L. (2003). *A Muslim Lobby at Whitehall? Examining the Role of the Muslim Minority in British Foreign Policymaking.* University of Oxford, Oxford.

Raedt, T. (2004). Muslims in Belgium: A Case Study of Emerging Identities. *Journal of Muslim Affairs, 24*(1), 9-30.

Ramadan, T. (1999). *To Be a European Muslim.* Leicester: The Islamic Foundation.

Ramadan, T. (2001). *Islam, the West and the Challenges of Modernity.* Leicester: The Islamic Foundation.

Ramadan, T. (2003, 6 June). *Islam, Citizenship and Social Justice.* Paper presented at the Islam and Social Justice, British Council in London.

Ramadan, T. (2004). *Western Muslims and the Future of Islam, .* Oxford: Oxford University Press.

Ramadan, T. (2006). *Manifesto for the new 'We',* from http://www.tariqramadan.com/article.php3?id_article=743&lang=en

Ramadan, T. (2006a) Być blisko Boga walcząc o swoje prawa. In: Pędziwiatr, K., Górak-Sosnowska, K., Kubicki, P. (Ed.). (2006). *Islam i obywatelskość w Europie (Islam and Citizenship in Europe).* Warszawa: Elipsa.

Rashid, A. A. (2007). Mission of the Reformed: The Founding of the Central Council of Ex-Muslims. *Qantara.de.*

Rath, J., Groenendijk, K., Penninx, R. (1991). The recognition and institutionalisation of Islam in Belgium, Great Britain and the Netherlands. *New Community, 18*(1), 101-114.

Rath, J., Penninx, K., Groenendijk i Mayer, A. (2001) Western Europe and Its Islam. The Social Reaction to the Institutionalization of a 'New' Religion in the Netherland, Belgium and United Kingdom. W: *International Comparative Studies Series.* 2. Leiden: Brill.

449

Rea, A. (1993). La construction de la politique d'integration des populations d'origine etrangere en Belgique. In M. Martiniello, Poncelet, M. (Ed.), *Migrations et minorite ethnique.*

Rea, A. (1995). Social Citizenship and Ethnic Minorities in the European Union. In M. Martiniello (Ed.), *Migration, Citizenship and Ethno-National Identities in the European Union.* Aldershot: Avebury.

Rea, A. (1997). Mouvements sociaux. In M. T. Coenen, and Lewin, R. (Ed.), *La Belgique et ses immigres - Les politiques monquees.* Bruxelles.

Rea, A. (1999). La reconnaissance et la représentation de l'Islam. *L'ANNÉE SOCIALE 1999.*

Rea, A. (2001). *Jeunes immigrés dans la cité: protestation collective, acteurs locaux et politiques publiques.* Bruxelles: Éditions Labor.

Rea, A. (2002). Les jeunes d'origine immigrés : intégrés et discriminés. *Working paper presented during the seminar at CEDEM.*

Rea, A. (2004). Les politiques d'integration des immigres dans la Region de Bruxelles-Capitale: entre social et securitaire. In P. Delwit, Rea, A., Swyngedouw, M. (Ed.), *Droits et devoirs de la citoyennete dans une societe interculturelle.*

Reid, A. (2006, 30th April). Britons Support Monarchy. *The Sun.*

Remennick, L. (2007). Transnationalism. In B. Ritzer (Ed.), *Blackwell Encyclopedia of Sociology*: Blackwell.

Renaerts, M. (1998). Belgique: l'enseignement de la religion islamique. In Messner, F., Vierling, J-M., *L'enseignement religieux à l'école publique.* Strasbourg: Oberlin. pp. 105-118

Renaerts, M. (1999) *Elections in the Muslim Community of Belgium,* ISIM Newsletter, 2, s. 26, Leiden.

Rex, J. (1991) *Ethnic Identity and Ethnic Mobilisation in Britain,* Research Monographs, Warwick, CRER, No. 5

Rex, J. (1998). Multiculturalism and political integration in Europe. In M. Martiniello (Ed.), *Multicultural policies and the state: a comparison of two European societies.* Utrecht: ERCOMER.

Richards, C. (2003). *Citizenship and Christianity.* London: Kevin Mayhew LTD.

Roald, A.-S. (2001). *Women in Islam: The Western Experience.* New York: Routledge.

Roberts, K.A. (1984) *Religion in Sociological Perspective.* California: The Dorsey Press.

Roosens, E. (1989). *Creating Ethnicity : The Process of Ethnogenesis.* Newbury Park: Sage Publications.

Roosens, E. (Ed.). (1995). *Rethinking Culture, 'Multicultural Society' and the School.* Oxford: Pergamon Press.

Roosens, E. (1998). Multicultural society : the case of Flemish Brussels. In M. Martiniello (Ed.), *Multicultural policies and the state: a comparison of two European societies.* Oxford: Oxford University Press.

Rosaldo, R. (1994). Cultural Citizenship and Educational Democracy. *Cultural Anthropology, 9*(3), 402-411.

Rosenblum, N. L. (Ed.). (2000). *Obligations of Citizenship and Demands of Faith: Religious Accommodation in Pluralist Democracies.* New Jersey: Princeton University Press.

Rossman, G. B., & Rallis, S. F. (2003). *Learning in the field: An introduction to qualitative research,* Thousand Oaks, CA: Sage Publications.

Roy, O. (1994). *The Failure of Political Islam.* Cambridge Massachusetts: Harvard University Press.

Roy, O. (1999). *Vers un islam européen.* Paris: Esprit.

Roy, O. (2000). L'individualisation de l'islam européen contemporain. In: Dassetto F., Ed., *Paroles de l'islam.* Paris: Maisonneuve & Larose.

Roy, O. (2002). *L'islam mondialisé.* Paris: Editions du Seuil.

Roy, O. (2003). EuroIslam: the jihad within? *National Interest* (Spring).

Roy, O. (2004). *Globalised Islam. The Search for a new Ummah.* London: Hurst & Company.

Runnymede Trust (1997). *Islamophobia a challenge for us all*. London
Rutledge, P. (1985). *The role of Religion in Ethnic Self Identity: A Vietnamese Community in Oklahoma*. New York: New York University Press.
Rzeczpospolita (2005a). *Europejczycy dyskryminują muzułmanów*, 8 marca.
Rzeczpospolita (2005b). „*Europejczycy dyskryminują muzułmanów*", 17 marca.
Sacranie, I. (2006). *Velidactory Speech of the Secretary General of the Muslim Council of Britain*, available on: http://www.mcb.org.uk/uploads/SECGEN.pdf
Saggar, S. (1998). A Late, Though Not Lost, Opportunity: Ethnic Minority Electors, Party Strategy and the Conservative Party. *The Political Quarterly, 69*(2), 148-159.
Said E. (1997). *Covering Islam: how the media and the experts determine how we see the rest of the world*, New York: Vintage Books.
Said, E. (2001). *Power, Politics, and Culture*. New York: Pantheon.
Samad, Y. (1996). The Politics of Islamic identity among Bangladeshis and Pakistanis in Britain. In T. Ranger, Samad, Y., Stuart, O. (Ed.), *Culture, Identity and Politics. Ethnic Minorities in Britain*. London: Avebury.
Sander, Å. (2003). Muslims in Sweden, Country report for the MusPol Research Project: *State policies towards Muslim minorities in the European Union*, available on http://www.emz-berlin.de/projekte/pdf/Muslims_in_Schweden.pdf
Sardar, Z. (2005). *Desperately Seeking Paradise: Journeys of a Sceptical Muslim*. London: Granta Books.
Sardar, Z. (2005a, 25 July). Beyond blame and shame: what we must do now. *New Statement*.
Sardar, Z., Davies, M.W. (1990) *Distorted Imagination: Lessons from the Rushdie Affair*. London: Berita.
Saroglou, V. (2007). *The attitudes of Belgians towards hijab*. Louvain-la-Neuve.
Sassen, S. (1991). *The Global City : New York, London, Tokyo*. New York: Princeton University Press.
Sassen, S. (2002). The Repositioning of Citizenship: Emergent Subjects and Spaces for Politics. *Berkeley Journal of Sociology, 46*, 4-25.
Saunders, P. (1996). *Unequal but Fair? A Study of Class Barriers in Britain*. London: IEA Health and Welfare Unit.
Sayad, A. (1984). Les effets culturels de l'émigration, un enjeu de luttes sociales. *Annuaire de l'Afrique du Nord, 23*, 383-397.
Sayad, A. (1988). La 'faute' de l'absence ou les effets de l'immigration. *Anthropologica medica, 4*, 5-69.
Sayad, A. (1991). *L'immigration ou Les paradoxes de l'altérité*. Bruxelles: De Boeck-Wesmael.
Sayad, A. (1999). *La Double absence: des illusions de l'émigré aux souffrances de l'immigré*. Paris: Editions du Seuil.
Sayad, A. (2004). *The Suffering of the Immigrant*. London: Polity.
Sayyid, B. (1997). *A Fundamental Fear: Eurocentrism and the Emergence of Islamism*. London: Zed Books.
Schiffauer, W. (1999). Islamism in the Diaspora: The Fascination of Political Islam Among Second Generation German Turks. *ESRC Transnational Communities Programme*
Schiffauer, W. (2000). *Die Gottesmänner. Türkische Islamisten in Deutschland. Eine Studie zur Herstellung religiöser Evidenz*. Frankfurt am Main: Suhrkamp.
Schiffauer, W. (2006). Enemies within the gates: The debate about the citizenship of Muslims in Germany. In T. Modood, Triandafyllidou, A., Zapata-Borrero, R. (Ed.), *Multiculturalism, Muslims and Citizenship: a European Approach*. London: Routledge.
Schmidt di Frieberg, O. (2002). Being Muslim in the Italian Public Sphere: Islamic Organisations in Turin and Trieste. In: Shadid, W.A.R., van Koningsveld S., red., *Intercultural Relations and Religious Authorities: Muslims in the European Union*, Leuven, Peeters.

451

Seddon, M., Hussain, D., Malik, N. (Ed.). (2003). *British Muslims: Loyalty and Belonging.* Leicester: The Islamic Foundation and Citizen Organising Foundation.

Seddon, M., Hussain, D., Malik, N. (Ed.). (2004). *British Muslims Between Assimilation and Segregation.* Leicester: The Islamic Foundation.

Sennett, R. (1998). *The corrosion of character : the personal consequences of work in the new capitalism.* New York: Norton.

Sennet, R. (2003). *Respect: The Formation of Character in an Age of Inequality.* London: Allen Lane.

Shadid, W. A. R., van Koningsveld, P.S. (Ed.). (1991). *The Integration of Islam and Hinduism in Europe.* Kampen: Kok Pharos.

Shadid, W. A. R., van Koningsveld, P.S. (Ed.). (1995). *Religious Freedom and the position of Islam in Western Europe. Opportunities and obstacles in the acquisition of equal rights.* Kampen: Kok Pharos.

Shadid, W. A. R., van Koningsveld, P.S. (Ed.). (1996). *Muslims in the Margin. Political Responses to the Presence of Islam in Western Europe.* Kampen: Kok Pharos.

Shadid, W. A. R., van Koningsveld, P.S. (Ed.). (2002). *Religious Freedom and the Neutrality of the State: the Position of Islam in the European Union.* Leuven: Peeters.

Shadid, W. A. R., van Koningsveld, P.S. (2005). Muslim dress in Europe: debates on the headscarf. *Journal of Islamic Studies, 16*(1), 35-61.

Siim, B. (2000). *Gender and Citizenship. Politics and Agency in France, Britain and Denmark.* Cambridge: Cambridge University Press.

Sikand, Y. (2002). *The Origins and Development of the Tablighi Jama'at (1920-2000). A cross-country comparative study.* New Delhi: Orient Longman.

Silvana da Rosa, A. (1994). From theory to metatheory in social representations: the lines of argument of a theoretical-methodological debate. *Social Science Information, 33*(2), 273-304.

Simmel, G.(1971). *On Individuality and Social Forms.* Chicago: University of Chicago Press.

Smith, G. (2000). Global Systems and Religious Diversity in the Inner City – Migrants in the East End of London. *International Journal on Multicultural Societies* (IJMS), *Vol. 2, No. 1, 2000: 17 - 40*

Smith, J. (1997). Characteristics of the modern transnational social movement sector. In: Jackie Smith, Charles Chatfield and Ron Pagnucco (eds), *Transnational Social Movements and Global Politics.* Syracuse: Syracuse University Press.

Soysal, Y.N. (1994). *Limits of Citizenship: Migrants and Postnational Membership in Europe.* Chicago: Chicago University Press.

Soysal, Y. N.(1997). Changing Parameters of Citizenship and Claims-Making : Organized Islam in European Public Spheres. In: *Theory and Society*, vol. 26, no. 4. Kluwer Academic Publishers.

Staszewski, M. (2006). Ecoles et foulards: le pourrissement. *Traces de Changement, 175,* 5.

Statham, P. (1999). Political Mobilisation by Minorities in Britain: a negative feedback of 'race relations'? *Journal of Ethnic and Migration Studies,* vol.25, no.4, pp.597-626.

Statham, P., Koopmans, R., Giugni, M., & Passy, F. (2005). Resilient or adaptable Islam? Multiculturalism, religion and migrants' claims-making for group demands in Britain, the Netherlands and France. *Ethnicities, 5*(4), 427-459.

Steenbergen van, B. (1994). *The Condition of Citizenship.* London: Sage.

Stern, J. (2004). *Terror in the Name of God: Why Religious Militants Kill.* New York: HarperCollins.

Stevenson, N. (Ed.). (2001). *Culture and Citizenship.* London: Sage.

Stürmer, S., Kampmeier, C. (2003). Active citizenship: The role of community identification in community volunteerism and local participation. *Psychologica Belgica* (Special Issue: Social Identity and Citizenship), 43, 103-122.

452

Styrdom, P. (1999). The Challenge of Collective Responsibility for Sociology. *Current Sociology, 47*(3), 65-82.

Surkyn, J., Reniers, G. (1997). Selecte gezelschappen – Over de migratiegeschiedenis en de interne dynamiek van migratieprocessen. In Lesthaeghe, R. (Ed.) *Diversiteit in sociale verandering – Turkse en Marokkaanse vrouwen in België*. Brussels, VUB Press. 41-72

Sutton, P. W., & Vertigans, S. (2005). *Resurgent Islam: A Sociological Approach*. London: Polity.

Swyngedouw, M. (2000). Belgium: explaining the relationship between Vlaams Blok and the city of Antwerp. In P. Hainsworth (Ed.), *The Politics of the Extreme Right*. London: A continuum imprint.

Swyngedouw, M., Phalet, K., Deschouwer, K. (1999). *Minderheden in Brussel*. Brussel: VUB Press.

Swyngedouw, M., Phalet, K., Jacobs, D.,. (2002, March). *Social Capital and Political Participation among Ethnic Minority Groups in Brussels. A Test of the Civic Community Argument of Fennema and Tillie*. Paper presented at the ECPR Workshop on Political Participation of Immigrants and their Descendants in Post-War Western Europe, Turin.

Sztompka, P. (1999). *Trust - A Sociological Theory*. Cambridge: Cambridge University Press.

Sztompka, P. (2002). *Socjologia - analiza społeczeństwa*. Kraków: Znak.

Sztompka, P. (2004). The Trauma of Social Change. In J. C. Alexander, R. Eyerman, B. Giesen, N. J. Smelser & P. Sztompka (Eds.), *Cultural Trauma and Collective Identity*. Berkeley: University of California Press.

Taj-Farouki, S. (2003). Islamists and the threat of jihad: Hizb ut-Tahrir and al Muhajiroun on Israel and the Jews. In B. S. Turner (Ed.), *Islam: Critical Concepts in Sociology* (Vol. IV). London: Routledge.

Tajfel, H. (1981). *Human groups and social categories*. Cambridge University Press

Taylor, C. (1989). *Sources of the Self: the Making of the Modern Identity*: Harvard University Press.

Taylor, C. (1992). *Multiculturalism and the 'Politics of Recognition'*: Princeton University Press.

Taylor, M. (2006, 5 October). BNP accused of exploiting cartoons row with Muslim leaflet. *The Guardian*.

Ternisien, X. (2005). *Les frères musulmans*. Paris: Fayard.

Ternisien, X. (2005a, May). La religion, l'orthodoxie, la femme et le sexe. *Le Monde*.

Tibi, B. (1998). *Europa ohne Identität, Die Krise der multikulturellen Gesellschaft*. Frankfurt am Main: Brandes & Apsel Verlag.

Tibi, B. (2002). A Plea for a Reform of Islam. In S. Stern, Seligmann, E. (Ed.), *The End of Tolerance?* London: Nicholas Brearley Publishing.

Tibi, B. (2006). Euro-islam jako europejski most między cywilizacjami. In K. Pędziwiatr, Górak-Sosnowska, K., Kubicki, P. (Ed.), *Islam i obywatelskość w Europie*. Warszawa: Elipsa.

Tietze, N. (2002). *Jeunes musulmans de France et d'Allemagne: Les contructions subjectives de l'identite*. Paris: L'Harmattan.

Tilleux, O. (2003). Contribution à l'étude des modes de fonctionnement des élites locales. *Recherches Sociologique, 1*, 3-28.

TimeOut. (2005). Top 20 movers and shakers 2005. *Time Out London*.

Timmerman, C. (1994). Jeunes filles de Turquie. Vie familiale et instruction scolaire. In: N. Bensalah, *Familles turques et maghrébines aujourd'hui. Evolution dans les espaces d'origine et en immigration*. Paris: Maisonneuve-Larose.

Timmerman, C. (1999a). *Onderwijs maakt het verschil. Socio-culturele praxis en etniciteitsbeleving bij Turkse jonge vrouwen*. Leuven: Acco.

Timmerman, C. (1999b). Islamism or the need for alternatives: the case of young Turkish women in Belgium. In M. L. Crul, F., Pang, Ch. (Ed.), *Culture, structure and beyond: Changing identities and social postitions of immigrants and their children*. Amsterdam.

Tribalat, M. (1995). *Faire France. Une grande enquête sur les immigrés et leurs enfants.* Paris: Broché.

Tocqueville de, A. (1999). *De la démocratie en Amérique.* Paris: Flammarion.

Torrekens, C. (2005). Le pluralisme religieux en Belgique. *Diversite Canadienne, 4*(3), 56-58.

Touraine, A. (1993). *La voix et le regard: Sociologie des mouvements sociaux.* Paris: Seuil.

Turam, B. (2004). The politics of engagement between Islam and secular state: ambivalences of 'civil society'. *The British Journal of Sociology, 55*(2).

Turner, B. S. (Ed.). (1993). *Citizenship and Social Theory.* London: Sage.

Turner, B. S. (1994). Postmodern Culture/Modern Citizens. In B. Steenbergen van (Ed.), *The Conditions of Citizenship.* London: Sage.

Turner, B. S. (1994a). *Orientalism, Postmodernism and Globalism.* London: Routledge.

Turner, B. S. (1997). Citizenship Studies: a General Theory. *Citizenship Studies, 1*(1), 5-18.

Turner, B. S. (2000). Globalization, religion and cosmopolitan virtue. *European Journal of Social Theory, 3*(2).

Turner, B. S. (2003). *Citizenship, Religion and Social Solidarity: Islam and European Integration.* Paper presented at the Trans-Islam Conference, Wolfson College, Oxford, November 2003.

Turner, B. S. (Ed.). (2003). *Islam.* London: Routledge.

Uslaner, E. M. (2002). Religion and Civic Engagement in Canada and the United States. *Journal for the Scientific Study of Religion, 41*(2), 239-254.

Van Der Veer, P., Munshi, S. (Ed.). (2004). *Media, War and Terrorism: Responses from the Middle East and Asia.* London: Taylor & Francis Group.

Van Loon, J. (2002). *Risk and Technological Culture. Towards a Sociology of Virulence.* London: Routledge.

Venel, N. (2004). *Musulmans et citoyens.* Paris: Presses Universitaires de France.

Verba, S., Schlozman, K.L., Brady, H.E. (1995). *Voice and Equality, Civic Voluntarism in American Politics.* Harvard: Harvard University Press.

Verheyden, L. (2006). Countering Radicalization and Recruitment – Belgian Perspective. Brussels.

Verhoeven, M. (1997). Minorite musulmane et ville. In F. Dassetto (Ed.), *Facettes de l'islam belge* (pp. 123-139). Louvain-la-Neuve: Bruylant.

Vertovec, S. (1998). Multi-multiculturalisms. In M. Martiniello (Ed.), *Multicultural policies and the state: a comparison of two European societies.* Oxford: Oxford University Press.

Vertovec, S. (2001). Transnationalism and Identity. *Journal of Ethnic and Migration Studies, 27*(4), 571-747.

Vertovec, S. (2004). Religion and Diaspora. In P. Antes, Geertz, A.M., Geertz, R., Warne, R. (Ed.), *New Approaches to the Study of Religion.* New York: Verlag de Gruyter.

Vertovec, S. (2006). *The Emergence of Super-Diversity in Britain:* Centre on Migration, Policy and Society.

Vertovec, S., Peach, C. (Ed.). (1997). *Islam in Europe.* London: Macmillan Press.

Vertovec, S., Cohen, R. (Ed.). (1999). *Migrations, Diasporas and Transnationalism.* Cheltenham: An Elgar Reference Collection.

Villalón, L. A. (1995). *Islamic Society and State Power in Senegal: Disciples and Citizens in Fatick.* Cambridge: Cambridge University Press.

Voet, R. (1998). *Feminism and Citizenship.* London: Sage.

Voyé, L. (1999). Secularization in a Context of Advanced Modernity. *Sociology of Religion, 60.*

Vuddamalay, V. (2002). Research on Immigration, Islam and Citizenship in Western Europe: How Far Has a Specific Transdisciplinary Domain Been Established? In R. Leveau, Withol de Wenden, C., Mohsen-Finan, K. (Ed.), *New European Identity and Citizenship.* Aldershot: Ashgate.

Waardenburg, J. (1983). The Right to Ritual. Mosquees in the Netherlands. *Nederlands Theologisch Tijdschrift,* 37 (3), pp. 253-264

Waardenburg, J. (1991). Muslim Associations and Official Bodies in Some European Countries. In: Shadid W.A,R and Konningsveld, P.S ed. *The Integration of Islam and Hinduism in Western Europe. Kampen:* Kok Pharos.

Wagner, P. (1994). *A Sociology of Modernity.* London: Routledge.

Wagner, W. (1994). Fields of research and socio-genesis of social representations: a discussion of criteria and diagnostics. *Social Science Information, 33*(2), 192-228.

Watson, H. (1994). Women and the Veil. In A. S. Ahmed, Donnan, H. (Ed.), *Islam, Globalization and Postmodernity.* London: Routledge.

Watson, J. (1977). *Between Two Cultures.* Oxford: Blackwell

Watt, M. (1999). Islamic Modernities? Citizenship, Civil Society, and Islamism in a Nigerian City. In Holsten (Ed.), *Cities and Citizenship.* Durham: NC: Duke University Press.

Weber, M. (1905, 2005). *Die protestantische Ethik und der' Geist' des Kapitalismus.* Berlin: Beltz-Athenaeum

Weber, M. (1958). *The City.* New York: Free Press.

Webb, J., Schirato, T., Danaher, G. (2002). *Understanding Bourdieu.* London: Sage.

Weekens-Bernard, D. (2007). *School Choice and Ethnic Segregation - Educational Decision-making Black and Minority Ethnic Parents.* London: Runnymede Trust.

Weithman, P. J. (2002). *Religion and the Obligations of Citizenship.* Cambridge: Cambridge University Press.

Weitzman, E. A. (2003). Software and Qualitative Research . In: Denzin, N. & Lincoln, Y. (Eds.), Collecting and Interpreting Qualitative Materials , 2nd edn. Sage , Thousand Oaks, CA,. In N. Denzin, Lincoln, Y. (Ed.), *Collecting and Interpreting Qualitative Materials.* Thousand Oaks: Sage.

Weitzman, E. A. (2007). Computer-Aided/Mediated Analysis. In B. Ritzer (Ed.), *Blackwell Encyclopedia of Sociology.* London: Blackwell Publishing House.

Welch, A. T. (1997). Islam. In J. R. Hinnells (Ed.), *A New Handbook of Living Religions.* London: Penguin.

Werbner, P. (1994). Islamic radicalism and the Gulf War: lay preachers and political dissent among British Pakistanis. In: Lewis, Ph. (ed.), Schnapper, Dominique (ed.), *Musulmans en Europe.* London: Pinter.

Werbner, P. (1996). The Making of Muslim Dissent: Hybridized Discourses, Lay Preachers, and Radical Rhetoric among British Pakistanis. In: *American Ethnologist,* col.23, No.1, pp.102 – 122

Werbner, P. (2002). *Imagined Diasporas Among Manchester Muslims.* Oxford: James Currey.

Werbner, P. (2004). The Predicament of Diaspora and Millennial Islam: Reflections on September 11, 2001. *Ethnicities, 4*(4), 451-476.

Whitley, P. (1999). The origins of Social Capital. In J. van Deth (Ed.) *Social Capital and European Democracy.* London: Routledge.

Wihtol de Wenden, C., Leveau, R. (2001). *La beurgeoisie: Les trois âges de la vie associative issue de l'immigration.* Paris: CNRS Editions.

Wiktorowicz, Q. (2005). *Radical Islam Rising: Muslim Extremism in the West.* Oxford: Rowman & Littlefield Publishers.

Wuthnow, R. (1991). *Acts of Compassion: Caring for Others and Helping Ourselves.* Princeton: Princeton University Press.

Wuthnow, R. (2002). Religious Involvement and Status-Bridging Social Capital. *Journal for the Scientific Study of Religion, 41*(4), 669-684.

Yaqoob, S. (2003). Global and local echoes of the anti-war movement: A British Muslim perspective,. *International Socialism Journal.*

Yaqoob, S. (2005, 15 July). Our leaders must speak up. *The Guardian.*

Yin, R. K. (1994). *Case Study Research: Design and Methods*. London: Sage.

Young, I. (1990). *Justice and the Politics of Difference*. Oxford: Princeton University Press.

YouGov (2001). *Perception of Muslims and Islam in the UK*, Results of the research are available of the website of the Islam Awareness Week http://www.iaw.org.uk

Yuval-Davis, N. (1992). Fundamentalism, multiculturalism and women in Britain. In R. Nile (Ed.), *Immigration and the Politics of Ethnicity and Race in Australia and Britain* (pp. 14-26). London: Institute of Commonwealth Studies.

Zemni, S. (2002). Islam, European Identity and the Limits of Multiculturalism. In Shahid, W.A.R.; Van Koningsveld, P.S. (Ed.) *Religious Freedom and the Neutrality of the State: the Position of Islam in the European Union*, Leuven: Peeters.

Zubaida, S. (1993). *Islam, the People and the State: Political Ideas and Movements in the Middle East*. London: I.B.Tauris.

APPENDIX I - KEY EVENTS IN THE HISTORY OF ISLAM IN BELGIUM, BRITAIN AND IN WIDER EUROPE SINCE 1973[419]

Year	Islam in Belgium	Islam in Britain	Islam in Europe (especially in France, Germany and Holland)
1973	- End of 'silent presence' of Muslims in the country.	- Establishment of the Islamic Foundation in Leicester (subsequently relocated in 1990 to Markfield).	- Establishment of the Islamic Council of Europe (headquarters in London, Secretary General: Salem Azzam).
1974	19 July – legal recognition of Islam.	- Publication of the 'Draft Prospectus of the Muslim Institute for Research and Planning', by Kalim Siddiqui. - Opening of the Deobandi seminar Dar-al-Uloom in Bury.	- Establishment of the *Federative van Moslim Organisaties in Nederland* – the first Muslim umbrella organisation in Holland.
1975	- First nominations of the teachers of Islam outside of the legal framework.		
1976		- Race Relations Act which recognizes the principle of 'racial equality' for individuals.	
1977	5 January – First Muslim manifestation in Brussels.	- Completion of the rebuilding of the Islamic Cultural Centre & London Central Mosque.	
1978	- Official introduction of the teaching of Islam in the state schools. The Islamic and Cultural Center of Belgium (Centre Islamique et Culturel de Belgique - CICB) is responsible for nominating the teachers.	- Completion of the new *markaz* of the Tablighi Jamaat in Dewsbury.	- Establishment of the *Unie van Marokkaanse Moslim Organisaties in Nederland* – one of the major Muslim organisations in Holland. - Opening of the first Muslim schools in Denmark.
1979			- Islam is formally recognized in Austria. Creation of the *Islamische Glaubensgemeinschatf in Österreich*.
1980	- Number of the prayer rooms in the country exceeds 100.		
1981			*Federative van Moslim Organisaties in Nederland* is replaced by *Moslim Organisaties in Nederland*.
1982		- Opening of the Deobandi seminar Dar-al-Uloom in Saville Town, Dewsbury.	- Opening of DITIB (*Diyanet Isleri Türk-Islam Birligi*) - the German branch of the Diyanet. - Establishment of the *Nederlandse Islamitische Federatie* – one of the major Muslim organisations in the Netherlands.
1983		- Yusuf Islam (Cat Stevens) starts the	- Establishment of the *Union des Organisations Islamiques de*

---

[419] Before 1973 the Muslim presence in Belgium and Britain had been rarely a topic of public debates. Since this time this largely 'silent presence' (Dassetto 1997) has started to become increasing 'visible'.

		Islamia School in North West London.	*France* – one of the biggest Muslim federations in France.
		- Union of Muslim Organisations presents Muslim concerns to Prime Minister Margaret Thatcher prior to the General Election.	
1984	- Religion of the Muslim immigrants presented as a key barrier in their integration.	- Foundation of the Islamic Relief by the Egyptian doctor Hany El Banna, in response to the famine in Africa.	
1985	- Two Brussels' mayors (Picqué and Nols) refuse to appoint the teachers of Islam in their communes.	- Launch of the Oxford Centre for Islamic Studies, Director Dr Farhan Nizami. - The Honeyford affair – headmaster suspended after objecting to multicultural policies in Bradford schools. - Official opening of the East London Mosque.	- Foundation of the *Fédération Nationale des Musulmans de France* – another major Muslim federation in France.
1986	20 May – Manifestation against the American bombardment of Libya. - Charles Picqué (the Mayor of St. Gilles) declares that 75% of Islamic teachers are 'dangerous fundamentalists'. He opposes to the establishment of the Iranian centre in his commune.		- Establishment of the *Islamrat für die Bundesrepublik Deutschland* – one of the major umbrella organisation in Germany.
1987		- The celebrations of Mawlid an-Nabi (Ar. مولد النبي) or the Prophet's birthday organized by pir Maruf Hussain Shah in the Hyde Park gather above 25,000 people from all over the country.	
1988		- Publication of 'The Satanic Verses' – beginning of the Rushdie affair. - Establishment of the Islamic Forum Europe.	
1989	- Assassination of the Director of the Islamic Centre. - Affaire des Foulards. - Proposition to set up Superior Council of Belgian Muslims rejected by the government.	- Large demonstrations calling for a ban on 'The Satanic Verses'. - Muslim delegation meets Mr. Patten, a Minister at the Home Office to press for legal redress against abuse and sacrilege.	- Headscarf affair in France.
1990	- Establishment by the government of the Provisional Council of Elders.	- Establishment of the Islamic Society of Britain.	- Establishment of the CORIF in France.
1991	- 'Black Sunday' - Elections to the Superior Council of Belgian Muslims rejected by the government. May - Riots in the Brussels' communes of Forest and Saint Gilles.	- Mobilisation of relief to help Bosnian Muslims.	- Beginning of the war in Yugoslavia.

1992		- Establishment of the Muslim Parliament of Great Britain by the Director of the Muslim Institute, Kalim Siddiqui.	- Agreement between the Muslim representative organisation and the state in Spain.
1993			- Creation of The Dutch Muslim Multimedia Company (*Nederlandse Moslim Omroep*) responsible for production of the Muslim material for the state television and radio.
1994		March – 6000 attend rally in London after Hebron mosque massacre.	
1995	April – Riots in Molenbeek (Commune of Brussels) sparked by racial tensions.		July/August/October- Bomb attacks on the Paris metro. The first attack on July 25th kills eight people.
1996	20 October – "White March". - Establishment of the *Présence Musulmane*. - Creation of the *Ligue Islamique Interculturelle de Belgique*.	- M. Sarwar (Govan, Glasgow) elected first Muslim MP (Labour).	- Establishment of the organisation Islam and Citizenship (*Islam en Burgerschap)* in the Netherlands.
1997	9 March – Funeral of Loubna Benaissa (9 year old child of Moroccan origin murdered by Patrick Derochette) in the midst Marc Dutroux trial. November – Riots in Anderlecht (Commune of Brussels) sparked by racial tensions.	- UK Action Committee on Islamic Affairs launch 'Elections 1997 & British Muslims' to help Muslim voters make an 'informed choice'. - Inaugural meeting of the Muslim Council of Britain (hereafter the MCB). - Setting up of the Muslim Association of Britain (hereafter the MAB). - Publication of the Runnymede Trust's report on Islamophobia.	
1998	13 December – Elections to Muslim General Assembly.	- First General Assembly Meeting of the Muslim Council of Britain at Brent Town Hall (Secretary General: Iqbal Sacranie). - Two Muslim peers appointed - Lord Nazir of Rotherham and Baroness Polla Uddin. - First Muslim school (Islamia Primary School) receives state founding.	
1999	May – establishment of the Executive of Muslims of Belgium (EMB*)*.	April – Blair attends first Muslim community reception for a Prime Minister organized by the MCB. - Bashir Khanbhai elected to European Parliament - Prison Service appoints first Muslim Advisor, Maqsood Ahmed.	

		- Creation of the City Circle.	
2000	February - Introduction of the new law enabling easier naturalisation of immigrants and persons of immigrant descent. - Setting up of the Arab European League (hereafter AEL) by Dyab Abou Jahjah.	- Launch of the annual Muslim News Awards for Excellence. - MCB joins inter faith lobbying against Government plans to repeal Section 28 of a local government act relating to sexuality teaching.	
2001	- Report of the 'Comité R' indicating links between the members of the EMB and foreign extremist movements. 9 September – Two Tunisians with fake Belgian passports kill Shah Masood in Afghanistan.	- Khalid Mahmood elected MP in June 2001 General Election. - Riots in the Northern towns (Oldham, Burnley and Bradford) sparked by racial tensions. - National Census includes a question on religion for the first time since 1851.	- Significant increase of Islamophobia in the aftermath of the 9/11.
2002	- The killing of the teacher of Islam (Mohamed Achrak) on the streets of Antwerp provokes riots. - The AEL calls the police racist and patrols the streets of Antwerp with video cameras to monitor police activity. - Establishment of the Party of Citizenship and Prosperity (Parti Citoyenneté et Prosperité) led by the Jean-François Abdullah Bastin.	- March of over 50,000 people in support of justice in Palestine.	
2003	September - Nizar Trabelsi is sentenced to 10 years for plotting a bomb attack against the NATO air base at Kleine Brogel. - The AEL participates in the federal elections under the umbrella RESIST with the PVDA (Dutch: *Partij van de Arbeid van België*) *or* the Workers' Party of Belgium. - Foundation by Diab Abou Jahjah of the Muslim Democratic Party or MDP (Dutch: *Moslim Democratische Partij*) to run in the next year's election.	- 3 March - Around a million demonstrators on the streets of London against the war in Iraq – demonstration co-organized by the Muslim Association of Britain. - High Street Banks start to sell Islamic products.	April – Establishment of the *Conseil Français du Cult Musulman* – an organisation that is supposed to represent French Muslims vis-à-vis the government.
2004	- Celebrations of the 40th anniversary of the Moroccan and Turkish presence in Belgium (bilateral agreements between the Belgian government and governments in Ankara and Rabat signed in 1964)	January - Kilroy-Silk affair. March – MCB sends a letter to the Mosques and Muslim Leaders urging them to more courageously "combat any threat to peace and stability".	11 March –Terrorist attacks in Madrid (Spain). French journalist taken hostage in Iraq. Their abductors demand the change of the newly introduced

- Vlaams Blok condemned for "repeated incitement to discrimination" and forced to start to function under a new name – Vlaams Belang. November – beginning of Naima Amzil affair. - According to the report published by the King Baudouin Foundation there are 328 mosques in Belgium.	May – first Muslim member of the Liberal Democrats (Mrs Kishwer Falkner) enters Parliament. July – visit of Qaradawi in London sparks hot debates. August – opening of the first Islamic bank in the country (Islamic Bank of Britain). - Official opening of the London Muslim Centre connected with the East London Mosque.	ban on 'the ostentatious religious signs'. October - France deports and Algerian imam for anti-Women statements. November – Assassination of Theo Van Gogh by a Dutch Muslim of Moroccan origin.
2005		
– Naima Amzil affair continues – the King Albert II pays a visit to the firm Rik Remmery to show his support for the owner and his Muslim employee. March – general elections aimed to renew the membership of the Muslim General Assembly and the Executive. December - Murielle Degauque, Belgian convert to Islam, becomes known as the first European Muslim female suicide bomber.	March – Establishment of the British Muslim Forum. May - George Galloway wins the elections in Tower Hamlets and as the only member from the Respect Party enters Parliament; two new Muslim MPs also elected: Shahid Malik and Sadiq Khan. 7 July - Terrorist attacks on the London Transport Network. 21 July – mock attacks on the London Transport Network. - 22 July – killing of Jean Charles de Menezes. August – Scotland Yard reports significant increase in religious hate crimes. October - Government's Task Group on tackling extremism publishes its report. - Government withdraws proposals for control orders on places of worship after concerted protests from faith organisations.	October/November – Civil unrest in the French suburbs.
2006		
- In the midst of the Danish cartoons affair the AEL launches 'Freedom of Speech Campaign' and publishes on its website cartoons on the subject of Holocaust denial arguing that they similarly to the newspapers republishing Danish cartoons have right to 'free speech'.	January/February – Danish cartoons affair – minor protests organized by Hizb ut-Tahrir. March - Britain's highest court rules that the school acted properly in refusing to allow a student to wear Muslim clothing of her choice (jilbab) rather than the attire permitted under school policy. June – creation of the Mosques and	January/February - The Cartoons Affair. June - North-Rhine Westphalia, joins seven other states in forbidding teachers in public schools from wearing the Muslim headscarf. September – Pope's Benedict XVI lecture at the University of

461

		Imams National Advisory Body (MINAB). July – creation of the Sufi Muslim Council. August – Disruption of the airlines terror plot.	Regensburg sparks Muslim protests against mischaracterization of Islam.
2007	19 June - The Walloon government officially recognises 43 mosques (out of 89 mosques in the region). - New Muslim school, Avicenna, opened by the Mosque al-Khalil in Molenbeek (Brussels) applies for the state founding. 13 December – official recognition of the first five mosques in the Capital-Region of Brussels. 22 December – official recognition of the fist six mosques in Flanders. - With a highly controversial verdict Dyab Abou Jahjah and Ahmed Azzuz from the AEL are sentenced to one year in prison for 'not using their authority to calm the protests' after the murder of Mohammed Achrak on the streets of Antwerp in 2002.	February - Disruption of the plot aimed at kidnapping and killing a Muslim soldier. May – publication of 'The Islamist' by Ed Husain provokes lively debates on Islamism in Britain. June - Salman Rushdie is knighted by the Queen. This provokes protests in Britain and outside of the country. June - Creation of Council of ex-Muslims of Britain. June/July- foiled bomb attacks in Glasgow and London.	May - Rachida Dati becomes first female Muslim Minister. She heads French Ministry of Justice. August - German State Court upholds headscarf ban for teachers. October - Rachid Ramda sentenced to life in prison for his role in financing the 1995 bomb attacks on the Paris metro.
2008	January – Petitions against the court decision to sentence the leaders of the AEL for a year of imprisonment. Ahmed Azzuz and Dyab Abou Jahjah appeal. February – resignation of Coskun Beyazgül from the post of the President of the EMB. March - cancellation of the ministerial subsidy to the EMB. - General Assembly of the EMB elects new governing board.	January – MCB stops boycotting Holocaust Memorial Day. February - Remarks on shariah made by Archbishop Rowan Williams speech during his speech on civil and religious law in England provokes hot debates on the status of Muslim law in Britain. - Sheikh Qaradawi is denied visa to the UK. MCB and some other organisations protest. April – Former members of the Hizb ut-Tahrir launch a Muslim thinktank - The Quilliam Foundation - aimed at 'improving relations with the West by challenging extremist ideologies'. June - 11th Annual General Meeting of the MCB concludes with the re-election of Dr Muhammad Abdul Bari for his second and final term as Secretary General.	February – Establishment of the European Assembly of Muslim Imams and Spiritual Guides in Brussels (led by Federation of Islamic Organisations in Europe or FIOE). March - A French Court of Appeals fines far-right leader Jean Marie Le Pen for discrimination and incitement to racial violence. - The leader of the Freedom Party in the Netherlands Geert Wilders releases an anti-Qur'an film 'Fitna'.

APPENDIX II - ORGANISATIONAL FACT SHEET

Astrolabe

The Astrolabe was set up in 2004 by a group of Muslim students and professionals. It wants to cater for the spiritual needs of Muslim youth while at the same time remains open for the co-operation with wider civil society. More specifically the Astrolabe aims to promote active citizenship and civic consciousness among the Muslim students and graduates and at the same time contribute to their religious self-development. The latter goal the organisation strives to attain inter alia by organising seminars on such topics as, for instance, 'Spirituality' (15 October 2006) 'Spirituality and knowledge of God' (11 February 2006) or 'The role of Muslim students and university graduates: spiritual and intellectual challenges' (10 April 2005). As one may read in the charter of the organisation the central objective of the Astrolabe is *'to promote an intellectual dynamism, which would enable Muslim students and university graduates to achieve a harmony between their spiritual belonging and their civic engagement'*. There are four 'committees' or working groups within the organisation reflecting its major preoccupations: the committee of spirituality, committee of identity, committee of citizenship and contemporary issues and committee of women. Each of the committees produces documents which are published on the website of the organisation. More information about the Astrolabe can be found on www.astrolabe.be

DéClik

The DéClik was established in April 2005 by Samira Benallal who is a sister of Nordine Benallal - a Belgian criminal famous for his numerous escapes from the country's high security prisons. It is the fate of her younger brother who very early in his life dropped out from school and socialized into the criminal world of the Brussels' inner city areas, that pushed her to set up the DéClik and through it try to avert other young persons of Maghrebi origin from pursuing the path of Nordine. The first and foremost goal of the association set up by Samira Benallal, and run by her and other Muslim and non-Muslim persons, is to improve the educational attainment of students from immigrant backgrounds, prevent their dropping out, and fight against their discrimination in the educational institutions. The DéClik is thus strongly lobbying against the educational exclusion of children of immigrant origin in the form of creation of the so called 'ghetto schools' and 'the educational system of two speeds'. The organization also carries out numerous projects informing young persons about the dangers of drugs for individuals and the whole social environments. Moreover, the DéClik strives to promote amongst the youth of the inner city areas active social citizenship. More information about the organisation can be found on www.declik.be

463

Federation of European Muslim Youth and Student Organisations (FEMYSO)

FEMYSO was established in 1996 by Muslim youth organisations from across Europe (with the key role of the French - *Jeunes Musulmans de France*, British - *Young Muslims UK*, and Swedish - *Sveriges Unga Muslimer*) to provide a social context in which they could come together, discuss different issues and act on matters of common interest. As one may read on its website *'Its mission is to be a platform for youth organisations to congregate, exchange information, gain experience and benefit from each other, to work for a better Europe.'* Some of the key goals of the FEMYSO are: to encourage the development of a European Muslim identity via the involvement of Muslim youth in discussions, educational and awareness programmes, highlighting their social responsibilities and contribution to Europe; to create a network within Europe to cater for youth exchange trips, transfer of experiences and cross-cultural exchange of information; to identify avenues of co-operation among its member organisations and other religious and non-religious youth bodies in Europe; to establish management and leadership programs to enhance the skills and potentials of youth; and finally to continuously review the problems and challenges that the Muslim youth are encountering in Europe and provide alternative solutions to their symptoms and causes. At present FEMYSO closely linked with the ikhwani Federation of Islamic Organisations in Europe (FIOE) has 37 member organisations bringing together Muslim youth from almost all European countries. The organisation has its office in Brussels only a few hundred metres from the buildings of the European Commission and the Council of European Union. Throughout the years it has established itself as a voice and resource for the generations of European Muslims, and has formed valuable linkages with inter alia the European Parliament and the European Commission. More information about the organisation can be found on www.femyso.net

Hizb ut-Tahrir (HT)

The Hizb ut-Tahrir (or the Party of Liberation) is an internationalist and pan-Islamist political organisation established in 1953 in Jerusalem by a Palestinian *qadi* (Islamic judge) Taqiuddin an-Nabhani. The major goal of the organisation which has a significant following amongst the young British Muslims is to unite all Muslim countries in a unitary Islamic state or caliphate, ruled by Islamic law and headed by an elected head of state *(caliph)*. The British branch of the organisation was set up in 1986 by Omar Bakri Mohammad and led by him till 1996 when he left the HT and relaunched a separate organisation al-Muhajiroun (ar. Emigrants). The HT urges British Muslims inter alia to choose whether they are Muslim or British, boycott all elections, reject the democratic process and campaign for the creation of a single, united Muslim state stretching from Morocco to Indonesia. The organisation has been banned in many Muslim countries. After the terrorist attacks of 7th July 2005 the British Prime Minister Tony Blair announced an intent to ban Hizb ut-Tahrir in Britain. This has not been done till now due to inter alia a failure to provide strong evidence linking the organisation with terrorist activities. More information about the organisation can be found on www.hizb.org.uk

Federation of Student Islamic Organisations (FOSIS)

Since its inception in 1962, FOSIS has developed into one of the leading Muslim student organisations in the UK. It has links with over 100 Islamic Societies and has established relationships with the National Union of Students and other key student organisations in the UK and Europe. As one of the oldest and most established organisations in the UK, FOSIS has developed a variety of resources (e.g. it owns two hostels in London) and specialised teams to assist and represent Muslim students within universities and other educational institutions making it an important source of reference for Muslim, as well as non-Muslim organisations. The key objectives of FOSIS are: to represent Muslim students and Islamic Societies at all levels; to protect and promote the interests of Muslim students; to encourage the formation of new Islamic societies on campuses and to support the activities of existing ones; to facilitate communication and co-ordination among Islamic Societies; to promote understanding of Islam and Muslims in an effort to eradicate intolerance and Islamophobia from campuses. The organisation claims to have more than 20000 members (out of around 30000 Muslim students studying at the British universities). Amongst its former members there were for example Dilwar Hussain from the Islamic Foundation and Tariq Ramadan. The FOSIS is extremely diverse both in ethnic and religious terms. One may find amongst its members the supporters of the isolationist Tablighi Jama'at, militant Hizb'ut Tahrir and Young Muslim advocating civic engagement. More information about the organisation can be found on www.fosis.org.uk

Islamic Society of Britain (ISB)

According to its former president Zahid Parvez and the author of the book '*Building a New Society: An Islamic Approach to Social Change*' the main idea behind the establishment of the ISB was to create an organisation for the growing Muslim youth population who did not feel comfortable in the languages of their parents, in which they could do something similar to their parents active in various ethno-religious organisations, but in the language in which they are comfortable with. The creation of the ISB, was also in his opinion an initiative influenced by the will of some committed British Muslims to play more active social and political role in the society. The membership of the organisation is ethnically-mixed. It draws from Pakistani, Bengali, Indian and other Muslim communities of the country, as well as, English converts (e.g. Sarah Joseph – the editor of the Muslim lifestyle magazine 'Emel'), both men and women. Currently the organisation has about 500 members, although some of the events it organises attract much wider audiences than its nominal membership. For example, its 'Living Islam' camp of 2003 gathered more than 3000 people. The ISB often describes itself as an organisation for a family. Its activities take place at local, regional and national levels and are designed to cater for the education and development of the whole family. The ISB tries to involve Muslims in addressing issues which they face or which they think are harmful to the society. The organisation has its branches in the major British cities. Each branch deals with different kinds of problems (e.g. drug addiction, Islamophobia, family problems) and works according to its own agenda. Since 1994 the ISB has also been organising Islam Awareness Week – an initiative that seeks to help

Muslims and non-Muslims to come together in a climate of understanding and appreciation. More information about the organisation can be found on www.isb.org.uk

Kawthar

The association Kawthar was set up in 1999 by a group of Muslim (Shia) women of different origins (Belgian, Moroccan, Turkish, Iranian and other) for two major reasons: firstly to promote emancipation of Muslim women and secondly to challenge some of the stereotypes of Muslim women and Muslims in general in the Belgian society. In order to achieve the aforementioned goals the association inter alia organizes numerous seminars and conferences. It does so often with assistance of other non-Muslim organizations. For instance, on 26th November 2005 the Kawthar organised a conference entitled 'Discrimination of Women: Who is Responsible?' in co-operation with the non-Muslim feminist organizations Vie Féminine and Association Sophia. At the same time the members of the organization have been strongly supporting the campaign for the right to wear a hijab in school and public spaces run together with other Muslim (e.g. LIIB and FEMYSO) and secular organizations (e.g. MRAX). The organisation publishes a quarterly Kawthar in which one may find not only articles on strictly religious issues but also commentaries of Muslim women on the contemporary politics and extensive articles on other non-religious subjects (e.g. on the history of feminism - no. 28, 2005, and on the natural disasters - no. 29, 2006). Some issues of this quarterly were sponsored by the King Baudouin Foundation. More information about the organisation can be found on www.bostani.com

L'Humanité Sans Frontiers (HSF)

The HSF (or Humanity Without Frontiers) was created in October 2002 by a group of young Muslims (active in other Muslim organisations – e.g. *LIIB* and *Présence Musulmane* – and non-affiliated ones) who decided to carry out their Ramadan initiative of feeding homeless people not only during the month of fasting but during a whole year. Today, every Sunday, the organisation prepares meals for around 120 homeless people and cooperates closely with other humanitarian organisations such as, for example, the Opération Thermos and Islamic Relief. In contrast to many other associations of this type, the HSF distributes food to the homeless not only during the winter time, but during the whole year. Its volunteers, both Muslims and non-Muslims, distribute meals prepared in the kitchen of the Belgian branch of Islamic Relief amongst the inhabitants of two centres for homeless: one for homeless men and the other for homeless families. Only about one-fourth of the people who are helped by the organisation are Muslims.

Muslim Association of Britain (MAB)

The Muslim Association of Britain was set up in 1997 by a group of Arab Muslims who felt largely left out in the country where Islam is dominated by people of South Asian origin. As one may read on its website yet a different reason for the inception of the organisation was *'to fill in the gap in terms of Islamic dawah work in Britain where the call for a comprehensive Islam that encompasses all aspects of life is lacking'*. The organisation which has about 1000 members co-organised demonstrations with the Stop the War coalition which in September 2002 and February 2003 brought to the streets of London hundred thousands of people. Among its aims and objectives are: to spread the teachings and culture of Islam, install the Islamic principles in the hearts of Muslim community and enhance the good morals within the British society, to assist the Muslim community in maintaining its integrity and foster in them good Islamic conduct, education and social relation especially ties of kinship. Its goal is also to make Muslims aware of their duties towards the society in which they are living and to promote an active role for the Muslim community in helping to solve different problems of the society (e.g. crime, drugs, unemployment and family disintegration). One of the most active members of the organisation is an Iraqi born Anas Osama Altikriti, an executive Board Member in charge of Media and Public Relations. In 2005 he set the Cordoba Foundation - an independent research and public relations organisation. More information about the MAB can be found on www.mabonline.net

Muslim Council of Britain (MCB)

There is no official Muslim representative organisation in Britain. However, since the New Labour came to power in 1997 the government has been tacitly supporting the Muslim Council of Britain (MCB), which strives to establish itself as a voice of Muslims in the country. The MCB was inaugurated - after 3 years of wide-ranging consultation - on 23rd November 1997 at the Brent Town Hall in Wembley by representatives of more than 250 Muslim organisations from all parts of Britain including Northern Ireland. Over the last years the organisation has strengthened and it is now considered one of the most representative organisations in the country. There are currently about 350 institutions affiliated to it including mosques, education and charitable institutions, women and youth organisations and professional bodies, both national and regional. The composition of the membership is ethnically mixed. The organisation is opposed to labels such as 'ethnic minority' clearly favouring religious identification. As one may read on its website the MCB's approach to dealing with civic affairs is one of participation, not agitation; in dealing with government, it is one of constructive engagement. The MCB strives to deal with problems and influence policies and outcomes through principled and effective participation, in conformity with Islamic norms and standards. Among its aims are inter alia: to promote cooperation, consensus and unity on Muslim affairs in the UK; to encourage and strengthen all existing efforts made for the benefit of the Muslim community; to work for a more enlightened appreciation of Islam and Muslims in the wider society; to establish a position for the Muslim community within British society that is fair and based on due rights; to work for the eradication of disadvantages and forms of discrimination faced by Muslims; to foster better community relations and work for the common good. More information about the organisation can be found on www.mcb.org.uk